ESSENTIALS OF

HUMAN SEXUALITY

ESSENTIALS OF

UMAN SEXUALITY

Spencer A. Rathus
Montclair State University

Jeffrey S. Nevid
St. John's University

Lois Fichner-Rathus
The College of New Jersey

ALLYN AND BACON

Boston
London
Toronto
Sydney
Tokyo
Singapore

Vice President and Editor-in-Chief, Social Sciences: Sean W. Wakely
Senior Editor: Carolyn Merrill
Editorial Assistant: Amy Goldmacher
Marketing Manager: Joyce Nilsen
Production Administrator: Deborah Brown
Editorial/Production Services: Colophon
Text Designer: Melinda Grosser for *silk*
Cover Administrator: Linda Knowles
Composition Buyer: Linda Cox
Manufacturing Buyer: Suzanne Lareau
Photo Researcher: Laurie Frankenthaler

Library of Congress Cataloging-in-Publication Data

Rathus, Spencer A.
    Essentials of human sexuality / Spencer A. Rathus, Jeffrey S.
Nevid, Lois Fichner-Rathus.
        p. cm.
    An abridged edition of the authors' Human sexuality in a world of
diversity.
    Includes bibliographical references and index.
    ISBN 0-205-27255-X
    1. Sex. I. Rathus, Spencer A. Human sexuality in a world of
diversity. II. Nevid, Jeffrey S. III. Fichner-Rathus, Lois, 1953-
IV. Title.
HQ21.R22   1997
306.7--dc21   97-18307
                                                CIP

Printed in the United States of America

10 9 8 7 6 5 4 3 2 1 RRDW 01 00 99 98 97

Photo Credits: Page 5, Lou Jones; Page 7, Corbis-Bettman; Page 10, Dan Habib/Impact Visuals; Page 17, Photo by Dellenback.
Reprinted by permission of Kinsey Institute for Research in Sex, Gender, and Reproduction, Inc.; Page 30, Catherine Leroy/SIPA Press;
Page 40, Susan Van Etten/The Picture Cube; Page 48, Thelma Shumsky/The Image Works; Page 63, Professor P. Motta/Dept. of Anatomy/
Rome University/Science Photo Library/Photo Researchers; Page 79, Willie Hill, Jr./The Image Works; Page 81, Alex Farnsworth/The Image
Works; Page 95, Laurie Platt Winfrey, Inc.; Page 98, Costa Manos/Magnum Photos; Page 114, 115 (both), From *Sex Errors of the Body*
© Dr. John Money; Page 118, Michael Edrington/The Image Works; Page 119, Bob Daemmrich/The Image Works; Page 125 (left), Larry
Kolvoord/The Image Works; Page 125 (right), Elizabeth Crews/The Image Works; Page 137, Guy Marineau/Black Star; Page 138 (both),
D. Perrett, K. May & S. Yoshikawa, University of St. Andrews/Science Photo Library/Photo Researchers; Page 142, Paul Fusco/Magnum
Photos; Page 149, Roy Morsch/The Stock Market; Page 159, Douglas Mason/Woodfin Camp & Associates; Page 162, Catherine Karnow/
Woodfin Camp & Associates; Page 167, Robert Harbison; Page 179, Donna Binder/Impact Visuals; Page 185, Catherine Noren/Stock,
Boston; Page 187, Rick Reinhard/Impact Visuals; Page 191, Stephen Marks; Page 202, Francis LeRoy/Bio Cosmos/Photo Researchers Science
Source; Page 209 (all), Petit Format/Nestle/Photo Researchers/Science Source; Page 219, Will & Demi McIntyre/Photo Researchers; Page 221
(all), SIU/Photo Researchers; Page 239, Courtesy of Wyeth-Ayerst Laboratories, Philadelphia, PA; Page 240 (left), Courtesy of Alza; Page 240
(right), Phototake; Page 256, David H. Hessell/Stock, Boston; Page 267, Rick Smolan/Stock, Boston; Page 276, Lawrence Migdale/Stock,
Boston; Page 280, David Wells/The Image Works; Page 286, Lou Jones; Page 290, Paul Fusco/Magnum Photos; Page 292, Christopher
Springman/The Stock Market; Page 306, Nicholas DeVore III/Photographers Aspen; Page 309, Roy Morsch/The Stock Market; Page 325,
Courtesy of Dr. Nicholas J. Fiumara; Page 329 (top), Custom Medical Stock Photo; Page 329 (bottom), C. James Webb/Phototake NYC;
Page 339, Contact/Alon Reininger/Woodfin Camp & Associates; Page 340, Phototake/CNRI; Page 342, Bio Photo Assoc/Photo Researchers;
Page 343, E. Gray/Science Photo Library/Photo Researchers; Page 344, James D. Wilson/Woodfin Camp & Associates; Page 351, Alon
Reininger/Contact/Woodfin Camp & Associates; Page 352, Donna Binder/Impact Visuals; Page 370, Steve McCurry/Magnum Photos;
Page 378, Rob Crandall/Stock, Boston; Page 379, Courtesy of the LaPorte County Child Abuse Prevention Council; Page 385, Archive
Photos/Fotos International; Page 394, Mike Yamashita/Woodfin Camp & Associates; Page 399, Paul Chesley/Photographers Aspen;
Page 401, Courtesy of Hammerhead Publishing; Page 405, J. Kirk Condyles/Impact Visuals.

Brief Contents

CHAPTER

1 What Is Human Sexuality? *1*

2 Female Sexual Anatomy and Physiology *27*

3 Male Sexual Anatomy and Physiology *57*

4 Sexual Response and Behavior *77*

5 Gender Identity and Gender Roles *109*

6 Attraction and Love *133*

7 Relationships, Intimacy, and Communication *155*

8 Sexual Orientation *177*

9 Conception, Pregnancy, and Childbirth *201*

10 Contraception and Abortion *233*

11 Sexuality Across the Life Span *265*

12 Sexual Dysfunctions *299*

13 Sexually Transmitted Diseases *323*

14 Atypical Sexual Variations *349*

15 Sexual Coercion *367*

16 Commercial Sex *392*

Contents

Preface *xii*

C H A P T E R

1 What Is Human Sexuality? *1*

Chapter Outline *1*

Did You Know That . . . ? *2*

What Is Human Sexuality? *2*

Thinking Critically About Human Sexuality *3*

Perspectives on Human Sexuality *3*

The Historical Perspective *3*

The Biological Perspective *9*

The Cross-Cultural Perspective *10*

Psychological Perspectives *11*

Sociocultural Perspectives *13*

Research Methods in Human Sexuality *15*

Populations and Samples: Representing the World of Diversity *15*

Methods of Observation *16*

A WORLD OF DIVERSITY
Around the World in Eighty Ways—A Preview *4*

C H A P T E R

2 Female Sexual Anatomy and Physiology *27*

Chapter Outline *27*

Did You Know That . . . ? *28*

The Female Sex Organs *28*

External Sex Organs *28*

Internal Sex Organs *34*

The Breasts *38*

Breast Cancer *39*

The Menstrual Cycle *42*

Regulation of the Menstrual Cycle *42*

Phases of the Menstrual Cycle *43*

Sex During Menstruation *47*

Menopause *47*

Menstrual Problems *49*

Dysmenorrhea *49*

Amenorrhea *50*

Premenstrual Syndrome (PMS) *50*

A WORLD OF DIVERSITY
Ritual Genital Mutilation *30*

APPLICATIONS
Preventing Vaginitis *35*
Breast Self-Examination *41*
Coping with Menstrual Discomfort *51*

C H A P T E R

3 Male Sexual Anatomy and Physiology *57*

Chapter Outline *57*

Did You Know That . . . ? *58*

The Male Sex Organs *58*

External Sex Organs *58*

Internal Sex Organs *61*

Diseases of the Urogenital System *65*

Urethritis *65*

Cancer of the Testes *65*

Disorders of the Prostate *66*

Male Sexual Functions *68*

Erection **68**

Spinal Reflexes and Sexual Response *69*

Ejaculation *71*

APPLICATIONS
Self-Examination of the Testes *66*

4 Sexual Response and Behavior 77

Chapter Outline   77

Did You Know That . . . ?   78

Making Sense of Sex: The Role of the Senses in Sexual Arousal   78

Vision: The Better to See You With   78

Smell: Does the Nose Know Best?   78

The Skin Senses: Sex as a Touching Experience   79

Taste: On Savory Sex   79

Hearing: The Better to Hear You With   80

Aphrodisiacs: Of Spanish Flies and Rhino Horns   80

Psychoactive Drugs   81

Sex Hormones: Do They "Goad" Us into Sex?   82

Sex Hormones and Sexual Behavior   82

The Sexual Response Cycle   83

Excitement Phase   84

Plateau Phase   84

Orgasmic Phase   85

Resolution Phase   87

Kaplan's Three Stages of Sexual Response: An Alternative Model   88

Controversies About Orgasm   88

Multiple Orgasms   88

How Many Kinds of Orgasms Do Women Have?   89

The G-Spot   90

Sexual Behavior   90

Solitary Sexual Behavior   91

Sex with Others   96

A WORLD OF DIVERSITY
Sociocultural Factors and Oral Sex   98

APPLICATIONS
Advantages and Disadvantages of Various Positions of Sexual Intercourse   104

5 Gender Identity and Gender Roles 109

Chapter Outline   109

Did You Know That . . . ?   110

Prenatal Sexual Differentiation   110

The Role of Sex Hormones in Sexual Differentiation   111

Descent of the Testes and the Ovaries   112

Sex Chromosomal Abnormalities   113

Prenatal Sexual Differentiation of the Brain   113

Gender Identity   113

Nature and Nurture in Gender Identity   113

Hermaphroditism   113

Transsexualism   116

Gender Roles and Stereotypes   118

Sexism   120

Gender Differences: *Vive la Différence or Vive la Similarité?*   120

Differences in Cognitive Abilities   120

Differences in Personality   121

On Becoming a Man or a Woman: Gender Typing   122

Biological Perspectives   122

Cross-Cultural Perspectives   123

Psychological Perspectives   124

Psychological Androgyny: The More Traits, the Merrier?   126

Psychological Androgyny, Psychological Well-Being, and Personal Development   127

Psychological Androgyny and Sexual Behavior   128

A WORLD OF DIVERSITY
Machismo/Marianismo Stereotypes and Hispanic Culture   119

APPLICATIONS
Challenging Gender Roles in Sexual Behavior   126

6 Attraction and Love 133

Chapter Outline   133

Did You Know That . . . ?   134

Attraction   135

Physical Attractiveness: How Important Is Looking Good?   135

The Matching Hypothesis: Who Is "Right" for You?   141

Similarity in Attitudes: Do Opposites Attract?   142

Reciprocity: If You Like Me, You Must Have Excellent Judgment   143

Love   143

The Greek Heritage   143

Romantic Love in Contemporary Western Culture   144

Contemporary Models of Love: Dare Science Intrude?   145

A WORLD OF DIVERSITY
Wide-Eyed with . . . Beauty? 138
Gender Differences in Preferences in Mates Across 37
Cultures 141

APPLICATIONS
Coping with Loneliness 150

CHAPTER

7 Relationships, Intimacy, and Communication 155

Chapter Outline 155

Did You Know That . . . ? 156

The ABC(DE)s of Romantic Relationships 156

The A's—Attraction 156

The B's—Building 157

The C's—Continuation 160

The D's—Deterioration 161

The E's—Ending 161

Intimacy 162

Knowing and Liking Yourself 162

Trusting and Caring 162

Being Honest 163

Making a Commitment 163

Maintaining Individuality When the *I* Becomes *We* 163

Communicating 163

Communication Skills for Enhancing Relationships and Sexual Relations 165

Common Difficulties in Sexual Communication 165

Getting Started 166

Listening to the Other Side 166

Learning About Your Partner's Needs 168

Providing Information 168

Making Requests 169

Handling Impasses 171

A WORLD OF DIVERSITY
Self-Disclosure: East May Be East and West May Be West, But Here, Perhaps, the Twain Do (Almost) Meet 159

APPLICATIONS
How to Improve Date-Seeking Skills 158
Delivering and Receiving Criticism 170

CHAPTER

8 Sexual Orientation 177

Chapter Outline 177

Did You Know That . . . ? 178

Coming to Terms with Terms 178

Classification of Sexual Orientation 179

The Kinsey Continuum 180

Bisexuality 183

Perspectives on Gay Male and Lesbian Sexual Orientations 183

Historical Perspectives 183

Cross-Cultural Perspectives 183

Attitudes Toward Sexual Orientation in Contemporary Society 184

Biological Perspectives 187

Psychological Perspectives 189

Adjustment of Gay Males and Lesbians 192

"Treatment" of Gay Male and Lesbian Sexual Orientations 192

Gay Male and Lesbian Sexual Behavior 194

Gay Lifestyles 194

Lifestyle Differences Between Gay Males and Lesbians 195

Variations in Gay Lifestyles 196

A WORLD OF DIVERSITY
Ethnicity and Sexual Orientation: A Matter of Belonging 185

APPLICATIONS
Coming Out: Coming to Terms with Being Gay 193

CHAPTER

9 Conception, Pregnancy, and Childbirth 201

Chapter Outline 201

Did You Know That . . . ? 202

Infertility and Alternative Ways of Becoming Parents 202

Male Fertility Problems 204

Female Fertility Problems 205

Pregnancy 206

Early Signs of Pregnancy 206

Pregnancy Tests 206

Early Effects of Pregnancy   207

Miscarriage   207

Sex During Pregnancy   207

Psychological Changes During Pregnancy   207

Prenatal Development   208

The Germinal Stage   209

The Embryonic Stage   209

The Fetal Stage   211

Environmental Influences on Prenatal Development   212

Chromosomal and Genetic Abnormalities   217

Childbirth   220

The Stages of Childbirth   220

Methods of Childbirth   222

Birth Problems   224

Anoxia   224

Preterm and Low-Birthweight Children   224

The Postpartum Period   226

Maternal Depression   226

Breast-Feeding Versus Bottle-Feeding   226

Resumption of Sexual Activity   227

A WORLD OF DIVERSITY
Ethnicity and Infant Mortality   225

APPLICATIONS
Optimizing the Chances of Conception   203
Averting Chromosomal and Genetic
Abnormalities   219

CHAPTER

10 Contraception and Abortion   233

Chapter Outline   233

Did You Know That . . . ?   234

Contraception   234

Oral Contraceptives ("the Pill")   234

Norplant   238

Intrauterine Devices (IUDs)   239

The Diaphragm   241

Spermicides   243

The Cervical Cap   244

Condoms   245

Douching   248

Withdrawal (Coitus Interruptus)   248

Fertility Awareness Methods (Rhythm Methods)   248

Sterilization   251

Other Devices   254

Abortion   255

Methods of Abortion   257

A WORLD OF DIVERSITY
Japan's Abortion Agony: In a Country That Prohibits the Pill, Reality Collides with Religion   256

APPLICATIONS
Selecting a Method of Contraception   238

CHAPTER

11 Sexuality Across the Life Span   265

Chapter Outline   265

Did You Know That . . . ?   266

Childhood   266

Infancy (0 to 2 Years)   266

Early Childhood (3 to 8 Years)   267

Preadolescence (9 to 13 Years)   267

Sex Education and Miseducation   268

Adolescence   270

Puberty   270

Sexual Behavior   274

Teenage Pregnancy   276

Adulthood   279

Singlehood   279

Cohabitation: Darling, Would You Be My POSSLQ?   280

Marriage   282

Marital Sexuality   283

Extramarital Sex   286

Divorce   287

Sex in the Later Years   288

Physical Changes   289

Sexual Behavior   291

Sex and Disability   291

Physical Disabilities   292

Psychological Disabilities   294

A WORLD OF DIVERSITY
Ethnic Differences in Premarital Intercourse, Adolescent Use of Contraception, and Resolution of Unwanted Pregnancies   276

APPLICATIONS
Talking to Your Children about Sex   269
Combating Teenage Pregnancy: A Role for the Schools?   278

CHAPTER
12 Sexual Dysfunctions   299

Chapter Outline   *299*

Did You Know That . . . ?   *300*

Types of Sexual Dysfunctions   *300*

Sexual Desire Disorders   *301*

Sexual Arousal Disorders   *302*

Orgasmic Disorders   *303*

Sexual Pain Disorders   *304*

Origins of Sexual Dysfunctions   *306*

Organic Causes   *306*

Psychosocial Causes   *308*

Treatment of Sexual Dysfunctions   *310*

The Masters and Johnson Approach   *311*

The Helen Singer Kaplan Approach   *311*

Treatment of Sexual Desire Disorders   *312*

Treatment of Sexual Arousal Disorders   *312*

Treatment of Orgasmic Disorders   *314*

Treatment of Sexual Pain Disorders   *317*

Evaluation of Sex Therapy   *317*

Biological Treatments of Premature Ejaculation and Erectile Disorder   *318*

A WORLD OF DIVERSITY
Inis Beag and Mangaia—Worlds Apart   *306*

APPLICATIONS
Finding a Qualified Sex Therapist   *319*

CHAPTER
13 Sexually Transmitted Diseases   323

Chapter Outline   *323*

Did You Know That . . . ?   *324*

Bacterial Diseases   *324*

Gonorrhea   *325*

Syphilis   *329*

Chlamydia   *330*

Other Bacterial Diseases   *331*

Vaginal Infections   *332*

Bacterial Vaginosis   *332*

Candidiasis   *332*

Trichomoniasis   *333*

Viral Diseases   *334*

AIDS   *334*

Herpes   *339*

Viral Hepatitis   *341*

Genital Warts   *341*

Ectoparasitic Infestations   *342*

Pediculosis   *342*

Scabies   *343*

A WORLD OF DIVERSITY
Ethnicity and AIDS in the United States   *336*

APPLICATIONS
How HIV Is Not Transmitted   *338*
Preventing AIDS and Other Sexually Transmitted Diseases   *343*

CHAPTER
14 Atypical Sexual Variations   349

Chapter Outline   *349*

Did You Know That . . . ?   *350*

Normal Versus Deviant Sexual Behavior   *350*

The Paraphilias   *350*

Fetishism   *351*

Transvestism   *351*

Exhibitionism   *352*

Obscene Telephone Calling   *354*

Voyeurism   *354*

Sexual Masochism   *355*

Sexual Sadism   *355*

Frotteurism   *357*

Other Paraphilias   *357*

Theoretical Perspectives   *358*

Biological Perspectives   *358*

Psychoanalytic Perspectives   *359*

Learning Perspectives   *360*

Sociological Perspectives   *361*

An Integrated Perspective: The "Lovemap"   *362*

Treatment of the Paraphilias   *362*

Psychotherapy   *362*

Behavior Therapy   *362*

Biochemical Approaches   *363*

A WORLD OF DIVERSITY
Nymphomania, Satyriasis, and the Sexual Double Standard   *359*

APPLICATIONS
How to Respond to an Exhibitionist   *353*

15 Sexual Coercion   367

Chapter Outline   *367*

Did You Know That . . . ?   *368*

Rape   *368*

Incidence of Rape   *368*

Types of Rapes   *369*

Social Attitudes and Myths That Encourage Rape   *371*

Sociocultural Factors in Rape   *371*

Psychological Characteristics of Rapists   *373*

Adjustment of Rape Survivors   *374*

Treatment of Rape Survivors   *376*

Sexual Abuse of Children   *378*

What Is Child Sexual Abuse?   *378*

Patterns of Abuse   *379*

Pedophilia   *380*

Incest   *381*

Effects of Child Sexual Abuse   *382*

Treatment of Survivors of Child Sexual Abuse   *384*

Treatment of Rapists and Child Molesters   *384*

Sexual Harassment   *385*

A WORLD OF DIVERSITY
Rape-Prone and Rape-Free Societies: Whither the United States?   *372*

APPLICATIONS
If You Are Raped . . .   *375*
Preventing Rape   *376*
Preventing Child Sexual Abuse   *383*
Resisting Sexual Harrassment   *386*

16 Commercial Sex   391

Chapter Outline   *391*

Did You Know That . . . ?   *392*

Prostitution   *392*

Types of Female Prostitutes   *393*

Characteristics of Female Prostitutes   *395*

Customers of Female Prostitutes   *396*

Male Prostitution   *397*

HIV, AIDS, and Prostitution   *398*

Pornography and Obscenity   *400*

What Is Pornographic?   *400*

Prevalence and Use of Pornography   *401*

Pornography and Sexual Coercion   *402*

Sex in Advertising   *405*

Advertising and Gender-Role Stereotypes   *406*

A WORLD OF DIVERSITY
'Tis a Puzzlement: On AIDS and Prostitution in Thailand   *399*

Glossary   *409*

References   *420*

Name Index   *437*

Subject Index   *442*

Preface

There are more things in heaven and earth, Horatio,
Than are dreamt of in your philosophy.

Hamlet, William Shakespeare

There are indeed more kinds of people in this world and more ways in which people experience their sexuality than most of us might imagine. Human sexuality may be intimately related to human biology, but it is embedded within the sociocultural fabric of human society. For this reason, a core theme of *Essentials of Human Sexuality* is its multicultural perspective. In this text, students learn to examine a broad view of sexual experience and the latest scientific findings in the field, and are encouraged to think about their own thoughts and perceptions about sexuality and sexual experience.

Essentials of Human Sexuality includes a built-in study system that is designed so that students may master difficult terms and fully understand key concepts. Each chapter ends with a carefully programmed, active review that contains unique prompts to help students prepare for class tests. The text is specifically designed to be accessible and useful, and, we hope, it will be compelling.

Themes of the Text

The four main themes that thread throughout *Essentials of Human Sexuality* are the rich diversity found in gender roles, sexual attitudes, and sexual behaviors and customs; critical thinking; making responsible sexual decisions; and sexual health.

Diversity

The majority of colleges and universities have as their mission to broaden students' perspectives so that they will appreciate and tolerate human diversity.

The United States is a nation of hundreds of different ethnic and religious groups, many of whom endorse culturally distinctive beliefs about appropriate gender roles for men and women and about sexual practices and customs.

Diversity is even greater within the global village of the world's more than 200 nations and each nation's distinctive subcultures. This text incorporates a multicultural, multiethnic perspective that reflects the diversity of sexual experience in our society and around the world and expands a student's understanding of the range of cultural differences in sexual attitudes and behavior. Discussion of diversity encourages respect for people holding distinctly diverse beliefs and attitudes. The book encourages students to question what is appropriate for women and men in terms of social roles and sexual conduct in light of cultural traditions and standards.

Critical Thinking

As we approach the new millennium, colleges and universities are encouraging students to become critical thinkers. Today's students are inundated with information about gender and sexuality so much so that it is difficult to sort out truth from fiction. Not only do politicians, theologians, and community leaders influence our gender- and sex-related attitudes and behaviors, but newspapers, television programs, and other media also brim with features about gender roles and issues concerning human sexuality.

Critical thinking means being skeptical of information that is presented in print or uttered by authority figures or celebrities. Critical thinking requires thoughtful analysis and probing the claims and arguments of others in light of evidence. Moreover, it requires a willingness to challenge conventional wisdom and common knowledge that many of us take for granted. It means scrutinizing definitions of terms and evaluating the premises or assumptions that underlie arguments.

"Thinking Critically About Human Sexuality" is addressed in a major section in Chapter 1. Throughout the book we continue to raise issues that demand critical thinking. These issues are intended to stimulate student interest in analyzing and evaluating their beliefs and attitudes toward gender roles and sexuality against accumulated scientific evidence.

Responsible Sexual Decision Making

Students are also encouraged to make responsible sexual decisions. There are psychological and physical dangers in "going with the flow" or being passive about one's sexuality. We do not encourage students to be sexually active (such a decision is personal). On the other hand, we do encourage students to actively make their own sexual decisions on the basis of accurate information.

Decision making is deeply intertwined with our sexual experience. For example, we need to decide:

Whom to date
How and when to become sexually intimate
Whether to practice contraception
Which contraception methods to use
How to protect ourselves against AIDS and other sexually transmitted diseases

Throughout the book students are provided with the information they need to make responsible decisions about their physical health, the gender roles they will enact, sexual practices, birth control, and prevention of sexually transmitted diseases.

Sexual Health

The text emphasizes issues relating to sexual health. There is extensive coverage of such topics as HIV/AIDS and other STDs, innovations in contraception and reproductive technologies, breast cancer, menstrual distress, and diseases that affect the reproductive tract. The text encourages students to take an active role in health promotion. For example, it includes applications that will help students examine their breasts and testes for abnormalities, reduce the risk of HIV infection, and cope with menstrual discomfort.

Coverage

Essentials of Human Sexuality provides a comprehensive review of the latest scientific findings in the field. It helps students acquire a broader view of human sexual experience by examining multiple perspectives on human sexuality—historical, biological, psychological, cultural, and sociological.

The Core of the Text

The text covers topics relating to human sexuality including research methods, sexual anatomy and physiology, sexual arousal and behavior, gender roles, attraction and love, intimate relationships and communication, sexual orientation, conception and contraception, prenatal development and childbirth, sexual behavior across the life span, sexual dysfunctions and sex therapy, sexually transmitted diseases, atypical variations in sexual behavior, sexual coercion, and commercial sex.

The text also emphasizes pressing issues that are likely to confront or concern today's students. These include sexual harrassment, date rape, interfaith couples, contraception, and the threat of AIDS.

Features

A World of Diversity

The feature A World of Diversity highlights the rich variety of human sexual customs and practices in our own society and around the world. Viewing human sexuality in a multicultural context helps students better understand how cultural beliefs, values, and attitudes can influence the expression of sexuality. Students may come to understand that their partners who may not share the same ethnic or religious heritages may feel differently than they do about sexual intimacy. Among many subject matters this feature includes are: "Around the World in 80 Ways— A Preview," "*Machismo/Marianismo* Stereotypes and Hispanic Culture," "Ritual Genital Mutilation," and " 'Tis a Puzzlement: On AIDS and Prostitution in Thailand."

Applications

Hands-on applications give students concrete advice for enhancing their sexual health and sexual experience. Useful information that is covered in this text includes "Breast Self-Examination," "Preventing Rape," "Preventing AIDS and Other Sexually Transmitted Diseases," "Self-Examination of the Testes," and "Talking to Your Children About Sex."

Learning Aids

Perhaps more than anything else a textbook is a teaching tool—a device for presenting material in a way that stimulates learning and critical thinking. *Essentials of Human Sexuality* was designed to maximize this goal by means of such pedagogical aids as the following:

Chapter Outlines

Each chapter begins with an outline that organizes the subject matter for the student. Heads were created to be succinct and to promote student interest in the topics they address.

"Did You Know That . . . ?"

Every chapter begins with a series of queries regarding sexual knowledge preceded by "Did You Know That . . . ?" For instance, "Did you know that the graham cracker came into being as a means to help young men control their sexual appetites?" "Did you know that opposites do not usually attract—we are more likely to be attracted to people who share our views and tastes than to people who disagree with them?" And so on.

This feature lays the groundwork for basics within a chapter's subject matter and at the same time erases some of the myths that have built up around the subject matter.

Running Glossary

Research shows that most students do not make use of glossaries in the endmatter of textbooks. Searching for the meaning of a term is often a cumbersome task and distracting, taking the reader away from the subject matter. This textbook has a running glossary—key terms are boldfaced within the text and defined in the margins where they appear. Meanings are immediately accessible and the reader can maintain concentration on the material.

Chapter Review (Interactive Summaries)

Chapter Review sections are, in effect, interactive summaries. They are carefully programmed to prompt students' memories of the key points covered in each chapter. They foster active learning by having students fill in missing information as they read. Prompts help students to complete the items.

Posttest with Answer Key

Most professors use multiple-choice questions in their assessment of student's mastery of a subject. For this reason each chapter concludes with a multiple-choice test that allows students to check their knowledge following the Chapter Review. This unique study system is designed to help students acquire complex terms and fully understand key concepts.

Acknowledgments

The authors owe a great debt of gratitude to the many researchers and scholars whose contributions to the body of knowledge in the field of human sexuality is represented in these pages. Underscoring the interdisciplinary nature of the field, we have drawn upon the work of scholars in such fields as psychology, sociology, medicine, anthropology, theology, and philosophy, to name a few. We are also indebted to the many researchers who have generously allowed us to quote from their work and reprint tabular material representing their findings.

Spencer A. Rathus
Jeffrey S. Nevid
Lois Fichner-Rathus

CHAPTER 1

What Is Human Sexuality?

What Is Human Sexuality?
Thinking Critically About Human Sexuality

Perspectives on Human Sexuality
The Historical Perspective
The Biological Perspective
The Cross-Cultural Perspective
Psychological Perspectives
Sociocultural Perspectives

Research Methods in Human Sexuality
Populations and Samples
Methods of Observation

Chapter Review

Chapter Quiz

A World of Diversity
Around the World in Eighty Ways—A Preview

- In ancient Greece, a mature man would take a sexual interest in an adolescent boy, often with the blessing of the boy's parents?
- The first illustrated sex manual was produced in China more than 2,000 years ago?
- The Hindus believed that sexual fulfillment was one way to become reincarnated at a higher level of existence?
- The graham cracker came into being as a means to help young men control their sexual appetites?
- You could study the sexual behavior of millions of Americans and still not obtain an accurate picture of the sexual behavior of the general U.S. population?
- Some sex researchers have engaged in "swinging" with the people they have studied?
- Masters and Johnson created a transparent artificial penis containing photographic equipment to study female sexual response?
- Regular churchgoers report higher levels of sexual satisfaction?

We are about to embark on the study of human sexuality. But why, you may wonder, do we need to *study* human sexuality? Isn't sex something to *do* rather than to *talk about?* Isn't sex a natural function? Don't we learn what we need to know from personal experience or from our parents or our friends?

Yes, we can learn how our bodies respond to sexual stimulation—what turns us on and what turns us off—through personal experience. Personal experience teaches us little, however, about the biological processes that bring about sexual response and orgasm. Nor does experience inform us about the variations in sexual behavior that exist around the world, or in the neighborhood. Experience does not prepare us to recognize the signs of sexually transmitted diseases or to evaluate the risks of pregnancy. Nor does experience help us deal with most sexual problems or dysfunctions.

Concerns about AIDS and unwanted teenage pregnancies have focused greater attention today on the importance of sex education. Many children receive some form of sex education as early as elementary school. You may know more about human sexuality than your parents or grandparents did at your age, or do today. But how much do you really know? What, for example, happens inside your body when you are sexually stimulated? What causes erection or vaginal lubrication? How do our sexual responsiveness and interests change as we age? Why does the United States have the highest incidence of rape in the industrialized world?

These are just a few of the issues we will explore in this book. We also expect to debunk some common but erroneous ideas about sex that you may have picked up before you began this course. Before we proceed further, let us define our subject. ■

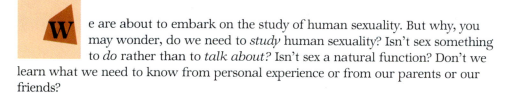 What Is Human Sexuality?

What *is* human sexuality? This is not a trick question. Consider the meaning, or rather meanings, of the word *sex.* One use of the term *sex,* then, refers to our **gender,** or state of being male or female. The word *sex* (or *sexual*) is also used to refer to anatomic structures, called sex (or sexual) organs, that play a role in reproduction or sexual pleasure. We may

Gender
One's personal, social, and legal status as male or female.

Coitus
(co-it-us or co-EET-us). Sexual intercourse.

Erotic
Arousing sexual feelings or desires. (From the Greek word for love, *eros.*)

Gender identity
The psychological sense of being male or female.

Gender roles
Complex clusters of ways in which males and females are expected to behave within a given culture.

Human sexuality
The ways in which we experience and express ourselves as sexual beings.

also speak of sex when referring to physical activities involving our sex organs for purposes of reproduction or pleasure: masturbation, hugging, kissing, **coitus,** and so on. Sex also relates to **erotic** feelings, experiences, or desires, such as sexual fantasies and thoughts, sexual urges, or feelings of sexual attraction to another person. We will use the term *gender* in this text to refer to the state of being male or female, as in **gender identity** and **gender roles.**

Human sexuality is defined as the ways in which we experience and express ourselves as sexual beings. Our awareness of ourselves as females or males is part of our sexuality, as is the capacity we have for erotic experiences and responses.

Human sexuality, like biology, psychology, and sociology, is also a *science*. It is an interdisciplinary enterprise that draws upon the scientific expertise of anthropologists, biologists, medical researchers, sociologists, and psychologists, to name but a few of the professional groups involved in the field. These disciplines all have contributions to make, since sexual behavior reflects our biological capabilities, our psychological characteristics, and social and cultural influences.

People's sexual attitudes, experiences, and behaviors are shaped to a large extent by their cultural traditions and beliefs. Consider some of the fascinating findings in this chapter's World of Diversity feature.

Thinking Critically About Human Sexuality

We are inundated with so much information about sex that it is difficult to separate truth from fiction. Newspapers, TV shows, and popular books and magazines contain features about sex that contradict one another, contain half-truths, or draw misleading conclusions. A scientific approach to human sexuality encourages people to think critically about the false claims and findings that are presented as truths.

To help students evaluate claims, arguments, and widely held beliefs, most colleges encourage *critical thinking*. One aspect of critical thinking is skepticism—not taking things for granted. It means being skeptical of things that are presented in print, uttered by authority figures or celebrities, or passed along by friends. Another aspect of critical thinking is thoughtful analysis and probing of claims and arguments. Critical thinking requires willingness to challenge the "common sense" that many of us take for granted. It means scrutinizing definitions of terms and evaluating the premises of arguments and their logic. It also means finding *reasons* to support your beliefs, rather than relying on feelings. When people think critically, they maintain open minds. They suspend their beliefs until they have obtained and evaluated the evidence.

Perspectives on Human Sexuality

Human sexuality is a complex topic. No single theory or perspective can capture all its nuances. In this book we explore human sexuality from many perspectives. In this section we introduce a number of perspectives—historical, biological, cross-cultural, psychological, and sociocultural.

The Historical Perspective

History places our sexual behavior in context. It informs us as to whether our sexual behavior reflects trends that have been with us through the millennia or the customs of a particular era.

Prehistoric Sexuality: From Female Idols to Phallic Worship

Information about life among our Stone Age ancestors is drawn largely from cave drawings, stone artifacts, and the customs of modern-day preliterate peoples. From such sources, historians and anthropologists infer a prehistoric division of labor. By and large,

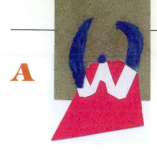 

A WORLD OF DIVERSITY

AROUND THE WORLD IN EIGHTY WAYS—A PREVIEW

Like other aspects of human behavior, sexual beliefs and behaviors vary widely around the world. The United States alone is a nation of hundreds of different ethnic and religious groups, which vary in their sexual customs, attitudes, and beliefs. This diversity extends to the entire "global village" of the world's nearly 200 nations and to each nation's own distinctive subcultures.

The World of Diversity features that appear throughout this text explore the rich variety of sexual expression found worldwide. Seeing sexuality in contexts other than our own can help us understand the role of a culture's beliefs, values, and attitudes on our own and others' expressions of sexuality. It can help us understand why our partners, who may not share the same ethnic or religious heritage, may have different beliefs about sexual intimacy. Exploring diversity can also help us understand cultural differences related to gender, sexual orientation, sexual attraction, sexual jealousy, premarital sex, teenage pregnancy, and risks of sexually transmitted diseases.

People in some societies believe, for instance, that a brother and sister who eat at the same table are engaging in a mildly erotic type of act. The practice is therefore forbidden (Davenport, 1977). In contemporary Islamic societies, female sexuality is often viewed as dangerous. If women's behavior and attire are not kept under strict control, they can be "fatal attractions" for men (Kammeyer et al., 1990). What is sexually arousing, too, varies from culture to culture. Among the Abkhasians in the southern part of what used to be the Soviet Union, men regard the female armpit as highly arousing. A woman's armpits are, therefore, a sight for her husband alone (Kammeyer et al., 1990).

Of course, one glaring reason for today's heightened interest in understanding sexuality in a broader perspective is the worldwide AIDS epidemic. Any effort to end this scourge requires that we open our eyes to cultural attitudes and traditions that may increase the risk of transmission of the disease.

If we take a quick tour of the world of diversity within our own borders and beyond, we find that:

- Kissing is practiced nearly universally as a form of petting in the United States, but it is unpopular in Japan and unknown among some cultures in Africa and South America.
- Some societies encourage sexual experimentation and even sexual intercourse among children and adolescents, while others punish any form of childhood sexual play.
- Marital fidelity is a prominent value in Western culture, but among some people of the Arctic it is considered hospitable for a man to offer his wife to a visiting tribesman.
- In the United States, there remains a tendency to blame the victims of crimes—especially rape victims—rather than the perpetrators. In the strongly patriarchal society of Islamic Pakistan, however, the so-called Hudood Ordinance has actually resulted in *prison sentences* for some women who have brought rape charges against men. Hudood, you see, grants more credibility to the testimony of men than to that of women. An accused man may claim that any sexual contact between himself and the woman making the accusations was consensual, and the court will be inclined to believe him. Women too are also frequently prevented from testifying in court. The result has been that some women who bring charges of rape are sometimes prosecuted for adultery and jailed if found guilty, while their assailants go free (Schork, 1990).
- Sex was typically considered "indecent and unmentionable" in

men hunted for game. Women nurtured children and gathered edible plants and nuts, and crabs and other marine life that wandered along the shore or swam in shallow waters.

Art produced in the Stone Age, some 20,000 years ago, suggests the worship of women's ability to bear children and perpetuate the species (Fichner-Rathus, 1995). Primitive statues and cave drawings portray women with large, pendulous breasts, rounded hips, and prominent sex organs. Most theorists regard the figurines as fertility symbols.

As the ice sheets of the last ice age retreated (about 11,000 B.C.) and the climate warmed, hunters and gatherers became farmers and herders. Villages sprang up around fields. Men tended the livestock. Women became farmers. As people grew aware of the male role in re-

Russia, according to Kon (1995), "a subject only for the degenerate underground." However, since the collapse of the Soviet Union, sex has apparently been escaping into the mainstream of Russian life. In today's Russia, newspapers and television regularly cover prostitution and pornography as well as the traditional bus accidents (Schillinger, 1995). As sex has grabbed the Russian imagination, the incidences of premarital sex and rape are also apparently on the rise (Kon, 1995).

- Although U.S. government officials may occasionally voice public condemnation of premarital sexual relations, the majority of people in the United States engage in them without fear of government reprisal. In China, however, where the results of a national survey showed that about half of the population engages in premarital relations, a male college student was expelled from a Beijing university when it became known that he had engaged in premarital sexual relations (Southerland, 1990). Other students report that the punishment was typical.

- Perhaps in response to feelings of guilt or remorse, many Japanese women who have abortions place miniature stone statues known as *mizuko-jizo* in Buddhist temples in memory of their aborted fetuses. They sometimes decorate the statues with bibs or little hats and surround them with little stuffed animals, baby food, and pacifiers—all in the belief that it keeps the souls of their aborted fetuses warm and entertained (Bumiller, 1990).

- The United States has its romantic Valentine's Day, but Japan has a blatantly erotic day: Christmas Eve. (Yes, Christmas Eve.) Whereas Christmas Eve is a time of religious devotion in many Western nations, it has become a time of sexual devotion in Japan. On Christmas Eve every single person must have a date—one that includes an overnight visit (Reid, 1990). The cost of a typical Christmas Eve date exceeds $1,000. Where do Tokyo singles like to go before their overnight visits? Tokyo Disneyland.

Kissing. Kissing is a nearly universal form of light petting in the United States, but it is unpopular in Japan and unknown in many African and South American cultures.

Phallic worship
Worship of the penis as a symbol of generative power.

Phallic symbols
Images of the penis.

Incest taboo
The prohibition against intercourse and reproduction among close blood relatives.

production, **phallic worship** sprang into being. The penis was glorified in art as a plough, an ax, or a sword. **Phallic symbols** played roles in religious ceremonies in ancient Egypt. Ancient Greek art revered phalluses, rendering them sometimes as rings and sometimes as necklaces. Some phalluses were given wings, suggesting the power ascribed to them. In ancient Rome, a large phallus was carried like a float in a parade honoring Venus, the goddess of love.

The **incest taboo** may have been the first human taboo (Tannahill, 1980). All human societies apparently have some form of incest taboo (Ember & Ember, 1990). Yet, brother–sister marriages were permitted among the rulers of ancient Egypt and among the royal families of the Incas and of Hawaii, even though they were generally prohibited among commoners.

The Ancient Hebrews

The ancient Hebrews viewed sex as a fulfilling experience intended to fulfill the divine injunction to "be fruitful and multiply." Childlessness and the development of a repulsive abnormality, such as a boil, were grounds for divorce. Male–male and female–female sexual behavior were strongly condemned. But sex within marriage was believed to strengthen marital bonds and solidify the family.

Women among the ancient Hebrews were expected to be good wives and mothers. A wife was considered the property of her husband. A wife could be stoned to death for adultery. She might also have had to share her husband with his secondary wives and concubines.

The Ancient Greeks

The classical or golden age of ancient Greece lasted for about 200 years, from about 500 B.C. to 300 B.C. Within this relatively short span lived the philosophers Socrates, Plato, and Aristotle; the playwrights Aristophanes, Aeschylus, and Sophocles; the natural scientist Archimedes; and the lawgiver Solon. Like the Hebrews, the Greeks valued family life. The Greeks expressed sexual interests openly. They admired the well-developed body and enjoyed nude wrestling among men in the arena. Erotic encounters and off-color jokes characterized the plays of Aristophanes and other playwrights. The Greeks held that the healthy mind must dwell in a healthy body. They cultivated muscle and movement along with mind.

Three aspects of Greek sexuality are of particular interest to our study of sexual practices in the ancient world: male–male sexual behavior, pederasty, and prostitution. The Greeks viewed men and women as **bisexual.** Male–male *sex* was deemed normal. However, only a few male–male *relationships,* such as relationships between soldiers and between adolescents and older men, received the stamp of social approval.

Pederasty means love of boys. Greek men might take on an adolescent male as a lover and pupil. Families were generally pleased if their adolescent sons attracted socially prominent mentors.

Prostitution flourished at every level of society. Prostitutes ranged from refined **courtesans** to **concubines** (slaves). Courtesans could play musical instruments, dance, engage in witty repartee, or discuss the latest political crisis. They were also skilled in the arts of love. No social stigma was attached to visiting a courtesan. Their clients included philosophers, playwrights, politicians, and generals.

Women in general held a low social status in society. The women of Athens had no more legal or political rights than slaves. They were subject to the authority of their male next-of-kin before marriage and to their husbands afterwards. They received no formal education and were consigned most of the time to women's quarters in their homes. All in all, the women of the ancient world were treated as *chattels*—property.

The Ancient Romans

Much is made of the sexual excesses of the Roman emperors and ruling families. The emperor Caligula sponsored orgies. Sexual excesses were found more often among the upper classes of palace society than among average Romans, however. Unlike their counterparts in ancient Greece, Romans viewed male–male sexual behavior as a threat to the integrity of the Roman family. Thus, it was not held in favor. Although Roman women were more likely than their Greek counterparts to share their husbands' social lives, they still were considered to be the property of their husbands.

The Early Christians

Early Christian views on sexuality were largely shaped by Saint Paul and the church fathers in the first century and by Saint Augustine in the latter part of the fourth century. The early Christians sought to restrict sex to marriage. They saw temptations of the flesh as distractions from spiritual devotion to God. Paul preached that celibacy was closer to the Christian ideal than marriage.

Christians, like Jews before them, demanded virginity of brides. Masturbation and prostitution were condemned as sinful. Early Christians taught that men should love their

Bisexual

Sexually responsive to either gender. (From the Latin *bi-,* meaning "two.")

Pederasty

Sexual love of boys. (From the Greek *paidos,* meaning "boy.")

Courtesan

A prostitute—especially the mistress of a noble or wealthy man. (From Italian roots meaning "court lady.")

Concubine

A secondary wife, usually of inferior legal and social status. (From Latin roots meaning "lying with.")

wives with restraint, not passion. The goal of procreation should govern sexual behavior—the intellect should rule the flesh. Divorce was outlawed. Masturbation, male–male sexual behavior, female–female sexual behavior, oral–genital contact, anal intercourse—all were viewed as abominations in the eyes of God.

Islam Islam, the dominant religion in the Middle East, was founded by the Prophet Muhammad. Muhammad was born in Mecca, in what is now Saudi Arabia, in about A.D. 570. The Islamic tradition treasures marriage and sexual fulfillment in marriage. Premarital intercourse invites shame and social condemnation. In some fundamentalist Islamic states, it incurs the death penalty.

The family is the backbone of Islamic society. Celibacy is frowned upon (Ahmed, 1991). Muhammad decreed that marriage represents the only road to virtue (Minai, 1981). Islamic tradition permits a sexual double standard, however. Men may take up to four wives, but women are permitted only one husband. Public social interactions between men and women are severely restricted. In traditional Islamic cultures, social dancing between the genders is shunned. Women are expected to keep their heads and faces veiled in public and to avoid all contact, even a handshake, with men other than their husbands.

The Far East In the cultures of the Far East, sexuality was akin to spirituality. To the Taoist masters of China, sex was a sacred duty. It was a form of worship that was believed to lead toward immortality. Sex was to be performed well and often if one was to achieve harmony with nature.

The Chinese culture was the first to produce a detailed sex manual, which came into use about 200 years before the birth of Jesus. The man was expected to extend intercourse as long as possible, thereby absorbing more of his wife's natural essence, or *yin*. Yin would enhance his own masculine essence, or *yang*. Taoists believed that it was wasteful for a man to "spill his seed." Masturbation, acceptable for women, was ruled out for men. The "good wife," like her Western counterparts, was limited largely to the domestic roles of child rearing and homemaking.

The ancient Hindus of India cultivated sexual pleasure as a spiritual ideal. From the fifth century onward, temples show sculptures of gods, heavenly nymphs, and ordinary people in erotic poses (Gupta, 1994). Hindu sexual practices were codified in a sex manual, the *Kama Sutra*. The *Kama Sutra* illustrates sexual positions, some of which would challenge a contortionist. It holds recipes for alleged aphrodisiacs. This manual remains the most influential sex manual ever produced. It is believed to have been written by the Hindu sage Vatsyayana sometime between the third and fifth centuries A.D., at about the time that Christianity was taking shape in the West as an organized religion.

An Illustration from the *Kama Sutra*. The *Kama Sutra*, an Indian sex manual believed to have been written sometime between the third and fifth centuries A.D., contains graphic illustrations of sexual techniques and practices.

The Hindus believed that sex was a religious duty, not a source of shame or guilt. In the Hindu doctrine of *karma* (the passage or transmigration of souls from one place to another), sexual fulfillment was regarded as one way to become reincarnated at a higher level of existence. Indian society grew more restrictive toward sexuality after about A.D. 1000 (Tannahill, 1980).

The Protestant Reformation   During the Reformation, Martin Luther (1483–1546) and other Christian reformers such as John Calvin (1509–1564) split off from the Roman Catholic Church and formed their own sects, which led to the development of the modern Protestant denominations. Luther disputed many Roman Catholic doctrines on sexuality. He believed that priests should be allowed to marry and rear children. Calvin rejected the Roman church's position that sex in marriage was permissible only for the purpose of procreation. To Calvin, sex strengthened the marriage bond and helped relieve the stresses of everyday life. The Protestant Reformation encouraged a more accepting view of sexuality, although it maintained strict adherence to the belief that sex was permissible only in the context of marriage.

Shaping the Present: From Repression to Revolution   Early settlers brought to the New World the religious teachings that had dominated Western thought and culture for centuries. Whatever their differences, each religion stressed the ideal of family life and viewed sex outside of marriage as immoral or sinful. A woman's place, by and large, was in the home and in the fields. Not until 1833, when Oberlin opened its doors to women, were women permitted to attend college in the United States. Not until the twentieth century did women gain the right to vote.

In this century, social change has swept through Western culture at a dizzying pace. Sexual behaviors and attitudes that would have been unthinkable a couple of generations ago—such as cohabitation ("living together")—have become commonplace. The social barriers that had restricted women's roles have largely broken down.

The middle and later parts of the nineteenth century are generally called the Victorian period, named after Queen Victoria of England. Victoria assumed the throne in 1837 and ruled until her death in 1901. Her name has become virtually synonymous with sexual repression. Victorian society in Europe and the United States, on the surface at least, was prim and proper. Even the legs of pianos were draped with cloth for the sake of modesty. Many women viewed sex as a marital duty to be performed for procreation or to satisfy their husbands' cravings. Consider the following quotation:

> I am happy now that Charles calls on my bed chamber less frequently than of old. As it is, I now endure but two calls a week and when I hear his steps outside my door I lie down on my bed, close my eyes, open my legs and think of England.
>
> (Attributed to Alice, Lady Hillingdon, wife of the second Baron Hillingdon)

Women were assumed not to experience sexual desires or pleasures. "I would say," observed Dr. William Acton (1814–1875), an influential English physician, in 1857, "that the majority of women (happily for society) are not much troubled with sexual feeling of any kind."

It was widely believed among medical authorities in England and the United States that sex drains the man of his natural vitality. Physicians thus recommended that intercourse be practiced infrequently, perhaps once a month or so. The Reverend Sylvester Graham (1794–1851) preached that ejaculation deprived men of the "vital fluids" they need to maintain health and vitality. Graham preached against "wasting the seed" by masturbation or frequent marital intercourse. (How frequent was frequent? In Graham's view, intercourse more than once a month could dangerously deplete the man's vital energies.) Graham recommended that young men control their sexual appetites by adopting a diet of simple foods based on whole-grain flours. To this day, his name is identified with a type of cracker he developed for this purpose in the 1830s, the graham cracker, derived from unbolted wheat (graham flour).

The Foundations of the Scientific Study of Sexuality   Against this backdrop of sexual repression, scientists and scholars first began to approach sexuality as an area of legitimate scientific study. An early important contributor to the science of human sexuality was the English physician Havelock Ellis (1859–1939). Ellis compiled a veritable encyclopedia of sexuality: *Studies in the Psychology of Sex*. Ellis challenged the prevailing view by arguing that sexual desires in women were natural and healthy. He argued that a gay male or lesbian sexual orientation was a naturally occurring variation within the spectrum of normal sexuality, and not an aberration.

Sexologist

A person who engages in the scientific study of sexual behavior.

Another influential **sexologist,** the German psychiatrist Richard von Krafft-Ebing (1840–1902), described individuals with sexual deviations in his book *Psychopathia Sexualis*. His writings contain vivid descriptions of deviations ranging from sadomasochism (sexual gratification through inflicting or receiving pain) and bestiality (sex with animals) to yet more bizarre and frightening forms, such as necrophilia (intercourse with dead people). Krafft-Ebing viewed sexual deviations as mental diseases that could be studied and perhaps treated by medical science.

At about the same time, a Viennese physician, Sigmund Freud (1856–1939), was developing a theory of personality that has had an enormous influence on modern culture and science. Freud believed that the sex drive is our principal motivating force.

Alfred Kinsey (1894–1956), an Indiana University zoologist, conducted the first large-scale studies of sexual behavior in the 1930s and 1940s. The results of his surveys were published in two volumes, *Sexual Behavior in the Human Male* (1948) and *Sexual Behavior in the Human Female* (1953). The publication of these books unleashed a torrent of criticism. A congressional committee in the 1950s went so far as to claim that Kinsey's work undermined the moral fiber of the nation, rendering it more vulnerable to a Communist takeover (Gebhard, 1976). Even so, Kinsey and his colleagues made sex a scientifically respectable field of study and helped lay the groundwork for greater openness in talking about sex.

The Sexual Revolution   The period of the mid-1960s to the mid-1970s is often referred to as the *sexual revolution*. Dramatic changes occurred in U.S. sexual attitudes and practices during the "Swinging Sixties." There was a major social upheaval, not only in sexual behavior, but also in science, politics, fashion, music, art, and cinema. The so-called Woodstock generation, disheartened by commercialism and the Vietnam War, tuned in (to rock music on the radio), turned on (to drugs), and dropped out (of mainstream society). The heat was on between the hippies and the hardhats. Long hair became the mane of men. Bell-bottomed jeans flared out. Films became sexually explicit. Hard rock music bellowed the message of rebellion and revolution.

The sexual revolution gained momentum from the war (in Vietnam), the bomb (fear of the nuclear bomb), the pill (the introduction of the birth-control pill), and the tube (TV, that is). The pill enabled people to engage in recreational or casual sex, rather than procreative sex (Asbell, 1995). Pop psychology movements, like the Human Potential Movement of the 1960s and 1970s (the "Me Decade"), spread the message that people should get in touch with and express their genuine feelings, including their sexual feelings. "Doing your own thing" became one catchphrase. "If it feels right, go with it" became another.

Popular books encouraged people to explore their sexuality. Film scenes of lovemaking became so commonplace that the movie rating system was introduced to alert parents. Protests against the Vietnam War and racial discrimination spilled over into broader protests against conventional morality and hypocrisy. Traditional prohibitions against drugs, casual sex, and even group sex crumbled. In addition to increased incidence of premarital sex, two other features of the sexual revolution have become permanent parts of our social fabric: the liberation of female sexuality and a greater willingness to discuss sex openly.

The Biological Perspective

The biological perspective focuses on the roles of genes, hormones, the nervous system, and other biological factors in human sexuality. Sex serves the biological function of re-

Are Today's Young People More or Less Liberal in the Expression of Their Sexuality than People in Earlier Generations? Today the threat of AIDS hangs over every sexual encounter. While many young people today are selective in their choice of partners and take precautions to make sex safer, more teenagers are engaging in sexual activity, and at younger ages, than in previous generations.

Sociobiology
The theory that dispositions toward behavior patterns that enhance reproductive success may be genetically transmitted.

Genes
The basic units of heredity, which consist of chromosomal segments of DNA.

production. People are endowed with anatomic structures and physiological capabilities that make sexual behavior possible—and, for most people, pleasurable.

The biology of sex informs us about the mechanisms of reproduction, sexual arousal, and sexual response. The biology of sex teaches that erection occurs when the penis becomes engorged with blood. It teaches that vaginal lubrication is the result of a "sweating" action of the vaginal walls. It teaches that orgasm is a spinal reflex as well as a psychological event.

Some scientists suggest that there is a genetic basis to social behavior, including sexual behavior, among humans and other animals. The theory of **sociobiology** proposes that dispositions toward *behavior* that enhances reproductive success—as well as physical traits that do so—may be transmitted by **genes.** Genes govern sexual maturation and the production of sex hormones. Hormones, in turn, are largely responsible for regulating the sexual behavior of other animal species. We may carry behavioral tendencies that helped our prehistoric ancestors survive and reproduce successfully, even if these traits are no longer adaptive in modern culture (Bjorklund & Kipp, 1996).

To what extent does biology govern sexual behavior? Is sex controlled by biological instincts? Or are psychosocial factors, such as culture, experience, and decision-making ability more important? The sexuality of other species is largely governed by biological processes, but *human* sexuality involves a complex interaction of biological and psychosocial factors. Biology indicates what is possible, and often, what is pleasurable or painful. Biology is not destiny, however. It does not imply what is proper and improper or determine our sexual decisions. Religious tradition, cultural and personal values, and learning and experience guide these decisions.

The Cross-Cultural Perspective

The cross-cultural perspective, like the historical perspective, provides insight into the ways in which cultural beliefs affect sexual behavior and attitudes. Historians are limited in their sources to the eyewitness accounts of others and the shards of information that can be gleaned from fading relics. Anthropologists, however, can observe other cultures firsthand. Interest in the cross-cultural perspective on sexuality was spurred by the early-twentieth-century work of the anthropologists Margaret Mead (1901–1978) and Bronislaw Malinowski (1884–1942).

In *Sex and Temperament in Three Primitive Societies* (1935), Mead laid the groundwork for recent psychological and sociological research challenging gender-role stereotypes. In most cultures characterized by a gender division of labor, men typically go to business or to the hunt, and—when necessary—to war. In such cultures, men are perceived as strong, active, independent, and logical. Women are viewed as passive, dependent, nurturant, and emotional. Mead concluded that these stereotypes are not inherent in our genetic heritage. Rather, men and women learn to behave in ways that are expected in their particular culture.

Malinowski lived on the Trobriand island of Boyawa in the South Pacific during World War I. There he gathered data on two societies of the South Pacific, the Trobrianders and the Amphett islanders. The Amphett islanders maintained strict sexual prohibitions, whereas the Trobrianders enjoyed greater freedom. Trobrianders, for example, encouraged their children to masturbate. Boys and girls were expected to begin to engage in intercourse when they were biologically old enough. According to custom, they would pair off, exchange a coconut, a bit of betel nut, a few beads, or some fruit from the bush. Then they would go off together and engage in intercourse (Malinowski, 1929, p. 488). Adolescents were expected to have multiple sex partners until they married.

Cross-Cultural Commonalities and Differences in Sexual Behavior   In 1951, Clellan Ford, an anthropologist, and Frank Beach, a psychologist, reviewed sexual behavior in nearly 200 preliterate societies around the world. They found great variety in sexual customs and beliefs. They also found some common threads. For example, kissing was quite common across the cultures they studied, although not universal. The Thonga of Africa were one society that did not practice kissing. Upon witnessing two European visitors kissing each other, members of the tribe commented that they could not understand why Europeans "ate" each other's saliva and dirt. The frequency of sexual intercourse also varies from culture to culture, but intercourse is relatively more frequent among young people everywhere.

Societies differ in their attitudes toward childhood masturbation. Some societies, such as the Hopi Native Americans of the southwest United States, ignore it. Trobrianders encourage children to stimulate themselves. Other societies condemn it.

The cross-cultural perspective illustrates the importance of learning in human sexual behavior. Societies differ widely in their sexual attitudes, customs, and practices. The members of all human societies share the same anatomic structures and physiological capacities for sexual pleasure, however. The same hormones flow through their arteries. Were human sexuality completely or predominantly determined by biology, we would not find such diversity.

Psychological Perspectives

Psychological perspectives focus on the many psychological influences—perception, learning, motivation, emotion, personality, and so on—that affect our sexual behavior and our experience of ourselves as female or male. Some psychological theorists, such as Sigmund Freud, focus on the motivational role of sex in human personality. Others focus on how our experiences and mental representations of the world affect our sexual behavior.

Sigmund Freud and Psychoanalytic Theory   Sigmund Freud, a Viennese physician, formulated a grand theory of personality termed **psychoanalysis.** Freud believed that we are all born with biologically based sex drives. These drives must be channeled through socially approved outlets if family and social life are to carry on without undue conflict. He hypothesized that conflicts between sexuality and society become internalized in the form of an inner conflict between two opposing parts of the personality—the **id,** which is the repository of biologically based drives or "instincts" (such as hunger, thirst, elimination, sex, and aggression), and the **ego,** which represents reason and good sense. The ego seeks socially appropriate outlets for satisfying the basic drives that arise from the id. Your id, for example, prompts you to feel sexual urges. Your ego attempts to find ways of satisfying those urges without incurring condemnation from others or from your own moral

Psychoanalysis
The theory of personality originated by Sigmund Freud, which proposes that human behavior represents the outcome of clashing inner forces.

Id
In Freud's theory, the mental structure that is present at birth, embodies physiological drives, and is fully unconscious.

Ego
In Freud's theory, the second mental structure to develop, which is characterized by self-awareness, planning, and delay of gratification.

Superego

In Freud's theory, the third mental structure, which functions as a moral guardian and sets forth high standards for behavior.

Unconscious mind

Those parts or contents of the mind that lie outside of conscious awareness.

Defense mechanisms

In psychoanalytic theory, automatic processes that protect the ego from anxiety by disguising or ejecting unacceptable ideas and urges.

Repression

The automatic ejection of anxiety-evoking ideas from consciousness.

Erogenous zones

Parts of the body, including but not limited to the sex organs, that are responsive to sexual stimulation.

Psychosexual development

In psychoanalytic theory, the process by which sexual feelings shift from one erogenous zone to another as a human being matures.

conscience, which Freud called the **superego.** How these internal conflicts are resolved, in Freud's view, largely determines our ability to love, work, and lead well-adjusted lives.

Freud proposed that the mind operates on conscious and unconscious levels. The conscious level corresponds to our state of present awareness. The **unconscious mind** refers to the darker reaches of the mind that lie outside our direct awareness. The ego shields the conscious mind from awareness of our baser sexual and aggressive urges by means of **defense mechanisms** such as **repression,** or motivated forgetting.

Although many sexual impulses are banished to the unconscious, they continue to seek expression. One avenue of expression is the dream, through which sexual impulses may be perceived in disguised, or symbolic, form. The therapists and scholars who follow in the Freudian tradition are quite interested in analyzing dreams, and the dream objects listed in Table 1.1 are often considered sexual symbols.

Freud introduced new and controversial ideas about ourselves as sexual beings. For example, he originated the concept of **erogenous zones**—the idea that many parts of the body, not just the genitals, are responsive to sexual stimulation.

According to Freud's theory of **psychosexual development,** children undergo five stages of development: oral, anal, phallic, latency, and genital, which are named according to the predominant erogenous zones of each stage. One of Freud's most controversial beliefs was that children normally harbor erotic interests. He theorized that it was normal for children to progress through stages of development in which the erotic interest shifts from one erogenous zone to another, as, for example, from the mouth to the anus. He believed

TABLE 1.1 Dream symbols in psychoanalytic theory*

Symbols for the Male Genital Organs

airplanes	fish	neckties	tools	weapons
bullets	hands	poles	trains	
feet	hoses	snakes	trees	
fire	knives	sticks	umbrellas	

Symbols for the Female Genital Organs

bottles	caves	doors	ovens	ships
boxes	chests	hats	pockets	tunnels
cases	closets	jars	pots	

Symbols for Sexual Intercourse

climbing a ladder	flying in an airplane
climbing a staircase	riding a horse
crossing a bridge	riding an elevator
driving an automobile	riding a roller coaster
entering a room	walking into a tunnel or down a hall

Symbols for the Breasts

apples	peaches

*Freud theorized that the content of dreams symbolized urges, wishes, and objects of fantasy that we would censor in the waking state.
Source: Adapted from Rathus, S. A. (1996). *Psychology in the New Millennium,* 6th ed. Ft. Worth: Harcourt Brace.

Oedipus complex
In psychoanalytic theory, a conflict of the phallic stage in which the boy wishes to possess his mother sexually and perceives his father as a rival in love. (The analogous conflict for girls is the *Electra complex.*)

Behaviorists
Learning theorists who argue that a scientific approach to understanding behavior must refer only to observable and measurable behaviors.

Social-learning theory
A cognitively oriented learning theory in which observational learning, values, and expectations play key roles in determining behavior.

Modeling
Acquiring knowledge and skills by observing others.

that the suckling of the infant in the oral stage was an erotic act. So too was learning to control the processes of elimation during the anal stage. Freud believed that it was normal for children to develop erotic feelings toward the parent of the other gender during the phallic stage. Freud termed these incestuous urges and feelings of rivalry the **Oedipus complex**.

Learning Theories   **Behaviorists** such as John B. Watson (1878–1958) and B. F. Skinner (1904–1990) emphasized the importance of rewards and punishments in the learning process. In psychology, events (such as rewards) that increase the frequency or likelihood of behavior are termed *reinforcements*. Children left to explore their bodies without parental condemnation will learn what feels good and tend to repeat it. The Trobriand child who is rewarded for masturbation and premarital coitus through parental praise and encouragement will be more likely to repeat these behaviors (at least openly!) than the child in a more sexually restrictive culture, who is punished for the same behavior. When sexual behavior (like masturbation) feels good, but parents connect it with feelings of guilt and shame, the child is placed in conflict and may vacillate between masturbating and swearing off it.

Social-learning theorists also use the concepts of reward and punishment, but they emphasize the importance of mental activity (anticipations, thoughts, plans, and so on) and learning by observation. Observational learning, or **modeling,** refers to acquiring knowledge and skills through observing others. Observational learning includes seeing models in films or on television, hearing about them, and reading about them.

Sociocultural Perspectives

Sexual behavior is determined not only by biological and psychological factors, but also by social factors. Social factors contribute to the shaping of our sexual attitudes, beliefs, and behavior. Whereas anthropologists contribute to our understanding of cross-cultural variance in sexuality, sociocultural theorists focus on differences in sexuality among the subgroups of a society, as defined, for example, by differences in religion, race/ethnicity, country of origin, socioeconomic status, marital status, age, educational level, and gender. Such a society is the United States.

Consider the issue of the numbers of sex partners people have. Table 1.2 reports the results of a national survey concerning the number of sex partners people report having since the age of 18. It considers the factors of gender, age, marital status, level of education, religion, and race/ethnicity (Laumann et al., 1994).

Consider gender. Males, according to the survey, report having greater numbers of sex partners than females do. For example, 1 male in 3 (33%) reports having 11 or more sex partners since the age of 18, as compared with fewer than 1 woman in 10 (9.2%). Throughout the text, we shall be focusing on gender differences and why men seem generally more likely than women to seek a wide range of sexual experience.

Concerning age, the numbers of sex partners appear to rise with age into the 40s. As people gain in years, they have had more opportunity to accumulate life experiences, including sexual experiences. But then the numbers of partners fall off among respondents in their 50s. Older respondents entered adulthood prior to the sexual revolution and were thus generally exposed to more conservative sexual attitudes. We shall find this sort of age difference, or age gradient, throughout the text as well.

Level of education is also connected with sexual behavior. Generally speaking, it would appear that education is something of a liberalizing influence. People with some college education, or who have completed college, are likely to have more sex partners than those who attended only grade school or high school.

If education is a liberating influence on sexuality, conservative religious experience would appear to be a restraining factor. In Table 1.2, those who report no religion and liberal Protestants (e.g., Methodists, Lutherans, Presbyterians, Episcopalians, and United Church of Christ) report higher numbers of sex partners than do Catholics and conservative Protestants (e.g., members of Baptist churches, Pentecostal churches, Churches of Christ, and Assemblies of God).

TABLE 1.2 Number of sex partners since age 18 as found in the NHSLS* study

Social Characteristics	Number of Sex Partners (%)					
	0	1	2–4	5–10	11–20	21+
Gender						
Male	3.4	19.5	20.9	23.3	16.3	16.6
Female	2.5	31.5	36.4	20.4	6.0	3.2
Age						
18–24	7.8	32.1	34.1	15.4	7.8	2.8
25–29	2.2	25.3	31.3	22.2	9.9	9.0
30–34	3.1	21.3	29.3	25.2	10.8	10.3
35–39	1.7	18.9	29.7	24.9	14.0	10.8
40–44	0.7	21.9	27.6	24.2	13.7	12.0
45–49	2.0	25.7	23.8	25.1	9.6	13.9
50–54	2.4	33.9	27.8	18.0	9.0	9.0
55–59	1.3	40.0	28.3	15.2	8.3	7.0
Marital Status						
Never married (not cohabiting)	12.3	14.8	28.6	20.6	12.1	11.6
Never married (cohabiting)	0.0	24.6	37.3	15.7	9.7	12.7
Married	0.0	37.1	28.0	19.4	8.7	6.8
Education						
Less than high school	4.2	26.7	36.0	18.6	8.8	5.8
High school graduate	3.4	30.2	29.1	20.0	9.8	7.4
Some college	2.1	23.9	29.4	23.3	11.9	9.3
College graduate	2.1	24.1	25.8	23.9	11.1	13.0
Advanced degree	3.5	24.6	26.3	22.8	9.6	13.2
Religion						
None	2.6	16.2	29.0	20.3	15.9	15.9
Liberal, moderate Protestant	2.3	22.8	31.2	23.0	12.4	8.3
Conservative Protestant	2.9	29.8	30.4	20.4	9.5	7.0
Catholic	3.8	27.2	29.2	22.7	8.1	9.1
Jewish[†]	0.0	24.1	13.0	29.6	16.7	16.7
Race/Ethnicity						
White (non-Hispanic)	3.0	26.2	28.9	22.0	10.9	9.1
African American	2.2	18.0	34.2	24.1	11.0	10.5
Hispanic American	3.2	35.6	27.1	17.4	8.2	8.5
Asian American[†]	6.2	46.2	24.6	13.8	6.2	3.1
Native American[†]	5.0	27.5	35.0	22.5	5.0	5.0

*National Health and Social Life Survey, conducted by a research team centered at the University of Chicago.
[†]These sample sizes are quite small.
Source: Adapted from Laumann, E. O., Gagnon, J. H., Michael, R. T., & Michaels, S. (1994). *The Social Organization of Sexuality: Sexual Practices in the United States.* Chicago: University of Chicago Press, Table 5.1C, p. 179.

Ethnicity is also connected with sexual behavior. The text's coverage of diversity addresses differences between non-Hispanic White Americans, African Americans, Hispanic Americans, Asian Americans, and Native Americans. The research findings listed in Table 1.2 suggest that White (non-Hispanic Americans) and African Americans have the highest numbers of sex partners. Hispanic Americans are mostly Catholic, and Catholicism, as noted, provides something of a restraint on sexual behavior. Asian Americans would appear to be the most sexually restrained ethnic group. However, as noted in the footnote to the table, the sample sizes of Asian Americans and Native Americans are relatively small.

Research Methods in Human Sexuality

Human sexuality is a science. Scientists base their knowledge on research evidence, rather than on intuition, faith, or superstition. Scientists are critical thinkers. They question prevailing assumptions and theories about sexual behavior. Scientists recognize that they cannot gain perfect knowledge. They know that one era's "truths" may become another era's ancient myths and fallacies.

Populations and Samples: Representing the World of Diversity

Population
A complete group of organisms or events.

Researchers undertake to learn about **populations.** Populations are complete groups of people or animals. Many researchers have attempted to learn about people in the United States, for example. (In 1998, there were about 270 million of them—a sizable population.) Other researchers may identify American adults, or American adolescents, as their population. Still other researchers attempt to compare the sexual behavior of African Americans to that of Hispanic Americans and other Americans. These are termed the *populations of interest,* or *target populations.* It would be expensive and difficult to try to study every individual in these populations.

Sample
Part of a population.

Generalize
To go from the particular to the general.

Because of the impossibility of studying all members of a population, scientists select individuals from the population and study them. The individuals who participate in research are said to comprise a **sample.** However, we cannot truly learn about the population of interest unless the sample *represents* that population. A *representative sample* is a research sample of participants who accurately represent the population of interest. If our samples do not represent the target populations, we cannot extend or **generalize** the results of our research to the populations of interest. If we wished to study the sexual behavior of Asian Americans, our population would consist of *all* Asian Americans. If we used only Asian American college students as our sample, our sample would not *represent* all Asian Americans.

Random sample
A sample in which every member of a population has an equal chance of participating.

Sampling Methods   One way of acquiring a representative sample is through random sampling. A **random sample** is one in which every member of the target population has an equal chance of participating.

Magazine editors may boast that they have surveyed samples of 20,000 or 30,000 readers, but size alone does not mean that a sample is representative. As an example, the *Literary Digest* magazine polled thousands of voters by telephone to predict the outcome of the 1936 presidential election. Based on the survey, the magazine predicted that Alfred Landon would defeat Franklin D. Roosevelt, but Roosevelt won by a landslide of nearly 11 million votes. The problem was that the election was held during the Great Depression, when only relatively affluent people could afford telephones. Those who could afford phones were also more likely to be Republicans and to vote for the Republican candidate, Landon. Thus, the *Digest* poll, although large, was biased. A sample of 30 million voters will not provide an accurate picture if it is biased.

Researchers overcome biased sampling by drawing *random* or *stratified random* samples of populations. In a random sample, every member of a population has an equal

Stratified random sample
A random sample in which known subgroups in a population are represented in proportion to their numbers in the population.

Volunteer bias
A slanting of research data that is caused by the characteristics of individuals who volunteer to participate, such as willingness to discuss intimate behavior.

Case study
A carefully drawn, in-depth biography of an individual or a small group of individuals that may be obtained through interviews, questionnaires, and historical records.

Survey
A detailed study of a sample obtained by means such as interviews and questionnaires.

chance of participating. In a **stratified random sample,** known subgroups of a population are represented in proportion to their numbers in the population. For instance, about 12% of the U.S. population is African American. Researchers could therefore decide that 12% of their sample must be African American if they are to represent all people in the United States.

Another problem is **volunteer bias.** That is, sexual research is almost invariably conducted with people who volunteer to participate. Volunteers may differ from people who refuse to participate. For example, volunteers tend to be more open about their sexuality than the general population. They may even tend to exaggerate behaviors that others might consider deviant or abnormal.

Methods of Observation

Once scientists have chosen those they will study, they observe them. In this section, we consider several methods of observation: the case-study method, the survey method, naturalistic observation, participant observation, and laboratory observation.

The Case-Study Method   A **case study** is a carefully drawn, in-depth biography of an individual or a small group. The focus is on understanding one or several individuals as fully as possible by unraveling the interplay of various factors in their backgrounds. In most case studies, the researcher comes to know the individual or group through interviews conducted over a prolonged period of time. The interviewing pattern tends to build upon itself with a good deal of freedom, as opposed to the one-shot, standardized set of questions used in survey questionnaires.

Researchers may also conduct case studies by interviewing people who have known the individuals or by examining public records. Sigmund Freud, for example, drew upon historical records in his case study of the Renaissance inventor and painter Leonardo da Vinci. Freud concluded that Leonardo's artistic productions represented the sublimating, or channeling, of male–male sexual impulses.

Despite the richness of material that may be derived from the case-study approach, people often have gaps in memory, especially for childhood events. Clinicians and interviewers may unintentionally guide people into saying what they expect to hear. Then, too, researchers may inadvertently color people's reports when they jot them down—shape them subtly in ways that reflect their own views.

The Survey Method   **Surveys** typically gather information about behavior through questionnaires or interviews. Researchers may interview or administer questionnaires to thousands of people from particular population groups to learn about their sexual behavior and attitudes. Interviews such as those used by Kinsey and his colleagues (1948, 1953) have the advantages of face-to-face contact and of giving the interviewer the opportunity to *probe*—that is, to follow up on answers that seem to lead toward useful information. A skilled interviewer may be able to set a respondent at ease and establish a sense of trust or *rapport* that encourages self-disclosure.

Questionnaires are less expensive than interviews. The major expenses in using questionnaires involve printing and distribution. Questionnaires can be administered to groups of people at once, and respondents can return them anonymously. Anonymity may encourage respondents to disclose intimate information. Questionnaires, of course, can be used only by people who can read and record their responses. Interviews can be used even with people who cannot read or write. But interviewers must be trained, sometimes extensively, and then paid for their time.

Some of the major surveys described in this book were conducted by Kinsey and his colleagues (1948, 1953), the Playboy Foundation (Hunt, 1974), Bell and his colleagues (1978, 1981), Coles and Stokes (1985), Wyatt and her colleagues (Wyatt, 1985, 1989; Wyatt et al., 1988a, 1988b), researchers at the Battelle Memorial Institute of Seattle (Billy et al., 1993; Tanfer et al., 1993), Janus and Janus (1993), and the University of Chicago group (Laumann et al., 1994).

Alfred Kinsey. Kinsey and his colleagues conducted the first large-scale scientific study of sexual behavior in the United States.

Many of these surveys have *something* to offer to our understanding of human sexuality, but some are more methodologically sound than others. None perfectly represents the U.S. population at large, however. Most people consider their sexuality to be among the most intimate, *private* aspects of their lives. People who willingly agree to be polled as to their political preferences may resist participation in surveys concerning their sexual behavior. Let us consider the techniques of the Kinsey studies and the NHSLS study in greater depth.

The Kinsey Reports Kinsey and his colleagues (1948, 1953) interviewed 5,300 males and 5,940 females in the United States between 1938 and 1949. They asked a wide array of questions on various types of sexual experiences, including masturbation, oral sex, and coitus that occurred before, during, and outside of marriage. For obvious reasons Kinsey could not use more direct observational methods, such as sending his researchers to peer through bedroom windows. Kinsey chose *not* to try to obtain a random sample. He believed that a high refusal rate would wreck the chances of accurately representing the general population. Instead, he adopted a *group sampling* approach. He recruited study participants from the organizations and community groups to which they belonged, such as college fraternities and sororities. He contacted representatives of groups in diverse communities and tried to persuade them to secure the cooperation of fellow group members. If he showed these individuals that they would not be subjected to embarrassment or discomfort, Kinsey hoped that they would persuade other members to participate. Kinsey understood that the groups he solicited were not necessarily representative of the general population. He believed, however, that his sampling approach was dictated by practical constraints. Even so, he made an attempt to sample as broadly as possible from the groups he solicited. In some cases he obtained full participation. In other cases he obtained a large enough proportion of the group membership to at least ensure representativeness of the group. Still, people of color, people in rural areas, older people, the poor, and Catholics and Jews were all underrepresented in Kinsey's samples.

To his credit, Kinsey took measures to instill candor in the people he interviewed. For one, study participants were assured of the confidentiality of their records. For another, Kinsey's interviewers were trained to conduct the interviews in an objective and matter-of-fact style. To reduce the tendency to slant responses in a socially desirable direction, participants were reassured that the interviewers were not passing judgment on them.

Kinsey checked the **reliability** of his data by evaluating the consistency of the responses given by several hundred interviewees who were reexamined after at least 18 months. Their reports of the **incidence** of sexual activities (for example, whether or not they had ever engaged in premarital or extramarital coitus) were highly reliable. That is, participants tended to give the same answers on both occasions. But reports of the **frequency** of sexual activities (such as the number of times one has masturbated to orgasm or the frequency of coitus in marriage) were less consistent. People find it more difficult to compute the frequencies of their activities than to answer whether or not they have ever engaged in them.

Kinsey recognized that consistency of responses across time did not guarantee their **validity.** He could not validate self-reports directly, as one might validate reports that one is drug-free by means of urine analysis. He could not send his investigators to peer through bedroom windows, so he had to use indirect means to validate the data. One indirect measure was comparison of the reports of husbands and wives. There was a remarkable consistency in the reports of 706 pairs of spouses. It thus appears that their self-reports were accurate.

The NHSLS Study The National Health and Social Life Survey was intended to provide general information about sexual behavior in the United States, and also specific information that might be used to predict and prevent the spread of AIDS. It was conducted by Edward O. Laumann of the University of Chicago and three colleagues—John H. Gagnon, Robert T. Michael, and Stuart Michaels—in the 1990s and published as *The Social Organization of Sexuality: Sexual Practices in the United States* in 1994. A compan-

Reliability
The consistency or accuracy of a measure.

Incidence
A measure of the occurrence or the degree of occurrence of an event.

Frequency
The number of times an action is repeated within a given period.

Validity
With respect to tests, the degree to which a particular test measures the constructs or traits it purports to measure.

ion volume authored by Michael, Gagnon, Laumann, and Gina Kolata—a *New York Times* science reporter—was also published: *Sex in America: A Definitive Survey*. *Sex in America* is a bit less technical in presentation but also offers some interesting data not found in the other version.

The sample included 3,432 people. Of this number, 3,159 were drawn from English-speaking adults living in households (not dormitories, prisons, and so forth), ages 18 to 59. The other 273 were purposely obtained by oversampling African American and Hispanic American households to obtain more information about these ethnic groups. The sample probably represents the overall U.S. population quite well. However, there may be too few Asian Americans, Native Americans, and Jews to offer much information about these groups.

The researchers identified samples of households in geographic areas—by addresses, not names. They sent a letter to each household, describing the purpose and methods of the study, and an interviewer visited each household one week later. The people targeted were assured that the purposes of the study were important and that the identities of participants would be kept confidential. Incentives of up to $100 were offered for cooperating. A high completion rate of close to 80% was obtained in this way. All in all, the NHSLS study could be the only one since Kinsey's day that offers a reasonably accurate picture of the sexual practices of the general population of the United States.

Magazine Surveys Major readership surveys have also been conducted by popular magazines, such as *Psychology Today, Redbook, Ladies' Home Journal, McCall's, Cosmopolitan,* and even *Consumer Reports*. Although these surveys all offer some useful information and may be commended for attaining large samples (ranging from 20,000 to 106,000!), their sampling techniques are inherently unscientific and biased. Each sample represents, at best, the readers of the magazine in which the questionnaire appeared. Moreover, we learn only about readers who volunteered to respond to these questionnaires. Volunteers tend to be more open and cooperative than people who do not volunteer. Finally, readers of these magazines are more affluent than the public at large, and readers of *Cosmopolitan, Psychology Today,* and even *Redbook* tend to be more liberal. So the samples may represent only those readers who were willing to complete and mail in the surveys.

Laumann and his colleagues (1994) are particularly harsh in their judgment of such surveys. They write that "such studies, in sum, produce junk statistics of no value whatsoever in making valid and reliable population projections" (p. 45).

In sum, the accuracy of surveys can be limited by factors such as these:

- Nonrepresentative sampling (Sampling may be biased.)
- Faulty memories of sexual behavior
- Distortion or concealment of information
- **Social desirability** (Some people try to ingratiate themselves with their interviewers by offering what they believe to be socially desirable answers.)
- Volunteer bias

Social desirability
A response bias to a questionnaire or interview, in which the person provides a socially acceptable response.

Naturalistic observation
A method in which organisms are observed in their natural environments.

Participant observation
A method in which observers interact with the people they study as they collect data.

The Naturalistic-Observation Method
In **naturalistic observation,** also called the *field study,* scientists directly observe the behavior of animals and humans where it happens. Anthropologists, for example, have lived among preliterate societies and reported on their social and sexual customs. Other disciplines, too, have adopted methods of naturalistic observation in their research on human sexuality. Sociologists have observed the street life of prostitutes. Psychologists have observed body language between couples in dating situations.

The Participant-Observation Method
In **participant observation,** the investigators learn about people's behavior by directly interacting with them. Participant observation has been used in studies of male–male sexual behavior and mate-swapping (swinging). In effect, participation has been the "price of admission" for observation.

The Laboratory-Observation Method
In *Human Sexual Response* (1966), William Masters and Virginia Johnson were among the first to report direct laboratory ob-

servations of individuals and couples engaged in sexual acts. In all, 694 people (312 men and 382 women) participated in the research. The women ranged from 18 to 78 in age; the men, from 21 to 80. There were 276 married couples, 106 single women, and 36 single men. The married couples engaged in intercourse and other forms of mutual stimulation, such as manual and oral stimulation of the genitals. The unmarried people participated in studies that did not require intercourse, such as measurement of female sexual arousal to insertion of a penis-shaped probe and male ejaculation during masturbation. Masters and Johnson performed similar laboratory observations of sexual response among gay people for their 1979 book, *Homosexuality in Perspective.*

Direct laboratory observation of biological processes was not invented by Masters and Johnson. However, they were confronting a society that was still unprepared to speak openly of sex, let alone to observe people engaged in sexual activity in the laboratory. Masters and Johnson were accused of immorality, voyeurism, and an assortment of other evils. Nevertheless, their methods offered the first reliable set of data on what happens to the body during sexual response. Their instruments permitted them to directly measure vasocongestion (blood flow to the genitals), myotonia (muscle tension), and other physiological responses. Perhaps their most controversial device was a "coition machine." This was a transparent artificial penis outfitted with photographic equipment. It enabled them to study changes in women's internal sexual organs as they became sexually aroused. From these studies, Masters and Johnson observed that it is useful to divide sexual response into four stages (their "sexual response cycle").

Limitations of Observational Research   One of the basic problems with naturalistic observation is the possibility that the behavior under study may be *reactive* to the measurement itself. This source of bias is referred to as the **observer effect.**

Observer effect

A distortion of individuals' behavior caused by the act of observation.

The ethnographer who studies a particular culture or subgroup within a culture may unwittingly alter the behavior of the members of the group by focusing attention on some facets of their behavior. Falling prey to social desirability, some people may "straighten out their act" while the ethnographer is present. Other people may try to impress the ethnographer by acting in ways that are more aggressive or sexually provocative than usual. In either case, people supply distorted or biased information. Ethnographers must corroborate self-reported information by using multiple sources. They must also consider whether their own behavior is more obtrusive than they think.

Observer bias can distort researchers' perceptions of the behaviors they observe. Observers who hold rigid sexual attitudes may be relatively unwilling to examine sexual activities that they consider to be offensive or objectionable. They may unwittingly (or intentionally) slant interviews in a way that presents a "sanitized" view of the behavior of those they study, or exaggerate or "sensationalize" certain sexual practices to conform to their preconceptions of the sexual behavior of the people they study.

The method of laboratory observation used by Masters and Johnson may be even more subject to distortion. Unlike animals, which naturalists may observe unobtrusively from afar, people who participate in laboratory observation know that they are being observed and that their responses are being measured. The problem of volunteer bias, troublesome for sex surveys, is even thornier in laboratory observation. How many of us would assent to performing sexual activities in the laboratory while we were connected to physiological monitoring equipment in full view of researchers? Some of the women observed by Masters and Johnson were patients of Dr. Masters who felt indebted to him and agreed to participate. Many were able to persuade their husbands to participate as well. Some were medical students and graduate students who may have been motivated to earn extra money (participants were paid for their time) as well as by scientific curiosity.

Another methodological concern of the Masters and Johnson approach is that observing people engaged in sexual activities may in itself alter their responses. People may not respond publicly in the same way that they would in private. The physiological monitoring equipment may also alter their natural responses. With these constraints in mind, it is perhaps remarkable that the people studied by Masters and Johnson were able to become sexually aroused and reach orgasm.

The Correlational Method

What are the relationships between age and frequency of coitus among married couples? What is the connection between socioeconomic status and teenage pregnancy? In each case, two variables are being related to one another: age and frequency of coitus, and socioeconomic status and rates of teenage pregnancy. Correlational research describes the relationship between variables such as these.

A **correlation** is a statistical measure of the relationship between two variables. In correlational studies, two or more variables are related, or linked to, one another by statistical means. The strength and direction (positive or negative) of the relationship between any two variables is expressed with a statistic called a **correlation coefficient.**

Research has shown relationships (correlations) between marital satisfaction and a host of variables: communication skills, shared values, flexibility, frequency of social interactions with friends, and churchgoing, to name a few. Although such research may give us an idea of the factors associated with marital satisfaction, the experimenters have not manipulated the variables of interest. For this reason we cannot say which, if any, of the factors is causally related to marital happiness. Consider the relationship between churchgoing and marital happiness. Couples who attend church more frequently report higher rates of marital satisfaction (Wilson & Filsinger, 1986). It is possible that churchgoing stabilizes marriages. It is also possible that people who attend church regularly are more stable and committed to marriage in the first place.

Correlations may be *positive* or *negative*. Two variables are positively correlated if one increases as the other increases. Frequency of intercourse, for example, has been found to be positively correlated with sexual satisfaction (Blumstein & Schwartz, 1983). That is, married couples who engage in coitus more frequently report higher levels of sexual satisfaction. However, the experimenters did not manipulate the variables. Therefore, we cannot conclude that sexual satisfaction *causes* high coital frequency. It could also be that frequent coitus contributes to greater sexual satisfaction. It is also possible that there is no causal relationship between the variables. Perhaps both coital frequency and sexual satisfaction are affected by other factors, such as communication ability, general marital satisfaction, health, and so on (see Figure 1.1). Similarly, height and weight are positively correlated but do not cause each other. Another factor, growth, contributes to both.

Limitations of the Correlational Method Correlation is not causation. Many variables are correlated but not causally related to one another.

Although correlations do not show cause and effect, they can be used to make predictions. For example, we can predict that people who were sexually traumatized as children are more likely to encounter psychological problems later on. They find it more difficult to establish intimate relationships in adulthood. However, we cannot demonstrate that sex-

Correlation

A statistical measure of the relationship between two variables.

Correlation coefficient

A statistic that expresses the strength and direction (positive or negative) of the relationship between two variables.

Figure 1.1. What Is the Relationship Between Frequency of Intercourse and Sexual Satisfaction?
Married couples who engage in coitus more frequently report higher levels of sexual satisfaction, but why? Since researchers have not manipulated the variables, we cannot conclude that sexual satisfaction *causes* high coital frequency. Nor can we say that frequent coitus causes greater sexual satisfaction. Perhaps both variables are affected by other factors, such as communication ability, general marital satisfaction, and general health.

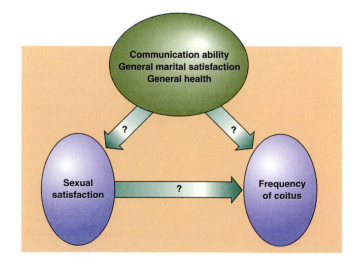

ual trauma directly causes these problems. Although correlation does not provide causal knowledge, it permits us to anticipate the needs of victims of sexual assault for treatment services. Knowledge of correlational relationships may also lead to controlled experiments that more directly address questions of cause and effect.

The Experimental Method　　The best (if not always feasible) method for studying *cause-and-effect relationships* is the **experiment.** Experiments permit scientists to draw conclusions about cause-and-effect relationships because the experimenter is able to control or manipulate the factors or variables of interest directly and to observe their effects.

In an experiment on the effects of alcohol on sexual arousal, for example, a group of participants would receive an intervention, called a **treatment,** such as a dose of alcohol. (In other experiments, the intervention or treatment might involve the administration of a drug, exposure to violent pornography, a program of sex education, etc.). They would then be carefully observed to learn whether this treatment made a difference in their behavior— in this case, their sexual arousal.

Independent and Dependent Variables　　In an experiment, the variables (treatments) that are hypothesized to have a causal effect are manipulated or controlled by the researcher. Consider an experiment designed to determine whether or not alcohol stimulates sexual arousal. The design might involve giving one group of participants a certain dosage of alcohol, and then measuring its effects. In such an experimental arrangement, the dosage of alcohol is considered an **independent variable,** whose presence and quantity is manipulated by the researchers. The measured results are called **dependent variables,** since changes in their values are believed to depend on the independent variable or variables. In this experiment, measures of sexual arousal would be the dependent variables. Dependent variables are outcomes; they are observed and measured by the researchers, but not manipulated. Sexual arousal might be measured by means such as physiological measurement (gauging the degree of penile erection in the male, for example) or self-report (asking participants to rate their sexual arousal on a rating scale).

In a study of the effects of sex education on teenage pregnancy, sex education would be the independent variable. The incidence of teenage pregnancy would be the dependent variable. Researchers would administer the experimental treatment (sex education) and track the participants for a period of time to determine their pregnancy rates. But how would experimenters know whether or not the treatment had made a difference in the pregnancy rate? One way is to randomly assign people or animals to experimental and control groups.

Experimental and Control Groups　　Participants in **experimental groups** receive the treatment. Participants in **control groups** do not. Every effort is made to hold all other conditions constant for both groups. By using random assignment and holding other conditions constant, researchers can be reasonably confident that the independent variable (treatment), and not extraneous factors (such as the temperature of the room in which the treatment was administered or differences between the participants in the experimental and control groups), brought about the results.

Random Assignment　　Why do experimenters assign individuals at random to experimental and control groups whenever possible? Consider a study conducted to determine the effects of alcohol on sexual arousal in response to sexually explicit material, such as adult films. If we permitted study participants to choose whether or not they would drink alcohol, we might not know if it was the alcohol itself that accounted for the results. Some other factor, called a **selection factor,** might discriminate between people who would or would not choose to drink alcohol. One difference might be that people who chose to drink might also have more permissive attitudes toward sexually explicit material than the others. Their permissiveness rather than the alcohol could affect their sexual responsiveness to these stimuli. If this were the case, experimental outcomes might reflect the effects of the selection factor rather than the alcohol.

Experiment
A scientific method that seeks to confirm cause-and-effect relationships by manipulating independent variables and observing their effects on dependent variables.

Treatment
In experiments, an intervention that is administered to participants (e.g., a test, a drug, or a sex education program) so that its effects may be observed.

Independent variable
A condition in a scientific study that is manipulated so that its effects may be observed.

Dependent variables
The measured results of an experiment, which are believed to be a function of the independent variables.

Experimental group
A group of study participants who receive a treatment.

Control group
A group of study participants who do not receive the experimental treatment. However, other conditions are held comparable to those of individuals in the experimental group.

Selection factor
A bias that may operate in research when people are allowed to determine whether or not they will receive a treatment.

Experimentation with Animals Researchers frequently undertake studies with other animal species that would be impractical or unethical with people. For example, it may be hypothesized that prenatal sexual hormones "feminize" or "masculinize" the brain to give rise to gender-typed behaviors or predispose the individual to a heterosexual, gay male, or lesbian sexual orientation. The ideal method for examining these hypotheses would be to alter the balance of sex hormones systematically at various stages of fetal development and then monitor individuals' behavior in subsequent years. However, neither parents nor researchers would be willing to risk the well-being of children through such an experiment. Therefore, studies of this kind have been conducted on animals to try to shed some light on similar processes in people.

To the extent that we share physiological processes with animals, experiments with other species may inform us about ourselves. Because of their physiological similarities to people, rats and monkeys are commonly used in laboratory experiments. But these animals are more similar to humans biologically than psychologically. Thus, we may make some generalizations from them to people concerning the effects of drugs and other biochemical treatments. We cannot, however, assume that their responses provide much of a clue to higher cognitive processes, such as thinking and reasoning.

Limitations of the Experimental Method Although scientists agree that the experimental method provides the strongest evidence of cause-and-effect relationships, experimenters cannot manipulate many variables of interest directly. We may suspect that sexual trauma in the form of rape or sexual assault is a causal factor in the development of psychological or emotional problems. However, we would not expose people to sexual trauma to observe its effects. In the absence of a direct manipulation of the presumed causal factor (rape), we cannot be sure that adjustment problems in rape victims are directly attributable to rape itself, especially when they occur years later. Other factors may be involved, such as insensitive treatment of rape victims by their families or by representatives of the criminal justice system.

Chapter Review

What Is Human Sexuality?

The word *sex* has (1: One *or* Many?) meanings. One use of the term *sex* refers to our (2) g_____, or state of being male or female. (3) H_____ sexuality is defined as the ways in which we experience and express ourselves as sexual beings. Human sexuality is an interdisciplinary (4) s_____ that draws upon the expertise of anthropologists, biologists, medical researchers, sociologists, and psychologists, to name but a few of the professional groups involved in the field. (5) _____ral theorists examine relationships between sexuality and factors such as culture, ethnicity, gender, and social class.

To help students evaluate claims, arguments, and widely held beliefs, colleges encourage (6) c_____ thinking. One aspect of critical thinking is (7) _____cism —not taking things for granted. When people think critically, they maintain (8) o_____ minds. They suspend their beliefs until they have evaluated the (9) _____ence.

Perspectives on Human Sexuality

(10) H_____ can show whether our sexual behavior reflects trends typical of human beings through the millennia or the customs of a particular time and place. Stone Age art suggests that people worshipped women's ability

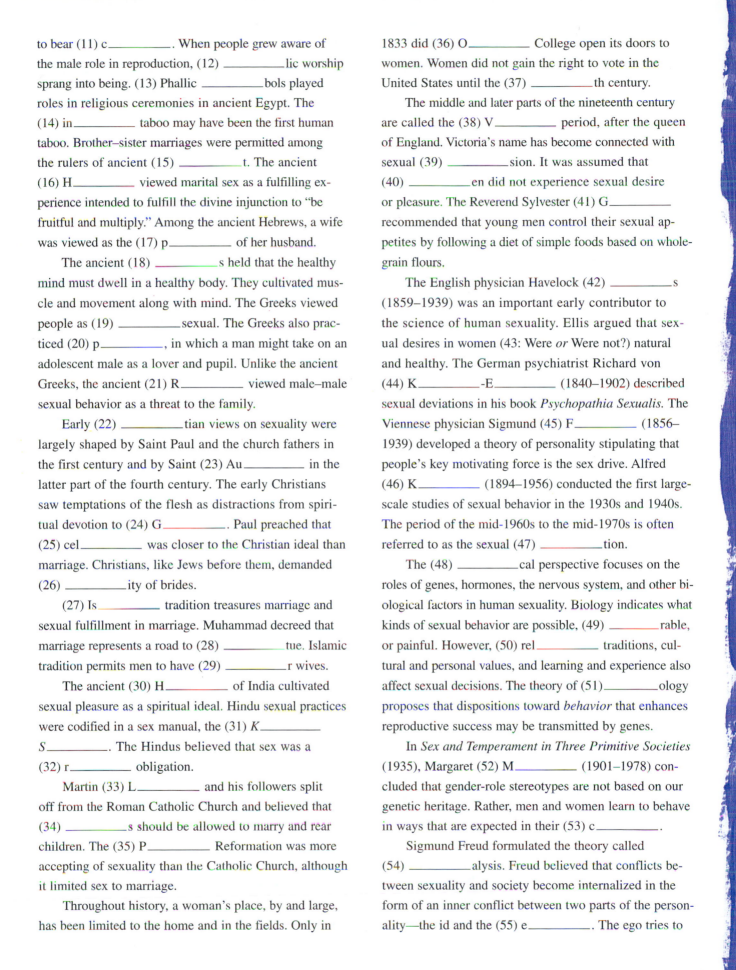

to bear (11) c_____. When people grew aware of the male role in reproduction, (12) _____lic worship sprang into being. (13) Phallic _____bols played roles in religious ceremonies in ancient Egypt. The (14) in_____ taboo may have been the first human taboo. Brother–sister marriages were permitted among the rulers of ancient (15) _____t. The ancient (16) H_____ viewed marital sex as a fulfilling experience intended to fulfill the divine injunction to "be fruitful and multiply." Among the ancient Hebrews, a wife was viewed as the (17) p_____ of her husband.

The ancient (18) _____s held that the healthy mind must dwell in a healthy body. They cultivated muscle and movement along with mind. The Greeks viewed people as (19) _____sexual. The Greeks also practiced (20) p_____, in which a man might take on an adolescent male as a lover and pupil. Unlike the ancient Greeks, the ancient (21) R_____ viewed male–male sexual behavior as a threat to the family.

Early (22) _____tian views on sexuality were largely shaped by Saint Paul and the church fathers in the first century and by Saint (23) Au_____ in the latter part of the fourth century. The early Christians saw temptations of the flesh as distractions from spiritual devotion to (24) G_____. Paul preached that (25) cel_____ was closer to the Christian ideal than marriage. Christians, like Jews before them, demanded (26) _____ity of brides.

(27) Is_____ tradition treasures marriage and sexual fulfillment in marriage. Muhammad decreed that marriage represents a road to (28) _____tue. Islamic tradition permits men to have (29) _____r wives.

The ancient (30) H_____ of India cultivated sexual pleasure as a spiritual ideal. Hindu sexual practices were codified in a sex manual, the (31) *K_____ S_____*. The Hindus believed that sex was a (32) r_____ obligation.

Martin (33) L_____ and his followers split off from the Roman Catholic Church and believed that (34) _____s should be allowed to marry and rear children. The (35) P_____ Reformation was more accepting of sexuality than the Catholic Church, although it limited sex to marriage.

Throughout history, a woman's place, by and large, has been limited to the home and in the fields. Only in 1833 did (36) O_____ College open its doors to women. Women did not gain the right to vote in the United States until the (37) _____th century.

The middle and later parts of the nineteenth century are called the (38) V_____ period, after the queen of England. Victoria's name has become connected with sexual (39) _____sion. It was assumed that (40) _____en did not experience sexual desire or pleasure. The Reverend Sylvester (41) G_____ recommended that young men control their sexual appetites by following a diet of simple foods based on whole-grain flours.

The English physician Havelock (42) _____s (1859–1939) was an important early contributor to the science of human sexuality. Ellis argued that sexual desires in women (43: Were *or* Were not?) natural and healthy. The German psychiatrist Richard von (44) K_____-E_____ (1840–1902) described sexual deviations in his book *Psychopathia Sexualis*. The Viennese physician Sigmund (45) F_____ (1856–1939) developed a theory of personality stipulating that people's key motivating force is the sex drive. Alfred (46) K_____ (1894–1956) conducted the first large-scale studies of sexual behavior in the 1930s and 1940s. The period of the mid-1960s to the mid-1970s is often referred to as the sexual (47) _____tion.

The (48) _____cal perspective focuses on the roles of genes, hormones, the nervous system, and other biological factors in human sexuality. Biology indicates what kinds of sexual behavior are possible, (49) _____rable, or painful. However, (50) rel_____ traditions, cultural and personal values, and learning and experience also affect sexual decisions. The theory of (51)_____ology proposes that dispositions toward *behavior* that enhances reproductive success may be transmitted by genes.

In *Sex and Temperament in Three Primitive Societies* (1935), Margaret (52) M_____ (1901–1978) concluded that gender-role stereotypes are not based on our genetic heritage. Rather, men and women learn to behave in ways that are expected in their (53) c_____.

Sigmund Freud formulated the theory called (54) _____alysis. Freud believed that conflicts between sexuality and society become internalized in the form of an inner conflict between two parts of the personality—the id and the (55) e_____. The ego tries to satisfy sexual urges without incurring the condemnation of the conscience, or (56) _____ ego. Freud proposed that the ego shields the conscious mind from awareness of sexual and aggressive urges by means of (57) d_____ mechanisms, such as repression.

According to Freud's theory of (58) _____ sexual development, children undergo five stages of development. The (59) O_____ complex concerns feelings of lust toward the parent of the other gender.

(60) Be_____ ists such as John B. Watson (1878–1958) and B. F. Skinner (1904–1990) emphasized the importance of rewards and (61) _____ ments in learning about our sexuality. Children who are allowed to explore their bodies will learn what feels good and tend to (62) _____ t it. (63) Social-_____ theorists emphasize the importance of learning by observation. Observational learning is also called (64) _____ ling.

(65) _____ cultural theorists focus on differences in sexuality among the subgroups of a society, as defined, for example, by differences in religion, race/ethnicity, country of origin, socioeconomic status, marital status, age, educational level, and gender. Such a society is the United States.

Research Methods in Human Sexuality

Scientists base their knowledge on research (66) _____ ence, rather than on intuition, faith, or superstition.

(67) _____ tions are complete groups of people or animals. The individuals who participate in research consist of a (68) s_____ of a population. We cannot learn about the population of interest unless the sample (69) _____ sents that population. If our samples represent the target populations, we can extend, or (70) _____ alize, the results of our research to those populations.

A (71) r_____ sample is one in which every member of the target population has an equal chance of participating. In a (72) _____ fied random sample, known subgroups of a population are represented in proportion to their numbers in the population.

A (73) c_____ study is a carefully drawn, in-depth biography of an individual or a small group.

(74) S_____ s are typically used to gather information about behavior through questionnaires or interviews. (75) _____ naires can be administered to groups of people at once. Respondents can return questionnaires unsigned, so that they are (76) _____ mous. Although many magazines have conducted large-scale surveys, none of them (77) _____ sent the U.S. population at large. Two other problems in using surveys are social (78) desir_____ and (79) vol_____ bias. Some people try to ingratiate themselves with their interviewers by offering (80) _____ ally desirable answers. Volunteers are usually (81: More or Less?) open about their sexuality than the population at large.

Naturalistic observation is also called the (82) f_____ study. In the field study, scientists directly (83) ob_____ the behavior of animals and humans where it happens. Scientists take precautions to keep their observations (84) un_____, so that they will not influence the behavior of the individuals they study.

In the (85) _____ pant observation, the investigators learn about people's behavior by directly interacting with them.

William (86) M_____ and Virginia Johnson were among the first to report direct (87) lab_____ observations of individuals and couples engaged in sexual acts. Their instruments permitted them to directly measure (88) vaso_____ (blood flow to the genitals), (89) myo_____ (muscle tension), and other physiological responses.

A (90) _____ ation is a statistical measure of the relationship between two variables. The strength and direction (positive or negative) of the relationship between any two variables is expressed with a statistic called a correlation (91) _____ cient. Correlations do not show cause and (92) _____ ct. However, correlations can be used to make (93) _____ tions.

The best method for studying (94) _____ -and-effect relationships is the experiment. Experiments permit scientists to draw conclusions about cause-and-effect relationships because they can manipulate the (95) v_____ s of interest and observe their effects. In an experiment, a group of participants receives an intervention called a (96) _____ ment.

In an experiment, the treatment is considered an (97) _____ dent variable. The measured results are called (98) _____ dent variables.

Well-designed experiments randomly assign people or animals to (99) _____tal and control groups. Participants in experimental groups (100: Do or Do not?) receive the treatment. Participants in control groups (101: Do or Do not?) receive the treatment. Every effort is made to hold all other conditions (102) co_____ for both groups.

Chapter Quiz

1. Critical thinking involves all of the following EXCEPT
   (a) skepticism.
   (b) challenging common sense.
   (c) evaluating the premises of logic.
   (d) accepting the opinions of authority figures.
2. According to the text, art produced in the Stone Age suggests that people worshipped
   (a) women's ability to bear children.
   (b) a scientific approach to human sexuality.
   (c) bisexuality in men.
   (d) men's ability to father children.
3. According to the text, which of the following is likely to have been the first human taboo?
   (a) The taboo against masturbation.
   (b) The taboo against incest.
   (c) The taboo against oral sex.
   (d) The taboo against anal intercourse.
4. Which of the following cultural groups first produced an illustrated sex manual?
   (a) The Greeks of the golden age.
   (b) The ancient Romans.
   (c) The ancient Chinese.
   (d) The ancient Indians.
5. According to the text, which of the following challenged the prevailing English view by arguing that sexual desires in women were natural and healthy?
   (a) Havelock Ellis.
   (b) Sylvester Graham.
   (c) Sigmund Freud.
   (d) Richard von Krafft-Ebing.
6. The theory of _____ proposes that dispositions toward behavior that enhances reproductive success—as well as physical traits that do so—may be transmitted by genes.

   (a) psychology
   (b) sociology
   (c) anthropology
   (d) sociobiology
7. One of Sigmund Freud's most controversial beliefs is that
   (a) children normally harbor erotic interests.
   (b) children tend to ignore unacceptable ideas and impulses.
   (c) children's dreams have symbolic meanings.
   (d) children tend to seek pleasure and avoid painful experiences.
8. Masters and Johnson are best known for using _____ in their research on human sexual response.
   (a) correlational coefficients
   (b) cross-cultural methods
   (c) the laboratory-observation method
   (d) the survey
9. People who agree to participate in psychological research may not represent the general population because of
   (a) obtrusive means of measurement.
   (b) volunteer bias.
   (c) random sampling.
   (d) level of education.
10. Most researchers agree that the best means of learning about cause and effect is
    (a) the experiment.
    (b) the correlational method.
    (c) the survey.
    (d) the case study.

Answers to Chapter Review

1. Many	9. Evidence	17. Property	25. Celibacy	33. Luther
2. Gender	10. History	18. Greeks	26. Virginity	34. Priests
3. Human	11. Children	19. Bisexual	27. Islamic	35. Protestant
4. Science	12. Phallic	20. Pederasty	28. Virtue	36. Oberlin
5. Sociocultural	13. Symbols	21. Romans	29. Four	37. Twentieth
6. Critical	14. Incest	22. Christian	30. Hindus	38. Victorian
7. Skepticism	15. Egypt	23. Augustine	31. *Kama Sutra*	39. Repression
8. Open	16. Hebrews	24. God	32. Religious	40. Women

41. Graham
42. Ellis
43. Were
44. Krafft-Ebing
45. Freud
46. Kinsey
47. Revolution
48. Biological
49. Pleasurable
50. Religious
51. Sociobiology
52. Mead
53. Culture

54. Psychoanalysis
55. Ego
56. Superego
57. Defense
58. Psychosexual
59. Oedipus
60. Behaviorists
61. Punishments
62. Repeat
63. Social-learning
64. Modeling
65. Sociocultural
66. Evidence

67. Populations
68. Sample
69. Represents
70. Generalize
71. Random
72. Stratified
73. Case
74. Surveys
75. Questionnaires
76. Anonymous
77. Represents
78. Desirability
79. Volunteer

80. Socially
81. More
82. Field
83. Observe
84. Unobtrusive
85. Participant
86. Masters
87. Laboratory
88. Vasocongestion
89. Myotonia
90. Correlation
91. Coefficient
92. Effect

93. Predictions
94. Cause
95. Variables
96. Treatment
97. Independent
98. Dependent
99. Experimental
100. Do
101. Do not
102. Constant

Answers to Chapter Quiz

1. (d)
2. (a)
3. (b)
4. (c)
5. (a)
6. (d)
7. (a)
8. (c)
9. (b)
10. (a)

CHAPTER 2

Female Sexual Anatomy and Physiology

O U T L I N E

The Female Sex Organs
External Sex Organs
Internal Sex Organs

The Breasts
Breast Cancer

The Menstrual Cycle
Regulation of the Menstrual Cycle
Phases of the Menstrual Cycle
Sex During Menstruation
Menopause

Menstrual Problems
Dysmenorrhea
Amenorrhea
Premenstrual Syndrome (PMS)

Chapter Review
Chapter Quiz

A World of Diversity
Ritual Genital Mutilation

Applications
Preventing Vaginitis
Breast Self-Examination
Coping with Menstrual Discomfort

- A name for the external female genitals is derived from Latin roots that mean "something to be shamed of"?
- Women, but not men, have a sex organ whose only known function is the experiencing of sexual pleasure?
- Cultures in some parts of Africa and the Middle East ritually mutilate or remove the clitoris?
- The hymen may be torn by horseback riding, strenuous exercise, or even by bicycle riding?
- Screening programs have greatly reduced the incidence of cervical cancer in the United States?
- The size of the breasts is largely determined by the amount of fatty tissue in them?
- About 80% of the women with breast cancer have no family history of the disease?
- Exercise and diet help many women cope with menstrual discomfort?

he French saying *Vive la différence!* ("Long live the difference!") celebrates the differences between men and women. In this chapter we tour the female sex organs. Even generally sophisticated students may fill in some gaps in their knowledge. Most of us know what a vagina is, but how many of us realize that only the female gender has an organ that is exclusively dedicated to pleasure? Or that a woman's passing of urine does not involve the vagina? How many of us know that a newborn girl already has all the **ova** she will ever produce? ■

Ova
Egg cells. (Singular: ovum.)

The Female Sex Organs

External Sex Organs

Pudendum
The external female genitals.

Vulva
The external sexual structures of the female.

The external sexual structures of the female are termed the **pudendum** or the **vulva.** *Pudendum* derives from the Latin term *pudendus.* It literally means "something to be ashamed of." *Vulva* is a Latin word that means "wrapper" or "covering." The vulva consists of the *mons veneris,* the *labia majora* and *minora* (major and minor lips), the *clitoris,* and the vaginal opening (see Figure 2.1). Figure 2.2 shows variations in the appearance of women's genitals.

Figure 2.1. Female External Sex Organs. This figure shows the vulva with the labia opened to reveal the urethral and vaginal openings.

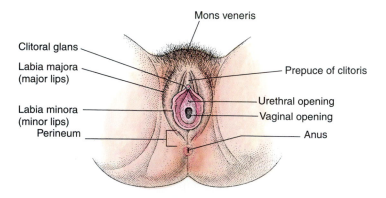

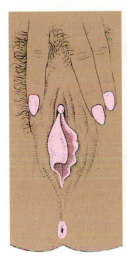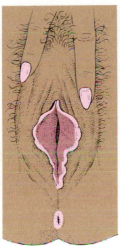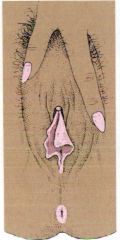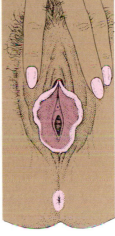

Figure 2.2. **Normal Variations in the Vulva.** The features of the vulva show a great deal of variation. A woman's attitude toward her genitals is likely to reflect her general self-concept and early childhood messages rather than the appearance of her vulva per se.

Mons veneris

A mound of fatty tissue that covers the joint of the pubic bones in front of the body, below the abdomen and above the clitoris. (The name is a Latin phrase meaning "hill" or "mount of Venus," the Roman goddess of love. Also known as the *mons pubis*, or simply *mons.*)

Labia majora

Large folds of skin that run downward from the mons along the sides of the vulva. (Latin for "large lips" or "major lips.")

Labia minora

Hairless, light-colored membranes, located between the labia majora. (Latin for "small lips" or "minor lips.")

Clitoris

A female sex organ consisting of a shaft and glans located above the urethral opening. It is extremely sensitive to sexual sensations.

Corpora cavernosa

Masses of spongy tissue in the clitoral shaft that become engorged with blood and stiffen in response to sexual stimulation. (Latin for "cavernous bodies.")

The Mons Veneris The **mons veneris** consists of fatty tissue that covers the joint of the pubic bones in front of the body, below the abdomen and above the clitoris. At puberty the mons becomes covered with pubic hair that is often thick and curly, but varies from person to person in waviness, texture, and color. The mons cushions a woman's body during sexual intercourse, protecting her and her partner from the pressure against the pubic bone caused by thrusting. There is an ample supply of nerve endings in the mons, so that caresses of the area can produce pleasurable sexual sensations.

The Labia Majora The **labia majora** are large folds of skin that run downward from the mons along the sides of the vulva. The labia majora of some women are thick and bulging. In other women, they are thinner, flatter, and less noticeable. When close together, they hide the labia minora and the urethral and vaginal openings.

The outer surfaces of the labia majora, by the thighs, are covered with pubic hair and darker skin than that found on the thighs or labia minora. The inner surfaces of the labia majora are hairless and lighter in color. They are amply supplied with nerve endings that respond to stimulation and can produce sensations of sexual pleasure. The labia majora also shield the inner portion of the female genitals.

The Labia Minora The **labia minora** are two hairless, light-colored membranes, located between the major lips. They surround the urethral and vaginal openings. The outer surfaces of the labia minora merge with the major lips. At the top they join at the prepuce (hood) of the clitoris. The labia minora differ markedly in appearance from woman to woman. Rich in blood vessels and nerve endings, the labia minora are highly sensitive to sexual stimulation. When stimulated they darken and swell, indicating engorgement with blood.

The Clitoris The clitoris is the only sex organ whose only known function is the experiencing of pleasure. **Clitoris** (see Figure 2.1) derives from the Greek word *kleitoris,* meaning "hill" or "slope." The clitoris receives its name from the manner in which it slopes upward in the shaft and forms a mound of spongy tissue at the glans. The body of the clitoris, termed the *clitoral shaft,* is about 1 inch long and ¼-inch wide. The clitoral shaft consists of erectile tissue that contains two spongy masses called **corpora cavernosa** ("cavernous bodies") that fill with blood (become engorged) and become erect in response to sexual stimulation. The stiffening of the clitoris is less apparent than the erection of the penis, because the clitoris does not swing free from the body as the penis does. The **prepuce** (meaning "before a swelling"), or hood, covers the clitoral shaft. It is a sheath of skin formed by the upper part of the labia minora.

The clitoral glans is a smooth, round knob or lump of tissue. It resembles a button and is situated above the urethral opening. The clitoral glans may be covered by the clitoral

A  WORLD OF  IVERSITY

RITUAL GENITAL MUTILATION

Despite hundreds of years of tradition, Hajia Zuwera Kassindja would not let it happen to her 17-year-old daughter, Fauziya. Hajia's own sister had died from it. So Hajia gave her daughter her inheritance from her deceased husband, which amounted to only $3,500 but left Hajia a pauper. Fauziya used the money to buy a phony passport and flee from the African country of Togo to the United States (Dugger, 1996a).

Upon arrival in the United States, Fauziya requested asylum from persecution. However, she was put into prison for more than a year. But then, in 1996, the Board of Immigration Appeals finally agreed that Fauziya was fleeing persecution, and she was allowed to remain in the United States. She now lives and studies near Washington, D.C.

From what had Hajia's sister died? From what was Fauziya escaping? *Ritual genital mutilation.*

Cultures in some parts of Africa and the Middle East ritually mutilate or remove the entire clitoris, not just the clitoral hood. Removal of the clitoris, or **clitoridectomy,** is a rite of initiation into womanhood in many of these predominantly Islamic cultures. It is often performed as a puberty rit-

ual in late childhood or early adolescence (not at birth, like male circumcision).

The clitoris gives rise to feelings of sexual pleasure in women. Its removal or mutilation represents an attempt to ensure the girl's chastity since it is assumed that uncircumcised girls are consumed with sexual desires (Ahmed,

1991). Cairo physician Said M. Thabit says, "With circumcision we remove the external parts, so when a girl wears tight nylon underclothes she will not have any stimulation" (cited in MacFarquhar, 1996, p. A3). Some groups in rural Egypt and in the northern Sudan, however, perform clitoridectomies primarily because it is a

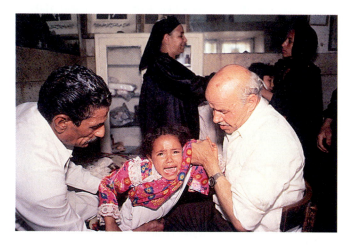

Ritual Genital Mutilation. Some predominantly Islamic cultures in Africa and the Middle East ritually mutilate or remove the clitoris as a rite of initiation into womanhood. Novelist Alice Walker drew attention to the practice in her novel *Possessing the Secret of Joy.* She has called for its abolition in her book and film *Warrior Marks.*

Prepuce
The fold of skin covering the glans of the clitoris (or penis). (From Latin roots meaning "before a swelling.")

Clitoridectomy
Surgical removal of the clitoris.

Homologous
Similar in structure; developing from the same embryonic tissue.

Analogous
Similar in function.

hood but is readily revealed by gently separating the labia minora and retracting the hood. It is highly sensitive to touch because of the rich supply of nerve endings. The clitoral glans is highly sensitive to touch. Women thus usually prefer to be stroked or stimulated on the mons, or on the clitoral hood, rather than directly on the glans.

In some respects, the clitoris is the female counterpart of the penis. Both organs develop from the same embryonic tissue, which makes them similar in structure, or **homologous.** They are not fully similar in function, or **analogous,** however. Both organs receive and transmit sexual sensations, but the penis is directly involved in reproduction and excretion by serving as a conduit for sperm and urine, respectively. The clitoris, however, is a unique sex organ. It serves no known purpose other than sexual pleasure.

Surgical removal of the clitoral hood is common among Muslims in the Near East and Africa. The nearby World of Diversity feature shows that this practice is an attempt to control female sexuality.

social custom that has been passed down from ancient times (Toubia, 1994). Some perceive it as part of their faith in Islam. However, neither Islam nor any other religion requires it (Mac-Farquhar, 1996). Ironically, many young women do not grasp that they are victims. They assume that clitoridectomy is part of being female (Rosenthal, 1994).

Clitoridectomies are performed under unsanitary conditions without benefit of anesthesia (Rosenthal, 1993). Medical complications are common, including infections, bleeding, tissue scarring, painful menstruation, and obstructed labor (Toubia, 1994). The procedure is psychologically traumatizing (Toubia, 1994). An even more radical form of clitoridectomy, called *infibulation* or pharaonic circumcision, is practiced widely in the Sudan. Pharaonic circumcision involves complete removal of the clitoris along with the labia minora and the inner layers of the labia majora. After removal of the skin tissue, the raw edges of the labia majora are sewn together. Only a tiny opening is left to allow passage of urine and menstrual discharge. The sewing together of the vulva may be intended to ensure the girls' chastity until marriage. Medical complications are common, including menstrual and urinary problems, and even death. After marriage, the opening is enlarged to permit intercourse. Enlargement is a gradual process that is often made difficult by scar tissue from the circumcision. Hemorrhaging and tearing of surrounding tissues are common consequences. It may take three months or longer before the opening is large enough to allow penile penetration. Mutilation of the labia is now illegal in the Sudan, although the law continues to allow removal of the clitoris. Some African countries have outlawed clitoridectomies, although such laws are rarely enforced (Rosenthal, 1993).

Millions of women in Africa and the Middle East—85 to 114 million by some estimates (Kaplan, 1993)—have undergone removal of the clitoris and the labia minora. Clitoridectomies remain common or even universal in nearly 30 countries in Africa, in many countries in the Middle East, and in parts of Malaysia, Yemen, Oman, Indonesia, and the India-Pakistan subcontinent (Rosenthal, 1995). Thousands of African immigrant girls living in European countries and the United States have also been mutilated (Dugger, 1996b).

Do not confuse male circumcision with the maiming inflicted on girls.

Former representative Patricia Schroeder of Colorado depicts the male equivalent of female genital mutilation as cutting off the penis (Dugger, 1996b). *The New York Times* columnist A. M. Rosenthal (1995) calls female genital mutilation the most widespread existing violation of human rights in the world. The Pulitzer Prize–winning, African American novelist Alice Walker has condemned it in her novel *Possessing the Secret of Joy* (1992). She called for its abolition in her book and movie *Warrior Marks*.

In 1996, the United States outlawed ritual genital mutilation within its borders. The government also directed U.S. representatives to world financial institutions to deny aid to countries that have not established educational programs to bring an end to the practice (Dugger, 1996b). Yet calls from Westerners to ban the practice in parts of Africa and the Middle East have sparked controversy on grounds of "cultural condescension"— that people in one culture cannot dictate the cultural traditions of another. Yet for Alice Walker, "torture is not culture." As the debate continues, some 2 million African girls continue to undergo ritual genital mutilations each year.

The Vestibule   The word *vestibule,* which means "entranceway," refers to the area within the labia minora that contains the openings to the vagina and the urethra. The vestibule is richly supplied with nerve endings and is very sensitive to tactile or other sexual stimulation.

The Urethral Opening   Urine passes from the female's body through the **urethral opening** (see Figure 2.1), which is connected by a short tube called the urethra to the bladder (see Figure 2.3 on page 32), where urine collects. The urethral opening lies below the clitoral glans and above the vaginal opening. The urethral opening, urethra, and bladder are unrelated to the reproductive system.

The proximity of the urethral opening to the external sex organs may pose some hygienic problems for sexually active women. The urinary tract, which includes the urethra, bladder, and kidneys, may become infected from bacteria that are transmitted from the

Urethral opening
The opening through which urine passes from the female's body.

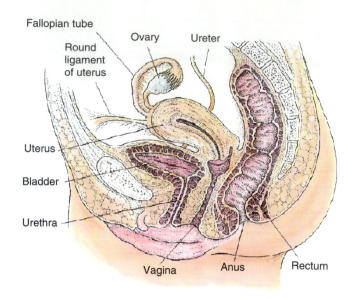

Figure 2.3. **The Female Reproductive System.** This cross-section locates many of the internal sex organs that compose the female reproductive system. Note that the uterus is normally tipped forward.

vagina or rectum. Infectious microscopic organisms may also pass from the male's sex organs to the female's urethral opening during sexual intercourse. Manual stimulation of the vulva with dirty hands may also transmit bacteria through the urethral opening to the bladder. Anal intercourse followed by vaginal intercourse may transfer microscopic organisms from the rectum to the bladder and cause infection. For similar reasons, women should first wipe the vulva, then the anus, when using the bathroom.

Cystitis

An inflammation of the urinary bladder. (From the Greek *kystis*, meaning "sac.")

Cystitis is a bladder inflammation that may stem from any of these sources. Its primary symptoms are burning and frequent urination (also called *urinary urgency*). Pus or a bloody discharge is common, and there may be an intermittent or persistent ache just above the pubic bone. These symptoms may disappear after several days, but consultation with a **gynecologist** is recommended, because untreated cystitis can lead to serious kidney infections. A few precautions may help women prevent serious inflammation of the bladder:

Gynecologist

A physician who treats women's diseases, especially of the reproductive tract. (From the Greek *gyne*, meaning "woman.")

- Drinking two quarts of water a day to flush the bladder
- Drinking orange or cranberry juice to maintain an acid environment that discourages growth of infectious organisms
- Decreasing use of alcohol and caffeine (from coffee, tea, or cola drinks) that may irritate the bladder
- Washing the hands prior to masturbation or self-examination
- Washing one's partner's and one's own genitals before and after intercourse
- Preventing objects that have touched the anus (fingers, penis, toilet tissue) from subsequently coming into contact with the vulva
- Urinating soon after intercourse to help wash away bacteria

Introitus

The vaginal opening. (From the Latin for "entrance.")

The Vaginal Opening   One does not see an entire vagina, but rather the vaginal opening, or **introitus,** when one parts the labia minora. The introitus lies below and is larger than the urethral opening. Its shape resembles that of the **hymen.**

Hymen

A fold of tissue across the vaginal opening that is usually present at birth and remains at least partly intact until a woman engages in coitus. (Greek for "membrane.")

The hymen is a fold of tissue across the vaginal opening that is usually present at birth and may remain at least partly intact until a woman engages in coitus. For this reason the hymen has been called the "maidenhead." Its presence has been taken as proof of virginity, and its absence as evidence of coitus. However, some women are born with incomplete hymens, and other women's hymens are torn accidentally, such as during horseback riding, strenuous exercise, or gymnastics—or even when bicycle riding. A punctured hymen is therefore poor evidence of coital experience. A flexible hymen may also withstand many coital experiences, so its presence does not guarantee virginity.

Figure 2.4 illustrates various vaginal openings. The first three show common shapes of hymens among women who have not had coitus. The fifth drawing shows a *parous*

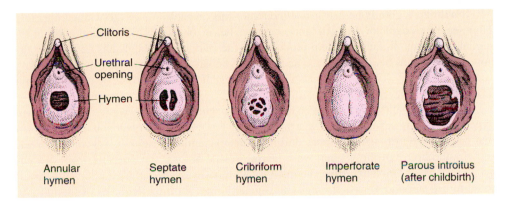

Figure 2.4. Appearance of Various Types of Hymens, and the Introitus (at right) As It Appears Following Delivery of a Baby.

("passed through") vaginal opening, typical of a woman who has delivered a baby. Now and then the hymen consists of tough fibrous tissue and is closed, or *imperforate,* as in the fourth drawing. An imperforate hymen may not be discovered until after puberty, when menstrual discharges begin to accumulate in the vagina. In these rare cases, a simple surgical incision will perforate the hymen.

The Perineum   The **perineum** incorporates the skin and underlying tissue between the vaginal opening and the anus. The perineum is rich in nerve endings. Stimulation of the area may heighten sexual arousal. Many physicians make a routine perineal incision during labor, called an **episiotomy,** to facilitate childbirth.

Structures That Underlie the External Sex Organs

Figure 2.5 shows what lies beneath the skin of the vulva. The vestibular bulbs and Bartholin's glands are active during sexual arousal and are found on both sides (shown on the right in Figure 2.5). Muscular rings (**sphincters**) that constrict bodily openings such as the vaginal and anal openings are also found on both sides.

The clitoral **crura** are wing-shaped, leglike structures that attach the clitoris to the pubic bone beneath. The crura contain corpora cavernosa, which engorge with blood and stiffen during sexual arousal.

The **vestibular bulbs** are attached to the clitoris at the top and extend downward along the sides of the vaginal opening. Blood congests them during sexual arousal, swelling the vulva and lengthening the vagina. This swelling contributes to coital sensations for both partners.

Perineum
The skin and underlying tissue that lie between the vaginal opening and the anus. (From Greek roots meaning "around" and "to empty out.")

Episiotomy
A surgical incision in the perineum that may be made during childbirth to protect the vagina from tearing. (From the Greek roots *epision*, meaning "pubic region," and *tome*, meaning "cutting.")

Sphincters
Ring-shaped muscles that surround body openings and open or close them by expanding or contracting. (From the Greek for "that which draws close.")

Crura
Anatomical structures resembling legs that attach the clitoris to the pubic bone. (Singular: crus. A Latin word meaning "leg" or "shank.")

Vestibular bulbs
Cavernous structures that extend downward along the sides of the introitus and swell during sexual arousal.

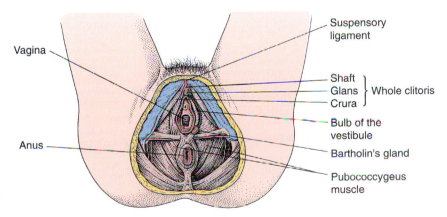

Figure 2.5.   Structures That Underlie the Female External Sex Organs. If we could see beneath the vulva, we would find muscle fibers that constrict the various body openings, plus the crura ("legs") of the clitoris, the vestibular bulbs, and Bartholin's glands.

THE FEMALE SEX ORGANS ~ **33**

Bartholin's glands
Glands that lie just inside the minor lips and secrete fluid just before orgasm.

Bartholin's glands lie just inside the minor lips on each side of the vaginal opening. They secrete a couple of drops of lubrication just before orgasm. This lubrication is not essential for coitus. In fact, the fluid produced by the Bartholin's glands has no known purpose. If the glands become infected and clogged, however, a woman may notice swelling and local irritation. It is wise to consult a gynecologist if these symptoms do not fade within a few days.

It was once believed that the source of the vaginal lubrication or "wetness" that women experience during sexual arousal was produced by the Bartholin's glands. It is now known that engorgement of vaginal tissues during sexual excitement results in a form of "sweating" by the lining of the vaginal wall. During sexual arousal the pressure from this engorgement causes moisture from the many small blood vessels that lie in the vaginal wall to be forced out and to pass through the vaginal lining, forming the basis of the lubrication. In less time than it takes to read this sentence (generally within 10 to 30 seconds), beads of vaginal lubrication or "sweat" appear along the interior lining of the vagina in response to sexual stimulation, in much the same way that rising temperatures cause water to pass through the skin as perspiration.

Pelvic floor muscles permit women to constrict the vaginal and anal openings. They contract automatically, or involuntarily, during orgasm, and their tone may contribute to coital sensations.

Internal Sex Organs

The internal sex organs of the female include the innermost parts of the vagina, the cervix, the uterus, and two ovaries, each connected to the uterus by a fallopian tube (see Figures 2.3, 2.6). These structures comprise the female reproductive system.

Vagina
The tubular female sex organ that contains the penis during sexual intercourse and through which a baby is born. (Latin for "sheath.")

The Vagina   The **vagina** extends back and upward from the vaginal opening (see Figure 2.3). It is usually 3 to 5 inches long at rest. Menstrual flow and babies pass from the uterus to the outer world through the vagina. During coitus, the penis is contained within the vagina.

The vagina is commonly pictured as a canal or barrel, but when at rest, it is like a collapsed muscular tube. Its walls touch like the fingers of an empty glove. The vagina expands in length and width during sexual arousal. The vagina can also expand to allow insertion of a tampon, as well as the passage of a baby's head and shoulders during childbirth.

The vaginal walls have three layers. The inner lining, or *vaginal mucosa,* is made visible by opening the labia minora. It is a mucous membrane similar to the skin that lines the inside of the mouth. It feels fleshy, soft, and corrugated. It may vary from very dry (especially if the female is anxious about something like examinations) to very wet, in which case fingers slide against it readily. The middle layer of the vaginal wall is muscular. The outer or deeper layer is a fibrous covering that connects the vagina to other pelvic structures.

Figure 2.6. **Female Internal Reproductive Organs.**
This drawing highlights the relationship of the uterus to the fallopian tubes and ovaries. Note the layers of the uterus, the ligaments that attach the ovaries to the uterus, and the relationship of the ovaries to the fimbriae of the fallopian tubes.

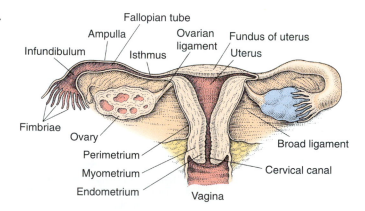

A P P L I C A T I O N S

PREVENTING VAGINITIS

Vaginitis refers to any vaginal inflammation, whether it is caused by an infection, an allergic reaction, or chemical irritation. Vaginitis may also stem from use of birth-control pills or antibiotics that alter the natural body chemistry, or from other factors, such as lowered resistance (from fatigue or poor diet). Changes in the natural body chemistry or lowered resistance permit microscopic organisms normally found in the vagina to multiply to infectious levels. Vaginitis may be recognized by abnormal discharge, itching, burning of the vulva, and, sometimes, urinary urgency. Women with vaginitis are advised to seek medical attention, but let us note some suggestions that may help prevent vaginitis (Boston Women's Health Book Collective, 1992):

- Wash your vulva and anus regularly with mild soap. Pat dry (taking care not to touch the vulva after dabbing the anus).
- Wear cotton panties. Nylon underwear retains heat and moisture that cause harmful bacteria to flourish.
- Avoid pants that are tight in the crotch.
- Be certain that sex partners are well-washed. Condoms may also reduce the spread of infections from one's sex partner.
- Use a sterile, water-soluble jelly such as K-Y jelly if artificial lubrication is needed for intercourse. Do *not* use Vaseline. Birth-control jellies can also be used for lubrication.
- Avoid intercourse that is painful or abrasive to the vagina.
- Avoid diets high in sugar and refined carbohydrates since they alter the normal acidity of the vagina.
- Women who are prone to vaginal infections may find it helpful to douche occasionally with plain water, a solution of 1 or 2 tablespoons of vinegar in a quart of warm water, or a solution of baking soda and water. Douches consisting of unpasteurized, plain (unflavored) yogurt may help replenish the "good" bacteria that are normally found in the vagina and that may be destroyed by use of antibiotics. Consult your physician before deciding to douche or to apply any preparations to the vagina.
- Watch your general health. Eating poorly or getting insufficient rest will reduce your resistance to infection.

Vaginitis
Vaginal inflammation.

The vaginal walls are rich with blood vessels but poorly supplied with nerve endings. Unlike the sensitive outer third of the vaginal barrel, the inner two thirds are so insensitive to touch that minor surgery may sometimes be performed on those portions without anesthesia. The entire vaginal barrel is sensitive to pressure, however, which can be experienced as sexually pleasurable.

The vaginal walls secrete substances that help maintain the vagina's normal acidity (pH 4.0 to 5.0). Normally the secretions taste salty. The odor and taste of these secretions may vary during the menstrual cycle. Although the evidence is not clear, the secretions are thought to contain substances that may act as sexual attractants. Women who frequently **douche** or use feminine deodorant sprays may remove or mask substances that may arouse sex partners. Douching or spraying may also alter the natural chemical balance of the vagina, which can increase the risk of vaginal infections. The normal, healthy vagina cleanses itself through regular chemical secretions that are evidenced by a mild white or yellowish discharge.

Douche
Application of a jet of liquid to the vagina as a rinse. (From the Italian *doccia*, meaning "shower bath.")

Cervix
The lower end of the uterus. (Latin for "neck.")

Os
The opening in middle of the cervix. (Latin for "mouth.")

The Cervix   The **cervix** is the lower end of the uterus. Its walls, like those of the vagina, produce secretions that contribute to the chemical balance of the vagina. The opening in the middle of the cervix, or **os,** is normally about the width of a straw, although it expands to permit passage of a baby from the uterus to the vagina during childbirth. Sperm pass from the vagina to the uterus through the cervical canal.

Cervical cancer is relatively uncommon in the United States, largely due to screening programs (Cannistra & Niloff, 1996). Nearly 16,000 new cases of cervical cancer are reported annually (American Cancer Society, 1995). Cervical cancer is more common among

Pap test

A test of a sample of cervical cells that screens for cervical cancer and other abnormalities. (Named after the originator of the technique, Dr. Papanicolaou.)

Radiotherapy

Treatment of a disease by X-rays or by emissions from a radioactive substance.

Uterus

The hollow, muscular, pear-shaped organ in which a fertilized ovum becomes implanted and develops until birth.

Fundus

The uppermost part of the uterus. (*Fundus* is a Latin word meaning "base.")

Endometrium

The innermost layer of the uterus. (From Latin and Greek roots meaning "within the uterus.")

Endometriosis

A condition caused by the growth of endometrial tissue in the abdominal cavity or elsewhere outside the uterus. Characterized by menstrual pain, it may cause infertility.

Myometrium

The middle, well-muscled layer of the uterus. (*Myo-* stems from the Greek *mys*, meaning "muscle.")

Perimetrium

The outer layer of the uterus. (From roots meaning "around the uterus.")

Hysterectomy

Surgical removal of the uterus.

Complete hysterectomy

Surgical removal of the ovaries, fallopian tubes, cervix, and uterus.

Fallopian tubes

Tubes that extend from the upper uterus toward the ovaries and conduct ova to the uterus. (After the Italian anatomist Gabriel Fallopio, who is credited with their discovery.)

women who have had many sex partners, who became sexually active at a relatively early age, who come from lower socioeconomic status, and who smoke. All women are at risk, however.

A **Pap test** examines a sample of cervical cells that are smeared on a slide to screen for cervical cancer and other abnormalities. The American Cancer Society (1995) recommends annual Pap tests along with a pelvic examination for women who are, or have been, sexually active or who have reached age 18. Most cases of cervical cancer can be successfully treated by surgery and **radiotherapy** if they are detected early. The five-year survival rate for women with cervical cancer is 67%. For women diagnosed with localized cancer, the survival rate is 90% (American Cancer Society, 1995). However, cervical cancer can also be prevented when precancerous changes are detected by Pap smear ("Panel Says," 1996). There are nearly 5,000 deaths from cervical cancer per year. The mortality rate is more than twice as high for African American women than for White women (American Cancer Society, 1995).

The Uterus   The **uterus,** or womb, (see Figures 2.3, 2.6) is the organ in which a fertilized ovum becomes implanted and develops until birth. The uterus usually slants forward (is *antroverted*), although about 10% of women have uteruses that tip backward (are *retroverted*). In most instances a retroverted uterus causes no problems, but some women with retroverted uteruses find coitus in certain positions painful. A retroverted uterus normally tips forward during pregnancy.

The uterus is suspended in the pelvis by flexible ligaments. In a woman who has not given birth, it is about 3 inches long, 3 inches wide, and 1 inch thick near the top. The uterus expands to accommodate a fetus during pregnancy and shrinks after pregnancy, though not to its original size.

The uppermost part of the uterus is called the **fundus** (see Figure 2.6). The uterus is shaped like an inverted pear. If a ceramic model of a uterus were placed on a table, it would balance on the fundus. The central region of the uterus is called the body. The narrow lower region is the cervix, which leads downward to the vagina.

Like the vagina, the uterus has three layers (also shown in Figure 2.6). The innermost layer, or **endometrium,** is richly supplied with blood vessels and glands. Its structure varies according to a woman's age and phase of the menstrual cycle. Endometrial tissue is discharged through the cervix and vagina at menstruation. For reasons not entirely understood, in some women endometrial tissue may also grow in the abdominal cavity or elsewhere in the reproductive system. This condition is called **endometriosis,** and the most common symptom is menstrual pain. If left untreated, endometriosis may lead to infertility.

Cancer of the endometrial lining is called endometrial cancer. Risk factors include obesity, a diet high in fats, early menarche or late menopause, history of failure to ovulate, and estrogen-replacement therapy (Rose, 1996). For women who obtain hormone-replacement therapy, combining estrogen with progestin mitigates the risk of endometrial cancer (Grodstein et al., 1996; Rose, 1996). Endometrial cancer is symptomized by abnormal uterine staining or bleeding, especially after menopause. The most common treatment is surgery (Rose, 1996). The five-year survival rate for endometrial cancer is up to 95% if it is discovered early and limited to the endometrium (Rose, 1996). (Endometrial cancer is usually diagnosed early because women tend to quickly report postmenopausal bleeding to their doctors.) The survival rate drops when the cancer invades surrounding tissues or metastasizes.

The second layer of the uterus, the **myometrium,** is well muscled. It endows the uterus with flexibility and strength, and creates the powerful contractions that propel a fetus outward during labor. The third or outermost layer, the **perimetrium,** provides an external cover.

One woman in three in the United States has a **hysterectomy** by the age of 60. Most hysterectomy patients are between the ages of 35 and 45. The hysterectomy is now the second most commonly performed operation on women in this country. (Cesarean sections are the most common.) A hysterectomy may be performed when women develop cancer of the uterus, ovaries, or cervix, or other diseases that cause pain or excessive uterine bleeding.

Isthmus
The segment of a fallopian tube closest to the uterus. (A Latin word meaning "narrow passage.")

Ampulla
The wide segment of a fallopian tube near the ovary. (A Latin word meaning "bottle.")

Infundibulum
The outer, funnel-shaped part of a fallopian tube. (A Latin word meaning "funnel.")

Fimbriae
Projections from a fallopian tube that extend toward an ovary. (Singular: fimbria. Latin for "fiber" or "fringe.")

Ectopic pregnancy
A pregnancy in which the fertilized ovum becomes implanted outside the uterus, usually in the fallopian tube. (*Ectopic* derives from Greek roots meaning "out of place.")

Ovaries
Almond-shaped organs that produce ova and the hormones estrogen and progesterone.

Estrogen
A generic term for female sex hormones (including estradiol, estriol, estrone, and others) or synthetic compounds that promote the development of female sex characteristics and regulate the menstrual cycle. (From the roots meaning "generating" [-*gen*] and "estrus.")

Progesterone
A steroid hormone secreted by the corpus luteum or prepared synthetically that stimulates proliferation of the endometrium and is involved in regulation of the menstrual cycle. (From the root *pro-*, meaning "promoting," and the words *gestation*, *steroid*, and *one*.)

Follicle
A capsule within an ovary that contains an ovum. (From a Latin word meaning "small bag.")

A hysterectomy may be partial or complete. A **complete hysterectomy** involves the surgical removal of the ovaries, fallopian tubes, cervix, and uterus. It is usually performed to reduce the risk of cancer spreading throughout the reproductive system. A partial hysterectomy removes the uterus but spares the ovaries and fallopian tubes. Sparing the ovaries allows the woman to continue to ovulate and produce adequate quantities of female sex hormones.

The hysterectomy has become steeped in controversy. In many cases it is possible that less radical medical interventions might successfully treat the problem (Bernstein et al., 1993). We advise women whose physicians recommend a hysterectomy to seek a second opinion before proceeding.

The Fallopian Tubes   Two uterine tubes, also called **fallopian tubes,** are about 4 inches in length and extend from the upper end of the uterus toward the ovaries (see Figure 2.6). The part of each tube nearest the uterus is the **isthmus,** which broadens into the **ampulla** as it approaches the ovary. The outer part, or **infundibulum,** has fringelike projections called **fimbriae** that extend toward, but are not attached to, the ovary.

Ova pass through the fallopian tubes on their way to the uterus. The fallopian tubes are not inert passageways. They help nourish and conduct ova. These tubes are lined with tiny hairlike projections termed cilia ("lashes") that help move ova through the tube. The exact mechanisms by which ova are guided are unknown, however. It is tempting to say that ova move at a snail's pace, but a snail would leave them far behind. They journey toward the uterus at about 1 inch per day. Since ova must be fertilized within a day or two after they are released from the ovaries, fertilization usually occurs in the infundibulum within a couple of inches of the ovaries. The form of sterilization called tubal ligation ties off the fallopian tubes, so that ova cannot pass through them or become fertilized.

In an **ectopic pregnancy,** the fertilized ovum implants itself outside the uterus, most often in the fallopian tube where fertilization occurred. Ectopic pregnancies can eventually burst fallopian tubes, causing hemorrhaging and death. Ectopic pregnancies are thus terminated before the tube ruptures. They are not easily recognized, however, because their symptoms—missed menstrual period, abdominal pain, irregular bleeding—suggest many conditions. Experiencing any of these symptoms is an excellent reason for consulting a gynecologist. Women who have had pelvic inflammatory disease (PID), undergone tubal surgery, or used intrauterine devices (IUDs) are at increased risk of developing ectopic pregnancies (Marchbanks, 1988).

The Ovaries   The two **ovaries** are almond-shaped organs that are each about 1½ inches long. They lie on either side of the uterus, to which they are attached by ovarian ligaments. The ovaries produce ova (egg cells) and the female sex hormones **estrogen** and **progesterone.**

Estrogen is a generic term for several hormones (such as estradiol, estriol, and estrone) that promote the changes of puberty and regulate the menstrual cycle. Estrogen also helps older women maintain cognitive functioning and feelings of psychological well-being (Sourander, 1994). Progesterone also has multiple functions, including regulating the menstrual cycle and preparing the uterus for pregnancy by stimulating the development of the endometrium (uterine lining). Estrogen and progesterone levels vary with the phases of the menstrual cycle.

The human female is born with all the ova she will ever have (about 2 million), but they are immature in form. Of these, about 400,000 survive into puberty, each of which is contained in the ovary within a thin capsule, or **follicle.** During a woman's reproductive years, from puberty to menopause, only 400 or so ripened ova, typically 1 per month, will be released by their rupturing follicles for possible fertilization. How these ova are selected is among the mysteries of nature.

The American Cancer Society (1995) estimates that each year some 27,000 women in the United States are diagnosed with ovarian cancer, and 14,500 die from it. It most often strikes women between the ages of 40 and 70 and ranks as the fourth leading cancer killer of women, behind lung cancer, breast cancer, and colon cancer. Women most at risk are those with blood relatives who had the disease, especially a first-degree relative (mother, sister, or daughter). Other risk factors are also important, since about 9 women in 10 who develop ovarian cancer do not have a family history of it. Researchers have identified several risk factors that increase the chances of developing the disease: never having given birth, prolonged use of talcum powder between the anus and the vagina, infertility, a history of breast cancer, and a diet rich in meat and animal fats. Questions have been raised as to whether the use of clomiphene, a fertility drug, increases the risk of ovarian cancer (Del Priore et al., 1995; Whittemore, 1994).

Early detection is the key to fighting ovarian cancer. When it is detected before spreading beyond the ovary, 90% of victims survive. However, the overall survival rate is only 42% (American Cancer Society, 1995). Unfortunately, ovarian cancer is often "silent" in the early stages, showing no obvious signs or symptoms. The most common sign is enlargement of the abdomen, which is caused by the accumulation of fluid. Periodic, complete pelvic examinations are important. The Pap test, which is useful in detecting cervical cancer, does not reveal ovarian cancer. The American Cancer Society (1995) advises women over the age of 40 to have a cancer-related checkup every year.

Surgery, radiation therapy, and drug therapy are treatment options. Surgery usually includes the removal of one or both ovaries, the uterus, and the fallopian tubes.

The Breasts

In some cultures the breasts are viewed merely as biological instruments for feeding infants. In our culture, however, breasts have taken on such erotic significance that a woman's self-esteem may become linked to her bustline.

The breasts are **secondary sex characteristics.** That is, like the rounding of the hips, they distinguish women from men, but they are not directly involved in reproduction. Each breast contains **mammary glands** (Figure 2.7). Each gland opens at the nipple through its own duct. The mammary glands are separated by soft, fatty tissue. It is the amount of this fatty tissue, not the amount of glandular tissue, that largely determines the size of the breasts. Women vary little in their amount of glandular tissue, so breast size does not determine the quantity of milk that can be produced.

The nipple, which lies in the center of the **areola,** contains smooth muscle fibers that make the nipple become erect when they contract. The areola, or area surrounding the nipple, darkens during pregnancy and remains darker after delivery. Oil-producing glands in the areola help lubricate the nipples during breast-feeding. Milk ducts conduct milk from the mammary glands through the nipples. Nipples are richly endowed with nerve endings, so that stimulation of the nipples heightens sexual arousal for many women. Figure 2.8 shows normal variations in the size and shape of the breasts of adult women.

Secondary sex characteristics

Physical traits that distinguish women from men but are not directly involved in reproduction.

Mammary glands

Milk-secreting glands. (From the Latin *mamma,* which means both "breast" and "mother.")

Areola

The dark ring on the breast that encircles the nipple.

Figure 2.7. A Breast of an Adult Woman. This drawing reveals the structures underlying the breast, including milk ducts and fat cells.

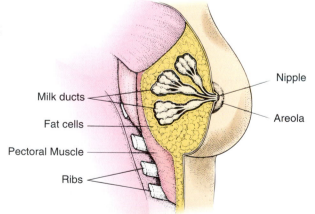

Milk ducts

Fat cells

Pectoral Muscle

Ribs

Nipple

Areola

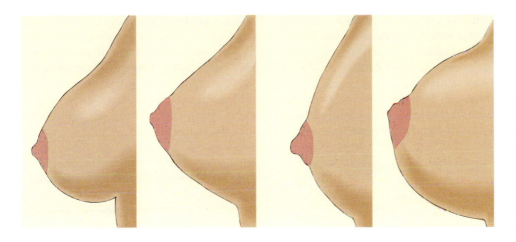

Figure 2.8. **Normal Variations in the Size and Shape of the Breasts of Adult Women.** The size and shape of the breasts have little bearing on ability to produce milk or on sensitivity to sexual stimulation. Breasts have become highly eroticized in our culture.

Women can prompt their partners to provide breast stimulation by informing them that their breasts are sensitive to stimulation. They can also guide a partner's hands in ways that provide the type of stimulation they desire. The breasts vary in sensitivity with the phases of the menstrual cycle, and some women appear less responsive to breast stimulation than others. However, some less sensitive women may learn to enjoy breast stimulation by focusing on breast sensations during lovemaking in a relaxed atmosphere.

Breast Cancer

Breast cancer strikes about 182,000 women and takes some 46,000 lives annually. It is the second leading cause of cancer deaths among women, after lung cancer (American Cancer Society, 1995). (An estimated 240 men also die of breast cancer annually.) The National Cancer Institute estimates that in the United States, 1 woman in 8 will develop breast cancer ("Chance of breast cancer," 1993). The disease takes the lives of nearly 3 of 10 women who develop it. It is not cancer in the breast that causes death, but rather its spread to vital body parts, such as the brain, the bones, the lungs, or the liver.

Despite the popular impression to the contrary, rates of breast cancer in the United States are not on the increase (American Cancer Society, 1995). Rather, more early cases of breast cancer are being detected because of an increased use of **mammography,** a specialized X-ray that detects cancerous lumps in the breast. Advances in early detection and treatment have led to increased rates of recovery. The five-year survival rate for women whose breast cancers have not metastasized—that is, spread beyond the breast—is 93%, up from 78% in the 1940s (Miller et al., 1996). The five-year survival rate drops to 69% if the cancer has spread to the surrounding region and to 18% if it has spread to distant sites in the body.

The risk of breast cancer increases sharply with age. About four of five cases develop in women over the age of 50 ("Chance of breast cancer," 1993). The National Cancer Institute (NCI) estimates that from birth to age 40, 1 in 217 women will develop breast cancer. From birth to age 50 the risk rises to 1 in 50. By age 60, the risk rises to 1 in 24, and by age 70, to 1 in 14 (Ochs, 1993a).

The risk of breast cancer is higher among women with a family history of the disease (Slattery & Kerber, 1993). A study of more than 100,000 women nurses showed that those with mothers or sisters who had breast cancer had nearly twice the chance of developing the disease themselves (Colditz et al., 1993). Women who had both a mother and a sister with the disease had between two and three times greater risk. Still, about 80% of women with breast cancer have no family history of the disease (Brody, 1995a). Only about 6% of the women with breast cancer in the nurses' study had either a mother or sister with the disease (Johnson & Williams, 1993).

Other risk factors include early onset of menstruation (before age 12), late menopause (after age 50), delayed childbearing (after age 30), never giving birth, and heavy drinking

Mammography
A special type of X-ray test that detects cancerous lumps in the breast.

of alcohol (American Cancer Society, 1994; Colditz et al., 1995; Fuchs et al., 1995). Many of these factors apparently create greater risk because of prolonged exposure to estrogen. Estrogen stimulates breast development in young women. Earlier onset of menstruation, later menopause, and delayed childbearing are all connected to longer, uninterrupted exposure to high levels of estrogen. Despite the fact that birth-control pills contain estogen, a review of 54 studies involving more the 150,000 women concluded that there is no connection between using the pill and breast cancer (Gilbert, 1996). Nor has it been shown that a diet high in fats contributes to breast cancer (Hunter et al., 1996).

Cysts
Saclike structures filled with fluid or diseased material.

Benign
Doing little or no harm.

Fibroadenoma
A benign, fibrous tumor.

Malignant
Lethal; causing or likely to cause death.

Lumpectomy
Surgical removal of a lump from the breast.

Mastectomy
Surgical removal of the entire breast.

Detection   Women with breast cancer have lumps in the breast, *but most lumps in the breasts are not cancerous.* Most are either **cysts** or **benign** tumors called **fibroadenomas.** Breast cancer involves lumps in the breast that are **malignant.**

There is no clear-cut way to prevent breast cancer, but early detection and treatment reduce the risk of mortality. The sooner cancer is detected, the less likely it is to have spread to critical organs.

Breast cancer may be detected in a number of ways, including breast self-examination, medical examination, and mammography. Through mammography, tiny, highly curable cancers can be detected—and treated—before they can be felt by touch (Brody, 1995a). By the time a malignant lump is large enough to be felt by touch, it may have metastasized—that is, splintered off to form colonies elsewhere in the body. A mammography can detect tiny tumors before metastasis. One study found that 82% of women whose breast cancers were detected early by mammography survived for at least five years following surgery, as compared to 60% of those whose cancers were discovered later. Early detection may offer another benefit. Smaller cancerous lumps can often be removed by **lumpectomy,** which spares the breast. More advanced cancers are likely to be treated by **mastectomy.**

The American Cancer Society recommends that women have a breast exam every three years when they are between 20 and 39 years of age, every one or two years between ages 40 and 49, and then annually thereafter ("Breast fears fade," 1993). They also recommend that young women receive a baseline mammogram for comparison with later tests. The mortality rate from breast cancer may be cut by 30% or more if women follow these guidelines (Brody, 1990b). Mammography is not foolproof, however. Thus, the chances of early detection are optimized through a combination of monthly breast self-examinations (see the nearby Application), annual breast examinations by a physician, and regular mammograms.

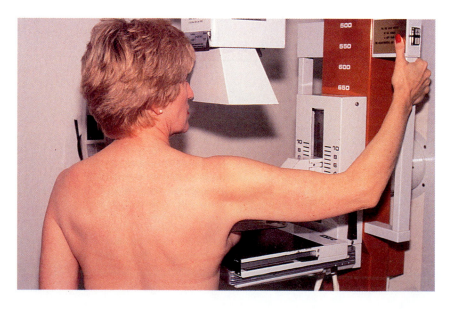

Mammography. Early detection is a key to effective treatment of cancer. Mammography uses specialized X-ray technology to detect cancerous lumps in the breast before they can be felt. The goal is to detect tumors before they have metastasized to other parts of the body.

APPLICATIONS

BREAST SELF-EXAMINATION

Regular breast self-examination and regular visits to a physician provide the best protection against breast cancer, since they may lead to early detection and treatment. A woman may wish to undertake an initial breast self-examination with a physician in order to determine the degree of "lumpiness" that seems normal for her. Then she should conduct a breast self-examination at least once a month, preferably about a week after her period ends (when the breasts are least influenced by hormones), so that any changes can be reported promptly to a physician (see Figure 2.9).

The following instructions for breast self-examination are based on American Cancer Society guidelines. Additional material on breast self-examination may be obtained from the American Cancer Society by calling this toll-free number: (800) ACS-2345.

1. *In the shower.* Examine your breasts during your bath or shower; hands glide more easily over wet skin. Keep your fingers flat, and move gently over every part of each breast. Use the right hand to examine the left breast and the left hand for the right breast. Check for any lump, hard knot, or thickening.

2. *Before a mirror.* Inspect your breasts with your arms at your sides. Next, raise your arms high overhead. Look for any changes in the contour of each breast, a swelling, dimpling of skin, or changes in the nipple. Then rest your palms on your hips and press down firmly to flex your chest muscles. Your left and right breasts will not exactly match—few women's breasts do. Regular inspection shows what is normal for you and will give you confidence in your examination.

3. *Lying down.* To examine your right breast, put a pillow or folded towel under your right shoulder. Place your right arm behind your head—this distributes breast tissue more evenly on the chest. With your left hand, fingers flat, press gently with the finger pads (the top thirds of the fingers) of the three middle fingers in small circular motions around an imaginary clock face. Begin at the outermost top of your right breast for 12 o'clock, then move to 1 o'clock, and so on around the circle back to 12. A ridge of firm tissue in the lower curve of each breast is normal. Then move in 1 inch, toward the nipple. Keep circling to examine *every part of your breast*, including the nipple. This requires at least three more circles. Now slowly repeat the procedure on your left breast. Place the pillow beneath your left shoulder, your left arm behind your head, and use the finger pads on your right hand.

After you examine your left breast fully, squeeze the nipple of each breast gently between your thumb and index finger. Any discharge, clear or bloody, should be reported to your doctor immediately.

Research shows that many women who know how to do breast self-examinations do not do them regularly. Why? There are many reasons, including fear of what one will find and doubts as to whether self-examination will make a difference. But the most frequently mentioned reasons are being too busy or forgetting (Friedman et al., 1994).

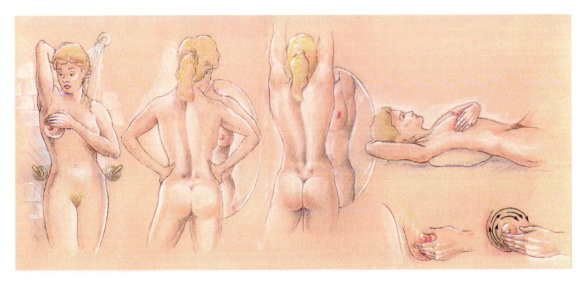

Figure 2.9. **Woman Examining Her Breasts for Lumps.**

The Menstrual Cycle

Menstruation
The cyclical bleeding that stems from the shedding of the uterine lining (endometrium).

Ovulation
The release of an ovum from an ovary.

Corpus luteum
The follicle that has released an ovum and then produces copious amounts of progesterone and estrogen during the luteal phase of a woman's cycle. (From Latin roots meaning "yellow body.")

Endocrine gland
A ductless gland that releases its secretions directly into the bloodstream.

Menarche
The onset of menstruation; first menstruation. (From Greek roots meaning "months" [*men*] and "beginning" [*arche*].)

Hypothalamus
A bundle of neural cell bodies near the center of the brain that are involved in regulating body temperature, motivation, and emotion.

Pituitary gland
The gland that secretes growth hormone, prolactin, oxytocin, and others.

Hormone
A substance secreted by an endocrine gland that regulates various body functions. (From the Greek *horman*, meaning "to stimulate" or "to excite.")

Testes
The male gonads. Singular: testis.

Testosterone
The male sex hormone that fosters the development of male sex characteristics and is connected with the sex drive.

Menstruation is the cyclical bleeding that stems from the shedding of the uterine lining (endometrium.) Menstruation takes place when a reproductive cycle has not led to the fertilization of an ovum. The word *menstruation* derives from the Latin *mensis,* meaning "month." The human menstrual cycle averages about 28 days in length.

The menstrual cycle is regulated by the hormones estrogen and progesterone, and can be divided into four phases. During the first phase of the cycle, the *proliferative phase,* which follows menstruation, estrogen levels increase, causing the ripening of perhaps 10 to 20 ova (egg cells) within their follicles and the proliferation of endometrial tissue in the uterus. During the second phase of the cycle, estrogen reaches peak blood levels, and **ovulation** occurs. Normally only 1 ovum reaches maturity and is released by an ovary during ovulation. Then the third phase—the *secretory,* or *luteal,* phase—of the cycle begins. The luteal phase begins right after ovulation and continues through the beginning of the next cycle.

The term *luteal phase* is derived from **corpus luteum,** the name given the follicle that releases an ovum. The corpus luteum functions as an **endocrine gland** and produces copious amounts of progesterone and estrogen. Progesterone causes the endometrium to thicken, so that it will be able to support an embryo if fertilization occurs. If the ovum goes unfertilized, however, estrogen and progesterone levels plummet. These falloffs provide the trigger for the fourth phase, the *menstrual phase,* which leads to the beginning of a new cycle.

Ovulation may not occur in every menstrual cycle. Anovulatory ("without ovulation") cycles are most common in the years just after **menarche.** They may become frequent again in the years prior to menopause, but they may also occur irregularly among women in their 20s and 30s.

Although the menstrual cycle averages about 28 days, variations among women, and in the same woman from month to month, are quite common. Girls' cycles are often irregular for a few years after menarche. Variations from cycle to cycle tend to occur during the proliferative phase that precedes ovulation. That is, menstruation tends to reliably follow ovulation by about 14 days. Variations of more than 2 days in the postovulation period are rare.

Although hormones regulate the menstrual cycle, psychological factors can influence the secretion of hormones. Stress can delay or halt menstruation. Anxiety that she may be pregnant and thus miss her period may also cause a woman to be late.

Regulation of the Menstrual Cycle

The menstrual cycle involves finely tuned relationships between structures in the brain—the **hypothalamus** and the **pituitary gland**—and the ovaries and uterus. All these structures are parts of the endocrine system, which means that they secrete chemicals directly into the bloodstream (see Figure 2.10). The ovaries and uterus are also reproductive organs. The chemicals secreted by endocrine glands are called **hormones.** (Other bodily secretions, such as milk, saliva, sweat, and tears, arrive at their destinations by passing through narrow, tubular structures in the body called ducts.)

Behavioral and social scientists are especially interested in hormones because of their behavioral effects. Hormones regulate bodily processes such as the metabolic rate, growth of bones and muscle, production of milk, metabolism of sugar, and storage of fats, among others. Several hormones play important roles in sexual and reproductive functions.

The gonads—the **testes** (or testicles) in the male and the ovaries in the female—secrete sex hormones directly into the bloodstream. The female gonads, the ovaries, produce the sex hormones estrogen and progesterone. The male gonads, the testes, produce the male sex hormone **testosterone.** Males and females also produce sex hormones of the other gender, but in relatively small amounts.

The hypothalamus is a pea-sized structure in the front part of the brain. It weighs about 4 to 5 grams and lies above the pituitary gland and below (hence the prefix *hypo-,* for "under") the thalamus. Despite its small size, it is involved in regulating many states of mo-

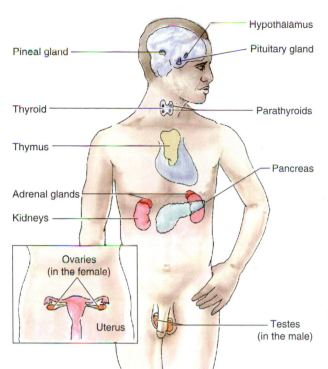

Figure 2.10. Major Glands of the Endocrine System. The endocrine system consists of glands that secrete chemicals called hormones directly into the bloodstream.

Prolactin

A pituitary hormone that stimulates production of milk.

Oxytocin

A pituitary hormone that stimulates uterine contractions in labor and the ejection of milk during nursing.

Gonadotropins

Pituitary hormones that stimulate the gonads. (Literally, "that which 'feeds' the gonads.")

Follicle-stimulating hormone (FSH)

A gonadotropin that stimulates development of follicles in the ovaries.

Luteinizing hormone (LH)

A gonadotropin that helps regulate the menstrual cycle by triggering ovulation.

Gonadotropin-releasing hormone (Gn-RH)

A hormone secreted by the hypothalamus that stimulates the pituitary gland to release gonadotropins.

Proliferative phase

The first phase of the menstrual cycle, which begins with the end of menstruation and lasts about 9 or 10 days. During this phase, the endometrium proliferates.

tivation, including hunger, thirst, aggression, and sex. For example, when the rear part of a male rat's hypothalamus is stimulated by an electric probe, the rat runs through its courting and mating sequence. It nibbles at a female's ears and at the back of her neck. When she responds, they copulate. Human sexuality is not so stereotyped or mechanical—although in the cases of some people who are highly routinized in their behavior, it may appear so.

The pituitary gland, which is about the size of a pea, lies below the hypothalamus at the base of the brain. Because many pituitary secretions regulate other endocrine glands, the pituitary has also been called the *master gland.* Pituitary hormones regulate bone and muscle growth and urine production. Two pituitary hormones are active during pregnancy and motherhood: **prolactin,** which stimulates production of milk; and **oxytocin,** which stimulates uterine contractions in labor and the ejection of milk during nursing. The pituitary gland also produces **gonadotropins** (literally, "that which 'feeds' the gonads") that stimulate the ovaries: **follicle-stimulating hormone (FSH)** and **luteinizing hormone (LH).** These hormones play central roles in regulating the menstrual cycle.

The hypothalamus receives information about bodily events through the nervous and circulatory systems. It monitors the blood levels of various hormones, including estrogen and progesterone, and releases a hormone called **gonadotropin-releasing hormone (Gn-RH),** which stimulates the pituitary to release gonadotropins. Gonadotropins, in turn, regulate the activity of the gonads. It was once thought that the pituitary gland ran the show, but it is now known that the pituitary gland is regulated by the hypothalamus. Even the "master gland" must serve another.

Phases of the Menstrual Cycle

We noted that the menstrual cycle has four stages or phases: proliferative, ovulatory, secretory, and menstrual (see Figure 2.11 on page 44).

The Proliferative Phase   The first phase, or **proliferative phase,** begins with the end of menstruation and lasts about 9 or 10 days in an average 28-day cycle (see Figure 2.11 and Figure 2.12 on page 45). During this phase the endometrium develops, or

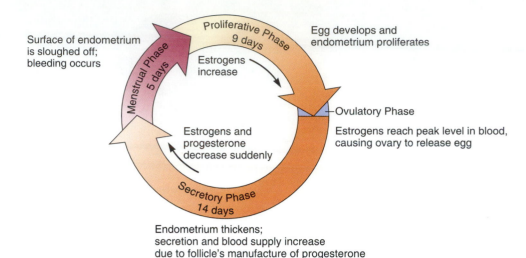

Figure 2.11. The Four Phases of the Menstrual Cycle. The menstrual cycle includes proliferative, ovulatory, secretory (luteal), and menstrual phases.

Surface of endometrium is sloughed off; bleeding occurs

Menstrual Phase 5 days

Proliferative Phase 9 days

Egg develops and endometrium proliferates

Estrogens increase

Ovulatory Phase

Estrogens reach peak level in blood, causing ovary to release egg

Estrogens and progesterone decrease suddenly

Secretory Phase 14 days

Endometrium thickens; secretion and blood supply increase due to follicle's manufacture of progesterone

---

Ovulatory phase

The second stage of the menstrual cycle, during which a follicle ruptures and releases a mature ovum.

Zygote

A fertilized ovum (egg cell).

Clomiphene

A synthetic hormone that is chemically similar to LH and induces ovulation.

Mittelschmerz

Pain that occurs during ovulation. (German for "middle pain," reflecting the fact that the pain occurs midway between menstrual periods).

Secretory phase

The third phase of the menstrual cycle, which follows ovulation. Also referred to as the *luteal phase,* after the *corpus luteum,* which begins to secrete large amounts of progesterone and estrogen following ovulation.

"proliferates." This phase is also known as the *preovulatory* or *follicular* phase, because certain ovarian follicles mature and the ovaries prepare for ovulation.

Low levels of estrogen and progesterone are circulating in the blood as menstruation draws to an end. When the hypothalamus senses a low level of estrogen in the blood, it increases its secretion of Gn-RH, which in turn triggers the pituitary gland to release FSH. When FSH reaches the ovaries, it stimulates some follicles (perhaps 10 to 20) to begin to mature. As the follicles ripen, they begin to produce estrogen. Normally, however, only one of them—called the *graafian follicle*—will reach full maturity in the days just preceding ovulation. As the graafian follicle matures, it moves toward the surface of the ovary, where it will eventually rupture and release a mature egg (see Figure 2.12 and Figure 2.13 on page 46).

Estrogen causes the endometrium in the uterus to thicken to about $\frac{1}{8}$-inch. Glands develop that would eventually nourish an embryo. Estrogen also stimulates the appearance of a thin cervical mucus. This mucus is alkaline and provides a hospitable, nutritious medium for sperm. The chances are thus increased that sperm that enter the female reproductive system at the time of ovulation will remain viable.

The Ovulatory Phase   During ovulation, or the **ovulatory phase,** the graafian follicle ruptures and releases a mature ovum *near* a fallopian tube—not actually *into* a fallopian tube (see Figure 2.13 on page 46). The other ripening follicles degenerate and are harmlessly reabsorbed by the body. If two ova mature and are released during ovulation, which happens occasionally, and both are fertilized, fraternal (nonidentical) twins will develop. Identical twins develop when one fertilized ovum divides into two separate **zygotes.**

Ovulation is set into motion when estrogen production reaches a critical level. The high level of estrogen is detected by the hypothalamus, which triggers the pituitary to release copious amounts of FSH and LH (see Figure 2.12). The surge of LH triggers ovulation, which usually begins 12 to 24 hours after the level of LH in the body has reached its peak.

The synthetic hormone **clomiphene** is chemically similar to LH and has been used by women who ovulate irregularly to induce reliable ovulation. The induction and accurate prediction of the timing of ovulation increase the chances of conceiving.

A woman's *basal body temperature,* taken by oral or rectal thermometer, dips slightly at ovulation (see Figure 2.12) and rises by about 1 degree Fahrenheit on the day following ovulation. Many women use this information to help them conceive or avoid conceiving. Note, however, that Figure 2.12 is idealized. Many women show greater fluctuations in daily temperature or gradual rises in temperature for about two days after ovulation.

Some women have discomfort or cramping during ovulation, termed **mittelschmerz.** Mittelschmerz is sometimes confused with appendicitis. Mittelschmerz, however, may occur on either side of the abdomen, depending on which ovary is releasing an ovum. A ruptured appendix always causes pain on the right side.

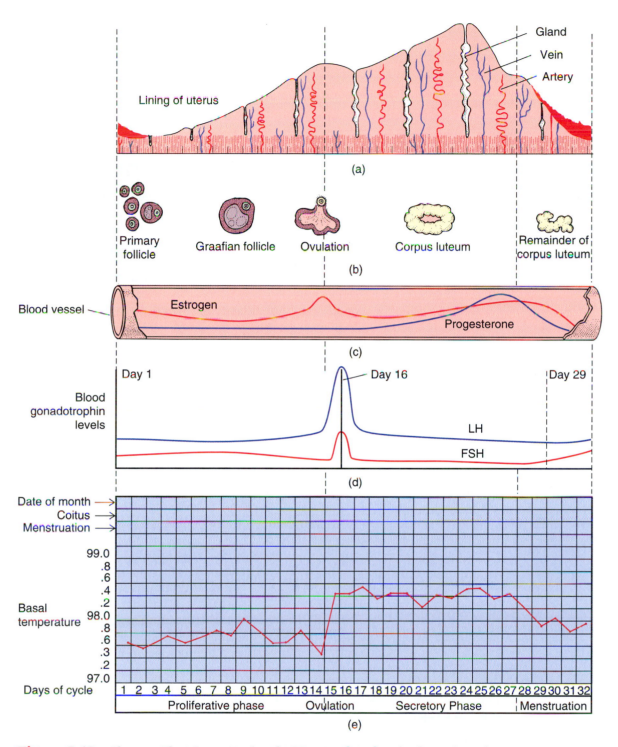

Figure 2.12. Changes That Occur During the Menstrual Cycle. This figure shows five categories of biological change: (a) changes in the development of the uterine lining (endometrium), (b) follicular changes, (c) changes in blood levels of ovarian hormones, (d) changes in blood levels of pituitary hormones, and (e) changes in basal temperature. Note the dip in temperature that is connected with ovulation.

The Secretory Phase The phase following ovulation is called the postovulatory or **secretory phase.** Some people refer to it as the *luteal phase,* which reflects the name given the ruptured (graafian) follicle—the *corpus luteum.* Figure 2.12 and Figure 2.13 on page 46 show the transformation of the graafian follicle into the corpus luteum.

Under the influence of LH, the corpus luteum, which has remained in the ovary, begins to produce large amounts of progesterone and estrogen. Levels of these hormones

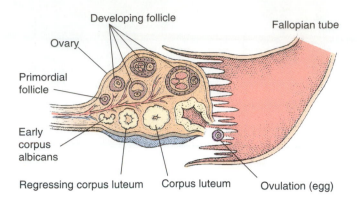

Figure 2.13. Maturation and Eventual **Decomposition of an Ovarian Follicle.** Many follicles develop and produce estrogen during the proliferative phase of the menstrual cycle. Usually only one, the graafian follicle, ruptures and releases an ovum. The graafian follicle then develops into the corpus luteum, which produces copious quantities of estrogen and progesterone. When fertilization does not occur, the corpus luteum decomposes.

peak at around the 20th or 21st day of an average cycle (see Figure 2.12). These hormones cause the glands in the endometrium to secrete nutrients to sustain a fertilized ovum that becomes implanted in the uterine wall.

If implantation does not occur, the hypothalamus responds to the peak levels of progesterone in the blood by signaling the pituitary to stop producing LH and FSH. Although certainly more complex, this feedback process is similar to that of a thermostat in a house reacting to rising temperatures by shutting down the furnace. The levels of LH and FSH decline rapidly, leading the corpus luteum to decompose. After its decomposition, levels of estrogen and progesterone fall precipitously. In this sense, the corpus luteum sows the seeds of its own destruction: Its hormones signal the brain to shut down secretion of substances that maintain it.

Menstrual phase
The fourth phase of the menstrual cycle, during which the endometrium is sloughed off in the menstrual flow.

The Menstrual Phase: An End and a Beginning   The **menstrual phase** is the sloughing off of the uterine lining (the endometrium) in the menstrual flow. Menstruation occurs when estrogen and progesterone levels decline to the point where they can no longer sustain the uterine lining. The lining then disintegrates and is discharged from the body along with the menstrual flow. Menstruation itself is the passing of the lining through the cervix and vagina.

The low estrogen levels of the menstrual phase signal the hypothalamus to release GnRH, which in turn stimulates the pituitary to secrete FSH. FSH, in turn, prompts ovarian secretion of estrogen and the onset of another proliferative phase. Thus a new cycle begins. The menstrual phase is a beginning as well as an end.

Menstrual flow contains blood from the endometrium (uterine lining), endometrial tissue, and cervical and vaginal mucus. Although the flow can appear persistent and last for five days or more, most women lose only a total of 2 or 3 ounces of blood (4 to 6 tablespoonfuls). A typical blood donor, by contrast, donates 16 ounces of blood at a sitting. A woman's blood loss through menstruation is thus usually harmless. Extremely heavy or prolonged (over a week) menstrual bleeding may reflect health problems and should be discussed with a health care provider.

Tampon
A cylindrical plug of cotton that is inserted into the vagina and left in place to absorb menstrual fluid. (A French word, meaning a gun barrel "plug.")

Prior to 1933, women generally used external sanitary napkins or pads to absorb the menstrual flow. In that year, however, **tampons** were introduced and altered the habits of millions of women. Women who use tampons can swim without concern while menstruating, wear more revealing or comfortable apparel, and feel generally less burdened.

Tampons are inserted into the vagina and left in place to absorb menstrual fluid. In recent years, questions have arisen about whether or not tampons cause or exacerbate infections. For example, tampon use has been linked to toxic shock syndrome (TSS), an infection that is sometimes fatal. Signs of TSS include fever, headache, sore throat, vomiting, diarrhea, muscle aches, rash, and dizziness. Peeling skin, disorientation, and a plunge in blood pressure may follow.

TSS is caused by the *Staphylococcus aureus* ("staph") bacterium. In 1980, the peak year for cases of TSS, there were 344 recorded cases of TSS and 28 fatalities. Proctor and

Gamble removed its "extra absorbent" tampon Rely from the market when it was discovered that 71% of these TSS victims had used the product. Plugging the vagina with a highly absorbent tampon that remains in place for six hours or more may create an ideal breeding ground for staph. The number of TSS cases has declined dramatically since then.

Some researchers believe that concern over TSS has been exaggerated. Nevertheless, many women now use regular rather than superabsorbent tampons to reduce the chance of creating a breeding ground for staph bacteria. Some women alternate tampons with sanitary napkins during each day of menstruation. Some change their tampons three or four times a day. Women are encouraged to consult their health care providers about TSS.

Sex During Menstruation

Many couples continue to engage in coitus during menstruation, but others abstain. One study found that people are less likely to initiate sexual activity during menstruation than during any other phase of the woman's cycle (Harvey, 1987). Some people abstain because of religious prohibitions. Others express concern about the "fuss" or the "mess" of the menstrual flow. Despite traditional attitudes that associate menstruation with uncleanliness, there is no evidence that coitus during menstruation is physically harmful to either partner. Ironically, menstrual coitus may be helpful to the woman. The uterine contractions that occur during orgasm may help relieve cramping by dispelling blood congestion. Orgasm achieved through masturbation may have the same effect.

Women may be sexually aroused at any time during the menstrual cycle. The preponderance of the research evidence, however, points to a peak in sexual desire in women around the time of ovulation (Kresin, 1993).

Human coital patterns during the phases of the menstrual cycle apparently reflect personal decisions, not hormone fluctuations. Some couples may decide to increase their frequency of coitus at ovulation in order to optimize the chances of conceiving, or to abstain during menstruation because of religious beliefs or beliefs linking menses with uncleanliness. Some may also increase their coital activity preceding menstruation to compensate for anticipated abstinence during menses, or increase coital activity afterwards to make up for deprivation.

Menopause

Menopause
The cessation of menstruation.

Climacteric
A long-term process, including menopause, that involves the gradual decline in the reproductive capacity of the ovaries.

Menopause, or the "change of life," is the cessation of menstruation. Menopause is a process that most commonly occurs between the ages of 46 and 50 and lasts for about two years. However, it may begin any time between the ages of 35 and 60. There is at least one case of a woman who became pregnant at age 61.

Menopause is a specific event in a long-term process known as the **climacteric** ("critical period"), which refers to the gradual decline in the reproductive capacity of the ovaries. The climacteric generally lasts for about 15 years, from ages 45 to 60 or so. After about the age of 35, the menstrual cycles of many women shorten, from an average of 28 days to 25 days at age 40 and to 23 days by the mid-40s. By the end of her 40s, a woman's cycles often become erratic, with some periods close together and others missed.

In menopause, the pituitary gland continues to pour normal levels of FSH and LH into the bloodstream, but for reasons that are not well understood, the ovaries gradually lose their capacity to respond. The ovaries no longer ripen egg cells or produce the sex hormones estrogen and progesterone.

The deficit in estrogen may lead to a number of unpleasant physical sensations, such as night sweats and hot flashes (suddenly feeling hot) and hot flushes (suddenly looking reddened). Hot flashes and flushes may alternate with cold sweats, in which a woman feels suddenly cold and clammy. Anyone who has experienced "cold feet" or hands from anxiety or fear will understand how dramatic the shifting patterns of blood flow can be. Hot flashes and flushes stem largely from "waves" of dilation of blood vessels across the face and upper body. All of these sensations reflect "vasomotor instability." That is, there are disruptions in the body mechanisms that dilate or constrict the blood vessels to maintain an even body tem-

Menopause and Sexuality
Menopause does not mark the end of a woman's sex life. Many women, in fact, feel sexually liberated by the biological severing of the traditional link between sexual activity and reproduction.

Osteoporosis
A condition caused by estrogen deficiency and characterized by a decline in bone density, such that bones become porous and brittle. (From the Greek *osteon*, meaning "bone," and the Latin *porus*, meaning "pore.")

Hormone-replacement therapy (HRT)
Replacement of naturally occurring estrogen or estrogen, and progesterone, with synthetic equivalents, following menopause.

perature. Additional signs of estrogen deficiency include dizziness, headaches, pains in the joints, sensations of tingling in the hands or feet, burning or itchy skin, and heart palpitations. The skin usually becomes drier. There is some loss of breast tissue and decreased vaginal lubrication during sexual arousal. Women may also encounter sleep problems, such as awakening more frequently at night and having difficulty falling back to sleep.

Long-term estrogen deficiency has been linked to brittleness and porosity of the bones (**osteoporosis**). In this condition, bones break more readily, and some women develop so-called dowager's hump. Osteoporosis is potentially severely handicapping, even life threatening. The increased brittleness of the bones increases the risk of serious fractures, especially of the hip, and many elderly women never recover from these fractures.

Estrogen deficiency also has psychological effects. It can impair cognitive functioning and feelings of psychological well-being (Sourander, 1994).

Some women who experience severe physical symptoms have been helped by **hormone-replacement therapy (HRT),** which typically consists of synthetic estrogen and progesterone. These synthetic hormones are used to offset the losses of their naturally occurring counterparts. HRT may help reduce the hot flushes and other symptoms brought about by hormonal deficiencies during menopause. It is especially helpful in protecting the woman against the development of osteoporosis (Davidson, 1995).

HRT is not without controversy. Although HRT has certainly been helpful to many menopausal women, some studies link use of estrogen to an increased risk of some kinds of cancer (Colditz et al., 1995). On the other hand, estrogen replacement lowers the woman's risk of cardiovascular disorders (heart and artery disease) (Grodstein et al., 1996), osteoporosis (Davidson, 1995; Everson et al., 1995), and colon cancer (Newcomb & Storer, 1995). HRT may reduce the risk of cardiovascular disease by lowering the levels of cholesterol in the bloodstream. A study of 49,000 postmenopausal nurses found that HRT was connected with 44% fewer heart attacks and a reduced risk of death from heart disease of

39% (Stampfer et al., 1991). Use of progestin along with estrogen does not mitigate the health benefits of estrogen on the heart (Grodstein et al., 1996).

Hormone-replacement therapy is not recommended for women whose medical conditions or family histories make it inadvisable for them (Brody, 1992b). It is usually not recommended, for example, for women with a family history of breast cancer. Women are advised to explore the health benefits and risks of HRT with their gynecologists.

Overall, fewer than one in five postmenopausal women receive hormone-replacement therapy (Brody, 1992b). For those who do not receive replacement hormones, other drugs are available, when they are needed, to help them deal with menopausal complaints, such as hot flashes.

Menstrual Problems

Although menstruation is a natural biological process, the majority of women experience some discomfort prior to or during menstruation. Table 2.1 contains a list of commonly reported symptoms of menstrual problems. The problems we explore in this section include dysmenorrhea; mastalgia; menstrual migraine headaches; amenorrhea; and premenstrual syndrome (PMS).

Dysmenorrhea

Dysmenorrhea
Pain or discomfort during menstruation.

Primary dysmenorrhea
Menstrual pain or discomfort that occurs in the absence of known organic problems.

Secondary dysmenorrhea
Menstrual pain or discomfort that is caused by identified organic problems.

Pain or discomfort during menstruation, or **dysmenorrhea,** is the most common type of menstrual problem. Most women at some time have at least mild menstrual pain or discomfort. Pelvic cramps are the most common manifestation of dysmenorrhea. They may be accompanied by headache, backache, nausea, or bloated feelings. Women who develop severe cases usually do so within a few years of menarche. **Primary dysmenorrhea** refers to menstrual pain or discomfort in the absence of known organic pathology. Women with **secondary dysmenorrhea** have identified organic problems that are believed to cause their menstrual problems. Their pain or discomfort is caused by, or is *secondary to,* these problems. Endometriosis, pelvic inflammatory disease, and ovarian cysts are just a few of the organic disorders that can give rise to secondary dysmenorrhea. Yet evidence is accumu-

TABLE 2.1 Common symptoms of menstrual problems

Physical Symptoms	Psychological Symptoms
Swelling of the breasts	Depressed mood, sudden tearfulness
Tenderness in the breasts	Loss of interest in usual social or recreational activities
Bloating	
Weight gain	Anxiety, tension (feeling "on edge" or "keyed up")
Food cravings	
Abdominal discomfort	Anger
Cramping	Irritability
Lack of energy	Changes in body image
Sleep disturbance, fatigue	Concern over skipping routine activities, school, or work
Migraine headache	
Pains in muscles and joints	A sense of loss of control
Aggravation of chronic disorders such as asthma and allergies	A sense of loss of ability to cope

lating that supposed primary dysmenorrhea is often *secondary* to hormonal changes, although the precise causes have not been delineated. For example, menstrual cramps sometimes decrease dramatically after childbirth, as a result of the massive hormonal changes that occur with pregnancy.

Painful menstruation was reported by nearly 75% of the participants in a sample of college women (Wildman & White, 1986). The symptoms varied not only from person to person but also according to whether or not the women had been pregnant. Women who had been pregnant reported a lower incidence of menstrual pain but a higher incidence of premenstrual symptoms and menstrual discomfort.

Biological Aspects of Dysmenorrhea   Menstrual cramps appear to result from uterine spasms that may be brought about by copious secretion of hormones called **prostaglandins.** Prostaglandins apparently cause muscle fibers in the uterine wall to contract, as during labor. Most contractions go unnoticed, but powerful, persistent contractions are discomfiting in themselves and may temporarily deprive the uterus of oxygen, another source of distress. Women with more intense menstrual discomfort apparently produce higher quantities of prostaglandins. Prostaglandin-inhibiting drugs, such as ibuprofen, indomethacin, and aspirin are thus often of help. Menstrual pain may also be secondary to endometriosis.

Pelvic pressure and bloating may be traced to pelvic edema (Greek for "swelling")—the congestion of fluid in the pelvic region. Fluid retention can lead to a gain of several pounds, sensations of heaviness, and **mastalgia**—a swelling of the breasts that sometimes causes premenstrual discomfort. Masters and Johnson (1966) noted that orgasm (through coitus or masturbation) can help relieve menstrual discomfort by reducing the pelvic congestion that spawns bloating and pressure. Orgasm may also increase the menstrual flow and shorten this phase of the cycle.

Headaches frequently accompany menstrual discomfort. Most headaches (in both sexes) stem from simple muscle tension, notably in the shoulders, the back of the neck, and the scalp. Pelvic discomfort may cause muscle contractions, thus contributing to the tension that produces headaches. Women who are tense about their menstrual flow are thus candidates for muscle tension headaches. Migraine headaches may arise from changes in the blood flow in the brain, however. Migraines are typically limited to one side of the head and are often accompanied by visual difficulties.

Amenorrhea

Amenorrhea is the absence of menstruation and is a primary sign of infertility. **Primary amenorrhea** describes the absence of menstruation in a woman who has not menstruated at all by about the age of 16 or 17. **Secondary amenorrhea** describes delayed or absent menstrual periods in women who have had regular periods in the past. Amenorrhea has various causes, including abnormalities in the structures of the reproductive system, hormonal abnormalities, growths such as cysts and tumors, and psychological problems, such as stress. Amenorrhea is normal during pregnancy and following menopause. Amenorrhea may also occur in women who exercise strenuously, such as competitive long-distance runners. It is unclear whether the cessation of menstruation in female athletes is due to the effects of strenuous exercise itself, to related physical factors such as low body fat, to the stress of intensive training, or to a combination of factors.

Premenstrual Syndrome (PMS)

The term **premenstrual syndrome (PMS)** describes the combination of bodily and psychological symptoms that may afflict women during the four- to six-day interval that precedes their menses each month (see Table 2.2). PMS also appears to be linked with imbalances in serotonin (Steiner et al., 1995), which is a chemical messenger in the nervous system. Serotonin imbalances are also linked to changes in appetite. In one study, women who suffered from PMS and nonsufferers alike showed increased appetite during

Prostaglandins
Hormones that cause muscle fibers in the uterine wall to contract, as during labor.

Mastalgia
A swelling of the breasts that sometimes causes premenstrual discomfort.

Amenorrhea
The absence of menstruation.

Primary amenorrhea
Lack of menstruation in a woman who has never menstruated.

Secondary amenorrhea
Lack of menstruation in a woman who has previously menstruated.

Premenstrual syndrome (PMS)
A combination of physical and psychological symptoms (e.g., anxiety, depression, irritability, weight gain from fluid retention, and abdominal discomfort) that regularly afflicts many women during the four- to six-day interval that precedes their menses each month.

the luteal phase, but the increases were greater for women with PMS (Both-Orthman et al., 1988). For many women, premenstrual symptoms persist during menstruation.

Nearly three women in four experience some form of PMS (Brody, 1989a). The great majority of cases involve mild to moderate levels of discomfort. Fewer than 10% of women report menstrual symptoms severe enough to impair their social, academic, or occupational functioning (Brody, 1996).

The causes of PMS are unclear, but evidence is accumulating for a biological basis to premenstrual symptoms (Asso & Magos, 1992). Researchers are looking to possible relationships between menstrual problems, including PMS, and chemical imbalances in the body. Researchers have yet to find differences in levels of estrogen or progesterone between women with severe PMS and those with mild symptoms or no symptoms (Rubinow & Schmidt, 1995). Perhaps it is not hormone levels themselves but the sensitivity of brain centers to these hormones that predisposes some women to PMS.

Treatments for PMS range from exercise and dietary control (for example, limiting salt and sugar), to use of vitamin supplements, to hormone treatments (usually progesterone), to drugs that increase the amount of serotonin in the nervous system (Steiner et al., 1995). Check with your physician about the most up-to-date research findings.

In this chapter we have explored female sexual anatomy and physiology. In the following chapter, we turn our attention to the male.

A P P L I C A T I O N S

COPING WITH MENSTRUAL DISCOMFORT

Only a generation ago, PMS was seen as something a woman must put up with. No longer. Today there are many treatment options. These include exercise, dietary control (for example, eating several small meals a day rather than two or three large meals; limiting salt and sugar; vitamin supplements), hormone treatments (usually progesterone), and medications that reduce anxiety or increase the amount of serotonin in the nervous system

(Brody, 1996; Steiner et al., 1995). If you have PMS, get in touch with the kinds of symptoms that affect you most through use of a PMS calendar or simply by paying close attention to what happens. Then check with your physician about the most up-to-date treatment approaches.

Women with persistent menstrual distress may profit from the suggestions listed below. Researchers are exploring the effectiveness of these techniques in

controlled studies. For now, you might consider running a personal experiment. Adopt the techniques that sound right for you—all of them, if you wish. Try them out for a few months to see if you reap any benefits.

1. Don't blame yourself! Menstrual problems were once erroneously attributed to women's "hysterical" nature. This is nonsense. Menstrual problems appear, in

large part, to reflect hormonal variations or chemical fluctuations in the brain during the menstrual cycle.

2. Keep a menstrual calendar, so that you can track your menstrual symptoms systematically and identify patterns (Figure 2.14). Clinicians often determine whether PMS is present by asking the woman to track her physical and emotional symptoms over at least two cycles.

3. Develop strategies for dealing with days that you experience the greatest distress—strategies that will help enhance your pleasure and minimize the stress affecting you on those days. Go see a movie or get into that novel you've been meaning to read.

4. Ask yourself whether you harbor any self-defeating attitudes toward menstruation that might be compounding distress. Do close relatives or friends see menstruation as an illness, a time of "pollution," a "dirty thing"? Have you adopted any of these attitudes—if not verbally, then in ways that affect your behavior, such as by restricting your social activities during your period?

5. See a doctor about your concerns, especially if you suffer severe symptoms. Severe menstrual symptoms are often secondary to medical disorders such as endometriosis and pelvic inflammatory disease (PID). Check it out.

6. Develop nutritious eating habits— and continue them throughout the entire cycle (that means always). Consider limiting intake of alcohol, caffeine, fats, salt, and sweets, especially during the days preceding menstruation.

7. Eat several smaller meals (or nutritious snacks) throughout the day, rather than a few highly filling meals.

8. Some women find that vigorous exercise—jogging, swimming, bicycling, fast walking, dancing, skating, even jumping rope— helps relieve premenstrual and menstrual discomfort. Evidence suggests that exercise helps to relieve and possibly prevent menstrual discomfort (Choi, 1992).

9. Check with your doctor about vitamin and mineral supplements (such as calcium and magnesium). Vitamin B6 appears to have helped some women.

10 Ibuprofen (brand names: Medipren, Advil, Motrin, etc.) and other medicines available over the counter may be helpful for cramping. Prescription drugs, such as antianxiety drugs or antidepressant drugs, may also be of help (Brody, 1996). Ask your doctor for a recommendation.

11. Remind yourself that menstrual problems are time-limited. Don't worry about getting through life or a career. Just get through the next couple of days.

PMS Calendar

Jane Doe

CYCLE DAY	1	2	3	4	5		24	25	26	27	28
Bleeding	X				X						
Date — March	3	4	5	6	7		26	27	28	29	30
Weight (Before Breakfast)	126	126	126	124	126		128	129	130	130	130

SYMPTOMS

	1	2	3	4	5		24	25	26	27	28
*Depression	2	1	1				2	2	2	1	2
*Anger, violent tendencies							2	2	1	2	3
*Irritability	1							2	2	2	2
*Anxiety, tension, nervousness	1						2	2	2	2	2
*Confusion, difficulty concentrating											
*Desire to be left alone											
*Tender breasts	1						2	2	3	3	3
*General bloated feeling							2	2	2	3	3
*Headaches	2	1					2	2	3	3	3
*Swelling of hands, ankles, or breasts	1						2	2	2	3	3
Acne	2	1	1				1	1	1	1	1
Dizziness											
Fatigue	2	2	1	1			2	2	2	2	2
Hot flashes											
Nausea, diarrhea, constipation										1	1
Racing or pounding heart											
Crying easily	2						2	2	1	2	3
Food cravings (sweet, salty)							1	1	1	1	1
Forgetfulness											
Increased appetite									1	1	1
Mood swings	1						1	2	2	2	2
Overly sensitive	1						2	2	2	3	3

a. None										
b.										

MEDICATIONS

a. None										
b.										

*Especially significant PMS symptoms.

Figure 2.14. The PMS Calendar. Keeping a PMS calendar may provide helpful information regarding the pattern of PMS symptoms that women may experience. Symptoms should be tracked for at least two cycles to reveal the pattern of complaints.

Chapter Review

The Female Sex Organs

The word (1) _____dum derives from a Latin root that means "something to be ashamed of." The external sexual structures of the female are termed the pudendum or the (2) v_____. The vulva consists of the mons (3) v_____, the labia majora and labia (4) _____a (major and minor lips), the clitoris, and the vaginal opening.

At puberty the mons becomes covered with (5) p_____ hair. The (6) m_____ cushions a woman during sexual intercourse. The (7) l_____ m_____ are large folds of skin that run downward from the mons along the sides of the vulva. The (8) l_____ m_____ are two hairless, light-colored membranes, located between the major lips. When the labia minora are stimulated, they darken and swell, indicating engorgement with (9) _____d.

The (10) _____is is the only sex organ whose only known function is the experiencing of pleasure. The clitoral shaft consists of erectile tissue that contains two spongy masses called (11) cor_____ cav_____ ("cavernous bodies") that become engorged and erect in response to sexual stimulation. The clitoral hood or (12) pre_____ covers the clitoral shaft. The clitoral (13) g_____ is covered by the clitoral hood but is readily revealed by separating the labia minora and retracting the hood.

The clitoris is the female counterpart of the (14) p_____. The clitoris and penis both develop from the same embryonic tissue, which makes them similar in structure, or (15) _____gous. But the two structures are not fully similar in function, or (16) _____gous. Surgical removal of the clitoral hood to control female sexuality is common among (17) _____lims in the Near East and Africa.

The (18) _____bule refers to the area within the labia minora that contains the openings to the vagina and the urethra. Urine passes from the female body through the (19) u_____ opening, which is connected by a short tube called the (20) u_____ to the bladder, where urine collects. The nearness of the (21) _____ral opening to the external sex organs may pose some hygienic problems for sexually active women. (22) _____tis is a bladder inflammation whose primary symptoms are burning and frequent (23) _____ation (also called *urinary urgency*). The vaginal opening is also known as the (24) _____tus. The (25) _____en is a fold of tissue that lies across the vaginal opening and is usually present at birth. The hymen has been of great cultural significance because its presence has been assumed to represent (26) vir_____. The (27) per_____ is the area between the vaginal opening and the anus. In an (28) _____tomy, a physician cuts the perineum during labor to facilitate childbirth.

The vestibular (29) _____s and Bartholin's (30) _____s lie beneath the vulva and are active during sexual arousal. Bartholin's glands secrete a couple of drops of lubrication just before orgasm. Vaginal (31) _____ation is caused by a form of "sweating" by the lining of the vaginal wall.

The internal sex organs of the female include the innermost parts of the vagina, the cervix, the uterus, and two (32) _____ies, each connected to the uterus by a fallopian tube. Menstrual flow and babies pass from the uterus to the outer world through the (33) _____a. The vaginal walls have (34: One, Two, *or* Three?) layer(s). (35) _____tis refers to a vaginal inflammation.

The (36) c_____ is the lower end of the uterus. A (37) P_____ test examines a sample of cervical cells that are smeared on a slide to screen for cervical cancer and other abnormalities.

A fertilized ovum becomes implanted and develops within the (38) u_____, or womb. Like the vagina, the uterus has (39: One, Two, *or* Three?) layer(s). Tissue from the innermost layer, or (40) _____ium, is discharged through the cervix and vagina at menstruation. Some women have (41) _____ osis, in which endometrial tissue also grows in the abdominal cavity or elsewhere in the reproductive system. Risk factors for endometrial cancer include obesity, a diet (42: Low *or* High?) in fats, early menarche or late (43) men_____, failure to ovulate, and estrogen-replacement therapy. Surgical removal of the uterus—called (44) _____ tomy —may be performed when women develop cancer of the uterus, ovaries, or cervix, or other diseases that cause pain or excessive uterine bleeding.

Two uterine tubes, also called (45) _____ ian tubes, extend from the upper end of the uterus toward the ovaries. Ova pass through the fallopian tubes on their way to the (46) _____ us. The fallopian tubes are lined with (47) c_____ that help move ova along. The form of sterilization called (48) _____ bal _____ tion ties off the fallopian tubes. In an (49) _____ ic pregnancy, the fertilized ovum becomes implanted outside the uterus.

The (50) _____ ries lie on either side of the uterus, to which they are attached by ovarian ligaments. The ovaries produce ova and the female sex hormones (51) _____ gen and (52) pro_____. Estrogen promotes the changes of puberty and regulates the (53) _____ ual cycle. Progesterone helps regulate the menstrual cycle and prepares the uterus for pregnancy by stimulating the development of the (54) en_____. Each ovum is contained within a thin capsule called a (55) _____ cle. Women who are at greatest risk of ovarian (56) c_____ are those with blood relatives who had the disease.

The Breasts

The breasts are (57) _____ ary sex characteristics. Each breast contains clusters of milk-producing (58) _____ ary glands. Each gland opens at the (59) _____ le through its own duct. The amount of (60) _____ ty tissue in the breasts, not the amount of glandular tissue, determines their size. The nipple lies in the center of the (61) _____ la. The nipple contains smooth muscle fibers that make it (62) e_____ when they contract.

(63) B_____ cancer is the second leading cause of cancer deaths among women. Many cases of breast cancer are detected early because of (64) _____ graphy, a specialized X-ray that detects cancerous lumps in the breast. The risk of breast cancer (65: Increases *or* Decreases?) sharply with age. The majority of women who develop breast cancer (66: Have *or* Do not have?) a family history of the disease. Other risk factors for breast cancer, such as early onset of menstruation and late menopause, seem to be due to prolonged exposure to (67) es_____. Most lumps that women find in the breasts (68: Are *or* Are not?) malignant.

The Menstrual Cycle

Menstruation is the cyclical bleeding that stems from the shedding of the (69) _____ ine lining (endometrium.) The menstrual cycle can be divided into (70: Two, Three, *or* Four?) phases. The first phase is the (71) _____ tive phase, which follows menstruation. Estrogen levels (72: Increase *or* Decrease?), causing the ripening of ova and the proliferation of endometrial tissue. During the second phase of the cycle, (73) _____ tion occurs. The third phase is the secretory, or (74) _____ al, phase. During the luteal phase, the (75) _____ us luteum produces progesterone and estrogen. Progesterone causes the (76) en_____ to thicken, so that it will be able to support an embryo. If fertilization does not occur, estrogen and progesterone levels (77: Increase *or* Decrease?). These declines trigger the fourth, or (78) men_____, phase of the cycle.

The menstrual cycle involves finely tuned relationships between structures in the brain—the (79) hypo_____ and the (80) pit_____ gland—and the ovaries and uterus. All these structures are parts of the endocrine system, which means that they secrete (81) _____ nes. The female (82) _____ ads are the ovaries.

Two pituitary hormones are active during pregnancy and motherhood: (83) _____ tin, which stimulates production of milk; and (84) _____ cin, which stimulates uterine contractions in labor and the ejection of milk during nursing. The pituitary gland also produces (85) _____ tropins. The gonadotropins include

(86) _____-stimulating hormone (FSH) and
(87) _____izing hormone (LH).

Many women insert (88) _____ons into the
vagina to absorb menstrual fluid. Tampon use has led to
some cases of (89) _____ _____ syndrome
(TSS), a sometimes fatal infection. TSS is caused by the
(90) *Staph*_____ *aureus* ("staph") bacterium. Many
women now use (91: Less *or* More?) absorbent tampons
to reduce the chance of breeding staph bacteria.

There (92: Is *or* Is not?) evidence that coitus during
menstruation is physically harmful.

(93) Men_____ is the cessation of menstruation. Menopause is part of a long-term process
known as the (94) _____ric ("critical period"),
which refers to the gradual decline in the reproductive
capacity and hormone production of the ovaries. The
deficit in (95) _____gen may lead to sensations
such as night sweats and hot flashes. Estrogen deficiency has also been linked to brittleness and porosity
of the bones, called (96) _____osis. Some women
with serious physical symptoms have been helped by
(97) _____-_____ment therapy (HRT),
which typically consists of synthetic estrogen and
progesterone. Some studies link use of estrogen to
an increased risk of some kinds of (98) _____cer.
On the other hand, estrogen replacement lowers
the woman's risk of (99) h_____ disease and
(100) osteo_____.

Menstrual Problems

Menstrual problems include (101) dysmenorrhea, mastalgia, menstrual (102) m_____ headaches, amenorrhea, and (103) _____ual syndrome (PMS).

Dysmenorrhea is (104) p_____ or discomfort
during menstruation. Pelvic (105) _____ps are
the most common symptom of dysmenorrhea. In
(106) _____ary dysmenorrhea, menstrual pain or
discomfort occurs in the absence of known biological
problems. In (107) _____ary dysmenorrhea, women
have identified biological problems that cause their discomfort. Secondary dysmenorrhea can be caused by
(108) _____metriosis, pelvic (109) _____tory
disease, ovarian cysts, and hormonal changes. Menstrual
cramps are uterine spasms that may be caused by hormones called (110) _____glandins. Retention of
(111) _____d can lead to bloating, weight gain, sensations of heaviness, and mastalgia.

PMS refers to symptoms that may affect women
during the four- to six-day interval that (112: Precedes
or Follows?) menstruation. Features of PMS include
(113) dep_____, (114) irri_____, cravings for
certain foods, feelings of being overwhelmed, and physical problems such as headaches, (115) ten_____ in
the breasts, joint or muscle pain, and weight gain or feeling bloated. (116: Only a few *or* Most?) women experience some dysmenorrhea or some form of PMS.

Chapter Quiz

1. The word(s) _____ derive(s) from roots that literally mean "something to be ashamed of."
   (a) clitoris
   (b) mons veneris
   (c) labia majora
   (d) pudendum
2. The _____ is the only sex organ whose only
   known function is the experiencing of pleasure.
   (a) labia minora
   (b) clitoris
   (c) Bartholin's gland
   (d) cervix
3. Which of the following is NOT a recommended pre-
   caution for preventing serious inflammation of the
   bladder?

   (a) Daily use of antibiotics.
   (b) Drinking two quarts of water a day.
   (c) Decreasing use of alcohol and caffeine.
   (d) Preventing objects that have touched the anus
       from coming into contact with the vulva.
4. An episiotomy is an incision in the
   (a) vulva.
   (b) uterus.
   (c) perineum.
   (d) corpora cavernosa.
5. A Pap test is used to help diagnose cancer of the
   (a) breast.
   (b) cervix.
   (c) endometrium.
   (d) ovaries.

6. A complete hysterectomy involves the surgical removal of all of the following EXCEPT FOR the
   - (a) vagina.
   - (b) ovaries.
   - (c) fallopian tubes.
   - (d) cervix.
7. The size of the breasts is largely determined by the
   - (a) size of the areola.
   - (b) amount of fatty tissue.
   - (c) number of mammary glands.
   - (d) width of the mammary glands.
8. The five-year survival rate for women whose breast cancers have not metastasized is nearly
   - (a) 63%.
   - (b) 73%.
   - (c) 83%.
   - (d) 93%.
9. Which of the following most directly stimulates follicles to begin to mature?
   - (a) Gn-RH.
   - (b) LH.
   - (c) FSH.
   - (d) Oxytocin.
10. Following menopause, estrogen-replacement therapy apparently lowers the risk of all of the following EXCEPT FOR
   - (a) cancer of the colon.
   - (b) low blood pressure.
   - (c) cardiovascular disorders.
   - (d) osteoporosis.

Answers to Chapter Review

1. Pudendum
2. Vulva
3. Veneris
4. Minora
5. Pubic
6. Mons
7. Labia majora
8. Labia minora
9. Blood
10. Clitoris
11. Corpora cavernosa
12. Prepuce
13. Glans
14. Penis
15. Homologous
16. Analogous
17. Muslims
18. Vestibule
19. Urethral
20. Urethra
21. Urethral
22. Cystitis
23. Urination
24. Introitus
25. Hymen
26. Virginity
27. Perineum
28. Episiotomy
29. Bulbs
30. Glands
31. Lubrication
32. Ovaries
33. Vagina
34. Three
35. Vaginitis
36. Cervix
37. Pap
38. Uterus
39. Three
40. Endometrium
41. Endometriosis
42. High
43. Menopause
44. Hysterectomy
45. Fallopian
46. Uterus
47. Cilia
48. Tubal ligation
49. Ectopic
50. Ovaries
51. Estrogen
52. Progesterone
53. Menstrual
54. Endometrium
55. Follicle
56. Cancer
57. Secondary
58. Mammary
59. Nipple
60. Fatty
61. Areola
62. Erect
63. Breast
64. Mammography
65. Increases
66. Do not have
67. Estrogen
68. Are not
69. Uterine
70. Four
71. Proliferative
72. Increase
73. Ovulation
74. Luteal
75. Corpus
76. Endometrium
77. Decrease
78. Menstrual
79. Hypothalamus
80. Pituitary gland
81. Hormones
82. Gonads
83. Prolactin
84. Oxytocin
85. Gonadotropins
86. Follicle
87. Luteinizing
88. Tampons
89. Toxic shock
90. *Staphylococcus*
91. Less
92. Is not
93. Menopause
94. Climacteric
95. Estrogen
96. Osteoporosis
97. Hormone-replacement
98. Cancer
99. Heart
100. Osteoporosis
101. Dysmenorrhea
102. Migraine
103. Premenstural
104. Pain
105. Cramps
106. Primary
107. Secondary
108. Endometriosis
109. Inflammatory
110. Prostaglandins
111. Fluid
112. Precedes
113. Depression
114. Irritability
115. Tenderness
116. Most

Answers to Chapter Quiz

1. (d)
2. (b)
3. (a)
4. (c)
5. (b)
6. (a)
7. (b)
8. (d)
9. (c)
10. (b)

CHAPTER 3

Male Sexual Anatomy and Physiology

O U T L I N E

The Male Sex Organs
External Sex Organs
Internal Sex Organs

Diseases of the Urogenital System
Urethritis
Cancer of the Testes
Disorders of the Prostate

Male Sexual Functions
Erection
Spinal Reflexes and Sexual Response
Ejaculation

Chapter Review

Chapter Quiz

Applications
Self-Examination of the Testes

- The penis contains neither bone nor muscle?
- Uncircumcised men may be at greater risk than circumcised men of becoming infected by the AIDS virus?
- The father determines the baby's gender?
- The testes churn out about 1,000 sperm per second?
- Morning erections have nothing to do with the need to urinate?
- Men cannot will themselves to have erections?
- African American men are at greater risk than White men to develop prostate cancer?
- Many men paralyzed below the waist can attain erection, engage in sexual intercourse, and ejaculate?
- Men can have orgasms without ejaculating?

In this chapter we examine male sexual anatomy and physiology, and we attempt to sort truth from fiction. We see, for example, that despite his lingering doubts, a man's capabilities as a lover do not depend on the size of his penis (at least within broad limits). For a man to judge his sexual prowess on the basis of locker-room comparisons makes about as much sense as choosing a balloon by measuring it when it is deflated.

In our exploration of male sexual anatomy and physiology, as in our exploration of female sexual physiology and anatomy, we begin with the external genitalia and then move inward. Once inside, we focus on the route of sperm through the male reproductive system. ■

The Male Sex Organs

External Sex Organs

The male external sex organs include the penis and the scrotum (see Figures 3.1, 3.2).

Penis
The male organ of sexual intercourse. (From the Latin for "tail.")

Corpora cavernosa
Cylinders of spongy tissue in the penis that become congested with blood and stiffen during sexual arousal.

Corpus spongiosum
The spongy body that runs along the bottom of the penis, contains the penile urethra, and enlarges at the tip of the penis to form the glans.

The Penis   At first glance, the structure of the **penis** may seem rather simple and obvious, particularly when compared to women's organs. This apparent simplicity may have contributed to cultural stereotypes that men are straightforward and aggressive, whereas women tend to be complicated, and perhaps, mysterious. Yet, as Figure 3.1 shows, the apparent simplicity of the penis is misleading. Much goes on below the surface. Gender stereotypes regarding anatomy are as misleading as those regarding personality (see Chapter 5).

The penis, like the vagina, is the sex organ used in sexual intercourse. Unlike the vagina, however, the penis serves as a conduit for urine. Semen and urine pass out of the penis through the urethral opening. The opening is called the urethral *meatus* (pronounced me-ATE-us), meaning "passage."

Despite the slang term "boner," the human penis contains no bones. Nor, despite another slang term, "muscle," does the penis contain muscle tissue. However, muscles at the base of the penis, like the muscles surrounding the vaginal and urethral openings in women, are involved in controlling urination and ejaculation.

Rather than bones or muscles, the penis contains three cylinders of spongy material that run its length. The larger two of these cylinders, the **corpora cavernosa** (see Figure 3.1), lie side by side and function like the cavernous bodies in the clitoris. These cylinders fill up with blood and stiffen during sexual arousal. In addition, a **corpus spongiosum** (spongy

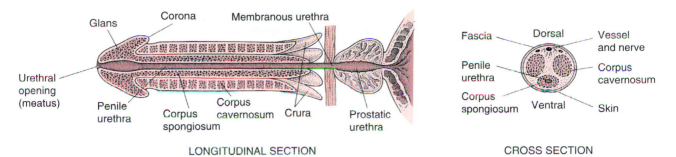

LONGITUDINAL SECTION   CROSS SECTION

Figure 3.1. **The Penis.** During sexual arousal the corpora cavernosa and corpus spongiosum become congested with blood, causing the penis to enlarge and stiffen.

Corona

The ridge that separates the glans from the body of the penis. (From the Latin for "crown.")

Frenulum

The sensitive strip of tissue that connects the underside of the penile glans to the shaft. (From the Latin *frenum*, meaning "bridle.")

Root

The base of the penis, which extends into the pelvis.

Shaft

The body of the penis, which expands as a result of vaso-congestion.

body) runs along the bottom, or ventral, surface of the penis. It contains the penile urethra that conducts urine through the penis to the urinary opening (urethral meatus) at the tip. At the tip of the penis, the spongy body enlarges to become the glans, or head, of the penis.

All three cylinders consist of spongy tissue that swells (becomes engorged) with blood during sexual arousal, resulting in erection. The urethra is connected to the bladder, which is unrelated to reproduction, and to those parts of the reproductive system that transport semen.

The glans of the penis, like the clitoral glans, is extremely sensitive to sexual stimulation. Direct, prolonged stimulation can become irritating, even painful. Men generally prefer to masturbate by stroking the shaft of the penis rather than the glans, although some prefer the latter. The **corona,** or coronal ridge, separates the glans from the body of the penis. It is also quite sensitive to sexual stimulation. After the glans, the parts of the penis that men tend to find most sensitive are the corona and an area on the underside of the penis called the **frenulum.** The frenulum is a thin strip of tissue that connects the underside of the glans to the shaft. Most men find the top part of the penis to be the least sensitive part.

The base of the penis, called the **root,** extends into the pelvis. It is attached to pelvic bones by leglike structures, called crura, that are like those that anchor the female's clitoris. The body of the penis is called the penile **shaft.** The penile shaft, unlike the clitoral shaft, is free-swinging. Thus, when sexual excitement engorges the penis with blood, the

Figure 3.2. **The Male Reproductive System.** The external male sex organs include the penis and the scrotum.

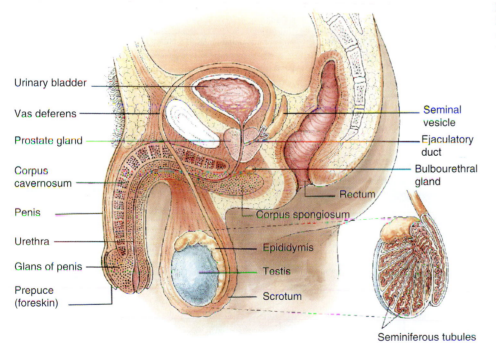

result—erection—is obvious. The expression "getting shafted," which means being taken advantage of, presumably refers to the penile shaft. Another phrase, "getting screwed," refers more directly to sexual intercourse.

The skin of the penis is hairless and loose, allowing expansion during erection. It is fixed to the penile shaft just behind the glans. Some of it, however, like the labia minora in the female, folds over to partially cover the glans. This covering is the prepuce, or **foreskin.** It covers part or all of the penile glans just as the clitoral prepuce (hood) covers the clitoral shaft. The prepuce consists of loose skin that freely moves over the glans. However, in the male, as in the female, smegma may accumulate below the prepuce, causing the foreskin to adhere to the glans.

Circumcision Circumcision is the surgical removal of the prepuce. Advocates of circumcision believe that it is hygienic because it eliminates a site where smegma might accumulate and bacteria might grow. Opponents of circumcision believe that it is unnecessary because regular cleaning is sufficient to reduce the risk of these problems.

Jews traditionally carry out male circumcision shortly after a baby is born. Circumcision is performed as a sign of the covenant between God and the people of Abraham—and for purposes of hygiene (see Figure 3.3). Muslims also have ritual circumcisions for religious reasons. Circumcision is common among Christians for hygienic reasons.

There is some evidence that penile cancer, a rare form of cancer, is slightly more common among uncircumcised men (Harahap & Siregar, 1988). Circumcision is the treatment of choice for **phimosis,** a condition in which it is difficult to retract the foreskin from the glans. Urinary tract infections are more common among uncircumcised male infants than among circumcised infants (Herzog, 1989; Wisell et al., 1987). Still, it has been argued that the risks associated with urinary tract infections in infancy are too low to justify routine circumcision (King, 1988; Lohr, 1989). Emerging evidence also suggests that uncircumcised men may be at greater risk than circumcised men of becoming infected by the AIDS virus. Certain cells in the foreskin may be especially susceptible to it (Touchette, 1991).

Questions have also been raised about the *sexual* effects of circumcision. One argument is that circumcised males may have more difficulty controlling ejaculation since the penile glans is directly exposed to sexual stimulation. As a result, the argument goes, such men would be more likely to suffer from **premature ejaculation.** Common sense—or should we say, common nonsense?—has actually had it both ways: that circumcised men are more *and* less sensitive to sexual stimulation than the uncircumcised. Perhaps the debate has continued this long because of the virtual absence of well-controlled scientific research comparing the sexual sensitivity of circumcised and uncircumcised men.

Penis Size The belief that the size of the man's penis determines his sexual prowess is based upon the assumption that men with bigger penises are better equipped to satisfy a woman sexually. Zilbergeld (1978) and others point out, however, that women rarely mention penis size as an important element in their sexual satisfaction. Quite regularly they *do*

Foreskin
The loose skin that covers the penile glans. Also referred to as the *prepuce.*

Circumcision
Surgical removal of the foreskin of the penis. (From the Latin *circumcidere,* meaning "to cut around.")

Phimosis
An abnormal condition in which the foreskin is so tight that it cannot be withdrawn from the glans. (From the Greek *phimos,* meaning "muzzle.")

Premature ejaculation
A sexual dysfunction in which the male persistently ejaculates too early to afford the couple adequate sexual gratification.

Figure 3.3. Circumcision. Circumcision is the surgical removal of the foreskin, or prepuce, of the penis. Circumcision has a long history as a religious rite among Jews. Many Christians also practice circumcision for hygienic reasons.

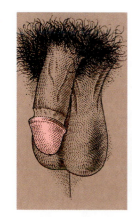  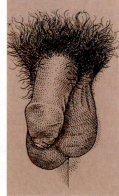 

Scrotum

The pouch of loose skin that contains the testes. (From the same linguistic root as the word *shred*, meaning "a long, narrow strip," and probably referring to the long furrows on the scrotal sac.)

Spermatic cord

The cord that suspends a testicle within the scrotum and contains a vas deferens, blood vessels, nerves, and the cremaster muscle.

Vas deferens

A tube that conducts sperm from the testicle to the ejaculatory duct of the penis. (From Latin roots meaning "a vessel" that "carries down.")

Cremaster muscle

The muscle that raises and lowers the testicle in response to temperature changes and sexual stimulation.

Dartos muscle

The muscle in the middle layer of the scrotum that contracts and relaxes in response to temperature changes.

Testes

The male gonads. (Singular: testis.)

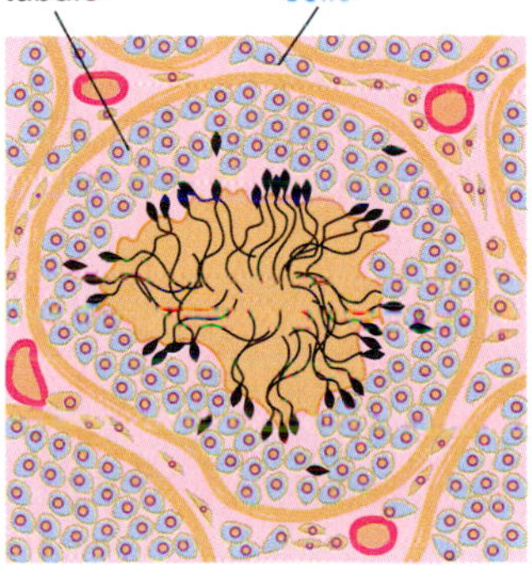

Seminiferous tubule   Interstitial cells

Figure 3.4. **Interstitial Cells.** Testosterone is produced by the interstitial cells, which lie between the seminiferous tubules in each testis. Sperm (seen in the middle of the diagram) are produced within the seminiferous tubules.

mention ability to communicate with partners, the emotional atmosphere of the relationship, and sensitivity to employing sexual techniques that enhance their partner's pleasure.

Masters and Johnson (1966) reported that the penises of the 312 male subjects they studied generally ranged in length from 3½ inches to a little more than 4 inches when flaccid (soft). The average erect penis ranges from 5 to 7 inches in length (Reinisch, 1990). Erect penises differ less in size than flaccid penises do (Jamison & Gebhard, 1988). Penises that are small when flaccid tend to gain more size when they become erect. Larger flaccid penises gain relatively less. Size differences in flaccid penises may thus be largely canceled out by erection. Nor is there a relationship between penis size and body weight, height, or build (Money et al., 1984).

Even when flaccid, the same penis can vary in size. Factors such as cold air or water, or emotions of fear or anxiety can cause the penis (along with the scrotum and testicles) to draw closer to the body, reducing its size. The flaccid penis may also grow in size in warm water or when the man is relaxed.

The Scrotum   The **scrotum** is a pouch of loose skin that becomes covered lightly with hair at puberty. The scrotum consists of two compartments that hold the testes. Each testicle is held in place by a **spermatic cord,** a structure that contains the **vas deferens,** blood vessels and nerves, and the cremaster muscle. The **cremaster muscle** raises and lowers the testicle within the scrotum in response to temperature changes and sexual stimulation. (The testes are drawn closer to the body during sexual arousal.)

Sperm production is optimal at a temperature that is slightly cooler than the 98.6 degrees Fahrenheit that is desirable for most of the body. Typical scrotal temperature is 5 to 6 degrees lower than body temperature. The scrotum is loose-hanging and flexible. It permits the testes and nearby structures to escape the higher body heat, especially in warm weather. In the middle layer of the scrotum is the **dartos muscle,** which (like the cremaster) contracts and relaxes reflexively in response to temperature changes. In cold weather, or when a man jumps into a body of cold water, it contracts to bring the testes closer to the body. In warm weather, it relaxes, allowing the testes to dangle farther from the body. The dartos muscle also increases or decreases the surface area of the scrotum in response to temperature changes. Smoothing allows greater dissipation of heat in hot weather. Tightening or constricting the skin surface helps retain heat and gives the scrotum a wrinkled appearance in the cold.

The scrotum is developed from the same embryonic tissue that becomes the labia majora of the female. Thus, like the labia majora, it is quite sensitive to sexual stimulation. It is somewhat more sensitive than the top side of the penis but less so than other areas of the penis.

Internal Sex Organs

The male internal sex organs consist of the testes, the organs that manufacture sperm and the male sex hormone testosterone; the system of tubes and ducts that conduct sperm through the male reproductive system; and the organs that help nourish and activate sperm and neutralize some of the acidity that sperm encounter in the vagina.

The Testes   The **testes** (or **testicles**) are the male gonads (*gonad* derives from the Greek *gone,* meaning "seed"). In slang the testes are frequently referred to as "balls" or "nuts." These terms are considered vulgar, but they are reasonably descriptive. They also make it easier for many people to refer to the testes in informal conversation.

The testes serve two functions analogous to those of the ovaries. They secrete sex hormones and produce mature **germ cells.** The germ cells are **sperm** and the sex hormones are **androgens.** The most important androgen is **testosterone.**

Testosterone   Testosterone is secreted by **interstitial cells,** which are also referred to as **Leydig's cells.** Interstitial cells lie between the seminiferous tubules and release testosterone directly into the bloodstream (see Figure 3.4). Testosterone stimulates prenatal differentiation of male sex organs, sperm production, and development of **secondary sex characteristics,** such as the beard, deep voice, and growth of the muscle mass.

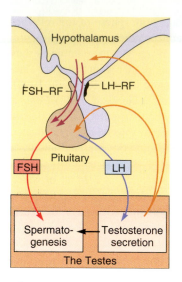

Figure 3.5. **Hormonal Control of the Testes.**
Several endocrine glands—the hypothalamus, the pituitary gland, and the testes—keep blood testosterone levels at a more or less constant level. Low testosterone levels signal the hypothalamus to secrete LH-releasing hormone (LH-RH). Like dominoes falling in a line, LH-RH causes the pituitary gland to secrete LH, which in turn stimulates the testes to release testosterone. Follicle-stimulating, hormone-releasing hormone (FSH-RH) from the hypothalamus causes the pituitary to secrete FSH, which in turn causes the testes to produce sperm cells.

Testicles
Testes.

Germ cell
A cell from which a new organism develops. (From the Latin *germen*, meaning "bud" or "sprout.")

Sperm
The male germ cell. (From a Greek root meaning "seed.")

Androgens
Male sex hormones. (From the Greek *andros*, meaning "man" or "males," and *-gene*, meaning "born.")

Testosterone
The male sex hormone that fosters the developement of male sex characteristics and is connected with the sex drive.

In men, several endocrine glands—the hypothalamus, pituitary gland, and testes (see Figure 3.5)—keep blood testosterone levels at a more or less even level. This contrasts with the peaks and valleys in levels of female sex hormones during the phases of the menstrual cycle. Testosterone levels vary slightly with stress, time of day or month, and other factors, but a feedback loop among the endocrine glands keeps them relatively stable.

The same pituitary hormones, FSH and LH, that regulate the activity of the ovaries also regulate the activity of the testes. FSH regulates the production of sperm by the testes. LH stimulates secretion of testosterone by the interstitial cells. Low testosterone levels signal the hypothalamus to secrete a hormone, called LH-releasing hormone (LH-RH). Like dominoes falling in a line, LH-RH causes the pituitary gland to secrete LH, which in turn stimulates the testes to release testosterone into the blood system. LH is also referred to as *interstitial-cell-stimulating hormone,* or ICSH.

When the level of testosterone in the blood system reaches a certain peak, the hypothalamus directs the pituitary gland *not* to secrete LH. This system for circling information around these three endocrine glands is called a *feedback loop.* This feedback loop is *negative.* That is, increases in hormone levels in one part of the system trigger another part to shut down, and vice versa.

The testes usually range between 1 and 1³/₄ inches in length. They are about half as wide and deep. The left testicle usually hangs lower, because the left spermatic cord tends to be somewhat longer.

Is There a Manopause? Men cannot undergo menopause; they have never menstruated. Yet one now and then hears of a so-called male menopause, occasionally referred to as "manopause." Women encounter relatively sudden age-related declines in sex hormones and fertility during menopause. Men experience a gradual decline in testosterone levels as they age, but nothing like the sharp plunge in estrogen levels that women experience during menopause. Testosterone levels begin to fall at about age 40 or 50 and may decline to one third or one half of their peak levels by age 80 (Brody, 1995c).

The drop in testosterone levels that occurs as men age may be connected to a variety of age-related symptoms, including reduced muscle mass and strength, accumulation of body fat, reduced energy levels, lowered fertility, and reduced erectile ability. However, despite a decline in testosterone levels, most men remain potent throughout their lives. Little is known about the critical levels of testosterone that are needed to maintain erectile ability. Certain age-related changes, such as reduced muscle mass and strength and increased body fat, may be due to other factors associated with aging rather than to declining testosterone production, such as a gradual loss of *human growth hormone,* which helps maintain muscle strength and may prevent fat buildup. Some experts believe that testosterone replacement may help avert erectile problems, bone loss, and frailty, in much the same way that estrogen replacement benefits postmenopausal women (Brody, 1995c). Others worry that excessive use of the hormone may increase the risks of prostate cancer and cardiovascular disease.

Although men do experience a gradual decline in the number and motility of sperm as they age, which reduces their fertility, some viable sperm continue to be produced even into late adulthood. Men can remain sexually active and father children at advanced ages. For both genders, marital satisfaction and attitudes toward aging can affect sexual behavior as profoundly as physical changes can.

Sperm Each testicle is divided into many lobes. The lobes are filled with winding **seminiferous tubules** (see Figure 3.2). Although packed into a tiny space, these tubules, placed end to end, would span the length of several football fields. Through a process called **spermatogenesis,** these threadlike structures produce and store hundreds of billions of sperm through the course of a lifetime.

Sperm cells develop through several stages. It takes about 72 days for the testes to manufacture a mature sperm cell (Leary, 1990). In an early stage, sperm cells are called

Interstitial cells
Cells that lie between the seminiferous tubules and secrete testosterone. (*Interstitial* means "set between.")

Leydig's cells
Another term for *interstitial cells.*

Secondary sex characteristics
Physical traits that distinguish men from women but are not directly involved in reproduction.

Seminiferous tubules
Tiny, winding, sperm-producing tubes that are located within the lobes of the testes. (From Latin roots meaning "seed bearing.")

Spermatogenesis
Process by which sperm cells are produced and developed.

Spermatocyte
An early stage in the development of sperm cells, in which each parent cell has 46 chromosomes, including one X and one Y sex chromosome.

Spermatids
Cells formed by the division of spermatocytes. Each spermatid has 23 chromosomes.

Spermatozoa
Mature sperm cells.

Epididymis
A tube that lies against the back wall of each testicle and serves as a storage facility for sperm. (From Greek roots meaning "upon testicles.")

Human Sperm Cells Magnified Many Times.

spermatocytes. Each one contains 46 chromosomes, including one X and one Y sex chromosome. Each spermatocyte divides into two **spermatids,** each of which has 23 chromosomes. Half the spermatids have X sex chromosomes, and the other half have Y sex chromosomes. Looking something like tadpoles when examined under a microscope, mature sperm cells, called **spermatozoa,** each have a head, a cone-shaped midpiece, and a tail. The head is about 5 microns ($\frac{1}{50,000}$ of an inch) long and contains the cell nucleus that houses the 23 chromosomes. The midpiece contains structures that provide the energy that the tail needs to lash back and forth in a swimming motion. Each sperm cell is about 50 microns ($\frac{1}{5,000}$ of an inch) long, one of the smallest cells in the body (Thompson, 1993).

During fertilization, the 23 chromosomes from the father's sperm cell combine with the 23 chromosomes from the mother's ovum, furnishing the standard ensemble of 46 chromosomes in the offspring. Among the 23 chromosomes borne by sperm cells is one sex chromosome—an X sex chromosome or a Y sex chromosome. Ova contain X sex chromosomes only. The union of an X sex chromosome and a Y sex chromosome leads to the development of male offspring. Two X sex chromosomes combine to yield female offspring. So the presence of an X or Y sex chromosome from the father determines the baby's gender.

The testes churn out about 1,000 sperm per second or about 30 billion—yes, *billion*— per year (Elmer-Dewitt, 1991). Mathematically speaking, 10 to 20 ejaculations hold enough sperm to populate Earth.

Sperm proceed from the seminiferous tubules through an intricate maze of ducts that converge in a single tube called the **epididymis.** The epididymis lies against the back wall of the testicle and serves as a storage facility for sperm. The epididymis, which is some 2 inches in length, consists of twisted passages that would be 10 to 20 feet in length if stretched end to end. Sperm are inactive when they enter the epididymis. They continue to mature as they slowly make their way through the epididymis for another two to four weeks.

The Vas Deferens   Each epididymis empties into a vas deferens (also called *ductus deferens*). The vas is a thin, cylindrical tube about 16 inches long that serves as a conduit for mature sperm. In the scrotum, the vas deferens lies near the skin surface within the

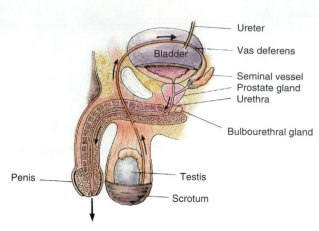

Figure 3.6. **Passage of Spermatozoa.** Each testicle is divided into lobes that contain threadlike seminiferous tubules. Through spermatogenesis, the tubules produce and store hundreds of billions of sperm over the course of a lifetime. During ejaculation, sperm cells travel through the vas deferens, up and over the bladder, into the ejaculatory duct, and then through the urethra. Secretions from the seminal vesicles and the bulbourethral glands join with sperm to compose semen.

Labels in figure: Ureter, Vas deferens, Seminal vessel, Prostate gland, Urethra, Bulbourethral gland, Testis, Scrotum, Penis, Bladder

Vasectomy

A sterilization procedure in which the vas deferens is severed, preventing sperm from reaching the ejaculatory duct.

Seminal vesicles

Small glands that lie behind the bladder and secrete fluids that combine with sperm in the ejaculatory ducts.

Ejaculatory duct

A duct formed by the convergence of a vas deferens with a seminal vesicle through which sperm pass through the prostate gland and into the urethra.

Cilia

Hairlike projections from cells that beat rhythmically to produce locomotion or currents.

Prostate gland

The gland that lies beneath the bladder and secretes prostatic fluid, which gives semen its characteristic odor and texture.

Cowper's glands

Structures that lie below the prostate and empty their secretions into the urethra during sexual arousal.

Bulbourethral glands

Another term for *Cowper's glands.*

spermatic cord. Therefore, a **vasectomy,** an operation in which the right and left vas deferens are severed, is a convenient means of sterilization. The tube leaves the scrotum and follows a circuitous path up into the abdominal cavity. Then it loops back along the rear surface of the bladder (see Figure 3.6).

The Seminal Vesicles

The two **seminal vesicles** are small glands, each about 2 inches long. They lie behind the bladder and open into the **ejaculatory ducts,** where the fluids they secrete combine with sperm (see Figure 3.6). A vesicle is a small cavity or sac; the seminal vesicles were so named because they were mistakenly believed to be reservoirs for semen, rather than glands.

The fluid produced by the seminal vesicles is rich in fructose, a form of sugar, which nourishes sperm and helps them become active, or motile. Sperm motility is a major factor in male fertility. Before reaching the ejaculatory ducts, sperm are propelled along their journey by contractions of the epididymis and vas deferens and by **cilia** that line the walls of the vas deferens. Once they become motile, they propel themselves by whipping their tails.

At the base of the bladder, each vas deferens joins a seminal vesicle to form a short ejaculatory duct that runs through the middle of the prostate gland (see Figure 3.6). In the prostate the ejaculatory duct opens into the urethra, which leads to the tip of the penis. The urethra carries sperm and urine out through the penis, but normally not at the same time.

The Prostate Gland

The **prostate gland** lies beneath the bladder and approximates a chestnut in shape and size (about $3/4$ inch in diameter). Note the spelling of the name of the gland—pros*tate,* not pros*trate.* (*Prostrate* means lying with one's face on the ground, as in some forms of prayer.) The prostate gland contains muscle fibers and glandular tissue that secrete prostatic fluid. Prostatic fluid is milky and alkaline. It provides the characteristic texture and odor of the seminal fluid. The alkalinity neutralizes some of the acidity of the vaginal tract, prolonging the life span of sperm as seminal fluid spreads through the female reproductive system. The prostate is continually active in mature males, but sexual arousal further stimulates secretions. Secretions are conveyed into the urethra by a sievelike duct system. There the secretions combine with sperm and fluid from the seminal vesicles.

A vasectomy prevents sperm from reaching the urethra but does not cut off fluids from the seminal vesicles or prostate gland. A man who has had a vasectomy thus emits an ejaculate that appears normal but contains no sperm.

Cowper's Glands

The **Cowper's glands** are also known as the **bulbourethral glands,** in recognition of their shape and location. These two structures lie below the prostate and empty their secretions into the urethra. During sexual arousal they secrete a drop or so of clear, slippery fluid that appears at the urethral opening. The functions of this fluid are not entirely understood. It may help buffer the acidity of the male's urethra and lubricate the urethral passageway to ease the passage of seminal fluid. The fluid is not produced in sufficient amounts to play a significant role in lubricating the vagina during intercourse.

Fluid from the Cowper's glands precedes the ejaculate and often contains viable sperm. Thus, coitus may lead to pregnancy even if the penis is withdrawn prior to ejaculation. This is one reason why people who practice the "withdrawal method" of birth control are frequently called "parents."

Semen   Sperm and the fluids contributed by the seminal vesicles, the prostate gland, and the Cowper's glands make up **semen**, or whitish seminal fluid, which is expelled through the tip of the penis during ejaculation. The seminal vesicles secrete about 70% of the fluid that constitutes the ejaculate. The remaining 30% of seminal fluid consists of sperm and fluids produced by the prostate gland and the Cowper's gland. Sperm themselves account for only about 1% of the volume of semen. This is why men with vasectomies continue to ejaculate about as much semen as before, although their ejaculates are devoid of sperm.

Semen is the medium that carries sperm through much of the male's reproductive system and the reproductive tract of the female. Semen contains water, mucus, sugar (fructose), acids, and bases. It activates and nourishes sperm, and the bases help shield sperm from vaginal acidity. The typical ejaculate contains between 200 and 400 million sperm and ranges between 3 and 5 milliliters in volume. (Five milliliters is equal to about 1 tablespoon.) The quantity of semen decreases with age and frequency of ejaculation.

Diseases of the Urogenital System

Because the organs that comprise the urinary and reproductive systems are near each other and share some "piping," they are referred to as the urinogenital or urogenital system. A number of diseases can affect the urogenital system. The type of physician who specializes in their diagnosis and treatment is a **urologist.**

Urethritis

Men, like women, are subject to bladder and urethral inflammations, which are generally referred to as **urethritis.** The symptoms include frequent urination (urinary frequency), a strong need to urinate (urinary urgency), burning during urination, and a penile discharge. People with symptoms of urinary frequency and urinary urgency feel the pressing need to urinate repeatedly, even though they may have just done so and may have but another drop or two to expel. The discharge may dry on the urethral opening, in which case it may have to be peeled off or wiped away before it is possible to urinate. The urethra also may become constricted when it is inflamed, slowing or halting urination. It is a frightening sensation for a male to feel the urine rush from his bladder and then suddenly stop at the urethral opening!

Preventive measures for urethritis parallel those suggested for cystitis (bladder infection): drinking more water, drinking cranberry juice (4 ounces, two or three times a day), and lowering intake of alcohol and caffeine. Cranberry juice is highly acidic, and acid tends to eliminate many of the bacteria that can give rise to urethritis.

Cancer of the Testes

Cancer of the testicles remains a relatively rare form of cancer, accounting for about 6,000 new cases annually, or about 1% of all new cancers in men (American Cancer Society, 1991). It is the most common form of solid-tumor cancer to strike men between the ages of 20 and 34, however (Vazi et al., 1989). It accounts for nearly 10% of all deaths from cancer among men in that age group.

Semen
The whitish fluid that constitutes the ejaculate, consisting of sperm and secretions from the seminal vesicles, prostate, and Cowper's glands.

Urologist
A physician who specializes in the diagnosis and treatment of diseases of the urogenital system.

Urethritis
An inflammation of the bladder or urethra.

A P P L I C A T I O N S

SELF-EXAMINATION OF THE TESTES

Self-examination (see Figure 3.7) is best performed shortly after a warm shower or bath, when the skin of the scrotum is most relaxed. The man should exam the scrotum for evidence of pea-sized lumps. Each testicle can be rolled gently between the thumb and the fingers. Lumps are generally found on the side or front of the testicle. The presence of a lump is not necessarily a sign of cancer, but it should be promptly reported to a physician for further evaluation. The American Cancer Society (1990) lists these warning signals:

1. A slight enlargement of one of the testicles.
2. A change in the consistency of a testicle.
3. A dull ache in the lower abdomen or groin.
   (Pain may be absent in cancer of the testes, however).
4. Sensation of dragging and heaviness in a testicle.

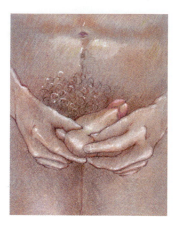

Figure 3.7.
Testicular Self-Examination.

Cryptorchidism
A condition in which one or two testicles fail to descend from the abdomen into the scrotum.

There is no evidence that testicular cancer results from sexual overactivity or masturbation. Men who had **cryptorchidism** as children (a condition in which one or both testicles fail to descend from the abdomen into the scrotum) stand about a 40 times greater chance of contracting testicular cancer. Undescended testicles appear to occur more commonly in boys born to mothers who used the hormone diethylstilbestrol (DES) during pregnancy. In the 1940s and 1950s, pregnant women were often prescribed DES to help prevent miscarriages.

Treatments include surgical removal of the diseased testis, radiation, and chemotherapy. The survival rate among cases that are detected early, before the cancer has spread beyond the testes, is 96% (American Cancer Society, 1991). Delayed treatment markedly reduces the chances of survival, because survival is connected with the extent to which the cancer has spread.

The early stages of testicular cancer usually produce no symptoms, other than the mass itself. Because early detection is crucial to survival, men are advised to examine themselves monthly, following puberty (Reinisch, 1990) and to have regular medical checkups. Self-examination may also reveal evidence of sexually transmitted diseases and other problems.

Disorders of the Prostate

The prostate gland is tiny at birth and grows rapidly at puberty. It may shrink during adulthood, but usually becomes enlarged past the age of 50.

Benign prostatic hyperplasia
Enlargement of the prostate gland due to hormonal changes associated with aging and characterized by symptoms such as urinary frequency, urinary urgency, and difficulty starting the flow of urine.

Benign Prostatic Hyperplasia   The prostate gland becomes enlarged in about one quarter of men past the age of 60 (Walsh, 1996). When enlargement is due to hormonal changes associated with aging rather than other causes, such as inflammation from sexually transmitted diseases, it is referred to as **benign prostatic hyperplasia.** Because the prostate surrounds the upper part of the urethra (see Figure 3.2), enlargement constricts the urethra. Symptoms such as urinary frequency (including increased frequency of nocturnal urination), urinary urgency, and difficulty starting the flow of urine result. At one time, surgical removal of part of the prostate was used to relieve the pressure on the urethra and increase the flow of urine. Today, chemotherapy is available to improve the flow of urine either by relaxing the smooth muscle of the prostate (with the drug terazosin) or by shrinking an enlarged prostate (with the drug finasteride) (Walsh, 1996). The use of microwave radiation is also under study.

Cancer of the Prostate   A more serious and life-threatening problem is prostate cancer. The American Cancer Society estimates that about one man in eight in the United States will develop prostate cancer (Ochs, 1993b). Prostate cancer is the second most common form of cancer among men, after skin cancer, and the second leading cause of cancer deaths in men, after lung cancer. According to the American Cancer Society (1995), there were 244,000 new cases of prostate cancer in the United States in 1995, and 40,400 men died from the disease.

Prostate cancer involves the growth of malignant prostate tumors that can metastasize to bones and lymph nodes if not detected and treated early. African American men are one-third more likely than White men to develop prostate cancer (American Cancer Society, 1995). African American men may also have less access to routine medical evaluations than White men do, so that disease is diagnosed at a later stage. Researchers have identified intake of animal fat as a potential risk factor. Men whose diets are rich in animal fats, especially fats from red meat, have a substantially greater chance of developing advanced prostate cancer than do men with a low intake of animal fat. The incidence of prostate cancer also increases with age. Over 80% of all prostate cancers are diagnosed in men over the age of 65 (American Cancer Society, 1995). Genetic factors may also be involved (Wilson, 1995).

The early symptoms of cancer of the prostate may mimic those of benign prostate enlargement: urinary frequency and difficulty in urinating. Later symptoms include blood in the urine, pain or burning on urination, and pain in the lower back, pelvis, or upper thighs (American Cancer Society, 1995). Most cases occur without noticeable symptoms in the early stages.

The American Cancer Society (1995) recommends that men receive annual rectal examinations beginning at about age 40. The physician inserts a finger into the rectum and feels for abnormalities in the prostate gland. The procedure may be uncomfortable, but it is brief and not particularly painful. Unfortunately, many men are reluctant to undergo a rectal examination, even though it is only mildly uncomfortable and may save their lives. Some are embarrassed or reluctant to discuss urinary problems with their physicians. Some may even resist the rectal examination because they associate rectal insertion with male–male sex. Still others are fearful that they may have cancer and choose to remain ignorant. Avoidance of, or ignorance of the need for, annual rectal exams among men is a major contributor to the death rate from prostate cancer.

A blood test can detect evidence of prostate cancer even among men whose prostates feel normal upon physical examination. A study of more than 10,000 men found that the blood test was about twice as successful in detecting early prostate cancer than were physical examinations (Catalona et al., 1993). The blood test measures prostate-specific antigen, or PSA, which is a type of protein that seeps out of the prostate gland when it is cancerous or enlarged. The American Cancer Society and other professional groups recommend that men of age 50 and above have an annual PSA blood test as well as a rectal examination (Morgan et al., 1996). African American men are encouraged to begin such screening at the age of 40 (Morgan et al., 1996).

When a cancerous growth is suspected on the basis of a rectal examination or a PSA blood test, further testing is usually done by ultrasound or biopsy. Early detection is important because treatment is most effective before the cancer has spread ("Early prostate surgery," 1996). Fifty-eight percent of cases of prostate cancer are discovered while they are still localized. The five-year survival rate is 94% for prostate cancer that has not metastasized (American Cancer Society, 1995). The survival rate drops dramatically if the cancer has metastasized. Still, the overall survival rate has improved in the past 30 years from 50% to 80% (American Cancer Society, 1995).

The most widely used treatment for prostate cancer is surgical removal of the prostate gland. However, surgical prostate removal may damage surrounding nerves, leading to problems in controlling the flow of urine or in erection or ejaculation. Recently introduced surgical techniques tend to spare the surrounding nerves and reduce, but not eliminate, the risk of complications. Other treatments include radiation, hormone treatment, and anti-cancer drugs. Hormone treatment and anticancer drugs may shrink the size of the tumor and relieve pain for long periods of time.

Among older men with slow-growing prostate cancer, physicians often prefer "watchful waiting" to surgery ("Early prostate surgery," 1996). The men frequently die first from causes other than cancer.

Prostatitis Many infectious agents can inflame the prostate, causing **prostatitis.** The chief symptoms are an ache or pain between the scrotum and anal opening and painful ejaculation. Prostatitis is usually treated with antibiotics. Although aspirin and ibuprofen may relieve the pain, men with these symptoms should consult a physician. Painful ejaculation may discourage masturbation or coitus, which is ironic, since regular flushing of the prostate through ejaculation may be helpful in the treatment of prostatitis.

Male Sexual Functions

The male sexual functions of erection and ejaculation provide the means for sperm to travel from the male's reproductive tract to the female's. There the sperm cell and ovum unite to conceive a new human being. Of course, the natural endowment of reproduction with sensations of pleasure helps ensure that it will take place with or without knowledge of these biological facts.

Erection

Erection is the engorgement of the penis with blood, such that the penis grows in size and stiffens. The erect penis is an efficient conduit, or funnel, for depositing sperm deep within the vagina.

In mechanical terms, erection is a hydraulic event. The spongy, cavernous masses of the penis are equipped to hold blood. Filling them with blood causes them to enlarge, much like a sponge swells as it absorbs water. Erection involves the cooperation of the vascular (blood) system and the nervous system.

In a few moments—as quickly as 10 or 15 seconds—the penis can double in length, become firm, and shift from a funnel for passing urine to one that expels semen. Moreover, the bladder is closed off when the male becomes sexually aroused, decreasing the likelihood that semen and urine will mix.

Yes, the blood that fills the penis during sexual arousal causes erectile tissue to expand. But what accounts for the firmness of an erection? A sponge that fills with water expands but does not grow hard. It turns out that the two corpora cavernosa are surrounded by a tough, fibrous covering called the *tunica albuginea*. As the rubber of a balloon resists the pressure of pumped-in air, this housing resists expansion, causing the penis to rigidify. The corpus spongiosum, which contains the penile urethra, also engorges with blood during erection. It does not become hard, however, since it lacks the fibrous casing. The penile glans, which is formed by the crowning of the spongiosum at the tip of the penis, turns a dark purplish hue as it becomes engorged, but it too does not stiffen.

Despite the advanced state of biological knowledge, some mechanics of erection are not completely understood. It is not entirely clear, for example, whether penile cavities become engorged because the veins that carry blood away from the penis do not keep pace with the rapid flow of blood entering the penis, or whether the returning blood flow is reduced by compression of the veins at the base of the penis (as stepping lightly on a hose slows the movement of water).

We do know that erection is reversed when more blood flows out of the erectile tissue than flows in, restoring the pre-erectile circulatory balance and shrinking the erectile tissue or spongy masses. The erectile tissue thus exerts less pressure against the fibrous cov-

Prostatitis
Inflammation of the prostate gland.

Erection
The enlargement and stiffening of the penis as a consequence of engorgement with blood.

ering, resulting in a loss of rigidity. Loss of erection occurs when sexual stimulation ceases, or when the body returns to a (sexual) resting state following orgasm. Loss of erection can also occur in response to anxiety or perceived threats. Loss of erection in response to threat can be abrupt, as when a man in the "throes of passion" suddenly hears a suspicious noise in the adjoining room, suggestive of an intruder. Yet the "threats" that induce loss of erection are more likely to be psychological than physical. In our culture, men often measure their manhood by their sexual performance. A man who fears that he will be unable to perform successfully may experience **performance anxiety** that can prevent him from achieving erection or lead to a loss of erection at penetration.

The male capacity for erection quite literally spans the life cycle. Erections are common in babies, even within minutes after birth. Evidence from ultrasound studies shows that male fetuses may even have erections months prior to birth. Men who are well into their 80s and 90s continue to experience erections and engage in coitus.

Nor are erections limited to the conscious state. Men have nocturnal erections every 90 minutes or so as they sleep. They generally occur during REM (rapid eye movement) sleep. REM sleep is associated with dreaming. It is so named because the sleeper's eyes dart about rapidly under the closed eyelids during this stage. Erections occur during most periods of REM sleep.

The mechanism of nocturnal erection appears to be physiologically based. That is, erections occur along with dreams that may or may not have erotic content. Morning erections are actually nocturnal erections. They occur when the man is awakened during REM sleep, as by an alarm clock. Men sometimes erroneously believe that a morning erection is caused by the need to urinate. When the man awakens with both an erection and the need to urinate, he may mistakenly assume that the erection was caused by the pressure of his bladder.

Spinal Reflexes and Sexual Response

Men may become sexually aroused by a range of stimulation, including tactile stimulation provided by their partners, visual stimulation (such as from scanning photos of nude models in men's magazines), or even mental stimulation from engaging in sexual fantasies. Regardless of the source of stimulation, the man's sexual responses, erection and ejaculation, occur by **reflex.** Erection and ejaculation are reflexes: automatic, unlearned responses to sexual stimulation. So too are vaginal lubrication and orgasm in women.

The reflexes governing erection and ejaculation are controlled at the level of the spinal cord. Thus, they are considered spinal reflexes. Erections may occur in response to different types of stimulation. Some occur from direct stimulation of the genitals, as from stroking, licking, or fondling the penis or scrotum. Erectile responses to such direct stimulation involve a simple spinal reflex that does not require the direct participation of the brain.

Erections can also be initiated by the brain, without the genitals being touched or fondled at all. Such erections may occur when a man has sexual fantasies, when he views erotic materials, or when he catches a glimpse of a woman in a bikini on a beach. In the case of the "no-hands" type of erections, stimulation from the brain travels to the spinal cord, where the erectile reflex is triggered. To better understand how this reflex works, we need to first explain the concept of the reflex arc.

The Reflex Arc   When you withdraw your hand from a hot stove or blink in response to a puff of air, you do so before you have any time to think about it. These responses, like erection, are reflexes that involve sensory neurons and effector neurons (see Figure 3.8 on page 70). In response to a stimulus like a touch or a change in temperature, sensory neurons or receptors in the skin "fire" and thereby send messages to the spinal cord. The message is then transmitted to effector neurons that begin in the spinal cord and cause muscles to contract or glands to secrete chemical substances. So if you accidentally touched a hot stove, sensory neurons in your fingers or hand would deliver a message to the spinal cord, which would trigger effector neurons to contract muscles that pull your hand away

Performance anxiety
Feelings of dread and foreboding experienced in connection with sexual activity (or any other activity that might be judged by another person).

Reflex
A simple, unlearned response to a stimulus that is mediated by the spine rather than the brain.

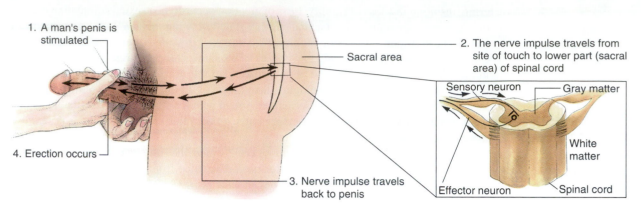

1. A man's penis is stimulated

4. Erection occurs

Sacral area

2. The nerve impulse travels from site of touch to lower part (sacral area) of spinal cord

3. Nerve impulse travels back to penis

Sensory neuron

Gray matter

White matter

Effector neuron

Spinal cord

Figure 3.8. **Reflexes.** Reflexes involve sensory neurons, effector neurons, and, sometimes, interneurons that connect the two in the spinal cord. Reflexes need not involve the brain, although messages to the brain may make us aware when reflexes are occurring. Reflexes are the product of "local government" in the spine. *(Source:* From *Human Sexuality* by S. A. Rathus. Copyright © 1983 by Holt, Rinehart & Winston, Inc. Reprinted by permission of the publisher.)

from the stove. The brain does not control this spinal reflex arc. That is not to say that the brain fails to "get the message" shortly afterwards. Sensory messages usually rise from the spinal cord to the brain to make us aware of stimulation. The experience of pain occurs when a message travels from the site of the injury to the spinal cord and then to receiving stations in the brain that "interpret" the message to produce the sensation of pain. The withdrawal of your hand from a harmful object begins before your brain even gets the message.

In some males, especially adolescents, the erectile reflex is so easily tripped that incidental rubbing of the genitals against his own undergarments, the sight of an attractive passer-by, or a fleeting sexual fantasy produces erection. Spontaneous erections may occur under embarrassing circumstances, such as before classes change in junior or senior high school, or on a public beach. In an effort to distract himself from erotic fantasies and to allow an erection to subside, many a male adolescent in the classroom has desperately renewed his interest in his algebra or foreign language textbook before the bell has rung.

As men mature they require more penile stimulation to achieve full erection. Partners of men in their 30s and 40s need not feel that their attractiveness has waned if their lovers no longer have instant "no-hands" erections when they disrobe. It takes men longer to achieve erection as they age, and direct penile stimulation becomes a more critical source of arousal.

The Role of the Autonomic Nervous System

Although stimulation that brings about an erection can originate in the brain, this does not mean that erection is a voluntary response, like raising your arm. Whatever the original or dominant source of stimulation—direct penile stimulation or sexual fantasy—erection remains an unlearned, automatic reflex.

Automatic responses, such as erection, involve the division of the nervous system called the **autonomic nervous system** (ANS). *Autonomic* means "automatic." The ANS controls automatic bodily processes such as heartbeat, pupil dilation, respiration, and digestion. In contrast, voluntary movement (like raising an arm) is under the control of the *somatic* division of the nervous system.

The ANS has two branches, the **sympathetic** and the **parasympathetic.** These branches have largely opposing effects; when they are activated at the same time, their effects become balanced out to some degree. In general, the sympathetic branch is in command during processes that involve a release of bodily energy from stored reserves, such as during running, performing some other athletic task, or being gripped by fear or anxiety. The sympathetic branch also governs the general mobilization of the body, such as by increasing the heart rate and respiration rate in response to threat.

Autonomic nervous system

The division of the nervous system that regulates automatic bodily processes, such as heartbeat, pupil dilation, respiration, and digestion. Abbreviated *ANS.*

Sympathetic

The branch of the ANS most active during emotional responses, such as fear and anxiety, that spend the body's reserves of energy. The sympathetic ANS largely controls ejaculation.

Parasympathetic

The branch of the ANS most active during processes that restore the body's reserves of energy, such as digestion. The parasympathetic ANS largely controls erection.

The parasympathetic branch is most active during processes that restore reserves of energy, such as digestion. When we experience fear or anxiety, the sympathetic branch of the ANS quickens the heart rate. When we relax, the parasympathetic branch curbs the heart rate. The parasympathetic branch activates digestive processes, but the sympathetic branch inhibits digestive activity. Since the sympathetic branch is in command when we feel fear or anxiety, such stimuli can inhibit the activity of the parasympathetic system, thereby slowing down digestive process and possibly causing indigestion.

The divisions of the autonomic nervous system play different roles in sexual arousal and response. The nerves that cause penile arteries to dilate during erection belong to the parasympathetic branch of the autonomic nervous system. It is thus the parasympathetic system that largely governs erection. The nerves governing ejaculation belong to the sympathetic branch, however. One implication of this division of neural responsibility is that intense fear or anxiety, which involves sympathetic nervous system activity, may inhibit erection by counteracting the activity of the parasympathetic nervous system. Since sympathetic arousal is involved in triggering the ejaculatory reflex, anxiety or fear may also accelerate ejaculation, causing premature ejaculation. Intense emotions like fear and anxiety can thus lead to problems in achieving or maintaining erection as well as causing hasty ejaculation.

Because erections seem spontaneous at times, and often occur when the man would rather not have them, it may seem to men that the penis has a mind of its own. Despite this common folk belief, however, the penis possesses no guiding intelligence. It consists of spongy masses of erectile tissue, not the lovely dense gray matter that renders your thought processes so incisive.

Erectile Abnormalities   Some men find that their erect penises are slightly curved or bent. Some degree of curvature is perfectly normal, but men with **Peyronie's disease** have excessive curvature that can make erections painful or make it difficult to enjoy coitus. The condition is caused by buildup of fibrous tissue in the penile shaft. Although some cases of Peyronie's disease appear to clear up on their own, most require medical attention.

Some men experience erections that persist for hours or days. This condition is called *priapism,* after Priapus of Greek myth, the son of Dionysus and Aphrodite who personified male procreative power. Priapism is often caused by leukemia, sickle cell anemia, or diseases of the spinal cord, although in some cases the cause remains unknown. Priapism occurs when the mechanisms that drain the blood that make the penis erect are damaged and so cannot return the blood to the circulatory system. The name of the disorder is truly a misnomer, because Priapus had a voracious sexual appetite. Men with priapism instead suffer from a painful condition that should receive medical attention. Priapism may become a medical emergency, since erection prolonged beyond six hours can starve penile tissues of oxygen, leading to tissue deterioration. Immediate medical intervention in the form of drugs or even surgery may be required to reverse the condition and allow blood to drain from the penis (Spark, 1991).

Ejaculation

Ejaculation, like erection, is a spinal reflex. It is triggered when sexual stimulation reaches a critical point or threshold. Ejaculation generally occurs together with **orgasm,** the sudden muscle contractions that occur at the peak of sexual excitement and result in the abrupt release of sexual tension that had built up during sexual arousal. Orgasm is accompanied by subjective sensations that are generally intensely pleasurable. Ejaculation, however, refers only to the expulsion of semen from the tip of the penis. Orgasm and ejaculation are *not* synonymous, however. Nor do they always occur simultaneously. For example, **paraplegics** can ejaculate if the area of the lower spinal cord that controls ejaculation is intact. They do not experience the subjective aspects of orgasm, however, since the sensations of orgasm do not reach the brain.

Conversely, prepubertal boys may experience orgasms even though they emit no ejaculate. Orgasms without ejaculate are termed "dry orgasms." Boys do not begin to produce seminal fluid (and sperm) until puberty. Mature men, too, can experience dry orgasms. They

Peyronie's disease
An abnormal condition characterized by an excessive curvature of the penis that can make erections painful.

Orgasm
The climax of sexual excitement.

Paraplegic
A person with sensory and motor paralysis of the lower half of the body.

Emission stage
The first phase of ejaculation, which involves contractions of the prostate gland, seminal vesicles, and the upper part of the vas deferens.

Ampulla
A sac or dilated part of a tube or canal.

Urethral bulb
The small tube that makes up the prostatic part of the urethral tract, which balloons out as muscles close at either end, trapping semen prior to ejaculation.

Expulsion stage
The second stage of ejaculation, during which muscles at the base of the penis and elsewhere contract rhythmically, forcefully expelling semen and providing pleasurable sensations.

Retrograde ejaculation
Ejaculation in which the ejaculate empties into the bladder. (From the Latin *retrogradi*, meaning "to go backward.")

can take the form of "little orgasms" preceding a larger orgasm, or they can follow "wet orgasms" when sexual stimulation is continued but seminal fluids have not been replenished.

Ejaculation occurs in two stages. The first phase, often called the **emission stage,** involves contractions of the prostate, seminal vesicles, and the upper part of the vas deferens (the **ampulla**). The force of these contractions propels seminal fluid into the prostatic part of the urethral tract—a small tube called the **urethral bulb**—which balloons out as muscles close at either end, trapping the semen.

The second stage, which is often referred to as the **expulsion stage,** involves the propulsion of the seminal fluid through the urethra and out of the urethral opening at the tip of the penis. In this stage, muscles at the base of the penis and elsewhere contract rhythmically, forcefully expelling semen. The second stage is generally accompanied by the highly pleasurable sensations of orgasm.

In ejaculation, the seminal fluid is released from the urethral bulb and expelled by forceful contractions of the pelvic muscles that surround the urethral channel and the crura of the penis. The first few contractions are most intense and occur at 0.8-second intervals. Subsequent contractions lessen in intensity. The interval between them gradually increases. Seminal fluid is expelled in spurts during the first few contractions. The contractions are so powerful that seminal fluid may be propelled to distances of 12 to 24 inches, according to observations made by Masters and Johnson. Some men, however, report that semen travels but a few inches or just oozes from the penile opening. The force of the expulsion varies with the condition of the man's prostate, his general health, and his age. More intense orgasms often accompany more forceful ejaculations.

Retrograde Ejaculation   Some men experience **retrograde ejaculation,** in which the ejaculate empties into the bladder rather than being expelled from the body. During normal ejaculation an external sphincter opens, allowing seminal fluid to pass out of the body. Another sphincter, this one internal, closes off the opening to the bladder, preventing the seminal fluid from backing up into the bladder. In retrograde ejaculation, the actions of these sphincters are reversed. The external sphincter remains closed, preventing the expulsion of the seminal fluid, while the internal sphincter opens, allowing the ejaculate to empty into the bladder. The result is a dry orgasm. No ejaculate is apparent because semen has backed up into the bladder. Retrograde ejaculation condition may be caused by prostate surgery (much less so now than in former years), drugs such as tranquilizers, certain illnesses, and accidents. Retrograde ejaculation is usually harmless in itself, since the seminal fluid is later discharged with urine. Infertility can result, however, and there may be some changes in the sensations associated with orgasm. Persistent dry orgasms should be medically evaluated, since their underlying cause may be a threat to health.

Chapter Review

The Male Sex Organs

The external male sex organs include the penis and the (1) _____um. The (2) p_____, like the vagina, is the sex organ used in sexual intercourse. Unlike the vagina, however, the penis also serves as a duct for (3) u_____. Semen and urine pass out of the penis through the (4) _____ral opening. The urethral opening is also called the urethral (5) m_____.

The human penis (6: *Does or* Does not?) contain bones. The human penis (7: *Does or* Does not?) contain muscle tissue.

The penis contains (8: One, Two, or Three?) cylinders of spongy material that run its length. The larger two cylinders are called (9) c_____ c_____. These cylinders fill with (10) _____d and stiffen during sexual arousal. The corpus (11) _____sum (spongy body) runs along the bottom and contains the urethra. The penile (12) g_____, like the clitoral glans, is extremely sensitive to sexual stimulation. The (13) c_____ separates the glans from the body of the penis. The (14) fr_____ is a strip of tissue that connects the underside of the glans to the penile shaft. The base of the penis is called the (15) r_____.

Some penile skin folds over to partially cover the glans; this covering is the (16) _____uce, or foreskin. (17) _____sion is the surgical removal of the prepuce. Research suggests that urinary tract infections are (18: Less or More?) common among uncircumcised male infants than among circumcised infants. Evidence also suggests that uncircumcised men are at (19: Lower or Greater?) risk than circumcised men of becoming infected by the AIDS virus.

Men commonly worry that their penises are too (20: Big or Small?).

The (21) sc_____ is a pouch of loose skin that holds the testes. Each testicle is held in place by a (22) _____ic cord, a structure that contains the vas (23) def_____, blood vessels and nerves, and the cremaster muscle.

Sperm production is optimal at a temperature (24: Cooler or Warmer?) than the 98.6 degrees Fahrenheit that is desirable for most of the body. The scrotum permits the testes to escape the (25: Higher or Lower?) body heat.

The (26) _____es are the male gonads. The testes serve functions analogous to those of the female (27) _____ies. They secrete sex hormones called (28) _____gens and produce germ cells called (29) s_____. The most important androgen is (30) _____rone.

Testosterone is secreted by (31) _____tial cells. Testosterone stimulates prenatal differentiation of male sex organs, sperm production, and development of (32) _____ary sex characteristics, such as the beard, deep voice, and muscle mass. In men, several (33) _____ine glands—the hypothalamus, pituitary gland, and testes—keep testosterone levels at a more or less even level. FSH regulates (34) s_____ production. LH stimulates secretion of (35) tes_____.

Men (36: Can or Cannot?) undergo menopause. (37: Men or Women?) encounter sudden age-related declines in sex hormones and fertility during menopause. Men experience a (38: Sudden or Gradual?) decline in testosterone levels as they age. Some experts believe that (39) _____rone replacement may help avert erectile problems, bone loss, and frailty, in much the same way that estrogen replacement benefits postmenopausal women. Others worry that testosterone replacement may increase the risks of (40) p_____ cancer and cardiovascular disease.

Lobes within each testicle are filled with winding (41) _____ferous tubules. The seminiferous tubules produce and store sperm through a process called (42) _____genesis. In an early stage, sperm cells are called (43) _____cytes and contain 46 chromosomes, including one X and one Y sex chromosome. Each spermatocyte divides into two (44) _____tids, each of which has 23 chromosomes. Half the spermatids have X sex chromosomes, and the other half have (45) _____ sex chromosomes. Ova contain (46) _____ sex chromosomes only.

Sperm proceed from the seminiferous tubules through ducts that converge in a tube called the (47) _____mis. Each epididymis empties into a (48) _____ deferens. A (49) _____my is a means of sterilization in which the right and left vas deferens are severed.

Two seminal vesicles are small glands that open into (50) _____tory ducts, where the fluids they secrete combine with sperm. The fluid produced by the seminal vesicles is rich in (51) _____ose. Once sperm become motile, they propel themselves by whipping their (52) _____ls.

The (53) pr_____ gland lies beneath the bladder and secretes prostatic fluid. Prostatic fluid is (54: Alkaline or Acidic?) and neutralizes some of the acidity of the vaginal tract. During sexual arousal, (55) C_____ glands secrete a drop or so of clear, slippery fluid that appears at the urethral opening. Fluid from the Cowper's glands often contains viable (56) _____m.

Sperm and the fluids contributed by the seminal vesicles, the prostate gland, and the Cowper's glands make up (57) s_____, the whitish fluid which is expelled during ejaculation. Semen activates and nourishes (58) s_____.

Diseases of the Urogenital System

Men, like women, are subject to bladder and urethral inflammations, which are generally referred to as (59) _____tis. The symptoms include frequent (60) _____tion, urinary urgency, burning urination, and a discharge.

Cancer of the (61) _____cles accounts for nearly 10% of all deaths from cancer among men of ages 20 to 34. Men who had (62) cryp_____ as children stand about a 40 times greater chance of contracting testicular cancer.

The prostate gland is tiny at birth and grows rapidly at puberty; it usually (63: Becomes enlarged or Shrinks?) past the age of 50. When enlargement is due to hormonal changes associated with aging rather than other causes, it is referred to as (64) be_____ prostatic (65) _____plasia. Prostate enlargement constricts the (66) ure_____. Symptoms such as urinary (67) fre_____, urinary (68) ur_____, and difficulty starting the flow of urine result.

Prostate cancer is the (69: First, Second, or Third?) most common form of cancer among men. It is the (70: First, Second, or Third?) leading cause of cancer deaths in men. African American men are (71: More or Less?) likely than White men to develop prostate cancer. Eating animal fat (72: Is or Is not?) a risk factor. The incidence of prostate cancer (73: Increases or Decreases?) with age. The American Cancer Society (1995) recommends that men receive annual rectal examinations beginning at about age (74) _____. A blood test that measures prostate-specific (75) _____gen, or PSA, can also detect evidence of prostate cancer. The American Cancer Society recommends that men of age (76) _____ and above have an annual PSA blood test.

(77) _____itis is inflammation of the prostate. The chief symptoms are pain between the scrotum and (78) a_____ opening and painful ejaculation.

Male Sexual Functions

(79) _____tion is the engorgement of the penis with blood, such that the penis grows in size and stiffens. When the male becomes sexually aroused, the (80) _____er is closed off so that semen and urine are unlikely to mix. A tough, fibrous covering called the tunica (81) _____nea accounts for the firmness of an erection. Loss of erection occurs when sexual stimulation stops or the body returns to a resting state following (82) _____sm. Loss of erection can also occur in response to feelings of (83) an_____. A man who fears that he will be unable to perform successfully may experience (84) per_____ anxiety that can interfere with erection.

Erections (85: Are or Are not?) common in babies. Men have (86) noc_____ erections as they sleep. Noctural erections generally occur during (87) r_____ _____ movement (REM) sleep. REM sleep is associated with (88) _____ing.

Erection and ejaculation are (89) _____xes—automatic, unlearned responses to sexual stimulation. Vaginal (90) _____tion and orgasm in women are also reflexes. The reflexes governing erection and ejaculation are controlled by the (91) s_____ cord.

Automatic responses, such as erection, involve the division of the nervous system called the (92) _____mic nervous system (ANS). The ANS has two branches, the sympathetic and the (93) _____pathetic. The (94) _____pathetic branch of the ANS largely governs erection. The nerves governing ejaculation belong to the (95) _____pathetic branch. Anxiety, which involves sympathetic nervous system activity, may (96: Trigger or Inhibit?) erection but (97: Trigger or Inhibit?) ejaculation.

Men with (98) _____nie's disease have excessively curved erection that can be painful. Men with (99) _____ism have erections that persist for hours or days.

Ejaculation, like erection, is a (100) s_____ reflex. Ejaculation generally occurs along with (101) o_____, but the term refers only to the expulsion of (102) _____en from the penis. Orgasms without ejaculate are termed (103) _____ orgasms.

Ejaculation occurs in (104: One, Two, or Three?) stages. The first phase, or (105) _____sion stage, involves contractions of the prostate, seminal vesicles, and the upper part of the vas deferens. The contractions propel seminal fluid into a tube called the (106) _____ al bulb. In the second stage, or (107) _____ sion stage, seminal fluid is propelled through the urethra and out of the penis. (108) _____ les at the base of the penis contract rhythmically, expelling semen. The first few contractions are (109: Most *or* Least?) intense and occur at 0.8-second intervals.

Chapter Quiz

1. The penis differs from the vagina in that
   (a) the penis is the sex organ used in sexual intercourse.
   (b) the penis serves as a duct for urine.
   (c) the penis develops from embryonic tissue.
   (d) the penis is found in mammals.
2. The penis contains _____ cylinder(s) of spongy material.
   (a) one
   (b) two
   (c) three
   (d) four
3. The condition in which it is difficult to retract the foreskin from the glans is called
   (a) phimosis.
   (b) circumcision.
   (c) priapism.
   (d) cryptorchidism.
4. The American Cancer Society estimates that about 1 man in _____ in the United States will develop prostate cancer.
   (a) 8
   (b) 80
   (c) 800
   (d) 8,000
5. The American Cancer Society and other professional groups recommend that men of age _____ and above have an annual PSA blood test as well as a rectal examination.
   (a) 40
   (b) 45

(c) 50
(d) 55

6. Erection is the engorgement of the penis with
   (a) semen.
   (b) blood.
   (c) sperm.
   (d) testosterone.
7. Erections generally occur during _____ sleep.
   (a) REM
   (b) non-REM
   (c) deepest
   (d) morning
8. In ejaculation, the seminal fluid is released from the
   (a) vas deferens
   (b) prostate gland
   (c) spinal cord
   (d) urethral bulb
9. The nerves that cause penile arteries to dilate during erection belong to the
   (a) sympathetic nervous system.
   (b) parasympathetic nervous system.
   (c) somatic nervous system.
   (d) central nervous system.
10. Men with _____ have excessive curvature of the penis that can make erections painful or make it difficult to enjoy sexual activity.
    (a) priapism
    (b) phimosis
    (c) Peyronie's disease
    (d) cryptorchidism

Answers to Chapter Review

1. Scrotum	10. Blood	19. Greater	28. Androgens	37. Women
2. Penis	11. Spongiosum	20. Small	29. Sperm	38. Gradual
3. Urine	12. Glans	21. Scrotum	30. Testosterone	39. Testosterone
4. Urethral	13. Corona	22. Spermatic	31. Interstitial	40. Prostate
5. Meatus	14. Frenulum	23. Deferens	32. Secondary	41. Seminiferous
6. Does not	15. Root	24. Cooler	33. Endocrine	42. Spermatogenesis
7. Does not	16. Prepuce	25. Higher	34. Sperm	43. Spermatocytes
8. Three	17. Circumcision	26. Testes	35. Testosterone	44. Spermatids
9. Corpora cavernosa	18. More	27. Ovaries	36. Cannot	45. Y

46. X
47. Epididymis
48. Vas
49. Vasectomy
50. Ejaculatory
51. Fructose
52. Tails
53. Prostate
54. Alkaline
55. Cowper's
56. Sperm
57. Semen
58. Sperm

59. Urethritis
60. Urination
61. Testicles
62. Cryptorchidism
63. Becomes enlarged
64. Benign
65. Hyperplasia
66. Urethra
67. Frequency
68. Urgency
69. Second
70. Second
71. More

72. Is
73. Increases
74. 40
75. Antigen
76. 50
77. Prostatitis
78. Anal
79. Erection
80. Bladder
81. Albuginea
82. Orgasm
83. Anxiety
84. Performance

85. Are
86. Nocturnal
87. Rapid eye
88. Dreaming
89. Reflexes
90. Lubrication
91. Spinal
92. Autonomic
93. Parasympathetic
94. Parasympathetic
95. Sympathetic
96. Inhibit
97. Trigger

98. Peyronie's
99. Priapism
100. Spinal
101. Orgasm
102. Semen
103. Dry
104. Two
105. Emission
106. Urethral
107. Expulsion
108. Muscles
109. Most

Answers to Chapter Quiz

1. (b)
2. (c)
3. (a)
4. (a)
5. (c)
6. (b)
7. (a)
8. (d)
9. (b)
10. (c)

CHAPTER 4

Sexual Response and Behavior

O U T L I N E

Making Sense of Sex: The Role of the Senses in Sexual Arousal

Vision: The Better to See You With

Smell: Does the Nose Know Best?

The Skin Senses: Sex as a Touching Experience

Taste: On Savory Sex

Hearing: The Better to Hear You With

Aphrodisiacs: Of Spanish Flies and Rhino Horns

Psychoactive Drugs

Sex Hormones: Do They "Goad" Us into Sex?

Sex Hormones and Sexual Behavior

The Sexual Response Cycle

Excitement Phase

Plateau Phase

Orgasmic Phase

Resolution Phase

Kaplan's Three Stages of Sexual Response: An Alternative Model

Controversies About Orgasm

Multiple Orgasms

How Many Kinds of Orgasms Do Women Have?

The G-Spot

Sexual Behavior

Solitary Sexual Behavior

Sex with Others

Chapter Review

Chapter Quiz

World of Diversity
Sociocultural Factors and Oral Sex

Applications
Advantages and Disadvantages of Various Positions of Sexual Intercourse

- "Spanish fly" is unlikely to turn your date on but may cure his or her warts?
- Normal men produce female sex hormones, and normal women produce male sex hormones?
- Orgasms attained through masturbation may be more intense than those attained through sexual intercourse?
- Married people often masturbate?
- Women are more likely to reach orgasm through masturbation than through sexual intercourse?
- Statistically speaking, oral sex is the norm for today's young married couples?
- White Americans are more likely than African Americans to engage in oral sex?
- Anal sex is more common among highly educated people?

What turns you on? What springs your heart into your mouth, tightens your throat, and opens the floodgates into your genitals? The sight of your lover undressing, a photo of Denzel Washington or Cindy Crawford, a sniff of some velvety perfume, a sip of wine?

Many factors contribute to sexual response and behavior. Although people's bodies are similar in their potential for sexual response, cultural influences affect sexual behavior. ■

Making Sense of Sex: The Role of the Senses in Sexual Arousal

We come to apprehend the world around us through our senses—vision, hearing, smell, taste, and the skin senses, which include that all-important sense of touch. Each of the senses plays a role in our sexual experience.

Vision: The Better to See You With

It was the face of Helen of Troy, not her scent or her melodic voice, that "launched a thousand ships." Men's and women's magazines are filled with pictures of comely members of the other gender. Visual cues can be sexual turn-ons. We may be turned on by the sight of a lover in the nude, disrobing, or dressed in evening wear. Some couples find it arousing to observe themselves making love in an overhead mirror or on videotape. Some people find sexually explicit movies arousing. Others are bored or offended by them.

Aphrodisiac
Any drug or other agent that is sexually arousing or increases sexual desire. (From *Aphrodite*, the Greek goddess of love and beauty.)

Smell: Does the Nose Know Best?

Odors can be sexual turn-ons or turn-offs. Most people in the United States prefer their lovers to be clean and fresh-smelling. People in our society learn to remove or mask odors by the use of soaps, deodorants, and so on. Inclinations to find underarm or genital odors offensive may reflect cultural conditioning and not biological predispositions. In some societies, genital secretions are considered **aphrodisiacs.**

Visual Cues Can Be Sexual Turn-Ons or Turn-Offs. Despite cross-cultural differences in standards of physical attractiveness, a clear complexion has universal appeal.

The Skin Senses: Sex as a Touching Experience

The sense of touch has the most direct effects on sexual arousal and response. Any region of the skin can become eroticized. **Erogenous zones** are parts of the body that are especially sensitive to tactile sexual stimulation—to strokes and other caresses. **Primary erogenous zones** are erotically sensitive because they are richly endowed with nerve endings. **Secondary erogenous zones** are parts of the body that become erotically sensitized through experience. For example, a woman might become sexually aroused when her lover gently caresses her shoulders, because such caresses have been incorporated as a regular feature of the couple's lovemaking.

Primary erogenous zones include the genitals; the inner thighs, perineum, buttocks, and anus; the breasts (especially the nipples); the ears (particularly the earlobes); the mouth, lips, and tongue; the neck; the navel; and, yes, the armpits. Preferences vary somewhat from person to person. Many women, for example, report little sensation when their breasts are stroked or kissed.

People are also highly responsive to images and fantasies. This is why the brain is sometimes referred to as the primary sexual organ, or an erogenous zone. Some women report reaching orgasm through fantasy alone (Kinsey et al., 1953). Men regularly experience erection and nocturnal emissions ("wet dreams") without direct stimulation of the genitals.

Technically, the brain is not an erogenous zone. It is not stimulated directly by touch. (The brain perceives touches of the skin, but it does not have sensory neurons to directly gather this information itself.)

Taste: On Savory Sex

Some people are sexually aroused by the taste of genital secretions, such as vaginal secretions or seminal fluid. We do not know, however, whether these secretions are laced with chemicals that have biologically arousing effects, or whether arousal reflects the meaning that these secretions have to the individual. Others are turned off by them.

Erogenous zones
Parts of the body that are especially sensitive to tactile sexual stimulation.

Primary erogenous zones
Erogenous zones that are particularly sensitive because they are richly endowed with nerve endings.

Secondary erogenous zones
Parts of the body that become erotically sensitized through experience.

Hearing: The Better to Hear You With

Sounds can be turn-ons or turn-offs. The sounds of one's lover, whether whispers, indications of pleasure, or animated sounds that may attend orgasm, may be arousing during the heat of passion. Many people are aroused when their lovers "talk dirty." Spoken vulgarities spur their sexual arousal. Others find vulgar language offensive. Music can contribute to sexual arousal. Music can relax us and put us "in the mood" or have pleasant associations ("They're playing our song!").

Do We Have a "Sixth Sense" for Sex?   For centuries, people have searched for a love potion—a magical formula that could make others fall in love with them or be strongly attracted to them. Some scientists believe that such potions exist in the form of chemical secretions known as **pheromones** (Berliner, 1993). Pheromones are odorless chemicals that in people would be detected through a "sixth sense"—the *vomeronasal organ*. This organ, located in the nose (hence, *nasal*), would detect these odorless chemicals and signal the brain to respond (Blakeslee, 1993b). Pheromones do trigger sexual behavior in many organisms, from insects to reptiles to mammals (Cobb & Jallon, 1990; Eggert & Muller, 1989; Mason et al., 1989). Pheromones are commonly contained in vaginal secretions and in urine. Chemicals in the urine of female dogs signal sexual receptivity.

Pheromones
Chemical substances secreted externally by certain animals, which convey information to, or produce specific responses in, other members of the same species. (From the Greek *pherien*, meaning "to bear [a message]" and *hormone*.)

Aphrodisiacs: Of Spanish Flies and Rhino Horns

An aphrodisiac is a substance that arouses or increases one's capacity for sexual pleasure or response. You may have heard of "Spanish fly," a supposed aphrodisiac once extracted from a Spanish beetle. (The beetle from which it was taken, *Lytta vesicatoria,* is near extinction.) A few drops in a date's drink were believed to make you irresistible. Spanish fly is toxic, however, not sexually arousing. The active ingredient, *cantharidin,* is a skin irritant that can burn off warts. It inflames the urethra, producing a burning sensation in the penis that is sometimes misinterpreted as sexual feelings.

Foods that resemble male genitals have been considered aphrodisiacs. They include oysters, clams, bull's testicles ("prairie oysters"), tomatoes, and "phallic" items such as celery stalks, bananas, and even ground-up rhinoceros, reindeer, and elephant horns (which is one derivation of the slang term "horny"). None of these foods or substances has been shown to be sexually stimulating, however.

Drugs and psychoactive substances may have certain effects on sexual arousal and response. The drug *yohimbine,* an extract from the African yohimbe tree, stimulates blood flow to the genitals (Brody, 1993b). Its aphrodisiac effects remain to be demonstrated, however.

The heart medicine amyl nitrate dilates blood vessels in the brain and genitals, producing sensations of warmth in the pelvis and possibly facilitating erection and prolonging orgasm. It is inhaled from ampules that "pop" open. "Poppers" can cause dizziness, fainting, and migraine-type headaches, however.

Certain drugs appear to have aphrodisiac effects by acting on the brain mechanisms controlling sex drive. For example, drugs that affect brain receptors for the neurotransmitter dopamine, such as the antidepressant drug *bupropion* (trade name: Wellbutrin) and the drug L-dopa used in the treatment of Parkinson's disease, can increase the sex drive (Brody, 1993b).

The most potent chemical aphrodisiac may be a naturally occurring substance in the body, the male sex hormone testosterone. It is the basic fuel of sexual desire in both genders (Brody, 1993b). In fact, **antiandrogen** drugs have **anaphrodisiac** effects.

The safest and perhaps most effective method for increasing the sex drive may be exercise. It boosts energy and increases the sex drive in both genders (Brody, 1993b). Perhaps the most potent aphrodisiac of all is novelty. Partners can make love in novel places, experiment with different techniques, wear provocative clothing, or share or enact fantasies.

Antiandrogen
A substance that decreases the levels of androgens in the bloodstream.

Anaphrodisiacs
Drugs or other agents that dull sexual arousal or sexual desire.

Some substances, such as potassium nitrate (saltpeter), have been considered anaphrodisiacs. Saltpeter is a diuretic that can increase the need for urination and thus make the thought of sex unappealing.

Tranquilizers and central nervous system depressants, such as barbiturates, can lessen sexual desire and impair sexual performance. These drugs may enhance sexual arousal in some people, however, by lessening sexual inhibitions. Antihypertensive drugs, which are used in the treatment of high blood pressure, may produce erectile and ejaculatory difficulties in men, and reduction of sexual desire in both genders. Certain antidepressant drugs, such as fluoxetine (brand name: Prozac), amitriptyline (brand name: Elavil), and imipramine (brand name: Tofranil) appear to dampen sex drive (Brody, 1993b; Meston & Gorzalka, 1992). Antidepressants may also impair erectile response and delay ejaculation in men and orgasmic responsiveness in women (Meston & Gorzalka, 1992). (Because they delay ejaculation, some of these drugs are being used to treat premature ejaculation.)

Nicotine, the stimulant in tobacco smoke, constricts the blood vessels. Thus it can impede sexual arousal by reducing the capacity of the genitals to become engorged with blood. Chronic smoking can also reduce the blood levels of testosterone in men, which can in turn lessen sex drive or motivation.

Psychoactive Drugs

Psychoactive drugs, such as alcohol and cocaine, are widely believed to have aphrodisiac effects. Yet their effects may reflect our expectations of them, or their effects on sexual inhibitions, rather than direct stimulation of sexual response.

Alcohol Small amounts of alcohol are stimulating, but large amounts curb sexual response. This fact should not be surprising because alcohol is a depressant. Alcohol reduces central nervous system activity. Large amounts of alcohol can severely impair sexual performance in both men and women.

Alcohol is connected with a liberated social role and thus provides an excuse for dubious behavior. "It was the alcohol," people can say, "not me." Alcohol can also induce feelings of euphoria. Euphoric feelings may enhance sexual arousal and also wash away qualms about expressing sexual desires. Alcohol also appears to impair the ability to weigh information ("information processing") that might otherwise inhibit sexual impulses (Steele & Josephs, 1990). When people drink, they may be less able to foresee the consequences of misconduct and less likely to ponder their standards of conduct.

Effects of Alcohol on Sexual Behavior— A Complex Picture. Small doses of alcohol can be stimulating and induce feelings of euphoria, both of which would appear to be connected with sexual interest. Alcohol can also reduce fear of consequences of engaging in risky behavior—sexual and otherwise. Drinkers sometimes say, "It was the alcohol, not me." Alcohol is also expected to be sexually liberating, and people often live up to social and cultural expectations. Yet, as a depressant drug, alcohol biochemically dampens sexual response.

Hallucinogenics　　There is no evidence that marijuana and other hallucinogenic drugs directly stimulate sexual response. However, fairly to strongly intoxicated marijuana users claim to have more empathy with others, to be more aware of bodily sensations, and to experience time as passing more slowly. These sensations could heighten subjective feelings of sexual response.

Stimulants　　Stimulants such as amphetamines ("speed," "uppers," "bennies," "dexies") have been reputed to heighten arousal and sensations of orgasm. These drugs generally activate the central nervous system but are not known to have specific sexual effects. Nevertheless, arousing the nervous system can contribute to sexual arousal (Palace, 1995). The drugs can also elevate the mood, and perhaps sexual pleasure is heightened by general elation. The downside is that high doses can give rise to irritability, restlessness, hallucinations, paranoid delusions, insomnia, and loss of appetite.

The stimulant cocaine produces a euphoric rush, which tends to ebb quickly. Physically, cocaine constricts blood vessels (reducing the oxygen supply to the heart), elevates the blood pressure, and accelerates the heart rate. Despite the popular belief that cocaine is an aphrodisiac, frequent use can lead to sexual dysfunctions, such as erectile disorder and failure to ejaculate among males, decreased vaginal lubrication in females, and lack of sexual desire (Weiss & Mirin, 1987).

Sex Hormones: Do They "Goad" Us into Sex?

Hormone

A substance secreted by an endocrine gland that regulates various body functions. (From the Greek *horman*, meaning "to stimulate" or "to excite.")

Hormones are chemical substances that are secreted by the ductless glands of the endocrine system and discharged directly into the bloodstream. The word *hormone* derives from the Greek *horman,* meaning "to stimulate" or "to excite." They very much goad us into sexual activity.

Both men and women produce small amounts of the sex hormones of the other gender in their bodies. Testosterone, the major form of androgen, or male sex hormone, is secreted in small amounts by the adrenal glands (located above the kidneys) in both genders, but in much larger amounts by the testes. The ovaries produce small amounts of androgens but much larger amounts of the female sex hormones, estrogen and progesterone. The testes similarly produce small amounts of estrogen and progesterone.

Sex Hormones and Sexual Behavior

Sex hormones have organizing and activating effects on behavior. That is, they exert an influence on the type of behavior that is expressed (an *organizing* effect) and the frequency or intensity of the drive that motivates the behavior and the ability to perform the behavior (*activating* effects). For example, sex hormones predispose lower animals and possibly people toward stereotypical masculine or feminine mating behaviors (an organizing effect). They also facilitate sexual response and influence sexual desire (activating effects). Testosterone activates the sex drive of both men and women.

Sex Hormones and Male Sexual Behavior　　Evidence of the role for hormones in sex drive is found among men who have declines in testosterone levels as the result of castration. Castration (removal of the testes) is sometimes performed as a medical treatment for cancer of the prostate or other diseases of the male reproductive tract, such as genital tuberculosis. Some convicted sex offenders have voluntarily undergone castration as a condition of release. Men who are castrated usually gradually lose sexual desire. They gradually lose the capacities to attain erection and to ejaculate—an indication that testosterone is important in maintaining sexual functioning as well as drive, at least in males.

Though minimal levels of androgens are critical to male sexuality, there is no one-to-one correspondence between hormone levels and the sex drive or sexual performance in adults. In men who have ample supplies of testosterone, sexual interest and functioning depend more on learning, fantasies, attitudes, memories, and other psychosocial factors than on hormone levels. At puberty, however, hormonal variations may play a more direct role in stimulating sexual interest and activity in males. Udry and his colleagues (Udry et al., 1985; Udry et al., 1986; Udry & Billy, 1987) found, for example, that testosterone levels predicted sexual interest, masturbation rates, and the likelihood of engaging in sexual intercourse among teenage boys. A positive relationship also has been found between testosterone levels in adult men and frequency of sexual intercourse (Dabbs & Morris, 1990; Knussman et al., 1986). Moreover, drugs that reduce the levels of androgen in the blood system, called *antiandrogens,* lead to reductions in sex drive and related fantasies and urges (Berlin, 1983; Money, 1987b).

Sex Hormones and Female Sexual Behavior   The female sex hormones estrogen and progesterone play prominent roles in promoting the changes that occur during puberty and in regulating the menstrual cycle. Female sex hormones do not appear to play a direct role in determining sexual motivation or response in human females, however. The human female is sexually responsive during all phases of the reproductive (menstrual) cycle—even during menstruation, when ovarian hormone levels are low—and after menopause.

There is some evidence, however, that sexual responsiveness in women is influenced by the presence of circulating androgens, or male sex hormones, in their bodies. The adrenal glands of women produce small amounts of androgens, just as they do in males. Women who receive **ovariectomies,** which are sometimes carried out when a hysterectomy is performed, no longer produce female sex hormones. Nevertheless, they continue to experience sex drives and interest as before. Loss of the ovarian hormone estradiol may cause vaginal dryness and make coitus painful, but it does not reduce sexual desire. (The dryness can be alleviated by a lubricating jelly or by estrogen-replacement therapy.) However, women whose adrenal glands *and* ovaries have been removed (so that they no longer produce androgens) gradually lose sexual desire. An active and enjoyable sexual history seems to ward off this loss, however, providing further evidence of the impact of mental and experiential factors on human sexual response.

A study was conducted with women whose ovaries had been surgically removed ("surgical menopause") as a way of treating disease. The ovaries supply major quantities of estrogen. Following surgery, the women in this study were treated either with estrogen-replacement therapy (ERT), with ERT *plus* androgens, or with a placebo (an inert substance made to resemble an active drug) (Sherwin et al., 1985). This was a double-blind study. Neither the women nor their physicians knew which drug the women were receiving. The results showed that the combination of androgens and ERT heightened sexual desire and sexual fantasies more than ERT alone or the placebo.

Ovariectomy
Surgical removal of the ovaries.

Sexual response cycle
Masters and Johnson's model of sexual response, which consists of four phases.

Vasocongestion
The swelling of the genital tissues with blood, which causes erection of the penis and engorgement of the area surrounding the vaginal opening.

Myotonia
Muscle tension.

The Sexual Response Cycle

Although we may be culturally attuned to focus on gender differences rather than similarities, Masters and Johnson (1966) found that the physiological responses of men and women to sexual stimulation (whether from coitus, masturbation, or other sources) are quite alike. The sequence of changes in the body that takes place as men and women become progressively more aroused is referred to as the **sexual response cycle.** Masters and Johnson divided the cycle into four phases: *excitement, plateau, orgasm,* and *resolution.* Figure 4.1 on page 84 suggests the levels of sexual arousal associated with each phase.

Both males and females experience **vasocongestion** and **myotonia** early in the response cycle. Vasocongestion is the swelling of the genital tissues with blood, which causes

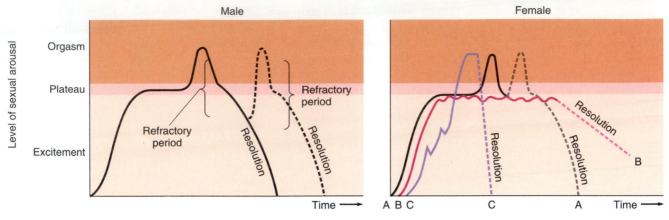

Figure 4.1. **Levels of Sexual Arousal During the Phases of the Sexual Response Cycle.**
Masters and Johnson divide the sexual response cycle into four phases: excitement, plateau, orgasm, and resolution. During the resolution phase, the level of sexual arousal returns to the prearoused state. For men there is a refractory period following orgasm. As shown by the broken line, however, men can become rearoused to orgasm once the refractory period is past and their levels of sexual arousal have returned to pre-plateau levels. Pattern A for women shows a typical response cycle, with the broken line suggesting multiple orgasms. Pattern B shows the cycle of a woman who reaches the plateau phase but for whom arousal is "resolved" without reaching the orgasmic phase. Pattern C shows the possibility of orgasm in a highly aroused woman who passes quickly through the plateau phase.

erection of the penis and engorgement of the area surrounding the vaginal opening. The testes, nipples, and even earlobes become engorged as blood vessels in these areas dilate.

Myotonia refers to muscle tension. Myotonia causes voluntary and involuntary muscle contractions, which produce facial grimaces, spasms in the hands and feet, and eventually, the spasms of orgasm. Let us follow these and the other bodily changes that constitute the sexual response cycle.

Excitement Phase

Excitement phase

The first phase of the sexual response cycle, which is characterized by erection in the male, vaginal lubrication in the female, and muscle tension and increases in heart rate in both males and females.

In younger men, vasocongestion during the **excitement phase** produces penile erection as early as 3 to 8 seconds after stimulation begins. Erection may occur more slowly in older men, but the responses are essentially the same. Erection may subside and return as stimulation varies. The scrotal skin thickens, losing its baggy appearance. The testes increase in size. The testes and scrotum become elevated.

In the female, vaginal lubrication may start 10 to 30 seconds after stimulation begins. Vasocongestion swells the clitoris, flattens the labia majora and spreads them apart, and increases the size of the labia minora. The inner two thirds of the vagina expand. The vaginal walls thicken, and because of the inflow of blood, turn from their normal pink to a deeper hue. The uterus becomes engorged and elevated. The breasts enlarge, and blood vessels near the surface become more prominent.

Sex flush

A reddish rash that appears on the chest or breasts late in the excitement phase of the sexual response cycle.

The skin may take on a rosy **sex flush** late in this phase. It varies with intensity of arousal and is more pronounced in women. The nipples may become erect in both genders, especially in response to direct stimulation. Men and women show some increase in myotonia, heart rate, and blood pressure.

Plateau Phase

Plateau phase

The second phase of the sexual response cycle, which is characterized by increases in vasocongestion, muscle tension, heart rate, and blood pressure in preparation for orgasm.

A plateau is a level region, and the level of arousal remains somewhat constant during the **plateau phase** of sexual response. Nevertheless, the plateau phase is an advanced state of arousal that precedes orgasm. Men in this phase show a slight increase in the circumference of the coronal ridge of the penis. The penile glans turns a purplish hue, a sign of vasocongestion. The testes are elevated further into position for ejaculation and may reach one and a half times their unaroused size. The Cowper's glands secrete a few droplets of fluid that are found at the tip of the penis (see Figure 4.2).

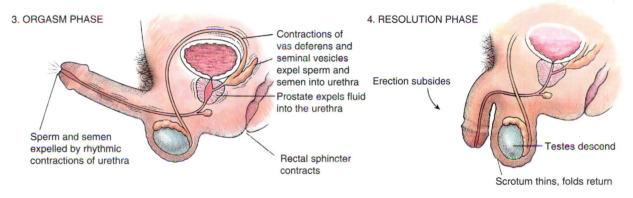

1. EXCITEMENT PHASE

Vasocongestion of penis results in erection

Meatus dilates

Testes begin elevation
Scrotal skin tenses, thickens

2. PLATEAU PHASE

The coronal ridge of the glans increases in diameter and turns a deeper reddish-purple

The Cowper's glands may release fluid

The testes become completely elevated and engorged when orgasm is imminent

Cowper's gland

3. ORGASM PHASE

Contractions of vas deferens and seminal vesicles expel sperm and semen into urethra

Prostate expels fluid into the urethra

Sperm and semen expelled by rhythmic contractions of urethra

Rectal sphincter contracts

4. RESOLUTION PHASE

Erection subsides

Testes descend

Scrotum thins, folds return

Figure 4.2. The Male Genitals During the Phases of the Sexual Response Cycle.

In women, vasocongestion swells the tissues of the outer third of the vagina, contracting the vaginal opening (thus preparing it to "grasp" the penis) and building the **orgasmic platform** (see Figure 4.3 on page 86). The inner part of the vagina expands fully. The uterus becomes fully elevated. The clitoris withdraws beneath the clitoral hood and shortens.

Coloration of the labia minora appears, which is referred to as the **sex skin.** Further engorgement of the areolas of the breasts may make it seem that the nipples have lost part of their erection (see Figure 4.4 on page 86). The Bartholin's glands secrete a fluid that resembles mucus.

About one man in four, and about three women in four, show a sex flush, which often does not appear until the plateau phase. Myotonia may cause spasmodic contractions in the hands and feet and facial grimaces. Breathing becomes rapid, like panting, and the heart rate may increase to 100 to 160 beats per minute. Blood pressure continues to rise. The increase in heart rate is usually less dramatic with masturbation than during coitus.

Orgasmic platform

The thickening of the walls of the outer third of the vagina, due to vasocongestion, that occurs during the plateau phase of the sexual response cycle.

Sex skin

Reddening of the labia minora that occurs during the plateau phase.

Orgasmic Phase

The orgasmic phase in the male consists of two stages of muscular contractions. In the first stage, contractions of the vas deferens, the seminal vesicles, the ejaculatory duct, and the prostate gland cause seminal fluid to collect in the urethral bulb at the base of the penis (see Figure 4.2). The internal sphincter of the urinary bladder contracts, preventing seminal fluid from entering the bladder in a backward, retrograde ejaculation. The closing off of the bladder also serves to prevent urine from mixing with semen. The collection of semen in the urethral bulb produces feelings of ejaculatory inevitability—the sensation that nothing will stop the ejaculate from "coming." This sensation lasts for about 2 to 3 seconds.

In the second stage, the external sphincter of the bladder relaxes, allowing the passage of semen. Contractions of muscles surrounding the urethra and urethral bulb and the base of the penis propel the ejaculate through the urethra and out of the body. Sensations of plea-

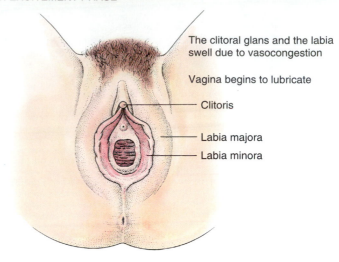

1. EXCITEMENT PHASE

The clitoral glans and the labia swell due to vasocongestion

Vagina begins to lubricate

Clitoris

Labia majora

Labia minora

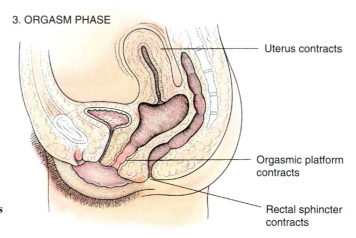

3. ORGASM PHASE

Uterus contracts

Orgasmic platform contracts

Rectal sphincter contracts

Figure 4.3. The Female Genitals During the Phases of the Sexual Response Cycle.

sure tend to be related to the strength of the contractions and the amount of seminal fluid. The first 3 to 4 contractions are generally most intense and occur at 0.8-second intervals (5 contractions every 4 seconds). Another 2 to 4 contractions occur at a somewhat slower pace. Rates and patterns vary somewhat from man to man.

Orgasm in the female is manifested by 3 to 15 contractions of the pelvic muscles that surround the vaginal barrel. The contractions first occur at 0.8-second intervals, producing, as in the male, a release of sexual tension. Another 3 to 6 weaker and slower contractions

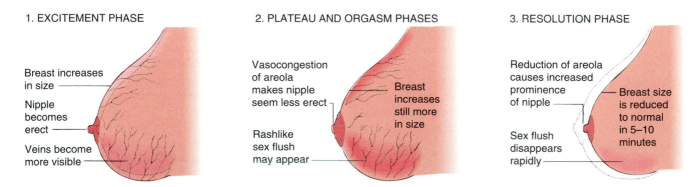

1. EXCITEMENT PHASE

Breast increases in size

Nipple becomes erect

Veins become more visible

2. PLATEAU AND ORGASM PHASES

Vasocongestion of areola makes nipple seem less erect

Breast increases still more in size

Rashlike sex flush may appear

3. RESOLUTION PHASE

Reduction of areola causes increased prominence of nipple

Breast size is reduced to normal in 5–10 minutes

Sex flush disappears rapidly

Figure 4.4. The Breast During the Phases of the Sexual Response Cycle.

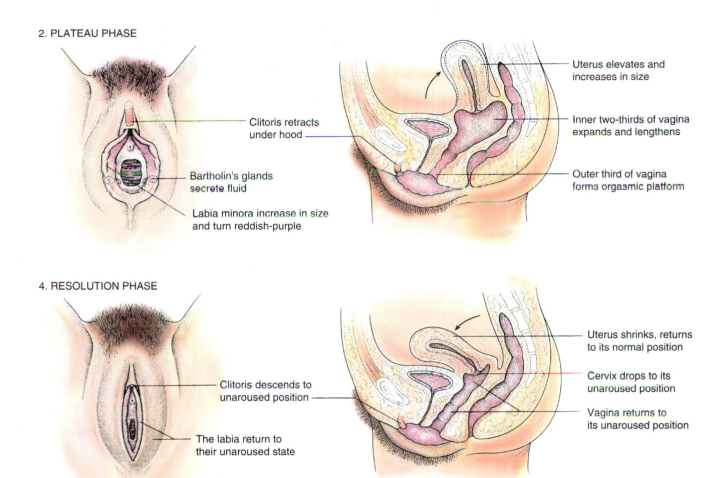

2. PLATEAU PHASE

Clitoris retracts under hood

Bartholin's glands secrete fluid

Labia minora increase in size and turn reddish-purple

Uterus elevates and increases in size

Inner two-thirds of vagina expands and lengthens

Outer third of vagina forms orgasmic platform

4. RESOLUTION PHASE

Clitoris descends to unaroused position

The labia return to their unaroused state

Uterus shrinks, returns to its normal position

Cervix drops to its unaroused position

Vagina returns to its unaroused position

follow. The spacing of these contractions is generally more variable in women than in men. The uterus and the anal sphincter also contract rhythmically. Uterine contractions occur in waves from the top to the cervix. In both genders, muscles go into spasm throughout the body. Blood pressure and heart rate reach a peak, with the heart beating up to 180 times per minute. Respiration may increase to 40 breaths per minute.

The sensations of orgasm have challenged the descriptive powers of poets. Words like "rush," "warmth," "explosion," and "release" do not adequately capture them. We may assume (rightly or wrongly) that others of our gender experience pretty much what we do, but can we understand the sensations of the other gender?

Several studies suggest that the orgasms of both genders may feel quite similar. In one, 48 men and women provided written descriptions of orgasms. The researchers (Proctor et al., 1974) modified the language (for example, changing "penis" to "genitals") so that the authors' genders would not be apparent. They then asked 70 "experts" (psychologists, gynecologists, etc.) to indicate the gender of each author. The ratings were no more reliable than guesswork.

Resolution Phase

Resolution phase
The fourth phase of the sexual response cycle, during which the body gradually returns to its prearoused state.

The period following orgasm, in which the body returns to its prearoused state, is called the **resolution phase.** Following ejaculation, the man loses his erection in two stages. The first occurs in about a minute. Half the volume of the erection is lost as blood from the corpora cavernosa empties into the other parts of the body. The second stage occurs over a period of several minutes: The remaining tumescence subsides as the corpus spongiosum empties. The testes and scrotum return to normal size, and the scrotum regains its wrinkled appearance.

In women orgasm also triggers release of blood from engorged areas. In the absence of continued stimulation, swelling of the areolas decreases; then the nipples return to normal size. The sex flush lightens rapidly. In about 5 to 10 seconds the clitoris descends to its normal position. The clitoris, vaginal barrel, uterus, and labia gradually shrink to their prearoused sizes. The labia minora turn lighter (the "sex skin" disappears) in about 10 to 15 seconds.

Most muscle tension (myotonia) tends to dissipate within 5 minutes after orgasm in both men and women. Blood pressure, heart rate, and respiration may also return to their prearousal levels within a few minutes. About 30% to 40% of men and women find their palms, the soles of their feet, or their entire bodies covered with a sheen of perspiration. Both men and women may feel relaxed and satiated.

Although the processes by which the body returns to its prearousal state are similar in men and women, there is an important gender difference. Unlike women, men enter a **refractory period** during which they are physiologically incapable of experiencing another orgasm or ejaculation. The refractory period of adolescent males may last only minutes, whereas that of men age 50 and above may last from several minutes (yes, "it could happen") to a day. Women do not undergo a refractory period and so can become quickly rearoused to the point of repeated (multiple) orgasm if they desire and receive continued sexual stimulation (see Figure 4.1).

Myotonia and vasocongestion may take an hour or more to dissipate in people who are aroused but who do not reach orgasm. Persistent pelvic vasocongestion may cause "blue balls" in males—the slang term for a throbbing ache. Women, too, may experience unpleasant pelvic throbbing if they have become highly aroused and do not find release.

Refractory period
A period of time following a response (e.g., orgasm) during which an individual is no longer responsive to stimulation (e.g., sexual stimulation).

Kaplan's Three Stages of Sexual Response: An Alternative Model

Whereas Masters and Johnson proposed a four-stage model of sexual response, Helen Singer Kaplan developed a three-stage model consisting of (1) desire, (2) excitement, and (3) orgasm. Kaplan's model makes it convenient for clinicians to classify sexual dysfunctions involving desire (low or absent desire), excitement (such as problems with erection in the male or lubrication in the female), and orgasm (such as premature ejaculation in the male or orgasmic dysfunction in the female).

Controversies About Orgasm

Are women capable of experiencing multiple orgasms? Are men? How many kinds of orgasm are there? Do women ejaculate during orgasm?

Few other topics in human sexuality have aroused more controversies over the years than orgasm. We do not have all the answers, but some intriguing research findings have shed light on some of these continuing controversies.

Multiple Orgasms

Masters and Johnson (1966) reported that most if not all women are capable of **multiple orgasms.** Though all women may have a biological capability for multiple orgasms, not all women report them. A recent survey of 720 nurses showed that only 43% reported experiencing multiple orgasms (Darling et al., 1991).

Masters and Johnson define *multiple orgasm* as the rapid occurrence of one or more *additional* orgasms following the first, before the body has returned to a pre-plateau level of arousal. By this definition, a person would not have experienced multiple orgasms if he or she had two or more successive orgasms that were separated by a return to a prearoused state or a pre-plateau (excitement stage) level of arousal. Yet the lines of demarcation between the excitement and plateau stages of arousal are not always obvious.

Multiple orgasms
One or more additional orgasms following the first, which occur within a short period of time and before the body has returned to a preplateau level of arousal.

By Masters and Johnson's definition, men are not capable of achieving multiple orgasms, because they enter a refractory period following ejaculation during which they are physiologically incapable of achieving another orgasm or ejaculation for a time. Women do not enter a refractory period. Women can continue to have orgasms if they continue to receive effective stimulation (and, of course, are interested in continuing).

Some men have two or more orgasms without ejaculation ("dry orgasms") preceding a final ejaculatory orgasm. These men may not enter a refractory period following their initial dry orgasms and may therefore be able to maintain their level of stimulation at near-peak levels. Some men report multiple orgasms in which dry orgasms follow an ejaculatory orgasm, with little or no loss of erection between orgasms (Dunn & Trost, 1989). Some men report more varied patterns, with ejaculatory orgasms and dry orgasms preceding or following each other in different sequences.

Masters and Johnson found that some women experienced 20 or more orgasms by masturbating. Still, few women have multiple orgasms during most sexual encounters, and many are satisfied with just one per occasion.

How Many Kinds of Orgasms Do Women Have?

The psychoanalyst Sigmund Freud proposed two types of female orgasm: the *clitoral orgasm* and the *vaginal orgasm*. Clitoral orgasms were achieved through direct clitoral stimulation, such as by masturbation. Clitoral orgasms were seen by psychoanalysts (mostly male psychoanalysts, naturally) as emblematic of a childhood fixation—a throwback to an erogenous pattern acquired during childhood masturbation.

The term *vaginal orgasm* referred to an orgasm achieved through deep penile thrusting during coitus and was theorized to be a sign of mature sexuality. Freud argued that women achieve sexual maturity when they forsake clitoral stimulation for vaginal stimulation. This view would be little more than an academic footnote but for the fact that some adult women who continue to require direct clitoral stimulation to reach orgasm, even during coitus, have been led by traditional (generally male) psychoanalysts to believe that they are sexually "fixated" at an immature stage, or are, at least, sexually inadequate.

Despite Freudian theory, Masters and Johnson (1966) were able to find only one kind of orgasm, physiologically speaking, regardless of the source of stimulation (manual–clitoral or penile–vaginal). By monitoring physiological responses to sexual stimulation, they found that the female orgasm involves the same biological events regardless of how it is attained.

Orgasms experienced through different means may also vary in physiological and subjective intensity. Masters and Johnson (1966) found that orgasms experienced during masturbation were generally more physiologically intense than those experienced during intercourse, perhaps because masturbation allows one to focus only on one's own pleasure and on ensuring that one receives effective stimulation to climax. This does not mean that orgasms during masturbation are more enjoyable or gratifying than those experienced through coitus, however. Given the emotional connectedness we may feel toward our lovers, we are unlikely to break off our relationships in favor of masturbation. Thus, "physiological intensity," as measured by laboratory instruments, does not translate directly into subjective pleasure or fulfillment.

The purported distinction between clitoral and vaginal orgasms also rests on an assumption that the clitoris is not stimulated during coitus. Masters and Johnson showed this to be a *false* assumption. Penile coital thrusting draws the clitoral hood back and forth against the clitoris. Vaginal pressure also heightens blood flow in the clitoris, further setting the stage for orgasm (Lavoisier et al., 1995).

The Singers' hypothesis of three distinct forms of female orgasm remains controversial. Researchers initially scoffed at the idea that orgasms could arise from vaginal stimulation alone. The vagina, after all, especially the inner two thirds of the vaginal cavity, is relatively insensitive to stimulation (erotic or otherwise). Proponents of the Singers' model counter that the type of uterine orgasm described by the Singers is induced more by pressure resulting from deep pelvic thrusting than by touch.

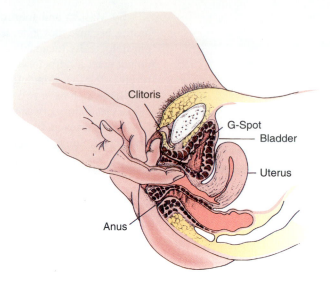

Figure 4.5. The Grafenberg Spot (G-Spot).

The G-Spot

A bean-shaped area within the anterior wall of the vagina may have special erotic significance. This area is believed to lie about 1 to 2 inches from the vaginal entrance and to consist of a soft mass of tissue that swells from the size of a dime to a half dollar when stimulated (Davidson et al., 1989). It has been called the **Grafenberg spot**—the "G-spot" for short (see Figure 4.5). The spot can be directly stimulated by the woman's or her partner's fingers or by penile thrusting in the rear entry or the female-superior positions. Some researchers suggest that stimulation of the spot produces intense erotic sensations and that with prolonged stimulation, a distinct form of orgasm occurs. This orgasm is characterized by intense pleasure and, in some cases, by a biological event earlier thought to be exclusively male in nature: ejaculation (Perry & Whipple, 1981; Whipple & Komisaruk, 1988). These claims, like other claims of distinct forms of female orgasm, are controversial.

The G-spot was named after a gynecologist, Ernest Grafenberg, who first suggested the erotic importance of this area. Grafenberg observed that orgasm in women could be induced by stimulating this area. He also claimed that such orgasms may be accompanied by the discharge of a milky fluid or "ejaculate" from the urethra. In a laboratory experiment, Zaviacic and his colleagues (1988a, 1988b) found evidence of an ejaculate in 10 of 27 women studied. Some researchers believe that this fluid is urine that some women release involuntarily during orgasm (Alzate, 1985). Other researchers believe that it differs from urine (Zaviacic et al., 1988; Zaviacic & Whipple, 1993).

The existence of the G-spot continues to be debated among researchers. A survey of 1,289 professional women in the health and counseling professions revealed that a majority believe that the G-spot exists and that they have experienced sexual pleasure when it has been stimulated (Davidson et al., 1989). Still, there was considerable confusion among these women as to the precise location of this sensitive area.

Sexual Behavior

This section describes sexual techniques and statistical breakdowns of "who does what with whom." There is great variety in human sexual expression. Some of us practice few, if any, of the techniques discussed here. Some of us practice most or all of them. Some of us practice some of them some of the time. Our knowledge of the prevalences of these techniques comes from sex surveys that began with Kinsey and have continued with the work of Hunt, the University of Chicago group, and others.

Grafenberg spot

A part of the anterior wall of the vagina, whose prolonged stimulation is theorized to cause particularly intense orgasms and a female ejaculation. Abbreviated *G-spot*.

The human body is sensitive to many forms of sexual stimulation. Yet biology is not destiny: A biological capacity does not impose a behavioral requirement. Cultural expectations, personal values, and individual experience—not only our biological capacities—determine our sexual behavior. What is right for you is right for you—not necessarily for your neighbor.

Solitary Sexual Behavior

Various forms of sexual expression do not require a partner. Masturbation is one of the principal forms of one-person sexual expression. Masturbation involves direct stimulation of the genitals. Other forms of individual sexual experience, such as sexual fantasy, may or may not be accompanied by genital stimulation.

Masturbation The word *masturbation* derives from the Latin *masturbari,* from the roots for "hand" and "to defile." The derivation provides clues to historical cultural attitudes toward the practice. **Masturbation** may be practiced by manual stimulation of the genitals, perhaps with the aid of artificial stimulation, such as a vibrator. It may employ an object, such as a pillow or a **dildo,** that touches the genitals. Even before we conceive of sexual experiences with others, we may learn early in childhood that touching our genitals can produce pleasure.

Pleasure is not the only reason that people masturbate. Table 4.1 lists reasons for masturbation, according to the findings of the NHSLS study.

Within the Judeo-Christian tradition, masturbation has been condemned as sinful. Until recent years masturbation was thought to be physically and mentally harmful, as well as degrading. Many clergy and medical authorities of the nineteenth century were persuaded that certain foods had a stimulating effect on the sex organs. So one form of advice to parents focused on modifying their children's diets to eliminate foods, notably meat, coffee, tea, and chocolate, that were believed to excite the sexual organs, and to substitute "unstimulating" foods in their place, most notably grain products.

You may have heard of the superintendent of the Battle Creek Sanatorium in Michigan, Dr. J. H. Kellogg (1852–1943). He is better known as the creator of the modern breakfast cereal. Kellogg identified 39 signs of masturbation, including acne, paleness, heart palpitations, rounded shoulders, weak backs, and convulsions. Kellogg believed that sexual desires

Masturbation
Sexual self-stimulation.

Dildo
A penis-shaped object used in sexual activity.

TABLE 4.1 Reasons for masturbation by respondents to NHSLS study

Reasons for Masturbation	Men (%)	Women (%)
To relax	26	32
To relieve sexual tension	73	63
Partners are unavailable	32	32
Partner does not want to engage in sexual activity	16	6
Boredom	11	5
To obtain physical pleasure	40	42
To help get to sleep	16	12
Fear of AIDS and other STDs	7	5
Other reasons	5	5

Source: Adapted from Laumann, E. O., Gagnon, J. H., Michael, R. T., & Michaels, S. (1994). *The Social Organization of Sexuality: Sexual Practices in the United States.* Chicago: University of Chicago Press, Table 3.3, p. 86.

could be controlled by a diet of simple foods, especially grains, including the corn flakes that have since borne his name.

Despite this history, there is no scientific evidence that masturbation is harmful. Masturbation does not cause insanity, grow hair on the hands, or cause warts or any of the other psychological and physical ills once ascribed to it. Masturbation is physically harmless, save for rare injuries to the genitals due to rough stimulation. Nor is masturbation in itself psychologically harmful, although people who consider masturbation wrong, harmful, or sinful may experience anxiety or guilt if they masturbate or wish to masturbate. These negative emotions are linked to their attitudes toward masturbation, not to masturbation per se (Michael et al., 1994).

Surveys indicate that most people masturbate at some time. The incidence of masturbation is generally greater among men than women. Nearly all of the adult men and about two thirds of the adult women in Kinsey's samples (Kinsey et al., 1948, 1953) reported that they had masturbated at some time. The NHSLS study also found a notable gender gap in reported frequencies of masturbation (Laumann et al., 1994). Table 4.2 shows how the sample group reported the frequency of masturbation during the past 12 months, broken down according to gender, age, marital status, level of education, religion, and race/ethnicity. Overall, 37% of the men and 58% of the women sampled reported that they had *not* masturbated during the past 12 months. Within every social category, men reported masturbating more frequently than women did. Despite the sexual revolution, women may still find masturbation less pleasurable or acceptable than men do (Leitenberg et al., 1993). Women may still be subject to traditional socialization pressures that teach that sexual activity for pleasure's sake is more of a taboo for women than for men. Then, too, women are more likely to pursue sexual activity within the context of a relationship.

Married people are less likely to have masturbated during the past 12 months than never married and formerly married people. Nevertheless, only 43% of the married men and 63% of the married women sampled said that they did not masturbate at all during the past year.

Education appears to be a liberating influence on masturbation. For both genders, people with more education reported more frequent masturbation. Perhaps better-educated people are less likely to believe the old horror stories about masturbation or to be subject to traditional social restrictions. Conservative religious beliefs appear to constrain masturbation. Conservative Protestants are apparently less likely to masturbate than liberal and moderate Protestants are. African Americans are notably less likely to report masturbating over a 12-month period than are other ethnic groups.

Masters and Johnson (1966) found that masturbation was a more reliable means for women to achieve orgasm than coitus, at least for women who accept masturbation as a sexual outlet.

Techniques of Male Masturbation

Sex is like bridge—if you don't have a good partner, you'd better have a good hand.

(Contemporary bathroom graffiti)

Although masturbation techniques vary widely, most men report that they masturbate by manual manipulation of the penis (see Figure 4.6 on page 94). Typically they take one or two minutes to reach orgasm (Hite, 1981; Kinsey et al., 1948). Men tend to grip the penile shaft with one hand, jerking it up and down in a milking motion. Some men move the whole hand up and down the penis, while others use just two fingers, generally the thumb and index finger. Men usually shift from a gentler rubbing action during the flaccid or semi-erect state of arousal to a more vigorous milking motion once full erection takes place. Men are also likely to stroke the glans and frenulum lightly at the outset, but their grip tightens and their motions speed up as orgasm nears. At orgasm, the penile shaft may be gripped tightly, but the glans has become sensitive, and contact with it is usually avoided. (Likewise, women usually avoid stimulating the clitoris directly during orgasm because of increased sensitivity.)

Some men use soapsuds (which may become irritating) as a lubricant for masturbation during baths or showers. Other lubricants, such as petroleum jelly or K-Y jelly, may also be used to reduce friction and to simulate the moist conditions of coitus.

TABLE 4.2 Sociocultural factors and frequency of masturbation during past 12 months, as found in the NHSLS study

		Frequency of Masturbation (%)			
		Not at All		At Least Once a Week	
Sociocultural Characteristics		**Men**	**Women**	**Men**	**Women**
Total population		36.7	58.3	26.7	7.6
Age	18–24	41.2	64.4	29.2	9.4
	25–29	28.9	58.3	32.7	9.9
	30–34	27.6	51.1	34.6	8.6
	35–39	38.5	52.3	20.8	6.6
	40–44	34.5	49.8	28.7	8.7
	45–49	35.2	55.6	27.2	8.6
	50–54	52.5	71.8	13.9	2.3
	55–59	51.7	77.6	10.3	2.4
Marital Status	Never married (not cohabiting)	31.8	51.8	41.3	12.3
	Married	42.6	62.9	16.5	4.7
	Formerly married (not cohabiting)	30.2	52.7	34.9	9.6
Education	Less than high school	54.8	75.1	19.2	7.6
	High school graduate	45.1	68.4	20.0	5.6
	Some college	33.2	51.3	30.8	6.9
	College graduate	24.2	47.7	33.2	10.2
	Advanced degree	18.6	41.2	33.6	13.7
Religion	None	32.6	41.4	37.6	13.8
	Liberal, moderate Protestant	28.9	55.1	28.2	7.4
	Conservative Protestant	48.4	67.3	19.5	5.8
	Catholic	34.0	57.3	24.9	6.6
Race/Ethnicity	White (non-Hispanic)	33.4	55.7	28.3	7.3
	African American	60.3	67.8	16.9	10.7
	Hispanic American	33.1	65.5	24.4	4.7
	Asian American	38.7	—*	31.3	—*
	Native American	—*	—*	—*	—*

*Sample sizes too small to report findings.

Source: Adapted from Laumann, E. O., Gagnon, J. H., Michael, R. T., & Michaels, S. (1994). *The Social Organization of Sexuality: Sexual Practices in the United States.* Chicago: University of Chicago Press, Table 3.1, p. 82.

A few men prefer to masturbate by rubbing the penis and testicles against clothing or bedding (Kinsey et al., 1948). A very few men rub their genitals against inflatable dolls sold in sex shops. These dolls may come with artificial mouths or vaginas that can be filled with warm water to mimic the sensations of coitus. Artificial vaginas are also for sale.

Some men strap vibrators to the backs of their hands. Most men rely heavily on fantasy or erotic photos or videos, but do not use sex-shop devices.

Figure 4.6. **Male Masturbation.** Masturbation techniques vary widely, but most men report that they masturbate by manual manipulation of the penis. They tend to grip the penile shaft with one hand and jerk it up and down in a milking motion.

Techniques of Female Masturbation Techniques of female masturbation also vary widely, but some general trends have been noted. Most women masturbate by massaging the mons, labia minora, and clitoral region with circular or back-and-forth motions (Hite, 1976; Kinsey et al., 1953). They may also straddle the clitoris with their fingers, stroking the shaft rather than the glans (see Figure 4.7). The glans may be lightly touched

Figure 4.7. **Female Masturbation.** Techniques of female masturbation vary so widely that Masters and Johnson reported never observing two women masturbating in precisely the same way. However, most women masturbate by massaging the mons, labia minora, and clitoral region, either with circular or back-and-forth motions.

early during arousal, but because of its exquisite sensitivity, it is rarely stroked for any length of time. Women typically achieve clitoral stimulation by rubbing or stroking the clitoral shaft or pulling or tugging on the vaginal lips. Some women also massage other sensitive areas, such as their breasts or nipples, with the free hand. Many women, like men, fantasize during masturbation (Leitenberg & Henning, 1995).

Women usually do *not* masturbate by simulating penile thrusting through the insertion of fingers or phallic objects into their vaginas (Hite, 1976; Kinsey et al., 1953). Hite reported that only 1.5% of her respondents exclusively relied on vaginal insertion as a means of masturbation. Kinsey and his colleagues found that only one in five women had sometimes used vaginal insertions of objects during masturbation.

Even when women do use insertion, they usually precede or combine it with clitoral stimulation. Sex shops sell dildos, which women can use to rub their vulvas or to insert them vaginally. Penis-shaped vibrators may be used in a similar fashion. Many women masturbate during baths, some by spraying their genitals with water-massage shower heads.

Handheld electrical vibrators provide a massaging action against the genitals that can be erotic. Some women find this type of stimulation too intense, however, and favor vibrators that strap to the back of the hand and cause the fingers to vibrate.

Sexual Fantasy   Sexual fantasies can occur without a partner, but many people also fantasize during lovemaking (Leitenberg & Henning, 1995). Some couples find it sexually arousing to share their fantasies or to enact them with their partners. Strictly speaking, however, a fantasy is a private mental experience. Sexual fantasies may be experienced without sexual behavior, as in erotic dreams or daydreams. Sexual fantasies can also be used to heighten sexual response during masturbation or sexual activity with another person. Masturbators often require some form of mental stimulation, such as fantasy or reading or viewing erotica, to reach orgasm.

Most men and women engage in sexual fantasies from time to time, especially during masturbation (Reinisch, 1990). Men fantasize more often than women do (Hsu et al., 1994). In their national survey, Laumann and his colleagues (1994) found that 54% of men and 19% of women said they thought about sex at least one time a day.

Sexual fantasies may be reasonably realistic, such as imagining sexual activity with an attractive classmate. They may involve flights of fancy, such as making love to a movie star. The most common fantasy theme reported among women involves someone they are or have

Sexual Fantasy. Sexual fantasies can be a powerful source of sexual stimulation, when people are masturbating or making love.

been involved with (Leitenberg & Henning, 1995). In contrast to men's fantasies, women are more likely to focus on the partner's feelings, touching, their own responses to what is happening, and the general feeling tone of the sexual encounter (Leitenberg & Henning, 1995).

The most common masturbation fantasy reported by both genders in the *Playboy* sample was "having intercourse with a loved one" (Hunt, 1974). But note some interesting gender differences: Men are more likely to assume aggressive, dominant roles. Women are more apt to enact passive, submissive roles (Leitenberg & Henning, 1995; Person et al., 1989). Women are more likely to connect sexual activity to relationships and emotional involvement than men are (Barbach, 1995; Leitenberg & Henning, 1995). Fantasizing about forcing someone into sexual activity, or about being victimized, does not mean that one wants these events to occur (Leitenberg & Henning, 1995; Reinisch, 1990). Women who imagine themselves being sexually coerced remain in control of their fantasies. Real assault victims are not.

Sex with Others

Partners' feelings for one another, and the quality of their relationships, may be stronger determinants of their sexual arousal and response than the techniques that they employ. As with other aspects of sharing relationships, communication is the most important "sexual" technique.

Foreplay Various forms of noncoital sex, such as cuddling, kissing, petting, and oral–genital contact, are used as **foreplay.** Women generally want longer periods of foreplay (and "afterplay") than men do (Denny et al., 1984). Since women usually require a longer period of stimulation during sex with a partner to reach orgasm, increasing the duration of foreplay may increase female coital responsiveness. Kissing, genital touching, and oral–genital contact may also be experienced as ends in themselves, not as preludes to coitus.

Foreplay
Mutual sexual stimulation that precedes sexual intercourse.

Kissing Couples may kiss for its own enjoyment or as a prelude to intercourse, in which case it is a part of foreplay. In *simple kissing,* the partners keep their mouths closed. Simple kissing may develop into caresses of the lips with the tongue, or into nibbling of the lower lip. In what Kinsey called *deep kissing,* which is also called French or soul kissing, the partners part their lips and insert their tongues into each other's mouths.

Kissing is not limited to the partner's mouth. Kinsey found that more than nine husbands in ten kissed their wives' breasts. Women usually prefer several minutes of body contact and gentle caresses before desiring to have their partner kiss their breasts, or suck or lick their nipples. Women also usually do not prefer a hard sucking action unless they are highly aroused. Other parts of the body are also often kissed, including the hands and feet, the neck and earlobes, the insides of the thighs, and the genitals themselves.

Touching Touching is a common form of foreplay. Both men and women generally prefer manual or oral stimulation of the genitals as a prelude to intercourse. Women generally prefer that direct caressing of the genitals be focused around the clitoris but not directly on the extremely sensitive clitoral glans. Men sometimes assume (often mistakenly) that their partners want them to insert their finger or fingers into the vagina as a form of foreplay. But not all women enjoy this form of stimulation.

Masters and Johnson (1979) noted gender differences with respect to preferences in foreplay. Men typically prefer direct stroking of their genitals by their partner early in lovemaking. Women, however, tend to prefer that their partners caress their genitals after a period of general body contact that includes holding, hugging, and nongenital massage.

Techniques of Manual Stimulation of the Genitals Here again, variability in technique is the rule, so partners need to communicate their preferences. The man's partner may use two hands to stimulate his genitals. One may be used to fondle the scrotum, by gently squeezing the skin between the fingers (taking care not to apply pressure to the testes themselves). The other hand may circle the coronal ridge and engage in gentle stroking of the penis, followed by more vigorous up and down movements as the man becomes more aroused.

The penis may also be gently rolled back and forth between the palms as if one were making a ball of clay into a sausage—increasing pressure as arousal progresses. Note that men who are highly aroused or who have just had an orgasm may find direct stimulation of the penile glans uncomfortable.

The woman may prefer that her partner approach genital stimulation gradually, following stimulation of other body parts. Genital stimulation may begin with light, stroking motions of the inner thighs and move on to the vaginal lips (labia) and the clitoral area. Women may enjoy pressure against the mons pubis from the heel of the hand, or stroking of the labia. Clitoral stimulation can focus on the clitoral shaft or the region surrounding the shaft, rather than the clitoris itself, because of the extreme sensitivity of the clitoral glans.

Some, but not all, women enjoy having a finger inserted into the vagina, which can stroke the vaginal walls or simulate thrusting of the penis. Vaginal insertion is usually not preferred, if at all, until the woman has become highly aroused. Many women desire that their partners discontinue stroking motions while they are experiencing orgasm, but others wish stimulation to continue. Men and women woman may physically guide their partners' hands or otherwise express their preferences as to the types of strokes they find most pleasurable.

If a finger is to be inserted into the vagina, it should be clean. Fingernails should be well trimmed. Inserting fingers that have been in the anus into the vagina is dangerous. The fingers may transfer microbes from the woman's digestive tract, where they do no harm, to the woman's reproductive tract, where they can cause serious infections.

Breast Stimulation   Men are more likely to stimulate women's breasts than to have their own breasts fondled, even though the breasts (and especially the nipples) are erotically sensitive in both genders. Most, but not all, women enjoy breast stimulation. Masters and Johnson report that some women are capable of achieving orgasm from breast stimulation alone.

The hands and the mouth can be used to stimulate the breasts and the nipples. Since the desired type and intensity of breast stimulation varies from person to person, partners need to communicate their preferences.

Fellatio
Oral stimulation of the male genitals.

Cunnilingus
Oral stimulation of the female genitals.

Oral–Genital Stimulation   Oral stimulation of the male genitals is called **fellatio.** Fellatio is referred to by slang terms such as "blow job," "sucking," "sucking off," or "giving head." Oral stimulation of the female genitals is called **cunnilingus,** which is referred to by slang expressions such as "eating" (a woman) or "going down" on her.

The popularity of oral–genital stimulation has increased dramatically since Kinsey's day, especially among young married couples. Kinsey and his colleagues (1948, 1953) found that at least 60% of married, *college-educated* couples had experienced oral–genital contact. Such experiences were reported by only about 20% of couples who had only a high school education and 10% who had only a grade school education.

According to the NHSLS study, the incidence of oral sex is somewhat lower in the 1990s (Laumann et al., 1994). About three of four men (77%) and two of three women (68%) report playing the active role in oral sex during their lifetimes. Nearly four men in five (79%) and three of four women (73%) report having been the recipients of oral–genital sex during their lifetimes. Among married couples, 80% of the men and 71% of the women have performed oral sex. Eighty percent of the men and 74% of the women have received oral sex. These are dramatic increases since Kinsey's day. Among young White women (ages 18 to 36) in Kinsey's sample, 48% reported ever engaging in fellatio. Fifty-one percent of their partners had engaged in cunnilingus.

Oral–genital stimulation can be a prelude to intercourse or a sexual end in itself. If orgasm is reached through oral–genital stimulation, a woman may be concerned about tasting or swallowing a man's ejaculate. There is no scientific evidence that swallowing semen is harmful to one's health unless the semen carries infectious microorganisms.

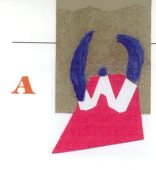 
SOCIOCULTURAL FACTORS AND ORAL SEX

Table 4.3 shows the incidence of oral sex among men and women with various levels of education and from different racial/ethnic backgrounds in the NHSLS survey. The incidence of oral sex correlates with level of education. That is, more highly educated individuals are more likely to have practiced oral sex. Why? Perhaps education encourages experimentation. Perhaps education dispels myths that nontraditional behavior patterns are necessarily harmful. Note also that African American men and women are less likely to have engaged in oral sex than people from other racial/ethnic backgrounds. African American men and women were also less likely than other ethnic groups to report masturbating during the past 12 months. African Americans may adhere more strictly to traditional ideas as to what kinds of sexual behavior are and are not proper.

Ethnicity and Oral Sex. According to the NHSLS study and others, African Americans report that they are less likely than people from other racial/ethnic backgrounds to engage in oral sex. Why do you think that this is so?

TABLE 4.3 NHSLS study respondents who report experience with oral sex

		Performed Oral Sex (%)		Received Oral Sex (%)	
		Men	Women	Men	Women
Education	Less than high school	59.2	42.1	60.7	49.6
	High school graduate	75.3	59.6	76.6	67.1
	Some college	80.0	78.2	84.0	81.6
	College graduate	83.7	78.9	84.6	83.1
	Advanced college degree	80.5	79.0	81.4	81.9
Race/Ethnicity	White	81.4	75.3	81.4	78.9
	African American	50.5	34.4	66.3	48.9
	Hispanic American	70.7	59.7	73.2	63.7
	Asian American	63.6	—*	72.7	—*

*There were not enough Asian-American women in the sample to allow for the reporting of meaningful findings.

Source: Adapted from Laumann, E. O., Gagnon, J. H., Michael, R. T., & Michaels, S. (1994). *The Social Organization of Sexuality: Sexual Practices in the United States.* Chicago: University of Chicago Press, Table 3.6, p. 98.

Techniques of Fellatio Although the word *fellatio* is derived from a Latin root meaning "to suck," a sucking action is generally not highly arousing. The up-and-down movements of the penis in the partner's mouth, or the licking of the penis, are generally the most stimulating. Gentle licking of the scrotum may also be highly arousing.

The mouth is stimulating to the penis because it contains warm, moist mucous membranes, as does the vagina. Muscles of the mouth and jaw can create varied pressure and movements. Erection may be stimulated by gently pulling the penis with the mouth (being careful never to touch the penis with the teeth) and simultaneously providing manual stimulation, as described earlier.

Higher levels of sexual arousal or orgasm can be promoted by moving the penis in and out of the mouth, simulating the motion of the penis in the vagina during intercourse. The speed of the motions can be varied, and manual stimulation near the base of the penis (firmly encircling the lower portion of the penis or providing pressure behind the scrotum) can also be stimulating.

Some people may gag during fellatio, a reflex that is triggered by pressure of the penis against the back of the tongue or against the throat. Gagging may be avoided if the man's partner grasps the shaft of the penis with one hand and controls the depth of penetration. Gagging is less likely to occur if the partner performing fellatio is on the top, rather than below, or if there is verbal communication about how deep the man may comfortably penetrate. Gagging may also be overcome by allowing gradually deeper penetrations of the penis over successive occasions while keeping the throat muscles relaxed.

Techniques of Cunnilingus Women can be highly aroused by their partner's tongue because it is soft, warm, and well lubricated. In contrast to a finger, the tongue can almost never be used too harshly. A woman may thus be more receptive to direct clitoral contact by a tongue. Cunnilingus provides such intense stimulation that many women find it to be the best means for achieving orgasm. Some women cannot reach orgasm in any other way (Hite, 1976).

In performing cunnilingus, the partner may begin by kissing and licking the woman's abdomen and inner thighs, gradually nearing the vulva. Gentle tugging at or sucking of the labia minora can be stimulating, but the partner should take care not to bite. Many women enjoy licking of the clitoral region, and others desire sucking of the clitoris itself. The tongue may also be inserted into the vagina where it may imitate the thrusts of intercourse.

"69" The term *sixty-nine,* or *soixante-neuf* in French (pronounced swah-sahnt nuff), describes simultaneous oral–genital stimulation (see Figure 4.8). The numerals 6 and 9 are used because they resemble two partners who are upside-down and facing each other.

Figure 4.8. **Simultaneous Oral–Genital Contact.** The "69" position allows partners to engage in simultaneous oral–genital stimulation.

The "69" position has the psychologically positive feature of allowing couples to experience simultaneous stimulation, but it can be an awkward position if two people are not similar in size. Some couples avoid 69 because it deprives each partner of the opportunity to focus fully on receiving or providing sexual pleasure. A person may find it distracting when receiving stimulation to have to focus on providing effective stimulation to someone else.

The 69 technique may be practiced side by side or with one partner on top of the other. But here again there are no strict rules, and couples often alternate positions.

Sexual Intercourse: Positions and Techniques

Sexual intercourse, or *coitus* (from the Latin *coire,* meaning "to go together"), is sexual activity in which the penis is inserted into the vagina. Intercourse may take place in many different positions. We focus on four commonly used positions: the male-superior (man-on-top) position, the female-superior (woman-on-top) position, the lateral-entry (side-entry) position, and the rear-entry position. Then we will discuss anal intercourse.

The Male-Superior (Man-on-Top) Position The male-superior position ("superiority" is used purely in relation to body position, but has sometimes been taken as a symbol of male domination) has also been called the **missionary position.** In this position the partners face one another. The man lies above the woman, perhaps supporting himself on his hands and knees rather than applying his full weight against his partner (see Figure 4.9). Still, movement is easier for the man than for the woman, which suggests that he is in charge.

Many students of human sexuality suggest that it is preferable for the woman to guide the penis into the vagina, rather than having the man do so. The woman can feel the location of the vaginal opening and determine the proper angle of entry. To accomplish this, the woman must feel comfortable "taking charge" of the couple's lovemaking. With the breaking down of the traditional stereotype of the female as passive, women are feeling more comfortable taking this role.

The Female-Superior (Woman-on-Top) Position In the female-superior position the couple face one another with the woman on top. The woman straddles the male from above, controlling the angle of penile entry and the depth of thrusting (see Figure

Missionary position

The coital position in which the man is on top. Also termed the *male-superior position.*

Figure 4.9. **The Male-Superior Coital Position.** In this position the couple face one another. The man lies above the woman, perhaps supporting himself on his hands and knees rather than allowing his full weight to press against his partner. The position is also referred to as the *missionary position.*

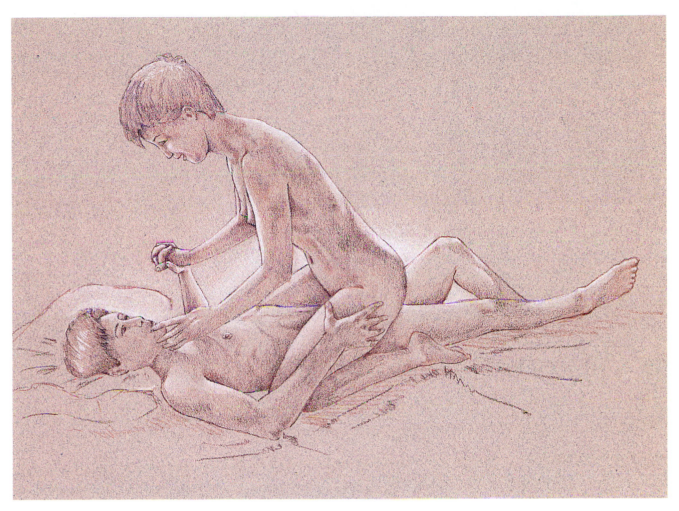

Figure 4.10. **The Female-Superior Coital Position.** The woman straddles the male from above, controlling the angle of penile entry and the depth of thrusting. The female-superior position puts the woman psychologically and physically in charge. The woman can ensure that she receives adequate clitoral stimulation from the penis or the hand. The position also tends to be less stimulating for the male and may thus help him to control ejaculation.

4.10). Some women maintain a sitting position; others lie on top of their partners. Many women vary their position.

The Lateral-Entry (Side-Entry) Position In the lateral-entry position, the man and woman lie side by side, facing one another (see Figure 4.11 on page 102).

The Rear-Entry Position In the rear-entry position, the man faces the woman's rear. In one variation (see Figure 4.12 on page 103), the woman supports herself on her hands and knees while the man supports himself on his knees, entering her from behind. In another, the couple lie alongside one another and the woman lifts one leg, draping it backward over her partner's thigh. The latter position is particularly useful during the later stages of pregnancy.

Use of Fantasy During Coitus Most married people have coital fantasies (Davidson & Hoffman, 1986). Fantasies allow couples to inject sexual variety, even offbeat sexual escapades, into their sexual activity without being unfaithful. There does not appear to be any connection between sexual dissatisfaction with one's relationship and the use of coital fantasies (Davidson & Hoffman, 1986). Thus they are not a form of compensation for an unrewarding sexual relationship.

Figure 4.11. **The Lateral-Entry Coital Position.** In this position the couple face each other side by side. Each partner has relatively free movement and easy access to the other. Because both partners rest easily on the bedding, it is an excellent position for prolonged coitus or for coitus when couples are fatigued.

Coital fantasies, like masturbation fantasies, are used to enhance sexual arousal and run a gamut of themes. They include making love to another partner, group sex, orgies, images of past lovers or special erotic experiences, and making love in fantastic and wonderful places.

Anal Intercourse Anal intercourse can be practiced by male–female couples and male–male couples. It involves insertion of the penis into the rectum. The rectum is richly endowed with nerve endings and is thus highly sensitive to sexual stimulation. Anal intercourse is also referred to as "Greek culture," or lovemaking in the "Greek style" because of bisexuality in ancient Greece among males. It is also the major act that comes under the legal definition of sodomy. Both women and men may reach orgasm through receiving the penis in the rectum and thrusting.

In anal intercourse, the penetrating male usually situates himself behind his partner. (He can also lie above or below his partner in a face-to-face position.) The receiving partner can supplement anal stimulation with manual stimulation of the clitoral region or penis to reach orgasm.

Women often report wanting their partner's fingers in the anus at the height of passion or at the moment of orgasm. A finger in the rectum at time of orgasm can heighten sexual sensation because the anal sphincters contract during orgasm. Although some men also want a finger in the anus, many resist because they associate anal penetration with the female role or with male–male sexual activity.

Many couples are repulsed by the idea of anal intercourse. They view it as unnatural, immoral, or risky. Yet others find anal sex to be an enjoyable sexual variation, though perhaps not a regular feature of their sexual diet.

The NHSLS survey found that 1 man in 4 (26%) and 1 woman in 5 (20%) reported having engaged in anal sex at some time during their lives (Laumann et al., 1994). Yet only about 1 person in 10 (10% of the men and 9% of the women) had engaged in anal sex during the

Figure 4.12. The Rear-Entry Coital Position. The rear-entry position is highly erotic for men who enjoy viewing and pressing their abdomens against their partners' buttocks. Some couples feel uncomfortable about the position because of its association with animal mating patterns. The position is also impersonal in that the partners do not face one another. Moreover, some couples dislike the feeling that the man is psychologically in charge because he can see his partner but she cannot readily see him.

past year. As with oral sex, there was a higher incidence of anal sex among more highly educated people in the NHSLS survey. For example, about 30% of the college graduates had engaged in anal sex, as compared with 20% of high school graduates. Education appears to be a liberating experience in sexual experimentation.

Religion appears to restrain anal sex. About 34% of the men and 36% of the women in the NHSLS survey who said they had no religion reported engaging in anal sex during their lifetimes. Percentage figures for male Christians ranged from the lower to upper 20s, and for female Christians, from the midteens to the lower 20s (Laumann et al., 1944, p. 99).

Anilingus
Oral stimulation of the anus.

Many couples kiss or lick the anus in their foreplay. This practice is called **anilingus.** Oral–anal sex carries a serious health risk, however. Microorganisms causing intestinal diseases and various sexually transmitted diseases can be spread through oral–anal contact.

Many couples today hesitate to engage in anal intercourse because of the fear of AIDS and other sexually transmitted diseases (STDs). The AIDS virus and other microorganisms causing STDs such as gonorrhea, syphilis, and hepatitis can be spread by anal intercourse, because small tears in the rectal tissues may allow the microbes to enter the recipient's blood system. Women also incur a greater risk of contracting HIV, the virus that causes AIDS, from anal intercourse than from vaginal intercourse—just as receptive anal intercourse in gay men carries a high risk of infection (Voeller, 1991). However, partners who are both infection-free are at no risk of contracting HIV or other STD-causing organisms through anal or vaginal intercourse, or any other sexual act.

ADVANTAGES AND DISADVANTAGES OF VARIOUS POSITIONS OF SEXUAL INTERCOURSE

Each of the coital positions has some advantages and disadvantages.

The Male-Superior (Man-on-Top) Position

The male-superior position has the advantage of permitting the couple to face one another so that kissing is easier. The woman may run her hands along her partner's body, stroking his buttocks and perhaps cupping a hand beneath his scrotum to increase stimulation as he reaches orgasm.

But the male-superior position makes it difficult for the man to caress his partner while simultaneously supporting himself with his hands. So the position may not be favored by women who enjoy having their partners provide manual clitoral stimulation during coitus. This position can be highly stimulating to the man, which can make it difficult for him to delay ejaculation. The position also limits the opportunity for the woman to control the angle, rate, and depth of penetration. It may thus be more difficult for her to attain the type of stimulation she may need to achieve orgasm, especially if she favors combining penile thrusting with manual clitoral stimulation. Finally, this position is not advisable during the late stages of pregnancy. At that time the woman's distended abdomen would force the man to arch severely above her, lest he place too much pressure against the woman's abdomen.

The Female-Superior (Woman-on-Top) Position

In the female-superior position the woman is psychologically, and to some degree physically, in charge. She can move as rapidly or as slowly as she wishes with little effort, adjusting her body so as to vary the angle and depth of penetration. She can reach behind her to stroke her partner's scrotum, or lean down to kiss him.

As in the male-superior position, kissing is relatively easy. This position has additional advantages. The man may readily reach the woman's buttocks or clitoris in order to provide manual stimulation. Assuming that the woman is shorter than he is, it is rather easy for him to stimulate her breasts orally (a pillow tucked behind his head may help). The woman can, in effect, guarantee that she receives adequate clitoral stimulation, either by the penis or manually by his hand or her own. This position thus facilitates orgasm in the woman.

The female-superior position tends to be less stimulating than the male-superior position for the male. While this is a disadvantage for some people, it can help him to control ejaculation. The position is commonly used by couples who are learning to overcome sexual difficulties.

The Lateral-Entry (Side-Entry) Position

This position has the advantages of allowing each partner relatively free movement and easy access to the other. The man and woman may kiss freely, and they can stroke each other's bodies with a free arm. The position is not physically taxing, because both partners are resting easily on the bedding. Thus it is an excellent position for prolonged coitus or for coitus when couples are somewhat fatigued.

There are disadvantages to this position. First, inserting the penis into the vagina while lying side by side may be awkward. Many couples thus begin coitus in another position and then change into the lateral-entry position—often because they wish to prolong coitus. Second, one or both partners may have an arm lying beneath the other that will "fall asleep" or become numb because of the constricted blood supply. Third, women

may not receive adequate clitoral stimulation from the penis in this position. Of course, such stimulation may be provided manually (by hand) or by switching to another position after a while. Fourth, it may be difficult to achieve deeper penetration of the penis. The lateral position is useful during pregnancy (at least until the final stages, when the distension of the woman's abdomen may make lateral entry difficult).

The Rear-Entry Position

The rear-entry position may be highly stimulating for both partners. Men may enjoy viewing, and pressing their abdomens against, their partner's buttocks. The man can reach around or underneath to provide additional clitoral or breast stimulation, and she may reach behind (if she is on her hands and knees) to stroke or grasp her partner's testicles. The version in which the couple lie alongside one another and the woman lifts one leg, draping it backward over her partner's thigh, is particularly useful during the later stages of pregnancy.

Potential disadvantages to this position include the following: First, this position is the mating position used by most other mammals, which is why it is sometimes referred to as *doggy style*. Some couples may feel uncomfortable about using the position because of its association with animal mating patterns. The position is also impersonal in the sense that the partners do not face one another, which may create a sense of emotional distance. Since the man is at the woman's back, the couple may feel that he is very much in charge—he can see her, but she cannot readily see him. Physically, the penis does not provide adequate stimulation to the clitoris. The penis also tends to pop out of the vagina from time to time.

Chapter Review

Making Sense of Sex: The Role of the Senses in Sexual Arousal

Vision (1: Is *or* Is not?) an important vehicle for sexual cues. Some researchers believe that people can be sexually aroused by odorless chemicals called (2) _____ mones. In many animals, pheromones are found in (3) _____ nal secretions and in (4) u _____ .

(5) _____ nous zones are parts of the body that are especially sensitive to touching. (6) _____ ary erogenous zones are sensitive because they are richly endowed with nerve endings. (7) _____ ary erogenous zones are parts of the body that become erotically sensitized through experience. Because people respond sexually to images and fantasies, the (8) b _____ is sometimes referred to as an erogenous zone. The brain (9: Is *or* Is not?) an erogenous zone because it not stimulated directly by touch.

Aphrodisiacs: Of Spanish Flies and Rhino Horns

An (10) _____ iac is a substance that arouses or increases one's capacity for sexual pleasure or response. (11) Sp _____ fly is a supposed aphrodisiac, but it inflames the urethra, producing a burning sensation that is sometimes misinterpreted as sexual feelings. Foods that resemble (12) _____ tals have been considered aphrodisiacs, including oysters, bananas, and even elephant horns.

The drug (13) _____ ine stimulates blood flow to the genitals. Amyl (14) _____ ate ("poppers") dilates blood vessels in the brain and genitals, producing sensations of warmth in the pelvis. The antidepressant drug (15) bu _____ (Wellbutrin) and the drug (16) L- _____ (used to treat Parkinson's disease) can increase the sex drive. These drugs affect brain receptors for the neurotransmitter (17) _____ ine. The most potent chemical aphrodisiac may be a naturally occurring substance—the male sex hormone (18) _____ rone.

The safest and perhaps most effective method for increasing the sex drive may be (19) _____ ise.

Some substances called (20) _____ siacs inhibit sexual response. (21) _____ peter, for example, indirectly dampens sexual arousal by increasing the need to urinate. Depressants such as tranquilizers and barbiturates usually (22: Lessen *or* Heighten?) sexual desire and impair sexual performance. Drugs used to treat high blood pressure may (23: Lessen *or* Heighten?) sexual performance in both genders. Antidepressant drugs such as (24) Pro _____ can dampen the sex drive and impair sexual performance. Nicotine constricts blood vessels and can thus (25: Increase *or* Decrease?) the capacity of the genitals to become engorged with blood. (26) _____ ogen drugs can lessen sexual response by lowering levels of testosterone.

Small amounts of alcohol are (27: Stimulating *or* Depressing?), but large amounts (28: Increase *or* Decrease?) sexual response. Alcohol tends to (29: Increase *or* Decrease?) sexual inhibitions. There (30: Is *or* Is not?) evidence that marijuana and other hallucinogenic drugs stimulate sexual response. Stimulants such as (31) _____ mines may contribute to sexual arousal and elevate the mood. Frequent use of (32) co _____ can lead to sexual dysfunctions and decreased sexual interest.

Sex Hormones: Do They "Goad" Us into Sex?

Hormones are secreted by the (33) _____ rine system and discharged into the bloodstream. Men and women (34: Do *or* Do not?) produce small amounts of the sex hormones of the other gender. Sex hormones have organizing and (35) _____ ting effects on behavior. Influencing the type of behavior that is expressed is an (36) _____ ing effect. Influencing the frequency or intensity of the sex drive is an (37) ac _____ effect.

Men who are (38) _____ated usually show a gradual loss of sexual desire. They also gradually lose the capacities to attain (39) _____tion and to ejaculate.

Female sex hormones (40: Do or Do not?) appear to play a direct role in sexual motivation or response in human females. Women's sexuality (41: Is or Is not?) clearly linked to hormonal fluctuations. There is evidence, however, that sexual response in women is influenced by the presence of (42) _____gens.

The Sexual Response Cycle

Masters and (43) J_____ term the changes that occur in the body during sexual arousal the sexual response cycle. Masters and Johnson divide the cycle into four phases: (44) _____ment, plateau, orgasm, and (45) _____tion. Both males and females experience (46) vaso_____ and (47) my_____ in the response cycle. Vasocongestion is the swelling of the genital tissues with (48) b_____. Myotonia refers to (49) m_____ _____sion.

The excitement phase is characterized by (50) _____tion in males and (51) _____al lubrication in females. The skin may take on a rosy sex (52) _____sh late in this phase. The plateau phase is an advanced state of arousal that precedes (53) _____sm. In women, vasocongestion builds the (54) or_____ _____form. Coloration of the (55) la_____ _____ra appears, which is referred to as the sex skin.

The orgasmic phase in males consists of two stages of muscular (56) _____tions. In the first stage, seminal fluid collects in the (57) _____thral _____lb. In the second stage, muscles propel the (58) _____late out of the body. Orgasm in the female is manifested by contractions of the (59) _____vic muscles that surround the vaginal (60) _____rel.

Following ejaculation, the man loses his erection in (61: One, Two, or Three?) stages. In women, orgasm triggers release of (62) _____d from engorged areas. Men enter a (63) _____tory period during which they are incapable of experiencing another orgasm or ejaculation.

Helen Singer Kaplan proposed a three-stage model of sexual response consisting of desire, (64) _____ement, and orgasm.

Controversies About Orgasm

Masters and Johnson found that (65: A few or Most?) women are capable of multiple orgasms. Masters and Johnson define multiple orgasm as the rapid occurrence of one or more *additional* orgasms following the first, before the body has returned to a (66) pre-_____ level of arousal.

The psychoanalyst Sigmund Freud proposed two types of female orgasm: the (67) _____ral orgasm and the (68) _____nal orgasm. Clitoral orgasms could be achieved through (69) _____ation. Vaginal orgasm could be achieved through deep (70) _____nile thrusting. Masters and Johnson found (71: One, Two, or Three?) kind(s) of orgasm.

A bean-shaped area within the anterior wall of the vagina—called the (72) _____berg spot—may have special erotic significance. The Grafenberg spot is usually referred to more simply as the (73) _____-_____. Some researchers suggest that stimulation of the G-spot produces orgasm and a form of female (74) _____tion. The existence of the G-spot is (75: Agreed upon or Debated?) among researchers.

Sexual Behavior

The word (76) _____tion derives from Latin roots for "hand" and "to defile." According to the NHSLS study, the main reason people masturbate is to relieve sexual (77) _____sion. Throughout history, masturbation (78: Has or Has not?) been seen as mentally and physically harmful. Dr. J. H. (79) K_____ developed the modern breakfast cereal to help people contain sexual impulses. There (80: Is or Is not?) scientific evidence that masturbation is harmful. Surveys indicate that (81: Most or Only a few?) people masturbate. Surveys report that men masturbate (82: More or Less?) frequently than women do. Education is a (83: Restraining or Liberating?) influence on masturbation. Conservative religious beliefs appear to (84: Constrain or Encourage?) masturbation. African Americans are (85: More or Less?) likely to report masturbating than are other ethnic groups.

Most men report that they masturbate by (86) _____ual manipulation of the penis. Techniques of female masturbation (87: Do or Do not?) vary widely. Most women (88: Do or Do not?) masturbate by massaging the clitoral glans. Women usually (89: Do or

Do not?) masturbate by inserting fingers or phallic objects into their vaginas.

Sexual fantasies are often used to (90: Lessen or Heighten?) sexual response during masturbation or sexual activity with another person. (91: Most or Only a few?) men and women have sexual fantasies from time to time. Men fantasize about sex (92: More or Less?) often than women do. In sexual fantasies, (93: Men or Women?) are more likely to assume aggressive, dominant roles. (94: Men or Women?) are more likely to connect sexual activity to relationships and emotional involvement. Fantasizing about forcing someone into sexual activity, or about being victimized, (95: Does or Does not?) mean that one wants these events to occur.

Women generally want (96: Longer or Shorter?) periods of foreplay (and "afterplay") than men do. Men and women generally (97: Do or Do not?) prefer manual or oral stimulation of the genitals as a prelude to intercourse. (98: Men or Women?) typically prefer direct stroking of their genitals by their partner earlier in lovemaking than the other gender does.

Oral stimulation of the male genitals is called (99) _____io. Oral stimulation of the female genitals is called (100) _____gus. According to the NHSLS study, (101: Only a few or Most?) men and women have played active and passive roles in oral sex. The mouth stimulates the penis because it contains

(102) _____us membranes. Women can be highly aroused by the tongue because it is soft, warm, and well (103) _____ted.

Sexual intercourse is also referred to as (104) _____us, (from the Latin coire, meaning "to go together"). The male-superior position has also been called the (105) _____ary position. In the (106) _____-superior position, the couple face one another with the woman on top. In the (107) _____-entry position, the man and woman lie side by side, facing one another. In the (108) _____-entry position, the man faces the woman's rear.

The male-superior position can be highly stimulating to the man, which can make it difficult for him to delay (109) _____tion. In the female-superior position, the (110: Man or Woman?) is psychologically, and to some degree physically, in charge. The position allows the woman to guarantee that she receives adequate (111) _____ral stimulation.

There (112: Does or Does not?) appear to be a connection between sexual dissatisfaction with one's relationship and the use of coital fantasies. (113: Only a few or Most?) married people engage in coital fantasies.

Anal intercourse is the major act that comes under the legal definition of (114) _____my. Kissing the anus is called (115) _____gus.

Chapter Quiz

1. According to the text, pheromones are detected through
   (a) vision.
   (b) tactile sensations.
   (c) the sense of taste.
   (d) the vomeronasal organ.
2. According to the text, the _____ is/are an example of a secondary erogenous zone.
   (a) earlobes
   (b) perineum
   (c) shoulders
   (d) genital organs
3. According to the text, the most potent chemical aphrodisiac may be
   (a) Spanish fly.
   (b) testosterone.
   (c) yohimbine.
   (d) amyl nitrate.
4. Erection first occurs during the _____ phase of Masters and Johnson's sexual response cycle.
   (a) excitement
   (b) plateau
   (c) desire
   (d) resolution
5. The sex skin occurs during the _____ phase of Masters and Johnson's sexual response cycle.
   (a) excitement
   (b) plateau
   (c) desire
   (d) resolution
6. According to Freudian theory, how many types of female orgasm are there?
   (a) One.
   (b) Two.
   (c) Three.
   (d) Four.

7. According to the NHSLS study, the main reason people give for masturbation is
   (a) to relax.
   (b) to release sexual tension.
   (c) partners are unavailable.
   (d) fear of AIDS and other sexually transmitted diseases.
8. Which of the following appears to be a restraining influence on oral and anal sex?
   (a) High level of education.
   (b) Sexual fantasies.
   (c) Marriage.
   (d) Conservative religious beliefs.
9. Which of the following coital positions is also known as the missionary position?
   (a) The male-superior position.
   (b) The female-superior position.
   (c) The lateral-entry position.
   (d) The rear-entry position.
10. Some couples may feel uncomfortable about using the _____ position because of its association with animal mating patterns.
   (a) male-superior position
   (b) female-superior position
   (c) lateral-entry position
   (d) rear-entry position

Answers to Chapter Review

1. Is
2. Pheromones
3. Vaginal
4. Urine
5. Erogenous
6. Primary
7. Secondary
8. Brain
9. Is not
10. Aphrodisiac
11. Spanish
12. Genitals
13. Yohimbine
14. Nitrate
15. Bupropion
16. L-dopa
17. Dopamine
18. Testosterone
19. Exercise
20. Anaphrodisiacs
21. Saltpeter
22. Lessen
23. Lessen
24. Prozac
25. Decrease
26. Antiandrogen
27. Stimulating
28. Decrease
29. Decrease
30. Is not
31. Amphetamines
32. Cocaine
33. Endocrine
34. Do
35. Activating
36. Organizing
37. Activating
38. Castrated
39. Erection
40. Do not
41. Is not
42. Androgens
43. Johnson
44. Excitement
45. Resolution
46. Vasocongestion
47. Myotonia
48. Blood
49. Muscle tension
50. Erection
51. Vaginal
52. Flush
53. Orgasm
54. Orgasmic platform
55. Labia minora
56. Contractions
57. Urethral bulb
58. Ejaculate
59. Pelvic
60. Barrel
61. Two
62. Blood
63. Refractory
64. Excitement
65. Most
66. Plateau
67. Clitoral
68. Vaginal
69. Masturbation
70. Penile
71. One
72. Grafenberg
73. G-spot
74. Ejaculation
75. Debated
76. Masturbation
77. Tension
78. Has
79. Kellogg
80. Is not
81. Most
82. More
83. Liberating
84. Constrain
85. Less
86. Manual
87. Do
88. Do not
89. Do not
90. Heighten
91. Most
92. More
93. Men
94. Women
95. Does not
96. Longer
97. Do
98. Men
99. Fellatio
100. Cunnilingus
101. Most
102. Mucous
103. Lubricated
104. Coitus
105. Missionary
106. Female
107. Lateral
108. Rear
109. Ejaculation
110. Woman
111. Clitoral
112. Does not
113. Most
114. Sodomy
115. Anilingus

Answers to Chapter Quiz

1. (d)
2. (c)
3. (b)
4. (a)
5. (b)
6. (b)
7. (b)
8. (d)
9. (a)
10. (d)

CHAPTER 5

Gender Identity and Gender Roles

OUTLINE

Prenatal Sexual Differentiation
The Role of Sex Hormones in Sexual Differentiation
Descent of the Testes and the Ovaries
Sex Chromosomal Abnormalities
Prenatal Sexual Differentiation of the Brain

Gender Identity
Nature and Nurture in Gender Identity
Hermaphroditism
Transsexualism

Gender Roles and Stereotypes

Sexism

Gender Differences: *Vive la Différence* or *Vive la Similarité?*
Differences in Cognitive Abilities
Differences in Personality

On Becoming a Man or a Woman: Gender Typing
Biological Perspectives
Cross-Cultural Perspectives
Psychological Perspectives

Psychological Androgyny: The More Traits, the Merrier?
Psychological Androgyny, Psychological Well-Being, and Personal Development
Psychological Androgyny and Sexual Behavior

Chapter Review

Chapter Quiz

A World of Diversity
Machismo/Marianismo Stereotypes and Hispanic Culture

Applications
Challenging Gender Roles in Sexual Behavior

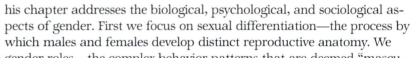
- If male sex hormones were not present during critical stages of prenatal development, we would all develop female sexual organs?
- Thousands of people have attempted to change their genders through gender-reassignment surgery?
- Women act as aggressively as men do when they are provoked and they believe that the social climate will accept aggressive behavior in them?
- One reason that women live longer than men do is that men often ignore physical symptoms until a readily treatable problem becomes serious or life threatening?
- The genitals of boys with Dominican Republic syndrome resemble those of girls at birth, but at puberty they quickly come to look like those of men?
- A 2½-year-old child may know that he is a boy but think that he can grow up to be a mommy?
- Adolescent girls who show a number of masculine traits are more popular than girls who thoroughly adopt the traditional feminine gender role?

This chapter addresses the biological, psychological, and sociological aspects of gender. First we focus on sexual differentiation—the process by which males and females develop distinct reproductive anatomy. We then turn to gender roles—the complex behavior patterns that are deemed "masculine" or "feminine" in a particular culture. The chapter examines empirical findings on actual gender differences, which may challenge some of the preconceptions that many of us hold regarding the differences between men and women. We next consider gender typing—the processes by which boys come to behave in line with what is expected of men (most of the time) and girls with what is expected of women (most of the time). We shall also explore the concept of psychological androgyny, which applies to people who display characteristics associated with both genders. ■

Prenatal Sexual Differentiation

Sexual differentiation
The process by which males and females develop distinct reproductive anatomy.

Chromosome
One of the rodlike structures, found in the nucleus of every living cell, that carries the genetic code in the form of genes.

Zygote
A fertilized ovum (egg cell).

Embryo
The stage of prenatal development that begins with implantation of a fertilized ovum in the uterus and concludes with development of the major organ systems at about two months after conception.

Let us trace the development of **sexual differentiation.** When a sperm cell fertilizes an ovum, 23 **chromosomes** from the male parent normally combine with 23 chromosomes from the female parent. The **zygote,** the beginning of a new human being, is only $\frac{1}{175}$ of an inch long. Yet, on this tiny stage, one's stamp as a unique individual has already been ensured—whether one will have black or blond hair, grow bald or develop a widow's peak, or become male or female.

The chromosomes from each parent combine to form 23 pairs. The 23rd pair are the sex chromosomes. An ovum carries an X sex chromosome, but a sperm carries either an X or a Y sex chromosome. If a sperm with an X sex chromosome fertilizes the ovum, the newly conceived person will normally develop as a female, with an XX sex chromosomal structure. If the sperm carries a Y sex chromosome, the child will normally develop as a male (XY).

After fertilization, the zygote divides repeatedly. After a few short weeks one cell has become billions of cells. At about 3 weeks a primitive heart begins to drive blood through the embryonic bloodstream. At about 5 to 6 weeks, when the **embryo** is only ¼ to ½ inch long, primitive gonads, ducts, and external genitals whose gender cannot be distinguished visually have formed (see Figure 5.1 on page 111 and Figure 5.2 on page 112). Each embryo possesses primitive external genitals, a pair of sexually undifferentiated gonads, and two sets of primitive duct structures, the Müllerian (female) ducts and the Wolffian (male) ducts.

During the first 6 weeks or so of prenatal development, embryonic structures of both genders develop along similar lines and resemble primitive female structures. At about the

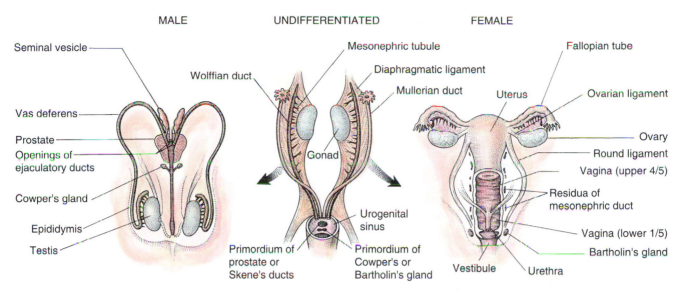

Figure 5.1. Development of the Internal Sexual Organs from an Undifferentiated Stage at About 5 or 6 Weeks Following Conception.

seventh week after conception, the genetic code (XX or XY) begins to assert itself, causing changes in the gonads, genital ducts, and external genitals. The Y sex chromosome causes the testes to begin to differentiate. Ovaries begin to differentiate if the Y chromosome is absent. Some rare individuals who have only one X sex chromosome instead of the typical XY or XX arrangement also become females, since they too lack the Y chromosome (Angier, 1990).

Thus, the basic blueprint of the human embryo is female. The genetic instructions in the Y sex chromosome cause the embryo to deviate from the female developmental course. "Adams" develop from embryos that otherwise would become "Eves."

By about the seventh week of prenatal development, the Y sex chromosome stimulates the production of *H-Y* antigen, a protein that fosters the development of testes. Strands of tissue begin to organize into seminiferous tubules. Female gonads begin to develop somewhat later than male gonads. The forerunners of follicles that will bear ova are not found until the fetal stage of development, about 10 weeks after conception. Ovaries begin to form at 11 or 12 weeks.

The Role of Sex Hormones in Sexual Differentiation

Androgens

Male sex hormones. (From the Greek *andros*, meaning "man" or "males," and *-gene*, meaning "born.")

Testosterone

The male sex hormone that fosters the development of male sex characteristics and is connected with the sex drive.

Without the influence of male sex hormones, or **androgens,** we would all develop into females (Angier, 1994; Federman, 1994). Once the testes develop in the embryo, they begin to produce androgens. The most important androgen, **testosterone,** spurs differentiation of the male (Wolffian) duct system (see Figure 5.1). Each Wolffian duct develops into an epididymis, vas deferens, and seminal vesicle. The external genitals, including the penis, begin to take shape at about the eighth week of development under the influence of another androgen, *dihydrotestosterone* (DHT). Yet another testicular hormone, one secreted during the fetal stage, prevents the Müllerian ducts from developing into the female duct system. It is appropriately termed the Müllerian inhibiting substance (MIS).

Small amounts of androgens are produced in female fetuses, but they are not normally sufficient to cause male sexual differentiation. In female fetuses, the relative absence of androgens causes degeneration of the Wolffian ducts and prompts development of female sexual organs. The Müllerian ducts evolve into fallopian tubes, the uterus, and the upper two thirds of the vagina. These developments occur even in the absence of female sex hor-

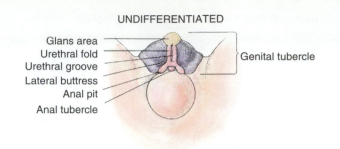

UNDIFFERENTIATED

Glans area
Urethral fold
Urethral groove
Lateral buttress
Anal pit
Anal tubercle

Genital tubercle

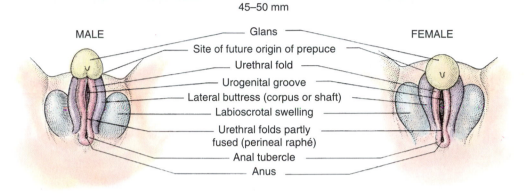

45–50 mm

MALE   Glans   FEMALE
Site of future origin of prepuce
Urethral fold
Urogenital groove
Lateral buttress (corpus or shaft)
Labioscrotal swelling
Urethral folds partly
fused (perineal raphé)
Anal tubercle
Anus

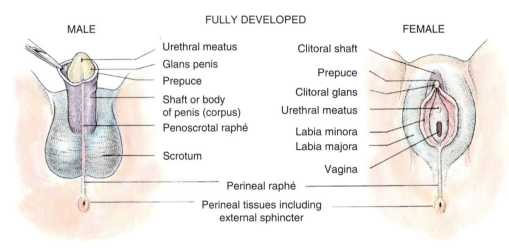

FULLY DEVELOPED

MALE   FEMALE

Urethral meatus   Clitoral shaft
Glans penis   Prepuce
Prepuce   Clitoral glans
Shaft or body   Urethral meatus
of penis (corpus)
Penoscrotal raphé   Labia minora
                         Labia majora
Scrotum   Vagina

Perineal raphé
Perineal tissues including
external sphincter

Figure 5.2. Development of the External Sexual Organs from an Undifferentiated Stage at About 5 or 6 Weeks Following Conception.

mones. Although female sex hormones are crucial in puberty, they are not involved in fetal sexual differentiation. If a fetus with an XY sex chromosomal structure failed to produce testosterone, it would develop female sexual organs.

Descent of the Testes and the Ovaries

The testes and ovaries develop from slender structures high in the abdominal cavity. By about 10 weeks after conception, they have descended so that they are almost even with the upper edge of the pelvis. The ovaries remain there for the rest of the prenatal period. Later they rotate and descend farther to their adult position in the pelvis. About four months after conception the testes normally descend into the scrotal sac through the **inguinal canal.** After their descent, this passageway is closed.

In a small percentage of males, one or both testes remain undescended. They remain in the abdomen at birth. The condition is termed **cryptorchidism.** In most cases of cryp-

Inguinal canal
A fetal canal that connects the scrotum and the testes, allowing their descent. (From the Latin *inguinus,* meaning "near the groin.")

Cryptorchidism
The condition in which one or two testicles fail to descend from the abdomen into the scrotum.

torchidism, the testes migrate to the scrotum during infancy. In still other cases the testes descend by puberty. Men with undescended testes are usually treated through surgery or hormonal therapy, since the condition places them at higher risk for cancer of the testes. Sperm production is also impaired because the undescended testes are subjected to a higher-than-optimal body temperature, causing sterility.

Sex Chromosomal Abnormalities

Klinefelter's syndrome
A sex-chromosomal disorder caused by an extra X sex chromosome.

Abnormalities of the sex chromosomes can have profound effects on sexual characteristics, physical health, and psychological development. **Klinefelter syndrome,** a condition that affects about 1 in 500 males, is caused by an extra X sex chromosome, so the man has an XXY rather than an XY pattern. Men with this pattern fail to develop appropriate secondary sex characteristics. They have enlarged breasts, poor muscular development, and, because they fail to produce sperm, they are infertile. They also tend to be mildly retarded.

Turner syndrome
A sex-chromosomal disorder caused by loss of some X chromosome material.

Turner syndrome, found only in women, occurs in 1 in 2,000–5,000 girls. It is caused by the loss of some X sex chromosome material. These girls develop typical external genital organs, but they are short in stature and their ovaries do not develop or function normally. Girls with Turner syndrome tend to be involved in fewer social activities and to have more academic problems relative to girls without Turner syndrome (Rovet & Ireland, 1994). However, they do not have major social or behavioral problems.

Prenatal Sexual Differentiation of the Brain

The brain, like the genital organs, undergoes prenatal sexual differentiation. Testosterone causes cells in the hypothalamus of male fetuses to become insensitive to the female sex hormone estrogen. In the absence of testosterone, as in female fetuses, the hypothalamus does develop sensitivity to estrogen.

Sensitivity to estrogen is important in the regulation of the menstrual cycle of women after puberty. The hypothalamus detects low levels of estrogen in the blood at the end of each cycle and initiates a new cycle by stimulating the pituitary gland to secrete FSH. FSH, in turn, stimulates estrogen production by the ovaries and the ripening of an immature follicle in an ovary. Sexual differentiation of the hypothalamus most likely occurs during the second trimester of fetal development (Pillard & Weinrich, 1986).

Gender Identity

Gender identity
The psychological sense of being male or female.

For all of us, our awareness of being male or being female—our **gender identity**—is one of the most obvious and important aspects of our self-concepts. Our gender identity is not an automatic extension of our anatomic gender. Gender identity is a psychological construct, a sense of being male or being female. **Gender assignment** reflects the child's anatomic gender and usually occurs at birth. Gender identity is so important to parents that they may want to know "Is it a boy or a girl?" before they begin to count fingers and toes.

Gender assignment
The labeling of a newborn as a male or female.

Most children first become aware of their anatomic gender by about the age of 18 months. By 36 months, most children have acquired a rather firm sense of gender identity (Etaugh & Rathus, 1995; McConaghy, 1979).

Nature and Nurture in Gender Identity

What determines gender identity? Are our brains biologically programmed along masculine or feminine lines by prenatal sex hormones? Does the environment, in the form of postnatal learning experiences, shape our self-concepts as males or females? Or does gender identity reflect an intermingling of biological and environmental influences?

Gender identity is almost always consistent with chromosomal gender. Such consistency does not certify that gender identity is biologically determined, however. We also tend to be reared as males or females, according to our anatomic genders. How, then, might we sort out the roles of nature and nurture, of biology and the environment?

Clues may be found in the experiences of rare individuals, **pseudohermaphrodites,** who possess the gonads of one gender but external genitalia that are ambiguous or typical of the other gender. Pseudohermaphrodites are sometimes reared as members of the other gender (the gender other than their chromosomal gender). Researchers wondered whether the gender identity of these children reflects their chromosomal and gonadal gender or the gender according to which they were reared. Before going further with this, let us distinguish between true hermaphroditism and pseudohermaphroditism.

Pseudohermaphrodites
People who possess the gonads of one gender but external genitalia that are ambiguous or typical of the other gender.

Hermaphroditism

Hormonal errors during prenatal development produce various congenital defects. Some individuals are born with both ovarian and testicular tissue. They are called **hermaphrodites,** after the Greek myth of the son of Hermes and Aphrodite, whose body became united with that of a nymph while he was bathing. True hermaphrodites may have one gonad of each gender (a testicle and an ovary), or gonads that combine testicular and ovarian tissue.

Hermaphrodites
People who possess both ovarian and testicular tissue. (From the names of the male and female Greek gods *Hermes* and *Aphrodite*.)

Regardless of their genetic gender, hermaphrodites usually assume the gender identity and gender role of the gender assigned at birth. Figure 5.3 shows a genetic female (XX) with a right testicle and left ovary. This person married and became a stepfather with a firm male identity. The roles of biology and environment remain tangled, however, since true hermaphrodites have gonadal tissue of both genders.

True hermaphroditism is extremely rare. More common is pseudohermaphroditism, which occurs in perhaps 1 infant in 1,000. The occurrence of pseudohermaphroditism has given scientists an opportunity to examine the roles of nature (biology) and nurture (environmental influences) in the shaping of gender identity.

Pseudohermaphroditism   *Pseudohermaphrodites* ("false" hermaphrodites) have testes or ovaries, but not both. Unlike true hermaphrodites, their gonads (testes or ovaries) match their chromosomal gender. Because of prenatal hormonal errors, however, their external genitals and sometimes their internal reproductive anatomy are ambiguous or resemble those of the other gender.

The most common form of female pseudohermaphroditism is **androgenital syndrome,** in which a genetic (XX) female has female internal sexual structures (ovaries), but masculinized external genitals (see Figure 5.4). The clitoris is so enlarged that it may resem-

Androgenital syndrome
A form of pseudohermaphroditism in which a genetic female has internal female sexual structures but masculinized external genitals.

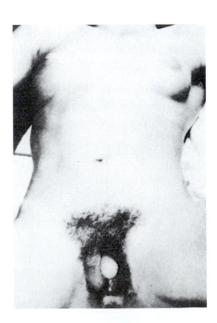

Figure 5.3. **A True Hermaphrodite.** This genetic (XX) female has one testicle and one ovary and the gender identity of a male.

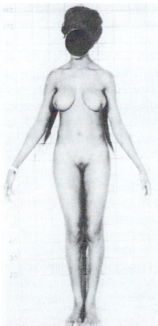

Figure 5.4. Pseudo-hermaphroditism. In androgenital syndrome (top photo), a genetic (XX) female has female internal sexual structures (ovaries) but masculinized external genitals. The bottom photo shows a genetic (XY) male with androgen-insensitivity syndrome. The external genitals are feminized, and the person has always lived as a female.

Androgen-insensitivity syndrome

A form of pseudohermaphroditism in which a genetic male is prenatally insensitive to androgens. As a result his genitals do not become normally masculinized.

ble a small penis. The syndrome occurs as a result of excessive levels of androgens. In some cases the fetus's own adrenal glands produce excess androgen (the adrenal glands usually produce low levels of androgen). In other cases mothers may have received synthetic androgens during their pregnancies. In the 1950s and 1960s, before these side effects were known, synthetic androgens were sometimes prescribed to help prevent miscarriages in women with histories of spontaneous abortions.

Another type of pseudohermaphroditism, **androgen-insensitivity syndrome,** describes genetic (XY) males who had lower-than-normal prenatal sensitivity to androgens. As a result their genitals did not become normally masculinized. At birth their external genitals are feminized, including a small vagina, and their testes are undescended. Because of insensitivity to androgens, the male duct system (epididymis, vas deferens, seminal vesicles, and ejaculatory ducts) fails to develop. Nevertheless, the fetal testes produce Müllerian inhibiting substance, preventing the development of a uterus or fallopian tubes.

A third type of pseudohermaphroditism is named **Dominican Republic syndrome** because it was first documented in a group of 18 affected boys in two rural villages in that nation (Imperato-McGinley et al., 1974). Dominican Republic syndrome is a genetic enzyme disorder that prevents testosterone from masculinizing the external genitalia. The boys were born with normal testes and internal male reproductive organs, but their external genitals were malformed. Their penises were stunted and resembled clitorises. Their scrotums were incompletely formed and resembled female labia. They also had partially formed vaginas.

Pseudohermaphroditism and Gender Identity The experiences of pseudohermaphrodites have provided insights into the origins of gender identity. The genitals of girls with androgenital syndrome are normally surgically feminized in infancy. The girls also receive hormone treatments to correct excessive adrenal output of androgens. As a result, they usually acquire a feminine gender identity and develop physically as normal females.

What if the syndrome is not identified early in life, however? Consider the cases of two children who were treated at Johns Hopkins University Hospital. The children both suffered from androgenital syndrome, but their treatments and the outcomes were very different. Each child was genetically female (XX). Each had female internal sex organs. Because of prenatal exposure to synthetic male sex hormones, however, each developed masculinized external sex organs (Money & Ehrhardt, 1972).

The problem was identified in one child (let's call her Abby) in infancy. Her masculinized sex organs were removed surgically when she was age 2. Like many other girls, Abby was tomboyish during childhood, but she was always feminine in appearance and had a female gender identity. She began to develop breasts by the age of 12, but did not begin to menstruate until age 20. She dated boys, and her fantasy life centered around marriage to a man.

The other child (let's call him James) was initially mistaken for a genetic male with stunted external sex organs. The error was discovered at the age of 3½. By then he had a firm male gender identity, so surgeons further masculinized his external sex organs rather than remove them. At puberty, hormone treatments stoked the development of body hair, male musculature, and other male secondary sex characteristics.

As an adolescent, James did poorly in school. Possibly in an effort to compensate for his poor grades, he joined a gang of semidelinquents. He became one of the boys. In contrast to Abby, James was sexually attracted to women.

Both children were pseudohermaphrodites. Both had internal female sexual organs and masculinized external organs, but they were treated and reared differently. In Abby's case, the newborn was designated female, surgically altered to remove the masculinized genitals, and reared as a girl. In James's case, the infant was labeled and reared as a boy. Each child acquired the gender identity of the assigned gender. Environmental influences appeared to play the critical role in shaping the gender identity of these children.

Further evidence for the importance of psychosocial influences on gender identity is found in studies of genetic (XY) males with androgen-insensitivity syndrome. They pos-

Dominican Republic syndrome

A form of pseudohermaphroditism in which a genetic enzyme disorder prevents testosterone from masculinizing the external genitalia.

sess testes but are born with feminine-appearing genitals and are typically reared as girls. They develop a female gender identity and stereotypical feminine interests. They show as much interest in dolls, dresses, and future roles as mothers and housewives as do genetic (XX) girls of the same ages and social class (Brooks-Gunn & Matthews, 1979; Money & Ehrhardt, 1972).

The boys with Dominican Republic syndrome also resembled girls at birth and were reared as females. At puberty, however, their testes swung into normal testosterone production, causing startling changes: their testes descended, their voices deepened, their musculature filled out, and their "clitorises" expanded into penises. Of the 18 boys who were reared as girls, 17 shifted to a male gender identity. Sixteen of the 18 assumed a stereotypical masculine gender role. Of the remaining 2, 1 adopted a male gender identity but continued to maintain a feminine gender role, including wearing dresses. The other maintained a female gender identity and later sought a sex-change operation to "correct" the pubertal masculinization.

The Dominican transformations suggest that gender identity is malleable. What of the roles of nature and nurture in the formation of gender identity, however? If environmental forces (nurture) were predominant, gender identity would be based on the gender in which the person is reared, regardless of biological abnormalities. With the Dominicans, however, pubertal biological changes led to changes in both gender identity and gender roles. Is nature (biology) then the primary determinant of gender identity? Unfortunately, the Dominican study does not allow clear separation of the effects of nature and nurture. One intriguing hypothesis is that the pubertal surges of testosterone may have activated brain structures that were masculinized during prenatal development. Prenatal testosterone levels in these boys were presumably normal and could have affected the sexual differentiation of brain tissue, even though the genetic defect prevented the hormone from masculinizing the external genitalia.

Consider some other possibilities: Did the children, seeing themselves transforming into men, begin to change their self-concepts to be consistent with their anatomic changes? Did the children choose to assume male gender identities because the masculine gender role was positively valued in their culture? Either possibility permits a psychological or cultural explanation of gender identity.

Most scientists conclude that gender identity is influenced by complex interactions between biological and psychosocial factors. Some place relatively greater emphasis on psychosocial factors (Money, 1987a; Money & Ehrhardt, 1972). Others emphasize the role of biological factors (Collaer & Hines, 1995). The debate over the relative contributions of nature and nurture is likely to continue.

Transsexualism

In 1953 an ex-GI who journeyed to Denmark for a "sex-change operation" made headlines. She became known as Christine (formerly George) Jorgensen. Since then, thousands of **transsexuals** have undergone gender-reassignment surgery. Among the better known is the tennis player Dr. Renée Richards, formerly Dr. Richard Raskin.

Gender-reassignment surgery cannot implant the internal reproductive organs of the other gender. Instead, it generates the likeness of external genitals typical of the other gender. This can be done more precisely with male-to-female than female-to-male transsexuals. After such operations, people can participate in sexual activity and even attain orgasm, but they cannot conceive or bear children.

Transsexuals experience **gender dysphoria.** That is, according to John Money (1994), they have the subjective experience of incongruity between their genital anatomy and their gender identity or role. They have the anatomic sex of one gender but feel that they are members of the other gender. As a result of this discrepancy, they wish to be rid of their own primary sex characteristics (their external genitals and internal sex organs) and to live as members of the other gender. Transsexualism is thought to be rare. Experts estimate the number of transsexuals in the United States to be about 25,000. Perhaps 6,000 to 11,000 of them have undergone gender-reassignment surgery (Selvin, 1993).

Transsexuals

People who have a gender-identity disorder in which they feel trapped in the body of the wrong gender.

Gender dysphoria

The subjective experience of incongruity between genital anatomy and gender identity or role.

Patterns of sexual attraction do not appear to be central in importance. Some transsexuals report never having had strong sexual feelings. Others are attracted to members of their own (anatomic) gender. They are unlikely to regard themselves as gay or lesbian, however. From their perspective, their lovers are members of the other gender. Still others are attracted to members of the other anatomic gender. Nonetheless, they all want to be rid of their own sex organs and to live as members of the other gender.

Theoretical Perspectives   No clear understanding of the nature or causes of transsexualism has emerged (Money, 1994). Views on its origins somewhat parallel those on the origins of a gay male or lesbian sexual orientation, which is surprising, given the fundamental differences that exist between the two.

Psychoanalytic theorists have focused on early parent–child relationships. Male transsexuals, in this view, may have had "close-binding mothers" (extremely close mother–son relationships) and "detached–hostile fathers" (fathers who were absent or disinterested) (Stoller, 1969). Such family circumstances may have fostered intense **identification** with the mother, to the point of an inversion of typical gender roles and identity. Girls with weak, ineffectual mothers and strong, masculine fathers may identify with their fathers, rejecting their own female identities.

There is some evidence that male transsexuals tend to have had unusually close relationships with their mothers during childhood. Female transsexuals tend to have identified more with their fathers and to have perceived their mothers as cold and rejecting (Pauly, 1974). Yet one problem with the psychoanalytic view is that the roles of cause and effect may be reversed. It could be that in childhood, transsexuals gravitate toward the parent of the other gender and reject the efforts of the parent of the same gender to reach out to them and engage them in gender-typed activities. These views also do not account for the many transsexuals whose family backgrounds fail to match these patterns. Moreover, these views lack predictive power. Most children—in fact, the vast majority!—with such family backgrounds do *not* become transsexuals.

Transsexuals may also be influenced by prenatal hormonal imbalances. The brain is in some ways "masculinized" or "feminized" by sex hormones during prenatal development. The brain could be influenced in one direction, even as the genitals are being differentiated in the other direction (Money, 1987a).

Gender Reassignment   Gender reassignment for transsexuals has been controversial since its inception. Yet psychotherapy is not considered a reasonable alternative, because it has been generally unsuccessful in helping transsexuals accept their anatomic genders (Roberto, 1983; Tollison & Adams, 1979).

Surgery is one element of gender reassignment. Since the surgery is irreversible, health professionals usually require that the transsexual live openly as a member of the other gender for a trial period of at least a year before surgery.

Once the decision is reached, a lifetime of hormone treatments is begun. Male-to-female transsexuals receive estrogen, which fosters the development of female secondary sex characteristics. It causes fatty deposits to develop in the breasts and hips, softens the skin, and inhibits growth of the beard. Female-to-male transsexuals receive androgens, which promote male secondary sex characteristics. The voice deepens, hair becomes distributed according to the male pattern, muscles enlarge, and the fatty deposits in the breasts and hips are lost. The clitoris may also grow more prominent.

Gender-reassignment surgery is largely cosmetic. Medical science cannot construct internal genital organs or gonads. Male-to-female surgery is generally more successful. The penis and testicles are first removed. Tissue from the penis is placed in an artificial vagina so that sensitive nerve endings will provide sexual sensations.

In female-to-male transsexuals, the internal sex organs (ovaries, fallopian tubes, uterus) are removed, along with the remaining fatty tissue in the breasts. The nipples are moved to keep them at the proper height on the torso. The urethra is rerouted through the enlarged clitoris, or an artificial penis and scrotum are constructed from tissue from the ab-

Identification

In psychoanalytic theory, the process of incorporating within ourselves our perceptions of the behaviors, thoughts, and feelings of others.

domen, the labia, and the perineum through a series of operations. In either case, the patient can urinate while standing, which appears to provide psychological gratification. Although the artificial penis does not stiffen and become erect naturally, a variety of methods, including implants, can be used to allow the artificial penis to approximate erection.

Outcomes of Gender-Reassignment Surgery   Following the introduction of gender-reassignment surgery in the the United States in 1960s, most reports of postoperative adjustment were positive (Pauly & Edgerton, 1986). Reviewers of the international literature reported in 1984 that about 90% of transsexuals who undergo gender-reassignment surgery experience positive results (Lundstrom et al., 1984). In Canada, a follow-up study of 116 transsexuals (female-to-male and male-to-female) at least one year after surgery found that most of them were content with the results and were reasonably well adjusted (Blanchard et al., 1985). Positive results for surgery were also reported in a study of 141 Dutch transsexuals (Kuiper & Cohen-Kettenis, 1988). Nearly 9 of 10 male-to-female and female-to-male transsexuals in a study of 23 transsexuals reported they were very pleased with the results of their gender-reassignment surgery (Lief & Hubschman, 1993).

Male-to-female transsexuals outnumber female-to-males, but postoperative adjustment is apparently more favorable for female-to-males. Nearly 10% of male-to-female cases, as compared to 4% to 5% of female-to-males, have had disturbing outcomes, such as severe psychological disorders, hospitalization, requests for reversal surgery, and even suicide (Abramowitz, 1986). One reason for the relatively better postoperative adjustment of the female-to-male transsexuals may be society's more accepting attitudes toward women who desire to become men (Abramowitz, 1986). Female-to-male transsexuals tend to be better adjusted socially before surgery as well (Kockott & Fahrner, 1988; Pauly, 1974), so their superior postoperative adjustment may be nothing more than a selection factor.

Stereotype
A fixed, conventional idea about a group of people.

Gender roles
Complex clusters of ways in which males and females are expected to behave within a given culture.

Gender Roles and Stereotypes

In our culture the **stereotypical** female exhibits traits such as gentleness, dependency, kindness, helpfulness, patience, and submissiveness (Cartwright et al., 1983). The masculine **gender-role** stereotype is one of toughness, gentlemanliness, and protectiveness (Myers & Gonda, 1982). Females are generally seen as warm and emotional; males as independent, assertive, and competitive. The times are a-changing, somewhat. Women, as well as men, now bring home the bacon, but women are still more often expected to fry it up in the pan

A Woman's Place? Contemporary men and women are entering occupations that had been traditionally associated with the other gender. Women fight fires and pilot aircraft; men pursue careers in nursing and primary education.

A WORLD OF DIVERSITY

MACHISMO/MARIANISMO *STEREOTYPES AND HISPANIC CULTURE**

Machismo is a cultural stereotype that defines masculinity in terms of an idealized view of manliness. To be *macho* is to be strong, virile, and dominant. Each Hispanic culture puts its own particular cultural stamp on the meaning of *machismo*, however. In the Spanish-speaking cultures of the Caribbean and Central America, the macho code encourages men to restrain their feelings and maintain an emotional distance. In my travels in Argentina and some other Latin American countries, however, I have observed that men who are sensitive and emotionally expressive are not perceived as compromising their macho code.

Marianismo

In counterpoint to the macho ideal among Hispanic peoples is the cultural idealization of femininity embodied in the concept of *marianismo.* The *marianismo* stereotype, which derives its name from the Virgin Mary, refers to the ideal of the virtuous woman as one who "suffers in silence," submerging her needs and desires to serve those of her husband and children. With the marianismo stereotype, the image of a woman's role as a martyr is raised to the level of a cultural ideal. According to this cultural stereotype, a woman is expected to demonstrate her love for her husband by waiting patiently at home and having dinner prepared for him at any time of day or night he happens to come home, to have his slippers ready for him, and so on. The feminine ideal is one of suffering in silence and being the provider of joy, even in the face of pain. Strongly influenced by the patriarchal Spanish tradition, the *marianismo* stereotype has historically been used to maintain women in a subordinate position in relation to men.

Acculturation: When Traditional Stereotypes Meet the Financial Realities of Life in the United States

Acculturation—the merging of cultures that occurs when immigrant groups become assimilated into the mainstream culture—has challenged this traditional *machismo/marianismo* division of marital roles among Hispanic couples in the United States. I have seen in my own work in treating Hispanic couples in therapy that marriages are under increasing strain from the conflict between traditional and modern expectations about marital roles. Hispanic American women have been entering the workforce in increasing numbers, usually in domestic or child-care positions, but they are still expected to assume responsibility for tending their own children, keeping the house, and serving their husbands' needs when they return home. In many cases, a reversal of traditional roles occurs, in which the wife works and supports the family while the husband remains at home because he is unable to find or maintain employment.

It is often the Hispanic American husband who has the greater difficulty accepting a more flexible distribution of roles within the marriage and giving up a rigid set of expectations tied to traditional *machismo/marianismo* gender expectations. Although some couples manage to reshape their expectations and marital roles in the face of changing conditions, many relationships buckle under the strain and are terminated in divorce. While I do not expect either the *machismo* or *marianismo* stereotype to disappear entirely, I would not be surprised to find a greater flexibility in gender-role expectations as a product of continued acculturation.

*This World of Diversity feature was written by Rafael Javier, Ph.D. Dr. Javier is associate clinical professor of psychology and director of the Center for Psychological Services and Clinical Studies at St. John's University in Jamaica, New York. Dr. Javier was born in the Dominican Republic and educated in philosophy in the Dominican Republic, Puerto Rico, and Venezuela, and in psychology and psychoanalysis at New York University. He is a practicing psychoanalyst and maintains a research interest in psycholinguistics and psychotherapy with ethnic minorities. All rights are reserved by Dr. Javier.

Hispanic American Women. Many Hispanic Americans adhere to the machismo stereotype of men as restraining their feelings and maintaining an emotional distance. The marianismo stereotype for women idealizes women who suffer in silence, who subordinate their needs to those of their husbands and children.

and bear the primary responsibility for child rearing (Deaux & Lewis, 1983). In some cultures, however, women are reared to be the hunters and food gatherers while men stay close to home and tend the children.

Sexism

Sexism

The prejudgment that because of gender, a person will possess negative traits.

We have all encountered the effects of **sexism**—the prejudgment that because of gender, a person will possess certain negative traits. These negative traits are assumed to disqualify the person for certain vocations or prevent him or her from performing adequately in these jobs or in some social situations.

Sexism may even lead us to interpret the same behavior in prejudicial ways when performed by women or by men. We may see the man as "self-assertive," but the woman as "pushy." We may look upon *him* as flexible, but brand *her* fickle and indecisive. *He* may be rational, whereas *she* is cold. *He* is tough when necessary, but *she* is bitchy. When the businesswoman engages in stereotypical masculine behaviors, the sexist reacts negatively by branding her abnormal or unhealthy.

Sexism may make it difficult for men to act in ways that are stereotyped as feminine. A "sensitive" woman is simply sensitive, but a sensitive man may be seen as a "sissy." A woman may be perceived as polite, whereas a man showing the same behavior seems passive or weak. Only recently have men begun to enter occupational domains previously restricted largely to women, such as secretarial work, nursing, and teaching in the primary grades. Only recently have the floodgates opened for women into traditionally masculine professions such as engineering, law, and medicine.

Although children of both genders have about the same general learning ability, stereotypes limit their horizons. Children tend to show preferences for gender-typed activities and toys by as early as 2 or 3 years of age. If they should stray from them, their peers are sure to remind them of the "errors of their ways." How many little girls are discouraged from considering professions like architecture and engineering because they are handed dolls, not blocks and fire trucks? How many little boys are discouraged from pursuing child-care and nursing professions because of the "funny" looks they get from others when they reach for dolls?

Children not only develop stereotyped attitudes about play activities; they also develop stereotypes about the differences between "man's work" and "woman's work." Women have been historically excluded from "male occupations," and stereotypical expectations concerning "men's work" and "women's work" filter down to the primary grades. For example, according to traditional stereotypes, women are *not expected* to excel in math. Exposure to such negative expectations may discourage women from careers in science and technology.

Gender Differences: *Vive la Différence* or *Vive la Similarité?*

If the genders were not anatomically different, this book would never have been written. How do the genders differ in cognitive abilities and personality, however?

Differences in Cognitive Abilities

A classic review by Eleanor Maccoby and Carol Nagy Jacklin (1974) found persistent evidence that females are somewhat superior to males in verbal ability. But a more recent review of the accumulated evidence found no overall gender differences in verbal abilities, with the exception that boys are more often slower to develop language skills (Hyde & Linn, 1988). Far more boys than girls have reading problems, ranging from reading below grade level to severe disabilities.

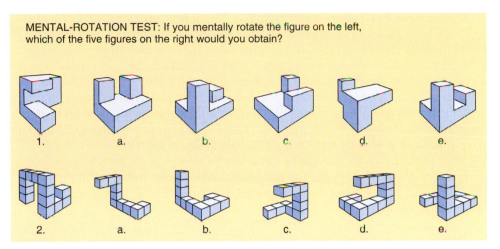

MENTAL-ROTATION TEST: If you mentally rotate the figure on the left, which of the five figures on the right would you obtain?

Figure 5.5. **Rotating Geometric Figures in Space.** Visual–spatial skills—for example, the ability to rotate geometric figures in space—have been considered part of the male gender-role stereotype. Gender differences in visual–spatial skills are small, however, and can be modified by training. (*Source:* From Rathus, S. A., et al. (1990). *Psychology.* [4th ed.]. Copyright © 1990 by Holt, Rinehart & Winston, Inc. Reprinted by permission of the publishers.)

Males generally exceed females in visual–spatial abilities (Voyer et al., 1995). Visual–spatial skills include the ability to follow a map when traveling to an unfamiliar location, to construct a puzzle or assemble a piece of equipment, and to perceive relationships between figures in space (see Figure 5.5).

Differences in math are small and narrowing at all ages (Hyde et al., 1990). Females excel in computational ability in elementary school, however. Males excel in mathematical problem solving in high school and in college (Hyde et al., 1990). Differences in problem solving are reflected on the mathematics test of the Scholastic Aptitude Test (SAT). The mean score is 500, and about two thirds of the test takers receive scores between 400 and 600. Boys outperform girls on SAT math items (Byrnes & Takahira, 1993). Twice as many boys as girls attain scores over 500. According to Byrnes and Takahira (1993), boys' superiority in math does not reflect gender per se. Instead, boys do well because of prior knowledge of math and their strategies for approaching math problems.

In our culture, then, girls are somewhat advanced in their development of verbal abilities. Boys apparently show greater math ability, beginning in adolescence. Three factors should caution us not to attach too much importance to these gender differences, however:

1. In most cases, the differences are small (Hyde & Plant, 1995; Maccoby, 1990; Voyer et al., 1995).
2. These gender differences are *group* differences. Variation in ability on tests of verbal or math skills is larger *within,* than between, the genders (Maccoby, 1990).
3. The small differences that may exist may largely reflect environmental influences and cultural expectations (Tobias, 1982). Spatial and math skills are stereotyped in our culture as masculine, whereas reading skills are stereotyped as feminine. In one study, however, female introductory psychology students who were given but three hours of training in performing visual–spatial skills such as rotating geometric figures performed these tasks as well as men (Stericker & LeVesconte, 1982).

Differences in Personality

There are also many gender differences in personality. According to a meta-analysis of the research literature, females exceed males in extraversion, anxiety, trust, and nurturance (Feingold, 1994). Males exceed females in assertiveness, tough-mindedness, and self-esteem. The assertiveness is connected with aggressiveness, as we see below. The tough-mindedness has unfortunate implications for men's health, as we also see. Two factors may largely account for the relatively lower self-esteem of females:

- Parents, on the average, prefer to have boys.
- Society has created an unlevel playing field in which females have to perform better than males to be seen as doing equally well.

Differences in Communication Styles: "He's Just an Old Chatterbox" We have been inundated with cartoons of suburban housewives gossiping across the fence or pouring endless cups of coffee when the "girls" drop by for a chat. Research has shown, however, that in many situations men spend more time talking than women do. Men are also more likely to introduce new topics and interrupt others (Brooks, 1982; Deaux, 1985; Hall, 1984). Girls tend to be more talkative during early childhood than boys. By the time they enter school, however, boys dominate classroom discussions (Sadker & Sadker, 1994). As girls mature, it appears that they learn to "take a back seat" to boys and let the boys do most of the talking when they are in mixed-gender groups (Hall, 1984).

Women are more willing than men to disclose their feelings and personal experiences, however (Dindia & Allen, 1992). The stereotype of the "strong and silent" male may not discourage men from hogging the conversation, but it may inhibit them from expressing their personal feelings.

Differences in Aggressiveness In almost all cultures (Ford & Beach, 1951; Mead, 1935), it is the males who march off to war and who battle for fame, glory, and shaving-cream-commercial contracts in stadiums and arenas. In most psychological studies on aggression, males have been found to behave more aggressively than females (Maccoby & Jacklin, 1980; White, 1983).

Differences in Willingness to Seek Health Care Men's life expectancies are seven years shorter, on the average, than women's. Part of the difference, according to a survey of 1,500 physicians, is due to women's greater willingness to seek health care ("Doctors tie male mentality," 1995). Men often let symptoms go until a problem that could have been prevented or readily treated becomes serious or life threatening. Women, for example, are much more likely to check themselves for breast cancer than men are to even recognize the symptoms of prostate cancer. Many men, according to the survey, have a "bullet-proof mentality." They are too strong to see the doctor in their 20s, too busy in their 30s, and too frightened later on.

On Becoming a Man or a Woman: Gender Typing

We have chronicled the biological process of sexual differentiation, and we have explored some gender differences in cognitive abilities and behavior. In this section we consider various explanations of **gender typing.**

Biological Perspectives

Biological views on gender typing tend to focus on the roles of genetics and prenatal influences in predisposing men and women to gender-linked behavior patterns. Biological perspectives have also focused on the possible role of hormones in sculpting the brain during prenatal development.

Sociobiology: It's Only Natural   To the sociobiologist, the story of the survival of our ancient ancestors is etched in our genes. Sociobiologists propose that those genes that bestow attributes that increase an organism's chances of surviving to produce viable offspring are most likely to be transmitted to future generations. We thus possess the genetic remnants of traits that helped our ancestors survive and reproduce (Bjorklund & Kipp, 1996). This heritage, according to sociobiologists, influences our social and sexual behavior as well as our anatomic features.

According to sociobiologists, men's traditional roles as hunters and warriors, and women's roles as caregivers and gatherers of fruits and vegetables, are bequeathed to us in our genes. Men are better suited to war and the hunt because of physical attributes passed

Gender typing
The process by which children acquire behavior that is deemed appropriate to their gender.

along since ancestral times. Upper-body strength, for example, would have enabled them to throw spears and overpower adversaries. Men also possess perceptual–cognitive advantages, such as superior visual–motor skills that favor aggression. Visual–motor skills would have enabled men to aim spears or bows and arrows.

Women, it is argued, are genetically predisposed to be empathic and nurturant because these traits enabled ancestral women to respond to children's needs and enhance the likelihood that their children would flourish and eventually reproduce, thereby transmitting their own genetic legacy to future generations. Prehistoric women thus tended to stay close to home, care for the children, and gather edible plants, whereas men ventured from home to hunt and raid their neighbors' storehouses.

Sociobiology is steeped in controversy. Although scientists do not dispute the importance of evolution in determining physical attributes, many are reluctant to attribute complex social behaviors, such as aggression and gender roles, to heredity. The sociobiological argument implies that stereotypical gender roles—men as breadwinners and women as homemakers, for example—reflect the natural order of things. Critics contend that biology is not destiny, that our behavior is not dictated by our genes.

Prenatal Brain Organization   Researchers have sought the origins of gender-typed behavior in the organization of the brain. Is it possible that the cornerstone of gender-typed behavior is laid in the brain before the first breath is taken?

The hemispheres of the brain are specialized to carry out certain functions (Levy, 1985). In most people, the right hemisphere ("right brain") appears to be specialized to perform visual–spatial tasks. The "left brain" appears to be more essential to verbal functions, such as speech, in most people.

We know that sex hormones are responsible for prenatal sexual differentiation of the genitals and for the gender-related structural differences in the hypothalamus of the developing prenatal brain. Sexual differentiation of the brain may also partly explain men's (slight!) superiority at spatial-relations tasks, such as interpreting road maps and visualizing objects in space. Testosterone in the brains of male fetuses spurs greater growth of the right hemisphere and slows the rate of growth of the left hemisphere. This difference may be connected with the ability to accomplish spatial-relations tasks.

Might boys' inclinations toward aggression and rough-and-tumble play also be prenatally imprinted in the brain? Some theorists argue that prenatal sex hormones may masculinize or feminize the brain by creating predispositions that are consistent with gender-role stereotypes, such as rough-and-tumble play and aggressive behavior in males (Collaer & Hines, 1995). Money (1987a) allows a role for prenatal dispositions but argues that social learning plays a stronger role in gender typing. He claims that social learning is even potent enough to counteract prenatal predispositions.

Cross-Cultural Perspectives

Sociobiology cannot account for differences in gender roles that exist across cultures, especially neighboring cultures. The anthropologist Margaret Mead (1935) lived among several tribes on the South Pacific island of New Guinea and found that gender roles in these tribes differed not only from those of Western culture, but also from one another.

Among the Mundugumor, a tribe of headhunters and cannibals, both men and women were warlike and aggressive. The women disdained bearing and rearing children because it interrupted participation in warring parties against neighboring villages. The men and women of the Arapesh tribe were gentle and peaceful, by contrast. Both genders nurtured the children. The Tchambuli were even more unusual in terms of what we consider stereotypical behavior in our society. The men spent most of their time caring for children, gossiping, bickering, primping and applying makeup, and haggling over prices. Fish was the staple diet of the Tchambuli, and women brought home the daily catch. Women kept their heads shaven, disdained ornaments, and were more highly sexed and aggressive than men.

Whatever the influence of biology on behavior, biological factors alone do not make men aggressive or independent, or women passive or submissive (Havemann & Lehtinen, 1990). Cultural expectations and learning play a large role.

Psychological Perspectives

Children acquire awareness of gender-role stereotypes by the tender ages of 2½ to 3½ (Kuhn et al., 1978). Both boys and girls generally agree, when asked to describe the differences between the genders, that boys build things, play with transportation toys such as cars and fire trucks, enjoy helping their fathers, and hit other children. Both boys and girls also agree that girls enjoy playing with dolls and helping their mothers cook and clean, and are talkative, dependent on others for help, and nonviolent. They perceive the label "cruel" to be a masculine trait, whereas "cries a lot" is perceived as a feminine trait. By the time they are age 3, most children have become aware of the differences in stereotypical ways men and women dress and the types of occupations that are considered appropriate for each gender (Ruble & Ruble, 1982). Psychologists have attempted to explain how children acquire such knowledge and adopt stereotypical behavior patterns in terms of psychoanalytic, social-learning, and cognitive–developmental theories.

Psychoanalytic Theory   Sigmund Freud explained gender typing in terms of identification. Appropriate gender typing, in Freud's view, requires that boys come to identify with their fathers and girls with their mothers. Identification is completed, in Freud's view, as children resolve the **Oedipus complex** (sometimes called the Electra complex in girls).

Oedipus complex

In psychoanalytic theory, a conflict of the phallic stage in which the boy wishes to possess his mother sexually and perceives his father as a rival in love. (The analogous conflict for girls is the *Electra complex.*)

According to Freud, the Oedipus complex occurs during the phallic period of psychosexual development, from the ages of 3 to 5. During this period the child develops incestuous wishes for the parent of the other gender and comes to perceive the parent of the same gender as a rival. The complex is resolved by the child's forsaking incestuous wishes for the parent of the other gender and identifying with the parent of the same gender. Through identification with the same-gender parent, the child comes to develop gender-typed behaviors that are typically associated with that gender. Children display stereotypical gender-typed behaviors earlier than Freud would have predicted, however. Even during the first year, boys are more independent than girls. Girls are more quiet and restrained. Girls show preferences for dolls and soft toys, and boys for hard transportation toys, by the ages of 1½ to 3.

Social-Learning Theory   Social-learning theorists explain the development of gender-typed behavior in terms of processes such as observational learning, identification, and socialization. Children can learn what is deemed masculine or feminine by observational learning, as suggested by the results of an experiment by Perry and Bussey (1979). In this study, 8- and 9-year-old boys and girls watched adult role models indicate their preferences for each of 16 pairs of items—pairs such as toy cows versus toy horses and oranges versus apples. What the children didn't know was that the expressed preferences were made arbitrarily. The children then were asked to indicate their own preferences for the items represented in the pairs. The boys' choices agreed with the adult men's an average of 14 out of 16 times. Girls chose the pair item selected by the men, on the average, only 3 out of 16 times.

Socialization

The process of guiding people into socially acceptable behavior patterns by means of information, rewards, and punishments.

Socialization also plays a role in gender typing. Almost from the moment a baby comes into the world, it is treated according to its gender. Parents tend to talk more to baby girls, and fathers especially engage in more roughhousing with boys (Jacklin et al., 1984). When children are old enough to speak, parents and other adults—even other children— begin to instruct children as to how they are expected to behave. Parents may reward children for behavior they consider gender-appropriate and punish (or fail to reinforce) them for behavior they consider inappropriate for their gender.

Parental roles in gender typing are apparently changing. With more mothers working outside the home, daughters today are exposed to more women who represent career-minded role models than was the case in earlier generations. More parents today are encouraging their daughters to become career-minded and to engage in strenuous physical activities, such as organized sports. Many boys today are exposed to fathers who take a larger role than men used to in child care and household responsibilities.

The popular media—books, magazines, radio, film, and especially television—also convey gender stereotypes (Remafedi, 1990). The media by and large portray men and women in traditional roles (Signorielli, 1990). Men more often play doctors, attorneys, and police officers. Working women are more likely than men to be portrayed as undergoing role conflict—being pulled in opposite directions by job and family. One study reported that despite current awareness of sexism, "Women are often still depicted on television as half-clad and half-witted, and needing to be rescued by quick-thinking, fully clothed men" (Adelson, 1990).

Social-learning theorists believe that aggression is largely influenced by learning. Boys are permitted, even encouraged, to engage in more aggressive behavior than girls. When girls act aggressively, they are often told that "this isn't the way girls act."

Cognitive–Developmental Theory

Psychologist Lawrence Kohlberg (1966) proposed a cognitive–developmental view of gender typing. From this perspective, children form concepts about gender and then make their behavior conform to their gender concepts. These developments occur in stages and are entwined with general cognitive development.

According to Kohlberg, gender typing entails the emergence of three concepts: *gender identity, gender stability,* and *gender constancy.* Gender identity is usually acquired by the age of 3. By the age of 4 or 5, most children develop a concept of **gender stability**—the recognition that people retain their genders for a lifetime. Prior to this age, boys may think that they will become mommies when they grow up, and girls, daddies.

The more sophisticated concept of **gender constancy** develops in most children by the age of 7 or 8. They recognize that gender does not change, even if people alter their dress or behavior. So gender remains constant even when appearances change. According to Kohlberg, children are motivated to behave in gender-appropriate ways once they have established the concepts of gender stability and gender constancy. They then make an active effort to obtain information as to which behavior patterns are considered "masculine" and which "feminine." Once they obtain this information, they imitate the "gender-appropriate" pattern.

Gender Schema Theory: An Information-Processing Approach

Gender schema theory proposes that children develop a **gender schema** as a means of organizing their perceptions of the world (Bem, 1981, 1985; Martin & Halverson, 1981). A gender schema is a cluster of mental representations about male and female physical qual-

Gender stability
The concept that people retain their genders for a lifetime.

Gender constancy
The concept that people's genders do not change, even if they alter their dress or behavior.

Gender schema
A cluster of mental representations about male and female physical qualities, behaviors, and personality traits.

Gender Typing. According to cognitive theories of gender typing, children are motivated to behave in ways that are consistent with their genders. Children seek information as to what behaviors are deemed appropriate for people of their gender.

CHALLENGING GENDER ROLES IN SEXUAL BEHAVIOR

If you are a man, do you feel that it is your responsibility to make dates and initiate sexual relationships? If you are a woman, do you feel that it is your responsibility to serve as the "gate-keeper" in romantic relationships? Regardless of your gender, how do you feel about sexually assertive women? About sexually passive men?

Gender roles have had a profound influence on dating practices and sexual behavior. Children learn early that women are expected to wait to be asked out and to screen suitors. Men are expected to make the first (sexual) move and women to determine how far advances will proceed. Regrettably, some men refuse to take no for an answer. They feel that they have the right to force their dates into sexual relations.

The view of men as initiators and women as gatekeepers is embedded within the larger stereotype that men are sexually aggressive and women are

sexually passive. Men feel pressed not only to initiate sexual encounters, but also to dictate all the "moves" thereafter, just as they are expected to take the lead on the dance floor. According to the stereotype, women are to let men determine the choice, timing, and sequence of sexual positions and techniques. Unfortunately, the stereotype favors men's sexual preferences. It denies women the opportunity to give and receive their preferred kinds of stimulation.

A woman may more easily reach orgasm in the **female-superior position,** but her partner may prefer the **male-superior position.** If the man is calling the shots, she may not have the opportunity to reach orgasm. Even the expression of her preferences may be deemed "unladylike."

The stereotypical masculine role also imposes constraints on men. Men are expected to take the lead in bringing their partners to orgasm,

but they should not ask their partners what they like because they are expected to be natural experts. ("Real men" not only don't eat quiche; they also need not ask women how to make love.)

Fortunately, more flexible attitudes are emerging. Women are becoming more sexually assertive, and men are becoming more receptive to expressing tenderness and gentleness.

According to another stereotype, men are always sexually ready. Women, however, discover their sexuality only when men ignite their sexual flames. The stereotype denies that "normal" women have spontaneous sexual desires or are readily aroused. Many people view women who are highly interested in sex as sluts or nymphomaniacs.

Are the traditional stereotypes preventing you from expressing your genuine sexual feelings and preferences? If so, what can you do about it?

Female-superior position
A coital position in which the woman is on top.

Male-superior position
A coital position in which the man is on top.

ities, behaviors, and personality traits. Once children acquire a gender schema, they begin to judge themselves according to traits considered relevant to their genders. In doing so, they blend their developing self-concepts with the prominent gender schema of their culture. Children with self-concepts that are consistent with the prominent gender schema of their culture are likely to develop higher self-esteem than children whose self-concepts are inconsistent.

According to gender schema theory, gender identity itself is sufficient to inspire gender-appropriate behavior. Once children develop a concept of gender identity, they begin to seek information concerning gender-typed traits and strive to live up to them. Research does suggest that children begin to imitate stereotypical masculine and feminine behavior patterns once they have developed gender identity. Gender stability and gender constancy are apparently not prerequisites for doing so.

Psychological Androgyny: The More Traits, the Merrier?

Most people think of masculinity and femininity as opposite ends of one continuum (Storms, 1980). People tend to assume that the more masculine a person is, the less feminine he or she must be, and vice versa. So a man who exhibits stereotypical feminine traits

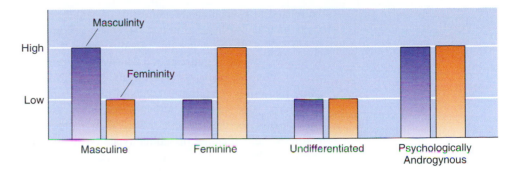

Figure 5.6. **A Model of Psychological Androgyny.** Some behavioral scientists argue that masculinity and femininity are independent personality dimensions. People who exhibit "masculine" assertiveness and instrumental skills along with "feminine" nurturance and cooperation are said to be psychologically androgynous. People high in assertiveness and instrumental skills fit only the masculine stereotype. People high in traits such as nurturance and cooperation fit only the feminine stereotype. People low in the stereotypical masculine and feminine patterns are considered undifferentiated. (*Source:* From Rathus, S. A. and Nevid, J. S. [1989]. *Psychology and the challenges: Adjustment and growth* [4th ed.]. Copyright © 1989 by Holt, Rinehart & Winston, Inc. Reprinted by permission of the publisher.)

of nurturance, tenderness, and emotionality is often considered less masculine than other men. Women who compete with men in business are perceived not only as more masculine but also as less feminine than other women.

Some behavioral scientists, such as Sandra Bem, argue that masculinity and femininity comprise separate personality dimensions. A person who is highly masculine, whether male or female, may also possess feminine traits—and vice versa. People who exhibit "masculine" assertiveness and instrumental skills (skills in the sciences and business, for example) along with "feminine" nurturance and cooperation fit both the masculine and feminine gender-role stereotypes. They are said to show **psychological androgyny** (see Figure 5.6). People high in assertiveness and instrumental skills fit only the masculine stereotype. People high in traits such as nurturance and cooperation fit only the feminine stereotype. People low in the stereotypical masculine and feminine patterns are considered "undifferentiated" according to gender-role stereotypes.

People who are psychologically androgynous may be capable of summoning a wider range of masculine and feminine traits to meet the demands of various situations and to express their desires and talents. Researchers, for example, have found psychologically androgynous persons of both genders to show "masculine" independence under group pressures to conform and "feminine" nurturance in interactions with a kitten or baby (Bem, 1975; Bem et al., 1976). Androgynous men and women are more apt to share leadership responsibilities in mixed-gender groups (Porter et al., 1985). By contrast, "masculine" men and women tend to dominate such groups, whereas "feminine" men and women are likely to take a back seat.

Many people who oppose the constraints of traditional gender roles may perceive psychological androgyny as a desirable goal. Some feminist writers, however, criticize psychological androgyny on grounds that the concept is defined in terms of, and thereby perpetuates, belief in the existence of masculine and feminine gender roles (Bem, 1993).

Psychological Androgyny, Psychological Well-Being, and Personal Development

Psychologically androgynous people tend to have higher self-esteem and to be generally better adjusted psychologically than people who are feminine or undifferentiated. Yet it appears that these benefits are more strongly related to the presence of masculine traits than to the combination of masculine and feminine traits (Whitley, 1983; Williams & D'Alessandro, 1994). That is, masculine traits such as assertiveness and independence may

Psychological androgyny Possession of stereotypical masculine traits, such as assertiveness and instrumental skills, along with stereotypical feminine traits, such as expressiveness, nurturance, and cooperation.

be related to psychological well-being, whether or not they are combined with feminine traits such as warmth, nurturance, and cooperation.

There is also evidence that feminine traits, such as nurturance and sensitivity, appear to predict success in intimate relationships—in *men* as well as in women. Marital happiness as rated by husbands is positively related to femininity in the wives (Antill, 1983). More interestingly, perhaps, ratings of marital happiness from the wives were also positively correlated with their husbands' femininity. Androgynous men are more likely to express tender feelings of love toward their partners and to be more accepting of their partner's faults than are masculine-typed ("macho") men (Coleman & Ganong, 1985). It seems that both genders appreciate spouses who are sympathetic, able to express warmth and tenderness, and nurturant toward children.

Masculine and androgynous adolescents of both genders tend to be more popular and to have higher self-esteem than other adolescents (Lamke, 1982b). We might not be surprised, given the prevalence of sexism, that adolescent boys fare better if they possess stereotypical masculine traits. What is more surprising is that adolescent girls also fare better when they exhibit stereotypical masculine traits, such as assertiveness and independence. It seems that young women do not risk having others question their femininity if they exhibit masculine traits, providing more evidence that the constellations of traits we call masculinity and femininity are independent clusters.

Psychological Androgyny and Sexual Behavior

Some evidence shows psychologically androgynous men and women to be more comfortable with their sexuality than are masculine men and feminine women (Walfish & Mayerson, 1980). Perhaps they can draw upon a broader repertoire of sexual behaviors. They may be comfortable with cuddling and tender holding, and also with initiating and directing sexual interactions. Researchers also find that androgynous women experience orgasm more frequently (Radlove, 1983) and express greater sexual satisfaction (Kimlicka et al., 1983) than feminine women do.

Chapter Review

Sexual (1) _____iation is the process by which males and females develop distinct reproductive anatomy. Gender (2) _____s are the behavior patterns that are deemed "masculine" or "feminine" in a particular culture. Gender (3) _____ing is the process by which boys come to behave in line with what is expected of men and girls with what is expected of women. Psychological (4) an_____ refers to people who have traits connected with both genders.

Prenatal Sexual Differentiation

When a sperm cell fertilizes an ovum, 23 (5) _____omes from the male parent nor-

mally combine with 23 chromosomes from the female parent. An ovum carries a(n) (6) _____ sex chromosome, but a sperm carries either an X or a Y sex chromosome. Females normally have a(n) (7) _____ sex chromosomal structure. Males normally have a(n) (8) _____ sex chromosomal structure.

At about (9) _____ weeks after conception, primitive gonads, ducts, and external genitals whose gender cannot be distinguished visually have formed. The embryo has two sets of primitive duct structures, the (10) M_____ (female) ducts and the (11) W_____ (male) ducts. During the first 6 weeks of prenatal development, embryonic structures of both genders resemble primitive (12: Male *or* Female?) The (13) _____ sex chromosome causes the testes to begin to differentiate. Ovaries begin to differentiate if the (14) _____ sex chromosome is absent. The H-Y antigen is a protein that fosters the development of (15) _____es.

(16) _____rone spurs differentiation of the male (Wolffian) duct system. Each Wolffian duct develops into an (17) _____ymis, vas (18) def_____, and seminal vesicle. Another androgen, (19) dihydro-_____ (DHT), spurs development of the external genitals, including the penis. Another testicular hormone, (20) M_____ inhibiting substance (MIS), prevents the Müllerian ducts from developing into the female duct system.

In female fetuses, the relative absence of (21) _____gens causes degeneration of the Wolffian ducts and prompts development of female sexual organs. The Müllerian ducts evolve into (22) _____ian tubes, the uterus, and the upper two thirds of the vagina.

About four months after conception, the testes normally descend into the scrotal sac through the (23) in_____ _____nal. In a few males, one or both testes remain in the abdomen at birth; the condition is termed (24) _____chidism.

(25) Kl_____ syndrome is caused by an extra X sex chromosome, resulting in an XXY rather than an XY pattern. Men with this pattern have enlarged (26) _____ts, poor muscle development, and are infertile. (27) _____ner syndrome, found only in women, is caused by the loss of some (28: X *or* Y?) sex chromosome material. The (29) _____ries of these girls do not develop or function normally.

The brain undergoes prenatal sexual differentiation. Testosterone causes cells in the (30) hypo_____ of male fetuses to become insensitive to estrogen. In female fetuses, the hypothalamus (31: Does *or* Does not?) develop sensitivity to estrogen. Sensitivity to estrogen is important in the regulation of the (32) men_____ cycle.

Gender Identity

One's gender (33) _____ty is one's awareness of being male or being female. Gender identity (34: Is *or* Is not?) an automatic extension of one's anatomic gender.

Gender (35) _____ment reflects the child's anatomic gender and usually occurs at birth.

(36) _____phrodites possess the gonads of one gender but external genitalia that are ambiguous or typical of the other gender. People who are born with both ovarian and testicular tissue are called (37) herma_____. The most common form of female pseudohermaphroditism is (38) _____ital syndrome, in which a genetic (XX) female has female internal sexual structures (ovaries), but masculinized external genitals. In (39) and_____-_____vity syndrome, genetic (XY) males have lower-than-normal prenatal sensitivity to androgens so that their genitals do not become normally masculinized. (40) D_____ Republic syndrome is a genetic enzyme disorder that prevents testosterone from masculinizing the external genitalia. Pseudohermaphrodites may be genetically male (XY) or female (XY), but assume the gender identity of the other gender because of the gender (41) _____ment at birth.

Boys with Dominican Republic syndrome are reared as (42: Males *or* Females?). At puberty, however, their (43) _____es descend, their voices deepen, and their "clitorises" expand into penises. Of the 18 boys who were reared as girls, (44) _____ later shifted to a male gender identity.

(45) _____uals are people with a gender-identity disorder in which they feel trapped in the body of the wrong gender. Transsexuals experience gender (46) _____ria. Transsexuals usually undergo (47) gender-_____ment surgery. Gender-reassignment surgery (48: Does *or* Does not?) implant the internal reproductive organs of the other gender. Gay men and lesbians (49: Do *or* Do not?) perceive their gender identities to be consistent with their anatomic gender. (50) P_____ theorists explain transsexualism in terms of early parent–child relationships in which children identify with the parent of the (51: Same *or* Other?) gender. Transsexuals may also be influenced by prenatal (52) _____nal imbalances. Transsexuals not only undergo gender-reassignment surgery, but also receive sex (53) hor_____ of the other gender for a lifetime. Most studies report that the adjustment of transsexuals who undergo gender reassignment is (54: Positive *or* Negative?).

Gender Roles and Stereotypes

A (55) _____ type is a fixed, oversimplified, and often severely distorted idea about a group of people. Cultures have broad expectations of men and women that are termed (56) gen_____ _____es. In our culture the stereotypical (57: Male *or* Female?) shows traits such as gentleness, dependency, kindness, helpfulness, patience, and submissiveness. The stereotypical (58: Male *or* Female?) shows toughness, gentlemanliness, and protectiveness. (59) _____mo is a Hispanic cultural stereotype of masculinity. To be (60) _____o is to be strong, virile, and dominant. Hispanic cultural idealization of femininity is termed (61) mar_____, viewing the virtuous woman as one who (62) "s_____ in silence," submerging her needs and desires to serve those of her family.

Sexism

(63) _____ism is the prejudgment that because of gender, a person will possess negative traits. Sexism has historically taken a greater toll on (64: Males *or* Females?). Sexism has generally (65: Expanded *or* Limited?) the horizons of both genders.

Gender Differences: *Vive la Différence or Vive la Similarité?*

A review by (66) M_____ and (67) J_____ found evidence that females are somewhat superior to males in verbal ability. More (68: Boys *or* Girls?) have reading problems. (69: Males *or* Females?) generally exceed the other gender in visual–spatial abilities and math. Gender differences in math are (70: Large *or* Small?). According to Byrnes and Takahira, (71: Girls *or* Boys?) do better in math because of prior knowledge of math and their strategies for approaching math problems.

(72: Males *or* Females?) exceed the other gender in extraversion, anxiety, trust, and nurturance. (73: Males *or* Females?) exceed the other gender in assertiveness, aggressiveness, tough-mindedness, and self-esteem. (74: Girls *or* Boys?) dominate classroom discussions. (75: Women *or* Men?) are more willing to disclose their feelings and personal experiences. (76: Men *or* Women?) are more willing than the other gender to seek health care.

On Becoming a Man or a Woman: Gender Typing

Biological views on gender typing tend to focus on the roles of (77) _____tics and prenatal influences in predisposing men and women to gender-linked behavior patterns. (78) _____gists propose that genes that bestow traits that increase an organism's chances of surviving to reproduce are most likely to be transmitted to future generations. According to sociobiologists, (79: Men's *or* Women's?) traditional roles as hunters and warriors, and (80: Men's *or* Women's?) roles as caregivers and gatherers of fruits and vegetables, are handed down to us in our genes.

Prenatal sex (81) hor_____ may partly explain men's slight superiority at spatial–relations tasks. Testosterone in the brains of male fetuses spurs greater growth of the (82: Left *or* Right?) hemisphere and slows the rate of growth of the other hemisphere. Some theorists argue that prenatal sex hormones may masculinize or feminize the brain by creating predispositions that are consistent with gender-role stereotypes, such as rough-and-tumble play and aggressive behavior in (83: Males *or* Females?).

Anthropologist Margaret Mead found that among the (84) Mun_____, a tribe of headhunters and cannibals, both men and women were warlike and aggressive. The men and women of the (85) Ara_____ were gentle and peaceful. Among the (86) _____buli, the men spent more time caring for children and applying makeup, and women were the more aggressive gender.

Psychological research shows that children become aware of gender-role stereotypes by the age of (87) _____. Sigmund (88) F_____ explained gender typing in terms of identification. Identification is completed, in Freud's view, as children resolve the (89) _____pus complex. During the (90) _____lic stage of psychosexual development, a child develops incestuous wishes for the parent of the other gender and comes to perceive the parent of the same gender as a rival. The complex is resolved when the child surrenders incestuous wishes for the parent of the other gender and (91) _____fies with the parent of the same gender.

Social-learning theorists explain the development of gender-typed behavior in terms of (92) ob_____ learning and (93) soc_____. People (94: Reward *or* Punish?*) children for behavior they consider gender-appropriate. However, more parents today are encouraging their (95: Daughters *or* Sons?*) to become career-minded and to engage in strenuous physical activities, such as sports. The popular media more often portray (96: Women *or* Men?*) as doctors, attorneys, and police officers. (97: Girls *or* Boys?*) are permitted, even encouraged, to engage in more aggressive behavior than the other gender.

Psychologist Lawrence (98) K_____ proposed a cognitive–developmental view of gender typing, which entails the emergence of three concepts: gender (99) id_____, gender (100) st_____, and gender (101) co_____. The concept of (102) gen_____ _____cy means that children recognize that gender does not change, even if people alter their dress or behavior. According to (103) cognitive–_____mental theory, children are motivated to behave in gender-appropriate ways once they have established the concepts of gender stability and gender constancy.

(104) Gen_____ _____ma theory proposes that children develop concepts about male and female physical qualities, behaviors, and personality traits as a means of organizing their perceptions of the world.

Once children acquire a gender (105) sch_____, they begin to judge themselves according to traits considered relevant to their gender. In doing so, they (106) bl_____ their developing self-concepts with the prominent gender schema of their culture.

Children learn at an early age that (107: Men *or* Women?*) men usually make dates and initiate sexual interactions. (108: Men *or* Women?*) usually serve as the "gatekeepers" in romantic relationships. According to another stereotype, (109: Women *or* Men?*) are always readily sexually aroused.

Psychological Androgyny: The More Traits, the Merrier?

Sandra Bem argues that masculinity and femininity make up (110: One *or* Two?*) personality dimension(s). People who show "masculine" and "feminine" traits are said to show psychological (111) _____gyny. Some feminist writers criticize psychological androgyny on grounds that the concept perpetuates belief in the existence of masculine and feminine (112) gen_____ _____ es. Psychologically androgynous people tend to have (113: Lower *or* Higher?*) self-esteem than people who are feminine or undifferentiated.

Chapter Quiz

1. In the embryo, ovaries begin to differentiate if the
   (a) X chromosome is present.
   (b) X chromosome is absent.
   (c) Y chromosome is present.
   (d) Y chromosome is absent.
2. In the embryo, each Wolffian duct develops into all of the following, EXCEPT for
   (a) an epididymis.
   (b) an ovary.
   (c) a vas deferens.
   (d) seminal vesicles.
3. Pseudohermaphrodites may possess the gonads
   (a) and external genitalia of males.
   (b) and external genitalia of females.
   (c) of one gender but external genitalia that are typical of the other gender.
   (d) and external genitalia that are typical of the other gender.
4. According to the text, _____ experience gender dysphoria.
   (a) people with Dominican Republic syndrome
   (b) hermaphrodites
   (c) psueodohermaphrodites
   (d) transsexuals
5. The *marianismo* stereotype is part of _____ culture.
   (a) Hispanic
   (b) Asian
   (c) Native American
   (d) African American
6. Which of the following is the most accurate statement about gender differences in mathematics?
   (a) Males excel in computational ability in elementary school.
   (b) Females excel in problem solving in high school and in college.
   (c) Girls outperform boys on SAT math items.
   (d) Differences in math are small and narrowing at all ages.

7. _____ propose that genes bestowing attributes that increase an organism's chances of surviving to produce viable offspring are most likely to be transmitted to future generations.
   (a) Psychologists
   (b) Sociobiologists
   (c) Anthropologists
   (d) Sociologists

8. Margaret Mead found that among the Mundugumor,
   (a) both men and women were warlike and aggressive.
   (b) neither men nor women were warlike and aggressive.
   (c) men but not women were warlike and aggressive.
   (d) women but not men were warlike and aggressive.

9. According to gender schema theory, children blend their developing _____ with the prominent gender schema of their culture.
   (a) embryonic structures
   (b) psychic structures
   (c) self-concepts
   (d) gender identities

10. Sandra Bem argues that masculinity and femininity are
   (a) opposite poles of a single personality dimension.
   (b) separate personality dimensions.
   (c) social requirements that promote the survival of a culture.
   (d) concepts found only in Western societies.

Answers to Chapter Review

1. Differentiation
2. Roles
3. Typing
4. Androgyny
5. Chromosomes
6. X
7. XX
8. XY
9. 5 or 6 (or 5 to 6)
10. Müllerian
11. Wolffian
12. Female
13. Y
14. Y
15. Testes
16. Testosterone
17. Epididymis
18. Deferens
19. Dihydrotestosterone
20. Müllerian
21. Androgens
22. Fallopian
23. Inguinal canal
24. Cryptorchidism
25. Klinefelter
26. Breasts
27. Turner
28. X
29. Ovaries
30. Hypothalamus
31. Does
32. Menstrual
33. Identity
34. Is not
35. Assignment
36. Pseudohermaphrodites
37. Hermaphrodites
38. Androgenital
39. Androgen-insensitivity
40. Dominican
41. Assignment
42. Females
43. Testes
44. 17
45. Transsexuals
46. Dysphoria
47. Reassignment
48. Does not
49. Do
50. Psychoanalytic
51. Other
52. Hormonal
53. Hormones
54. Positive
55. Stereotype
56. Gender roles
57. Female
58. Male
59. *Machismo*
60. Macho
61. *Marianismo*
62. Suffers
63. Sexism
64. Females
65. Limited
66. Maccoby
67. Jacklin
68. Boys
69. Males
70. Small
71. Boys
72. Females
73. Males
74. Boys
75. Women
76. Women
77. Genetics
78. Sociobiologists
79. Men's
80. Women's
81. Hormones
82. Right
83. Males
84. Mundugumor
85. Arapesh
86. Tchambuli
87. 2½ to 3½
88. Freud
89. Oedipus
90. Phallic
91. Identifies
92. Observational
93. Socialization
94. Reward
95. Daughters
96. Men
97. Boys
98. Kohlberg
99. Identity
100. Stability
101. Constancy
102. Gender constancy
103. Cognitive–developmental
104. Gender schema
105. Schema
106. Blend
107. Men
108. Women
109. Men
110. Two
111. Androgyny
112. Gender roles
113. Higher

Answers to Chapter Quiz

1. (d)
2. (b)
3. (c)
4. (d)
5. (a)
6. (d)
7. (b)
8. (a)
9. (c)
10. (b)

CHAPTER 6

Attraction and Love

OUTLINE

Attraction
Physical Attractiveness: How Important Is Looking Good?
The Matching Hypothesis: Who Is "Right" for You?
Similarity in Attitudes: Do Opposites Attract?
Reciprocity: If You Like Me, You Must Have Excellent Judgment

Love
The Greek Heritage
Romantic Love in Contemporary Western Culture
Contemporary Models of Love: Dare Science Intrude?

Chapter Review

Chapter Quiz

A World of Diversity
Wide-Eyed with . . . Beauty?
Gender Differences in Preferences in Mates Across
    37 Cultures

Applications
Coping with Loneliness

- Beauty is *not* simply "in the eye of the beholder"—there appear to be some universal standards for beauty?
- College women believe that college men would like them to be thinner than men actually want them to be?
- People are regarded as more attractive when they are smiling?
- Women who are assigned names like Kathy and Jennifer *at random* are rated as more attractive then women assigned names like Harriet and Gertrude?
- Opposites *do not usually* attract—we are more likely to be attracted to people who share our views and tastes then to people who disagree with them?
- It is possible to be in love with someone who is not also a friend?
- Many people are lonely because they fear being rejected by others?

andy and Stretch. A new technique for controlling weight gain? No, these are the names of a couple who have just met at a camera club that doubles as a meeting place for singles.

Candy and Stretch stand above the crowd—literally. She is almost 6 feet tall, an attractive woman in her early 30s. He is more plain looking, but "wholesome." He is in his late 30s and 6 feet 5 inches tall. Stretch has been in the group for some time. Candy is a new member. Let us follow them as they meet during a coffee break. As you will see, there are some differences between what they say and what they think (Bach & Deutsch, 1970).

	THEY SAY	THEY THINK
STRETCH:	Well, you're certainly a welcome addition to our group.	(Can't I ever say something clever?)
CANDY:	Thank you. It certainly is friendly and interesting.	(He's cute.)
STRETCH:	My friends call me Stretch. It's left over from my basketball days. Silly, but I'm used to it.	(It's safer than saying my name is David Stein.)
CANDY:	My name is Candy.	(At least my nickname is. He doesn't have to hear Hortense O'Brien.)
STRETCH:	What kind of camera is that?	(Why couldn't a girl named Candy be Jewish? It's only a nickname, isn't it?)
CANDY:	Just this old German one of my uncle's. I borrowed it from the office.	(He could be Irish. And that camera looks expensive.)
STRETCH:	May I? (He takes her camera, brushing her hand and then tingling with the touch.) Fine lens. You work for your uncle?	(Now I've done it. Brought up work.)
CANDY:	Ever since college.	(Okay, so what if I only went for a year?)
	It's more than being just a secretary. I get into sales, too.	(If he asks what I sell, I'll tell him anything except underwear.)
STRETCH:	Sales? That's funny. I'm in sales, too, but mainly as an executive. I run our department.	(Is there a nice way to say used cars? I'd better change the subject.)
	I started using cameras on trips. Last time I was in the Bahamas, I took—	(Great legs! And the way her hips move—)
CANDY:	Oh! Do you go to the Bahamas, too? I love those islands.	(So I went just once, and it was for the brassiere manufacturers' convention. At least we're off the subject of jobs.)

THEY SAY	THEY THINK
STRETCH:	(She's probably been around. Well, at least we're off the subject of jobs.)
I did a little underwater work there last summer. Fantastic colors. So rich in life.	(And lonelier than hell.)
CANDY:	(Look at that build. He must swim like a fish. I should learn.)
I wish I'd had time when I was there. I love the water.	(Well, I do. At the beach, anyway, where I can wade in and not go too deep.)

So begins a relationship. Candy and Stretch have a drink and talk, talk, talk—sharing their likes and dislikes. Amazingly, they seem to agree on everything, from clothing to cars to politics. The attraction they feel is very strong, and neither of them is willing to turn the other off by disagreeing.

They fall in love. Weeks later they still agree on everything, even though there is one topic they avoid scrupulously: religion. Their different backgrounds became apparent once they exchanged last names. That doesn't mean they have to talk about it, however.

They delay introductions to their parents. The O'Briens and the Steins are narrow-minded about religion. If the truth be known, so are Candy and Stretch. Candy errs by telling Stretch, "You're not like other Jews I know." Stretch also voices his feelings now and then. After Candy has nursed him through a cold, he remarks, "You know, you're very Jewish." Candy and Stretch play the games required to maintain the relationship. They tell themselves that their remarks were mistakes, and, after all, anyone can make mistakes. They were meant as compliments, weren't they? Yet each is becoming isolated from family and friends.

One of the topics they ignore is birth control. As a Catholic, Candy does not take oral contraceptives. (Stretch later claimed that he had assumed she did.) Candy becomes pregnant, and they get married. Only through professional help do they learn each other's genuine feelings. And on several occasions, the union comes close to dissolving.

How do we explain the goings-on in this tangled web of deception? Candy and Stretch felt strongly attracted to each other. What determines who is attractive? Why did Candy and Stretch pretend to agree on everything? Why did they put off introductions to their parents?

Two possible consequences of attraction are friendship and love. Candy and Stretch "fell in love." What *is* love? When the first author was a teenager, the answer was, "Five feet of heaven in a ponytail." However, this answer may lack scientific merit. We see that there are different forms of love and that our concepts of love are far from universal. ■

Attraction

Let us explore some of the factors that determine interpersonal attraction.

Physical Attractiveness: How Important Is Looking Good?

We might like to think of ourselves as so sophisticated that physical attractiveness does not move us. We might like to claim that sensitivity, warmth, and intelligence are more important to us. However, we may never learn about other people's personalities if they do not meet our minimal standards for physical attractiveness. Research shows that physical attractiveness is a major determinant of interpersonal and sexual attraction (Hensley, 1992). In fact, physical appearance is the key factor in consideration of partners for dates, sex, and marriage (Hatfield & Sprecher, 1986).

Is Beauty in the Eye of the Beholder? What determines physical attractiveness? Are our standards fully subjective, or is there broad agreement on what is attractive? Cross-cultural studies show that people universally want physically appealing partners (Ford & Beach, 1951). However, is that which appeals in one culture repulsive in others?

In certain African tribes, long necks and round, disklike lips are signs of feminine beauty. Women thus stretch their necks and lips to make themselves more appealing. Women of the Nama tribe persistently tug at their labia majora to make them "beautiful"— that is, prominent and elongated (Ford & Beach, 1951).

In our culture, taller men are considered to be more attractive by women (Hensley, 1994; Sheppard & Strathman, 1989). Undergraduate women prefer their dates to be about 6 inches taller than they are. Undergraduate men, on the average, prefer women who are about 4½ inches shorter (Gillis & Avis, 1980). Tall women are not viewed so positively. Shortness, though, is perceived to be a liability for both men and women (Jackson & Ervin, 1992).

Some women of Candy's stature find that shorter men are discouraged from asking them out. Some walk with a hunch, as if to minimize their height. A neighbor of the first and third authors refers to herself as 5 feet 13 inches tall.

Female plumpness is valued in many, perhaps most, preliterate societies (Anderson et al., 1992; Frayser, 1985). Wide hips and a broad pelvis are widely recognized as sexually appealing. In our culture, however, slenderness is in style. Some young women suffer from an eating disorder called **anorexia nervosa,** in which they literally starve themselves to conform to the contemporary ideal. Both genders find slenderness (though not anorexic thinness) attractive, especially for females (Fallon & Rozin, 1985; Franzoi & Herzog, 1987; Rozin & Fallon, 1988).

The hourglass figure is popular in the United States. In one study, 87 African American college undergraduates—both male and female—rated women of average weight with a waist-to-hip ratio of 0.7 to 0.8 as most attractive and desirable for long-term relationships (Singh, 1994a). Neither very thin nor obese women were found to be as attractive, regardless of the waist-to-hip ratio. Findings were similar for a sample of 188 White students (Singh, 1994b).

Do men idealize the *Penthouse* centerfold? What size busts do men prefer? Women's beliefs that men prefer large breasts may be somewhat exaggerated. The belief that men want women to have bursting bustlines leads many women to seek breast implants in the attempt to live up to an ideal that men themselves don't generally hold (Rosenthal, 1992). Researchers in one study showed young men and women (ages 17 to 25 years) a continuum of male and female figures that differed only in the size of the bust for the female figures and of the pectorals for the male figures (Thompson & Tantleff, 1992). The participants were asked to indicate the ideal size for their own gender and the size they believed the average man and woman would prefer.

The results show some support for the "big is better" stereotype—for both men and women. Women's conception of ideal bust size was greater than their actual average size. Men preferred women with still larger busts, but not nearly as large as the busts women *believed* that men prefer. Men believed that their male peers preferred women with much bustier figures than their peers themselves said they preferred. Ample breast or chest sizes may be preferred by the other gender, but people seem to have an exaggerated idea of the sizes the other gender actually prefers.

Both genders find obese people unattractive, but there are gender differences in impressions of the most pleasing body shape. On the average, college men think that their present physiques are close to ideal and appealing to women (Fallon & Rozin, 1985). College women generally see themselves as much heavier than the figure that is most alluring to men, and heavier still than the figure they perceive as the ideal feminine form. Both genders are wrong about the preferences of the other gender, however. Men actually prefer

Anorexia nervosa
A potentially life-threatening eating disorder characterized by refusal to maintain a healthy body weight, intense fear of being overweight, a distorted body image, and, in females, lack of menstruation (amenorrhea).

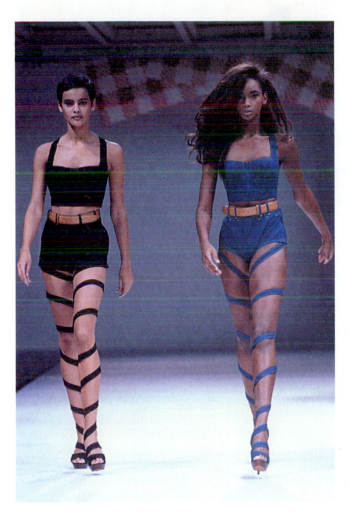

Slim Is In. Pressure to conform to an idealized slender image plays a key role in the development of eating disorders among young women.

women to be somewhat heavier than the women imagine they would. Women prefer their men to be a bit leaner than the men would have expected.

Traits and Perceptions of Attractiveness
Both genders rate the attractiveness of faces higher when they are shown smiling in photographs than when they are shown in a nonsmiling pose (Mueser et al., 1984). (Photographers are not ignorant of this fact.) So there is reason to "put on a happy face" when you meet people socially or ask someone out on a date. Context is important, however. It may be more appropriate in a business context to maintain a more serious countenance. The effects of a smile may also be a greater determinant of attractiveness in women than in men (Deutsch et al., 1987).

Gender-role expectations may affect perceptions of attractiveness. Women who viewed videos of prospective dates found men who acted outgoing and self-expressive more appealing than men who were passive (Riggio & Woll, 1984). Another study found that highly feminine women are more likely to be attracted to dominant "macho" men than less feminine women are (Maybach & Gold, 1994). Yet men who viewed videos in the Riggio and Woll (1984) study were put off by outgoing, self-expressive behavior in women. In yet another study, women rated videos of dominant college men (defined in this study as social control over a troublesome interaction with an instructor) as more appealing than submissive men. Again, male viewers were put off by similarly dominant women (Sadalla et al., 1987). Despite recent changes in traditional gender-role stereotypes, many men in the United States still prefer demure women. This is not to suggest that dominant, self-expressive women should stifle themselves to attract traditional men; the relationships would probably rub them both the wrong way.

WIDE-EYED WITH . . . BEAUTY?

Some aspects of beauty seem to be largely cross-cultural. Research suggests that White people, African Americans, Asian Americans, and Hispanic Americans tend to agree on the facial features that they find to be attractive (Cunningham et al., 1995). They all prefer female faces with large eyes; greater distance between the eyes; small noses; narrower faces with smaller chins; high, expressive eyebrows; larger lower lips; and a well-groomed, full head of hair.

Consider the methodology of a study that compares the facial preferences of people in Japan and England. Perrett (1994) created computer composites of the faces of 60 women. Part A of Figure 6.1 is a composite of the 15 women who were rated the most attractive. He then used computer enhancement to exaggerate the differences between the composite of

the 60—that is, the average face—and the composite of the 15 most attractive women. He found that both Japanese and British men deemed women with large eyes, high cheekbones, and narrow jaws to be the most attractive (Perrett, 1994). Computer enhancement resulted in the image shown in Part B of Figure 6.1. The enhanced composite has still higher cheekbones and a narrower jaw than Part A. Part B was then rated as the most attractive image. Similar results were found for the image of a Japanese woman.

Cunningham and his colleagues (1995) reported historical anecdotes that suggest that the facial preferences of people as diverse as Europeans, Black Africans, Native Americans, Indians (in India, that is), and Chinese are quite consistent. They quoted from Charles Darwin's 1871 treatise, *The*

Descent of Man, and Selection in Relation to Sex:

> Mr. Winwood Reade . . . who has had ample opportunities for observation [with Black Africans] who have never associated with Europeans is convinced that their ideas of beauty are, on the whole, the same as ours; and Dr. Rohlfs writes to me the same effect with respect to Borneo and the countries inhabited by the Pullo tribes. . . . Capt. Burton believes that a woman whom we consider beautiful is admired throughout the world.

Darwin believed that our physical preferences were largely inborn and related to survival of our species. What do you think? Do you believe that "their ideas of beauty are, on the whole, the same as ours"? Or do you think that research hasn't yet ferreted out significant cultural or ethnic differences that might exist? If there is ethnic consistency in these preferences, how would you explain them? For example, do you believe

- that they are coincidental?
- that there has been more exchange of ideas among cultures than has been believed?
- that there is something instinctive about them?

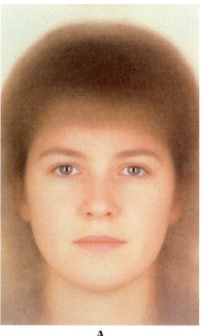

A

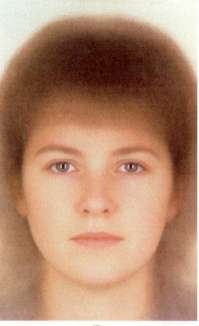

B

Figure 6.1. **What Features Contribute to Facial Attractiveness?** In both England and Japan, features such as large eyes, high cheekbones, and narrow jaws contribute to perceptions of the attractiveness of women. Part A is a computer composite of the faces of 15 women rated as the most attractive of a group of 60. Part B is a computer composite that exaggerates the features of these 15 women. That is, they are developed further in the direction that separates them from the average of the full group.

Names and Perceptions of Attractiveness   Names also may affect perceptions of physical appeal. In one study, women who were randomly assigned names like Kathy, Jennifer, and Christine were rated more attractive than women assigned the names Harriet, Gertrude, and Ethel (Garwood et al., 1980). Seems silly, does it not? After all, our parents name us, and there need be no relationship between our names and our physical appeal. On the other hand, we may choose to keep our names or to use nicknames. So if you are unhappy with your name, why not assume a more popular nickname? Beginning college or a new job is an ideal time for doing so. Men, too, can doff their Sylvesters and Ernests, if they prefer. If you have an unusual name and are content with it, be yourself, however.

What Do You Look for in a Long-Term, Meaningful Relationship?

Your second author conducted a survey of college men and women in the early 1980s and found that psychological characteristics such as warmth, fidelity, honesty, and sensitivity were rated higher in importance than physical attractiveness as desirable qualities in a prospective partner for a meaningful, long-term relationship (Nevid, 1984). Physical attractiveness won out when students were asked to consider the qualities that are most important in a partner for a sexual relationship. Overall, however, men placed greater emphasis on the physical characteristics of their partners for both types of relationships than did women. Women placed more value on qualities such as warmth, assertiveness, wit, and ambition. The single most highly desired quality students wanted in long-term partners was honesty. Honestly.

Although personal qualities may assume more prominent roles in determining partner preferences in long-term relationships, physical appeal probably plays a "filtering" role. Unless a prospective date meets minimal physical standards, we might not look beneath the surface for "more meaningful" traits.

Nevid's results have been replicated in studies on initial attraction and on choice of mates. Women place relatively greater emphasis than men on traits like vocational status, earning potential, expressiveness, kindness, consideration, dependability, and fondness for children. Men give relatively more consideration to youth, physical attractiveness, cooking ability (can't they switch on the microwave by themselves?), and frugality (Howard et al., 1987; Sprecher et al., 1994). When it comes to mate selection, females in a sample of students from Germany and the Netherlands also emphasized the financial prospects and status of a potential mate, whereas males emphasized the importance of physical attractiveness (de Raad & Doddema-Winsemius, 1992). A study of more than 200 Korean college students found that in mate selection, women placed relatively more emphasis on education, jobs, and family of origin than men did (Brown, 1994). Men placed relatively more emphasis on physical attractiveness and affection. (Yes, men were more "romantic." Women were more pragmatic.)

Susan Sprecher and her colleagues (1994) surveyed a national probability sample of 13,017 English- or Spanish-speaking people, age 19 or above, living in households in the United States. In one section of their questionnaire, they asked respondents how willing they would be to marry someone who was older, younger, of a different religion, not likely to hold a steady job, not good-looking, and so forth. Each item was followed by a 7-point scale in which 1 meant "not at all" and 7 meant "very willing." As shown in Table 6.1 on page 140, women were more willing than men to marry someone who was not good-looking. On the other hand, women were less willing to marry someone not likely to hold a steady job.

Are Attractiveness Preferences Inherited?

On the surface, gender differences in perceptions of attractiveness seem unbearably sexist—and perhaps they are. Yet some sociobiologists believe that evolutionary forces favor the continuation of gender differences in preferences for mates because certain preferred traits provide reproductive advantages (Bjorklund & Kipp, 1996). Some physical features, like cleanliness, good complexion, clear eyes, good teeth, good hair, firm muscle tone, and a steady gait are universally appealing to both genders (Ford & Beach, 1951). Perhaps they are markers of reproductive potential (Symons, 1995). Age and health may be relatively more important to

TABLE 6.1 Gender differences in mate preferences

How willing would you be to marry someone who ...	Men	Women
• was not "good-looking"?	3.41	4.42†
• was older than you by 5 or more years?	4.15	5.29†
• was younger than you by 5 or more years?	4.54	2.80†
• was not likely to hold a steady job?	2.73	1.62†
• would earn much less than you?	4.60	3.76†
• would earn much more than you?	5.19	5.93†
• had more education than you?	5.22	5.82†
• had less education than you?	4.67	4.08†
• had been married before?	3.35	3.44
• already had children?	2.84	3.11*
• was of a different religion?	4.24	4.31
• was of a different race?	3.08	2.84†

Based on a 7 point scale where 1 = not at all, and 7 = very willing.
*Difference statistically significant at the .01 level of confidence.
†Difference statistically significant at the .001 level of confidence.

Source: Based on information in Susan Sprecher, Quintin Sullivan, & Elaine Hatfield (1994). Mate Selection Preferences: Gender Differences Examined in a National Sample. *Journal of Personality and Social Psychology, 66* (6), 1074–1080.

a woman's appeal, since these characteristics tend to be associated with her reproductive capacity: the "biological clock" limits her reproductive potential. Physical characteristics associated with a woman's youthfulness, such as smooth skin, firm muscle tone, and lustrous hair, may thus have become more closely linked to a woman's appeal (Buss, 1994). A man's reproductive value, however, may depend more on how well he can provide for his family than on his age or physical appeal. The value of men as reproducers, therefore, is more intertwined with factors that contribute to a stable environment for child rearing—such as economic status and reliability. Sociobiologists argue that these gender differences in mate preferences may have been passed down through the generations as part of our genetic heritage (Buss, 1994; Symons, 1995).

Men's interest in younger women is apparently universal. It occurs in both preliterate and industrialized societies (Buss, 1994; Symons, 1979). Female jealousy of younger women is another thread that spans cultures. Sexual competition, according to Margaret Mead, generally involves

> the struggle between stronger older men and weaker younger men or between more attractive younger women and more entrenched older ones.
>
> (Mead, 1967, p. 198)

Sociobiological views of gender differences in mate preferences are largely speculative and not fully consistent with the evidence. Despite gender differences, both men and women report that they place greater weight on personal characteristics than on physical features in judging prospective mates (Buss, 1994). Many women, like men, still prefer physically appealing partners (Bixler, 1989). Women also tend to marry men similar to themselves in physical attractiveness as well as socioeconomic standing. Note also that older men are more likely than younger men to die from natural causes. From the standpoint of reproductive advantages, women would thus achieve greater success by marrying fit, younger males who are likely to survive during the child-rearing years than by marrying older, higher-status males. Moreover, similar cultural influences, rather than inherited dispositions, may ex-

A WORLD OF DIVERSITY

GENDER DIFFERENCES IN PREFERENCES IN MATES ACROSS 37 CULTURES

What do men in Nigeria, Japan, Brazil, Canada, and the United States have in common? For one thing, men in these countries report that they prefer mates who are younger than themselves. Buss (1994) reviewed survey evidence on the preferred age difference between one-self and one's mate in 37 cultures (representing 33 countries) in Europe, Africa, Asia, Australia, New Zealand, and North and South America. Women, however, preferred older mates (the range was from 1.82 years to 5.1 years).

Gender differences in the preferred age of mates paralleled actual differences in age of men and women at the time of marriage. Men were between two and five years older on the average than their brides at the time of marriage. The smallest age difference at marriage, 2.1 years, was found in

Poland. The largest difference, 4.92 years, was found in Greece. Men in the mainland United States are 2.71 years older than women at the time of marriage. In Canada, men are 2.51 years older than their mates, on the average.

Buss finds that in all 37 cultures, men placed greater value on a prospective partner's "good looks" than did women. On the other hand, women in 36 of 37 cultures placed greater value on "good earning capacity" of prospective mates.

The consistency of Buss's findings lends credence to the notion that there are widespread gender differences in preferences with respect to age, physical characteristics, and financial status of prospective mates. Generally speaking, men across cultures place greater value on the physical attractiveness and relative youth of prospective

mates, whereas women place relatively greater value on the earning capacity of prospective mates. Buss interprets women's preferences for relatively older mates as additional evidence that women appraise future mates on the basis of their ability to provide for a wife and family, since age and income tend to be linked among men.

Despite these gender differences in preferences for mates, Buss finds that both men and women placed greater weight on personal qualities than on looks or income potential of prospective mates. In *all* 37 cultures, the characteristics "kind, understanding" and "intelligent" were rated higher than earning power or physical attractiveness.

plain commonalities across cultures in gender differences in mate preferences. For example, in societies in which women are economically dependent on men, a man's appeal may depend more on his financial resources than on his physical appeal.

The Matching Hypothesis: Who Is "Right" for You?

Matching hypothesis
The concept that people tend to develop romantic relationships with people who are similar to themselves in attractiveness.

Do not despair if you are less than exquisite in appearance, along with most of us mere mortals. You may be saved from permanently blending in with the wallpaper by the effects of the **matching hypothesis.** This concept holds that people tend to develop romantic relationships with people who are similar to themselves in physical attractiveness rather than the local Denzel Washington or Cindy Crawford look-alike.

Researchers have found that people who are dating steadily, engaged, or married tend to be matched in physical attractiveness (Kalick, 1988). Young married couples even tend to be matched in weight (Schafer & Keith, 1990). The central motive for seeking "matches" seems to be fear of rejection by more appealing people (Bernstein et al., 1983).

There are exceptions to the matching hypothesis. Now and then we find a beautiful woman married to a plain or ugly man (or vice versa). How do we explain it? What, after all, would *she* see in *him?* According to one study (Bar-Tal & Saxe, 1976), people judging "mismatched" pairs may tend to ascribe wealth, intelligence, or success to the man. We seek an unseen factor that will balance the physical attractiveness of one partner. For some "mismatched" couples, similarities in attitudes and personalities may balance out differences in physical attractiveness.

More Than Beauty   Matching applies not only to physical appeal. Our sex and marital partners tend to be like us in race and ethnicity, age, level of education, and religion. Consider some findings of the NHSLS study (Michael et al., 1994, pp. 45–47):

- The sex partners of nearly 94% of unmarried White men are White women. About 2% of single White men are partnered with Hispanic American women, 2% with Asian American women, and less than 1% with African American women.
- The sex partners of nearly 82% of African American men are African American women. Nearly 8% of African American men are partnered with White women. Under 5% are partnered with Hispanic American women.
- About 83% of the women and men in the study chose partners within 5 years of their own age and of the same or a similar religion.
- Of all the women in the study, *not one* with a graduate college degree had a partner who had not finished high school.
- Men with a college degree almost never had sexual relationships with women with much more or much less education than they had.

Similarity in Attitudes: Do Opposites Attract?

Why do the great majority of us have partners from our own backgrounds? One reason is that marriages are made in the neighborhood and not in heaven (Michael et al., 1994). That is, we tend to live among people who are similar to us in background, and thus come into contact with them. Another is that we are drawn to people who are similar in their attitudes. People similar in background are more likely to be similar in their attitudes. Similarity in attitudes and tastes is a key contributor to attraction, friendships, and love relationships (Cappella & Palmer, 1990; Griffin & Sparks, 1990; Laumann et al., 1994).

Let us also note a gender difference. Evidence shows that women place greater weight on attitude similarity as a determinant of attraction to a stranger of the other gender than do men, whereas men place more value on physical attractiveness (Feingold, 1991).

We also tend to *assume* that people we find attractive share our attitudes (Dawes, 1989; Marks et al., 1981). The physical attraction between Candy and Stretch motivated them to pretend that their preferences, tastes, and opinions coincided. They entered into a nonspoken agreement not to discuss their religious differences. When sexual attraction is strong,

Who Is Right for You? Research shows that people tend to pair off with others who are similar in physical characteristics and personality traits.

perhaps we want to think that the kinks in the relationship will be small or that we can iron them out. Let us also note that though similarity may be important in determining initial attraction, compatibility appears to be an even stronger determinant of maintaining an enduring intimate relationship (Vinacke et al., 1988).

Reciprocity: If You Like Me, You Must Have Excellent Judgment

Has anyone told you that you are good-looking, brilliant, and emotionally mature to boot? That your taste is elegant? Ah, what superb judgment!

When we feel admired and complimented, we tend to return these feelings and behaviors. This is called **reciprocity.** Reciprocity is a potent determinant of attraction (Condon & Crano, 1988). We tend to be much more warm, helpful, and candid when we are with strangers whom we believe like us (Clark et al., 1989; Curtis & Miller, 1986). We even tend to welcome positive comments from others when we know them to be inaccurate (Swann et al., 1987).

Perhaps the power of reciprocity has enabled many couples to become happy with one another and reasonably well adjusted. By reciprocating positive words and actions, a person can perhaps stoke neutral or mild feelings into robust, affirmative feelings of attraction.

Attraction can lead to feelings of love. Let us now turn to that most fascinating topic.

Reciprocity
Mutual exchange.

Love

For thousands of years, poets have sought to capture love in words. A seventeenth-century poet wrote that his love was like "a red, red rose." In Sinclair Lewis's novel *Elmer Gantry,* love is "the morning and the evening star." Love is beautiful and elusive. It shines, brilliant and heavenly. Passion and romantic love are also earthy and sexy, brimming with sexual desire.

Romantic love is hardly unique to our culture. Researchers report finding evidence of romantic love in 147 of the 166 different cultures they studied in a recent cross-cultural comparison (Jankowiak & Fischer, 1992). Romantic love occurs even in most preliterate societies. The absence of romantic love in the remaining 19 cultures, the investigators suspect, was most probably due to the limitations of their study methods (Gelman, 1993).

Our culture idealizes the concept of romantic love. Thus we readily identify with the plight of the "star-crossed" lovers in *Romeo and Juliet* and *West Side Story,* who sacrificed for love. We learn that "love makes the world go round" and that "love is everything." Virtually all of the participants in the Janus and Janus nationwide survey (96% of the men and 98% of the women) reported that love is important to them (Janus & Janus, 1993). Like other aspects of sexual and social behavior among humans, the concept of love must be understood within a cultural context. Luckily (or miserably), we have such a context in Western culture. . . .

The Greek Heritage

The concept of love can be traced back at least as far as the classical age of Greece. The Greeks distinguished four concepts related to the modern meanings of love: *storge, agape, philia,* and *eros.*

Storge is loving attachment, deep friendship, or nonsexual affection. It is the emotion that binds friends and parents and children. Some scholars believe that even romantic love is a form of attachment that is similar to the types of attachments infants have to their mothers (Hazan & Shaver, 1987).

Agape is similar to generosity and charity. It implies the wish to share one's bounty, and is epitomized by anonymous donations of money. In relationships, it is characterized by selfless giving (Lee, 1988). Agape, according to Lee's research, is the kind of love least frequently found between adults in committed relationships.

Storge
(STORE-gay) Loving attachment and nonsexual affection; the type of emotion that binds parents to children.

Agape
(AH-gah-pay) Selfless love; a kind of loving that is similar to generosity and charity.

Philia

(FEEL-yuh) Friendship love, which is based on liking and respect rather than sexual desire.

Eros

The kind of love that is closest in meaning to the modern-day concept of passion.

Philia is closest in meaning to friendship. It is based on liking and respect, rather than sexual desire. It involves the desire to do and enjoy things with the other person, and to see him or her when one is lonely or bored.

Eros is closest in meaning to our concept of passion. Eros was a character in Greek mythology (transformed in Roman mythology into Cupido, now called Cupid) who would shoot unsuspecting people with his love arrows, causing them to fall madly in love with the person who was nearest to them at the time. Erotic love embraces sudden passionate desire: "love at first sight" and "falling head over heels in love." Passion can be so gripping that one is convinced that life has been changed forever. This feeling of sudden transformation was captured by the Italian poet Dante Alighieri (1265–1321), who exclaimed upon first beholding his beloved Beatrice, *"Incipit vita nuova,"* which can be translated as "My life begins anew." Romantic love can also be earthy and sexy. In fact, sexual arousal and desire may be the strongest component of passionate or romantic love (Berscheid, 1988). Romantic love begins with a powerful physical attraction or feelings of passion, and is associated with strong physiological arousal (Lee, 1988).

Unlike the Greeks, we tend to use the word *love* to describe everything from feelings of affection toward another to romantic ardor to sexual intercourse ("making love"). Still, different types or styles of love are recognized in our own culture, as we shall see.

Romantic Love in Contemporary Western Culture

The experience of *romantic love*, as opposed to loving attachment or sexual arousal per se, occurs within a cultural context in which the concept is idealized. Western culture has a long tradition of idealizing the concept of romantic love, as represented, for instance, by romantic fairy tales that have been passed down through the generations. In fact, our exposure to the concept of romantic love may begin with hearing the fairy tales of Sleeping Beauty, Cinderella, and Snow White—along with their princes charming. Later perhaps, the concept of romantic love blossoms with exposure to romantic novels, television and film scripts, and the heady tales of friends and relatives.

During adolescence, strong sexual arousal along with an idealized image of the object of our desires leads us to label our feelings as love. We may learn to speak of "love" rather than "lust," because sexual desire in the absence of a committed relationship might be viewed as primitive or animalistic. Being "in love" ennobles attraction and sexual arousal, not only to society but also to oneself. Unlike lust, love can even be discussed at the dinner table. If others think we are too young to experience "the real thing"—which presumably includes knowledge of and respect for the other person's personality traits—our feelings may be called "puppy love" or a "crush."

Western society maintains much of the double standard toward sexuality. Thus, women are more often expected to justify sexual experiences as involving someone they love. Young men usually need not attribute sexual urges to love. So men are more apt to deem love a "mushy" concept. The vast majority of people in the United States nonetheless believe romantic love is a prerequisite for marriage. Romantic love is rated by young people as the single most important reason for marriage (Roper Organization, 1985). Over 80% of college men and women subscribe to the belief that "being in love" is a precondition for marriage (Berscheid, 1988; Simpson et al., 1986). More than half also believe that falling out of love justifies divorce.

Which is the more romantic gender? Although the question may well incite an argument in mixed company, the Janus and Janus (1993) nationwide survey of adult Americans found that a slightly greater percentage of the single men (82%) perceived themselves as being romantic than did single women (77%). Yet among married people, the figures were reversed, with 79% of the women describing themselves as romantic as compared to 72% of the men. Perhaps there is some truth to the stereotype that men are more romantic during the courtship stage of relationships than the marriage stage. Then again, maybe self-perceptions of being romantic don't quite jibe with the reality.

When reciprocated, romantic love is usually a source of deep fulfillment and ecstasy (Hatfield, 1988). How wonderful when love meets its match. When love is unrequited, however, it can lead to emptiness, anxiety, or despair. Romantic love can thus teeter between states of ecstasy and misery (Hatfield, 1988). Perhaps no other feature of our lives can lift us up as high or plunge us as low as romantic love.

Infatuation Versus "True Love": Will Time Tell?   Perhaps you first noticed each other when your eyes met across a crowded room, like the star-crossed lovers in *West Side Story*. Or perhaps you met when you were both assigned to the same Bunsen burner in chemistry lab—less romantic, but closer to the flame. However it happened, the meeting triggered such an electric charge through your body that you could not get him (or her) out of your mind. Were you truly in love, however, or was it merely a passing fancy? Was it infatuation or the "real thing"—a "true," lasting, and mutual love? How do you tell them apart?

Perhaps you don't, at least not at first. **Infatuation** is a state of intense absorption in or focus on another person. It is usually accompanied by sexual desire, elation, and general physiological arousal or excitement. Some refer to passion as infatuation. Others dub it a "crush." Both monickers suggest that it is a passing fancy. In infatuation, your heart may pound whenever the other person draws near or enters your fantasies.

For the first month or two, infatuation and the more enduring forms of romantic love are essentially indistinguishable (Gordon & Snyder, 1989). At first, both may be characterized by intense focusing or absorption. Infatuated people may become so absorbed that they cannot sleep, work, or carry out routine chores. Logic and reason are swept aside. Infatuated people hold idealized images of their love objects and overlook their faults. Caution may be cast to the winds. In some cases, couples in the throes of infatuation rush to get married, only to find a few weeks or months later that they are not well suited.

As time goes on, signs that distinguish infatuation from a lasting romantic love begin to emerge. The partners begin to view each other more realistically and determine whether or not the relationship should continue.

Infatuation has been likened to a state of passionate love (Sternberg, 1986) that is based on intense feelings of passion but not on the deeper feelings of attachment and caring that typify a more lasting mutual love. Although infatuation may be a passing fancy, it can be supplanted by the deeper feelings of attachment and caring that characterize more lasting love relationships.

Note, too, that infatuation is not a necessary first step on the path to a lasting mutual love. Some couples develop deep feelings of love without ever experiencing the fireworks of infatuation (Sternberg, 1986). Or sometimes one partner is infatuated while the other manages to keep his or her head below the clouds.

Contemporary Models of Love: Dare Science Intrude?

Despite the importance of love, scientists have historically paid little attention to it. Some people believe that love cannot be analyzed scientifically. Love, they maintain, should be left to the poets, philosophers, and theologians. Yet researchers are now applying the scientific method to the study of love. They recognize that love is a complex concept, involving many areas of experience—emotional, cognitive, and motivational (Sternberg & Grajck, 1984). They have reinforced the Greek view that there are different kinds and styles of love. Let us consider some of the views of love that have emerged from modern theorists and researchers.

Love as Appraisal of Arousal   Social psychologists Ellen Berscheid and Elaine Hatfield (Berscheid & Walster, 1978; Walster & Walster, 1978) define **romantic love** in terms of a state of intense physiological arousal and the cognitive appraisal of that arousal as love. The physiological arousal may be experienced as a pounding heart, sweaty palms, and butterflies in the stomach when one is in the presence of or thinking about one's love

---

Infatuation

A state of intense absorption in or focus on another person, which is usually accompanied by sexual desire, elation, and general physiological arousal or excitement; passion.

Romantic love

A kind of love characterized by feelings of passion and intimacy.

interest. Cognitive appraisal of the arousal means attributing it to some cause, such as fear or love. The perception that one has fallen in love is thus derived from several simultaneous events: (1) a state of intense physiological arousal that is connected with an appropriate love object (that is, a person, not an event like a rock concert), (2) a cultural setting that idealizes romantic love, and (3) the attribution of the arousal to feelings of love toward the person.

Styles of Love   Some psychologists speak in terms of *styles* of love. Clyde and Susan Hendrick (1986) developed a love attitude scale that suggests the existence of six styles of love among college students. The following is a list of the styles. Each one is exemplified by statements similar to those on the original scale. As you can see, the styles owe a debt to the Greeks:

1. *Romantic love (eros):* "My lover fits my ideal." "My lover and I were attracted to one another immediately."
2. *Game-playing love (ludus):* "I keep my lover up in the air about my commitment." "I get over love affairs pretty easily."
3. *Friendship (storge, philia):* "The best love grows out of an enduring friendship."
4. *Logical love (pragma):* "I consider a lover's potential in life before committing myself." "I consider whether my lover will be a good parent."
5. *Possessive, excited love (mania):* "I get so excited about my love that I cannot sleep." "When my lover ignores me, I get sick all over."
6. *Selfless love (agape):* "I would do anything I can to help my lover." "My lover's needs and wishes are more important than my own."

Most people who are "in love" experience a number of these styles, but the Hendricks (1986) found some interesting gender differences in styles of love. College men are significantly more likely to develop game-playing and romantic love styles. College women are more apt to develop friendly, logical, and possessive love styles. (There were no gender differences in selfless love.) The Hendricks and their colleagues (1988) have also found that romantically involved couples tend to experience the same kinds of love styles. They also showed that couples with romantic and selfless styles of love are more likely to remain together. A game-playing love style leads to unhappiness, however, and is one reason that relationships come to an end.

Sternberg's Triangular Theory of Love   Psychologist Robert Sternberg (1986, 1987, 1988) offers a triangular theory of love. In his view there are three distinct components of love:

1. *Intimacy:* the experience of warmth toward another person that arises from feelings of closeness, bondedness, and connectedness to the other. Intimacy also involves the desire to give and receive emotional support and to share one's innermost thoughts with the other.
2. *Passion:* an intense romantic or sexual desire for another person, which is accompanied by physiological arousal.
3. *Decision/commitment:* a component of love that involves both short-term and long-term issues. In the short term there is the issue of deciding that one loves the other person. In the long term there is the issue of one's willingness to make a *commitment* to maintain the relationship through good times and bad. Decision and commitment need not go hand in hand. Although decision generally precedes commitment, some people become committed to a relationship before they even decide whether they love the other person. Others, however, never make a lasting commitment or openly acknowledge loving the other person.

According to Sternberg's model, love can be conceptualized in terms of a triangle in which each vertex represents one of these basic elements of love (see Figure 6.2). The way the components are balanced can be represented by the shape of the triangle. For example, a love in which all three components were equally balanced would be represented by an equilateral triangle, as in Figure 6.2.

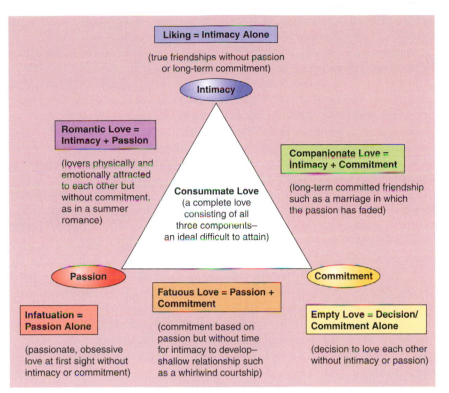

Figure 6.2. The Triangular Model of Love. According to psychologist Robert Sternberg, love consists of three components, as shown by the vertices of this triangle. Various kinds of love consist of different combinations of these components. Romantic love, for example, consists of passion and intimacy. Consummate love—a state devoutly to be desired—consists of all three.

Sternberg believes that couples are well matched if they possess corresponding levels of passion, intimacy, and commitment. Compatibility can be represented visually in terms of the congruence of the love triangles. Figure 6.3(A) on page 148 shows a perfect match, in which the triangles are congruent. Figure 6.3(B) depicts a good match; the partners are similar in the three dimensions. Figure 6.3(C) shows a mismatch; major differences exist between the partners on all three components. Relationships may run aground when partners are mismatched. A relationship may fizzle, rather than sizzle, when one partner experiences more passion than the other, or when one wants a long-term commitment when the other's idea of commitment is to stay the night.

According to the Sternberg model, various combinations of the three elements of love characterize different types of love relationships (Sternberg, 1986, 1988) (see Figure 6.3 and Table 6.2 on page 148). For example, *infatuation* (passionate love) is typified by strong sexual desire, but not by intimacy and commitment. The partners may each feel passionate love for the other, or such feelings may go unrequited.

Liking is very much like friendship. It consists of feelings of closeness and emotional warmth without passion or decision/commitment. Liking is not felt toward passing acquaintances. It is reserved for people to whom one feels close enough to share one's innermost feelings and thoughts. We sometimes develop these intimate relationships without making the commitment to maintaining a long-term relationship that typifies other types of love, however. Liking may develop into a passionate love, however, or into a more committed form of friendship (called *companionate love* in Sternberg's model).

Should lovers also be friends, or are lovers and friends part of the twain that never meet? Candy and Stretch's relationship lacked the quality most often associated with true friendship: the willingness to share confidences. Despite their physical intimacy, their relationship remained so superficial that they couldn't even share information about their religious backgrounds.

Candy and Stretch were "in love" although they were far from friends. Friendship and passionate love do not necessarily overlap. There is nothing that prevents people in love from becoming good friends, however—perhaps even the best of friends. Sternberg's model recognizes that the intimacy we find in true friendships and the passion we find in

A

Intimacy

Self   Other

Passion   Decision/Commitment

Perfectly matched involvements

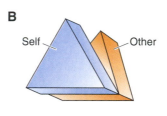

B

Self   Other

Closely matched involvements

C

Other   Self

Severely mismatched involvements

Figure 6.3. Compatibility and Incompatibility, According to the Triangular Model of Love. Compatibility in terms of Sternberg's types of love can be represented as triangles. Part A shows a perfect match, in which triangles are congruent. Part B depicts a good match; the partners are similar according to the three dimensions. Part C shows a mismatch. Major differences exist between the partners on all three components.

love are blended in two forms of love—romantic love and consummate love. These love types differ along the dimension of decision/commitment, however.

Romantic love has both passion and intimacy but lacks commitment. Romantic love may burn brightly and then flicker out. Or it may develop into a more complete love, called *consummate love,* in which all three components flower. Desire is accompanied by a deeper intimacy and commitment. The flames of passion can be stoked across the years, even if they do not burn quite as brightly as they once did. Consummate love is most special, and certainly an ideal toward which many Westerners strive. In *empty love,* by contrast, there is nought but commitment. Neither the warm emotional embrace of intimacy nor the flame of passion exists. With empty love, one's lover is a person whom one tolerates and remains with because of a sense of duty.

Sometimes a love relationship has both passion and commitment but lacks intimacy. Sternberg calls this *fatuous (foolish) love.* Fatuous love is associated with whirlwind courtships that burn brightly but briefly as the partners come to the realization that they are not well matched. Intimacy can develop in such relationships, but couples who rush into marriage often find that the realities of marriage give the lie to their expectations.

In *companionate love,* finally, intimacy and commitment are strong, but passion is lacking. This form of love typifies long-term (so-called Platonic) friendships and marriages in which passion has ebbed but a deep and abiding friendship remains.

Although romantic love may become transformed into companionate love, the process by which this transformation takes place remains vague (Shaver et al., 1988). Companionate love need not be sexless or lacking in romance, however. Although passion may have ebbed, the giving and receiving of sexual pleasure can help strengthen bonds.

TABLE 6.2   Types of love according to Sternberg's triangular model

1. Nonlove	A relationship in which all three components of love are absent. Most of our personal relationships are of this type—casual interactions or acquaintances that do not involve any elements of love.
2. Liking	A loving experience with another person or friendship in which intimacy is present but passion and commitment are lacking.
3. Infatuation	A kind of "love at first sight" in which one experiences passionate desires for another person in the absence of both intimacy and decision/commitment components of love.
4. Empty love	A kind of love characterized by the decision (to love) and the commitment (to maintain the relationship) in the absence of either passion or intimacy. Stagnant relationships that no longer involve the emotional intimacy or physical attraction that once characterized them are of this type.
5. Romantic love	A loving experience characterized by the combination of passion and intimacy, but without decision/commitment components of love.
6. Companionate love	A kind of love that derives from the combination of intimacy and decision/commitment components of love. This kind of love often occurs in marriages in which passionate attraction between the partners has died down and has been replaced by a kind of committed friendship.
7. Fatuous love	The type of love associated with whirlwind romances and "quicky marriages" in which the passion and decision/commitment components of love are present, but intimacy is not.
8. Consummate love	The full or complete measure of love involving the combination of passion, intimacy, and decision/commitment. Many of us strive to attain this type of complete love in our romantic relationships. Maintaining it is often harder than achieving it.

Source: Adapted from Sternberg, 1988.

Consummate Love. According to Sternberg, romantic love may develop into a more complete love, called consummate love, in which desire is accompanied by deep intimacy and commitment. Consummate love is the special ideal toward which many Westerners strive.

Partners may feel that their sex lives have even become more deeply satisfying as they seek to please each other by practicing what they have learned about each other's sexual needs and wants.

The balance among Sternberg's three aspects of love is likely to shift through the course of a relationship. A healthful dose of all three components—found in consummate love—typifies, for many of us, an ideal marriage. At the outset of marriage, passions may be strong but intimacy weak. Couples may only first be getting to know each other's innermost thoughts and feelings. Time alone does not cause intimacy and commitment to grow, however. Some couples are able to peer into each other's deeper selves and form meaningful commitments at relatively early stages in their relationships. Yet some long-married couples may remain distant or waver in their commitment. Some couples experience only a faint flickering of passion early in the relationship. Then it becomes quickly extinguished. For some the flames of passion burn ever brightly. Yet many married couples find that passion tends to fade while intimacy and commitment grow stronger.

Knowing about these components of love may help couples avoid pitfalls. Couples who recognize that passion exerts a strong pull early in a relationship may be less likely to let passion rush them into marriage. Couples who recognize that it is normal for passions to fade may avoid assuming that their love is at an end when it may, in fact, be changing into a deeper, more intimate and committed form of love. This knowledge may also encourage couples to focus on finding ways of rekindling the embers of romance, rather than looking to escape at the first signs that the embers have cooled.

Researchers have tested some facets of the triangular model. One study reported mixed results. As the model would predict, married adults reported higher levels of commitment to their relationships than did unmarried adults (Acker & Davis, 1992). Yet the expected decline in passion over time was found only for women. Critics contend that Sternberg's model does not account for all the nuances and complexities of love (Murstein, 1988). The model tells us little, for example, about the *goals* of love or the *sources* of love. In fairness, Sternberg's model is a major contribution to the scientific study of love, which is only now beginning. Poets, philosophers, and theologians, by comparison, have been writing about love for millennia.

In this chapter we have discussed interpersonal attraction—the force that initiates social contact. In the next chapter we follow the development of social contacts into intimate relationships.

A P P L I C A T I O N S

COPING WITH LONELINESS

In this chapter we have explored feelings of attraction and love. Unfortunately, many people do not experience these feelings. Or, if they do, the feelings are not reciprocated. As a result, many people are lonely.

The causes of loneliness are many and complex. Lonely people tend to have several of the following characteristics:

1. *Lack of social skills.* Lonely people often lack the interpersonal skills needed to make friends or to cope with disagreements.
2. *Lack of interest in other people.*
3. *Lack of empathy.*
4. *Fear of rejection.* This fear is often connected with self-criticism of social skills and expectations of failure in relating to others (Schultz & Moore, 1984).
5. *Failure to disclose personal information to potential friends* (Solano et al., 1982).
6. *Cynicism about human nature* (e.g., seeing people as only out for themselves).
7. *Demanding too much too soon.* They perceive other people as cold and unfriendly in the early stages of a relationship.
8. *General pessimism.* When we expect the worst, we often get . . . you guessed it.
9. *An external locus of control.* That is, they do not see themselves as capable of taking their lives into their own hands and achieving their goals.

Psychologists have helped people cope with loneliness by fostering more adaptive ways of thinking and behaving. Lonely people often have distorted views of other people. They may have one or two unfortunate experiences and jump to the conclusion that people are generally selfish and not worth the effort of getting involved. Let's face it: some people *are* basically out for themselves, but the expectation that everyone is can perpetuate loneliness by motivating avoidance of social activities.

What can you do to deal with loneliness in your own life? We are all different, and the methods that might help one person may not aid another. But here is a list of suggestions (Rathus & Fichner-Rathus, 1994):

1. *Challenge your feelings of pessimism.* Adopt the attitude that things happen when you make them happen.
2. *Challenge your cynicism about human nature.* Yes, lots of people are selfish and not worth knowing, but if you assume that all people are like that, you can doom yourself to a lifetime of loneliness. Your task is to find people who possess the qualities that you value.
3. *Challenge the idea that failure in social relationships is awful and is thus a valid reason for giving up on them.* Sure, social rejection can be painful, but unless you happen to be Harrison Ford or Julia Roberts, you may not appeal to everyone. We must all learn to live with some rejection. But keep looking for the people who possess the qualities you value and who will find things of equal value in you.
4. *Follow the suggestions for improving your date-seeking skills spelled out in the Applications in Chapter 7.* Sit down at a table with people in the cafeteria, not off in a corner by yourself. Smile and say hi to people who interest you. Practice opening lines for different occasions—and a few follow-up lines. Try them out in the mirror.
5. *Make numerous social contacts.* Join committees for student activities. Try intramural sports. Join social-action groups, such as environmental groups and community betterment groups. Join clubs, such as the photography club or the ski club. Get on the school yearbook or newspaper staff.
6. *Be assertive.* Express your genuine opinions.
7. *Become a good listener.* Ask people how they're doing. Ask them for their opinions about classes, politics, the campus events of the day. Then actually *listen* to what they have to say. Tolerate diverse opinions; remember that no two of us are identical in our outlooks. Maintain eye contact. Keep your face friendly. (No, you don't have to remain neutral and friendly if someone becomes insulting toward a religious or ethnic group.)
8. *Give people the chance to know you.* Exchange opinions and talk about your interests. Yes, you'll turn some people off—who doesn't?—but how else will you learn whether you and another person share common ground?
9. *Fight fair.* Friends will inevitably disappoint you, and you'll want to tell them about it. Do so, but fairly. You can start by asking if it's okay to be open about something. Then say, "I feel upset because you . . ." You can ask your friend if he or she realized that his or her behavior upset you. Try to work together to find a way to avoid recurrences. Finish by thanking your friend for helping you resolve the problem.
10. *Remember that you're worthy of friends.* It's true—warts and all. None of us is perfect. We're all unique, but you may connect with more people than you imagine. Give people a chance.
11. *Use your college counseling center.* Many thousands of students are lonely but don't know what to do about it. Others just cannot find the courage to approach others. College counseling centers are very familiar with the problem of loneliness, and you should consider them a valuable resource. You might even ask if there's a group at the center for students seeking to improve their dating or social skills.

Chapter Review

Attraction

Research shows that (1) _____ical attractiveness is a major determinant of interpersonal and sexual attraction. (2) Cross-_____ studies show that people universally want physically appealing partners. However, what is considered attractive in one culture (3: Is *or* May not be?) attractive in another.

In our culture, (4: Shorter *or* Taller?) men are considered to be more attractive by women. Female plumpness (5: Is *or* Is not?) valued in many preliterate societies. In our culture, female (6: Slenderness *or* Plumpness?) is in style. The (7) _____ glass figure is idealized in the United States. Women's ideas of the ideal bust size are (8: Larger *or* Smaller?) than their actual average size. Men prefer women with (9: Larger *or* Smaller?) busts than women consider ideal. (10: Men, Women, *or* Men and women?) find obese people unattractive. Most college men (11: Do *or* Do not?) think that their present physiques are close to ideal and appeal to women. Most college women see themselves as (12: Lighter *or* Heavier?) than the most alluring figure. Men prefer women to be somewhat (13: Lighter *or* Heavier?) than the women imagine they would. Women prefer their men to be (14: Lighter *or* Heavier?) than the men expect.

People rate others as (15: More *or* Less?) attractive when they are smiling. Women find men who act outgoing and self-expressive to be (16: More *or* Less?) appealing than passive men. Most men appear (17: To be *or* Not to be?) attracted to outgoing, self-expressive women. Women with popular names such as Jennifer and Christine (18: Are *or* Are not?) rated as more attractive than women with names such as Harriet and Ethel.

Nevid surveyed college students and found that psychological characteristics such as warmth, fidelity, honesty, and sensitivity were rated as (19: More *or* Less?) important than physical attractiveness in a partner for a meaningful, long-term relationship. Physical attractiveness (20: Is *or* Is not?) considered relatively more important in a partner for a sexual relationship. Overall, (21: Men *or*

Women?) place greater emphasis on the physical traits of their partners. The single most highly desired trait students wanted in long-term partners was (22) h_____.

In choice of mates, men place (23: Greater *or* Less?) emphasis than the other gender on traits like vocational status, earning potential, expressiveness, kindness, consideration, dependability, and fondness for children. (24: Men *or* Women?) place more emphasis on youth, physical attractiveness, and cooking ability.

Susan Sprecher and her colleagues found that (25: Men *or* Women?) were more willing to marry someone who was not good-looking. (26: Men *or* Women?) were less willing to marry someone who was not likely to hold a steady job.

Buss's study of 37 cultures finds that most men prefer mates who are (27: Younger *or* Older?) than themselves. Buss also found that (28: Men *or* Women?) placed more value on a partner's "good looks." (29: Men *or* Women?) in 36 of 37 cultures placed greater value on "good earning capacity" of prospective mates. Some (30) _____logists believe that evolutionary forces favor the continuation of gender differences in preferences for mates because they provide reproductive advantages.

The (31) _____ing hypothesis holds that people tend to develop romantic relationships with people who are similar to themselves in physical attractiveness. Researchers find that people in prolonged relationships tend to be (32: Similar *or* Dissimilar?) in physical attractiveness and weight. The key motive for seeking "matches" seems to be fear of (33) _____tion by more appealing people. In the United States, the sex partners of (34: Less than *or* More than?) 90% of unmarried White men are White women. People with college degrees usually (35: Do *or* Do not?) choose sex partners with college educations.

Similarity in attitudes and tastes (36: Is *or* Is not?) a key contributor to attraction, friendships, and love relationships. (37: Men *or* Women?) place greater weight on attitude similarity as a determinant of attraction to a stranger than does the other gender. People also tend to assume that the people they find to be attractive share their (38) _____ udes.

(39) _____ city is the tendency to return feelings of admiration and liking.

Love

Romantic love (40: Is _or_ Is not?) unique to Western culture. (41: More _or_ Less?) than 80% of the participants in the Janus and Janus survey reported that love is important to them.

The ancient Greeks distinguished four concepts related to the modern meanings of love: (42) st_____, agape, philia, and (43) er_____. (44) _____ ge is the emotion that binds friends and parents and children. (45) _____ pe is similar to generosity and charity. Philia is closest in meaning to (46) _____ ship. Eros is closest in meaning to the concept of (47) _____ sion.

Romantic love occurs within a cultural context in which the concept is (48) _____ ized. Because Western society maintains much of the (49) d_____ standard toward sexuality, women are more often expected to justify sexual experiences as involving someone they love. (50: Only a few _or_ Most?) people in the United States believe that romantic love is a prerequisite for marriage. (51: Men _or_ Women?) tend to be more romantic than the other gender.

(52) _____ tion is a state of intense absorption in or focusing on another person. Infatuation is usually accompanied by (53) _____ ual desire, elation, and excitement. At first, infatuation and (54) _____ tic love are indistinguishable. Sternberg likens infatuation to intense feelings of passion but not the deeper feelings of (55) _____ ment and caring that typify a more lasting mutual love.

Social psychologists Ellen Berscheid and Elaine Hatfield define romantic love in terms of a state of intense (56) _____ gical arousal and the cognitive (57) ap_____ of that arousal as love. Arousal may be experienced as a pounding (58) _____ t, sweaty (59) _____ s, and butterflies in the stomach. Cognitive appraisal means attributing arousal to love.

Clyde and Susan Hendrick developed a love attitude scale that suggests the existence of (60) _____ styles of love among college students: romantic love (eros), (61) g_____-_____ ing love (ludus), friendship (storge, philia), (62) l_____ love (pragma), possessive, excited love (mania), and selfless love (agape). The Hendricks found that college (63: Men _or_ Women?) are significantly more likely to develop romantic love.

Psychologist Robert (64) S_____ offers a triangular theory of love. In his view there are three distinct components of love: (65) _____ macy, passion, and (66) d_____/commitment. Sternberg believes that couples are (67: Poorly _or_ Well?) matched if they possess corresponding levels of passion, intimacy, and commitment. According to Sternberg, (68) _____ tion (passionate love) is typified by strong sexual desire, but not by intimacy and commitment. Friendship and passionate love (69: Do _or_ Do not?) necessarily overlap. According to Sternberg, romantic love has passion and intimacy but lacks (70) _____ ment. Romantic love may develop into more complete love, called (71) _____ ate love, in which all three components flower. In (72) _____ ate love, intimacy and commitment are strong, but passion is lacking. The balance among Sternberg's three aspects of love is likely to (73: Remain stable _or_ Shift?) through the course of a relationship.

Chapter Quiz

1. Which of the following is the key factor in choosing dating partners?
   (a) Attitudinal similarity.
   (b) Physical appearance.
   (c) Reciprocity of feelings.
   (d) Propinquity.

2. Which of the following is found universally attractive in women?
   (a) A good complexion.
   (b) Slenderness.
   (c) Plumpness.
   (d) Self-assertive behavior.

3. Which of the following statements about body shape is true of college students?
   (a) College men generally think that they are too heavy.
   (b) College men prefer women to be more slender than the women imagine.
   (c) College women see their own body shapes as being close to ideal.
   (d) College women prefer men to be more slender than the men imagine.
4. What is the connection beween names and perceptions of attactiveness?
   (a) There is no connection beween names and perceptions of attactiveness.
   (b) Women with unusual names are found to be most attractive.
   (c) Women with popular names are found to be most attractive.
   (d) Women with old-fashioned names are found to be most attractive.
5. The central motive for seeking "matches" seems to be
   (a) desire for compatibility.
   (b) reciprocity of feelings.
   (c) the attempt to avoid cognitive dissonance.
   (d) fear of rejection by more appealing people.
6. Loving attachment, deep friendship, or nonsexual affection describes the concept of
   (a) agape.
   (b) eros.
   (c) storge.
   (d) philia.
7. _____ is a state of intense absorption in or focusing on another person.
   (a) Intimacy
   (b) Infatuation
   (c) Romantic love
   (d) Companionate love
8. People who say "I keep my lover up in the air about my commitment," or "I get over love affairs pretty easily" appear to be "in" the _____ style of love.
   (a) game-playing
   (b) romantic
   (c) logical
   (d) possessive
9. Which of the following is NOT one of Sternberg's components of love?
   (a) Passion.
   (b) Mania.
   (c) Intimacy.
   (d) Decision/commitment.
10. According to Sternberg, romantic love involves
    (a) passion and intimacy.
    (b) ludus and mania.
    (c) eros and storge.
    (d) agape and philia.

Answers to Chapter Review

1. Physical
2. Cultural
3. May not be
4. Taller
5. Is
6. Slenderness
7. Hourglass
8. Larger
9. Larger
10. Men and women
11. Do
12. Heavier
13. Heavier
14. Lighter
15. More
16. More
17. Not to be
18. Are
19. More
20. Is
21. Men
22. Honesty
23. Less
24. Men
25. Women
26. Women
27. Younger
28. Men
29. Women
30. Sociobiologists
31. Matching
32. Similar
33. Rejection
34. More than
35. Do
36. Is
37. Women
38. Attitudes
39. Reciprocity
40. Is not
41. More
42. Storge
43. Eros
44. Storge
45. Agape
46. Friendship
47. Passion
48. Idealized
49. Double
50. Most
51. Men
52. Infatuation
53. Sexual
54. Romantic
55. Attachment
56. Physiological (Biological)
57. Appraisal
58. Heart
59. Palms
60. Six
61. Game-playing
62. Logical
63. Men
64. Sternberg
65. Intimacy
66. Decision
67. Well
68. Infatuation
69. Do not
70. Commitment
71. Consummate
72. Companionate
73. Shift

Answers to Chapter Quiz

1. (b)
2. (a)
3. (d)
4. (c)
5. (d)
6. (c)
7. (b)
8. (a)
9. (b)
10. (a)

C HAPTER 7

Relationships, Intimacy, and Communication

O U T L I N E

The ABC(DE)s of Romantic Relationships

The A's—Attraction
The B's—Building
The C's—Continuation
The D's—Deterioration
The E's—Ending

Intimacy

Knowing and Liking Yourself
Trusting and Caring
Being Honest
Making a Commitment
Maintaining Individuality When the *I* Becomes *We*
Communicating

Communication Skills for Enhancing Relationships and Sexual Relations

Common Difficulties in Sexual Communication
Getting Started

Listening to the Other Side
Learning About Your Partner's Needs
Providing Information
Making Requests
Handling Impasses

Chapter Review

Chapter Quiz

Applications
How to Improve Date-Seeking Skills
Delivering and Receiving Criticism

A World of Diversity
Self-Disclosure: East May Be East and West May Be West,
    But Here, Perhaps, the Twain Do (Almost) Meet

DID YOU KNOW THAT . . .

- Small talk is a very important "audition" for the formation of a relationship?
- Married people are most likely to have met their spouses through mutual friends?
- It is useful to practice opening lines when you want to develop a relationship?
- You should be careful not to disclose too much too soon with new people?
- People can have intimate relationships without being sexually intimate?
- Men do not naturally know what is pleasing to a woman?
- If you are criticized, the best course may be to acknowledge the criticism and avoid retaliation?
- Disagreements are not necessarily the death knell of a relationship?

ill you, won't you, will you, won't you, will you join the dance?

(Lewis Carroll, *Alice in Wonderland*)

No man is an island, entire of itself.

(John Donne)

In this chapter we first define the stages that lead to intimacy in relationships. We see that not all relationships achieve this level of interrelatedness, even some supposedly deep and permanent relationships such as marriage. Finally, we discuss the ways that communication contributes to relationships and sexual satisfaction, and we enumerate ways of enhancing communication skills. ■

The ABC(DE)s of Romantic Relationships

Social-exchange theory

The view that the development of a relationship reflects the unfolding of social exchanges—that is, the rewards and costs of maintaining the relationship as opposed to ending it.

ABCDE model

Levinger's view, which approaches romantic relationships in terms of five stages: attraction, building, continuation, deterioration, and ending.

Romantic relationships, like people, undergo stages of development. According to **social-exchange theory,** the development reflects the unfolding of social exchanges, which involve the rewards and costs of maintaining the relationship as opposed to dissolving it. During each stage, positive factors sway partners toward maintaining and enhancing their relationship. Negative factors incline them toward letting it deteriorate and end (Karney & Bradbury, 1995).

George Levinger (1980) proposes an **ABCDE model** to describe the stages of romantic relationships: (1) *A*ttraction, (2) *B*uilding, (3) *C*ontinuation, (4) *D*eterioration, and (5) *E*nding.

The A's—Attraction

Attraction occurs when two people become aware of each other and find one another appealing or enticing. We may find ourselves attracted to an enchanting person "across a crowded room," in a nearby office, or in a new class. We may meet others through blind dates, introductions by mutual friends, computer match-ups, or by "accident." Initial feelings of attraction are largely based on visual impressions, though we may also form initial impressions by overhearing people speak or hearing others talk about them.

According to the NHSLS study (Michael et al., 1994), married people are most likely to have met their spouses through mutual friends (35%) or by self-introductions (32%) (see Figure 7.1). Other sources of introductions are family members (15%) and coworkers, classmates, or neighbors (13%). Mutual friends and self-introductions are also the most common ways of meeting for unmarried couples (Michael et al., 1994).

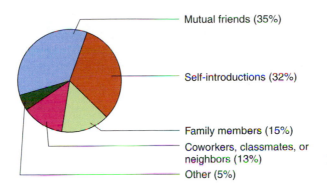

Figure 7.1. How Married People Met Their Partners.

Pie chart labels: Mutual friends (35%), Self-introductions (32%), Family members (15%), Coworkers, classmates, or neighbors (13%), Other (5%)

The B's—Building

Building a relationship follows initial attraction. Factors that motivate us to try to build relationships include similarity in the level of physical attractiveness, similarity in attitudes, and mutual liking and positive evaluations. Factors that may deter us from trying to build relationships include lack of physical appeal, dissimilarity in attitudes, and negative mutual evaluations.

Not-So-Small Talk: An Audition for Building a Relationship

In the early stages of building a relationship, we tend to look for overlapping attitudes and interests, and we check out our feelings of attraction. At this point the determination of whether to strive to develop the relationship is often made, at least in part, on the basis of **small talk.** Small talk allows an exchange of information but stresses breadth of topic coverage rather than in-depth discussion. Engaging in small talk may seem "phony," but premature self-disclosure of intimate information may repel the other person, as we shall see.

Small talk is a trial balloon for friendship. Successful small talk encourages a couple to venture beneath the surface. At a cocktail party, people may flit about from person to person, exchanging small talk, but now and then a couple finds common ground and pairs off.

The "Opening Line": How Do You Get Things Started?

One kind of small talk is the greeting, or opening line. We usually precede verbal greetings with eye contact and decide to begin talking if eye contact is reciprocated. Avoidance of eye contact may mean that the person is shy, but it could also signify lack of interest. If you would like to progress from initial attraction to surface contact, try a smile and direct eye contact. If the eye contact is reciprocated, choose an opening line, or greeting:

Verbal salutes, such as "Good morning."
Personal inquiries, such as "How are you doing?"
Compliments, such as "I like your outfit."
References to your mutual surroundings, such as "What do you think of that painting?" or "This is a nice apartment house, isn't it?"
References to people or events outside the immediate setting, such as "How do you like this weather we've been having?"
References to the other person's behavior, such as "I couldn't help noticing you were sitting alone," or "I see you out on this track every Saturday morning."
References to your own behavior, or to yourself, such as "Hi, my name is Allan Felix" (feel free to use your own name, if you prefer).

The simple "Hi" or "Hello" is very useful. A friendly glance followed by a cheerful hello ought to give you some idea of whether the attraction is reciprocated. If the hello is returned with a friendly smile and inviting eye contact, follow it up with another greeting, such as a reference to your surroundings, the other person's behavior, or your name.

Exchanging "Name, Rank, and Serial Number"

Early exchanges are likely to include name, occupation, marital status, and hometown. This has been likened to

Small talk
A superficial kind of conversation that allows exchange of information but stresses breadth of topic coverage rather than in-depth discussion.

exchanging "name, rank, and serial number" with the other person. Each person seeks a sociological profile of the other to discover common ground that may provide a basis for pursuing the conversation. An unspoken rule seems to be at work: "If I provide you with some information about myself, you will reciprocate by giving me an equal amount of information about yourself. Or . . . 'I'll tell you my hometown if you tell me yours' " (Knapp, 1978, p. 114). If the other person is unresponsive, she or he may not be attracted to you, and you may wish to try someone else. But you may also be awkward in your approach or perhaps turn the other person off by disclosing too much about yourself at once. The Applications box below suggests ways of improving date-seeking skills.

APPLICATIONS

HOW TO IMPROVE DATE-SEEKING SKILLS

All right, you know that Mr. or Ms. Right exists. So what do you do? How do you go about making a date?

You can enhance social skills, including date-seeking skills, through the technique of *successive approximations*. That means practicing a series of tasks that are graded in difficulty. You will gain skills and self-confidence as you tackle smaller challenges and progress to more difficult ones. Friends can help you polish your date-seeking skills. They can role-play the prospective date and give honest feedback about your behavior.

Here is a series of tasks that may help you sharpen your skills. After you achieve success with the easier ones, move on to the more challenging practice levels.

Easy Practice Level

Select a person with whom you are friendly, but one whom you have no desire to date. Practice making small talk about the weather, new films, TV shows, concerts, museum shows, political events, and personal hobbies.

Select a person you might have some interest in dating. Smile when you pass this person at work, school, or elsewhere, and say "Hi." Engage in this activity with other people of both genders to increase your skills at greeting others.

Speak into your mirror, using behavior rehearsal and role playing. Pretend you are in the process of sitting next to the person you would like to date, say, at lunch or in the laundry room. Say "Hello" with a broad smile, and introduce yourself. Work on the smile until it looks inviting and genuine. Make some comment about the food or the setting—the cafeteria, the office, whatever. Use a family member or confidant to obtain feedback about the effectiveness of your smile, tone of voice, posture, and choice of words.

Medium Practice Level

Sit down next to the person you want to date, and engage in small talk. If you are in a classroom, talk about a homework assignment, the seating arrangement, or the instructor (be kind). If you are at work, talk about the building or some recent interesting event in the neighborhood. Ask your intended date how he or she feels about the situation. If you are at a group meeting, such as Parents Without Partners, tell the other person that you are there for the first time and ask for advice on how to relate to the group.

Engage in small talk about the weather and local events. Channel the conversation into an exchange of personal information. Give your "name, rank, and serial number"—who you are, your major field or your occupation, where you're from, why or how you came to the school or company. The other person is likely to reciprocate and provide equivalent information. Ask how he or she feels about the class, place of business, city, hometown, and so on.

Rehearse asking the person out before your mirror, a family member, or a confidant. You may wish to ask the person out for a cup of coffee or to a film. It is somewhat less threatening to ask someone out to a gathering at which "some of us will be getting together." Or you may rehearse asking the person to accompany you to a cultural event, such as an exhibition at a museum or a concert—it's "sort of" a date, but also less anxiety inducing.

Target Behavior Level

Ask the person out on a date in a manner consistent with your behavior rehearsal. If the person says he or she has a previous engagement or can't make it, you may wish to say something like, "That's too bad," or "I'm sorry you can't make it," and add something like, "Perhaps another time." You should be able to get a feeling for whether the person you asked out was just seeking an excuse or has a genuine interest in you and, as claimed, could not in fact accept the specific invitation.

Before asking the date out again, pay attention to his or her apparent comfort level when you return to small talk on a couple of occasions. If there is still a chance, the person should smile and return your eye contact. The other person may also offer you an invitation. In any event, if you are turned down twice, do not ask a third time. And don't make a catastrophe out of the refusal. Look up. Note that the roof hasn't fallen in. The birds are still chirping in the trees. You are still paying taxes. Then give someone else a chance to appreciate your fine qualities.

A WORLD OF DIVERSITY

SELF-DISCLOSURE: EAST MAY BE EAST AND WEST MAY BE WEST, BUT HERE, PERHAPS, THE TWAIN DO (ALMOST) MEET

Research suggests that we should refrain from disclosing certain types of information too rapidly if we want to make a good impression. In one study, confederates of the experimenters (Wortman et al., 1976) engaged in 10-minute conversations with study participants. Some confederates were "early disclosers," who shared intimate information early. Others, "late disclosers," shared intimate information toward the end of the conversation only. In either case, the information was identical. Study participants then rated the disclosers. Early disclosers were rated less mature, secure, well adjusted, and genuine than the late disclosers. Study participants also preferred to continue relationships with the late disclosers. We may say we value "openness" and "honesty" in our relationships, but it may be a social mistake to open up too soon.

A Japanese study showed similar results. Japanese college students rated actors in a mock conversation more favorably when they disclosed less about themselves (Nakanishi, 1986). Chinese people also responded negatively to others who are prone to early self-disclosure.

Despite such cross-cultural similarities, self-disclosure in general may be viewed less favorably in Eastern cultures. In Japanese society, for example, self-disclosure is often seen as inappropriate in social relationships (Nakanishi, 1986). Not surprisingly, researchers find that people in the United States tend to disclose much more about themselves in social interactions than do the Japanese (Gudykunst & Nishida, 1984).

Do You Dare Let It All Hang Out? Despite the common belief that one should be honest and open, research suggests that people who self-disclose too much too soon are seen as socially inept. Researchers find that people in Japan tend to disclose less personal information in social interactions than people in the United States do.

Self-disclosure

The revelation of personal, perhaps intimate, information.

Self-Disclosure: You Tell Me and I'll Tell You . . . Carefully

Opening up, or **self-disclosure,** is central to building intimate relationships. But just what sort of information is safe to disclose upon first meeting someone? If you refuse to go beyond name, rank, and serial number, you may look uninterested or as if you are trying to keep things under wraps. If, on the other hand, you spill out the fact that you have a terrible rash on your thigh, it's likely that you have disclosed too much too soon.

If the contact provided by small talk and initial self-disclosure has been mutually rewarding, partners in a relationship tend to develop deeper feelings of liking for each other (Collins & Miller, 1994). Self-disclosure may continue to build gradually through the course of a relationship as partners come to trust each other enough to share confidences and more intimate feelings.

Gender Differences in Self-Disclosure

A woman complains to a friend: "He never opens up to me. It's like living with a stone wall." Women commonly declare that men are loath to express their feelings (Tannen, 1990). Researchers find that men tend to be less willing to disclose their feelings, perhaps in adherence to the traditional "strong and silent" male stereotype (see Chapter 5).

Yet gender differences in self-disclosure tend to be small. Overall, researchers find that women are only slightly more revealing about themselves than men (Dindia & Allen, 1992). We should thus be careful not to rush to the conclusion that men are always more "tight-lipped." The belief that there are large gender differences in self-disclosure appears to be something of a myth.

Stereotypes are also a-changing—somewhat. We now see depictions in the media of the "new" man as someone who is able to express feelings without compromising his masculinity. We shall have to wait to see whether this "new" sensitive image replaces the rugged, reticent stereotype, or is a passing fancy.

Mutuality: When the "We," Not the "I's," Have It   When feelings of attraction and the establishment of common ground lead a couple to regard themselves as "we"—not just two "I's" who happen to be in the same place at the same time—they have attained what Levinger terms a state of **mutuality.** The development of mutuality favors the continuation and further deepening of the relationship.

Mutuality

A phase in building a relationship in which members of a couple come to regard themselves as "we," no longer two "I's" who happen to be in the same place at the same time.

The C's—Continuation

Once a relationship has been established, the couple embarks upon the stage of continuation. Factors that encourage continuation include seeking ways to introduce variety and maintain interest (such as trying out new sexual practices and social activities), showing evidence of caring and positive evaluation (such as sending birthday or Valentine's Day cards), showing lack of jealousy, perceiving fairness in the relationship, and experiencing mutual feelings of general satisfaction.

Factors in this stage that can throw the relationship into a downward spiral include boredom (e.g., falling into a rut in leisure activities, sexual practices, etc.), displaying evidence of negative evaluation (such as bickering, and forgetting anniversaries and other important dates or pretending that they do not exist), perceiving a lack of fairness in the relationship (such as one partner's always deciding how the couple will spend their free time), or experiencing feelings of jealousy and general dissatisfaction.

Jealousy

> O! beware, my lord, of jealousy;
> It is the green-ey'd monster . . .
>
> (William Shakespeare, *Othello*)

Thus was Othello, the Moor of Venice, warned of jealousy in the Shakespearean play that bears his name. Yet Othello could not control his feelings and slew his beloved Desdemona. The English poet John Dryden labeled jealousy a "tyrant of the mind." Anthropologists find evidence of jealousy in all cultures, although it may vary in amount and intensity across and within cultures. It appears to be more common and intense among cultures with a stronger *machismo* tradition, in which men are expected to display their virility.

Sexual jealousy is aroused when we suspect that an intimate relationship is threatened by a rival. Lovers can become jealous when others show sexual interest in their partners or when their partners show an interest (even a casual or nonsexual interest) in another. Jealousy can impair a relationship and produce feelings of mistrust of one's partner or toward potential rivals.

Sexual jealousy may be associated with a range of negative emotions, including fear of losing the loved one and anger toward the rival, the loved one, or both. Feelings of possessiveness, which are related to jealousy, can also stress a relationship. In extreme cases jealousy can cause depression or give rise to spouse abuse, suicide, or, as with Othello, murder. But milder forms of jealousy are not necessarily destructive to a relationship. They may even serve the positive function of revealing how much one cares for one's partner.

How common is sexual jealousy? Common. In a survey of 103 women at various stages of involvement in an intimate relationship, 3 out of 4 reported feelings of jealousy (Pines & Aronson, 1983). Fifty-four percent described themselves as jealous. Women who were in nonmonogamous relationships or were dissatisfied with their relationships were more likely to describe themselves as jealous. A typical situation that prompted jealousy was a party at which the woman's partner spent time talking to, or dancing or flirting with, other women.

What causes jealousy? In some cases, people become mistrustful of their current partners because their former partners had cheated. Jealousy may also derive from low self-esteem or a lack of self-confidence. People with low self-esteem may experience sexual jealousy because they become overly dependent on their partners. They may also fear that they will not be able to find another partner if their present lover leaves.

White (1981) has concluded from his research on jealousy that feelings of inadequacy lead to jealousy in women. In men, the reverse seems to be the case. For men, that is, feelings of jealousy tend to give rise to feelings of inadequacy. It is as if jealousy leads them to question whether they are worthy of their partners' affections. For both men and women, however, feelings of jealousy can lead to perceiving anyone as a rival, which can make them continually mistrustful.

Unfortunately many lovers—including many college students—play jealousy games. They let their partners know that they are attracted to other people. They flirt openly and even manufacture tales to make their partners pay more attention to them, to test the relationship, to inflict pain, or to take revenge for a partner's disloyalty.

The D's—Deterioration

Deterioration is the fourth stage of a relationship. It is not necessarily a stage that we seek, and certainly not an inevitability. Positive factors that can deter or slow deterioration include putting time and energy into the relationship, striving to cultivate the relationship, and showing patience—for example, giving the relationship a reasonable opportunity to improve. Negative factors that foster deterioration include failure to invest time and energy in the relationship, deciding to put an end to it, or simply permitting deterioration to proceed unchecked.

A relationship begins to deteriorate when one or both partners deem the relationship to be less enticing or rewarding than it had been. Couples who work toward maintaining and enhancing their relationships may find that they become stronger and more meaningful.

Active and Passive Responses to Deterioration   When a couple perceives their relationship to be deteriorating, they can respond in active or passive ways. Active means of response include doing something that may enhance the relationship (such as working on improving communication skills, negotiating differences, or seeking professional help) or making a decision to end the relationship. Passive methods of responding are basically characterized by waiting for something to happen, by just doing nothing. People can sit back passively and wait for the relationship to improve on its own (once in a great while, it does) or for the relationship to deteriorate to the point where it ends. ("Don't look at me; these things happen.")

It is irrational (and damaging to a relationship) to assume that suitable relationships require no investment of time and effort. No two of us are matched perfectly. Unless one member of a couple does double duty as a doormat, inevitable frictions will surface. When problems arise, it is better to work to resolve them than to act as if they don't exist and hope that they will disappear of their own accord.

The E's—Ending

Ending is the fifth and final stage of a relationship. Although it may be the ultimate stage of development, like deterioration, it need not be inevitable or desirable. Various factors can prevent a deteriorating relationship from ending. For example, people who continue to find some sources of satisfaction, who are committed to maintaining the relationship, or who believe that they will eventually be able to overcome their problems are more likely to invest what they must to prevent the collapse.

According to social-exchange theory, relationships draw to a close when negative forces are in sway—when the partners find little satisfaction in the affiliation, when the barriers to leaving the relationship are low (that is, the social, religious, and financial constraints are manageable), and especially when alternative partners are available (Karney & Bradbury, 1995).

The swan song of a relationship is not always a bad thing. When people are definitely incompatible, and when genuine attempts to preserve the relationship have faltered, ending the relationship can offer each partner a chance for happiness with someone else.

Intimacy

Intimacy
Feelings of closeness and connectedness that are marked by sharing of inmost thoughts and feelings.

Intimacy involves feelings of emotional closeness and connectedness with another person and the desire to share each other's inmost thoughts and feelings. Intimate relationships are also characterized by attitudes of mutual trust, caring, and acceptance.

Sternberg's (1986) triangular theory of love (see Chapter 6) regards intimacy as a basic component of romantic love. But people can be intimate and not in love, at least not in romantic love. Close friends and family members become emotionally intimate when they care deeply for each other and share their private feelings and experiences. It is not necessary for people to be *sexually* intimate to have an emotionally intimate relationship. Nor does sexual intimacy automatically produce emotional intimacy. People who are sexually involved may still fail to touch each other's lives in emotionally intimate ways. Even couples who fall in love may not be able to forge an intimate relationship because of unwillingness or inability to exchange inmost thoughts and feelings. Sometimes husbands or wives share greater emotional intimacy with friends than with their spouses.

Let us now consider some of the factors that are involved in building and maintaining intimate relationships.

Knowing and Liking Yourself

Some social scientists suggest that an initial step toward intimacy with others is getting to know and like yourself. By coming to know and value yourself, you identify your inmost feelings and needs and develop the security to share them.

Trusting and Caring

Two of the most important ingredients of an intimate relationship are trust and caring. When trust exists in a relationship, partners feel secure that disclosing intimate feelings

Building Intimacy. Intimate couples share each other's inmost thoughts and feelings. Intimacy also involves mutual trust, caring, and acceptance.

will not lead to ridicule, rejection, or other kinds of harm. Trust usually builds gradually, as partners learn whether or not it is safe to share confidences. Caring is an emotional bond that allows intimacy to develop. In caring relationships, partners seek to gratify each other's needs and interests.

Tenderness is expressed by putting one's arm around a partner's shoulder to offer support, or by verbalizations of love, caring, and appreciation. In romantic relationships, tenderness also takes the form of kissing, hugging, cuddling, and holding hands.

Being Honest

Since intimacy involves the sharing of one's inmost thoughts and feelings, honesty is a core feature of intimacy. Without honesty, partners see only each other's facades. A person need not be an "open book" to develop and maintain intimacy, however. Some aspects of experience are kept even from one's most intimate partners, for they may be too embarrassing or threatening to reveal (Kammeyer et al., 1990). For example, we would not expect partners to disclose every passing sexual fantasy.

Intimate relationships thus usually involve balances in which some things are revealed and others are not. Total honesty could devastate a relationship. It would not be reasonable, for example, to expect intimate partners to divulge the details of past sexual experiences. The recipient may wonder: "Why is Kimball telling me this? Am I as good a lover as _____ ? Is Kimball still in love with _____ ? What else did Kimball do with _____ ?" Discretion thus also buttresses intimate relationships. Honesty does not require revealing every detail. Nor is intimacy established by brutal criticism, even if it is honest.

Making a Commitment

Have you ever noticed that people may open up to strangers on airplanes or trains, yet find it hard to talk openly with people to whom they are closest? An intimate relationship involves more than the isolated act of baring one's soul to a stranger. Truly intimate relationships are marked by commitment or resolve to maintain the relationship through thick and thin. When we open up to strangers on a plane, we know it is unlikely that we will have to face them again.

This does not mean that intimate relationships require indefinite or lifelong commitments. A commitment, however, carries an obligation that the couple will work to overcome problems in the relationship rather than run for the exit at the first sign of trouble.

Maintaining Individuality When the *I* Becomes *We*

In committed relationships, a delicate balance exists between individuality and mutuality. In healthy unions, a strong sense of togetherness does not eradicate individuality. Partners in such relationships remain free to be themselves. Neither seeks to dominate or submerge himself or herself into the personality of the other. Each partner maintains individual interests, likes and dislikes, needs and goals.

Communicating

Good communication is another hallmark of an intimate relationship. Partners are able to share their most personal thoughts and feelings clearly and honestly. Communication is a two-way street. It embraces sending and receiving messages. The good communicator is thus a skilled listener as well as a clear speaker (Tannen, 1990). We generally associate communication with *talk*, which involves the use of verbal messages to convey a thought or a feeling. Through talk, the speaker *encodes* a thought or a feeling into words. The listener *decodes* the words to extract the meaning of the message. Problems in verbal communication can arise at several levels:

1. *The speaker may use words differently than the listener, leading to misunderstandings or miscommunication.* For example, the speaker might say, "You look really cute

tonight." The listener might object, saying, "You think I look *cute*? What's wrong with the way I look?" The speaker protests, "No, I didn't mean it that way. I meant you look good. Yes, good."

2. *The speaker's words may not match his or her tone of voice, facial expression, or body gestures.* For example, the speaker says, "Darling, I really *don't mind* if we visit your mother this weekend." But the speaker did not say, "I really *want* to visit your mother," so the words "don't mind" come across as a kind of snarl. In such cases, the listener is likely to place greater weight on *how* something is said rather than on *what* is said.

3. *The speaker may not be able to put into words what he or she truly means or feels.* Sometimes we grasp for words to express our feelings, but they do not come, or those that do come miss the mark.

Nonverbal Communication: The Body Speaks   Though the spoken word is a primary form of communication, we often express our feelings through nonverbal channels as well, such as by tone of voice, gestures, body posture, and facial expressions (Tannen, 1990). People may place more weight on how words are said than on their denotative meaning. People also accentuate the meaning of their words through gestures, raising or lowering their voices, or using a sterner or softer tone of voice.

Nonverbal communication is used not only to accentuate the spoken word, but also to directly express feelings. We sometimes are better able to convey our feelings through body language than by the use of words. A touch or a gaze into someone's eyes may express more about our feelings than words can. Parents express feelings of tenderness and caring toward infants by hugging, holding, and caressing them, and by speaking in a gentle and soothing tone of voice, even though the meanings of the words cannot yet be grasped.

Let us examine some aspects of nonverbal communication:

On "Being Uptight" and "Hanging Loose"   The ways that people carry themselves offer cues about their feelings and potential actions. People who are emotionally "uptight" often stand or sit rigidly and straight-backed. People who feel more relaxed literally "hang loose."

People who face us and lean toward us are in effect saying that they like us or care about what we are saying. If we overhear a conversation between a couple and see that the woman is leaning toward the man, but he is leaning back and playing with his hair, we tend to infer that he is not accepting what she is saying or has lost interest.

Touching   Touching is a powerful form of communication. Women are more apt than men to touch the people with whom they interact. When touching suggests too much intimacy, however, it can be annoying. Touching may also establish "property rights" over one's partner. People may touch their partners in public or hold their hands, not as a sign of affection, but as a signal to others that their partners are taken and that others should keep a respectful distance. Similarly, the wearing of an engagement or wedding ring signals unavailability.

Gazing and Staring: The Look of Love?   We gather information about the motives, feelings, and attitudes of others through eye contact. In Western culture, looking other people "squarely in the eye"—at least among men—is positively valued. People who do so appear self-assertive, direct, and candid. When people look away, they may be perceived as shy, deceitful, or depressed. In some Asian cultures, however, looking other people directly in the eye may seem an aggressive invasion.

Unaggressive gazing into another person's eyes—especially the eyes of a person whom one considers attractive—can create deep feelings of intimacy in our culture. In a laboratory study, couples who had just met were instructed to gaze into each other's eyes for two minutes. Afterwards, many reported experiencing feelings of passion (Kellerman et al., 1989). Is this what is meant by "the look of love"?

All in all, there are many ways in which we communicate with others through verbal and nonverbal channels. Let us now look at ways in which partners can learn to communicate better with each other, especially about sex. Many couples, even couples who are able to share deepest thoughts and feelings, may flounder at communicating their sexual needs and preferences. Couples who have lived together for decades may know each other's tastes in food, music, and movies about as well as they know their own but still be hesitant to share their sexual likes and dislikes (Havemann & Lehtinen, 1990). They may also be reluctant, for fear of opening wounds in the relationship, to exchange their feelings about other aspects of their relationship, including each other's habits, appearance, and gender-stereotypical attitudes.

Communication Skills for Enhancing Relationships and Sexual Relations

Marital counselors and sex therapists might be as busy as the proverbial Maytag repair-person if more couples communicated with each other about their sexual feelings. Unfortunately, when it comes to sex, *talk* may be the most overlooked four-letter word.

Many couples suffer for years because one or both partners are unwilling to speak up. Or problems arise when one partner misinterprets the other. One partner might interpret the other's groans or grimaces of pleasure as signs of pain and pull back during sex, leaving the other frustrated. Improved communication may be no panacea, but it helps. Clear communication can take the guesswork out of relationships, avert misunderstandings, relieve resentments and frustrations, and increase both sexual and general satisfaction with the relationship.

Common Difficulties in Sexual Communication

Why is it so difficult for couples to communicate about sex? Here are some possibilities:

On "Making Whoopie"—Is Sex Talk Vulgar?   Vulgarity, like beauty, is to some degree in the eye of the beholder. One couple's vulgarity may be another couple's love talk. Some people may maintain a Victorian belief that any talk about sex is not fit for mixed company, even between intimate partners. Sex, that is, is something you may do, but not something to be talked about. Other couples may be willing in principle to talk about sex, but find the reality difficult because of the lack of an agreeable, common language.

How, for example, are they to refer to their genitals or to sexual activities? One partner may prefer to use coarse four-letter (or five-letter) words to refer to them. The other might prefer more clinical terms. A partner who prefers slang for the sexual organs might be regarded by the other as vulgar or demeaning. (But as the forbidden fruit is often the sweetest, some people feel sexually aroused when they or their partners "talk dirty.") One who uses clinical terms, such as fellatio or coitus, might be regarded as, well, clinical. Some couples try to find a common verbal ground, one that is not vulgar at one extreme, or clinical at the other. They might speak, for example, of "doing it" rather than "engaging in sexual intercourse." (The title of the Eddie Cantor musical of the 1930s suggests that some people once spoke of "making whoopie.") Or they might speak of "kissing me down there" rather than practicing fellatio or cunnilingus.

In some cases of gross mismatch in partners' choices for the language of love, the differences run much deeper than choice of words.

On Irrational Beliefs   Many couples also harbor irrational beliefs about relationships and sex, such as the notion that people should somehow *know* what their partners want, without having to ask. The common misconception that people should know what pleases their partners undercuts communication. Men, in particular, seem burdened with the stereotype that they should have a natural expertise at sex. Women may feel it is "unladylike" to talk openly about their sexual needs and feelings. Both partners may hold the idealized romantic notion that "love is all you need" to achieve sexual happiness. But such knowledge does not arise from instinct nor love. It is learned—or it remains unknown.

A related irrational belief is that "my partner will read my mind." We may erroneously assume that if our partners truly loved us, they would somehow "read our minds" and know what types of sexual stimulation we desire. Unfortunately, or fortunately, others cannot read our minds. We must assume the responsibility for communicating our preferences.

Some people communicate more effectively than others, perhaps because they are more sensitive to others' needs or because their parents served as good models as communicators. But communication skills can be acquired at any time. Learning takes time and work, but the following guidelines should prove helpful. These skills can also improve communication in areas of intimate relationships other than the sexual.

Getting Started

How do you broach tough topics? Here are some ideas.

Talking About Talking   You can start by talking about talking. You can inform your partner that it is difficult for you to talk about problems and conflicts: "You know, I've always found it awkward to find a way of bringing things up," or, "You know, I think other people have an easier time than I do when it comes to talking about some things." You can allude to troublesome things that happened in the past when you attempted to resolve conflicts. This approach encourages your partner to invite you to proceed.

Broaching the topic of sex is perhaps the most difficult step in communicating with your partner. Couples who gab endlessly about their finances, their children, their work, and so on, suddenly clam up when sex comes up. So it may be helpful for you and your partner to first agree to talk about talking about sex. You can begin by admitting that it is hard or embarrassing for you to talk about sex. You can say that your sexual relationship is important to you and that you want to do everything you can to enhance it. Gently probe your partner's willingness to set aside time to talk about sex, preferably when you can dim the lights and not be interrupted.

The "right time" may be when you are both relaxed, rested, and unpressed for time. The "right place" can be any place where you can enjoy privacy and go undisturbed. Sex talk need not be limited to the bedroom. Couples may feel more comfortable talking about sex over dinner, when cuddling on the sofa, or when just relaxing together.

Requesting Permission to Bring Up a Topic   Another possibility is to request permission to raise an issue. You can say something like this: "There's something on my mind. Do you have a few minutes? Is now a good time to tell you about it?" Or you can say, "There's something that we need to talk about, but I'm not sure how to bring it up. Can you help me with it?"

Giving Your Partner Permission to Say Something That Might Be Upsetting to You   You can tell your partner that it is okay to point out ways in which you can become a more effective lover. For example, you can say, "I know that you don't want to hurt my feelings, but I wonder if I'm doing anything that you'd rather I didn't do?"

Listening to the Other Side

Skilled listening involves skills such as active listening, paraphrasing, the use of reinforcement, and valuing your partner even when the two of you disagree.

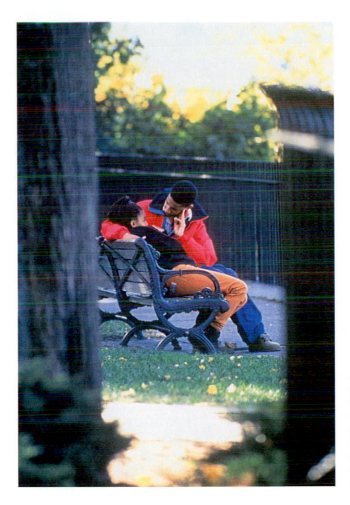

Active Listening. Effective communication requires listening to the other person's side. We can listen actively rather than passively by maintaining eye contact and showing that we understand the other person's feelings and ideas.

Listening Actively   To listen actively rather than passively, first adopt the attitude that you may actually learn something—or perceive things from another vantage point—by listening. Second, recognize that even though the other person is doing the talking, you need not sit back passively. In other words, it is not helpful to stare off into space while your partner is talking, or to offer a begrudging "mm-hmm" now and then to be "polite." Instead, you can listen actively by maintaining eye contact and modifying your facial expression to show that you understand his or her feelings and ideas. For example, nod your head when appropriate.

Listening actively also involves asking helpful questions, such as "Would you please give me an example?" or "Was that good for you?"

An active listener does not simply hear what the other person is saying, but also focuses attentively on the speaker's words and gestures to grasp meaning. Nonverbal cues may reveal more about the speaker's inner feelings than the spoken word. Good listeners do not interrupt, change the topic, or walk away when their partners are speaking.

Paraphrasing   Paraphrasing shows that you understand what your partner is trying to say. In paraphrasing, you recast or restate the speaker's words to confirm your comprehension. For example, suppose your partner says, "You hardly ever say anything when we're making love. I don't want you to scream or make obligatory grunts, or do something silly, but sometimes I wonder if I'm trying to make love to a brick wall." You can paraphrase it by saying something like this: "So it's sort of hard to know if I'm really enjoying it."

Reinforcing the Other Person for Communicating   Even when you disagree with what your partner is saying, you can maintain good relations and keep channels of communication open by saying something like "I really appreciate your taking the time to try to work this out with me" or "I hope you'll think it's okay if I don't see things entirely in the same way, but I'm glad that we had a chance to talk about it."

Showing That You Value Your Partner, Even When the Two of You Disagree   When you disagree with your partner, do so in a way that shows that you still value your partner as a person. In other words, say something like "I love you very much, but it annoys me when you . . . " rather than "You're really contemptible for doing . . . " By so doing, you encourage your partner to disclose sensitive material without fear of personal attack or the risk of losing your love or support.

Learning About Your Partner's Needs

Listening is basic to learning about another person's needs, but sometimes it helps to go a few steps further.

Asking Questions to Draw the Other Person Out   You can ask open-ended questions that allow for a broader exploration of issues, such as these:

> "What do you like best about the way we make love?"
> "Do you think that I do things to bug you?"
> "Does it bother you that I go to bed later than you do?"
> "Does anything disappoint you about our relationship?"
> "Do you think that I do things that are inconsiderate when you're studying for a test?"

Closed-ended questions that call for a limited range of responses would be most useful when you're looking for a simple yes-or-no type of response, such as "Would you rather make love with the stereo off?"

Using Self-Disclosure   Self-disclosure is essential to developing intimacy. You can also use self-disclosure to learn more about your partner's needs, because communicating your own feelings and ideas invites reciprocation. For example, you might say, "There are times when I feel that I disappoint you when we make love. Should I be doing something differently?"

Granting Permission for the Other Person to Say Something That Might Upset You   You can ask your partner to level with you about an irksome issue. You can say that you recognize that it might be awkward to discuss it, but that you will try your best to listen conscientiously and not get too disturbed. You can also limit communication to one such difficult issue per conversation. If the entire emotional dam were to burst, the job of mopping up could be overwhelming.

Providing Information

There are many skillful ways of communicating information, including "accentuating the positive" and using verbal and nonverbal cues. When you want to get something across, remember that it is irrational to expect that your partner can read your mind. He or she can tell when you're wearing a grumpy face, but your expression does not provide much information about your specific feelings. When your partner asks, "What would you like me to do?" responding with "Well, I think you can figure out what I want" or "Just do whatever you think is best" is not very helpful. Only you know what pleases you. Your partner is not a mind-reader.

Accentuating the Positive   Let your partner know when he or she is doing something right! Speak up or find another way to express your appreciation. Accentuating the positive is rewarding and also informs your partner about what pleases you. In other words, don't just wait around until your partner does something wrong and then seize the opportunity to complain!

Using Verbal Cues   Sexual activity provides an excellent opportunity for direct communication. You can say something like "Oh, that's great" or "Don't stop." Or you can ask for feedback, as in "How does that feel . . . ?"

Feedback provides direct guidance about what is pleasing. Partners can also make specific requests and suggestions.

Using Nonverbal Cues   Sexual communication also occurs without words. Couples learn to interpret each other's facial expressions as signs of pleasure, boredom, even disgust. Our body language also communicates our likes and dislikes. Our partners may lean toward us or away from us when we touch them, or relax or tense up; in any case, they speak volumes in silence.

The following exercises may help couples use nonverbal cues to communicate their sexual likes and dislikes. Similar exercises are used by sex therapists to help couples with sexual dysfunctions.

1. *Taking turns petting.* Taking turns petting can help partners learn what turns one another on. Each partner takes turns caressing the other, stopping frequently enough to receive feedback by asking questions like "How does that feel?" The recipient is responsible for giving feedback, which can be expressed either verbally ("Yes, that's it— yes, just like that" or "No, a little lighter than that") or nonverbally, as by making certain appreciative or disapproving sounds. Verbal feedback is usually more direct and less prone to misinterpretation. The knowledge gained through this exercise can be incorporated into the couple's regular pattern of lovemaking.

2. *Directing your partner's hand.* Gently guiding your partner's hand—to show your partner where and how you like to be touched—is a most direct way of communicating sexual likes. While taking turns petting, and during other acts of lovemaking, one partner can gently guide the other's fingers and hands through the most satisfying strokes and caresses. Women might show partners how to caress the breasts or clitoral shaft in this manner. Men might cup their partners' hands to show them how to stroke the penile shaft or caress the testes.

3. *Signaling.* Couples can use agreed-upon nonverbal cues to signal sexual pleasure. For example, one partner may rub the other in a certain way, or tap the other, to signal that something is being done right. The recipient of the signal takes mental notes and incorporates the pleasurable stimulation into the couple's lovemaking. This is a sort of "hit or miss" technique, but even near misses can be rewarding.

Making Requests

A basic part of improving relationships or lovemaking is asking partners to change their behavior—to do something differently or to stop doing something that hurts or is ungratifying. The skill of making requests now comes to the fore.

Being Specific   Be specific in requesting changes. Telling your partner something like "I'd like you to be nicer to me" may accomplish little. Your partner may not know that his or her behavior is *not* nice and may not understand how to be "nicer." It is better to say something like "I would appreciate it if you would get coffee for yourself, or at least ask me in a more pleasant way." Or, "I really have a hard time with the way you talk to me in front of your friends. It's as if you're trying to show them that you have control over me or something." Similarly, it may be less effective to say "I'd like you to be more loving" than to say, "When we make love, I'd like you to kiss me more and tell me how you care about me."

Of course, you can precede your specific requests with openers such as "There's something on my mind. Is this a good time for me to bring it up with you?"

Using "I-Talk"   Using the word *I* is an excellent way of expressing your feelings. Psychologists who help people become more assertive often encourage them to use the words *I, me,* and *my* in their speech, not just to express their feelings, but to buttress their sense of self-worth.

DELIVERING AND RECEIVING CRITICISM

> Honest criticism is hard to take, particularly from a relative, a friend, an acquaintance, or a stranger.
>
> Franklin P. Jones

It is difficult enough to be critical of, or to be criticized by, people at work, in school, or casual acquaintances. It is much more difficult to deal with criticism with an intimate partner. The ways in which we criticize loved ones, or respond to criticism from them, can truly make or break love relationships. Here are some hints for delivering and receiving criticism in ways that can enhance rather than destroy relationships.

DELIVERING CRITICISM

Delivering criticism effectively is a skill. It requires focusing partners' attention on the problem without inducing resentment or defensiveness, or reducing them to trembling masses of guilt or fear.

Evaluating Your Motives

First, weigh your goals forthrightly. Is your primary intention to punish your partner, or are you more interested in gaining cooperation? If your goal is punishment, you may as well be coarse and disparaging, but expect to invite reprisals. If your goal is to improve the relationship, however, a tactful approach may be in order.

Picking the Right Time and Place

Deliver criticism privately—not in front of friends or family members. Your partner has a right to be upset when you make criticism public. Making private matters public induces indignation and cuts off communication.

Being Specific

Being specific may be even more important when delivering criticism than when making requests. By being specific about the *behavior* that disturbs you, you bypass the trap of disparaging your partner's personality or motives. For example, you may be more effective by saying "I could lose this job because you didn't write down the message" than by saying "You're completely irresponsible" or "You're a flake." Similarly, you may achieve better results by saying "The bathroom looks and smells dirty when you throw your underwear on the floor" rather than "You're a filthy pig." It is more to the point (and less intimidating) to complain about specific, modifiable behavior than to try to overhaul another person's personality.

Expressing Displeasure in Terms of Your Own Feelings

Your partner is likely to feel less threatened if you express displeasure in terms of your own feelings than by directly attacking his or her personality. Attacks often arouse defensive behavior, and sometimes retaliation, rather than enhance relationships. When confronting your partner for failing to be sensitive to your sexual needs when making love, it may be more effective to say "You know, it really *upsets* me that you don't seem to care about my feelings when we make love" than "You're so wrapped up in yourself that you never think about anyone else."

Keeping Criticism and Complaints to the Here and Now

How many times have you been in an argument and heard things like "You never appreciated me!" or "Last summer you did the same thing!" Bringing up the past during conflicts muddles current issues and heightens resentments. When your partner forgets to jot down the details of the telephone message, it is more useful to note that "This was a vital phone call" than "Three weeks ago you didn't tell me about the phone call from Chris and as a result I missed out on seeing *Home Alone: The College Years.*" It's better to leave alone who did what to whom last year (or even last week). Focus on the present.

Expressing Criticism Constructively

Be sensitive to your partner's needs by avoiding blunt criticisms or personal attacks and by suggesting constructive alternatives. Avoid saying things like "You're really a lousy lover." Say instead, "Can I take your hand and show you what I'd like?" As a rule of thumb, unless you can criticize your partner constructively, it may be best not to criticize at all.

Expressing Criticism Positively

Whenever possible, express criticism positively, and combine it with a concrete request. When commenting upon the lack of affection your partner displays during lovemaking, say, "I love it when you kiss me. Please

You are more likely to achieve desired results by framing requests in *I*-talk than by heaping criticisms on your partner. For example, "I would like it if we spent some time cuddling after sex" is superior to "You don't seem to care enough about me to want to hold me after we make love." Saying "I find it very painful when you use a harsh voice with me" is probably more effective than "Sometimes people's feelings get hurt when their boyfriends [girlfriends] speak to them harshly in front of their friends or families."

You may find it helpful to try out *I*-talk in front of a mirror or with a confidant before using it with your partner. In this way, you can see whether your facial expression and tone kiss me more" rather than "You never kiss me when we're in bed and I'm sick of it."

RECEIVING CRITICISM

Delivering criticism can be tricky, especially when you want to inspire cooperation. Receiving criticism can be even trickier. Nevertheless, the following suggestions offer some help.

Clarifying Your Goals

When you hear "It's time you did something about . . . ," it is understandable if the hair on the backs of your arms does a headstand. After all, it's a blunt challenge. When we are confronted harshly, we are likely to become defensive and think of retaliating. But if your objective is to enhance the relationship, take a few moments to stop and think. To resolve conflicts, we need to learn about the other person's concerns, keep lines of communication open, and find ways of changing problem behavior.

So when your partner says, "It's about time you did something about the bathroom," stop and think before you summon up your most menacing voice and say, "Just what the hell is that supposed to mean?" Ask yourself what you want to find out.

Asking Clarifying Questions

Just as it's important to be specific when delivering criticism, it helps if you encourage the other person to be specific when you are on the receiving end of criticism. In the example of the complaint about the bathroom, you can help your partner be specific and, perhaps, avert the worst by asking

clarifying questions, such as "Can you tell me exactly what you mean?" or "The bathroom?"

Consider a situation in which a lover says something like "You know, you're one of the most irritating people I know." Rather than retaliate and perhaps hurt the relationship further, you can say something like "How about forgoing the character assassination and telling me what I did that's bothering you?" This response assertively requests an end to insults and asks that your partner be specific.

Acknowledging the Criticism

Even when you disagree with a criticism, you can keep lines of communication open and show some respect for your partner's feelings by acknowledging and paraphrasing the criticism.

On the other hand, if you are at fault, you can acknowledge that forthrightly. For example, you can say, "You're right. It was my day to clean the bathroom and it totally slipped my mind" or "I was so busy, I just couldn't get to it." Now the two of you should look for a way to work out the problem. When you acknowledge criticism, you cue your partner to back off a bit and look for ways to improve the situation. But what if your partner then becomes abusive and says something like "So you admit you blew it?" You might then try a little education in conflict resolution. You could say, "I admitted that I was at fault. If you're willing to work with me to find a way to handle it, great; but I'm not going to let you pound me into the ground over it."

Rejecting the Criticism

Now, if you think that you were not at fault, express your feelings. Use *I*-talk, and be specific. Don't seize the opportunity to angrily point out your partner's shortcomings. By doing so, you may shut down lines of communication.

Negotiating Differences

Negotiate your differences if you feel that there is merit on both sides of the argument. You may want to say something like "Would it help if I . . . ?" And if there's something about your obligation to clean the bathroom that seems totally out of place, perhaps you and your partner can work out an exchange—that is, you get relieved of cleaning the bathroom in exchange for tackling a chore that your partner finds equally odious.

If none of these approaches helps resolve the conflict, consider the possibility that your partner is using the comment about the bathroom as a way of expressing anger over other issues. You may find out by saying something like "I've been trying to find a way to resolve this thing, but nothing I say seems to be helping. Is this really about the bathroom, or are there other things on your mind?"

And notice that we haven't suggested that you seize the opportunity to strike back by saying "Who're you to complain about the bathroom? What about your breath and that pig sty you call your closet?" Retaliation is tempting and may make you feel good in the short run, but it can do a relationship more harm than good in the long run.

of voice are consistent with what you are saying. Friends may also provide pointers on the content of what you are saying.

Handling Impasses

Communication helps build and maintain relationships, but sometimes partners have profound, substantial disagreements. In fact, it is normal to have disagreements from time to time. Even when their communication skills are superbly tuned, partners now and then reach an impasse.

Opening the lines of communication may also elicit hidden frustrations. These frustrations can lead partners to seriously question the value of continuing the relationship or to agree to consult a helping professional. Though some people feel it is best to "let sleeping dogs lie," the *skillful* airing of underlying dissatisfactions can be healthful for a relationship. Couples who reach an impasse can follow several courses of action that may be helpful:

Looking at the Situation from the Other Person's Perspective
Some of the conflict may be resolved by (honestly!) saying something like "I still disagree with you, but I can understand why you take your position." In this way, you recognize your partner's goodwill and, perhaps, lessen tensions.

Seeking Validating Information
On the other hand, if you do not follow your partner's logic, you can say something like "Please believe me: I'm trying very hard to look at this from your point of view, but I can't follow your reasoning. Would you try to help me understand your point of view?"

Taking a Break
Sometimes when you reach a stalemate, it helps to allow the problem to "incubate" for a while. If you and your partner put the issue aside for a while, perhaps a resolution will dawn on one of you later on. If you wish, schedule a follow-up discussion so that the issue won't be swept under the rug.

Tolerating Differentness
Although we tend to form relationships with people who share similar attitudes, there is never a perfect overlap. A partner who pretends to be your clone will most likely become a bore. Assuming that your relationship is generally rewarding and pleasurable, you may find it possible to tolerate certain differences between yourself and your partner. Respecting other people in part means allowing them to be who they are. When we have a solid sense of who we are as individuals and what we stand for, we are more apt to tolerate differentness in our partners.

Agreeing to Disagree
When all else fails, you can agree to disagree on various issues. You can remain a solid, respected individual, and your partner can remain a worthwhile, effective person even if the two of you disagree from time to time.

Disagreement is not necessarily destructive to a relationship—unless you are convinced that it must be. Two people cannot see everything in the same way. Failure to ever disagree will have to leave at least one partner feeling frustrated now and then.

You can handle an impasse by focusing on the things that you and your partner have in common. Presumably there will be a number of them—some of them with little feet.

Chapter Review

The ABC(DE)s of Romantic Relationships

According to (1) so_____-_____nge theory, the development of romantic relationships reflects the unfolding of social exchanges, which involve the rewards and costs of maintaining the relationship as opposed to dissolving it. During each stage, (2) _____tive factors sway partners toward maintaining and enhancing their relation-

ship. (3) _____tive factors incline partners toward letting it deteriorate and end. George (4) Le_____ proposes an ABCDE model to describe the stages of romantic relationships: *A*ttraction, (5) _____ing, (6) _____tion, *D*eterioration, and *E*nding.

According to the NHSLS study, married people are most likely to have met their spouses through mutual (7) _____nds or by (8) self-_____tions. Factors that motivate us to try to build relationships include (9) _____rity in level of physical attractiveness, similarity in (10) _____udes, mutual liking, and positive evaluations. In the early stages, people often decide whether to try to develop the relationship on the basis of (11) s_____ talk. Small talk allows people to exchange (12) _____tion and stresses (13: Breadth of topic coverage *or* In-depth discussion?). Premature (14) self-_____sure of intimate information may repel another person.

One kind of small talk is the greeting, or (15) _____ing line. The simple (16) "H_____" is a very useful greeting. Researchers find that (17: Men or Women?) are more willing to disclose their feelings than the other gender. When a couple regards themselves as "we"—not two "I's"—they have attained a state of (18) _____ity. Factors that encourage continuation of a relationship include (19) va_____ in activities, evidence of caring and positive (20) _____tion, and fairness.

Anthropologists find evidence of jealousy in (21: All *or* Only a few?) cultures. Jealousy occurs when people feel that a relationship is (22) _____ned by a rival. Jealousy (23: Is *or* Is not?) necessarily harmful to a relationship. Jealousy may derive from low (24) self-_____.

A relationship begins to deteriorate when one or both partners deem the relationship to be less (25) _____ing than it had been. A(n) (26) _____ive response to a deteriorating relationship means doing something that may enhance the relationship or deciding to end the relationship. (27) _____ive responding means waiting for something to happen.

According to social-exchange theory, relationships draw to a close when the partners find little (28) _____tion in the affiliation, when the barriers to leaving the relationship are low (that is, the social, religious, and financial constraints are manageable), and especially when alternative (29) _____ners are available.

Intimacy

Intimacy involves feelings of emotional (30) _____ness with another person. (31) _____berg's triangular theory of love regards intimacy as a basic component of romantic love. It (32: Is *or* Is not?) necessary for people to be sexually intimate to have an emotionally intimate relationship.

Two of the most important ingredients of an intimate relationship are (33) t_____ and caring. When trust exists in a relationship, partners feel that they can disclose their (34) in_____ feelings. Caring is an (35) _____nal bond that allows intimacy to develop. Since intimacy involves the sharing of one's inmost thoughts and feelings, (36) _____ty is a core feature of intimacy. However, (37) to_____ honesty could devastate a relationship. Truly intimate relationships are marked by (38) _____ment to maintain the relationship through thick and thin. In committed relationships, a delicate balance exists between (39) _____lity and mutuality.

The good (40) _____cator is a skilled listener as well as a clear speaker. Though speech is a primary form of communication, we often express our feelings through (41) _____al channels such as tone of voice, gestures, body posture, and facial expressions. Women are (42: More *or* Less?) apt than men to touch the people with whom they interact.

In Western culture, looking other people "squarely in the eye" is (43: Positively *or* Negatively?) valued. In our culture, gazing into another person's eyes—especially the eyes of a person whom one considers attractive—can create deep feelings of (44) _____.

Communication Skills for Enhancing Relationships and Sexual Relations

Many couples have (45) _____nal beliefs about relationships and sex, such as the notion that people should *know* what their partners want. (46: Men *or* Women?) seem burdened with the stereotypical notion that they should have a natural expertise at sex.

One way to get started talking about sex is to talk about (47) _____ing, by saying, for example, "You know, I've always found it awkward to find a way of bringing things up." Another possibility is to request (48) _____sion to raise an issue, by saying something like "There's something on my mind. Do you have a few minutes? Is now a good time to tell you about it?"

Skilled listening involves skills such as (49) _____ive listening, (50) _____sing, the use of reinforcement, and valuing your partner even when the two of you disagree.

One way to learn about your partner's needs is to ask (51) _____tions. Questions may be

(52) _____-ended or closed-ended. You can also use (53) self-_____ure to learn more about your partner's needs, because communicating your own feelings and ideas invites reciprocation. One can communicate one's sexual preferences by using (54) _____bal cues, such as "Oh, that's great" or (55) non_____ cues, such as body language.

It is helpful to be (56) spe_____ in requesting changes. Using the word (57) _____ is an excellent way of expressing your feelings.

Delivering (58) _____cism effectively requires focusing partners' attention on the problem without inducing resentment. Deliver criticism (59) _____tely —not in front of friends or family members—and be spe-cific. When delivering criticism, focus on the (60: Past or Present?). Try to suggest (61) _____tive alterna-tives. When you are receiving criticism, it helps to ask (62) _____ing questions. Even when you disagree with a criticism, you can keep lines of communication open by (63) _____ging the criticism.

When communication does not help resolve prob-lems, partners are at an (64) im_____. It may be possible to get by an impasse by looking at the situation from the other person's (65) _____tive. It also helps to take a (66) br_____ for a while or to toler-ate the other person's (67) _____ness. When all else fails, partners can agree to (68) dis_____ on various issues.

Chapter Quiz

1. The view that the development of relationships de-pends on the balance of the rewards of maintaining it and the costs of dissolving it is termed
   (a) social-exchange theory.
   (b) the ABCDE model.
   (c) stimulus-response theory.
   (d) operant conditioning.
2. According to the text, small talk
   (a) is an insincere way to begin a relationship.
   (b) is an in-depth discussion of important issues.
   (c) promotes premature disclosure of intimate information.
   (d) stresses breadth of topic coverage.
3. Which of the following most accurately describes gen-der differences in self-disclosure?
   (a) Men are always reluctant to disclose their feelings.
   (b) Women are always willing to disclose their feelings.
   (c) Gender differences in self-disclosure tend to be small.
   (d) Men are usually more willing than women to dis-close their feelings.
4. According to the text, jealousy appears to be more common in cultures
   (a) that are wealthy.
   (b) with a stronger *machismo* tradition.
   (c) that are primitive.
   (d) that stress the value of male–female relationships for reproductive purposes.
5. According to the text, it is irrational (incorrect) to as-sume that
   (a) suitable relationships require no investment of time and effort.

   (b) small talk will lead to the development of a good relationship.
   (c) partners need to work at maintaining good rela-tionships.
   (d) communication skills are important to relation-ships.
6. Which of the following contributes to the ending of a relationship?
   (a) The partners believe in a religious tradition that encourages maintaining relationships.
   (b) The partners find the relationship to be satisfy-ing.
   (c) The barriers to leaving the relationship are high.
   (d) Alternative partners are available.
7. Which of the following is the most accurate statement about intimacy and relationships?
   (a) It is not necessary for people to be sexually intimate to have an emotionally intimate relationship.
   (b) It is necessary for people to be sexually intimate to have an emotionally intimate relationship.
   (c) People cannot be intimate with one another un-less they are in love.
   (d) Intimacy is best established by complete honesty.
8. In healthy, committed relationships.
   (a) a delicate balance exists between individuality and mutuality.
   (b) a strong sense of togetherness eliminates individuality.
   (c) partners seek to submerge their own personalities into the personalities of their partners.
   (d) partners do whatever they can to meet all of their partners' sexual desires.

9. According to the text, which of the following is NOT an irrational belief about relationships and sex?
   (a) Men should have a natural expertise about sex.
   (b) People should know what their partners want without having to communicate.
   (c) Sexual knowledge is learned.
   (d) It is unladylike for women to express their feelings about sex.

10. The communications skill of active listening includes all of the following EXCEPT
   (a) nodding your head when appropriate.
   (b) interrupting the speaker.
   (c) maintaining eye contact.
   (d) asking helpful questions.

Answers to Chapter Review

1. Social-exchange
2. Positive
3. Negative
4. Levinger
5. Building
6. Continuation
7. Friends
8. Self-introductions
9. Similarity
10. Attitudes
11. Small
12. Information
13. Breadth of topic coverage
14. Self-disclosure
15. Opening
16. "Hi" or "Hello"
17. Women
18. Mutuality
19. Variety
20. Evaluation
21. All
22. Threatened
23. Is not
24. Self-esteem or Self-confidence
25. Enticing or Rewarding
26. Active
27. Passive
28. Satisfaction
29. Partners
30. Closeness or Connectedness
31. Sternberg's
32. Is not
33. Trust
34. Intimate or Inmost
35. Emotional
36. Honesty
37. Total
38. Commitment
39. Individuality
40. Communicator
41. Nonverbal
42. More
43. Positively
44. Intimacy
45. Irrational
46. Men
47. Talking
48. Permission
49. Active
50. Paraphrasing
51. Questions
52. Open
53. Self-disclosure
54. Verbal
55. Nonverbal
56. Specific
57. *I*
58. Criticism
59. Privately
60. Present
61. Constructive
62. Clarifying
63. Acknowledging
64. Impasse
65. Perspective
66. Break
67. Differentness
68. Disagree

Answers to Chapter Quiz

1. (a)
2. (d)
3. (c)
4. (b)
5. (a)
6. (d)
7. (a)
8. (a)
9. (c)
10. (b)

CHAPTER 8

Sexual Orientation

OUTLINE

Coming to Terms with Terms
Classification of Sexual Orientation
The Kinsey Continuum
Bisexuality

Perspectives on Gay Male and Lesbian Sexual Orientations
Historical Perspectives
Cross-Cultural Perspectives
Attitudes Toward Sexual Orientation in Contemporary Society
Biological Perspectives
Psychological Perspectives

Adjustment of Gay Males and Lesbians
"Treatment" of Gay Male and Lesbian Sexual Orientations

Gay Male and Lesbian Sexual Behavior

Gay Lifestyles
Lifestyle Differences Between Gay Males and Lesbians
Variations in Gay Lifestyles

Chapter Review

Chapter Quiz

A World of Diversity
Ethnicity and Sexual Orientation: A Matter of Belonging

Applications
Coming Out: Coming to Terms with Being Gay

- Sexual feelings involving people of one's own gender are common in adolescence and do not mean that one will be gay in adulthood?
- Some people are equally attracted to men and women?
- Jews and Christians have traditionally referred to male–male sexual activity as the sin of Sodom?
- Among the warlike Sambian people of New Guinea, young males perform fellatio on older males in the belief that it will enable them to acquire the fierce manhood of the headhunter?
- Two out of three Americans favor health insurance and inheritance rights for gay spouses?
- Some heterosexuals seem to hate gay people because they are threatened by the possibility of discovering male–male sexual impulses within themselves?
- Many gay couples have lifestyles similar to those of married heterosexual couples and are as well adjusted?

Sexual orientation

The direction of one's sexual interests—toward members of the same gender, the other gender, or both genders.

Heterosexual orientation

Erotic attraction to, and preference for, developing romantic relationships with members of the other gender.

Homosexual orientation

Erotic attraction to, and preference for, developing romantic relationships with members of one's own gender. (From the Greek *homos*, meaning "same," not the Latin *homo*, which means "man").

Gay males

Males who are erotically attracted to and desire to form romantic relationships with other males.

Lesbians

Females who are erotically attracted to and desire to form romantic relationships with other females. (After *Lesbos*, the Greek island on which, legend has it, female–female sexual activity was idealized.)

Bisexuality

Erotic attraction to, and interest in developing romantic relationships with, both males and females.

 exual orientation refers to one's erotic attractions toward, and interests in developing romantic relationships with, members of one's own or the other gender. A **heterosexual orientation** refers to an erotic attraction to, and preference for developing romantic relationships with, members of the other gender. (Many gay people refer to heterosexual people as being *straight,* or as *straights.*) Notice that we say *other gender,* not *opposite gender.* Social critics note that many of the problems that arise between men and women are based on the notion that men and women are polar opposites (Bem, 1993). Research and common sense both support the view that men and women are more alike in personality and behavior than they are different, however. ■

Coming to Terms with Terms

A **homosexual orientation** refers to an erotic attraction to, and interest in forming romantic relationships with, members of one's own gender. The term *homosexuality* denotes sexual interest in members of one's own gender and applies to both men and women. Homosexual men are often referred to as **gay males.** Homosexual women are also called **lesbians** or *gay women.* Gay males and lesbians are also referred to collectively as "gays" or "gay people." The term **bisexuality** refers to an orientation in which one is sexually attracted to, and interested in forming romantic relationships with, both males and females.

Now that we have defined the term *homosexuality,* let us note that we will use it only sparingly. Many gay people object to the term *homosexual* because they feel that it draws too much attention to sexual behavior. Moreover, the term bears a social stigma. As noted by the American Psychological Association's (1991) Committee on Lesbian and Gay Concerns, the word *homosexual* has also been historically associated with concepts of deviance and mental illness. Many gays would prefer terms such as *gay male* or *lesbian sexual orientation,* or a term such as *homophile,* if a term must be used to set them apart. The Greek root *philia* suggests love and friendship rather than sexual behavior. Thus, a homophile is a person who develops romantic love for and emotional commitment to members of her or his own gender. Sexual activity is secondary. Also, the term is often used to refer to men only. It thus renders lesbians invisible.

A Slice of Contemporary Life. Some gay couples consider themselves to be married, although their unions are not legally recognized in nearly all jurisdictions.

Then, too, the word *homosexual* is ambiguous in meaning—that is, does it refer to sexual behavior or sexual orientation? In this book, your authors speak of male–female sexual behavior (not *heterosexual* behavior), male–male sexual behavior, and female–female sexual behavior.

Classification of Sexual Orientation

Determining a person's sexual orientation might seem to be a clear-cut task. Some people are exclusively gay and limit their sexual activities to partners of their own gender. Others are strictly heterosexual and limit their sexual activities to partners of the other gender. Many people fall somewhere in between, however. Where might we draw the line between a gay male and lesbian sexual orientation, on the one hand, and a heterosexual orientation, on the other? Where do we draw the line between these orientations and bisexuality?

It is possible, indeed not unusual, for heterosexual people to have had some sexual experiences with people of their own gender. Consider a survey of more than 7,000 male readers of *Playboy* magazine. Among those reporting sexual experiences with both men and women in adulthood, more than 2 out of 3 perceived themselves to be heterosexual rather than bisexual (Lever et al., 1992). For many of these men, sexual experiences with other men were limited to a brief period of their lives and did not alter their sexual orientations. Lacking heterosexual outlets, prison inmates may have sexual experiences with people of their own gender while they maintain their heterosexual identities. Inmates would form sexual relationships with people of the other gender if they were available, and they return to male–female sexual behavior upon release from prison. Physical affection also helps some prisoners, male and female, cope with loneliness and isolation. Males who engage in prostitution with male clients may separate their sexual orientation from their "trade." Many fantasize about a female when permitting a client to fellate them. The behavior is male–male. The person's sexual *orientation* may be heterosexual.

Gay males and lesbians, too, may engage in male–female sexual activity while maintaining a gay sexual orientation. Some gay males and lesbians marry members of the other gender but continue to harbor unfulfilled desires for members of their own gender. Then, too, some people are bisexual but may not have acted upon their attraction to members of their own gender.

Sexual orientation is not necessarily expressed in sexual behavior. Many people come to perceive themselves as gay or heterosexual long before they ever engage in sexual activity. Some people, gay and heterosexual alike, adopt a celibate lifestyle for religious or ascetic reasons.

Attraction to people of the other gender and people of one's own gender may thus not be mutually exclusive. People may have various degrees of sexual interest in, and sexual experience with, people of either gender. Kinsey and his colleagues recognized that the boundaries between gay male and lesbian sexual orientations, on the one hand, and a heterosexual orientation, on the other, are sometimes blurry. They thus proposed a continuum of sexual orientation rather than two poles.

The Kinsey Continuum

Kinsey and his colleagues (1948, 1953) conceived a 7-point "heterosexual–homosexual continuum" (see Figure 8.1). People are located on the continuum according to their patterns of sexual attraction and behavior. People in category 0 are considered exclusively heterosexual. People in category 6 are considered exclusively gay.

What percentage of the population, then, is gay? The percentages depend on the criteria one uses. Kinsey and his colleagues reported that about 4% of men and 1% to 3% of women in their samples were exclusively gay (6 on their scale). A larger percentage of people were considered predominantly gay (scale points 4 or 5) or predominantly heterosexual (1 or 2 on their scale). Some were classified as equally gay and heterosexual in orientation and could be labeled bisexual (scale point 3). Most people were classified as exclusively heterosexual (scale point 0). Table 8.1 indicates the percentage of people who were classified according to the seven categories in Figure 8.1. Percentages varied according to marital status, age, level of education, and other factors. This particular table is based on people ages 20 to 35.

Between the poles of the continuum lie people with various degrees of sexual interest in, and sexual experience with, people of their own gender. Thirty-seven percent of men and 13% of the women told interviewers they had reached orgasm through sexual activity with someone of their own gender at some time after puberty. Fifty percent of men who remained single until age 35 reported they had reached orgasm through sexual activity with other males.

Kinsey's figures for male–male sexual activity may have been exaggerated. For instance, his finding that 37% of males had reached orgasm through sexual activity with other males was based on a sample that included a high proportion of former prisoners. Findings may also have been distorted by the researchers' efforts to recruit known gay people into their samples. Once these sources of possible bias are corrected, the incidence of male–male sexual activity drops from 37% to about 25%.

Figure 8.1. **The Kinsey Continuum.** Kinsey and his colleagues conceived a 7-point heterosexual–homosexual continuum that classifies people according to their homosexual behavior and the magnitude of their attraction to members of their own gender. People in category 0, who accounted for most of Kinsey's study participants, were considered exclusively heterosexual. People in category 6 were considered exclusively homosexual.

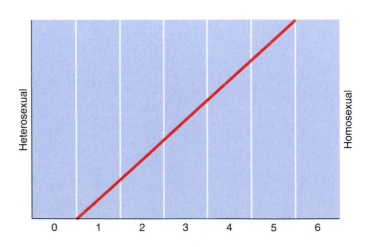

TABLE 8.1 Percentages of respondents ages 20 to 35 at each level of the Kinsey Continuum of Sexual Orientation

Rating Category	Females (%)	Males (%)
0: *Entirely heterosexual experience*		
Single	61–72	53–78
Married	89–90	90–92
Previously married	75–80	
1–6: *At least some sexual experience with people of one's own gender*	11–20	18–42
2–6: *More than incidental sexual experience with people of one's own gender*	6–14	13–38
3–6: *Homosexual as much or more than heterosexual*	4–11	9–32
4–6: *Mostly homosexual*	3–8	7–26
5–6: *Almost exclusively homosexual*	2–6	5–22
6: *Exclusively homosexual*	1–3	3–16

Adapted from Kinsey, A. C., et al. (1953). *Sexual Behavior in the Human Female.* Philadelphia: W. B. Saunders, p. 488. Reprinted by permission of the Kinsey Institute for Research in Sex, Gender, and Reproduction, Inc.

Kinsey's research also showed that sexual behavior patterns could shift during a person's lifetime, sometimes dramatically so (Sanders et al., 1990). Sexual experiences or feelings involving people of one's own gender are common, especially in adolescence, and do not mean that one will engage in sexual activity exclusively with people of one's own gender in adulthood (Bullough, 1990).

What did Kinsey find with respect to more enduring patterns of male–male and female–female sexual activity? Estimates based on an analysis of Kinsey's data (Gebhard, 1977) suggest that 13% of the men and 7% of the women, or 10% for both genders combined, were either predominantly or exclusively interested in, and sexually active with, people of their own gender for at least three years between the ages of 16 and 55.

Current estimates generally find lower percentages of gay people in the population than Kinsey did. Research in the United States, Britain, France, and Denmark finds that about 3% of men surveyed *identify* themselves as gay (Hamer et al., 1993; Laumann et al., 1994). About 2% of the U.S. women surveyed *identify* themselves as having a lesbian sexual orientation (Janus & Janus, 1993; Laumann et al., 1994). Surveys in the United States, Britain, and France find that larger numbers of men (5% to 11%) and women (2% to 4%) report *engaging in sexual behavior* with members of their own gender within the past five years (Sell et al., 1995). Surveys show that still larger numbers of men (8% to 9%) and women (8% to 12%) report some *sexual attraction* to members of their own gender, but no sexual interaction since the age of 15 (Sell et al., 1995).

Sex surveys reveal the percentages only of people *willing to admit* to certain behaviors or sexual orientations (Cronin, 1993; Isay, 1993). Surveys may omit gay people who hesitate to proclaim their sexual orientation because of social stigma or repression of their sexual feelings.

Challenges to the Kinsey Continuum

Challenges to the Kinsey Continuum   Although the Kinsey continuum has been widely adopted by sex researchers, it is not universally accepted. Kinsey believed that exclusive heterosexual and gay sexual orientations lay at opposite poles of one continuum. Therefore, the more heterosexual a person is, the less gay that person is, and vice versa (Sanders et al., 1990).

Viewing gay and heterosexual orientations as opposite poles of one continuum is akin to the traditional view of masculinity and femininity as opposite poles of one continuum, such that the more masculine one is, the less feminine, and vice versa. But we may also regard masculinity and femininity as independent personality dimensions. Similarly, we can regard the sexual orientations of gay people and heterosexuals as separate dimensions, rather than opposites.

Psychologist Michael Storms (1980) suggests that gay and heterosexual orientations are independent dimensions. Thus, one can be high or low on both dimensions simultaneously. Storms (1980) suggests that there are separate dimensions of responsiveness to male–female (**heteroerotic**) stimulation and sexual stimulation that involves someone of the same gender (**homoerotic** stimulation), as shown in Figure 8.2. According to this model, bisexuals are high in both dimensions, whereas people who are low in both are essentially asexual. According to Kinsey, bisexual individuals would be *less* responsive to stimulation by people of the other gender than heterosexual people are, but *more* responsive to stimulation by people of their own gender. According to the two-dimensional model, however, bisexual people may be as responsive to stimulation by people of the other gender as heterosexual people are, and as responsive to stimulation by people of their own gender as gay people are.

Kinsey had argued that the content of erotic fantasies was an excellent gauge of sexual orientation. To test this formulation, Storms (1980) investigated the erotic fantasies of heterosexual, gay, and bisexual people. Kinsey might have predicted that bisexual individuals would have *fewer* heteroerotic fantasies than heterosexual people, and *more* homoerotic fantasies than heterosexual people. But Storms predicted that "bisexuals will report *as much* heteroerotic fantasy as heterosexual people and *as much* homoerotic fantasy as homosexuals" (p. 786).

Storms found that heterosexual students reported significantly more fantasies about the other gender than their own gender. Gay students reported more frequent fantasies about their own gender. Bisexuals, as predicted, reported a high level of both kinds of fan-

Heteroerotic

Of an erotic nature and involving members of the other gender.

Homoerotic

Of an erotic nature and involving members of one's own gender.

Figure 8.2. **Heterosexuality and Homosexuality as Separate Dimensions.** According to this model, homosexuality and heterosexuality are independent dimensions. One can thus be high or low on both dimensions at the same time. Most people are high in one dimension. Bisexuals are high in both dimensions. People who are low in both are considered *asexual.*

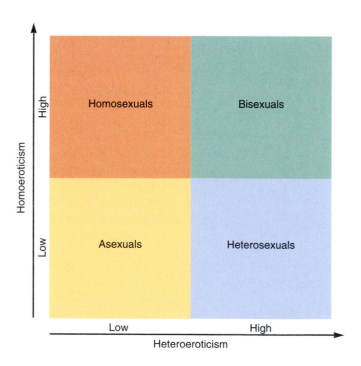

tasies. Because Storms did find that many bisexual people show a high level of sexual interest in both men and women, it may be that sexual interest in the other gender and in one's own gender are independent dimensions rather than opposite poles of one continuum.

Bisexuality

Bisexual people are sexually attracted to both males and females. Kinsey and his colleagues considered people rated as 3s to be bisexual (see Figure 8.1). Depending on how one defines bisexuality, perhaps 1% to 4% of the population is bisexual. About 1% of the people (0.8% of the men and 0.9% of the women) surveyed in the NHSLS study (Laumann et al., 1994) reported having a bisexual *identity*. However, about 4% (3.9% of the men and 4.1% of the women) reported that they were sexually attracted to both women and men.

Bisexual people are sometimes said to "swing both ways," or to be "A/C–D/C" (as in "alternating current" and "direct current"). Some gay people (and some heterosexual people) believe that claims to bisexuality are a "cop-out" that people use to deny being gay. Perhaps they fear leaving their spouses or "coming out" (declaring their gay male or lesbian sexual orientation publicly). Others view bisexuality as a form of sexual experimentation with people of one's own gender by people who are predominantly heterosexual. But many avowed bisexual people disagree. They report that they can maintain erotic interests in, and romantic relationships with, members of both genders. Some authors (e.g., Garber, 1995; Weinberg et al., 1994) insist that bisexuality is an authentic sexual orientation and not simply a "cover" for a gay male or lesbian sexual orientation.

Perspectives on Gay Male and Lesbian Sexual Orientations

Gay male and lesbian sexual orientations have existed throughout history. In this section we review historical and other perspectives on gay male and lesbian sexual orientations.

Historical Perspectives

In Western culture, few sexual practices have met with such widespread censure as sexual activities with members of one's own gender. Within the Judeo-Christian tradition, male–male and female–female sexual behavior has been deemed criminal and sinful—an outrage against God and humanity. Most states, grounded in this religious tradition, pose criminal penalties for sexual practices commonly associated with male–male and female–female sex, such as anal and oral sex.

Jews and Christians have traditionally referred to male–male sexual activity as the sin of Sodom. Hence the origins of the term *sodomy,* which generally alludes to anal intercourse (and sometimes to oral–genital contact). According to the Book of Genesis, the city of Sodom was destroyed by God.

Cross-Cultural Perspectives

Ford and Beach (1951) found that in nearly two thirds of the preliterate societies they studied, male–male sexual interactions were viewed as normal and deemed socially acceptable for some people. The other societies had sanctions against male–male sexual behavior.

Sexual activities between males are sometimes limited to rites that mark the young male's initiation into manhood. In some preliterate societies, semen is believed to boost strength and virility. Older males thus transmit semen to younger males through oral or anal sexual activities. Among the Sambian people of New Guinea, a tribe of warlike headhunters, 9- to 12-year-old males leave their parents' households and live in a "clubhouse" with other prepubertal and adolescent males. There they undergo sexual rites of passage. To acquire the fierce manhood of the headhunter, they perform fellatio on older males and drink "men's milk" (semen) (Herdt, 1981; Money, 1990; Stoller & Herdt, 1985). The initiate is enjoined to ingest as much semen as he can, "as if it were breast milk or food" (Herdt, 1981, p. 235). Ingestion of semen is believed to give rise to puberty. Following puberty, adolescents are fellated by younger males (Baldwin & Baldwin, 1989). By the age of 19, however, young men are expected to take brides and enter exclusively male–female sexual relationships.

These practices of Sambian culture might seem to suggest that the sexual orientations of males are fluid and malleable. The practices involve *behavior,* however, and not *sexual orientation.* Male–male sexual behavior among Sambians takes place within a cultural context that bears little resemblance to consensual male–male sexual activity in Western society. The prepubertal Sambian male does not *seek* sexual liaisons with other males. He is removed from his home, by force if necessary, and thrust into male–male sexual encounters by older males (Baldwin & Baldwin, 1989).

Little is known about female–female sexual activity in non-Western cultures. Evidence of female–female sexual behavior was found by Ford and Beach in only 17 of the 76 societies they studied. This cross-cultural evidence is consistent with data from our own culture. Here, too, males are more likely than females to develop sexual interests in, or romantic relationships with, members of their own genders (Katz, 1995; Laumann et al., 1994).

Attitudes Toward Sexual Orientation in Contemporary Society

Negative attitudes toward gay people pervade our society (Katz, 1995). A national survey of men of ages 15 to 19 showed that 9 of 10 felt that sex between men was "disgusting." Three of five could not even see themselves being friends with a gay man (Marsiglio, 1993b).

Seventy-five percent of respondents to a 1987 survey felt that sexual relations between members of the same gender are "always wrong" (Davis & Smith, 1987). Forty percent would bar gay people from teaching in a college or university. A 1992 national Gallup poll found that the great majority (78%) of Americans favor equal employment opportunities for gay people ("Job rights," 1992). Two out of three Americans favor health insurance and inheritance rights for gay spouses. Yet fewer than one in three favors legally sanctioned gay marriages. Only about a third supported the right of gay couples to adopt children. Americans were about equally split on the issues of whether gay people should be permitted to teach in elementary schools or become members of the clergy.

Some of those who would bar gay people from teaching and other activities believe that gay people, given the chance, will seduce and recruit children into a gay lifestyle. Such beliefs have been used to prevent gay couples from becoming adoptive or foster parents and to deny them custody or visitation rights to their own children, following divorce. Some people who would bar gay people from interactions with children fear that the children will be molested. Yet more than 90% of cases of child molestation involve heterosexual male assailants (Gelles & Cornell, 1985; Gordon & Snyder, 1989). Nor are children who are reared or taught by gay men or lesbians more likely to become gay themselves. One study found that 36 of 37 children who were reared by lesbian or transsexual couples developed a heterosexual orientation (Green, 1978).

Homophobia

A cluster of negative attitudes and feelings toward gay people, including intolerance, hatred, and fear. (From Greek roots meaning "fear" [of members of the] "same" [gender].)

Gay bashing

Violence against homosexuals.

Homophobia   Homophobia takes many forms, including

- use of derogatory names (such as *queer, faggot,* and *dyke*).
- telling disparaging "queer jokes."
- barring gay people from housing, employment, or social opportunities.
- taunting (verbal abuse).
- **gay bashing** (physical abuse).

Homophobia derives from root words meaning "fear of homosexuals." Although some psychologists link homophobia to fears of a gay male or lesbian sexual orientation within

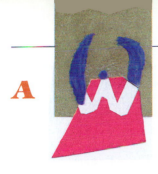 
ETHNICITY AND SEXUAL ORIENTATION: A MATTER OF BELONGING

Lesbians and gay men frequently suffer the slings and arrows of an outraged society. Because of societal prejudices, it is difficult for many young people to come to terms with an emerging lesbian or gay male sexual orientation. You might assume that people who have been subjected to prejudice and discrimination—members of ethnic minority groups in the United States—would be more tolerant of a lesbian or gay male sexual orientation. However, according to Greene (1994), such an assumption might not be warranted.

Greene (1994) notes that it is difficult to generalize about ethnic groups in the United States. For example, African Americans may find their cultural origins in the tribes of West Africa, but they have also been influenced by Christianity and the local subcultures of their North American towns and cities. Native Americans represent hundreds of tribal groups, languages, and cultures. By and large, however, a lesbian or gay male sexual orientation is rejected by ethnic minority groups in the United States. Lesbians and gay males are pressured to keep their sexual orientations a secret or to move to communities where they can live openly without sanction.

Within traditional Hispanic American culture, the family is the primary social unit. Men are expected to support and defend the family, and women are expected to be submissive, respectable, and deferential to men (Morales, 1992). Because women are expected to remain virgins until marriage, men sometimes engage in male–male sexual behavior without considering themselves gay (Greene, 1994). Hispanic American culture frequently denies the sexuality of women. Thus, women who label themselves lesbians are doubly condemned—because they are lesbians and because they are confronting others with their sexuality. Because lesbians are independent of

men, most Hispanic American heterosexual people view Hispanic American lesbians as threats to the tradition of male dominance (Trujillo, 1991).

Asian American cultures emphasize respect for one's elders, obedience to parents, and sharp distinctions in masculine and feminine gender roles (Chan, 1992). The topic of sex is generally taboo within the family. Asian Americans, like Hispanic Americans, tend to assume that sex is unimportant to women. Women are also considered to be less important than men. Open admission of a lesbian or gay male sexual orientation is seen as a rejection of one's traditional cultural roles and a threat to the continuity of the family line (Chan, 1992; Garnets & Kimmel, 1991).

Because many African American men have had difficulty finding jobs, gender roles among African Americans have been more flexible than those found among white Americans and most other ethnic minority groups (Greene, 1994). Nevertheless, the African American community appears to strongly reject gay men and lesbians, pressuring them to remain secretive about their sexual orientations (Gomez & Smith, 1990; Poussaint, 1990). Greene (1994) hypothesizes a

number of factors that influence African Americans to be hostile toward lesbians and gay men. One is strong allegiance to Christian beliefs and biblical scripture. Another is internalization of the dominant culture's stereotyping of African Americans as highly sexual beings. That is, many African Americans may feel a need to assert their sexual "normalcy" or even a sense of sexual superiority.

Prior to the European conquest, sex may not have been discussed openly by Native Americans, but sex was generally seen as a natural part of life. Individuals who incorporated both traditional feminine and masculine styles were generally accepted and even admired. The influence of the religions of colonists led to greater rejection of lesbians and gay men, and pressure to move off the reservation to the big city (Greene, 1994). Native American lesbians and gay men, like Asian American lesbians and gay men, thus often feel doubly removed from their families.

If any generalization is possible, it may be that lesbians and gay men find more of a sense of belonging in the gay community than in their ethnic communities.

A Matter of Belonging. Gay couples who are members of ethnic minority groups often report that they feel more a part of the gay community than of their ethnic group.

oneself, homophobic attitudes may also be embedded within a cluster of stereotypical gender-role attitudes toward family life (Kerns & Fine, 1994). These attitudes support male dominance and the belief that it is natural and appropriate for women to sacrifice for their husbands and children (Katz, 1995; Marsiglio, 1993b).

Homophobic attitudes are more common among males who identify with a traditional male gender role and those who hold a fundamentalist religious orientation (Kerns & Fine, 1994; Marsiglio, 1993b). Similarly, researchers find that college students who hold a conservative political orientation tend to be more accepting of negative attitudes toward gay people than are liberal students (Lottes & Kuriloff, 1992). Generally speaking, heterosexual men are relatively less tolerant of gay people than are heterosexual women (Kerns & Fine, 1994; Seltzer, 1992; Whitley & Kite, 1995).

Perhaps some heterosexual men are threatened by the possibility of discovering male–male sexual impulses within themselves (Freiberg, 1995). Research by Henry Adams and his colleagues (1996) supports this possibility. The Adams group showed men sexually explicit videotapes of male–female, female–female, and male–male sexual activity and measured their sexual response by means of the penile plethysmograph. The plethysmograph measures penile circumference (size of erection). Partcipants were also asked to report how sexually aroused they felt in response to the videos. The men were also evaluated for their attitudes toward gay males. Nonhomophobic viewers were sexually aroused, according to their penile circumference, only by videos of male–female and female–female sexual activity. The homophobic viewers were also aroused in terms of penile circumference by the video of male–male sexual activity. However, the homophobic men also reported that they did not *feel* aroused by the male–male sexual activity, suggesting that they were out of touch with their biological response.

Gay Bashing and the AIDS Epidemic   When AIDS first appeared, it primarily struck the gay male community. Some people believed that the epidemic was a God-sent plague intended to punish gay people for sinful behavior.

The advent of the epidemic has been accompanied by a dramatic rise in the incidence of gay bashing (Freiberg, 1995; Katz, 1995). However, the percentage of gay men who account for new cases of AIDS has been steadily declining (see Chapter 13).

Sexual Orientation and the Law   During the past generation, gay people have organized effective political groups to fight discrimination and to overturn the sodomy laws that have traditionally targeted them. Despite their success, sodomy laws are still on the books in about half of our states. Sodomy laws prohibit "unnatural" sexual acts, even between consenting adults. A gay male or lesbian sexual orientation is not illegal in itself. However, certain sexual acts that many gay people (and heterosexual people) practice, such as anal intercourse and oral–genital contact, fall under the legal definition of sodomy in many states. Sodomy laws also typically prohibit sexual contacts with animals. Although sodomy laws are usually intended to apply equally to all adults, married or unmarried, heterosexual or gay, the vast majority of prosecutions have been directed against gay people.

Many other countries, including Mexico, Holland, Italy, Spain, England, France, and the Scandinavian countries, have decriminalized male–male and female–female sexual activity (Carrera, 1981). In Canada, a consensual sexual act is prosecutable under sodomy laws only if one of the participants is under 21 years of age or the act is performed in public.

As this book goes to press, gay marriages may soon be permitted in a number of states. In 1996, however, the U. S. Senate voted 85–14 that states would not have to recognize gay marriages permitted in other states (Schmitt, 1996).

Gay Activism   Nowhere in the United States have gay people been more politically effective than in San Francisco. They are well represented on the city police force and in other public agencies. The coming out of many gay people, and their flocking to more tolerant urban centers have rendered them formidable political forces in these locales.

The Mattachine Society, named after gay medieval court jesters, was the first powerful gay rights organization. At first, membership was kept secret to protect members' so-

Gay Rights. Gay men, lesbians, and those who care about them have participated in demonstrations demanding equal access to housing, jobs, and other opportunities.

cial standing in the community. Today, however, members' names are published, and many heterosexual supporters are listed in their ranks. Founded in Los Angeles in 1950, the Mattachine Society now has chapters in most metropolitan areas. The society publishes the *Mattachine Newsletter* and *Homosexual Citizen.* Another newsletter, the *Advocate,* has become the nation's best-known gay newsletter.

The largest lesbian organization is the Daughters of Bilitis, named after the Greek courtesan who was loved by the lesbian poet Sappho. Founded in 1956, the group provides a forum for sharing social experiences and pursuing equal rights. The organization's newsletter is the *Ladder.*

Stereotypes and Sexual Behavior

Among heterosexual people, sexual aggressiveness is linked to the masculine gender role. Sexual passivity is linked to the feminine role. Some heterosexual people assume (often erroneously) that in gay male and lesbian relationships, one partner consistently assumes the masculine role in sexual relations, and the other, the feminine.

Many gay couples vary the active and passive roles, however. Among gay male couples, for example, roles in anal intercourse (*inserter* versus *insertee*) and in fellatio are often reversed. Contrary to popular assumptions, sexual behavior between lesbians seldom reflects distinct **butch–femme** gender roles. Most lesbians report providing and receiving oral–genital stimulation. Typically, partners alternate roles or simultaneously perform and receive oral stimulation. Many gay people claim that the labels of *masculine* and *feminine* only represent the "straight community's" efforts to pigeonhole them in terms "straights" can understand.

Biological Perspectives

Is sexual orientation an *inborn* trait that is transmitted genetically, like eye color or height? Does it reflect hormonal influences? Biological perspectives focus on the role of genetics and hormonal influences in shaping sexual orientation.

Genetics and Sexual Orientation

Considerable evidence exists that gay male and lesbian sexual orientations run in families (Bailey et al., 1993; Pillard, 1990). In one study, for example, 22% of the brothers of a sample of 51 predominantly gay men were either gay or bisexual themselves. This is nearly four times the proportion expected in the general population (Pillard & Weinrich, 1986). Although such evidence is consistent with a genetic explanation, families also share a common environment.

Twin studies also shed light on the possible role of heredity (Rose, 1995). **Monozygotic (MZ) twins,** or identical twins, develop from a single fertilized ovum and share 100% of

Butch

A lesbian who assumes a traditional masculine gender role.

Femme

A lesbian who assumes a traditional feminine gender role.

Monozygotic (MZ) twins

Twins who develop from the same fertilized ovum; identical twins.

Dizygotic (DZ) twins
Twins who develop from different fertilized ova; fraternal twins.

Concordance
Agreement.

their heredity. **Dizygotic (DZ) twins,** or fraternal twins, develop from two fertilized ova. Like other brothers and sisters, DZ twins share only 50% of their heredity. Thus if a gay male or lesbian sexual orientation were transmitted genetically, it should be found about twice as often among identical twins of gay people as among fraternal twins. Since MZ and DZ twins who are reared together share similar environmental influences, differences in the degree of **concordance** for a given trait between the types of twin pairs are further indicative of genetic origins.

Several studies have identified gay men who had either identical (MZ) or fraternal (DZ) twin brothers in order to examine the prevalences of a gay male sexual orientation in their twin brothers (Rose, 1995). Consistent with a genetic explanation, MZ twins do appear to have a higher concordance rate for a gay male sexual orientation than DZ twins. Bailey and Pillard (1991) reported a 52% concordance rate among MZ twin pairs versus a 22% rate among DZ twin pairs in their sample. In another study, researchers reported a concordance rate for a gay sexual orientation of 66% in MZ twins, as compared to 30% among DZ twins (Whitam et al., 1993). But bear in mind that MZ twins are more likely to be dressed alike and treated alike than DZ twins. Thus, their greater concordance for a gay sexual orientation may at least in part reflect environmental factors. The greater concordance between MZ twins may only signify that MZ twins are likely to react more similarly than DZ twins to the same *environmental* influences (Bancroft, 1990).

Researchers at the National Cancer Institute have found evidence linking a region on the X sex chromosome to a gay male sexual orientation (Hamer et al., 1993). The researchers cautioned that they had not found a particular gene linked to sexual orientation, just a general location of where the gene may be found. Nor do scientists know how such a gene, or combination of genes, might account for sexual orientation.

Sexologist John Money (1994) agrees that genetic factors may play a role in the development of sexual orientation. However, genetic factors do not fully govern sexual orientation. Most researchers believe that sexual orientation is affected by a complex interplay of biological and psychosocial influences (Barlow & Durand, 1995).

Hormonal Influences and Sexual Orientation

Sex hormones strongly influence the mating behavior of other species (Crews, 1994). Researchers have thus looked into possible hormonal factors in determining sexual orientation in humans.

Testosterone is essential to male sexual differentiation. Thus, the levels of testosterone and its by-products in the blood and urine have been suspected as a possible influence of sexual orientation, at least in males. Research has failed to connect sexual orientation in either gender with differences in the levels of either male or female sex hormones in adulthood (Friedman & Downey, 1994). In adulthood, testosterone appears to have **activating effects.** That is, it affects the intensity of sexual desire, but not the preference for partners of the same or the other gender (Whalen et al., 1990).

Activating effects
Those effects of sex hormones that influence the level of the sex drive but not sexual orientation.

What of the possible *prenatal* effects of sex hormones? Experiments have been performed in which pregnant rats were given antiandrogen drugs that block the effects of testosterone. When the drugs were given during critical periods in which the fetuses' brains were becoming sexually differentiated, male offspring were likely to show feminine mating patterns as adults (Ellis & Ames, 1987). The adult males became receptive to mounting attempts by other males and failed to mount females.

Do prenatal sex hormones play a similar role in determining sexual orientation in people? There is suggestive evidence. For example, Meyer-Bahlburg and his colleagues (1995) interviewed groups of women exposed prenatally to DES—a synthetic estrogen. They found that these women were more likely to be rated as lesbian or bisexual than women who were not exposed to DES. We do know that the genitals of gay people differentiate prenatally in accord with their chromosomal gender (Whalen et al., 1990). It remains possible that imbalances in prenatal sex hormones may cause brain tissue to be sexually differentiated in one direction even though the genitals are differentiated in the other (Collaer & Hines, 1995).

The Structure of the Brain

Evidence suggests that there may be structural differences between the brains of heterosexual and gay men. In 1991, Simon LeVay, a neurobiologist at the Salk Institute in La Jolla, California, carried out autopsies on the brains of 35 AIDS victims—19 gay men and 16 (presumably) heterosexual men. He found that a segment of the hypothalamus in the brains of the gay men was less than half the size of the same segment in the heterosexual men. The same brain segment was larger in the brain tissues of heterosexual men than in brain tissues obtained from a comparison group of 6 presumably heterosexual women. No significant differences in size were found between the brain tissues of the gay men and the women, however.

LeVay's findings are intriguing, but they are preliminary. We do not know, for example, whether the structural differences found by LeVay are innate. Nor should LeVay's findings be taken to mean that biology is destiny. As Richard Nakamura, a scientist with the National Institute of Mental Health, commented, "This [LeVay's findings] shouldn't be taken to mean that you're automatically [gay] if you have a structure of one size versus a structure of another size" (Angier, 1991).

Psychological Perspectives

Do family relationships play a role in the origins of sexual orientation? What are the effects of childhood sexual experiences? Psychoanalytic theory and learning theory provide two of the major psychological approaches to understanding the origins of sexual orientation.

Psychoanalytic Views

Polymorphously perverse
In psychoanalytic theory, being receptive to all forms of sexual stimulation.

Displacement
In psychoanalytic theory, a defense mechanism that allows one to transfer unacceptable wishes or desires onto more appropriate or less threatening objects.

Castration anxiety
In psychoanalytic theory, a man's fear that his genitals will be removed. Castration anxiety is an element of the Oedipus complex and is implicated in the directionality of erotic interests.

Penis envy
In psychoanalytic theory, the girl's wish to have a penis.

Sigmund Freud, the originator of psychoanalytic theory, believed that children enter the world **polymorphously perverse.** That is, prior to internalizing social inhibitions, children are open to all forms of sexual stimulation. However, through proper resolution of the Oedipus complex, a boy will forsake his incestuous desires for his mother and come to identify with his father. As a result, his erotic attraction to his mother will eventually be transferred, or **displaced,** onto more appropriate *female* partners. A girl, through proper resolution of her Electra complex, will identify with her mother and seek erotic stimulation from men when she becomes sexually mature.

In Freud's view, a gay male or lesbian sexual orientation results from failure to successfully resolve the Oedipus complex by identifying with the parent of the same gender. In men, faulty resolution of the Oedipus complex is most likely to result from the so-called classic pattern of an emotionally "close-binding" mother and a "detached–hostile" father. A boy reared in such a family may come to identify with his mother and even to "transform himself into her" (Freud, 1922/1959, p. 40). He may thus become effeminate and develop sexual interests in men.

Freud believed that the mechanism of unresolved **castration anxiety** plays a role in a gay male sexual orientation. By the time the Oedipus complex takes effect, the boy will have learned from self-stimulation that he can obtain sexual pleasure from his penis. In his youthful fantasies, he associates this pleasure with mental images of his mother. He is also likely to have learned that females do not possess a penis. Somewhere along the line the psychoanalyst theorizes that the boy may also have been warned that his penis will be removed if he plays with himself. From all this, the boy may surmise that females—including his mother—once had penises, but that they were removed.

During the throes of the Oedipus complex, the boy unconsciously comes to fear that his father, his rival in love for the mother, will retaliate by removing the organ that the boy has come to associate with sexual pleasure. His fear causes him to repress his sexual desire for his mother and to identify with the potential aggressor—his father. The boy thus overcomes his castration anxiety and is headed along the path of adult heterosexuality.

If the Oedipus complex is not successfully resolved, castration anxiety may persist. When sexually mature, the man will not be able to tolerate sex with women. Their lack of a penis will arouse unconscious castration anxiety within himself. According to psychoanalytic theory, the boy may unconsciously associate the vagina with teeth, or other sharp instruments, and be unable to perform sexually with a woman.

The Electra complex in little girls follows a somewhat different course. Freud believed that little girls become envious of boys' penises, since they lack their own. This concept of **penis envy** was one of Freud's most controversial beliefs. In Freud's view, jealousy leads little girls to resent their mothers, whom they blame for their anatomic "deficiency," and to turn from their mothers to their fathers as sexual objects. They now desire to possess the father, because the father's penis provides what they lack. But incestuous desires bring the girl into competition with her mother. Motivated by fear that her mother will withdraw her love if the desires persist, the girl normally represses them and identifies with her mother. She then develops traditional feminine interests and eventually seeks erotic stimulation from men. She supplants her childhood desire for a penis with a desire to marry a man and bear children. The baby, emitted from between her legs, serves as the ultimate penis substitute.

A girl who does not resolve her penis envy in childhood may "manifest homosexuality, . . . exhibit markedly masculine traits in the conduct of her later life, choose a masculine vocation, and so on" (Freud, 1922/1959, p. 50). The residue of this unresolved complex is continued penis envy, the striving to become a man by acting like a man and seeking sexual satisfaction with women: lesbianism.

In Freud's view, a gay male or lesbian sexual orientation is one result of assuming the gender role normally taken up by the other gender. The gay male is expected to be effeminate; the lesbian, masculine. But, as noted in research into gender-typed behavior and sexual orientation, this stereotypical view of gay people is far from universal. Nor do the behaviors stereotypical of the other gender found in some adult gay men or women necessarily derive from Oedipal problems. Biological and other psychosocial factors may be involved.

A nagging problem of Freudian theory is that many of its concepts, such as castration anxiety and penis envy, are believed to operate at an unconscious level. As such, they lie beyond the scope of scientific observation and measurement. We cannot learn whether boys experience castration anxiety by asking them, since the theory claims that **repression** will keep such anxieties out of awareness. Nor can we directly learn about penis envy by interviewing girls.

Repression
The automatic ejection of anxiety-evoking ideas from consciousness.

Research on Psychoanalytic Theories of Sexual Orientation

Psychoanalysts—psychotherapists trained in the Freudian tradition—have researched sexual orientation largely through case studies. These studies have been carried out almost exclusively with gay males who were in therapy at the time.

In 1962, psychoanalyst Irving Bieber reported the results of questionnaires filled out by 77 psychiatrists on 106 gay male clients. In 1976, he reported the results of similar surveys of gay men in therapy.

Bieber claimed to find the "classic pattern" among gay males—their orientation was determined by having a dominant, "smothering" mother and a passive, detached father. As the clients described them, the mothers were overprotective, seductive, and jealous of their sons. The fathers were aloof, unaffectionate, and hostile toward them. The father, being detached, may have failed to buffer the close mother–son relationship. The mother's relationship with the father was typically disturbed, and the mother may have substituted a "close-binding" relationship with her son. This classic pattern was believed to result in the boy's developing a fear of sexual contacts with women. Though he would be unconscious of this dynamic, for him, any female partner would represent his mother. Desire for her would stir unconscious fears of retaliation by the father—that is, castration anxiety.

Bieber's findings may be criticized on several grounds:

1. The study participants were all in analysis, and many wanted to become heterosexual. Thus we cannot generalize the results to well-adjusted gay men.
2. The analysts may have chosen cases that confirmed their theoretical perspectives.
3. No clear evidence exists that gay males either fear or are repulsed by female genitalia.
4. Many *heterosexual* men have family backgrounds that fit the classic pattern, and the families of many gay men do *not* fit the pattern.
5. Retrospective accounts of childhood relationships with parents are subject to gaps in memory and distortions.

More recent evidence has brought the issue of familial closeness between gay men and their parents into closer perspective. Richard Pillard and his colleagues (Pillard & Weinrich, 1986; Pillard, 1990) found that gay males described themselves as more distant from

Father–Son Relationship. Does the quality of the father–son relationship play a role, as some theorists suspect, in the development of homosexuality in men? According to a recent study, gay men perceived themselves as having been more distant from their fathers during childhood than did heterosexual men. The question is, why?

their fathers during childhood than did either heterosexual controls or the gay men's own heterosexual brothers. The gay men in their sample also reported greater closeness to their mothers. Still, the father's psychological distance from the son may have reflected the *son's* alienation from him, not the reverse. That is, the son may have been so attached to his mother, or so uninterested in traditional masculine activities, that he rebuffed paternal attempts to engage him in conventional father–son activities.

In sum, family characteristics may play a role in the development of sexual orientation. However, there is great variation among the families of gay males and lesbians. No single pattern applies in all cases (Isay, 1990). Family dynamics may be one of many factors that shape sexual orientation.

Learning Theories   Learning theorists agree with Freud that early experiences play an important role in the development of sexual orientation. They focus on the role of reinforcement of early patterns of sexual behavior, however, rather than on the resolution of unconscious conflicts. People generally repeat pleasurable activities and discontinue painful ones. Thus, people may learn to engage in sexual activity with people of their own gender if childhood sexual experimentation with them is connected with sexual pleasure.

If sexual motivation is high, as it tends to be during adolescence, and the only outlets are with others of one's own gender, adolescents may experiment sexually with them. If these encounters are pleasurable, and heterosexual experiences are unpleasant, a firmer gay male or lesbian sexual orientation may develop (Gagnon & Simon, 1973). Conversely, pain, anxiety, or social disapproval may be connected with early contacts with people of one's own gender. In such cases, the child may learn to inhibit feelings of attraction to people of his or her own gender and develop a firmer heterosexual orientation.

Although learning may play a role in the development of a gay male or lesbian sexual orientation, most adolescent encounters with people of the same gender, even if pleasurable, do not lead to an adult gay male or lesbian sexual orientation. Many heterosexual people have had adolescent encounters with members of their own gender without being swayed in their adult orientations. Moreover, the overwhelming majority of gay males and lesbians were aware of sexual interest in people of their own gender *before* they had sexual encounters with them, pleasurable or otherwise (Bell et al., 1981).

All in all, the origins of sexual orientation remain mysterious and complex. Perhaps sexual orientation springs from multiple origins, including biological and psychosocial factors (Strickland, 1995). Genetic and biochemical factors (such as hormone levels) may affect the prenatal organization of the brain (Money, 1994). These factors may predispose people to a certain sexual orientation. But it may be that early socialization experiences are also involved. The precise effects of these factors have so far eluded researchers.

Adjustment of Gay Males and Lesbians

Despite the widespread belief that there is something wrong with gay men and lesbians, evidence has failed to show that they are more emotionally unstable or more subject to psychological disorders (such as anxiety and depression) than other people (Reiss, 1980). Nor have researchers been able to distinguish between gay and heterosexual people on the basis of psychological tests (Reiss, 1980). A gay male or lesbian sexual orientation is no longer itself considered a form of mental illness. In 1973 the American Psychiatric Association voted to drop a gay male or lesbian sexual orientation from its list of mental disorders, although a diagnostic category remains for people with persistent and marked distress about their sexual orientation (American Psychiatric Association, 1994, p. 538).

Gay men, lesbians, and bisexuals occupy all socioeconomic and vocational levels and follow a variety of lifestyles. Researchers find gay men and lesbians overall to be more highly educated than most Americans (Cronin, 1993). Bell and Weinberg (1978) found variations in adjustment in the gay community that seem to mirror the variations in the heterosexual community. Gay people who lived with partners in stable, intimate relationships—so-called close couples—were about as well adjusted as married people. Older gay people who lived alone and had few sexual contacts were more poorly adjusted. So, too, are many heterosexual people who have similar lifestyles. All in all, differences in adjustment seem more likely to reflect the lifestyle than the sexual orientation.

"Treatment" of Gay Male and Lesbian Sexual Orientations

Despite the judgment of the American Psychiatric Association, some people still view a gay male or a lesbian sexual orientation as an illness. If it is an illness, then it is something to be "cured," perhaps by medical or psychological means. However, the great majority of gay men and lesbians do not seek professional assistance to change their sexual orientations.

A few gay men and women do express an interest in changing their orientations, however. Helping professionals have tried to help them do so in a variety of ways. At one time, when it was commonly believed that hormonal imbalances influenced one's sexual orientation, hormone treatments were in vogue. There is no evidence that they were effective.

A few psychotherapists have reported changing the sexual orientations of some individuals. For example, Bieber (1976) claimed that about one in four clients changed his or her sexual orientation through psychoanalytic psychotherapy. But critics charge that these clients were highly motivated to change. Moreover, some of them began therapy as bisexuals. Their change in lifestyle may be attributable to their initial motivation to change and not to the therapy itself.

Masters and Johnson (1979) employed methods used to treat sexual dysfunctions (see Chapter 12) to "reverse" patients' gay male or lesbian sexual orientations. For example, they involved gay males in a graded series of pleasurable activities with women, such as massage and genital stimulation. Masters and Johnson reported a failure rate of 20% for the gay men and 23% for the lesbians they treated in their therapy program. At a five-year follow-up, more than 70% of the clients continued to engage in male–female sexual activity (Schwartz & Masters, 1984). For many reasons, however, these patients do not seem to represent the general gay population:

- Most of them were bisexuals. Only about one in five engaged exclusively in male–male or female–female sexual activities.
- More than half were married.
- They all were motivated to switch their sexual orientations.

COMING OUT: COMING TO TERMS WITH BEING GAY

Because of the backdrop of social condemnation and discrimination, gay males and lesbians in our culture often struggle to come to terms with their sexual orientation. Gay men and lesbians usually speak of the process of accepting their sexual orientation as "coming out" or as "coming out of the closet." Coming out is a two-pronged process: coming out to oneself (recognizing one's gay male or lesbian sexual orientation) and coming out to others (declaring one's orientation to the world). Coming out can create a sense of pride in one's sexual orientation and foster the ability to form emotionally and sexually satisfying relationships with gay male or lesbian partners.

Coming Out to Oneself

Many gay people have a difficult time coming to recognize, let alone accept, their sexual orientation. Some have even considered or attempted suicide because of problems in self-acceptance:

> It (suicidal thinking) was because of my homosexuality. I was completely depressed that my homosexuality was leading me nowhere. My life seemed to be going around in a circle. I was still fighting against recognition of my homosexuality. I knew what I was but I didn't want to be.
>
> [I had] the feeling that homosexuality was a hopeless existence. I felt there was no future in it, that I was doomed to be alone. And from my Catholic background, I felt that homosexuality was very evil.
>
> (Bell & Weinberg, 1978, p. 202)

Consider the experience of a New Zealand gay adolescent who was subjected to merciless taunting until his parents pulled him out of school. "He threw a ball like a girl does," said a hotline worker (cited in Shenon, 1995), "and the hassling just wouldn't stop. He was hassled nonstop from the day he got to that school until the day he left."

"You're judged constantly on your maleness," adds a Roman Catholic priest in New Zealand (cited in Shenon,

1995). "It can be a very intolerant country. You must worship rugby and beer. And if you don't, God help you. I think we've just been dreadful about this macho-ness."

For some people, coming to recognize and accept a gay male or lesbian sexual orientation involves gradually stripping away layers of denial. For others it may be a sudden awakening. Long-standing sexual interests in members of one's own gender may rush into focus on a particular person, as happened with a graduate student named David:

> In college [David's] closest friend was gay. Although this friend had wanted to have sex with David and the attraction was mutual, David still could not associate this attraction with a sexuality that was not acceptable to him. In his first year of graduate school, when he was about 23, he fell in love and then suddenly and with a great sense of relief recognized and acknowledged to himself that he was homosexual. He then had sex for the first time and has subsequently been . . . open about his sexuality.
>
> (Isay, 1990, p. 295)

Recognition of a gay sexual orientation may be only the first step in a lifelong process of sexual identity formation. Acceptance of being gay becomes part of one's self-definition (Isay, 1990). The term *gay*, or *homosexual*, *identity* refers to the subjective or psychological sense of being gay.

Some gay men and lesbians who have not yet come to recognize or accept their gay sexual orientation get married. For some, marriage is a means of testing feelings toward people of the other gender. For others, marriage represents an attempt to conceal or overcome their sexual orientation (Buxton, 1994; Gabriel, 1995a). Perhaps 20% of gay males and a higher percentage of lesbians get married at least once (Bell & Weinberg, 1978). But such marriages tend to be unhappy and short-lived. They

may be strained by one partner's concealing her or his gay sexual orientation. Alternatively, they may buckle from the open acknowledgment of being gay. Virtually all such marriages in Bell and Weinberg's study eventually ended in separation or divorce.

In the 1990s, many American couples have a gay or lesbian spouse. Thousands of gay men and lesbians who had conformed to social pressures by getting married are now coming out of the closet and sometimes leaving home (Buxton, 1994; Gabriel, 1995a).

Coming Out to Others

There are different patterns of coming out to others. Coming out occasionally means an open declaration to the world. More often a person may inform only one or a few select people. The person might tell friends but not family members.

Many gay men and lesbians remain reluctant to declare their sexual orientation, even to friends and family. Disclosure is fraught with the risk of loss of jobs, friendships, and social standing (Padesky, 1988). A social worker who counsels lesbians described some fears of coming out to others expressed by her clients:

> Will I lose my job, will I lose my house, will I lose my children, will I be attacked? I've seen people lose a job. Even if you don't lose it, you become marginal, excluded either actively or through uncomfortable vibes.
>
> (Cited in Barrett, 1990, p. 470)

Gay men and lesbians often anticipate negative reactions from informing family members, including denial, anger, and rejection. Family members and loved ones may refuse to hear or be unwilling to accept reality. Other families are more accepting. They may in fact have had suspicions and prepared themselves for such news. Then, too, many families are initially rejecting but often eventually come to at least grudging acceptance that their child is gay.

Regardless of these people's changes in sexual behavior, remember that sexual behavior is not the equivalent of sexual orientation. (It was thus inaccurate for Masters and Johnson to claim that they had reversed an individual's sexual *orientation*.) That is, many gay people engage in sexual activities with people of the other gender. Nevertheless, they still prefer to have such relationships with people of their own gender.

Isay (1990), a psychoanalyst, argues that gay men and women often enter therapy because of conflicts that arise from social pressure and prejudice. Such pressures can create problems in the acceptance of one's gay male or lesbian sexual orientation. The role of the therapist, he argues, should be to help unburden the client of conflict and promote a more gratifying life as a gay person.

Gay Male and Lesbian Sexual Behavior

Generally speaking, gay couples express themselves sexually through as wide a range of activities as heterosexual couples, with the exception of vaginal intercourse. But there are shades of difference between gay and heterosexual couples in sexual techniques.

Gay male couples tend to engage in sexual activities such as kissing, hugging, petting, mutual masturbation, fellatio, and anal intercourse. Laboratory observations of sexual relations between gay males by Masters and Johnson (1979) showed that gay males spent a good deal of time caressing their partners' bodies before approaching the genitals. After hugging and kissing, 31 of 42 gay male couples observed by Masters and Johnson used oral or manual nipple stimulation.

Not all gay males enjoy or practice anal intercourse. Of those who do, most alternate between being the inserter and the insertee. The frequency of anal intercourse among gay males is apparently declining in the face of the AIDS epidemic (Catania et al., 1991; Centers for Disease Control, 1990a; Sonenstein et al., 1989).

Risks of infection and of injury to the rectum or anus are associated with another sexual practice called "fisting." Fisting is the insertion of the fist or hand into the rectum, usually after the bowels have been evacuated with an enema.

Sexual techniques practiced by lesbians vary. Lesbian couples report kissing, manual and oral breast stimulation, and manual and oral stimulation of the genitals (Kinsey et al., 1953). Manual genital stimulation is the most common and frequent sexual activity among lesbian couples (Bell & Weinberg, 1978). Most lesbian couples also engage in genital apposition. That is, they position themselves so as to rub their genitals together rhythmically (Kinsey et al., 1953). Like gay males, lesbians spend a good deal of time holding, kissing, and caressing each other's bodies before they approach the breasts and genitals. By contrast, heterosexual males tend to move quickly to stimulate their partners' breasts or start directly with genital stimulation (Masters & Johnson, 1979).

Like heterosexual women, lesbians are less genitally oriented and less fixated on orgasm than men. Lesbians generally begin stimulating their partners with more general genital stimulation rather than direct clitoral stimulation, whereas heterosexual males often begin by stimulating the clitoris (Masters & Johnson, 1979). Nor do lesbian couples generally engage in deep penetration of the vagina with fingers. Rather, they may use more shallow vaginal penetration, focusing stimulation on the vaginal lips and entrance. The emotional components of lovemaking—gentle touching, cuddling, and hugging—are important elements of sexual sharing in lesbian relationships.

Gay Lifestyles

One of the mistakes that lay people (and some researchers) make is to treat gay people as if they were all the same. According to Bell and Weinberg (1978), gay people do not adopt a single, stereotypical lifestyle. That is why the authors termed their report *Homosexualities: A Study of Diversity Among Men and Women.* Variations in sexual expression exist within and across sexual orientations. Descriptions of gay and heterosexual lifestyles must consider individual differences.

Gay men and lesbians in larger U.S. urban centers can usually look to gay communal structures to provide services and support. These include gay rights organizations and gay-oriented newspapers, magazines, bookstores, housing cooperatives, medical services, and other support services (Gagnon, 1990). The gay community provides a sense of acceptance and belonging that gay people do not typically find in society at large. Gay people still encounter discrimination in the workplace, in housing, and in the military.

Restrictions on gay males participating in the armed services has been a continuing controversy. In 1993, President Bill Clinton encountered stiff opposition when he sought to follow through on his campaign pledge to permit openly gay men and women to serve in the military. As a compromise measure, he instituted a "don't ask, don't tell" policy. It permits gay males and lesbians to serve so long as they do not publicly express or reveal their sexual orientation. Moreover, military officials are prohibited from inquiring about the sexual orientation of recruits or initiating investigations in the absence of a public display or disclosure of a gay male or lesbian sexual orientation ("Defense dept. suspends," 1993). The constitutionality of this policy has been challenged since it may restrict free speech.

Gay rights organizations fight for rights for gay people to participate fully in society—to teach in public schools, to adopt children, to live together in sanctioned relationships, and to serve openly and proudly in the military. Cafés and social clubs provide places where gay men and lesbians can socialize and be open about their sexual orientations. Organizations such as New York's Gay Men's Health Crisis (GMHC) provide medical, social, and psychological assistance to gay males who have been afflicted by AIDS.

Not all gay people feel that they are a part of the "gay community" or participate in gay rights organizations, however. For many, their sexual orientation is a part of their identity, but not a dominant theme that governs their social and political activities.

Lifestyle Differences Between Gay Males and Lesbians

Much of our knowledge of lifestyle patterns among gay males and lesbians comes from research that predates the AIDS epidemic. Researchers in the 1970s found that gay males were more likely than lesbians to engage in casual sex with many partners. Lesbians more often confined their sexual activity to a committed, affectionate relationship (Bell & Weinberg, 1978). Bell and Weinberg reported that 84% of gay males, as compared to about 7% of lesbian women, reported having more than 50 partners in their lifetimes. Seventy-nine percent of gay males in their study, as compared to only 6% of lesbians, reported that more than half of their partners had been strangers.

Even in this age of AIDS, a recent survey found that only about half of gay men (40% to 60%), but about three in four lesbians, are currently involved in a steady relationship (Peplau & Cochran, 1990). Even gay males within committed relationships have more permissive attitudes toward extracurricular sexual activity than lesbians do (Blumstein & Schwartz, 1990; Peplau & Cochran, 1990).

Cruising
The name that gay people give to searching for a sex partner.

Traditionally, the gay bar was an arena for making sexual contacts (Bell & Weinberg, 1978). **Cruising** is the name gay people give to searching for a sex partner, principally for casual sex. One can "cruise," and one can "be cruised." Today, with the threat of AIDS hanging over every casual sexual encounter, cruising has lost popularity. Many gay baths, long a setting for casual sexual contacts, have closed down—or been closed down by authorities—because of AIDS. Many gay males have changed their behavior to prevent contracting or spreading AIDS. Gay males are more likely to limit or avoid anal and oral sex, especially with new partners. They are now more likely to use latex condoms when they do practice these techniques, to limit their sexual contacts to partners they know, and to rely more on masturbation as a sexual outlet (Centers for Disease Control, 1990a, 1990b; Siegel et al., 1988).

Research also shows that extracurricular sexual activity continues to be commonplace among gay male couples. One study surveyed 943 gay males and 1,510 married heterosexual males who had been living with a partner for 2 to 10 years. Four of five (79%) of the gay males reported sex with another partner during the preceding year, as compared to only 11% of the heterosexual males (Blumstein & Schwartz, 1990). Among couples who had been together for longer than 10 years, 94% of gay men reported extracurricular activity at some time during their primary relationships.

Variations in Gay Lifestyles

Close couples

Bell and Weinberg's term for gay couples whose relationships resemble marriage in their depth of commitment and exclusiveness.

Open couples

Bell and Weinberg's term for gay couples who live together but engage in secret affairs.

Functionals

Bell and Weinberg's term for gay people who live alone, have adapted well to a swinging lifestyle, and are sociable and well adjusted.

Dysfunctionals

Bell and Weinberg's term for gay people who live alone and have sexual, social, or psychological problems.

Asexuals

Bell and Weinberg's term for gay people who live alone and have few sexual contacts.

Bell and Weinberg (1978) found that about 3 out of 4 gay couples they studied could be classified according to 1 of 5 lifestyles: *close couples, open couples, functionals, dysfunctionals,* and *asexuals.* **Close couples** strongly resembled married couples. They evidenced deep emotional commitment and few outside sexual relationships. Almost three times as many lesbians (28%) as gay males (10%) lived in such committed, intimate relationships. Gay people living in close relationships showed fewer social and psychological problems than those with any other lifestyle.

Partners in **open couples** lived together but engaged in clandestine affairs. Gay people in open couples were not as well adjusted as those in close couples. Nevertheless, their overall adjustment was similar to that of heterosexual people. Still other gay people lived alone and had sexual contacts with numerous partners—a kind of "swinging singles" gay lifestyle. Some of those who lived alone, **functionals,** appeared to have adapted well to their swinging lifestyle and were sociable and well adjusted. Others, called **dysfunctionals,** had sexual, social, or psychological problems. Dysfunctionals were often anxious, unhappy, and found it difficult to form intimate relationships. **Asexuals** also lived alone but were distinguished by having few sexual contacts. Asexuals tended to be older than gay people in the other groups. Although they did not have the adjustment problems of dysfunctionals, they too did not form intimate relationships. Despite being largely asexual in terms of their behavior, their sexual orientation was clearly gay.

The Bell and Weinberg study described diversity of lifestyles in the gay community in the 1970s, before the AIDS epidemic struck. Although such lifestyles continue today to a certain extent, the AIDS epidemic has inhibited promiscuous sex within the gay community. The specter of AIDS has had a more profound effect on the lifestyles and sexual practices of gay males than on any other group in society.

Chapter Review

Classification of Sexual Orientation

Sexual (1) _____tion refers to one's erotic attractions toward, and interests in developing romantic relationships with, members of one's own or the other gender. A (2) _____sexual orientation refers to an erotic attraction to, and preference for developing romantic relationships with, members of the other gender. A (3) _____sexual orientation refers to an erotic attraction to, and interest in forming romantic relationships

with, members of one's own gender. The term *homosexuality* applies to (4: Men, Women, *or* Both men and women?). Homosexual men are often referred to as (5) _____ males. Homosexual women are also called (6) l_____ or gay women. The term (7) _____ity refers to an orientation in which one is sexually attracted to, and interested in forming romantic relationships with, both males and females. Gay people have a gender identity that (8: Is *or* Is not?) consistent with their anatomic gender.

Heterosexual people (9: Always, Sometimes, *or* Never?) have sexual experiences with people of their own gender. Males who engage in prostitution with male clients are (10: Always, Sometimes, *or* Never?) heterosexual.

Kinsey and his colleagues proposed a (11) _____ um of sexual orientation rather than two poles. (12) Bi_____ represents a midpoint on the Kinsey continuum. People in category 0 of the continuum are considered exclusively (13) _____sexual. People in category 6 are considered exclusively (14) _____. Kinsey and his colleagues reported that about (15) _____% of men and 1% to 3% of women in their samples were exclusively gay. Statistics concerning past sexual activity with a member of one's own gender can be misleading because they may represent a (16) s_____ episode or a brief period of experimentation. Kinsey's research also showed that sexual behavior patterns (17: Could *or* Could not?) shift during a person's lifetime.

Current estimates generally find (18: Lower *or* Higher?) percentages of gay people in the population than Kinsey did. Research in the United States, Britain, France, and Denmark finds that about (19) _____% of men surveyed identify themselves as gay. A (20: Lower *or* Higher?) percentage of U.S. women surveyed identify themselves as lesbians.

Kinsey believed that exclusive heterosexual and gay sexual orientations lay at (21: The same *or* Opposite?) poles of one continuum. Michael Storms suggests that gay and heterosexual orientations are independent (22) _____sions. According to Storms, bisexuals are (23: High *or* Low?) in both dimensions. Storms found that many bisexual people show a (24: High *or* Low?) level of sexual interest in both men and women.

(25: Less *or* More?) than 5% of the population is bisexual. Bisexual people are sometimes said to (26) "s_____ both ways," or to be (27) "A/C-_____."

Perspectives on Gay Male and Lesbian Sexual Orientations

Within the Judeo-Christian tradition, male–male sexual activity (28: Is *or* Is not?) regarded as sinful. Jews and Christians traditionally refer to male–male sexual activity as the sin of (29) _____om. The term *sodomy* generally alludes to (30) a_____ _____course.

In their review of the literature on 76 preliterate societies, Ford and Beach found that male–male sexual interactions were viewed as normal and socially acceptable (31: In most *or* In only a few?) of the societies for some members of the group. In some preliterate societies, (32) s_____ is believed to boost strength and virility. Among the (33) _____ian people of New Guinea, young males perform fellatio on older males and drink "men's milk" as a rite of passage into manhood. By the age of 19, young Sambian men are expected to begin exclusive (34: Male–male *or* Male–female?) sexual relationships.

Negative attitudes toward gay people are (35: Common *or* Uncommon?) in our society. A 1992 national Gallup poll found that (36: Most *or* Only a few?) Americans favor equal employment opportunities for gay people. A (37: Majority *or* Minority?) of Americans favor gay marriages. More than 90% of cases of child molestation involve (38) _____sexual male assailants. Children who are reared or taught by gay men or lesbians (39: Are *or* Are not?) likely to become gay themselves.

(40) H_____ derives from roots meaning "fear of homosexuals." Physical abuse of gay people is termed (41) g_____ _____ing. Homophobic attitudes appear to be connected with (42: Traditional *or* Nontraditional?) gender-role attitudes toward family life. These attitudes support (43: Male *or* Female?) dominance. College students with a conservative political orientation are (44: More *or* Less?) accepting of gay people than are liberal students. Male college students tend to be (45: More *or* Less?) homophobic than college women.

Research by Henry Adams and his colleagues suggests that some homophobic men have (46: Heteroerotic *or* Homoerotic?) impulses of which they are unaware. Male homophobic viewers of male–male sexual activity were (47: More *or* Less?) sexually aroused in terms of penile circumference than were male viewers who were not homophobic.

Strides toward social acceptance of gay people (48: Have *or* Have not?) been made since Kinsey's day. However, the advent of the AIDS epidemic has been accompanied by a(n) (49: Increase *or* Decrease?) in gay bashing. The percentage of gay men who account for new cases of AIDS has been (50: Increasing *or* Decreasing?) in recent years.

Sodomy laws are on the books in about (51: 25, 50, or 75?)% of states. A gay male or lesbian sexual orientation (52: Is or Is not?) illegal in itself. The vast majority of prosecutions under (53) _____ my laws have been directed against gay people. In 1996, the U.S. Senate voted 85–14 that states (54: Would or Would not?) have to recognize gay marriages permitted in other states.

Gay activists in the United States have been most politically effective in the city of (55) S_____ _____. The (56) _____chine Society was the first powerful gay rights organization. *The* (57) _____ate has become the nation's best-known gay newsletter. The largest lesbian organization is the Daughters of (58) B_____. The organization is named after the Greek courtesan who was loved by the lesbian poet (59) S_____.

Many gay couples vary the (60) _____ive and passive sexual roles. Sexual behavior between lesbians seldom reflects distinct (61) bu_____–_____me gender roles.

Gay male and lesbian sexual orientations (62: Do or Do not?) appear to run in families. Monozygotic (MZ) twins, or identical twins, develop from a single fertilized ovum and share (63) _____% of their heredity. Dizygotic (DZ) twins, or (64) _____nal twins, develop from two fertilized ova. DZ twins share (65) _____% of their heredity. If a gay sexual orientation is transmitted genetically, it should be found about twice as often among (66) _____cal twins of gay people as among fraternal twins. Recent studies (67: Do or Do not?) find that MZ twins have a higher concordance rate for a gay male sexual orientation than DZ twins do. Researchers at the National Cancer Institute have found evidence linking a region on the (68) _____ sex chromosome to a gay male sexual orientation.

Research has (69: Connected or Not connected?) sexual orientation in either gender with differences in the levels of either male or female sex hormones in adulthood. However, it may be that (70) pre_____ sex hormones play a role in determining sexual orientation in people.

Research by Simon (71) Le_____ suggests that there may be structural differences between the brains of heterosexual and gay men. He found that a segment of the (72) hypo_____ in the brains of the gay men was less than half the size of the same segment in the heterosexual men. Scientist Richard Nakamura comments that one (73: Is or Is not) automatically gay if one has a brain structure of one size versus another.

Sigmund Freud, the originator of (74) psycho-_____ theory, believed that children enter the world (75) poly_____ _____verse. That is, prior to internalizing social inhibitions, children are open to (76: All or Only a few?) forms of sexual stimulation. However, through proper resolution of the (77) O_____ _____plex, a boy will identify with his father. A girl, through proper resolution of the (78) E_____ _____plex, will identify with her mother. In men, faulty resolution of the Oedipus complex is most likely to result from the so-called classic pattern of an emotionally (79) "c_____-_____ing" mother and a "detached–hostile" father. Freud believed that unresolved (80) cas_____ _____ty plays a role in a gay male sexual orientation. According to Freud, the Electra complex involves (81) p_____ _____vy. Psychoanalyst Irving (82) B_____ claimed to find a dominant, "smothering" mother and a passive, detached father as parents of gay males. However, all of Bieber's study participants were in analysis, and many wanted to become (83) het_____.

Learning theorists focus on the role of (84) _____ment of early patterns of sexual behavior. Evidence shows, however, that adolescent encounters with members of one's own gender usually (85: Do or Do not?) affect adult sexual orientation. Moreover, (86: Most or Only a few?) gay males and lesbians become aware of sexual interest in people of their own gender before they have sexual encounters with them. All in all, it is likely that sexual orientation (87: Has or Does not have?) a simple, single cause.

Adjustment of Gay Males and Lesbians

Evidence shows that gay men and lesbians (88: Are or Are not?) more emotionally unstable or subject to psychological problems than other people. The American Psychiatric Association (89: Does or Does not?) consider a gay male or lesbian sexual orientation to be a form of mental illness. Gay people occupy all (90) _____-economic and vocational levels and follow a variety of lifestyles. Gay (91) c_____ _____ples are about as well adjusted as married people.

Most gay men and lesbians (92: Do *or* Do not?) wish to change their sexual orientations. (93) M_____ and Johnson tried to reverse sexual orientation by involving gay males in a graded series of pleasurable activities with women. The people that they worked with do not represent the general gay population because they all (94: Were *or* Were not?) motivated to switch their sexual orientations. Isay argues that the role of a therapist should be to help unburden the client of conflict and promote a more gratifying life as a (95: Gay *or* Heterosexual?) person.

Gay men and lesbians usually speak of the process of accepting their sexual orientation as "coming out" or "coming out of the (96) _____ et." Coming out is a two-pronged process: coming out to oneself and coming out to (97) _____rs.

Bell and Weinberg found that about (98) _____% of gay males and a higher percentage of lesbians get married to heterosexuals at least once. A (99: Minority *or* Majority?) of such marriages eventually end in separation or divorce.

Gay Male and Lesbian Sexual Behavior

Gay couples engage in behaviors similar to those of heterosexual couples, with the exception of (100) _____nal intercourse. Gay males tend to spend (101: More *or* Less?) time than heterosexual males in caressing their partners' bodies before approaching the genitals. The frequency of anal intercourse among gay males is apparently (102: Rising *or* Declining?) in the face of the AIDS epidemic. (103) _____ing is the insertion of the fist or hand into the rectum. (104) _____al genital stimulation is the most common and frequent sexual activity among lesbian couples.

Gay Lifestyles

According to Bell and Weinberg, gay people (105: Do *or* Do not?) adopt a single, stereotypical lifestyle. In 1993, President Clinton instituted a (106) "Don't ask, _____ _____" policy that permits gay males and lesbians to serve in the military so long as they do not publicly express their sexual orientation. Gay rights organizations fight for rights for gay people to teach in public schools, to adopt children, to get married, to obtain health (107) _____nce through a partner's place of work, and to serve openly in the military.

(108: Gay males *or* Lesbians?) are more likely to engage in casual sex with many partners. A higher percentage of (109: Gay males *or* Lesbians?) is currently involved in a steady relationship. (110) _____ing is the name gay people give to searching for a sex partner. Because of fear of AIDS, gay males have become (111: More *or* Less?) likely to limit or avoid anal and oral sex and to use condoms when they do practice these techniques.

Bell and Weinberg classified gay people's relationships as close couples, (112) o_____ couples, functionals, (113) dys_____, and asexuals.

Chapter Quiz

1. What is the usual relationship between sexual orientation and gender identity?
   - (a) Bisexuals have a confused gender identity.
   - (b) Gender identity develops later than usual among gay males and lesbians.
   - (c) There is no research on the relationship between sexual orientation and gender identity.
   - (d) Gay people have a gender identity that is consistent with their anatomic gender.
2. In a survey of male readers of *Playboy* magazine, of those who had sexual experiences with both men and women in adulthood, _____ reported themselves to be heterosexual rather than bisexual.
   - (a) none
   - (b) one-third
   - (c) one-half
   - (d) more than two thirds
3. Kinsey and his colleagues conceived a _____-point "heterosexual–homosexual continuum."
   - (a) 2
   - (b) 5
   - (c) 7
   - (d) 10
4. The term *sodomy* most commonly refers to
   - (a) anal intercourse.
   - (b) masturbation.
   - (c) oral–anal sexual activity.
   - (d) sexual activity with three or more partners.
5. Why do young Sambian males perform fellatio on older males?
   - (a) They have Dominican Republic syndrome and spend their early years as females.
   - (b) They are attempting to achieve the fierce manhood of the headhunter.

(c) Sexual orientation changes frequently during childhood and adolescence.

(d) They are paid to do so as part of a religious ritual.

6. Research conducted by Henry Adams and his colleagues (1996) suggests that many men may be homophobic because
   (a) they drink (alcohol) excessively.
   (b) they have sexual interest in other men but are unaware of it.
   (c) of the AIDS epidemic.
   (d) the Judeo-Christian tradition frowns on male–male sexual behavior.

7. Which of the following statements about genetics and sexual orientation is most accurate?
   (a) A gay male orientation is not found among MZ and DZ twins.
   (b) The concordance rate for a gay male orientation is equal among MZ and DZ twins.
   (c) The concordance rate for a gay male orientation is higher among MZ than DZ twins.
   (d) The concordance rate for a gay male orientation is higher among DZ than MZ twins.

8. Simon LeVay conducted research on sexual orientation through

(a) the survey method.

(b) autopsies of the brains of people who died from AIDS.

(c) studies of the genetic makeup of heterosexuals and gay people.

(d) cross-cultural research.

9. According to _____, sexual orientation in males is connected with the resolution of the Oedipus complex.
   (a) Michael Storms
   (b) Alfred Kinsey
   (c) Alan Bell
   (d) Sigmund Freud

10. Which of the following statements about gender and sexual orientation appears to be best supported by research reported in the text?
   (a) Lesbians are more likely than gay males to have many sex partners.
   (b) Gay males are more likely than lesbians to have many sex partners.
   (c) Heterosexual males are more likely than gay males to have many sex partners.
   (d) Heterosexual females are more likely than lesbians to have many sex partners.

Answers to Chapter Review

1. Orientation
2. Heterosexual
3. Homosexual
4. Both men and women
5. Gay
6. Lesbians
7. Bisexuality
8. Is
9. Sometimes
10. Sometimes
11. Continuum
12. Bisexuality
13. Heterosexual
14. Gay or Homosexual
15. 4
16. Single
17. Could
18. Lower
19. 3
20. Lower
21. Opposite
22. Dimensions
23. High
24. High
25. Less
26. Swing
27. D/C
28. Is
29. Sodom
30. Anal intercourse
31. In most
32. Semen
33. Sambian
34. Male–female
35. Common
36. Most
37. Minority
38. Heterosexual
39. Are not
40. *Homophobia*
41. Gay bashing
42. Traditional
43. Male
44. Less
45. More
46. Homoerotic
47. More
48. Have
49. Increase
50. Decreasing
51. 50
52. Is not
53. Sodomy
54. Would not
55. San Francisco
56. Mattachine
57. *Advocate*
58. Bilitis
59. Sappho
60. Active
61. Butch–femme
62. Do
63. 100
64. Fraternal
65. 50
66. Identical
67. Do
68. X
69. Not connected
70. Prenatal
71. LeVay
72. Hypothalamus
73. Is not
74. Psychoanalytic or Psychodynamic
75. Polymorphously perverse
76. All
77. Oedipus complex
78. Electra complex
79. Close-binding
80. Castration anxiety
81. Penis envy
82. Bieber
83. Heterosexual
84. Reinforcement
85. Do not
86. Most
87. Does not have?
88. Are not
89. Does not
90. Socioeconomic
91. Close couples
92. Do not
93. Masters
94. Were
95. Gay
96. Closet
97. Others
98. 20
99. Majority
100. Vaginal
101. More
102. Declining
103. Fisting
104. Manual
105. Do not
106. Don't tell
107. Insurance
108. Gay males
109. Lesbians
110. Cruising
111. More
112. Open
113. Dysfunctionals

Answers to Chapter Quiz

1. (d)
2. (d)
3. (c)
4. (a)
5. (b)
6. (b)
7. (c)
8. (b)
9. (d)
10. (b)

CHAPTER 9

Conception, Pregnancy, and Childbirth

O U T L I N E

Infertility and Ways of Becoming Parents
Male Fertility Problems
Female Fertility Problems

Pregnancy
Early Signs of Pregnancy
Pregnancy Tests
Early Effects of Pregnancy
Miscarriage
Sex During Pregnancy
Psychological Changes During Pregnancy

Prenatal Development
The Germinal Stage
The Embryonic Stage
The Fetal Stage
Environmental Influences on Prenatal Development
Chromosomal and Genetic Abnormalities

Childbirth
The Stages of Childbirth
Methods of Childbirth

Birth Problems
Anoxia
Preterm and Low-Birthweight Children

The Postpartum Period
Maternal Depression
Breast-Feeding Versus Bottle-Feeding
Resumption of Sexual Activity

Chapter Review

Chapter Quiz

Applications
Optimizing the Chances of Conception
Averting Chromosomal and Genetic Abnormalities

A World of Diversity
Ethnicity and Infant Mortality

- Fertilization normally occurs in a fallopian tube, not the uterus?
- Prolonged athletic activity can decrease fertility in the male?
- A human embryo can be removed from one woman and implanted in the uterus of another?
- Morning sickness can actually occur throughout the day?
- In most cases, sexual intercourse is safe throughout the course of pregnancy?
- For the first week following conception, a fertilized egg cell is not attached to its mother's body?
- The placenta is unique in that it develops from material supplied by both mother and embryo?
- The majority of babies born to mothers who are infected with HIV do not become infected themselves?
- Most women who have had cesarean deliveries can subsequently have vaginal deliveries?
- Only a minority of women in the United States breast-feed their children?

Zona pellucida

A gelatinous layer that surrounds an ovum. (From roots meaning "zone that light can shine through.")

Hyaluronidase

An enzyme that briefly thins the zona pellucida, enabling one sperm to penetrate. (From roots meaning "substance that breaks down a glasslike fluid.")

Infertility

Inability to conceive a child.

Figure 9.1. **Human Sperm Swarming Around an Ovum in a Fallopian Tube.** Fertilization normally occurs in a fallopian tube, not in the uterus.

Conception is the union of a sperm cell and an ovum. On one hand, conception is the beginning of a new human life. Conception is also the end of a fantastic voyage, however, in which a viable ovum, one of only several hundred that will mature and ripen during a woman's lifetime, unites with one of several hundred *million* sperm produced by the man in the average ejaculate.

Ova carry X sex chromosomes. Sperm carry either X or Y sex chromosomes. Girls are conceived from the union of an ovum and an X-bearing sperm, boys from the union of an ovum and a Y-bearing sperm.

The 200 to 400 million sperm in an average ejaculate may seem excessive, since only 1 can fertilize an egg. Only 1 in 1,000 will ever arrive in the vicinity of an ovum, however. Millions deposited in the vagina simply flow out of the woman's body because of gravity, unless she remains prone for quite some time. Normal vaginal acidity kills many more. Many surviving sperm swim against the current of fluid coming from the cervix, through the os and into the uterus. Surviving sperm may reach the fallopian tubes 60 to 90 minutes after ejaculation. About half the sperm end up in the wrong tube—that is, the one not containing the egg. Perhaps some 2,000 sperm find their way into the right tube. Fewer still manage to swim the final 2 inches against the currents generated by the cilia that line the tube.

Fertilization normally occurs in a fallopian tube. (Figure 9.1 shows sperm swarming around an egg in a fallopian tube.) Ova are surrounded by a gelatinous layer called the **zona pellucida.** Sperm that have completed their journey secrete the enzyme **hyaluronidase,** which briefly thins the zona pellucida, enabling one sperm to penetrate. Once a sperm has entered, the zona pellucida thickens, locking other sperm out. The corresponding chromosomes in the sperm and ovum line up opposite each other. Conception occurs as the chromosomes from the sperm and ovum combine to form 23 new pairs, which carry a unique set of genetic instructions. ■

Infertility and Ways of Becoming Parents

The term **infertility** is usually not applied until the failure to conceive has persisted for more than a year. Infertility concerns millions of Americans. Because the incidence of in-

OPTIMIZING THE CHANCES OF CONCEPTION

Some couples may wish to optimize their chances of conceiving during a particular month so that birth occurs at a desired time. Others may have difficulty conceiving and wish to maximize their chances for a few months before consulting a fertility specialist. Some fairly simple procedures can dramatically increase the chances of conceiving for couples without serious fertility problems.

The ovum can be fertilized for about 4 to 20 hours after ovulation. Sperm are most active within 48 hours after ejaculation. So one way of optimizing the chances of conception is to engage in coitus within a few hours of ovulation. There are a number of ways to predict ovulation.

Using the Basal Body Temperature Chart

Few women have perfectly regular cycles, so they can only guess when they are ovulating. A basal body temperature (BBT) chart (see Figure 9.2) may help provide a more reliable estimate.

Body temperature is fairly even before ovulation, and early morning body temperature is generally below 98.6 degrees Fahrenheit. But just prior to ovulation, basal temperature dips. On the day following ovulation, temperature tends to rise by about 0.4 to 0.8 degrees and to remain higher until menstruation. In using the BBT method, a women attempts to detect these temperature changes by tracking her temperature just after awakening each morning but before rising from bed. The couple record the woman's temperature and the day of the cycle (as well as the day of the month) and indicate whether they have engaged in coitus. With regular charting for six months, the woman may learn to predict the day of ovulation more accurately—assuming that her cycles are fairly regular.

Analyzing Urine for Luteinizing Hormone

Over-the-counter kits are more accurate than the BBT method. They predict ovulation by analyzing the woman's urine for the surge in luteinizing hormone (LH) that precedes ovulation.

Tracking Vaginal Mucus

Women can track the thickness of their vaginal mucus during the phases of the menstrual cycle by rolling it between their fingers and noting changes in texture. The mucus is thick, white, and cloudy during most phases of the cycle. It becomes thin, slippery, and clear for a few days preceding ovulation. A day or so after ovulation the mucus again thickens and becomes opaque.

Additional Considerations

Coitus in the male-superior position allows sperm to be deposited deeper in the vagina and minimizes leakage of sperm out of the vagina due to gravity. Women may improve their chances of conceiving by lying on their backs and drawing their knees close to their breasts following ejaculation. This position makes gravity work for, rather than against, conception. Women may also lie still for about 30 to 60 minutes following ejaculation.

The man should penetrate the woman as deeply as possible just prior to ejaculation, hold still during ejaculation, then withdraw slowly in a straight line to avoid dispersing the pool of semen.

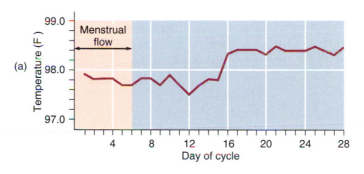

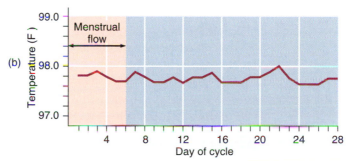

Figure 9.2. **A Basal Body Temperature (BBT) Chart.** Body temperature dips slightly just prior to ovulation, rises about 0.4 to 0.8 of a degree following ovulation, and remains elevated through the course of the cycle. Part (a) represents a cycle in which a sustained elevation in temperature occurred following ovulation on day 15. Part (b) shows no sustained temperature rise, which is indicative of an absence of ovulation in this cycle. *Source:* Adapted from Kolodny, R. C., Masters, W. H., and Johnson, V. E. (1979). *Textbook of sexual medicine.*

fertility increases with age, it is partially the result of a rise in couples who postpone child-bearing until their 30s and 40s (Sheehy, 1995). All in all, about 15% of American couples have fertility problems (Howards, 1995). However, about half of them eventually succeed in conceiving a child (Jones & Toner, 1993). Many treatment options are available, ranging from drugs to stimulate ovulation to newer reproductive technologies, such as in vitro fertilization.

Male Fertility Problems

Although most concerns about fertility have traditionally centered on women, the problem lies with the man in about 30% of cases (Howards, 1995). In about 20% of cases, problems are found in both partners (Hatcher et al., 1990; Howards, 1995).

Fertility problems in the male reflect abnormalities such as these:

1. Low sperm count
2. Irregularly shaped sperm—for example, malformed heads or tails
3. Low sperm **motility**
4. Chronic diseases such as diabetes, as well as infectious diseases such as sexually transmitted diseases
5. Injury to the testes
6. An **auto-immune response,** in which antibodies produced by the man deactivate his own sperm
7. A pituitary imbalance and/or thyroid disease

Motility
Self-propulsion. A measure of the viability of sperm cells.

Auto-immune response
The production of antibodies that attack naturally occurring substances that are (incorrectly) recognized as being foreign or harmful.

Problems in producing normal, abundant sperm may be caused by genetic factors, advanced age, hormonal problems, diabetes, injuries to the testes, varicose veins in the scrotum, drugs (alcohol, narcotics, marijuana, tobacco), antihypertensive medications, environmental toxins, excess heat, and emotional stress.

Low sperm count is the most common problem. Sperm counts of 40 million to 150 million sperm per milliliter of semen are considered normal. A count of fewer than 20 million is generally regarded as low. Sperm production may be low among men with undescended testes that were not surgically corrected prior to puberty. Frequent ejaculation can reduce sperm counts. Sperm production may also be impaired in men whose testicles are consistently 1 or 2 degrees above the typical scrotal temperature of 94 to 95 degrees Fahrenheit (Leary, 1990). Frequent hot baths and tight-fitting underwear can also reduce sperm production, at least temporarily. Some men may encounter fertility problems from prolonged athletic activity, use of electric blankets, or even long, hot baths. In such cases the problem can be readily corrected. Male runners with fertility problems are often counseled to take time off to increase their sperm counts.

Sometimes the sperm count is adequate, but prostate, hormonal, or other factors deprive sperm of motility or deform them. Motility can also be hampered by scar tissue from infections. Scarring may prevent sperm from passing through parts of the male reproductive system, such as the vas deferens. To be considered normal, sperm must be able to swim for at least two hours following coitus, and most (60% or more) must be normal in shape.

Sperm counts have been increased by surgical repair of the varicose veins in the scrotum. Microsurgery can open blocked passageways that prevent the outflow of sperm (Howards, 1995). Most men whose infertility is due to higher-than-normal scrotal temperatures show increased sperm count and quality with the wearing of cooling undergarments (Leary, 1990; Silber, 1991).

Artificial Insemination   The sperm of men with low sperm counts can be collected and quick-frozen. The sperm from multiple ejaculations can then be injected into a woman's uterus at the time of ovulation. This is one kind of **artificial insemination.** The sperm of men with low sperm motility can also be injected into their partners' uteruses, so that the sperm begin their journey closer to their destination. Sperm from a donor can be used to artificially inseminate a woman whose partner is infertile. The child then bears the genes of one of the parents, the mother. A donor can be chosen who resembles the man in physical traits and ethnic background.

Artificial insemination
The introduction of sperm in the reproductive tract through means other than sexual intercourse.

Female Fertility Problems

Major causes of infertility in women include the following:

1. Irregular ovulation, including failure to ovulate
2. Obstructions or malfunctions of the reproductive tract
3. Endometriosis
4. Declining hormone levels that occur with aging and may prevent the ovum from becoming fertilized or remaining implanted in the uterus

Ten percent to 15% of female infertility problems stem from failure to ovulate. Many factors can play a role in failure to ovulate, including hormonal irregularities, malnutrition, genetic factors, stress, and disease. Failure to ovulate may occur in response to extreme dieting, as in the case of the eating disorder *anorexia nervosa*.

Ovulation may often be induced by the use of fertility drugs such as *clomiphene* (Clomid). Clomiphene stimulates the pituitary gland to secrete FSH and LH, which in turn stimulate maturation of ova. Clomiphene leads to conception in the majority of cases of infertility that are due *solely* to irregular or absent ovulation (Reinisch, 1990). But since infertility can have multiple causes, only about 50% of women who use clomiphene become pregnant. Another infertility drug, Pergonal, contains a high concentration of FSH, which directly stimulates maturation of ovarian follicles. Like clomiphene, Pergonal has high success rates with women whose infertility is due to lack of ovulation. Clomiphene and Pergonal have been linked to multiple births, including quadruplets and even quintuplets.

Local infections that scar the fallopian tubes and other organs impede the passage of sperm or ova. Such infections include pelvic inflammatory disease—an inflammation of the woman's internal reproductive tract that can be caused by various infectious agents, such as the bacteria responsible for gonorrhea and chlamydia (see Chapter 13).

In **endometriosis,** cells break away from the uterine lining (the endometrium) and become implanted and grow elsewhere. When they develop on the surface of the ovaries or fallopian tubes, they may block the passage of ova or impair conception. About one case in six of female sterility is believed to be due to endometriosis. Hormone treatments and surgery sometimes reduce the blockage to the point that women can conceive. A physician may suspect endometriosis during a pelvic exam, but it is diagnosed with certainty by **laparoscopy.** A long, narrow tube is inserted through an incision in the navel, permitting the physician to inspect the organs in the pelvic cavity visually. The incision is practically undetectable.

Several new methods help many couples with problems, such as blocked fallopian tubes, bear children.

In Vitro Fertilization

In the method of **in vitro fertilization** (IVF), conception takes place in a laboratory dish (not a test tube). Fertility drugs may be used to ripen ova. Ripe ova are then surgically removed from an ovary and placed in a laboratory dish along with the father's sperm. The fertilized egg is then placed in the mother's uterus, where it must become implanted to develop to term.

GIFT

In **gamete intrafallopian transfer,** or GIFT, sperm and ova are inserted together into a fallopian tube for fertilization. Unlike in vitro fertilization, conception occurs in a fallopian tube rather than a laboratory dish.

ZIFT

ZIFT (**zygote intrafallopian transfer**) involves a combination of IVF and GIFT. Sperm and ova are combined in a laboratory dish. Following fertilization, the **zygote** is placed in the mother's fallopian tube to begin its journey to the uterus for implantation. ZIFT has an advantage over GIFT in that the fertility specialists can ascertain that fertilization has occurred before insertion is performed.

Donor IVF

Donor IVF is a variation of the IVF procedure in which the ovum is taken from another woman, fertilized, and then injected into the uterus or fallopian tube of the intended mother. The procedure is used in cases in which the intended mother does not produce ova.

Endometriosis

A condition caused by the growth of endometrial tissue in the abdominal cavity or elsewhere outside the uterus. Characterized by menstrual pain, it may cause infertility.

Laparoscopy

A medical procedure in which a long, narrow tube (laparoscope) is inserted through an incision in the navel, permitting the visual inspection of organs in the pelvic cavity. (From the Greek *lapara*, meaning "flank.")

In vitro fertilization

A method of conception in which mature ova are surgically removed from an ovary and placed in a laboratory dish along with sperm.

Gamete intrafallopian transfer (GIFT)

A method of conception in which sperm and ova are inserted into a fallopian tube to encourage conception.

Zygote intrafallopian transfer (ZIFT)

A method of conception in which an ovum is fertilized in a laboratory dish and then placed in a fallopian tube.

Zygote

A fertilized ovum (egg cell).

Donor IVF

A variation of in vitro fertilization in which the ovum is taken from one woman, fertilized, and then injected into the uterus or fallopian tube of another woman.

Embryonic transfer
A method of conception in which a woman volunteer is artificially inseminated by the male partner of the intended mother, after which the embryo is removed from the volunteer and inserted within the uterus of the intended mother.

Intracytoplasmic injection
A method of conception in which sperm is injected directly into an ovum.

Surrogate mother
A woman who is impregnated through artificial insemination, with the sperm of a prospective father, carries the embryo and fetus to term, and then gives the child to the prospective parents.

Embryonic Transfer   A similar method for women who do not produce ova of their own is **embryonic transfer.** In this method a woman volunteer is artificially inseminated by the male partner of the infertile woman. Five days later the embryo is removed from the volunteer and inserted within the uterus of the mother-to-be.

In vitro and transfer methods are costly. Success with in vitro fertilization drops from nearly 30% in women in their mid-20s to 10% to 15% in women in their late 30s (Toner et al., 1991). As success remains elusive in many cases, frustration and lack of hope often lead couples to consider dropping out of infertility treatment programs (Blenner, 1992).

Intracytoplasmic Injection   **Intracytoplasmic injection** has been used when the man has too few sperm for IVF, or when IVF fails (Howards, 1995). In this method, sperm is injected directly into an ovum. To date, the method has resulted in pregnancy in about 35% of cases (Van Steirteghem et al., 1993).

Surrogate Motherhood   A **surrogate mother** is artificially inseminated by the husband of the infertile woman and carries the baby to term. The surrogate signs a contract to turn the baby over to the infertile couple. Such contracts have been invalidated in some states, however, so that surrogate mothers in these states cannot be compelled to hand over the babies.

Adoption   Adoption is yet another way for people to obtain children. Despite the occasional conflicts in which adoptive parents are pitted against biological parents who change their minds about giving their children up for adoption, most adoptions result in the formation of loving new families. Many people in the United States find it easier to adopt infants from other countries, infants with special needs, or older children.

Pregnancy

In this section we examine biological and psychological aspects of pregnancy: signs of pregnancy, prenatal development, complications, effects of drugs and sex, and the psychological experiences of pregnant women and fathers.

Early Signs of Pregnancy

For many women the first sign of pregnancy is missing a period. But some women have irregular menstrual cycles or miss a period because of stress. Missing a period is thus not a fully reliable indicator. Some women also experience cyclic bleeding or spotting during pregnancy, although the blood flow is usually lighter than normal. If a woman's basal body temperature remains high for about three weeks after ovulation, there is reason to suspect pregnancy even if she spots two weeks after ovulation.

Pregnancy Tests

Human chorionic gonadotropin
A hormone produced by women shortly after conception, which stimulates the corpus luteum to continue to produce progesterone. The presence of HCG in a woman's urine indicates that she is pregnant.

Hegar's sign
Softness of a section of the uterus between the uterine body and the cervix, which indicates that a woman is pregnant.

Pregnancy tests rely on the fact that women produce **human chorionic gonadotropin** (HCG) shortly after conception. Tests can detect HCG in the urine as early as the third week of pregnancy. A blood test can detect HCG in the woman's blood as early as the eighth day of pregnancy, about five days preceding her expected period.

Over-the-counter home pregnancy tests are also available. They too test the woman's urine for HCG and are intended to be used as early as one day after a missed period. Laboratory-based tests are considered 98% or 99% accurate. Home-based tests performed by lay people are somewhat less accurate. Women are advised to consult their physicians if they suspect that they are pregnant or wish to confirm a home pregnancy test result.

About a month after a woman misses her period, a health professional may be able to confirm pregnancy by pelvic exam. Women who are pregnant usually show **Hegar's sign.**

Hegar's sign is softness of a section of the uterus between the uterine body and the cervix, which may be palpated (felt) by the woman's physician by placing a hand on the abdomen and two fingers in the vagina.

Early Effects of Pregnancy

Just a few days after conception, a woman may note tenderness of the breasts. Hormonal stimulation of the mammary glands may make the breasts more sensitive and cause sensations of tingling and fullness.

Morning sickness, which may actually occur throughout the day, refers to the nausea, food aversions, and vomiting experienced during pregnancy. About half of all pregnant women experience morning sickness during the first few months of pregnancy (Thompson, 1993). In some cases, morning sickness is so severe that the woman cannot eat regularly and must be hospitalized to ensure that she and the fetus receive adequate nutrition. Morning sickness usually subsides by about the twelfth week of pregnancy. Pregnant women may also experience greater-than-normal fatigue during the early weeks, so that they sleep longer and fall asleep more readily than usual. Frequent urination, which may also be experienced, is caused by pressure from the swelling uterus on the bladder.

Morning sickness
Symptoms of pregnancy, including nausea, aversions to specific foods, and vomiting.

Miscarriage

Miscarriages have many causes, including chromosomal defects in the fetus and abnormalities of the placenta and uterus. About three in four miscarriages occur in the first 16 weeks of pregnancy, and the great majority of these occur in the first 7 weeks. Some miscarriages occur so early that the woman is not aware that she was pregnant. In most cases women who miscarry can carry subsequent pregnancies to term.

Miscarriage
A spontaneous abortion.

Sex During Pregnancy

Most health professionals concur that coitus is safe throughout the course of pregnancy until the start of labor, provided that the pregnancy is developing normally and the woman has no history of miscarriages. Women who experience bleeding or cramps during pregnancy may be advised by their obstetricians not to engage in coitus (Samuels & Samuels, 1986).

Many women show declines in sexual interest and activity during the first trimester because of fatigue, nausea, or misguided concerns that coitus will harm the embryo or fetus. Also during the first trimester, vasocongestion may cause tenderness of the breasts, discouraging fondling and sucking. Researchers in Israel reported a gradual decline in sexual interest and frequency of intercourse and orgasm during pregnancy among a sample of 219 women. The greatest decline occurred during the third trimester (Hart et al., 1991). Pain during intercourse is also commonly reported, especially in the third trimester (Ulbrich et al., 1990).

As the woman's abdominal region swells, the popular male-superior position becomes unwieldy. The female-superior, lateral-entry, and rear-entry positions are common alternatives. Of course, manual and oral sex can continue as usual.

Some women are concerned that the uterine contractions of orgasm may dislodge an embryo. Such concerns are usually unfounded, unless the woman has a history of miscarriage or is presently at risk of miscarriage. Women may also be concerned that orgasmic contractions during the final month may induce labor. Evidence on the issue is mixed, however. Women and their partners are advised to consult their obstetricians.

Psychological Changes During Pregnancy

A woman's psychological response to pregnancy reflects her desire to be pregnant, her physical changes, and her attitudes toward these changes. Women with the financial, social, and psychological resources to meet the needs of pregnancy and child rearing may welcome pregnancy. Other women may question their ability to handle their pregnancies and childbirth. Or they may fear that pregnancy will interfere with their careers or their mates' feelings about them. In general, women who want to have a baby are better adjusted during their pregnancies.

The first trimester may be difficult for women who are ambivalent about pregnancy. At that stage symptoms like morning sickness are most pronounced, and women must come to terms with being pregnant. The second trimester is generally less tempestuous. Morning sickness and other symptoms have largely vanished. It is not yet difficult to move about, and the woman need not yet face the delivery. Women first note fetal movement during the second trimester, and for many the experience is stirring:

> I was lying on my stomach and felt—something, like someone lightly touching my deep insides. Then I just sat very still and . . . felt the hugeness of having something living growing in me. Then I said, No, it's not possible, it's too early yet, and then I started to cry. . . . That one moment was my first body awareness of another living thing inside me.
>
> (*The New Our Bodies, Ourselves,* 1992)

During the third trimester it is normal, especially for first-time mothers, to worry about the mechanics of delivery and whether the child will be normal. The woman becomes increasingly heavy and literally "bent out of shape." It may become difficult to get up from a chair or out of bed. She must sit farther from the steering wheel when driving. Muscle tension from supporting the extra weight in her abdomen may cause backaches. She may feel impatient in the days and weeks just prior to delivery.

Men, like women, respond to pregnancy according to the degree to which they want the child. Many men are proud and look forward to the child with great anticipation. In such cases, pregnancy may bring parents closer together. But fathers who are financially or emotionally unprepared may consider the pregnancy a "trap." Now and then an expectant father experiences some signs of pregnancy, including morning sickness and vomiting. This reaction is termed a **sympathetic pregnancy.**

Sympathetic pregnancy
The experiencing of a number of signs of pregnancy by the father.

Prenatal Development

We can date pregnancy from the onset of the last menstrual cycle before conception, which makes the normal gestation period 280 days. We can also date pregnancy from the date at which fertilization was assumed to have taken place, which normally corresponds to two weeks after the beginning of the woman's last menstrual cycle. In this case, the normal gestation period is 266 days.

Once pregnancy has been confirmed, the delivery date may be calculated by *Nagele's rule:*

- Jot down the date of the first day of the last menstrual period.
- Add seven days.
- Subtract three months.
- Add one year.

For example, if the last period began on November 12, 1999, adding seven days yields November 19, 1999. Then subtracting three months yields August 19, 1999. Adding one year gives a "due date" of August 19, 2000. Few babies are born exactly when they are due, but the great majority are delivered during a ten-day period that spans the date.

Shortly following conception, the single cell that results from the union of sperm and egg begins to multiply—becoming two cells, then four, then eight, and so on. During the weeks and months that follow, tissues, structures, and organs begin to form, and the fetus gradually takes on the shape of a human being. By the time the fetus is born, it consists of hundreds of billions of cells—more cells than there are stars in the Milky Way galaxy. Prenatal development can be divided into three periods: the *germinal stage,* which corresponds to about the first two weeks, the *embryonic stage,* which coincides with the first two months, and the *fetal stage.* We also commonly speak of prenatal development in terms of three trimesters of three months each.

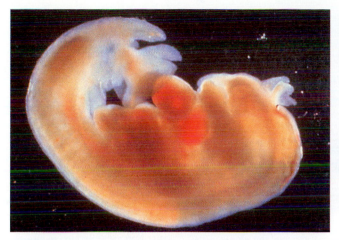

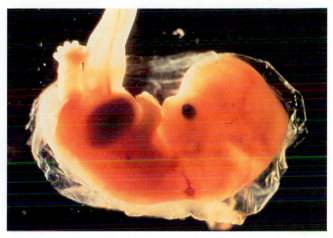

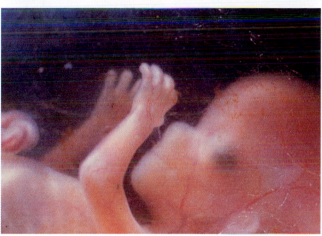

Prenatal Development. The rates of human growth and development are most dramatic prior to birth. Within a few months, a human fetus advances from weighing a fraction of an ounce to several pounds, and from one cell to billions of cells.

Germinal stage
The period of prenatal development prior to implantation in the uterus.

Period of the ovum
Germinal stage.

Blastocyst
A stage within the germinal stage of prenatal development, in which the embryo is a sphere of cells surrounding a cavity of fluid.

Embryonic stage
The stage of prenatal development that lasts from implantation through the eighth week and is characterized by the differentiation of the major organ systems.

Cephalocaudal
From the head downward. (From Latin roots meaning "head" and "tail.")

The Germinal Stage

Within 36 hours after conception, the zygote divides into 2 cells. It then divides repeatedly, becoming 32 cells within another 36 hours as it continues its journey to the uterus. It takes the zygote perhaps three or four days to reach the uterus. This mass of dividing cells then wanders about the uterus for perhaps another three or four days before it begins to become implanted in the uterine wall. The process of implantation takes about another week. This period from conception to implantation is termed the **germinal stage,** or the **period of the ovum** (see Figure 9.3 on page 210).

Several days into the germinal stage, the cell mass takes the form of a fluid-filled ball of cells, which is called a **blastocyst.** Already some cell differentiation has begun. Cells begin to separate into groups that will eventually become different structures.

Implantation may be accompanied by some bleeding, which results from the usual rupturing of some small blood vessels that line the uterus. Bleeding can also be a sign of a miscarriage—though most women who experience implantation bleeding do not miscarry but go on to have normal pregnancies and deliver healthy babies.

The Embryonic Stage

The period from implantation to about the eighth week of development is called the **embryonic stage.** The major organ systems of the body begin to differentiate during this stage.

Development of the embryo follows two trends—**cephalocaudal** and **proximodistal.** The apparently oversized heads depicted in Figure 9.4 on page 211 represent embryos and fetuses at various stages of prenatal development. Growth of the head (the cephalic region)

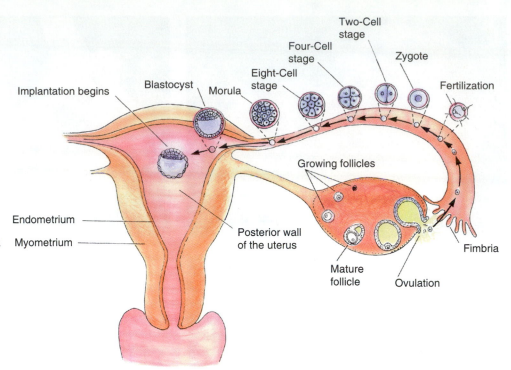

Figure 9.3. **The Ovarian Cycle, Conception, and the Early Days of the Germinal Stage.** The zygote first divides about 36 hours after conception. Continuing division creates the hollow sphere of cells termed the blastocyst. The blastocyst normally becomes implanted in the wall of the uterus.

Figure labels: Implantation begins · Blastocyst · Morula · Eight-Cell stage · Four-Cell stage · Two-Cell stage · Zygote · Fertilization · Growing follicles · Endometrium · Myometrium · Posterior wall of the uterus · Mature follicle · Ovulation · Fimbria

Proximodistal

From the central axis of the body outward. (From Latin roots meaning "near" and "far.")

Amniotic sac

The sac containing the fetus.

Amniotic fluid

Fluid within the amniotic sac that suspends and protects the fetus.

Placenta

An organ connected to the fetus by the umbilical cord. The placenta serves as a relay station between mother and fetus, allowing the exchange of nutrients and wastes.

Umbilical cord

A tube that connects the fetus to the placenta.

takes precedence over the growth of the lower parts of the body. You can also think of the body as containing a central axis that coincides with the spinal cord. The growth of the organ systems that lie close to this axis (that is, *proximal* to the axis) takes precedence over the growth of those that lie farther away toward the extremities (that is, *distal* to the axis). Relatively early maturation of the brain and organ systems that lie near the central axis allows these organs to facilitate further development of the embryo and fetus.

During the third week of development, the head and blood vessels begin to form. By the fourth week, a primitive heart begins to beat and pump blood in an embryo that measures but a fifth of an inch in length. The heart will normally continue to beat without rest for every minute of every day for the better part of a century. By the end of the first month of development we can see the beginnings of the arms and legs—"arm buds" and "leg buds." The mouth, eyes, ears, and nose begin to take shape. The brain and other parts of the nervous system begin to develop.

The arms and legs develop in accordance with the proximodistal principle. First the upper arms and legs develop. Then the forearms and lower legs. Then the hands and feet form, followed by webbed fingers and toes by about six to eight weeks into development. The webbing is gone by the end of the second month. By this time the head has become rounded, and the limbs have elongated and separated. Facial features are visible. All this has occurred in an embryo that is about 1 inch long and weighs 1/30 of an ounce.

The Amniotic Sac   The embryo—and later on, the fetus—develops within a protective environment in the mother's uterus called the **amniotic sac,** which is surrounded by a clear membrane. The embryo and fetus are suspended within the sac in **amniotic fluid.** The amniotic fluid acts like a shock absorber. It cushions the embryo from damage that might result from the mother's movements. The fluid also helps maintain a steady temperature.

The Placenta   Nutrients and waste products are exchanged between mother and embryo (or fetus) through a mass of tissue called the **placenta.** The placenta is unique in origin. It develops from material supplied by both mother and embryo. Toward the end of the first trimester, it becomes a flattish, round organ about 7 inches in diameter and 1 inch thick—larger than the fetus itself. The fetus is connected to the placenta by the **umbilical cord.** The mother is connected to the placenta by the system of blood vessels in the uter-

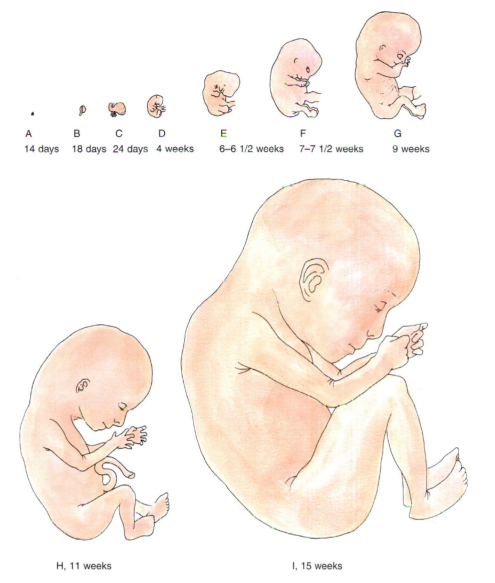

A
14 days   B
18 days   C
24 days   D
4 weeks   E
6–6 1/2 weeks   F
7–7 1/2 weeks   G
9 weeks

H, 11 weeks   I, 15 weeks

Figure 9.4. **Human Embryos and Fetuses.** Development is cephalocaudal and proximodistal. Growth of the head takes precedence over the growth of the lower parts of the body.

ine wall. The umbilical cord develops about five weeks after conception and reaches 20 inches in length. It contains two arteries through which maternal nutrients reach the embryo. A vein transports waste products back to the mother.

The circulatory systems of mother and embryo do not mix. A membrane in the placenta permits only certain substances to pass through, such as oxygen (from the mother to the fetus); carbon dioxide and other wastes (from the embryo or fetus to the mother, to be eliminated by the mother's lungs and kidneys); nutrients; some microscopic disease-causing organisms; and some drugs, including aspirin, narcotics, alcohol, and tranquilizers.

The placenta is also an endocrine gland. It secretes hormones that preserve the pregnancy, stimulate the uterine contractions that induce childbirth, and help prepare the breasts for breast-feeding. The placenta itself secretes increasing amounts of estrogen and progesterone. The placenta passes from the woman's body after delivery. For this reason it is also called the "afterbirth."

The Fetal Stage

The fetal stage begins by the ninth week and continues until birth. By about the ninth or tenth week, the fetus begins to respond to the outside world by turning in the direction of external stimulation. By the end of the first trimester, the major organ systems, the fingers and toes, and the external genitals have been formed. The gender of the fetus can be determined visually. The eyes have become clearly distinguishable.

During the second trimester the fetus increases dramatically in size, and its organ systems continue to mature. The brain now contributes to the regulation of basic body functions. The fetus increases in weight from 1 *ounce* to 2 *pounds* and grows from about 4 to 14 inches in length. Soft, downy hair grows above the eyes and on the scalp. The skin turns ruddy because of blood vessels that show through the surface. (During the third trimester, layers of fat beneath the skin will give the red a pinkish hue.)

By the middle of the fourth month, the mother can usually feel the first fetal movements. By the end of the second trimester, the fetus moves its limbs so vigorously that the mother may complain of being kicked—often at 4:00 A.M. It opens and shuts its eyes, sucks its thumb, alternates between periods of wakefulness and sleep, and perceives lights and sounds. The fetus also does somersaults, which the mother will definitely feel. Fortunately, the umbilical cord will not break or strangle the fetus, no matter what acrobatic feats the fetus performs.

Near the end of the second trimester the fetus approaches the **age of viability.** Still, only a minority of babies born at the end of the second trimester who weigh under 2 pounds will survive—even with intense medical efforts.

During the third trimester, the organ systems continue to mature and enlarge. The heart and lungs become increasingly capable of maintaining independent life. Typically, during the seventh month the fetus turns upside down in the uterus so that it will be headfirst, or in a **cephalic presentation,** for delivery. But some fetuses do not turn during this month. If such a fetus is born prematurely it can have either a **breech presentation** (bottom first) or a shoulder-first presentation, which can complicate problems of prematurity. The closer to term (the full nine months) the baby is born, the more likely it is that the presentation will be cephalic. If birth occurs at the end of the eighth month, the odds are overwhelmingly in favor of survival.

During the final months of pregnancy, the mother may become concerned that the fetus seems to be less active than before. Most of the time the change in activity level is normal. The fetus has grown so large that it is cramped, and its movements are restricted.

Environmental Influences on Prenatal Development

Environmental factors that affect prenatal development include the mother's diet, maternal diseases and disorders, and the mother's use of drugs.

The Mother's Diet   It is a common misconception that the fetus will take what it needs from its mother. Actually, malnutrition in the mother can adversely affect fetal development. Maternal malnutrition during the third trimester, when the fetus normally makes sharp gains in weight, is linked to low birthweight and increased infant mortality. Pregnant women who are well nourished are more likely to deliver babies of average or above average size. Their infants are also less likely to develop colds and serious respiratory disorders.

A woman can expect to gain at least 20 pounds during pregnancy because of the growth of the placenta, amniotic fluid, and the fetus itself. Most women will gain about 25 pounds or so (Thompson, 1993). Overweight women may gain less. Slender women may gain 30 pounds. Regular weight gains are most desirable, about ½ pound a week during the first half of pregnancy and about 1 pound a week during the second half.

Maternal Diseases and Disorders   Environmental influences or agents that can harm the embryo or fetus are called **teratogens.** These include drugs taken by the mother, such as alcohol and even aspirin, as well as substances produced by the mother's body, such as Rh-positive antibodies. Other teratogens include the metals lead and mer-

Age of viability
The age at which a fetus can sustain independent life.

Cephalic presentation
Emergence of the baby headfirst from the womb.

Breech presentation
Emergence of the baby feet first from the womb.

Teratogens
Environmental influences or agents that can damage an embryo or fetus. (From the Greek *teras*, meaning "monster.")

cury, radiation, and disease-causing organisms such as viruses and bacteria. Although many disease-causing organisms cannot pass through the placenta to infect the embryo or fetus, some extremely small organisms, such as those causing syphilis, measles, mumps, and chicken pox, can. Some disorders such as toxemia are not transmitted to the embryo or fetus but can adversely affect the environment in which it develops.

Critical period of vulnerability

A period of time during which an embryo or fetus is vulnerable to the effects of a teratogen.

Critical Periods of Vulnerability   The times at which exposure to particular teratogens can cause the greatest harm are termed **critical periods of vulnerability.** Critical periods correspond to the times at which the structures most affected by the teratogens are developing (see Figure 9.5). The heart, for example, develops rapidly from the third to the fifth week following conception. It may be most vulnerable to certain teratogens at this time. The arms and legs, which develop later, are most vulnerable from the fourth through the eighth week of development. Since the major organ systems differentiate during the embryonic stage, the embryo is most vulnerable to the effects of teratogens during this stage.

Let us now consider some of the most damaging effects of specific maternal diseases and disorders.

Rubella

A viral infection that can cause mental retardation and heart disease in an embryo. Also called *German measles*.

Rubella (German Measles)   Rubella is a viral infection. Women who contract rubella during the first month or two of pregnancy, when rapid differentiation of major organ systems is taking place, may bear children who are deaf or who develop mental retardation, heart disease, or cataracts. Risk of these defects declines as pregnancy progresses.

Nearly 85% of women in the United States had rubella as children and so acquired immunity. Women who do not know whether they have had rubella may be tested; if they are

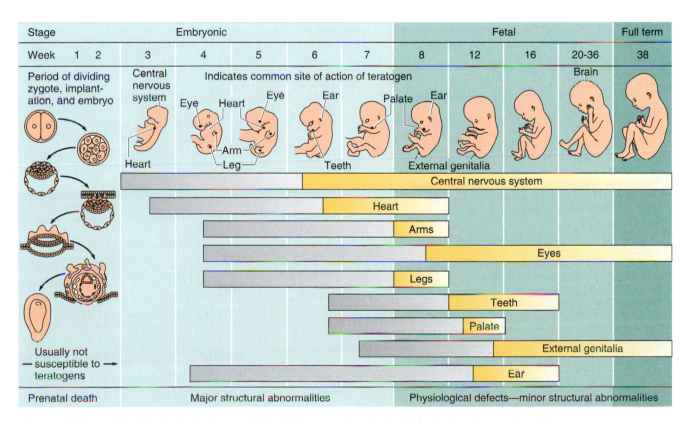

Figure 9.5.   Critical Periods in Prenatal Development. The developing embryo is most vulnerable to teratogens when the organ systems are taking shape. The periods of greatest vulnerability of organ systems are shown in blue. Periods of lesser vulnerability are shown in yellow. *Source: Rathus, S. A. (1988). Understanding Child Development.* Copyright © 1988 by Holt, Rinehart, & Winston, Inc. Reprinted with permission.

not immune, they can be vaccinated *prior to pregnancy.* Inoculation during pregnancy is considered risky because the vaccine causes a mild case of the disease in the mother, which can affect the embryo or fetus. Increased awareness of the dangers of rubella during pregnancy, and of the preventive effects of inoculation, has led to a dramatic decline in the number of children born in the United States with defects caused by rubella.

Syphilis
A sexually transmitted disease caused by a bacterial infection.

Stillbirth
The birth of a dead fetus.

Acquired immunodeficiency syndrome (AIDS)
A sexually transmitted disease that destroys white blood cells in the immune system, leaving the body vulnerable to various "opportunistic" diseases.

Toxemia
A life-threatening condition that is characterized by high blood pressure.

Sexually Transmitted Diseases   Maternal **syphilis** may cause miscarriage or **stillbirth,** or be passed along to the child in the form of congenital syphilis. Congenital syphilis can impair the vision and hearing, damage the liver, or deform the bones and teeth.

Routine blood tests early in pregnancy can diagnose syphilis and other problems. Because the bacteria that cause syphilis do not readily cross the placental membrane during the first months of pregnancy, the fetus will probably not contract syphilis if an infected mother is treated successfully with antibiotics before the fourth month of pregnancy.

Acquired immunodeficiency syndrome (AIDS) is caused by the *human immunodeficiency virus* (HIV). HIV is blood-borne and is sometimes transmitted through the placenta to infect the fetus. The rupturing of blood vessels in mother and baby during childbirth provides another opportunity for transmission of HIV (Peckham & Gibb, 1995). *However, the majority of babies born to mothers who are infected with HIV do not become infected themselves.* Chapter 13 describes measures that can be taken to minimize the probability of transmission. HIV can also be transmitted to children by breast-feeding.

Toxemia   Toxemia is a life-threatening condition characterized by high blood pressure that may afflict women late in the second or early in the third trimester of pregnancy. The first stage is termed *preeclampsia.* It is diagnosed by protein in the urine, swelling from fluid retention, and high blood pressure, and may be relatively mild. As preeclampsia worsens, the mother may have headaches and visual problems from the raised blood pressure, along with abdominal pain. If left untreated, the disease may progress to the final stage, termed *eclampsia.* Eclampsia can lead to maternal or fetal death. Babies born to women with toxemia are often undersized or premature.

Toxemia appears to be linked to malnutrition. Ironically, undernourished women may gain weight rapidly through fluid retention, but their swollen appearance may discourage them from eating. Pregnant women who gain weight rapidly but have not increased their food intake should consult their obstetricians.

Ectopic pregnancy
A pregnancy in which the fertilized ovum becomes implanted outside the uterus, usually in the fallopian tube. (*Ectopic* derives from Greek roots meaning "out of place.")

Rh incompatibility
A condition in which antibodies produced by a pregnant woman are transmitted to the fetus and may cause brain damage or death.

Ectopic Pregnancy   In an **ectopic pregnancy,** the fertilized ovum implants itself someplace other than the uterus. Most ectopic pregnancies occur in a fallopian tube ("tubal pregnancies") when the ovum is prevented from moving into the uterus because of obstructions caused by infections. If ectopic pregnancies do not abort spontaneously, they must be removed by surgery or use of medicines such as methotrexate (Hausknecht, 1995), since the fetus cannot develop to term. Delay in removal may cause hemorrhaging and the death of the mother. A woman with a tubal pregnancy will not menstruate, but may notice spotty bleeding and abdominal pain.

Rh Incompatibility   In **Rh incompatibility,** antibodies produced by the mother are transmitted to a fetus or newborn infant. *Rh* is a blood protein found in some people's red blood cells. Rh incompatibility occurs when a woman who does not have this blood factor, and is thus *Rh-negative,* is carrying an *Rh-positive* fetus, which can happen if the father is Rh-positive. The negative–positive combination is found in about 10% of U.S. marriages. However, it becomes a problem only in a minority of the resulting pregnancies. In such cases the mother's antibodies attack the red blood cells of the fetus, which can cause brain damage or death. Rh incompatibility does not usually adversely affect a first child because women will usually not yet have formed antibodies to the Rh factor.

Since mother and fetus have separate circulatory systems, it is unlikely that Rh-positive fetal red blood cells will enter the Rh-negative mother's body. The probability of an exchange of blood increases during childbirth, however, especially when the placenta becomes detached from the uterine wall. If an exchange of blood occurs, the mother will then produce antibodies to the baby's Rh-positive blood. The mother's antibodies may enter the fetal bloodstream and cause a condition called *fetal erythroblastosis,* which can result in anemia, mental deficiency, or even the death of the fetus or newborn infant.

Blood-typing of pregnant women significantly decreases the threat of erythroblastosis. If an Rh-negative mother is injected with the vaccine Rhogan within 72 hours after delivery of an Rh-positive baby, she will not develop the dangerous antibodies and thus will not pass them on to the fetus in a subsequent pregnancy. A fetus or newborn child at risk for erythroblastosis may also receive a preventive blood transfusion, in order to remove the mother's Rh-positive antibodies from its blood.

Drugs Taken by the Mother (and the Father) Some widely used drugs, including nonprescription drugs like aspirin, are linked with birth abnormalities. In the 1960s the drug thalidomide was marketed to pregnant women as a presumably safe treatment for nausea and insomnia. However, the drug caused birth deformities, including stunted or missing limbs. Maternal use of illegal drugs such as cocaine and marijuana may also place the fetus at risk.

Paternal use of certain drugs also may endanger the fetus. One question is whether drugs alter the genetic material in the father's sperm. The use of certain substances by those who come into contact with a pregnant woman can harm the fetus. For example, the mother's inhalation of second-hand tobacco or marijuana smoke can hurt the fetus.

Several antibiotics may harm a fetus, especially if they are taken during certain periods of fetal development. Tetracycline may yellow the teeth and deform the bones. Other antibiotics have been implicated in deafness and jaundice.

Acne drugs can cause physical and mental handicaps in the children of women who use them during pregnancy (Mills, 1995). Antihistamines, used commonly for allergies, may deform the fetus.

If you are pregnant, or suspect that you are, it is advisable to consult your obstetrician before taking any and all drugs, not just prescription drugs. Your obstetrician can usually direct you to a safe and effective substitute for a drug that could harm a fetus.

Hormones The hormones progestin and DES have sometimes been used to help women at risk of miscarriage maintain their pregnancies. When taken at about the time that sex organs differentiate, progestin—which is similar in composition to male sex hormones—can masculinize the external sex organs of embryos with female (XX) sex chromosomal structures. Progestin taken during the first trimester has also been linked to increased levels of aggressive behavior during childhood.

DES
Diethylstilbestrol: an estrogen that was once given to women at risk for miscarriage to help maintain pregnancy.

DES (short for *diethylstilbestrol*), a powerful estrogen, was given to many women at risk for miscarriage from the 1940s through the 1960s to help maintain their pregnancies. DES is suspected of causing cervical and testicular cancer in some of the children whose mothers used it when pregnant. Other problems have been reported as well. Daughters whose mothers used DES during their pregnancies have a higher-than-expected rate of miscarriages and premature deliveries. It was once suspected that men who were exposed prenatally to DES had higher than expected rates of infertility. However, research reveals no connection between in utero exposure to DES and male infertility (Wilcox et al., 1995).

Vitamins Many pregnant women are prescribed daily doses of multivitamins to maintain their own health and to promote the development of a healthy pregnancy. "Too much of a good thing" may be hazardous, however. High doses of vitamins such as A, B_6, D, and K have been linked to birth defects. Vitamin A excesses have been linked with cleft palate and eye damage, whereas excesses of vitamin D are linked to mental retardation.

Narcotics Narcotics such as heroin and methadone can readily pass from mother to fetus through the placental membrane. Narcotics are addictive. Fetuses of mothers who use them regularly during their pregnancies can become addicted in utero. At birth, such babies may undergo withdrawal and show muscle tension and agitation. Women who use narcotics are advised to notify their obstetricians so that measures can be taken to aid the infants prior to and following delivery.

Tranquilizers and Sedatives   The tranquilizers Librium and Valium cross the placental membrane and may cause birth defects such as harelip. Sedatives, such as the barbiturate *phenobarbital,* are suspected of decreasing testosterone production and causing reproductive problems in the sons of women who use them during pregnancy.

Hallucinogenics   Use of hallucinogenic drugs such as marijuana and LSD during pregnancy has been linked to chromosomal damage in fetuses (National Academy of Sciences, 1982). The active ingredient in marijuana, THC, readily crosses the placenta, as does LSD. Use of marijuana can lead to decreased androgen production in male fetuses, which can interfere with the process of sexual differentiation. Research provides evidence that preschoolers whose mothers used marijuana during their pregnancies suffered more neurological and visual problems than did children of nonusers (Fried, 1986).

Fetal alcohol syndrome
A cluster of symptoms caused by maternal drinking, in which the child shows developmental lags and characteristic facial features such as an underdeveloped upper jaw, flattened nose, and widely spaced eyes.

Alcohol   Mothers who drink heavily during pregnancy expose the fetus to greater risk of birth defects, infant mortality, sensory and motor problems, and mental retardation (Barr et al., 1990; Coles, 1994). Nearly 40% of children whose mothers drank heavily during pregnancy develop **fetal alcohol syndrome** (FAS). FAS is a cluster of symptoms typified by developmental lags and characteristic facial features, such as an underdeveloped upper jaw, flattened nose, and widely spaced eyes. Infants with FAS are often smaller than average and have smaller than average brains. They may be mentally retarded, lack coordination, and have deformed limbs and heart problems.

Although research suggests that light drinking is unlikely to harm the fetus in most cases (Jacobson & Jacobson, 1994), FAS has been found even among the children of mothers who drank only two ounces of alcohol a day during the first trimester (Astley et al., 1992). Moreover, individual sensitivities to alcohol may vary widely (Jacobson & Jacobson, 1994). The critical period for the development of the facial features associated with FAS seems to be the first two months of prenatal development, when the head is taking shape (Coles, 1994).

Cigarette Smoking   Maternal smoking increases the risk of miscarriage and complications during pregnancy such as premature rupturing of the amniotic sac, stillbirth, premature birth, low birthweight, and early infant mortality (English & Eskenazi, 1992; Floyd et al., 1993; USDHHS, 1992a). Women who smoke less than a pack a day stand a higher risk of pregnancy and birth complications than do nonsmokers (Floyd et al., 1993; Mayer et al., 1990). The health risks generally increase with the amount smoked.

Maternal smoking may also impair intellectual development. In one study, women who smoked during pregnancy were 50% more likely than nonsmokers to have children whose intelligence test scores placed them in the mentally retarded range (that is, beneath an IQ score of 70) when the children were 10 years old (Drews et al., 1996).

Low birthweight is the most common risk factor for infant disease and mortality (USDHHS, 1992a). Maternal smoking during pregnancy more than doubles the risk of low birthweight (Mayer et al., 1990). The combination of smoking and drinking alcohol places the child at greater risk of low birthweight than either practice alone (Day & Richardson, 1994). As many as 1 in 4 cases of low birthweight could be prevented if mothers-to-be quit smoking during pregnancy (USDHHS, 1990). The earlier the pregnant smoker quits, the better for the baby (and herself!). Simply cutting down on smoking during pregnancy may not offer much protection in preventing low birthweight, however (USDHHS, 1990).

Maternal smoking also has important acute effects on fetal heart rate (Graca et al., 1991) and increases the risk of sudden infant death syndrome (SIDS) (Feng, 1993; Haglund & Cnattingius, 1990; Malloy et al., 1992; Schoendorf & Kiely, 1992; Zhang & Fried, 1992). Maternal smoking has also been linked to reduced lung function in newborns (Hanrahan et al., 1992) and asthma in childhood (Martinez et al., 1992). Evidence also points to reduced attentions spans, hyperactivity, and lower IQs and achievement test scores in children exposed to maternal smoking during and following pregnancy (Barr et al., 1990).

Smoking by the father (or other household members) may be dangerous to a fetus because secondary smoke (smoke exhaled by the smoker or emitted from the tip of a lit cigarette) may be absorbed by the mother and passed along to the fetus. Passive exposure to second-hand smoke during infancy is also linked to increased risk of SIDS (Schoendorf & Kiely, 1992).

Other Agents   X-rays increase the risk of malformed organs in the fetus, especially within a month and a half following conception. (Ultrasound has *not* been shown to harm the embryo or fetus.)

Chromosomal and Genetic Abnormalities

Not all of us have the normal complement of chromosomes. Some of us have genes that threaten our health or our existence (see Table 9.1).

Down syndrome

A chromosomal abnormality that leads to mental retardation, caused by an extra chromosome on the 21st pair.

Down Syndrome   Children with **Down syndrome** have characteristic round faces; wide, flat noses; and protruding tongues. They often suffer from respiratory problems and heart malformations, problems that tend to claim their lives by middle age—the "prime of life" when most of us are reaching our vocational heights. People with Down syndrome are also moderately mentally retarded, but they usually can learn to read and write. With a little help from family and social agencies, they may hold jobs and lead largely independent lives.

The risk of a child's having Down syndrome increases with the mother's age (see Table 9.2 on page 218). Down syndrome is usually caused by an extra chromosome on the 21st pair. In about 95% of cases, Down syndrome is transmitted by the mother (Antonarakas et al., 1991). The inner corners of the eyes of people with the syndrome have a downward-sloping crease of skin that gives them a superficial likeness to Asians. This is why the syndrome was once dubbed *mongolism,* a moniker that has since been rejected because of its racist overtones.

TABLE 9.1   Some chromosomal and genetic abnormalities

Cystic fibrosis	A genetic disease in which the pancreas and lungs become clogged with mucus, which impairs the processes of respiration and digestion.
Down syndrome	A condition characterized by a 3rd chromosome on the 21st pair. The child with Down syndrome has a characteristic fold of skin over the eye and mental retardation. The risk of a child's exhibiting the syndrome increases as parents increase in age.
Hemophilia	A sex-linked disorder in which the blood fails to clot properly.
Huntington's chorea	A fatal neurological disorder whose onset occurs in middle adulthood.
Neural-tube defects	Disorders of the brain or spine, such as *anencephaly,* in which part of the brain is missing, and *spina bifida,* in which part of the spine is exposed or missing. Anencephaly is fatal shortly after birth, but some spina bifida victims survive for a number of years, albeit with severe handicaps.
Phenylketonuria	A disorder in which children cannot metabolize phenylalanine, which builds up in the form of phenylpyruvic acid and causes mental retardation. The disorder can be diagnosed at birth and controlled by diet.
Retina blastoma	A form of blindness caused by a dominant gene.
Sickle cell anemia	A blood disorder that mostly afflicts African Americans, in which deformed blood cells obstruct small blood vessels, decreasing their capacity to carry oxygen and heightening the risk of occasionally fatal infections.
Tay-Sachs disease	A fatal neurological disorder that primarily afflicts Jews of European origin.

Source: Etaugh & Rathus (1995).

TABLE 9.2 Risk of giving birth to an infant with Down syndrome, according to age of the mother

Age of Mother	Probability of Down Syndrome
30	1/885
31	1/826
32	1/725
33	1/592
34	1/465
35*	1/365
36	1/287
37	1/225
38	1/176
39	1/139
40	1/109
41	1/85
42	1/67
43	1/53
44	1/41
45	1/32
46	1/25
47	1/20
48	1/16
49	1/11

*Age at which testing for Down syndrome is usually first recommended.
Source: Adapted from Samuels & Samuels, 1986, p. 240. Reprinted with permission.

Sickle Cell Anemia and Tay-Sachs Disease

Sickle cell anemia and Tay-Sachs disease are genetic disorders that are most likely to afflict certain racial and ethnic groups. Sickle cell anemia is most prevalent in the United States among African Americans. One of every 375 African Americans is affected by the disease, and 8% are carriers of the sickle cell trait (Leary, 1993). In sickle cell anemia, the red blood cells assume a sickle shape—hence the name—and they form clumps that obstruct narrow blood vessels and diminish the supply of oxygen. As a result, victims can suffer problems ranging from swollen, painful joints to potentially lethal problems such as pneumonia and heart and kidney failure. Infections are a leading cause of death among those with the disease (Leary, 1993).

Tay-Sachs disease is a fatal neurological disease of young children. Only 1 in 100,000 people in the United States is affected, but among Jews of Eastern European background the figure rises steeply to 1 in 3,600 (Hubbard & Wald, 1993). The disease is characterized by degeneration of the central nervous system and gives rise to retardation, loss of muscle control and paralysis, blindness, and deafness. Victims seldom live beyond the age of 5.

Sex-Linked Genetic Abnormalities

Some genetic defects, such as hemophilia, are sex linked, in that they are carried only on the X sex chromosome. They are transmitted from generation to generation as **recessive traits.** Females, each of whom has two X sex chromosomes, are less likely than males to be afflicted by sex-linked disorders,

Recessive trait
A trait that is not expressed when the gene or genes involved have been paired with dominant genes. Recessive traits are transmitted to future generations, however, and are expressed if they are paired with other recessive genes.

AVERTING CHROMOSOMAL AND GENETIC ABNORMALITIES

Based upon information about a couple's medical background and family history of genetic defects, genetic counselors help couples appraise the risks of passing along genetic defects to their children. Some couples facing a high risk of passing along genetic defects to their children decide to adopt. Other couples decide to have an abortion if the fetus is determined to have certain abnormalities.

Various medical procedures are used to detect the presence of these disorders in the fetus. **Amniocentesis** is usually performed about four months into pregnancy but is sometimes done earlier. Fluid is drawn from the amniotic sac (or "bag of waters") with a syringe. Fetal cells in the fluid are grown in a culture and examined under a microscope for the presence of biochemical and chromosomal abnormalities. *Chorionic villus sampling (CVS)* is performed several weeks earlier. A narrow tube is used to snip off material from the chorion, which is a membrane that contains the amniotic sac and fetus. The material is analyzed. CVS is somewhat riskier than amniocentesis, so most obstetricians prefer to use the latter. The tests detect Down syndrome, sickle cell anemia, Tay-Sachs disease, spina bifida, muscular dystrophy, Rh incompatibility, and other conditions. The tests also identify the gender of the fetus.

In ultrasound, high-pitched sound waves are bounced off the fetus, like radar, revealing a picture of the fetus on a TV monitor and allowing the obstetrician to detect certain abnormalities. Obstetricians also use ultrasound to locate the fetus during amniocentesis in order to lower the probability of injuring it with the syringe.

Parental blood tests can suggest the presence of problems such as sickle cell anemia, Tay-Sachs disease, and neural-tube defects. Still other tests examine fetal DNA and can indicate the presence of Huntington's chorea, cystic fibrosis, and other disorders.

Amniocentesis
A procedure for drawing off and examining fetal cells in the amniotic fluid to determine the presence of various disorders in the fetus.

because the genes that carry the disorder would have to be present on both of their sex chromosomes for the disorder to be expressed. Sex-linked disorders are more likely to afflict sons of female carriers because they have only one X sex chromosome, which they inherit from their mothers. England's Queen Victoria was a hemophilia carrier and transmitted the condition to many of her children, who in turn carried it into several ruling houses of Europe. For this reason hemophilia has been dubbed the "royal disease."

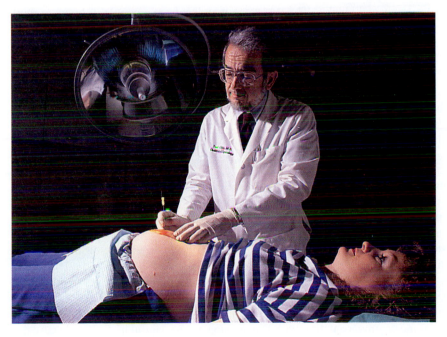

Amniocentesis. In this form of prenatal testing, cells sloughed off by the fetus into amniotic fluid are withdrawn by a syringe and examined for genetic and chromosomal abnormalities.

Childbirth

Early in the ninth month of pregnancy, the fetus's head settles in the pelvis. This shift is called "dropping" or "lightening." The woman may actually feel lighter because of lessened pressure on the diaphragm. About a day or so before the beginning of labor, the woman may notice blood in her vaginal secretions because fetal pressure on the pelvis may rupture superficial blood vessels in the birth canal. Tissue that had plugged the cervix, possibly preventing entry of infectious agents from the vagina, becomes dislodged. There is a resultant discharge of bloody mucus. At about this time one woman in ten also has a rush of warm "water" from the vagina. The "water" is amniotic fluid, and it means that the amniotic sac has burst. Labor usually begins within a day after rupture of the amniotic sac. For most women the amniotic sac does not burst until the end of the first stage of childbirth. Other signs of impending labor include indigestion, diarrhea, abdominal cramps, and an ache in the small of the back. Labor begins with the onset of regular uterine contractions.

The first uterine contractions are relatively painless and are called **Braxton-Hicks contractions,** or "false" labor contractions. They are false because they do not widen the cervix or advance the baby through the birth canal. They tend to increase in frequency but are less regular than labor contractions. "Real" contractions, by contrast, become more intense when the woman moves around or walks.

The initiation of labor may involve the secretion of hormones by the fetal adrenal and pituitary glands that stimulate the placenta and mother's uterus to secrete **prostaglandins.** Prostaglandins stimulate the uterine musculature to contract. It would make sense for the fetus to have a mechanism for signaling the mother that it is mature enough to sustain independent life. The mechanisms that initiate and maintain labor are not fully understood, however. Later in labor the pituitary gland releases **oxytocin,** a hormone that stimulates contractions strong enough to expel the baby.

The Stages of Childbirth

Childbirth begins with the onset of labor and progresses through three stages.

The First Stage   In the first stage uterine contractions **efface** and **dilate** the cervix to about 4 inches (10 cm) in diameter, so that the baby may pass. Stretching of the cervix causes most of the pain of childbirth. A woman may experience little or no pain if her cervix dilates easily and quickly. The first stage may last from a couple of hours to more than a day. Twelve to 24 hours of labor is considered about average for a first pregnancy. In later pregnancies labor takes about half this time.

The initial contractions are usually mild and spaced widely, at intervals of 10 to 20 minutes. They may last 20 to 40 seconds. As time passes, contractions become more frequent, long, strong, and regular.

Transition is the process that occurs when the cervix becomes nearly fully dilated and the baby's head begins to move into the vagina, or birth canal. Contractions usually come quickly during transition. Transition usually lasts about 30 minutes or less and is often accompanied by feelings of nausea, chills, and intense pain.

The Second Stage   The second stage of childbirth follows transition and begins when the cervix has become fully dilated and the baby begins to move into the vagina and first appears at the opening of the birth canal (see Figure 9.6 on page 221). The woman may be taken to a delivery room for the second stage of childbirth. The second stage is shorter than the first stage. It lasts from a few minutes to a few hours and ends with the birth of the baby.

Each contraction of the second stage propels the baby farther along the birth canal (vagina). When the baby's head becomes visible at the vaginal opening, it is said to have *crowned.* The baby typically emerges fully a few minutes after crowning.

An **episiotomy** may be performed on the mother when the baby's head has crowned. Episiotomies are controversial, however. The incision can be painful in itself and cause dis-

---

Braxton-Hicks contractions
So-called false labor contractions that are relatively painless.

Prostaglandins
Hormones that cause muscle fibers in the uterine wall to contract, as during labor.

Oxytocin
A pituitary hormone that stimulates uterine contractions in labor and the ejection of milk during nursing.

Efface
To become thin.

Dilate
To open or widen.

Transition
The process during which the cervix becomes nearly fully dilated and the head of the fetus begins to move into the birth canal.

Episiotomy
A surgical incision in the perineum that may be made during childbirth to protect the vagina from tearing. (From Greek roots *epision*, meaning "pubic region," and *tome*, meaning "cutting.")

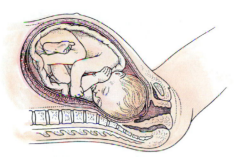

1. The second stage of labor begins

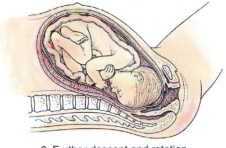

2. Further descent and rotation

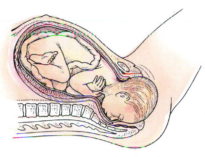

3. The crowning of the head

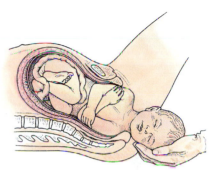

4. Anterior shoulder delivered

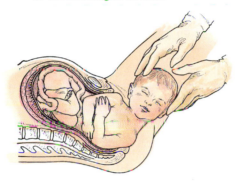

5. Posterior shoulder delivered

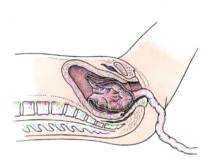

6. The third stage of labor begins with separation of the placenta from the uterine wall

Figure 9.6. **The Stages of Childbirth.** In the first stage, uterine contractions efface and dilate the cervix to about 4 inches so that the baby may pass. The second stage begins with movement of the baby into the birth canal and ends with birth of the baby. During the third stage the placenta separates from the uterine wall and is expelled through the birth canal.

Perineum
The skin and underlying tissue that lie between the vaginal opening and the anus. (From Greek roots meaning "around" and "to empty out.")

comfort and itching as it heals. In some cases the discomfort interferes with coitus for months. Many obstetricians no longer perform episiotomies routinely. However, most health professionals concur that an episiotomy is preferable to the random tearing that can occur if the tissues of the **perineum** become extremely effaced.

With or without an episiotomy, the baby's passageway to the external world is a tight fit at best. As a result, the baby's facial features and the shape of its head may be temporarily distended. The baby may look as if it has been through a prizefight. Its head may be elongated, its nose flattened, and its ears bent. Although parents may be concerned about whether the baby's features will assume a more typical shape, they almost always do.

The Third Stage The third, or placental, stage of childbirth may last from a few minutes to an hour or more. During this stage, the placenta is expelled. Detachment of the placenta from the uterine wall may cause some bleeding. The uterus begins the process of contracting to a smaller size. The attending physician sews up the episiotomy or any tears in the perineum.

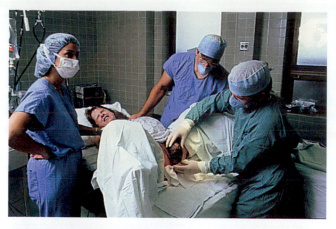

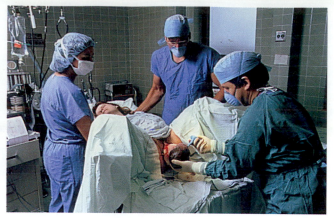

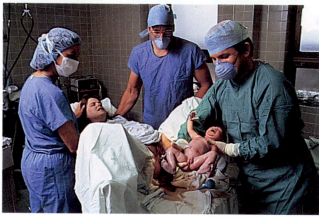

Coming into the World. Childbirth progresses through three stages. In the first stage, uterine contractions efface and dilate the cervix so that the baby may pass. The second stage lasts from a few minutes to a few hours and ends with the birth of the baby. During the third stage the placenta is expelled.

In the New World As the baby's head emerges, mucus is cleared from its mouth by means of suction aspiration to prevent the breathing passageway from being obstructed. Aspiration is often repeated once the baby is fully delivered. (Newly delivered babies are no longer routinely held upside down to help expel mucus. Nor is the baby slapped on the buttocks to stimulate breathing, as in old films.)

Once the baby is breathing adequately, the umbilical cord is clamped and severed about 3 inches from the baby's body. The stump of the umbilical cord dries and falls off in its own time, usually in seven to ten days.

While the mother is in the third stage of labor, the nurse may perform procedures on the baby, such as placing drops of silver nitrate or an antibiotic ointment into the eyes. This procedure is required by most states to prevent bacterial infections in the newborn's eyes. Typically the baby is also footprinted and (if the birth has taken place in a hospital) given an identification bracelet. Since neonates do not manufacture vitamin K on their own, the baby may also receive an injection of the vitamin to ensure that her or his blood will clot normally in case of bleeding.

Methods of Childbirth

Until this century childbirth was usually an event that happened at home and involved the mother, a midwife, family, and friends. These days women in the United States and Canada typically give birth in hospitals, attended by obstetricians who use surgical instruments and anesthetics to protect mothers and children from infection, complications, and pain. Medical procedures save lives but also make childbearing more impersonal. Social critics argue that these procedures have "medicalized" a natural process. They have usurped control over women's bodies and, through the use of drugs, denied many women the experience of giving birth.

The degree to which a new product has each of these characteristics affects the speed of diffusion. It may take years for a market to widely adopt a new product. Let's take a closer look at the humble microwave oven—a product that was highly innovative in its early days but now is generally a low-priced staple of every kitchen (and every college apartment and dorm)—as an example to better understand why each of these five factors is important:

- **Relative advantage** describes the degree to which a consumer perceives that a new product provides superior benefits. In the case of the microwave oven, consumers in the 1960s did not believe that the product provided important benefits that would improve their lives. But by the late 1970s, that perception had changed because more women had entered the workforce. In the 1960s, a woman had all day to prepare the evening meal, so she didn't need the microwave (yes, at that time there were very few males in the "househusband" role—that's really changed today!). In the 1970s, however, when many women left home for work at 8:00 A.M. and returned home at 6:00 P.M., an appliance that would "magically" defrost a frozen chicken and cook it in 30 minutes provided a genuine advantage.

- **Compatibility** is the extent to which a new product is consistent with existing cultural values, customs, and practices. Did consumers see the microwave oven as being compatible with existing ways of doing things? Hardly. Cooking on paper plates? If you put a paper plate in a conventional oven, you'll likely get a visit from the fire department. By anticipating compatibility issues early in the new-product-development stage, marketing strategies can address such problems in planning communications and consumer education programs, or there may be opportunities to alter product designs to overcome some consumer objections.

- **Complexity** is the degree to which consumers find a new product or its use difficult to understand. Many microwave users today haven't a clue about how a microwave oven cooks food. When appliance manufacturers introduced the first microwaves, they explained that this new technology causes molecules to move and rub together, which creates friction that produces heat. Voilà! Cooked pot roast. But that explanation was too complex and confusing for the homemaker of the Beaver Cleaver days back in the 1960s.

- **Trialability** is the ease of sampling a new product and its benefits. Marketers took an important step in the 1970s to speed up adoption of the microwave oven product trial. Just about every store that sold microwaves invited shoppers to visit the store and sample an entire meal a microwave cooked. Finally, consumers began to understand what the product even was and what it could do!

- **Observability** refers to how visible a new product and its benefits are to others who might adopt it. The ideal innovation is easy to see. For example, for a generation of kids, scooters like the Razor became the hippest way to get around as soon as one preteen saw his or her friends flying by. That same generation observed its friends trading Pokémon cards and wanted to join in (were you part of this craze when you were younger?). In the case of the microwave, it wasn't quite so readily observable for its potential adopters—only close friends and acquaintances who visited someone's home would likely see an early adopter using it. But the fruits of the microwave's labors—tasty food dishes—created lots of buzz at office watercoolers and social events, and its use spread quickly. Too bad they didn't have social media back then—if they had, it's a sure bet that the rate of adoption of microwaves would have been a whole lot faster.

relative advantage
The degree to which a consumer perceives that a new product provides superior benefits.

compatibility
The extent to which a new product is consistent with existing cultural values, customs, and practices.

complexity
The degree to which consumers find a new product or its use difficult to understand.

trialability
The ease of sampling a new product and its benefits.

observability
How visible a new product and its benefits are to others who might adopt it.

Objective Summary ➡ Key Terms ➡ Apply

8.1 Objective Summary (pp. 234–237)

Explain how value is derived through different product layers.

Products can be physical goods, services, ideas, people, or places. A good is a *tangible* product, something that we can see, touch, smell, hear, taste, or possess. In contrast, *intangible* products—services, ideas, people, and places—are products that we can't always see, touch, taste, smell, or possess. Marketers think of the product as more than just a thing that comes in a package. They view it as a bundle of attributes that includes the packaging, brand name, benefits, and supporting features in addition to a physical good. The key issue is the marketer's role in creating the value proposition to develop and market products appropriately.

The core product is the basic product category benefits and customized benefit(s) the product provides. The actual product is the physical good or delivered service, including the packaging and brand name. The augmented product includes both the actual product and any supplementary services, such as warranty, credit, delivery, installation, and so on.

Key Terms

attributes, p. 235

good, p. 235

core product, p. 235

actual product, p. 236

augmented product, p. 237

8.2 Objective Summary (pp. 237–241)

Describe how marketers classify products.

Marketers generally classify goods and services as either consumer or B2B products. They further classify consumer products according to how long they last and by how they are purchased. Durable goods provide benefits for months or years, whereas nondurable goods are used up quickly or are useful for only a short time. Consumers purchase convenience products frequently with little effort. Customers carefully gather information and compare different brands on their attributes and prices before buying shopping products. Specialty products have unique characteristics that are important to the buyer. Customers have little interest in unsought products until a need arises. Business products are for commercial uses by organizations. Marketers classify business products according to how they are used, for example, equipment: maintenance, repair, and operating (MRO) products; raw materials; processed materials; specialized services; and component parts.

Key Terms

durable goods, p. 237

nondurable goods, p. 237

convenience product, p. 238

staple products, p. 239

consumer packaged good (CPG) or fast-moving consumer good (FMCG), p. 239

impulse products, p. 239

emergency products, p. 239

shopping products, p. 239

specialty products, p. 240

unsought products, p. 240

equipment, p. 240

maintenance, repair, and operating (MRO) products, p. 240

raw materials, p. 240

processed materials, p. 241

specialized services, p. 241

component parts, p. 241

8.3 Objective Summary (pp. 241–243)

Understand the importance and types of product innovations.

Innovations are anything consumers perceive to be new. Understanding new products is important to companies because of the fast pace of technological advancement, the high cost to companies of developing new products, and the contributions to society that new products can make. Marketers classify innovations by their degree of newness. A continuous innovation is a modification of an existing product, a dynamically continuous innovation provides a greater change in a product, and a discontinuous innovation is a new product that creates major changes in people's lives.

Key Terms

innovation, p. 241

creativity, p. 241

continuous innovation, p. 242

knockoff, p. 242

dynamically continuous innovation, p. 243

discontinuous innovation, p. 243

convergence, p. 243

8.4 Objective Summary (pp. 244–249)

Show how firms develop new products.

In new product development, marketers generate product ideas from which product concepts are first developed and then screened. Next, they develop a marketing strategy and conduct a business analysis to estimate the profitability of the new product. Technical development includes planning how the product will be manufactured and may mean obtaining a patent. Next, an actual or a simulated test market may be conducted to assess the effectiveness of the new product in the market. Finally, in the commercialization phase the product is launched, and the entire marketing plan is implemented.

Key Terms

research and development (R&D), p. 244

new product development (NPD), p. 244

idea generation (ideation), p. 244

value co-creation, p. 244

product concept development and screening, p. 245

technical success, p. 245

commercial success, p. 245

business analysis, p. 246

technical development, p. 246

prototypes, p. 247

patent, p. 247

market test (or test market), p. 247

simulated market test, p. 248

commercialization, p. 248

crowdfunding, p. 248

8.5 Objective Summary (pp. 249–255)

Explain the process of product adoption and the diffusion of innovations.

Product adoption is the process by which an individual begins to buy and use a new product, whereas the diffusion of innovations is how a new product spreads throughout a population. The stages in the adoption process are awareness, interest, trial, adoption, and confirmation. To better understand the diffusion process, marketers classify consumers—according to their readiness to adopt new products—as innovators, early adopters, early majority, late majority, and laggards.

Five product characteristics that have an important effect on how quickly (or if) a new product will be adopted by consumers are relative advantage, compatibility, product complexity, trialability, and observability. Similar to individual consumers, organizations differ in their readiness to adopt new products based on characteristics of the organization, its management, and characteristics of the innovation.

Key Terms

product adoption, p. 249

diffusion, p. 249

tipping point, p. 249

adoption pyramid, p. 249

media blitz, p. 250

impulse purchase, p. 251

beta test, p. 252

bleeding edge technology, p. 252

innovators, p. 253

early adopters, p. 253

early majority, p. 253

late majority, p. 253

laggards, p. 254

relative advantage, p. 255

compatibility, p. 255

complexity, p. 255

trialability, p. 255

observability, p. 255

Chapter **Questions** and **Activities**

MyMarketingLab™

Go to **mymktlab.com** to watch this chapter's Rising Star video(s) for career advice and to respond to questions.

Concepts: Test Your Knowledge

8-1. What is a good? What are the differences between tangible and intangible products?

8-2. What is the difference between the core product, the actual product, and the augmented product?

8-3. What is the difference between a durable good and a nondurable good? What are the main differences among convenience, shopping, and specialty products?

8-4. What is an unsought product? How do marketers make such products attractive to consumers?

8-5. What types of products are bought and sold in B2B markets?

8-6. What is a new product? Why is understanding new products so important to marketers? What are the types of innovations?

8-7. What is R&D, and what is its importance to marketers and the product development process?

8-8. List and explain the steps marketers undergo to develop new products.

8-9. What is a test market? What are some pros and cons of test markets?

8-10. Explain the stages a consumer goes through in the adoption of a new product.

8-11. List and explain the categories of adopters.

8-12. What product factors affect the rate of adoption of innovations?

Activities: Apply What You've Learned

8-13. *Creative Homework/Short Project* Assume that you are employed in the marketing department of a firm that is producing an electric scooter. In developing this product, you realize that it is important to provide a core product, an actual product, and an augmented product that meets the needs of customers. Develop an outline of how your firm might provide these three product layers in the electric scooter.

8-14. *In Class, 10–25 Minutes for Teams* Firms go to great lengths to develop new product ideas. Sometimes new ideas come from brainstorming, in which groups of individuals get together and try to think of as many different, novel, creative, and, it is hoped, profitable ideas for a new product as possible. With a group of other students, participate in brainstorming for new product ideas for one of the following (or some other product of your choice):
a. An exercise machine with some desirable new features
b. A combination shampoo and body wash
c. A new type of university
Then, with your class, screen one or more of the ideas for possible further product development.

8-15. *In Class, 10–25 Minutes for Teams* As an entrepreneur, you know that innovation will play a huge role in your new business. With your team, brainstorm briefly to define what your new business will be—let the sky be your limit. Then create a short outline that defines the various types of innovations—continuous, dynamically continuous, and discontinuous—and give examples of each. Which innovation type would be the easiest when starting out? Which innovation type brings the greatest reward? Which innovation type ultimately makes the most sense for your new business?

8-16. *Creative Homework/Short Project* As a member of a new product team with your company, you are working to develop an electric car jack that would make changing car tires easier. You are considering conducting a test market for this new product. Outline the pros and cons for test marketing this product. What are your recommendations?

8-17. *For Further Research (Individual)* Every year, marketers come out with many new or new and improved products. Using the web, research a new or new and improved product and summarize either how marketers developed and tested that product before taking it to market or how they created awareness about that new product once they developed it.

8-18. *Creative Homework/Short Project* Select a company and identify an existing product sold by that company that could potentially be further developed to meet new consumer needs. Using the selected product, develop an approach to engage consumers in the process of value co-creation with the objective of developing a new version of the selected product.

8-19. *For Further Research (Individual)* Select a recently successful product that you believe is innovative and do some research on how the product was introduced. Using the adopter categories in the chapter, identify adopters of the product that you consider to be innovators and provide evidence of specific behaviors and characteristics that support the placement of these consumers within that adopter category.

8-20. *For Further Research (Individual)* Identify an innovative product that was just recently introduced into the market and using the five characteristics that affect the rate of adoption (relative advantage, compatibility, complexity, trialability, and observability) evaluate the product on each respective characteristic. Based on your evaluation state whether you believe the innovation will be quickly adopted, slowly adopted, or adopted at a rate somewhere in between. Use your best judgment in making this determination.

8-21. *For Further Research (Individual)* Sometimes products are massively successful because consumers find a use for them separate from what the developing company initially envisioned. Find two products online that fit this description and identify their initial intended

Anesthetized Childbirth

In sorrow thou shalt bring forth children.

(Genesis 3:16)

The Bible suggests that the ancients saw suffering as a woman's lot. But during the past two centuries, science and medicine have led to the expectation that women should experience minimal discomfort during childbirth. Today some anesthesia is used to minimize or eliminate pain in most U.S. deliveries.

General anesthesia induces unconsciousness. The drug sodium pentothal, a barbiturate, induces general anesthesia when it is injected into a vein. Barbiturates may also be taken orally to reduce anxiety while the woman remains awake. Women may also receive tranquilizers like Valium or narcotics like Demerol to help them relax and to blunt pain without inducing sleep.

Anesthetic drugs, as well as tranquilizers and narcotics, decrease the strength of uterine contractions during delivery. They may thus delay the process of cervical dilation and prolong labor. They also weaken the woman's ability to push the baby through the birth canal. Because they cross the placental membrane, they also lower the newborn's overall responsiveness.

Regional or **local anesthetics** block pain in parts of the body without generally depressing the mother's alertness or putting her to sleep. In a *pudendal block,* the external genitals are numbed by local injection. In an *epidural block* and a *spinal block,* an anesthetic is injected into the spinal canal, which temporarily numbs the mother's body below the waist. To prevent injury, the needles used for these injections do not come into contact with the spinal cord itself. Although local anesthesia decreases the responsiveness of the newborn baby, there is little evidence that medicated childbirth has serious, long-term consequences on children (Ganitsch, 1992).

Natural Childbirth   Partly as a reaction against the use of anesthetics, English obstetrician Grantly Dick-Read endorsed **natural childbirth** in his 1944 book *Childbirth Without Fear.* Dick-Read argued that women's labor pains were heightened by their fear of the unknown and resultant muscle tensions. Many of Dick-Read's contributions came to be regarded as accepted practice in modern childbirth procedures, such as the emphasis on informing women about the biological aspects of reproduction and childbirth, the encouragement of physical fitness, and the teaching of relaxation and breathing exercises.

Prepared Childbirth: The Lamaze Method   The French obstetrician Fernand Lamaze visited the Soviet Union in 1951 and found that many Russian women bore babies without anesthetics and without reporting a great deal of pain. Lamaze returned to western Europe with some of the techniques the women used, and they are now usually termed the **Lamaze method,** or *prepared childbirth.* Lamaze (1981) argued that women can learn to conserve energy during childbirth and reduce the pain of uterine contractions by associating the contractions with other responses, such as thinking of pleasant mental images such as beach scenes, or engaging in breathing and relaxation exercises.

A pregnant woman typically attends Lamaze classes with a "coach"—usually the father—who will aid her in the delivery room by timing contractions, offering emotional support, and coaching her in the breathing and relaxation exercises. The woman and her partner also receive more general information about childbirth. The father is integrated into the process, and many couples report that their marriages are strengthened as a result.

The Lamaze method is flexible concerning the use of anesthetics. Many women report some pain during delivery and obtain anesthetics. However, the Lamaze method appears to enhance women's self-esteem by helping them gain a greater sense of control over the delivery process.

Cesarean Section   In a **cesarean section,** the baby is delivered through surgery rather than naturally through the vagina. The term is derived from the Latin for "to cut." In a cesarean section (C-section for short) the woman is anesthetized, and incisions are made in the abdomen and uterus so that the surgeon can remove the baby. The incisions

---

General anesthesia
The use of drugs to put people to sleep and eliminate pain, as during childbirth.

Local anesthesia
Anesthesia that eliminates pain in a specific area of the body, as during childbirth.

Natural childbirth
A method of childbirth in which women use no anesthesia but are given other strategies for coping with discomfort and are educated about childbirth.

Lamaze method
A childbirth method in which women learn about childbirth, learn to relax and to breathe in patterns that conserve energy and lessen pain, and have a coach (usually the father) present at childbirth. Also termed *prepared childbirth.*

Cesarean section
A method of childbirth in which the fetus is delivered through a surgical incision in the abdomen.

are then sewn up and the mother can begin walking, often on the same day, although generally with some discomfort for a while.

C-sections are most likely to be advised when normal delivery is difficult or threatening to the health of the mother or child. Vaginal deliveries can become difficult if the baby is large or the mother's pelvis is small or misshapen, or if the mother is overly tired or weakened. Herpes and HIV infections in the birth canal can be bypassed by C-section. C-sections are also likely to be performed if the baby presents for delivery in the breech position (feet downward) or the **transverse position** (lying crosswise), or if the baby is in distress.

Use of the C-section has mushroomed. Today nearly 1 of every 4 births is by C-section (DiMatteo et al., 1996; Paul, 1996). Compare this figure to about 1 in 10 births in 1975. The increased rate of C-sections reflects advances in medical technology (such as use of fetal monitors that allow doctors to detect fetal distress), fear of malpractice suits, financial incentives for hospitals and physicians, and simply the current medical practice patterns (DiMatteo et al., 1996). Critics claim that many C-sections are unnecessary and reflect overly aggressive medical practices. Even the Centers for Disease Control and Prevention hopes to lower the rate of cesareans in the United States to 15 per 100 births by the year 2000, a level the agency considers to be medically appropriate (Paul, 1996).

Medical opinion once held that after a woman had a C-section, subsequent deliveries also had to be performed by C-section. Otherwise, uterine scars might rupture during labor. Research has shown that rupture is rare, however. In one study, only 10 of 3,249 women who chose to try vaginal delivery after a previous C-section had a uterine rupture (McMahon et al., 1996). Moreover, there were no maternal deaths.

Birth Problems

Most deliveries are uncomplicated, or "unremarkable" in the medical sense—although childbirth is the most remarkable experience of many parents' lives. Problems can and do occur, however. Some of the most common birth problems are anoxia and the birth of preterm and low-birthweight babies.

Anoxia

Prenatal **anoxia** can cause various problems in the neonate and affect later development. It leads to complications such as brain damage and mental retardation. Prolonged anoxia during delivery can also result in cerebral palsy and possibly death.

The baby is supplied with oxygen through the umbilical cord. Passage through the birth canal squeezes the umbilical cord. Temporary squeezing, like holding one's breath for a moment, is unlikely to cause problems. (In fact, slight oxygen deprivation at birth is not unusual because the transition from receiving oxygen through the umbilical cord to breathing on its own may not happen immediately after the baby emerges.) Anoxia can result if constriction of the cord is prolonged, however. Prolonged constriction is more likely to occur with a breech presentation, because the baby's head presses the umbilical cord against the birth canal during delivery. Fetal monitoring can help detect anoxia early, however, before damage occurs. A C-section can be performed if the fetus appears to be in distress.

Preterm and Low-Birthweight Children

A neonate is considered to be premature, or **preterm,** if it is born before 37 weeks of gestation. The normal period of gestation is 40 weeks. Prematurity is generally linked with low birthweight, since the fetus normally makes dramatic gains in weight during the last weeks of pregnancy. Regardless of the length of its gestation period, a newborn baby is considered to have a low birthweight if it weighs less than 5 pounds (about 2,500 grams).

Preterm or low-birthweight babies face a heightened risk of infant mortality (Singh & Yu, 1995). A birthweight of 3¼ pounds (1,500 grams) is considered to be the cutoff with respect to the likelihood of mortality.

Transverse position
A crosswise birth position.

Anoxia
Oxygen deprivation.

Preterm
Born prior to 37 weeks of gestation.

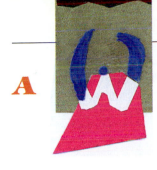

A WORLD OF DIVERSITY

ETHNICITY AND INFANT MORTALITY

Back in 1950, there were more than 25 infant deaths per 1,000 live births in the United States. Because the United States now has some of the world's most sophisticated medical technology, that number has been dropping sharply, to 8.5 in 1992 and 7.9 in 1994. Yet within the United States, there are also dramatic ethnic differences in rates of infant mortality. Infant mortality rates are lowest for Chinese Americans and Japanese Americans (Singh & Yu, 1995). Hispanic Americans of Cuban, Mexican, or Central or South American descent have the next lowest infant mortality rates. Non-Hispanic White Americans follow, and then come African Americans. The infant mortality rate for African Americans is about twice that for non-Hispanic White Americans (Singh & Yu, 1995). In the year 1992, African Americans made up about 12% of the U.S. population. However, they accounted for about 17% of the live births and one third of the infant deaths in the nation (Singh & Yu, 1995).

Much of the ethnic difference in infant mortality can apparently be attributed to differences in prenatal health care. Table 9.3 shows 1990 infant health statistics obtained from public records in New York City. Residents of the affluent White Kips Bay–Yorkville area have healthier newborns than residents of East Harlem (a low-income neighborhood made up mostly of African Americans) or of middle-income and mainly White Astoria–Long Island City. East Harlem mothers, like other low-income mothers (McLaughlin et al., 1992), were more likely than their middle- and upper-income counterparts to have babies with low birthweights and babies who died during infancy. Maternal malnutrition and use of chemical substances such as alcohol and tobacco during pregnancy have all been linked to low birthweights and increased mortality during the first year of life (Barr et al., 1990; McLaughlin et al., 1992).

The differences in infant health shown in the table are also connected with the incidence of prenatal care received by the mothers in the three neighborhoods. According to 1990 New York City Department of Health records, nearly 36% of East Harlem mothers received either late prenatal care or none, as compared with about 6% in Kips Bay–Yorkville and about 10% in Astoria–Long Island City. Research has shown that comprehensive prenatal care is connected with higher birthweights (McLaughlin et al., 1992).

TABLE 9.3 Infant health statistics for three New York City neighborhoods

Infant Health Statistics	East Harlem	Astoria–Long Island City	Kips Bay–Yorkville
Infant deaths per 1,000 live births	23.4	14.9	7.3
Low birthweight babies per 100 live births (less than 5.5 pounds)	18.5	6.1	6.0
Very low birthweight babies per 100 live births (less than 3.3 pounds)	3.8	0.98	0.87
Live births per 100 in which mothers received late or no prenatal care	35.8	10.4	6.1

This table shows infant health statistics for three New York City neighborhoods. East Harlem is a heavily studied inner-city area characterized by poverty, a high proportion of minority residents, and many teenage pregnancies. The Astoria–Long Island City area is populated by middle-income residents. Kips Bay–Yorkville is a high-income area.
Source: Department of Health, City of New York, 1990.

Surfactants
Substances that prevent the walls of the airways from sticking together.

Preterm babies are relatively thin because they have not yet formed the layer of fat that accounts for the round, robust appearance of most full-term babies. Their muscles are immature, which weakens their sucking and breathing reflexes. Also, in the last weeks of pregnancy fetuses secrete **surfactants** that prevent the walls of their airways from sticking together. Muscle weakness and incomplete lining of the airways with surfactants can cause a cluster of problems known as **respiratory distress syndrome,** which is responsible for many neonatal deaths. Preterm babies may also suffer from underdeveloped immune systems, which leave them more vulnerable to infections.

Preterm infants usually remain in the hospital for a time. There they can be monitored and placed in incubators that provide a temperature-controlled environment and offer some protection from disease. If necessary, they may also receive oxygen.

The Postpartum Period

The weeks following delivery are called the **postpartum** period. The first few days postpartum are frequently happy ones. The long wait is over, as are the discomforts of childbirth. A sizable number of women experience feelings of depression, however, in the days and sometimes weeks and months following childbirth.

Maternal Depression

Mood changes following childbirth are experienced by many new mothers. During the days or weeks following the delivery of their babies, anywhere from 50% to 80% of new mothers (Harding, 1989) experience periods of sadness, tearfulness, and irritability that are commonly called the "postpartum blues," the "maternity blues," or the "baby blues." The baby blues usually last about 48 hours and are generally believed to be a normal response to hormonal and psychological changes that attend childbirth (Harding, 1989; Samuels & Samuels, 1986).

Some mothers experience more persistent and severe mood changes, called **postpartum depression** (PPD) (Whiffen, 1992). PPD may last a year or even longer. PPD can involve extreme sadness or despair, apathy, changes in appetite and sleep patterns, low self-esteem, and difficulty concentrating. A study of 1,033 married, middle-class, first-time mothers from the Pittsburgh area who had full-term, healthy infants found that 9.3% of them had experienced PPD (Campbell & Cohn, 1991). Some researchers (e.g., Gitlin & Pasnau, 1989) estimate that PPD affects up to 15% of new mothers.

PPD may reflect a combination of physiological and psychological factors. Hormonal changes may play a role in PPD, but women with PPD are more likely than those with the "maternity blues" to have been susceptible to depression before and during their pregnancies (O'Hara et al., 1984). Psychosocial factors such as stress, a troubled marriage, or the need to adjust to an unwanted or sick baby may all increase a woman's susceptibility to PPD (Gitlin & Pasnau, 1989; O'Hara et al., 1984, 1991). Adjusting to a new baby imposes inevitable changes on parents, and change is usually stressful in itself. Depression is likely to be prolonged in women who feel helpless in meeting the demands they face (Cutrona, 1983). First-time mothers, single mothers, and mothers who lack social support from their partners or family members face the greatest risk of PPD (Gitlin & Pasnau, 1989).

New fathers may also have bouts of depression. New mothers are not the only ones who must adjust to the responsibilities of parenthood. Fathers too may feel overwhelmed or unable to cope. Perhaps more fathers might experience the "paternity blues" but for the fact that mothers generally shoulder the lion's share of child-rearing chores.

Breast-Feeding Versus Bottle-Feeding

Only a minority of U.S. women breast-feed their children. One reason is that many women return to the workforce shortly following childbirth. Some choose to share feeding chores with the father, who is equally equipped to prepare and hold a bottle, but not to breast-feed. Other women find breast-feeding inconvenient or unpleasant. Long-term comparisons of breast-fed and bottle-fed children show few, if any, significant differences. Breast-feeding does reduce the general risk of infections to the baby, however, by transmitting the mother's antibodies to the baby. Breast-feeding also reduces the incidence of allergies in babies, particularly in allergy-prone infants.

Prolactin
A pituitary hormone that stimulates production of milk.

Lactation
Production of milk by the mammary glands.

The hormones prolactin and oxytocin are involved in breast-feeding. **Prolactin** stimulates production of milk, or **lactation,** two to three days after delivery. Oxytocin causes the breasts to eject milk and is secreted in response to suckling. When an infant is weaned, secretion of prolactin and oxytocin is discontinued, and lactation comes to an end.

Uterine contractions that occur during breast-feeding help return the uterus to its typical size. Breast-feeding also delays resumption of normal menstrual cycles. Breast-feeding is not a perfectly reliable birth-control method, however. (But nursing women are advised not to use birth-control pills, since the hormone content of the pills is passed to the infant through the milk.)

Should a woman breast-feed her baby? Although breast-feeding has benefits for both mother and infant, each woman must weigh these benefits against the difficulties breast-feeding may pose for her. These include assuming the sole responsibility for nighttime feedings, the physical demands of producing and expelling milk, tendency for soreness in the breasts, and the inconvenience of being continually available to meet the infant's feeding needs. Women should breast-feed because they want to, not because they feel they must.

Resumption of Sexual Activity

The resumption of coitus depends on a couple's level of sexual interest, the healing of episiotomies or other injuries, fatigue, the recommendations of obstetricians, and, of course, tradition. Obstetricians usually advise a six-week waiting period for safety and comfort.

Women will typically prefer to delay coitus until it becomes physically comfortable, generally when the episiotomy or other lacerations have healed and the lochia has ended. This may take several weeks. Women who breast-feed may also find they have less vaginal lubrication, which can cause some discomfort during coitus. K-Y jelly or other lubricants may help in such cases.

The return of sexual interest and resumption of sexual activity may take longer for some couples than for others. Sexual interest depends more on psychological than on physical factors. Many couples encounter declining sexual interest and activity in the first year following childbirth, generally because child care can sap energy and limit free time. Generally speaking, couples whose sexual relationships were satisfying before the baby arrived tend to show greater sexual interest and to resume sexual activity earlier than those who had less satisfying relationships beforehand. (No surprise.)

Chapter Review

(1) _____tion is the union of a sperm cell and an ovum. Ova carry (2) _____ sex chromosomes. Sperm carry either X or Y sex (3) _____omes. Girls are conceived from the union of an ovum and an X-bearing sperm, boys from the union of an ovum and a (4) _____-bearing sperm.

There are 200 to 400 (5) _____ion sperm in an average ejaculate. Fertilization normally occurs in a (6) _____ian tube. Ova are surrounded by a gelatinous layer called the (7) z_____ _____cida. Sperm secrete the enzyme (8) hyal_____, which thins the zona pellucida, enabling one sperm to penetrate.

Conception occurs as the chromosomes from the sperm and ovum combine to form (9) _____ pairs.

One way of optimizing the chances of conception is to engage in coitus within a few hours of (10) _____tion. People can predict ovulation by using the basal body temperature chart, analyzing urine or saliva for (11) _____ing hormone, or tracking vaginal mucus.

Infertility and Ways of Becoming Parents

The term (12) *in*_____ is usually not applied until the failure to conceive has persisted for more than a year. The incidence of infertility (13: Increases *or* Decreases?) with age. About (14) _____% of American couples have fertility problems.

The fertility problem lies with the man in about (15) _____% of cases. In about (16) _____% of cases, problems are found in both partners. Fertility problems in the male reflect abnormalities such as (17: High *or* Low?) sperm count, irregularly shaped sperm, low sperm (18) mo_____, disease, injury to the testes, hormonal problems, varicose veins in the (19) _____um, drugs, environmental toxins, excess heat, and stress. Low (20) _____m count is the most common problem. To be considered normal, sperm must be able to swim for at least (21) _____ hour(s) following coitus, and most must be normal in shape. In one kind of (22) ar_____ _____tion, the sperm of men with low sperm counts is collected and injected into the uterus at the time of ovulation. Sperm from a (23) d_____ who resembles the man can be used to artificially inseminate a woman whose partner is infertile.

Major causes of infertility in women include irregular (24) _____tion, malfunctions of the reproductive tract, (25) endo_____, and declining levels of sex hormones that occur with aging. Ovulation is sometimes induced by fertility drugs such as (26) _____phene (Clomid). It stimulates the (27) pi_____ gland to secrete FSH and LH, which in turn stimulate the maturation of ova.

Local infections such as pelvic (28) _____tory disease can scar the fallopian tubes and other organs and impede the passage of sperm or ova. In endometriosis, cells break away from the (29) _____ine lining and become implanted and grow elsewhere, impeding conception.

In the method of (30) in v_____ _____-tion, conception takes place in a laboratory dish and the embryo is injected into the mother's uterus to become implanted and develop to term. In (31) g_____ intra_____ _____fer, or GIFT, sperm and ova are inserted together into a fallopian tube for fertilization. In (32) z_____ intrafallopian transfer, sperm fertilize an ovum in a laboratory dish and the zygote is placed in a fallopian tube to journey to the uterus for implantation. In (33) d_____ IVF, an ovum is taken from another woman, fertilized, and injected into the uterus or fallopian tube of the intended mother. In (34) _____nic transfer, a woman is artificially inseminated by the male partner of the infertile woman, after which the embryo is removed from the volunteer and inserted for implantation in the intended mother.

Pregnancy

For many women the first sign of pregnancy is missing a (35) _____d. Pregnancy tests rely on the fact that women produce (36) human chor_____ _____pin (HCG) shortly after conception. Women who are pregnant usually show (37) _____r's sign—softness of a section of the uterus between the uterine body and the cervix—which may be detected by a physician.

Soon after conception, a woman may note (38) _____ness of the breasts. About half of pregnant women have nausea, food aversions, and vomiting, which is termed (39) mor_____ _____ness, although it may occur throughout the day. Pregnant women may also experience fatigue and have (40) fre_____ _____tion, caused by pressure on the bladder.

Miscarriages may be caused by (41) _____mal defects in the fetus and tend to occur (42: Early *or* Late?) in pregnancy. Most health professionals agree that coitus (43: Is *or* Is not?) usually safe throughout pregnancy. Most women show (44: More *or* Less?) interest in sexual activity during the first trimester of pregnancy. Now and then an expectant father experiences some signs of pregnancy, a reaction that is called a (45) sym_____pregnancy.

Prenatal Development

If we date pregnancy from the onset of the last menstrual cycle before conception, the normal gestation period is (46) _____ days. The delivery date is usually calculated by (47) _____'s rule. Prenatal development can be divided into three periods: the (48) _____nal stage, which corresponds to about the first two weeks, the (49) _____nic stage, which coincides with the first two months, and the (50) _____tal stage.

After conception, it takes the zygote three or four days to reach the (51) _____us. (52) _____tation takes about another week. Several days into the germinal stage, the cell mass becomes a fluid-filled ball called a (53) _____cyst. The major organ systems of the body begin to differentiate during the (54) em_____ stage. Embryonic development follows two trends: (55) _____caudal and (56) prox_____. The heart begins to beat by the (57) _____th week following conception.

The embryo and fetus develop the (58) am_____ sac. Nutrients and waste products are exchanged between mother and embryo (or fetus) through the (59) pl_____. The fetus is connected to the placenta by the (60) _____al cord. The circulatory systems of mother and embryo (61: Do or Do not?) mix. The placenta also secretes (62) _____nes that preserve the pregnancy, stimulate uterine contractions that induce childbirth, and prepare the breasts for breast-feeding. The placenta is also called the (63) _____birth.

The mother usually feels the first fetal movements by the middle of the (64) f_____ month. The fetus typically turns upside down in the uterus during the seventh month so that it will be in a head-first, or (65) _____lic, presentation for delivery.

Maternal malnutrition during the third trimester is linked to (66: Low or High?) birthweight and (67: Increased or Decreased?) infant mortality. Environmental agents that can harm the fetus are called (68) _____gens. The times at which exposure to particular teratogens causes the greatest harm are termed (69) cr_____ _____ods of vulnerability. Women who contract (70) r_____ (German measles) during the first month or two of pregnancy may bear children who are deaf or who develop mental retardation. The rupturing of (71) b_____ vessels during childbirth provides an opportunity for transmission of HIV from mother to baby. The majority of babies born to mothers who are infected with HIV (72: Do or Do not?) become infected themselves.

Toxemia is a life-threatening condition characterized by (73: High or Low?) blood pressure, that may afflict women in pregnancy. Babies born to women with toxemia are often small or (74) _____ture. In an (75) _____ic pregnancy, the fertilized ovum implants itself someplace other than the uterus, most often a fallopian tube. In Rh incompatibility, (76) _____dies produced by the mother can be transmitted to a fetus or

newborn infant. Rh incompatibility occurs when a woman who is Rh- (77: Positive or Negative?) is carrying an Rh- (78: Positive or Negative?) fetus.

In the 1960s the drug (79) _____mide, which was intended to help pregnant women with nausea and insomnia, caused birth deformities. The antibiotic (80) tet_____ may yellow the teeth and deform the bones. (81) Di_____bestrol (DES), a powerful estrogen, was once given to women at risk for miscarriage to help maintain their pregnancies. DES is suspected of causing (82) _____cal and testicular cancer in some of the children whose mothers used it.

Nearly 40% of children whose mothers drink heavily during pregnancy develop (83) fe_____ _____ol syndrome (FAS). The critical period for the development of the facial features associated with FAS seems to be the first (84) _____ months of prenatal development, when the head is taking shape. Maternal smoking (85: Increases or Decreases?) the risk of spontaneous abortion, stillbirth, premature birth, low birthweight, and early infant mortality. Low (86) birth_____ is the most common risk factor for infant disease and mortality.

Children with (87) D_____ syndrome have characteristic round faces; wide, flat noses; and protruding tongues. People with Down syndrome are also moderately (88) men_____ _____ded. The risk of a child's having Down syndrome (89: Increases or Decreases?) with the mother's age.

(90) S_____ cell anemia is most prevalent in the United States among African Americans. (91) Tay-_____ disease is most common among Jews of Eastern European background.

Some genetic defects, such as hemophilia, are sex linked, in that they are carried only on the (92: X or Y?) sex chromosome. Sex-linked disorders are more likely to afflict sons of (93: Male or Female) carriers because they have only one X sex chromosome, which they inherit from their mothers.

In (94) _____tesis, fluid is drawn from the amniotic sac, and fetal cells are examined for the presence of biochemical and chromosomal abnormalities. (95) Cho_____ _____us sampling (CVS) can be performed several weeks earlier. In (96) _____nd, high-pitched sound waves are bounced off the fetus, revealing a picture of the fetus on a TV monitor. Parental

(97) _____ od tests can suggest the presence of problems such as sickle cell anemia, Tay-Sachs disease, and neural tube defects.

Childbirth

The first uterine contractions are relatively painless and are called (98) Br_____-Hicks contractions, or "false" labor contractions. The initiation of labor may involve the secretion of hormones that stimulate the placenta and mother's uterus to produce (99) pr_____dins. They stimulate the (100) _____ine muscles to contract. Later in labor the pituitary gland releases (101) _____cin, a hormone that stimulates contractions strong enough to expel the baby.

There are (102: One, Two, or Three?) stages of childbirth. In the first stage uterine contractions efface and dilate the (103) c_____. (104) _____tion occurs when the cervix becomes nearly fully dilated and the baby's head begins to move into the vagina. The (105: First, Second, or Third?) stage of childbirth begins when the cervix has become fully dilated and the baby first appears at the opening of the birth canal. When the baby's head becomes visible at the vaginal opening, it is said to have (106) _____ed. During the third, or (107) _____tal, stage of childbirth, the placenta is expelled.

Today some (108) _____sia is used to minimize or eliminate pain in most deliveries in the United States. (109) G_____ anesthesia induces unconsciousness. Women may receive (110) _____izers such as Valium or narcotics such as Demerol to help them relax and to blunt pain without inducing sleep. Regional, or (111) _____al, anesthetics block pain in certain parts of the body.

In the (112) L_____ method, women may learn to conserve energy during childbirth and reduce the pain of uterine contractions by engaging in breathing and relaxation exercises. A woman typically attends Lamaze classes with a (113) c_____ who will help her in the delivery room by timing contractions, offering emotional support, and coaching her in the breathing and relaxation exercises.

In a (114) ce_____ section, the baby is delivered through surgery rather than naturally through the vagina. C-sections are likely to be performed if the baby presents for delivery in the (115) b_____ position (feet downward) or if the baby is in distress. Today nearly 1 of every (116) _____ births in the United States is by C-section.

Birth Problems

Prenatal (117) an_____ leads to complications such as brain damage and mental retardation. The baby is supplied with oxygen through the (118) um_____ cord.

A neonate is considered to be premature, or preterm, if it is born before (119) _____ weeks of gestation. Preterm or low-birthweight babies are at greater risk of infant (120) _____lity.

Infant mortality rates in the United States are lowest for Chinese Americans and (121) _____ese Americans. (122) _____ic Americans have the next lowest infant mortality rates. (123) _____an Americans have the highest infant mortality rates. Much of the ethnic difference in infant mortality can be attributed to differences in prenatal (124) h_____ care.

The Postpartum Period

The weeks following delivery are called the (125) _____tum period. During the days or weeks following the delivery of their babies, half or more of new mothers experience periods of sadness that are called the "postpartum (126) _____es." The blues are generally believed to be a normal response to (127) _____nal and psychological changes that attend childbirth. Some mothers experience more persistent and severe mood changes, called (128) post_____ _____sion (PPD).

A (129: Minority or Majority?) of U.S. women breast-feed their children. Breast-feeding reduces the risk of infections to the baby by transmitting the mother's (130) _____dies to the baby. The hormone (131) _____tin stimulates production of milk two to three days after delivery. Obstetricians usually advise a (132) _____-week waiting period before resuming coitus for reasons of safety and comfort.

Chapter Quiz

1. The enzyme hyaluronidase
   (a) stimulates production of milk.
   (b) passes through the placenta.
   (c) stimulates contractions of labor.
   (d) thins the zona pellucida.
2. The most common cause of male infertility is
   (a) low sperm motility.
   (b) low sperm count.
   (c) injury to the testes.
   (d) higher-than-normal scrotal temperature.
3. The presence of human chorionic gonadotropin is assessed to determine
   (a) blocked fallopian tubes.
   (b) sickle-cell anemia.
   (c) pregnancy.
   (d) Down syndrome.
4. If we date pregnancy from the onset of the last menstrual cycle before conception, the normal gestation period is _____ days.
   (a) 266
   (b) 272
   (c) 280
   (d) 288
5. In the method of _____, an ovum is fertilized in a laboratory dish and then placed in a fallopian tube.
   (a) ZIFT
   (b) GIFT
   (c) embryonic transfer
   (d) intracytoplasmic injection
6. The umbilical cord contains
   (a) one artery and one vein.
   (b) two arteries and two veins.
   (c) two arteries and one vein.
   (d) one artery and two veins.
7. A breech presentation is
   (a) bottom first.
   (b) head first.
   (c) sideways.
   (d) shoulder first.
8. Preeclampsia is a stage of
   (a) sickle-cell anemia.
   (b) Tay-Sachs disease.
   (c) rubella.
   (d) toxemia.
9. The critical period for the development of the facial features associated with FAS seems to be the first _____ of prenatal development.
   (a) week
   (b) two weeks
   (c) month
   (d) two months
10. The pudendal block is an example of
    (a) general anesthesia.
    (b) local anesthesia.
    (c) use of a tranquilizer.
    (d) use of a narcotic.

Answers to Chapter Review

1. Conception
2. X
3. Chromosomes
4. Y
5. Million
6. Fallopian
7. Zona pellucida
8. Hyaluronidase
9. 23
10. Ovulation
11. Luteinizing
12. *Infertility*
13. Increases
14. 15
15. 30
16. 20
17. Low
18. Motility
19. Scrotum
20. Sperm
21. Two
22. Artificial insemination
23. Donor
24. Ovulation
25. Endometriosis
26. Clomiphene
27. Pituitary
28. Inflammatory
29. Uterine
30. In vitro fertilization
31. Gamete intrafallopian transfer
32. Zygote
33. Donor
34. Embryonic
35. Period (menstrual period)
36. Human chorionic gonadotropin
37. Hegar's
38. Tenderness
39. Morning sickness
40. Frequent urination
41. Chromosomal
42. Early
43. Is
44. Less
45. Sympathetic
46. 280
47. Nagele's
48. Germinal
49. Embryonic
50. Fetal
51. Uterus
52. Implantation
53. Blastocyst
54. Embryonic
55. Cephalocaudal
56. Proximodistal
57. Fourth
58. Amniotic
59. Placenta
60. Umbilical
61. Do not
62. Hormones
63. Afterbirth
64. Fourth
65. Cephalic
66. Low
67. Increased
68. Teratogens
69. Critical periods
70. Rubella
71. Blood
72. Do not
73. High
74. Premature
75. Ectopic
76. Antibodies
77. Negative
78. Positive
79. Thalidomide
80. Tetracycline
81. Diethylstilbestrol
82. Cervical
83. Fetal alcohol
84. Two
85. Increases
86. Birthweight
87. Down
88. Mentally retarded
89. Increases
90. Sickle
91. Tay-Sachs
92. X
93. Female
94. Amniocentesis
95. Chorionic villus
96. Ultrasound
97. Blood
98. Braxton
99. Prostaglandins
100. Uterine
101. Oxytocin
102. Three
103. Cervix
104. Transition
105. Second
106. Crowned
107. Placental
108. Anesthesia
109. General
110. Tranquilizers

111. Local
112. Lamaze
113. Coach
114. Cesarean
115. Breech

116. 4
117. Anoxia
118. Umbilical
119. 37
120. Mortality

121. Japanese
122. Hispanic
123. African
124. Health
125. Postpartum

126. Blues
127. Hormonal
128. Postpartum
     depression
129. Minority

130. Antibodies
131. Prolactin
132. Six

Answers to Chapter Quiz

1. (d)
2. (b)

3. (c)
4. (c)

5. (a)
6. (c)

7. (a)
8. (d)

9. (d)
10. (b)

CHAPTER 10

Contraception and Abortion

OUTLINE

Contraception
Oral Contraceptives ("the Pill")
Norplant
Intrauterine Devices (IUDs)
The Diaphragm
Spermicides
The Cervical Cap
Condoms
Douching
Withdrawal (Coitus Interruptus)
Fertility Awareness Methods (Rhythm Methods)
Sterilization
Other Devices

Abortion
Methods of Abortion

Chapter Review

Chapter Quiz

Applications
Selecting a Method of Contraception

A World of Diversity
Japan's Abortion Agony: In a Country That Prohibits the Pill, Reality Collides with Religion

- Most contraceptives provide little or no protection against sexually transmitted diseases?
- Many birth-control pills fool the brain into acting as though the woman is already pregnant? Therefore, no additional ova mature or are released.
- Many birth-control pills have healthful side effects? For example, the combination pill reduces the risks of ovarian and endometrial cancer.
- There is an oral contraceptive that can be taken the morning after intercourse?
- Many sterilization operations can be surgically reversed?
- Testosterone can be used as a male *contraceptive* device?
- Vacuum aspiration is now the most widely used abortion method in the United States?

Methods of birth control include contraception and abortion. Contraception refers to techniques that prevent conception. Abortion refers to the termination of a pregnancy before the embryo or fetus is capable of surviving outside the womb. ■

Contraception

There are many methods of contraception, including oral contraceptives (the pill), Norplant, intrauterine devices (IUDs), diaphragms, cervical caps, spermicides, condoms, douching, withdrawal (coitus interruptus), timing of ovulation (rhythm method), and some devices under development.

Oral Contraceptives ("the Pill")

Oral contraceptive
A contraceptive, consisting of sex hormones, which is taken by mouth.

Combination pill
A birth-control pill that contains synthetic estrogen and progesterone.

Minipill
A birth-control pill that contains synthetic progesterone but no estrogen.

An **oral contraceptive** is commonly referred to as a birth-control pill, or simply "the pill." However, there are many kinds of birth-control pills that vary in the type and dosages of hormones they contain. Birth-control pills fall into two major categories: combination pills and minipills.

Combination pills (such as Ortho-Novum, Ovcon, and Loestrin) contain a combination of synthetic forms of the hormones estrogen and progesterone (progestin). Most combination pills provide a steady dose of synthetic estrogen and progesterone. Other combination pills, called *multiphasic* pills, vary the dosage of these hormones across the menstrual cycle to reduce the overall dosages to which the woman is exposed and possible side effects. The **minipill** contains synthetic progesterone (progestin) only.

Available only by prescription, oral contraceptives are used by 28% of women in the United States who use reversible (nonsterilization) forms of contraception, or some 19 million women (Angier, 1993a). Birth-control pills are the most popular forms of contraception among single women of reproductive age (Gilbert, 1996).

How They Work   Women cannot conceive when they are already pregnant because their bodies suppress maturation of egg follicles and ovulation. The combination pill fools the brain into acting as though the woman is already pregnant, so that no additional ova mature or are released. If ovulation does not take place, a woman cannot become pregnant.

The estrogen in the combination pill inhibits FSH production, so follicles do not mature. The progesterone (progestin) inhibits the pituitary's secretion of LH, which would otherwise lead to ovulation. The woman continues to have menstrual periods, but there is no unfertilized ovum to be sloughed off in the menstrual flow.

The combination pill is taken for 21 days of the typical 28-day cycle. Then, for 7 days, the woman either takes no pill at all or an inert placebo pill to maintain the habit of taking a pill a day. The sudden drop in hormone levels causes the endometrium to disintegrate and menstruation to follow 3 or 4 days after the last pill has been taken. Then the cycle is repeated.

The progestin in the combination pill also increases the thickness and acidity of the cervical mucus. The mucus thus becomes a more resistant barrier to sperm and inhibits development of the endometrium. Therefore, even if an egg were somehow to mature and become fertilized in a fallopian tube, sperm would not be likely to reach it. Even if sperm were to fertilize an egg, the failure of the endometrium to develop would mean that the fertilized ovum could not become implanted in the uterus. Progestin may also impede the progress of ova through the fallopian tubes and make it more difficult for sperm to penetrate ova.

The minipill contains progestin but no estrogen. Minipills are taken daily through the menstrual cycle, even during menstruation. They thicken the cervical mucus and render the inner lining of the uterus less receptive to a fertilized egg. Thus, even if the woman does conceive, the fertilized egg will pass from the body rather than becoming implanted in the uterine wall. Since it contains no estrogen, the minipill does not usually prevent ovulation. The combination pill, by contrast, prevents ovulation. Since ovulation and fertilization may occur in women who use the minipill, some people see use of the minipill as an early abortion method.

Effectiveness   The failure rate of the birth-control pill associated with perfect use is very low—0.5% or less, depending on the type of pill (see Table 10.1 on page 236). The failure rate increases to 3% in typical use. Failures can occur when women forget to take the pill for two days or more, when they do not use backup methods when they first go on the pill, and when they switch from one brand to another. But forgetting to take the pill even for one day may alter the woman's hormonal balance, allowing ovulation—and fertilization—to occur.

Reversibility   Use of oral contraceptives may temporarily reduce fertility after they are discontinued but is not associated with permanent infertility (Mishell, 1989). Nine of ten women begin ovulating regularly within three months of suspending use (Reinisch, 1990). When a woman appears not to be ovulating after going off the pill, a drug like clomiphene is often used to induce ovulation.

Advantages and Disadvantages   Oral contraception, used properly, is nearly 100% effective. It does not interfere with sexual spontaneity or diminish sexual sensations.

Birth-control pills may also have some *healthful* side effects. They appear to reduce the risk of pelvic inflammatory disease (PID), benign ovarian cysts, and fibrocystic (benign) breast growths (Gilbert, 1996). They regularize menstrual cycles and reduce menstrual discomfort. The pill may also be helpful in the treatment of iron-deficiency anemia and facial acne. The combination pill reduces the risks of ovarian and endometrial cancer (Gilbert, 1996; Hatcher et al., 1994).

The pill does have some disadvantages. It confers no protection against STDs. Moreover, it may reduce the effectiveness of antibiotics used to treat STDs. Going on the pill requires medical consultation, so a woman must plan to begin using the pill at least several weeks before becoming sexually active and must incur the expense of medical visits.

The main drawbacks of birth-control pills are potential side effects and possible health risks. The estrogen in combination pills may produce side effects such as nausea and vomiting, fluid retention (feeling "bloated"), weight gain, increased vaginal discharge, headaches, tenderness in the breasts, and dizziness. Many of these side effects are temporary. Weight gain can result from estrogen (through fluid retention) or progestin (through increased appetite and development of muscle). Oral contraceptives may also increase blood

Method	Women Experiencing an Accidental Pregnancy within the First Year of Use (%)		Women Continuing Use at One Year[3] (%)	Reversibility	Protection Against Sexually Transmitted Diseases (STDs)
	Typical Use[1]	Perfect Use[2]			
Chance[4]	85	85		Yes (unless fertility has been impaired by exposure to STDs)	No
Spermicides[5]	21	6	43	Yes	Some
Periodic Abstinence	20		67	Yes	No
Calendar		9			
Ovulation Method		3			
Sympto-Thermal[6]		2			
Postovulation		1			
Withdrawal	19	4		Yes	No
Cervical Cap[7]					
Parous Women*	36	26	45	Yes	Some[8]
Nulliparous† Women	18	9	58	Yes	Some[8]
Diaphragm[7]	18	6	58	Yes	Some[8]
Condom Alone					
Female (Reality)	21	5	56	Yes	Yes[8]
Male	12	3	63	Yes	Yes[8]
Pill	3		72	Yes	No, but may reduce the risk of PID[9]
Progestin Only		0.5			
Combined		0.1			
IUD					
Progestasert T	2.0	1.5	81	Yes, except if fertility is impaired	No, and may increase the risk of PID
Copper T 380A	0.8	0.6	78		
LNg 20	0.1	0.1	81		

pressure in some women, but serious elevations are rare in women using the low-dose pills that are available today (Hatcher et al., 1994).

Many women have avoided using the pill because of the risk of blood clots. The lower dosages of estrogen found in most types of birth-control pills today are associated with much lower risk of blood clots than was the case in the 1960s and 1970s, when higher dosages were typically used (Gilbert, 1996). Still, women who are at increased risk for blood clotting problems, such as those with a history of circulatory problems or stroke, are typically advised not to use the pill.

Because of their increased risk of cardiovascular problems, caution should be exercised when the combination pill is used by women over 35 years of age who are heavy smokers (15 or more cigarettes daily) (Hatcher et al., 1994). Nursing mothers should also avoid using the pill, as the hormones may be passed to the baby in the mother's milk. But for the great majority of healthy women in their 20s and 30s, there is very little chance of developing blood clots or other cardiovascular problems from using the pill (Hatcher et al.,

Method	Women Experiencing an Accidental Pregnancy within the First Year of Use (%)		Women Continuing Use at One Year[3] (%)	Reversibility	Protection Against Sexually Transmitted Diseases (STDs)
	Typical Use[1]	Perfect Use[2]			
Depo-Provera	0.3	0.3	70	Yes	No
Norplant (6 capsules)	0.09	0.09	85	Yes	No
Female Sterilization	0.4	0.4	100	Not usually	No
Male Sterilization	0.15	0.10	100	Not usually	No

[1]Among typical couples who initiate use of a method (not necessarily for the first time), the percentage who experience an accidental pregnancy during the first year if they do not stop use for any other reason.

[2]Among couples who initiate use of a method (not necessarily for the first time) and who use it perfectly (both consistently and correctly), the percentage who experience an accidental pregnancy during the first year if they do not stop use for any other reason.

[3]Among couples attempting to avoid pregnancy, the percentage who continue to use a method for one year.

[4]The percentages failing in columns 2 and 3 are based on data from populations in which contraception is not used and from women who cease using contraception in order to become pregnant. Among such populations, about 89% become pregnant within one year. This estimate was lowered slightly (to 85%) to represent the percentage who would become pregnant within one year among women now relying on reversible methods of contraception if they abandoned contraception altogether.

[5]Foams, creams, gels, vaginal suppositories, and vaginal film.

[6]Cervical mucus (ovulation) method supplemented by calendar in the preovulatory and basal body temperature in the postovulatory.

[7]With spermicidal cream or jelly.

[8]These methods provide better protection against STDs if a spermicide such as nonoxynol-9 is used simultaneously.

[9]Pelvic inflammatory disease.

*Women who have borne children.

†Women who have not borne children.

Sources: For failure rates and percentages of women discontinuing use, adapted from Hatcher et al. (1994). For reversibility and protection against sexually transmitted diseases, adapted from Reinisch (1990).

1994). Many health professionals, including the American College of Obstetricians and Gynecologists, believe that healthy nonsmokers age 35 to 44 can continue to use oral contraceptives safely (Mishell, 1989).

The pill may also have psychological effects. Some users report depression or irritability. Switching brands or altering doses may help.

Progestin fosters male secondary sex characteristics, so women who take the minipill may develop acne, facial hair, thinning of scalp hair, reduction in breast size, vaginal dryness, and missed or shorter periods. Irregular or so-called breakthrough bleeding between menstrual periods is a common side effect of the minipill (Reinisch, 1990). Irregular bleeding should be brought to the attention of a health professional. Because they can produce vaginal dryness, minipills can hinder vaginal lubrication during intercourse, decreasing sexual sensations and rendering sex painful.

Researchers have also examined suspected links between the use of the pill and certain forms of cancer, especially breast cancer, since breast cancer is sensitive to hormonal

APPLICATIONS

SELECTING A METHOD OF CONTRACEPTION

Is it time for you and your partner to use a method of contraception? If so, how will you determine which one is right for you? There is no simple answer. What is right for your friends may be wrong for you. Here are some issues to consider:

1. *Convenience.* Is the method convenient? Does it require a device that must be purchased in advance? If so, can it be purchased over the counter, or is a prescription required? Will the method impair sexual spontaneity or sexual sensations?

2. *Moral acceptability.* A method that is morally acceptable to one person may be objectionable to another. Some oral contraceptives permit fertilization but then prevent implantation of the fertilized ovum in the uterus. These oral contraceptives could be considered a method of early abortion.

3. *Cost.* Methods vary in cost. Some require medical visits in addition to the cost of the devices. Other methods, such as rhythm methods, are essentially free.

4. *Sharing responsibility.* Most forms of birth control place the burden of responsibility on the woman. The woman must consult with her doctor to obtain birth-control pills or check that her IUD remains in place. Some couples prefer methods that allow for greater sharing of responsibility, such as alternating use of the condom and diaphragm.

5. *Safety.* What are the side effects? Can your or your partner's health or comfort be affected by its use?

6. *Reversibility.* The effects of most birth-control methods are reversed when they are discontinued. In other cases reversibility may take a while, as with oral contraceptives. Sterilization should be considered irreversible, although many attempts at reversal are successful.

7. *Protection against STDs.* Some birth-control methods, such as using condoms, afford protection against STDs as well as pregnancy.

8. *Effectiveness.* Techniques and devices vary widely in their effectiveness in actual or typical use. Table 10.1 shows the failure rates, reversibility, and degree of protection against STDs afforded by different contraceptive methods.

---

changes. The evidence linking use of the pill with increased risk of cervical cancer is mixed, with some studies showing such a link and others showing none (Hatcher et al., 1994). Women who begin to use the pill, regardless of their age or risk status, should pay attention to changes in their physical condition, have regular checkups, and promptly report any physical complaints or unusual symptoms to their physicians.

"Morning-After" Pills   The so-called morning-after pill, or postcoital contraceptive, actually refers to several types of pills that have high doses of estrogen and progestin. Since they are not taken regularly, they do not prevent ovulation from occurring. Instead, they stop fertilization from taking place or prevent the fertilized egg from implanting itself in the uterus (Hoffman, 1993). In that respect, then, some people consider them an early abortion technique. Morning-after pills are most effective when taken within 72 hours after ovulation. Women who wait to see whether they have missed a period are no longer candidates for the morning-after pill. Depending on the brand, four, six, or eight pills are prescribed.

Morning-after pills have a higher hormone content than most birth-control pills. For this reason, nausea is a common side effect (Hatcher et al., 1994). Because of the strength of the dosage, the morning-after pill is not recommended as a regular form of birth control. We also know little about possible long-term health complications. Morning-after pills are *one-time* forms of "emergency" protection (Hatcher et al., 1994).

Norplant

The contraceptive implant *Norplant* consists of six matchstick-sized silicone tubes that contain progestin and are surgically embedded in a woman's upper arm. About 1 million women in the United States have received Norplant since FDA approval in 1990 (Kolata, 1995).

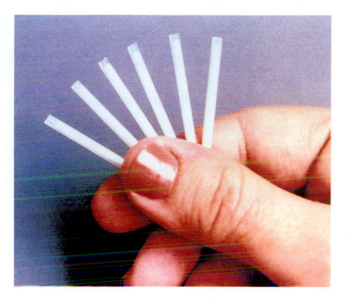

Norplant. Norplant consists of silicone rods that are surgically implanted in the woman's arm. They gradually dispense progestin, the same female sex hormone found in the minipill. Their effectiveness lasts about five years.

How It Works   Norplant, like the pill, relies on female sex hormones to suppress fertility. But rather than taking a pill once a day, tubes implanted in the woman's body release a small, steady dose of progestin into her bloodstream, providing continuous contraceptive protection for as long as five years (Hatcher et al., 1994). The progestin in the Norplant system suppresses ovulation and thickens the cervical mucus so that sperm cannot pass. After five years the tubes are replaced. An alternative implant, Norplant-2, consists of two hormone-releasing tubes that provide at least three years of protection. Implantation takes a few minutes in a doctor's office and is carried out under local anesthesia.

Effectiveness   Norplant is reported to have an extremely low failure rate of less than 1% per year across five years (see Table 10.1).

Reversibility   Although the failure rate of Norplant approximates that of sterilization, Norplant is fully reversible.

Advantages and Disadvantages   The key advantage of Norplant is its convenience. The most commonly reported side effect is abnormal menstrual bleeding (Hatcher et al., 1994; Mishell, 1989).

Intrauterine Devices (IUDs)

Intrauterine device

A small object that is inserted into the uterus and left in place to prevent conception. Abbreviated *IUD*.

Camel drivers setting out on long desert journeys placed round stones in the uteruses of female camels to prevent them from becoming pregnant and lost to service. The stones may have acted as primitive **intrauterine devices** (IUDs). IUDs are small objects of various shapes that are inserted into the uterus. IUDs have been used by humans since the time of ancient Greece. Today, they are inserted into the uterus by a physician or nurse practitioner and usually left in place for a year or more. Fine plastic threads or strings hang down from the IUD into the vagina, so that the woman can check to see that it remains in place.

IUDs are used by about 1.5 million women in the United States and more than 80 million women around the world (Altman, 1991). Married women in the United States are more than twice as likely as single women to use an IUD (U.S. Bureau of the Census, 1990b).

Figure 10.1 on page 240 shows two IUDs: the Progestasert T, which releases small quantities of progesterone (progestin) daily, and the Copper T 380A (ParaGard), a T-shaped, copper-based device. Because the Progestasert T must be replaced annually, and any insertion carries some risk of infection, health authorities recommend the use of the ParaGard device, which can be used for upwards of eight years, unless the woman is allergic to copper (Hatcher et al., 1994).

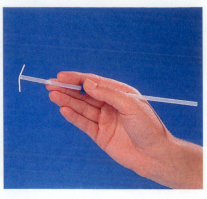

Figure 10.1. Two IUDs: The Progestasert T and the Copper T 380A (ParaGard). The Progestasert T releases small quantities of progesterone (progestin) daily. The Copper T 380A is a T-shaped, copper-based device.

How It Works   We do not know exactly how IUDs work. A foreign body, such as the IUD, apparently irritates the uterine lining. This irritation gives rise to mild inflammation and the production of antibodies that may be toxic to sperm or to fertilized ova and/or may prevent fertilized eggs from becoming implanted. Inflammation may also impair proliferation of the endometrium—another impediment to implantation. Progestin released by the Progestasert T also has effects like the progestin-only minipill: It lessens the likelihood of fertilization and implantation. Action on fertilized ova may be considered to constitute an early abortion. Since IUDs may not prevent fertilization, people who oppose abortion, regardless of how soon it occurs after conception, also oppose the IUD.

Effectiveness   The failure rate associated with typical use of the Progestasert T is about 2% (see Table 10.1). Most failures occur within three months of insertion, often because the device shifts position or is expelled. ParaGard is the most effective IUD. The first-year failure rate in typical use is 0.8%.

The IUD may irritate the muscular layer of the uterine wall, causing contractions that expel it through the vagina. The device is most likely to be expelled during menstruation, so users are advised to check their sanitary napkins or tampons before discarding them. Women who use IUDs are advised to check the string several times a month to ensure that the IUD is in place. Spontaneous expulsions occur in 2% to 10% of users within the first year of use (Hatcher et al., 1994). Some family-planning clinics advise women to supplement their use of IUDs with other devices for the first three months, when the risks of a shift in position or expulsion are greatest.

Reversibility   IUDs may be removed readily by professionals. Nine out of ten former IUD users who wish to do so become pregnant within a year (Reinisch, 1990).

Advantages and Disadvantages   The IUD has three major advantages: (1) it is highly effective; (2) it does not diminish sexual spontaneity or sexual sensations; and (3) once in place, the woman need not "do anything" more to prevent pregnancy (other than check that it remains in place).

The IUD also does not interfere with the woman's normal hormonal production. Users continue to produce pituitary hormones that stimulate ovarian follicles to mature and rupture, thereby releasing mature ova and producing female sex hormones.

If IUDs are so effective and relatively "maintenance free," why are they not more popular? One reason is that insertion can be painful. Another reason is side effects. The most common side effects are excessive menstrual cramping, irregular bleeding (spotting) between periods, and heavier than usual menstrual bleeding (Reinisch, 1990). A more serious concern is the possible risk of pelvic inflammatory disease (PID), a serious disease that can become life threatening if left untreated (Hatcher et al., 1994).

PID can scar the fallopian tubes, causing infertility. Women with pelvic infections should not use an IUD (Hatcher et al., 1994).

Another risk in using an IUD is that the device may perforate (tear) the uterine or cervical walls, which can cause bleeding, pain, and adhesions and become life threatening. Perforations are usually caused by improper insertion and occur in perhaps 1 case in 1,000 (Reinisch, 1990). IUD users are also at greater risk for ectopic pregnancies and for miscarriage.

Despite the fact that the IUD irritates uterine tissues, there is no evidence that IUD users run a greater risk of cancer. Long-term data on the health effects of IUD use are limited, however.

Another drawback to the IUD is its cost. The typical cost of an IUD insertion in a family-planning clinic ranges from $200 to $300 (Hatcher et al., 1994). Potential expulsion of the IUD presents yet another disadvantage. Moreover, the IUD, like the pill, offers no protection against STDs. Finally, like the pill, IUDs place the burden of contraception entirely on the woman.

The Diaphragm

Diaphragm

A shallow rubber cup or dome, fitted to the contour of a woman's vagina, that is coated with a spermicide and inserted prior to coitus to prevent conception.

Diaphragms were once used by about one third of U.S. couples who practiced birth control. When invented in 1882, they were a breakthrough. Their popularity declined only in the 1960s with the advent of the pill and the IUD. Today, only 1 married White woman in 20 and 1 married African American woman in 50 under the age of 44 regularly use the diaphragm (U.S. Bureau of the Census, 1990b).

The diaphragm is a shallow cup or dome made of thin latex rubber (see Figure 10.2). The rim is a flexible metal ring covered with rubber. Diaphragms come in different sizes, to allow a precise fit.

Diaphragms are available by prescription and must be fitted to the contour of the vagina by a health professional. Several sizes and types of diaphragms may be tried during a fitting. Women practice insertion in a health professional's office so they can be guided as needed.

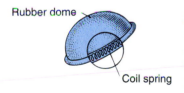

How It Works   The diaphragm is inserted and removed by the woman, much like a tampon. It is akin to a condom in that it forms a barrier against sperm when placed snugly over the cervical opening. Yet it is unreliable as a barrier alone. Thus, the diaphragm should be used in conjunction with a spermicidal cream or jelly. The diaphragm's main function is to keep the spermicide in place.

How It Is Used   The diaphragm should be inserted no more than two hours before coitus, since the spermicides that are used may begin to lose effectiveness beyond this time. Some health professionals, however, suggest that the diaphragm may be inserted up to six hours preceding intercourse. (It seems reasonable to err on the side of caution and assume that there is a two-hour time limit.) The woman or her partner places a tablespoonful of spermicidal cream or jelly on the inside of the cup and spreads it inside the rim. (Cream spread outside the rim might cause the diaphragm to slip.) The woman opens the inner lips of the vagina with one hand and folds the diaphragm with the other by squeezing the ring. She inserts the diaphragm against the cervix, with the inner side facing upward (see Figure 10.3 on page 242). Her partner can help insert the diaphragm, but the woman is advised to check its placement. Some women prefer a plastic insertion device, but most find it easier to insert the diaphragm without it. The diaphragm should be left in place *at least six hours* to allow the spermicide to kill any remaining sperm in the vagina (Hatcher et al., 1994). It should not be left in place for longer than 24 hours, to guard against toxic shock syndrome.

After use, the diaphragm should be washed with mild soap and warm water and stored in a dry, cool place. When cared for properly, a diaphragm can last about two years. Women may need to be refitted after pregnancy or a change in weight of about ten pounds or more.

Figure 10.2.   A Diaphragm. The diaphragm is a shallow cup or dome made of latex. Diaphragms must be fitted to the contour of the vagina by a health professional. The diaphragm forms a barrier to sperm but should be used in conjunction with a spermicidal cream or jelly.

Rubber dome

Coil spring

Spermicide

Diaphragm

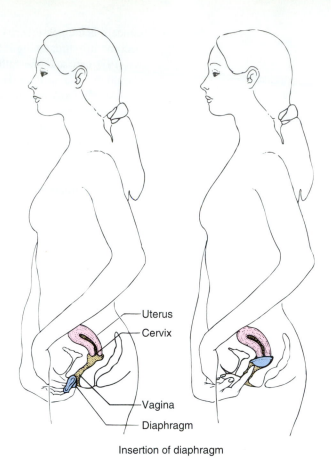

Insertion of diaphragm

Figure 10.3. **Insertion and Checking of the Diaphragm.**
Women are instructed in insertion of the diaphragm by a health
professional. In practice, a woman and her partner may find
joint insertion an erotic experience.

Effectiveness   If used consistently and correctly, the failure rate of the diaphragm
is estimated to be 6% during the first year of use (see Table 10.1). In typical use, however,
the failure rate is believed to be three times as high—18%. Some women become pregnant
because they do not use the diaphragm during every coital experience. Others may insert
it too early or not leave it in long enough. The diaphragm may not fit well, or it may slip—
especially if the couple is acrobatic. A diaphragm may develop tiny holes or cracks.
Women are advised to inspect the diaphragm for signs of wear and consult their health professionals when in doubt. Effectiveness also is seriously compromised when the diaphragm
is not used along with a correctly applied spermicide (Trussell et al., 1993).

Reversibility   The effects of the diaphragm are fully reversible. In order to become
pregnant, the woman simply stops using it. The diaphragm has not been shown to influence subsequent fertility.

Advantages and Disadvantages   The major advantage of the diaphragm is
that when used correctly it is a safe and effective means of birth control and does not alter
the woman's hormone production or reproductive cycle. The diaphragm can be used as
needed, whereas the pill must be used daily and the IUD remains in place whether or not
the woman engages in coitus. Another advantage is the virtual absence of side effects. The
few women who are allergic to the rubber in the diaphragm can switch to a plastic model.
Another advantage is that spermicides that contain nonoxynol-9 may provide some, but not
total, protection against STDs, including AIDS, genital herpes, trichomoniasis ("trich"),
syphilis, and perhaps chlamydia (Reinisch, 1990).
    The major disadvantage is the high pregnancy rate associated with typical use. Nearly
1 in 5 typical users (18%) of the diaphragm combined with spermicidal cream or jelly be-

comes pregnant during the first year of use (Hatcher et al., 1994). Another disadvantage is the need to insert the diaphragm prior to intercourse, which the couple may find disruptive. Another disadvantage is that the woman's partner may find the taste of the spermicides used in conjunction with the diaphragm to be unpleasant during oral sex. The pressure exerted by the diaphragm against the vaginal and cervical walls may also irritate the urinary tract and cause urinary or even vaginal infections. Switching to a different size diaphragm or one with a different type of rim may help alleviate this problem. About 1 woman or man in 20 may develop allergies to the particular spermicide that is used, which can lead to irritation of the genitals. This problem may also be alleviated by switching to another brand.

Spermicides

Spermicides are chemical agents that kill sperm. They come in different forms, including jellies and creams, suppositories, aerosol foam, and a contraceptive film. Spermicides should be left in place in the vagina (no douching) for *at least 6–8 hours* after coitus (Hatcher et al., 1994).

Spermicidal jellies, creams, foam, and suppositories should be used no more than 60 minutes preceding coitus to provide for maximum effectiveness (Hatcher et al., 1994). Spermicidal jellies and creams come in tubes with plastic applicators that introduce the spermicide into the vagina (see Figure 10.4). Spermicidal foam is a fluffy white cream with the consistency of shaving cream. It is contained in a pressurized can and is introduced with a plastic applicator in much the same way as spermicidal jellies and creams.

Vaginal suppositories are inserted into the upper vagina, near the cervix, where they release spermicide as they dissolve. Unlike spermicidal jellies, creams, and foam, which become effective immediately when applied, suppositories must be inserted no less than 10 to 15 minutes before coitus so that they have sufficient time to dissolve (Hatcher et al., 1994).

Spermicidal film consists of thin, 2-inch-square sheets that are saturated with spermicide. When placed in the vagina, they dissolve into a gel and release the spermicide. The spermicidal film should be inserted at least five minutes before intercourse to allow it time to melt and for the spermicide to be dispersed (Hatcher et al., 1994). It remains effective for upwards of one hour (Hatcher et al., 1994). One disadvantage of the film that some users have noted is a tendency for it to adhere to the fingertips, which makes it difficult to insert correctly.

How They Work   Spermicides coat the cervical opening, blocking the passage of sperm and killing sperm by chemical action.

Effectiveness   In typical use, the first-year failure rate of spermicides used alone is 21 pregnancies per year per 100 users (Hatcher et al., 1994; Reinisch, 1990). When used correctly and consistently, the failure rate is estimated to drop to about 6 pregnancies per 100 users in the first year. All forms of spermicide are more effective when they are combined with other forms of contraception, such as the condom.

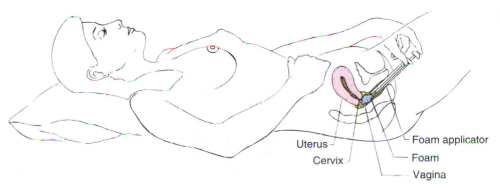

Figure 10.4. The Application of Spermicides. Spermicidal jellies and creams come in tubes with plastic applicators. Spermicidal foam comes in a pressurized can and is applied with a plastic applicator in much the same way as spermicidal jellies and creams.

Uterus
Cervix
Foam applicator
Foam
Vagina

Reversibility   Spermicides have not been linked with any changes in reproductive potential. Couples who wish to become pregnant simply stop using them.

Advantages and Disadvantages   The major advantages of spermicides are that they do not alter the woman's natural biological processes and are applied only as needed. Unlike a diaphragm, they do not require a doctor's prescription or a fitting. They can be bought in virtually any drugstore, and the average cost per use of the foam variety is modest—about 50 cents. Spermicides that contain nonoxynol-9 may also provide some protection against organisms that give rise to STDs.

The major disadvantage is the high failure rate among typical users. Foam often fails when the can is not shaken enough, when too little is used, when it is not applied deeply enough within the vagina near the cervix, or when it is used after coitus has begun.

Spermicides are generally free of side effects but occasionally cause vaginal or penile irritation. Irritation is sometimes alleviated by changing brands. Some partners find the taste of spermicides unpleasant. (Couples can engage in oral sex before applying spermicides.) Spermicides may pose a danger to an embryo, so women who suspect they are pregnant are advised to suspend use until they find out for certain.

The Cervical Cap

The cervical cap, like the diaphragm, is a dome-shaped rubber cup. It comes in different sizes and must be fitted by a health professional. It is smaller than the diaphragm, however—about the size of a thimble—and is meant to fit snugly over the cervical opening.

How It Is Used   Like the diaphragm, the cap is intended to be used with a spermicide applied inside it (Hatcher et al., 1994). When inserting it, the woman (or her partner) fills the cap about a third full of spermicide. Then, squeezing the edges together, the woman inserts the cap high in the vagina, so that it presses firmly against the cervix. The woman can test the fit by running a finger around the cap to ensure that the cervical opening is covered. It should be left in place for at least 8 hours after intercourse. The cap provides continuous protection for upwards of 48 hours without the need for additional spermicide. To reduce the risk of toxic shock syndrome, the cap should not be left in place longer than 48 hours.

How It Works   Like the diaphragm, the cervical cap forms a barrier and also holds spermicide in place against the cervix. It prevents sperm from passing into the uterus and fallopian tubes and kills sperm by chemical action.

Effectiveness   The failure rate in typical use is estimated to be high, ranging from 18% in women who have not borne children to 36% in women who have (Hatcher et al., 1994). Failures may be attributed, at least in part, to the cap's becoming dislodged and to changes in the cervix during the menstrual cycle, which can cause the cap to fit less snugly over the cervix.

Reversibility   There is no evidence that the cervical cap affects fertility.

Advantages and Disadvantages   Like the diaphragm, the cap is a mechanical device that does not affect the woman's hormonal production or reproductive cycle. The cap may be especially suited to women who cannot support a diaphragm because of lack of vaginal muscle tone. Because of concern that the cap may irritate cervical tissue, however, Mishell (1989) recommends that repeat Pap tests be performed with users.

Some women find the cap uncomfortable. The cap can also become dislodged during sexual activity or lose its fit as the cervix changes over the menstrual cycle. Reported side effects include urinary tract infections and allergic reactions or sensitivities to the rubber or spermicide.

The effectiveness of the cervical cap is considerably greater among women who have not given birth (Trussell et al., 1993). Women who have given birth may wish to consult their gynecologists concerning the suitability of the cap.

Condoms

Condom

A sheath made of animal membrane or latex that covers the penis during coitus and serves as a barrier to sperm following ejaculation.

Prophylactic

An agent that protects against disease.

Condoms are also called "rubbers," "safes," **prophylactics** (because latex condoms protect against STDs), and "skins" (referring to those that are made from lamb intestines). Condoms lost popularity with the advent of the pill and the IUD. They are less effective than the pill or IUD, may disrupt sexual spontaneity, and can decrease coital sensations because they prevent the penis from actually touching the vaginal wall.

Condoms have been making a comeback, however, because those made of latex rubber can help prevent the spread of the AIDS virus (the *human immunodeficiency virus* [HIV]) and other STDs and, to a lesser extent, because of concerns about side effects of the pill and the IUD. Largely because of concerns about AIDS and other STDs, use of condoms among unmarried women jumped from 18% in 1987 to 33% in 1992 (Forrest & Fordyce, 1993). Unmarried women are more likely to report using condoms than are married women (33% vs. 19%). Overall, 17% of U.S. women who use reversible forms of contraception use condoms (Angier, 1993b).

Condom advertisements have appeared in mainstream media, including magazines such as *People* and *Cosmopolitan,* and on major TV networks. In a TV commercial, a man and a woman are shown hurriedly undressing. The man tells the woman that he forgot to bring a condom with him. She then tells him that he'd best forget it (making love, that is). Whether the media campaign will increase condom usage remains to be seen.

The renewed popularity of condoms has also been spurred by the increased assertiveness of contemporary women. They make the point (which should be obvious, but all too often is not) that contraception is as much the man's responsibility as the woman's. Condoms alter the psychological aspect of sexual relations. By using a condom the man assumes much of the responsibility for contraception. Condoms are the only contraceptive device worn by men, and the only readily reversible method of contraception that is available to men. Condoms are inexpensive and can be obtained without prescription from pharmacies, family-planning clinics, rest rooms, and even from vending machines in some college dormitories.

Some condoms are made of latex rubber. Thinner, more expensive condoms ("skins") are made from the intestinal membranes of lambs. The latter allow greater sexual sensation but do not protect as well against STDs. Only latex condoms are effective against the tiny AIDS virus. Condoms made of animal intestines have pores large enough to permit the AIDS virus and other viruses, such as the one that causes hepatitis B, to slip through (Consumer's Union, 1995). A few condoms are made from other materials, such as plastic (polyurethane). Questions remain about the effectiveness of polyurethane condoms (Consumer's Union, 1995). Some condoms have plain ends. Others have nipples or reservoirs (see Figure 10.5 on page 246) that catch semen and may help prevent the condom from bursting during ejaculation.

How It Works A condom is a cylindrical sheath that serves as a barrier, preventing the passage of sperm and disease-carrying microorganisms from the man to his partner. It also helps prevent infected vaginal fluids (and microorganisms) from entering the man's urethral opening or from penetrating through small cracks in the skin of the penis.

How It Is Used The condom is rolled onto the penis once erection is achieved and before contact between the penis and the vagina (see Figure 10.6 on page 246). If the condom is *not* used until moments before the point of ejaculation, sperm-carrying fluid from the Cowper's glands or from preorgasmic spasms may already have passed into the vagina. Nor does the condom afford protection against STDs if it is fitted after penetration.

Condoms sometimes fall off or break. Between 1% and 2% of condoms break or fall off during intercourse or when withdrawing the penis afterward (Cates & Stone, 1992a;

Figure 10.5. **Condoms.** Some condoms are plain-tipped, whereas others have nipples or reservoirs that catch semen and may help prevent the condom from bursting during ejaculation. Latex condoms form effective barriers to the tiny AIDS virus.

Trussell et al., 1992). Condoms also sometimes slip down the shaft of the penis without falling off. The following guidelines[1] will help couples use condoms effectively:

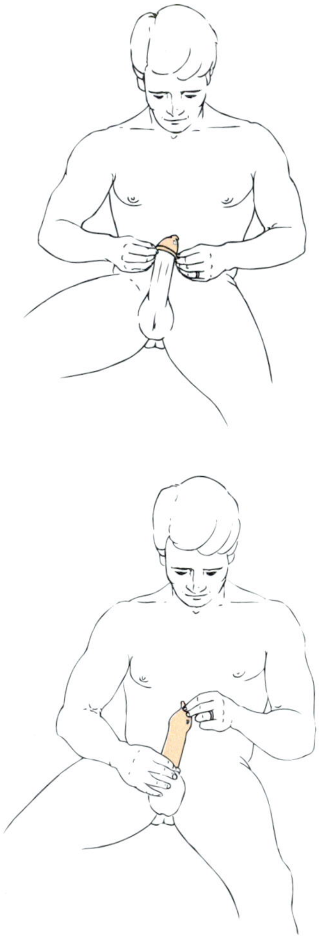

- Use a condom each and every time you have intercourse. Inexperienced users should also practice putting on a condom before they have the occasion to use one with a partner.
- Handle the condom carefully, making sure not to damage it with your fingernail, teeth, or sharp objects.
- Place the condom on the erect penis before it touches the vulva.
- Uncircumcised men should pull back the foreskin before putting on the condom.
- If you use a spermicide, place some inside the tip of the condom before placing the condom on the penis. You may also wish to use additional spermicide applied by an applicator inside the vagina to provide extra protection, especially in the event of breakage of the condom.
- Do not pull the condom tightly against the tip of the penis.
- For a condom without a reservoir tip, leave a small empty space—about a half-inch—at the end of the condom to hold semen, yet do not allow any air to be trapped at the tip. Some condoms come equipped with a reservoir (nipple) tip that will hold semen.
- Unroll the condom all the way to the bottom of the penis.
- Ensure that adequate vaginal lubrication during intercourse is present, possibly using lubricants if necessary. But use only water-based lubricants such as contraceptive jelly or K-Y jelly. Never use an oil-based lubricant that can weaken the latex material, such as petroleum jelly (Vaseline), cold cream, baby oil or lotion, mineral oil, massage oil, vegetable oil, Crisco, hand or body lotions, and most skin creams. Do not use saliva as a lubricant because it may contain infectious organisms, such as viruses.
- If the condom breaks during intercourse, withdraw the penis immediately, put on a new condom, and use more spermicide.
- After ejaculation, carefully withdraw the penis while it is still erect.
- Hold the rim of the condom firmly against the base of the penis as the penis is withdrawn, to prevent the condom from slipping off.
- Remove the condom carefully from the penis, making sure that semen doesn't leak out.
- Check the removed condom for tears or cracks. If any are found, immediately apply a spermicide containing nonoxynol-9 directly to the penis and within the vagina. Wrap the used condom in a tissue, and discard it in the garbage. Do not flush it down the toilet, as condoms may cause problems in the sewers. Wash your hands thoroughly with soap and water.

Figure 10.6. **Applying a Condom.** First the rolled-up condom is placed on the head of the penis, and then it is rolled down the shaft of the penis. If a condom without a reservoir tip is used, a ½-inch space should be left at the tip for the ejaculate to accumulate.

[1]Adapted from the Centers for Disease Control pamphlet *Condoms and Sexually Transmitted Diseases . . . Especially AIDS* (HHS Publication FDA 90–4329) and other sources.

Since condoms can be eroded by exposure to body heat or other sources of heat, they should not be kept for any length of time in a pocket or the glove compartment of a car. Nor should a condom be used more than once. Here are some other things you should *never* do with a condom:

- Never use teeth, scissors, or sharp fingernails to open a package of condoms. Open the condom package carefully to avoid tearing or puncturing the condom.
- Never test a condom by inflating it or stretching it.
- Never use a condom after its expiration date.
- Never use damaged condoms. Condoms that are sticky, gummy, discolored, brittle, or appear otherwise damaged, or that show signs of deterioration should be considered damaged.
- Never use a condom if the sealed packet containing the condom is damaged, cracked, or brittle, as the condom itself may be damaged or defective.
- Do not open the sealed packet until you are ready to use the condom. A condom contained in a packet that has been opened can become dry and brittle within a few hours, causing it to tear more easily. The box that contains the condom packets, however, may be opened at any time.
- Never use the same condom twice. Use a new condom if you switch the site of intercourse, such as from the vagina to the anus, or from the anus to the mouth, during a single sexual act.
- If you want to carry a condom with you, place it in a loose jacket pocket or purse, not in your pant's pocket or in a wallet held in your pant's pocket, where it might be exposed to body heat.
- Never buy condoms from vending machines that are exposed to extreme heat or placed in direct sunlight.

Effectiveness   In typical use, the failure rate of the male condom is estimated at 12% (see Table 10.1). That is, 12 out of 100 women whose partners rely on condoms alone for contraception can expect to become pregnant during the first year of use. This rate can be reduced to perhaps 2% or 3% if the condom is used correctly and combined with the use of a spermicide (Hatcher et al., 1994; Reinisch, 1990). The effectiveness of a condom and spermicide combined rivals that of the birth-control pill when used correctly and consistently.

Reversibility   The condom is simply a mechanical barrier to sperm and does not compromise fertility. Therefore, a couple who wish to conceive a child simply discontinue its use.

Advantages and Disadvantages   Condoms have the advantage of being readily available. They can be purchased without prescription. They require no fitting and can remain in sealed packages until needed. They are readily discarded after use. The combination of condoms and spermicides containing the ingredient nonoxynol-9 increases contraceptive effectiveness and protection against various STD-causing organisms, including HIV. Some condoms contain this spermicidal agent as a lubricant. When in doubt, ask the pharmacist.

Condoms do not affect production of hormones, ova, or sperm. Women whose partners use condoms ovulate normally. Men who use them produce sperm and ejaculate normally. With all these advantages, why are condoms not more popular?

One disadvantage of the condom is that it may render sex less spontaneous. The couple must interrupt lovemaking to apply the condom. Condoms may also lessen sexual sensations, especially for the man. Latex condoms do so more than animal membrane sheaths. Condoms also sometimes slip off or tear, allowing sperm to leak through.

On the other hand, condoms are almost entirely free of side effects (an advantage reported by 70% of female respondents to a *Consumer Reports* survey). They offer protection against STDs that is unparalleled among contraceptive devices. They can also be used without prior medical consultation. Both partners can share putting on the condom, which makes it an erotic part of their lovemaking, not an intrusion. The use of textured or ultrathin condoms may increase sensitivity, especially for the male. Thus many couples find that advantages outweigh disadvantages. Sex in the age of AIDS has given condoms a new respectability, even a certain trendiness. Notice, for example, the new "designer colors" and styles on display at your local pharmacy. Advertisers now also target women in their ads, suggesting that women, like men, can come prepared with condoms.

It is tempting to claim that the condom has a perfect safety record and no side effects. Let us settle for "close to perfect." Some people may have allergic reactions to the spermicides with which some lubricated condoms are coated or that the woman may apply. In such cases the couple may need to use a condom without a spermicidal lubricant or stop using supplemental spermicides. Some people are allergic to latex.

Women have an absolute right to insist that their male sex partners wear latex condoms, assuming that their partners are not latex-sensitive. STDs such as gonorrhea and chlamydia (see Chapter 13) do far more damage to a woman's reproductive tract than to a man's. Condoms can help protect women from vaginitis, pelvic inflammatory disease (PID), infections that can harm a fetus or cause infertility, and most important, AIDS.

Douching

Douche
Application of a jet of liquid to the vagina as a rinse.

Many couples believe that if a woman **douches** shortly after coitus, she will not become pregnant. Women who douche for contraceptive purposes often use syringes to flush the vagina with water or a spermicidal agent. The water is intended to wash sperm out; the spermicides, to kill them. Douching is ineffective, however, because large numbers of sperm move beyond the range of the douche seconds after ejaculation. In addition, squirting a liquid into the vagina may even propel sperm *toward* the uterus. Douching, at best, has a failure rate among typical users of 40% (Reinisch, 1990), too high to be considered reliable.

Regular douching may also alter the natural chemistry of the vagina, increasing the risk of vaginal infection. In short, douching is a "nonmethod" of contraception.

Withdrawal (Coitus Interruptus)

Coitus interruptus
The practice of withdrawing the penis prior to ejaculation during sexual intercourse.

Withdrawal (**coitus interruptus**) means that the man removes his penis from the vagina before ejaculating. Withdrawal has a first-year failure rate among typical users ranging from 19% to 23% (Hatcher et al., 1994; Reinisch, 1990). There are several reasons for these failures. The man may not withdraw in time. Even if the penis is withdrawn just before ejaculation, some ejaculate may still fall on the vaginal lips, and sperm may find their way to the fallopian tubes. Active sperm may also be present in the *pre*-ejaculatory secretions of fluid from the Cowper's glands, a discharge of which the man is usually unaware and cannot control. These sperm are capable of fertilizing an ovum even if the man withdraws before orgasm. Because of its unreliability and high failure rate, withdrawal, like douching, is also a non-method of contraception.

Fertility Awareness Methods (Rhythm Methods)

Fertility awareness, or *rhythm,* methods rely on awareness of the fertile segments of the woman's menstrual cycle. Terms such as *natural birth control* or *natural family planning* also refer to these methods. The essence of such methods is that coitus is avoided on days when conception is most likely. Fertility awareness methods are used by about 3% of married women ages 15 to 44, but by less than 1% of single women (U.S. Bureau of the Census, 1990b). Women of ages 25 to 44 are more than twice as likely as 15- to 24-year-olds to use rhythm methods. Since the rhythm method does not employ artificial devices, it is acceptable to the Roman Catholic Church.

How They Work   A number of rhythm methods are used to predict the likelihood of conception. They are the mirror images of the methods that couples use to increase their chances of conceiving (see Chapter 9). Methods for enhancing the chances of conception seek to predict time of ovulation so the couple can arrange to have sperm present in the woman's reproductive tract at about that time. As methods of *birth control,* rhythm methods seek to predict ovulation so that the couple can *abstain* from coitus when the woman is fertile.

Calendar method

A fertility awareness (rhythm) method of contraception that relies on prediction of ovulation by tracking menstrual cycles, typically for a 10- to 12-month period, and assuming that ovulation occurs 14 days prior to menstruation.

The Calendar Method   The **calendar method** assumes that ovulation occurs 14 days prior to menstruation. The couple abstains from intercourse during the period that begins 3 days prior to day 13 (because sperm are unlikely to survive for more than 72 hours in the female reproductive tract) and ends 2 days after day 15 (because an unfertilized ovum is unlikely to remain receptive to fertilization for longer than 48 hours). The period of abstention thus covers days 10 to 17 of the woman's cycle.

When a woman has regular 28-day cycles, predicting the period of abstention is relatively straightforward. Women with irregular cycles are generally advised to chart their cycles for 10 months to a year to determine their shortest and longest cycles. The first day of menstruation counts as day 1 of the cycle. The last day of the cycle is the day preceding the onset of menstruation.

Consider a woman whose cycles vary from 23 to 33 days. In theory she will ovulate 14 days before menstruation begins. (To be safe she should assume that ovulation will take place anywhere from 13 to 15 days before her period.) Applying the rule of "three days before" and "two days after," she should avoid coitus from day 5 of her cycle, which corresponds to 3 days before her earliest expected ovulation (computed by subtracting 15 days from the 23 days of her shortest cycle and then subtracting 3 days), through day 22, which corresponds to 2 days after her latest expected ovulation (computed by subtracting 13 days from the 33 days of her longest cycle and then adding 2 days). Another way of determining this period of abstention would be to subtract 18 days from the woman's shortest cycle to determine the start of the "unsafe" period and 11 days from her longest cycle to determine the last "unsafe" day. The woman in the example has irregular cycles. She thus faces an 18-day abstention period each month—quite a burden for a sexually active couple.

Most women who follow the calendar method need to abstain from coitus for at least 10 days during the middle of each cycle (Reinisch, 1990). Moreover, the calendar method cannot ensure that the woman's longest or shortest menstrual cycles will occur during the 10- to 12-month period of baseline tracking. Some women, too, have such irregular cycles that the range of "unsafe" days cannot be predicted reliably even if baseline tracking is extended.

Basal body temperature (BBT) method

A fertility awareness method of contraception that relies on prediction of ovulation by tracking the woman's temperature during the course of the menstrual cycle.

The Basal Body Temperature (BBT) Method   In the **basal body temperature (BBT) method,** the woman tracks her body temperature upon awakening each morning to detect the small changes that occur directly before and after ovulation. A woman's basal body temperature sometimes dips slightly just before ovulation and then tends to rise between 0.4 and 0.8 degrees Fahrenheit just before, during, and after ovulation. It remains elevated until the onset of menstruation. (The rise in temperature is caused by the increased production of progesterone by the corpus luteum during the luteal phase of the cycle.) Thermometers that provide finely graded readings, such as electronic thermometers, are best suited for determining minor changes. A major problem with the BBT method is that it does not indicate the several *unsafe* preovulatory days during which sperm deposited in the vagina may remain viable. Rather, the BBT method indicates when a woman *has* ovulated. Thus, many women use the calendar method to predict the number of "safe" days prior to ovulation and the BBT method to determine the number of "unsafe" days after. A woman would avoid coitus during the "unsafe" preovulatory period (as determined by the calendar method) and then for three days when her temperature rises and remains elevated. A drawback of the BBT method is that changes in body temperature may also result from factors unrelated to ovulation, such as infections, sleeplessness, or stress. So some women triple-check themselves by also tracking their cervical mucus.

Ovulation method
A fertility awareness method of contraception that relies on prediction of ovulation by tracking the viscosity of the cervical mucus.

Viscosity
Stickiness, consistency.

Peak days
The days during the menstrual cycle during which a woman is most likely to be fertile.

The Cervical Mucus (Ovulation) Method   The **ovulation method** tracks changes in the **viscosity** of the cervical mucus. Following menstruation, the vagina feels rather dry. There is also little or no discharge from the cervix. These dry days are relatively safe. Then a mucous discharge appears in the vagina that is first thick and sticky, and white or cloudy in color. Coitus (or unprotected coitus) should be avoided at the first sign of any mucus. As the cycle progresses, the mucous discharge thins and clears, becoming slippery or stringy, like raw egg white. These are the **peak days.** This mucous discharge, called the *ovulatory mucus,* may be accompanied by a feeling of vaginal lubrication or wetness. Ovulation takes place about a day after the last peak day (about four days after this ovulatory mucus first appears). Then the mucus becomes cloudy and tacky once more. Intercourse may resume four days following the last peak day.

One problem with the mucus method is that some women have difficulty detecting changes in the mucous discharge. Such changes may also result from infections, certain medications, or contraceptive creams, jellies, or foam. Sexual arousal may also induce changes in viscosity.

Ovulation-Prediction Kits   Predicting ovulation is more accurate with an ovulation-prediction kit. Kits allow women to test their urine daily for the presence of luteinizing hormone (LH). LH levels surge about 12 to 24 hours prior to ovulation. Ovulation-prediction kits are more accurate than the BBT method. Some couples use the kits to enhance their chances of conceiving a child by engaging in coitus when ovulation appears imminent. Others use them as a means of birth control to find out when to avoid coitus. When used correctly, ovulation-predicting kits are between 95% to 100% accurate (Reinisch, 1990).

Ovulation kits are expensive and require that the woman's urine be tested each morning. Nor do they reveal the full range of the unsafe *pre*ovulatory period during which sperm may remain viable in the vagina. A couple might thus choose to use the kits to determine the unsafe period following ovulation, and the calendar method to determine the unsafe period preceding ovulation.

Effectiveness   The estimated first-year failure rate in typical use is 20%, which is high but no higher than the use of contraceptive devices such as the cervical cap or the female condom (see Table 10.1). Still, perhaps one in five typical users will become pregnant during the first year of use. (You may have heard the joke "What do you call people who use the rhythm method? Parents!") Fewer failures occur when these methods are applied conscientiously, when a combination of rhythm methods is used, and when the woman's cycles are quite regular. Restricting coitus to the postovulatory period can reduce the pregnancy rate to 1% (Hatcher et al., 1994). The trick is to be able to reliably determine when ovulation occurs. The pregnancy rate can be reduced to practically zero if rhythm methods are used with other forms of birth control, such as the condom or diaphragm.

Advantages and Disadvantages   Because they are a natural form of birth control, rhythm methods appeal to many people who, for religious or other reasons, prefer not to use artificial means. Since no devices or chemicals are used, there are no side effects. Nor do they cause any loss of sensation, as condoms do. Nor is there disruption of lovemaking, as with condoms, diaphragms, or foam, although lovemaking could be said to be quite "disrupted" during the period of abstention. Rhythm methods are inexpensive, except for ovulation-prediction kits. Both partners may share the responsibility for rhythm methods. The man, for example, can take his partner's temperature or assist with the charting. All rhythm methods are fully reversible.

A disadvantage is the fact that the reliability of rhythm methods is low. Rhythm methods may be unsuitable for women with irregular cycles. Women with irregular cycles who ovulate as early as a week after their menstrual flows can become pregnant even if they engage in unprotected intercourse only when they are menstruating, since some sperm remaining in a woman's reproductive tract may survive for up to eight days and fertilize an ovum that is released at that time (Reinisch, 1990). Moreover, the rhythm method requires abstaining from coitus for several days, or perhaps weeks, each month. Rhythm methods also require that records of the menstrual cycle be kept for many months prior to implementation. Unlike diaphragms, condoms, or spermicides, rhythm methods cannot be used at a moment's notice. Finally, rhythm methods do not offer any protection against STDs.

Sterilization

Sterilization
Surgical procedures that render people incapable of reproduction without affecting sexual activity.

Many people decide to be sterilized when they plan to have no children or no more children. With the exception of abstinence, sterilization is the most effective form of contraception. Yet the prospect of **sterilization** arouses strong feelings because a person is transformed all at once, and presumably permanently, from someone who might be capable of bearing children to someone who cannot. This transformation often involves a profound change in self-concept. These feelings are especially strong in men and women who link fertility to their sense of masculinity or femininity.

Still, more than a million sterilizations are performed in the United States each year. It is the most widely used form of birth control among married couples age 30 and above (Reinisch, 1990). Nineteen percent of the respondents in a 1992 national sample of nearly 7,000 women ages 15 to 50 reported being sterilized; 12% reported having partners who had undergone a vasectomy. Married women were far more likely to rely on a permanent method of contraception (tubal sterilization or vasectomy) than were single women (48% vs. 11%).

Vasectomy
A sterilization procedure in which the vas deferens is severed, preventing sperm from reaching the ejaculatory duct.

Male Sterilization   The male sterilization procedure used today is the **vasectomy.** About 500,000 vasectomies are performed each year in the United States (Altman, 1993b). More than 15% of men in the United States have had vasectomies.

A vasectomy is usually carried out in a doctor's office, under local anesthesia, in 15 to 20 minutes. Small incisions are made in the scrotum. Each vas is cut, a small segment is removed, and the ends are tied off or cauterized (to prevent them from growing back together) (see Figure 10.7). Now sperm can no longer reach the urethra. Instead, they are harmlessly reabsorbed by the body.

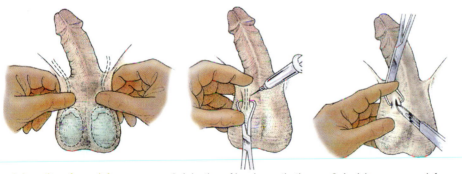
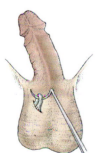
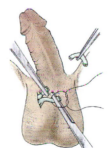
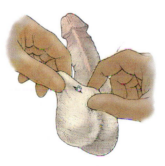
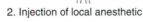

1. Location of vas deferens

2. Injection of local anesthetic

3. Incision over vas deferens

4. Isolation of vas from surrounding tissue

5. Removal of segment of vas; tying of ends

6. Return of vas to position; incision is closed and process is repeated on the other side

Figure 10.7. **Vasectomy.** The male sterilization procedure is usually carried out in a doctor's office, using local anesthesia. Small incisions are made in the scrotum. Each vas deferens is cut, and the ends are tied off or cauterized to prevent sperm from reaching the urethra. Sperm are harmlessly reabsorbed by the body after the operation.

The man can usually resume sexual relations within a few days. Since some sperm may be present in his reproductive tract for a few weeks, however, he is best advised to use an additional contraceptive method until his ejaculate shows a zero sperm count. Some health professionals recommend that the man have a follow-up sperm count a year after his vasectomy, to ensure that the cut ends of the vas deferens have not grown together—a complication that occurs in about 1% of cases (Reinisch, 1990).

Vasectomy does not diminish sex drive or result in any change in sexual arousal, erectile or ejaculatory ability, or sensations of ejaculation. Male sex hormones and sperm are still produced by the testes. Without a passageway to the urethra, however, sperm are no longer expelled with the ejaculate. Since sperm account for only about 1% of the ejaculate, the volume of the ejaculate is not noticeably different.

Though there are no confirmed long-term health risks of vasectomy (Reinisch, 1990), two recent studies of more than 73,000 men who had undergone vasectomies raise concerns that the procedure may not be as risk-free as people generally believe. The studies showed that men who had had vasectomies more than 20 years earlier faced a slightly increased risk of prostate cancer (Altman, 1993a; Giovannucci et al., 1993a, 1993b). The studies found a correlation between vasectomies and the risk of prostate cancer, but did not establish a causal connection. It is possible that other factors than the vasectomy itself may explain the greater risk faced by vasectomized men. The results also conflict with earlier studies showing either no link between vasectomies and the risk of prostate cancer or even a *lower* risk among vasectomized men. More research is needed to clarify the relationship between vasectomy and prostate cancer. In the meantime, medical experts recommend that men who have had vasectomies get annual checkups for signs of prostate cancer (Altman, 1993a).

The vasectomy is nearly 100% effective. Fewer than 2 pregnancies occur during the first year among 1,000 couples in which the man has undergone a vasectomy (see Table 10.1). The few failures stem from sperm remaining in the male's genital tract shortly after the operation, or the growing together of the segments of a vas deferens.

Reversibility is simple in concept but not in practice. Thus, vasectomies should be considered permanent. In an operation to reverse a vasectomy, called a **vasovasotomy,** the ends of the vas deferens are sewn together, and in a few days they grow together. Estimates of success at reversal, as measured by subsequent pregnancies, range from 16% to 79% (Hatcher et al., 1994). Some vasectomized men develop antibodies that attack their own sperm. The production of antibodies does not appear to endanger the man's health (Hatcher et al., 1994), but it may contribute to infertility following reconnection (Reinisch, 1990).

Major studies conducted over a 15-year period revealed no deaths due to vasectomy in the United States (Reinisch, 1990). Few documented complications of vasectomies have been reported in the medical literature. Minor complications are reported in 4% or 5% of cases, however. They typically involve temporary local inflammation or swelling after the operation. Ice packs and anti-inflammatory drugs, such as aspirin, may help reduce swelling and discomfort. More serious but rarer medical complications include infection of the epididymis (Reinisch, 1990).

Female Sterilization   Nearly four in ten (39%) married women under the age of 45 have been surgically sterilized (U.S. Bureau of the Census, 1990b). **Tubal sterilization,** also called *tubal ligation,* is the most common method of female sterilization. Tubal sterilization prevents ova and sperm from passing through the fallopian tubes. About 650,000 tubal sterilizations are performed each year in the United States (Altman, 1993c).

The two main surgical procedures for tubal sterilization are *minilaparotomy* and *laparoscopy.* In a **minilaparotomy,** a small incision is made in the abdomen, just above the pubic hairline, to provide access to the fallopian tubes. Each tube is cut and either tied back or clamped with a clip. In a **laparoscopy** (see Figure 10.8), sometimes called "belly button surgery," the fallopian tubes are approached through a small incision in the abdomen just below the navel. The surgeon uses a narrow, lighted viewing instrument called a *laparoscope* to locate the tubes. A small section of each of the tubes is cauterized, cut, or clamped. The woman usually returns to her daily routine in a few days and can resume

Vasovasotomy
The surgical method of reversing vasectomy in which the cut or cauterized ends of the vas deferens are sewn together.

Tubal sterilization
The most common method of female sterilization, in which the fallopian tubes are surgically blocked to prevent the meeting of sperm and ova. Also called *tubal ligation.*

Minilaparotomy
A kind of tubal sterilization in which a small incision is made in the abdomen to provide access to the fallopian tubes.

Laparoscopy
Tubal sterilization by means of a *laparoscope,* which is inserted through a small incision just below the navel and used to cauterize, cut, or clamp the fallopian tubes. Sometimes referred to as "belly button surgery."

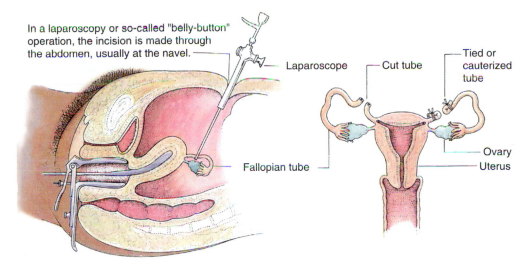

In a laparoscopy or so-called "belly-button" operation, the incision is made through the abdomen, usually at the navel.

Laparoscope

Cut tube

Tied or cauterized tube

Fallopian tube

Ovary

Uterus

Figure 10.8. Laparoscopy. In this method of female sterilization, the surgeon approaches the fallopian tubes through a small incision in the abdomen just below the navel. A narrow instrument called a *laparoscope* is inserted through the incision, and a small section of each fallopian tube is cauterized, cut, or clamped to prevent ova from joining with sperm.

Culpotomy
A kind of tubal sterilization in which the fallopian tubes are approached through an incision in the back wall of the vagina.

Hysterectomy
Surgical removal of the uterus.

coitus when it becomes comfortable. In an alternative sterilization procedure, a **culpotomy,** the fallopian tubes are approached through an incision in the back wall of the vagina.

None of these methods disrupts sex drive or sexual response. Surgical sterilization does not induce premature menopause or alter the woman's production of sex hormones. The menstrual cycle is undisturbed. The unfertilized egg is simply reabsorbed by the body, rather than being sloughed off in the menstrual flow.

A **hysterectomy** also results in sterilization. A hysterectomy is a major operation that is commonly performed because of cancer or other diseases of the reproductive tract; it is inappropriate as a method of sterilization. Hysterectomy carries the risks of major surgery and, when the ovaries are removed along with the uterus, it induces a "surgical menopause" because the woman no longer produces female sex hormones.

Female sterilization is highly effective in preventing pregnancy, although slightly less effective than male sterilization. Overall, about 1 women in 200 (0.4%) is likely to become pregnant in the first year following a tubal sterilization (Hatcher et al., 1994), most likely the result of a failed surgical procedure or an undetected pregnancy at the time of the procedure. Like vasectomy, tubal ligation should be considered irreversible. Reversals are successful, as measured by subsequent pregnancies, in 43% to 88% of cases (Hatcher et al., 1994). Reversal is difficult and costly, however.

About 2% to 11% of sterilized women incur medical complications (Reinisch, 1990). The most common complications are abdominal infections, excessive bleeding, inadvertent punctures of nearby organs, and scarring. The use of general anesthesia (typical in laparoscopies and in some minilaparotomies) poses additional risks, as in any major operation. (Most of the deaths that are attributed to tubal sterilization actually result from the anesthesia [Reinisch, 1990]. The overall death rate is quite small, however—2 to 5 deaths per 100,000 operations.)

Advantages and Disadvantages of Sterilization The major advantages of sterilization are effectiveness and permanence. Sterilization is nearly 100% effective. Following surgery the couple need not do anything more to prevent conception. The permanence is also its major drawback, however. People sometimes change their minds about wanting to have children.

Sterilization procedures create varying risks of complications following surgery, with women generally incurring greater risks than men. Another disadvantage of sterilization is that it affords no protection against STDs (Cates & Stone, 1992b). People who are sterilized may still wish to use condoms and spermicides for protection against STDs.

Other Devices

A number of other contraceptive devices have recently been introduced or are under development.

The Female Condom   The female condom consists of a polyurethane (plastic) sheath that is used to line the vagina during intercourse. It is held in place at each end by a flexible plastic ring. The female condom provides a secure but flexible shield that barricades against sperm but allows the penis to move freely within the vagina during coitus. It can be inserted as long as eight hours preceding intercourse but should be removed immediately afterward (Hatcher et al., 1994). A new one must be used for each act of intercourse.

Like the male condom, the female condom may offer some protection against STDs. Dr. Mary E. Guinan (1992) of the Centers for Disease Control points out that women can use the female condom if their partners refuse to wear a male condom. Cynthia Pearson (1992) of the National Women's Health Network notes that the female condom "for the first time [gives] women control over exposure to sexually transmitted disease, including AIDS."

The female condom (brand name: Reality) was approved in 1993 with the provision that it carry a warning on its label stating that it appears to be less effective than the male latex condom in preventing pregnancies and transmission of STDs. During test trials, the pregnancy rate was estimated to range between 21% and 26%, but is estimated to be as low as 5% among cautious users (Hatcher et al., 1994). Evidence concerning the effectiveness of the female condom in providing protection against STDs is scarce (Centers for Disease Control, 1993a).

Many women also complain that the female condom is bulky and difficult to insert (Stewart, 1992). Still, it is the first barrier method of contraception that women control themselves. Naming the device *Reality* suggests that it may be used most widely by women faced with the reality of male partners who refuse to use condoms themselves or who fail to use them consistently or properly. The female condom costs several times as much as the male condom.

The Contraceptive Sponge   The contraceptive sponge (brand name: Today) was taken off the market by the manufacturer in 1995 (*Self,* 1995). FDA inspectors had found some problems in production, including bacterial contamination. The manufacturer decided that it would be too costly to modify procedures to meet FDA objections. As of this writing, therefore, the contraceptive sponge is no longer available. Nevertheless, we will provide a brief description. Times change, and the sponge could make a comeback.

The contraceptive sponge was a soft, disposable device. Unlike the diaphragm, the sponge did not need to be fitted. Like the diaphragm, it provided a barrier that held a spermicide. But the sponge could be inserted into the vagina up to 18 hours before coitus and had the additional effect of absorbing sperm. It was odorless and tasteless, and users found it less drippy than the diaphragm. On the negative side, about 1 user in 20 (male and female) was mildly irritated by the spermicide. There was also a remote chance of toxic shock syndrome: 1 case arose for every 4 *million* days of use.

The Vaginal Ring   The vaginal ring can be worn in the vagina for three months before replacement. Shaped like a diaphragm, the ring contains either a combination of estrogen and progestin or progestin only. The hormones are slowly released and pass into the bloodstream through the mucosal lining of the vagina. The vaginal ring is a convenient means of receiving a continuous dose of hormones without having to remember to take a pill. Research on the effectiveness of the vaginal ring is underway.

Depo-Provera   Depo-Provera (medroxyprogesterone acetate) is a long-acting, synthetic form of progesterone that works as a contraceptive by inhibiting ovulation. The progesterone signals the pituitary gland in the brain to stop producing hormones that would lead to the release of mature ova by the ovaries. Administered by injection once every three months, Depo-Provera is an effective form of contraception, with reported failure rates of less than 1 pregnancy per 100 women during the first year of use (Hatcher et al., 1994). Depo-Provera has been used by more than 30 million women in more than 90 countries worldwide since it was first marketed in 1969. However, approval in the United States was held up because of concerns over side effects, including the risk of breast cancer. A review by the Food and Drug Administration (FDA) finally found the cancer risk to be minimal and approved Depo-Provera as a contraceptive in 1992. A World Health Organization study of 12,000 women found no links between the drug and the risk of ovarian or cervical cancer (Walt, 1993). Yet the drug may produce side effects such as weight gain, menstrual irregularity, and spotting between periods (Hatcher et al., 1994). Use of Depo-Provera has also been linked to *osteoporosis,* a condition involving bone loss that can cause bones to become brittle and fracture easily.

Under Development   Other methods of contraception are in experimental stages, including sterilization techniques that promise greater reversibility. Also in the experimental stage is a so-called male pill, an oral contraceptive for men. The male sex hormone testosterone has shown promise in reducing sperm production ("Male birth control," 1995). The pituitary gland normally stimulates the testes to produce sperm. Testosterone suppresses the pituitary, in turn suppressing sperm production. Men who have received testosterone injections have shown declines in sperm production. Potential complications include an increased risk of prostate cancer. Testosterone also appears to increase cholesterol levels in the bloodstream, which may heighten the risk of cardiovascular disease.

Another approach was suggested when investigators in China found extremely low birth rates in communities in which cottonseed oil was used in cooking. They extracted a drug from the cotton plant, *gossypol,* which shows promise as a male contraceptive. Chinese studies reveal the drug to be nearly 100% effective in preventing pregnancies. The drug appears to nullify sperm production without affecting hormone levels or the sex drive. However, toxic effects of gossypol have limited its acceptability as a male contraceptive.

Some men are infertile because they produce antibodies that destroy their own sperm. It is also speculated that vasectomy causes some men's bodies to react to their own sperm as foreign substances and produce antibodies. This is an immunological response to sperm. Some researchers have suggested that it may be possible to develop ways to induce the body to produce such antibodies. Ideally this procedure would be reversible.

Applying ultrasound waves to the testes has been shown to produce reversible sterility in laboratory rats, dogs, and monkeys. No one is quite certain how ultrasound works in inducing temporary sterilization. Moreover, its safety has not been demonstrated.

Abortion

Induced abortion
The purposeful termination of a pregnancy before the embryo or fetus is capable of sustaining independent life. (From the Latin *abortio,* meaning "that which is miscarried.")

An **induced abortion** (in contrast to a spontaneous abortion, or miscarriage) is the purposeful termination of a pregnancy. Perhaps more than any other contemporary social issue, induced abortion (hereafter referred to simply as abortion) has divided neighbors and family members into opposing camps.

Thirty-seven million abortions worldwide, including more than 1.5 million in the United States, are performed each year (Smolowe, 1993; U.S. Bureau of the Census, 1990b). The great majority of abortions in the United States—nearly 90%—occur during the first trimester. This is when they are safest to the woman and least costly (Centers for Disease Control, 1992a). Most women who have abortions are unmarried.

Women of color in the United States have proportionally more abortions than White women (Centers for Disease Control, 1992a). There are about 55 abortions per 1,000 women of color reported each year, as compared to 23 for White women. These statistics may underestimate the rates of abortion, especially for higher-income women who have greater access to private health care providers. Many abortions performed in private settings are reported under a medical classification other than abortion.

JAPAN'S ABORTION AGONY: IN A COUNTRY THAT PROHIBITS THE PILL, REALITY COLLIDES WITH RELIGION

Yuka Sugimoto winds her way among thousands of miniature stone statues in a hillside Buddhist temple (WuDunn, 1996). She finds the one she is seeking—the proper *mizuko jizo*—and lingers to ponder the clandestine act that resulted in this.

Buddhists come to the temples to pray for health, wealth, or a wife or husband. Not Ms. Sugimoto. She comes to this ancient temple once a month as a way of making amends with the fetus she aborted 2 years earlier, when she was an unmarried student.

Japan may be the richest, most technologically advanced nation in the world, but its abortion rate is one of the highest among the world's industrialized nations. One reason for this is the lack of birth-control alternatives. The government bans the use of the birth-control pill as a contraceptive, and doctors do not encourage the use of sterilization, IUDs, or diaphragms. Nearly 75% of Japanese continue to use condoms and rhythm methods despite their high failure rate.

Offerings Made at a Buddhist Temple in Japan by Women Who Have Had Abortions. Japan prohibits women from using the birth-control pill, thereby increasing the incidence of abortion.

Over the years Japanese officials defended the ban against the pill by arguing that oral contraceptives are unsafe and would promote promiscuity ("Still no pill for Japan," 1992). In 1992, a review by the Health and Welfare Ministry found birth-control pills to be safe, but decided to uphold the ban because of concerns about AIDS. Though Japan has had relatively few

---

There are many reasons why women have abortions, including psychological factors as well as external circumstances. Abortion is often motivated by a desire to reduce the risk of physical, economic, psychological, and social disadvantages that the woman perceives for herself and her present and future children should she take the pregnancy to term (Russo et al., 1992).

The national debate over abortion has been played out in recent years against a backdrop of demonstrations, marches, and occasional acts of violence, such as firebombings of abortion clinics and even murder. The right-to-life (pro-life) movement asserts that human life begins at conception and thus views abortion as the murder of an unborn child (Sagan & Dryan, 1990). Some in the pro-life movement brook no exception to their opposition to abortion. Others would permit abortion to save the mother's life or when a pregnancy results from rape or incest.

The pro-choice movement contends that abortion is a matter of personal choice and that the government has no right to interfere with a woman's right to terminate a pregnancy. Pro-choice advocates argue that women are free to control what happens within their bodies, including pregnancies.

Most people in the United States favor legalized abortion but not under all circumstances. A 1993 ABC News/*Washington Post* poll found that a woman's right to have an

AIDS cases by international standards (fewer than 500 by mid-1991), the health ministry feared that lifting the ban on the pill might discourage condom use and lead to an epidemic of AIDS. Some women in Japan are able to skirt the ban by consulting sympathetic physicians who are willing to prescribe them presumably to treat gynecological complaints.

In part because of limited contraceptive options, the Japanese use condoms more than any other people in the world. They are widely available in drugstores, supermarkets, and vending machines; embarrassed housewives can buy them from door-to-door saleswomen. Abortion is the widely used backup for failed contraception. And yet, although abortions have now been legal and easily accessible in Japan for over 40 years, women who have them feel stigmatized because abortion is regarded by many Japanese, even those who accept it, as "killing a baby."

The majority of Japanese draw little distinction between a fetus and an infant. According to Samuel Coleman, the author of *Family Planning in Japanese Society*, the reasons lie at least partially in Shinto and Buddhism, Japan's two major religions. Although neither religion promotes active opposition to abortion, Buddhism is based on the ideal of overcoming one's sense of ego. In this context, a woman who aborts wrongly puts her ego before her fetus. Shinto, an ancient religion based on ancestor and nature worship, holds that an aborted fetus can place a curse on the woman who aborts.

Offerings at the Temple

Hiroshi Hihara is a gynecologist in Tokyo. He makes his living on infertility work and abortions, many of them for married women whose method of contraception has failed. Although Hihara is a member of a Buddhist temple, he does not consider himself religious. But he says he is not comfortable with abortion. "Abortion is legal and approved of by the government, and if a patient wants it, I can't turn her down," he says. "She's entitled to it. But I am not happy to do it." And yet, he performs some 200 abortions a year and quietly admits, when asked, that his fees from abortion represent "a large portion of my income."

Caught in this moral and economic trap, he resolves his feelings in a uniquely Japanese way. First, he tells each abortion patient to make an offering after the operation at any of the Buddhist temples selling miniature stone statues, or *mizuko jizo*, which women can buy in memory of an aborted fetus. Thousands of such statues stand on display at temples these days, and although some are for miscarriages and stillborn children, the vast majority are for abortions. Many of the statues are decorated with crocheted hats, plastic bibs, and little pinwheels, all put there by women to keep the soul of the aborted fetus warm and amused.

Debate is going on over whether to legalize the pill and promote other forms of birth control such as the diaphragm. Whether Japanese women will use the pill if legalized is an open question. In a June 1990 survey released by one of Japan's largest newspapers, results showed that fewer than 10% of Japanese women would use it even if it were available.

abortion was approved by a margin of 2 to 1, 65% versus 33%. Yet, according to a 1989 Gallup poll, only 27% of Americans believe that a woman should have a right to an abortion for any reason. A large majority believe that women should be permitted to have an abortion if the pregnancy results from rape or incest, if the woman's life or health is threatened, or if the child is likely to be born seriously deformed. A majority feel that abortion should be illegal, however, for a woman who does not want or cannot afford a child. Even a great majority of American Catholics and Protestants endorse abortion under certain conditions, such as when the woman's health is endangered, when there is chance of birth defects, or when a woman becomes pregnant as the result of rape.

Vacuum aspiration
Removal of the uterine contents by suction. An abortion method used early in pregnancy. (From the Latin *aspirare*, meaning "to breathe upon.")

Methods of Abortion

Many abortion methods are in use today.

Vacuum Aspiration   Vacuum aspiration, or suction curettage, is the safest and most common method of abortion. It accounts for more than 90% of abortions in the United States. It is relatively painless and inexpensive. It can be done with little or no anesthesia in a medical office or clinic, but only during the first trimester. Later, thinning of the uterine walls increases the risks of perforation and bleeding.

In the procedure the cervix is usually dilated first by insertion of progressively larger curved metal rods, or "dilators," or by insertion, hours earlier, of a stick of seaweed called *Laminaria digitata. Laminaria* expands as it absorbs cervical moisture, providing a gentler means of opening the os. Then an angled tube connected to an aspirator (suction machine) is inserted through the cervix into the uterus. The uterine contents are then evacuated (emptied) by suction (see Figure 10.9). Possible complications include perforation of the uterus, infection, cervical lacerations, and hemorrhaging, but these are rare.

D&C

Abbreviation for *dilation and curettage*, an operation in which the cervix is dilated and uterine contents are then gently scraped away.

Dilation and Curettage (D&C)

The **D&C** was once the customary method of performing abortions. It now accounts for only a small number of abortions in the United States. It is usually performed 8 to 20 weeks following the last menstrual period (LMP). Once the cervix has been dilated, the uterine contents are scraped from the uterine lining with a blunt scraping tool.

D&C's are carried out in a hospital, usually under general anesthesia. The scraping increases the chances of hemorrhaging, infection, and perforation. Because of these risks, D&C's have largely been replaced by the vacuum aspiration method. D&C's are still used to treat various gynecological problems, however, such as abnormally heavy menstrual bleeding.

D&E

Abbreviation for *dilation and evacuation*, an abortion method in which the cervix is dilated prior to vacuum aspiration.

Dilation and Evacuation (D&E)

The **D&E** is used most commonly during the second trimester, when vacuum aspiration alone would be too risky. The D&E combines suction and the D&C. First the cervix is dilated. The cervix must also be dilated more fully than with vacuum aspiration to allow for passage of the larger fetus. Then a suction tube is inserted to remove some of the contents of the uterus. But suction alone cannot safely remove all uterine contents. So the remaining contents are removed with forceps. A blunt scraper may also be used to scrape the uterine wall to make sure that the lining has been removed fully. Like the D&C, the D&E is usually performed in the hospital under general anesthesia. Most women recover quickly and relatively painlessly. In rare instances, however, complications can arise. These include excessive bleeding, infection, and perforation of the uterine lining (Thompson, 1993).

Intra-amniotic infusion

An abortion method in which a substance is injected into the amniotic sac to induce premature labor. Also called *instillation*.

Inducing Labor by Intra-amniotic Infusion

Second-trimester abortions are sometimes performed by chemically inducing premature labor and delivery. The procedure, which must be performed in a hospital, is called instillation, or **intra-amniotic infusion**. It is usually performed when fetal development has progressed beyond the point at which other methods are deemed safe. A saline (salt) solution or a solution of prostaglandins (hormones that stimulate uterine contractions during labor) is injected into the

Figure 10.9. **Vacuum Aspiration.** This is the safest and most common method of abortion, but it can be performed only during the first trimester. An angled tube is inserted through the cervix into the uterus, and the uterine contents are then evacuated (emptied) by suction.

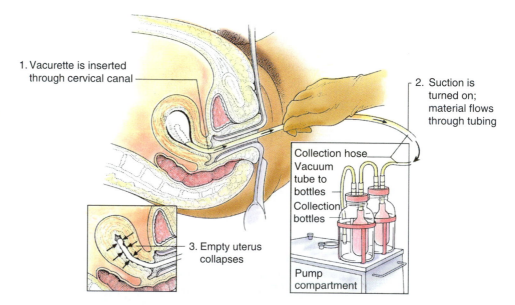

1. Vacurette is inserted through cervical canal

2. Suction is turned on; material flows through tubing

Collection hose
Vacuum tube to bottles
Collection bottles

3. Empty uterus collapses

Pump compartment

amniotic sac. Prostaglandins may also be administered by vaginal suppository. Uterine contractions (labor) begin within a few hours after infusion. The fetus and placenta are expelled from the uterus within the next 24 or 48 hours.

Intra-amniotic infusion accounts for only a small number of abortions. Medical complications, risks, and costs are greater with this procedure than with other methods of abortion. Overly rapid labor can tear the cervix, but previous dilation of the cervix with *Laminaria* lessens the risk. Perforation, infection, and hemorrhaging are rare if prostaglandins are used, but about half the recipients experience nausea and vomiting, diarrhea, or headaches. Saline infusion can cause shock and even death if the solution is carelessly introduced into the bloodstream.

Hysterotomy   The **hysterotomy** is, in effect, a cesarean section. Incisions are made in the abdomen and uterus, and the fetus and uterine contents are removed. Hysterotomy may be performed during the late second trimester, between the 16th and 24th weeks LMP. It is performed very rarely, usually only when intra-amniotic infusion is not advised. A hysterotomy is major surgery that must be carried out under general anesthesia in a hospital. Hysterotomy involves risks of complications from the anesthesia and the surgery itself.

Abortion Drugs   Most early abortions are accomplished by vacuum aspiration, which is a surgical technique. Although vacuum aspiration is safe enough for the woman, 60% to 70% of women in the United States would prefer a drug-induced abortion if it were available (Population Council, 1995).

RU-486 is an abortion pill that was given a "tentative seal of approval" by the U.S. Food and Drug Administration in September 1996 (Reuter, 1996). It contains *mifepristone,* a chemical that induces early abortion by blocking the effects of progesterone. Progesterone is the hormone that stimulates proliferation of the endometrium, allowing implantation of the fertilized ovum and, subsequently, development of the placenta. The pill was developed in France. Today, nearly half of French women seeking abortion prefer RU-486 to surgical methods, including vacuum aspiration.

Supporters of RU-486 argue that it offers a safe, noninvasive substitute for more costly and unpleasant abortion procedures (Reuter, 1996).

RU-486's introduction in the United States has been delayed largely because of opposition by pro-life groups (Hausknecht, 1995). Opponents argue that RU-486 makes abortions more accessible and difficult to regulate (Smolowe, 1993). Pro-life groups consider abortion murder, whether induced by surgery or a pill.

As the abortion debate continues, so does research into the use of other drugs. A combination of the cancer drug *methotrexate* and the ulcer drug *misoprostol,* for example, can be used to terminate early pregnancy. Methotrexate is toxic to the trophoblastic tissue of the embryo, and misoprostol causes uterine contractions. Hausknecht (1995) reported a pilot study in which an injection of methotrexate followed by a vaginal suppository with misoprostol led to successful abortions in 171 of 178 women. (The remaining 7 subsequently underwent aspiration.) Moreover, it would appear that the combination of methotrexate and misoprostol has fewer side effects than RU-486.

Hysterotomy
An abortion method in which the fetus is removed by cesarean section.

Chapter Review

The term (1) _____tion refers to techniques that prevent conception. The term (2) _____tion refers to the termination of a pregnancy before the fetus is capable of surviving outside the womb.

Contraception

An (3) _____l contraceptive is commonly referred to as a birth-control pill, or simply "the pill." (4) _____tion pills contain a combination of estrogen and progesterone (progestin). (5) _____ sic combination pills vary the dosage of these hormones across the menstrual cycle. The minipill contains (6) _____ tin only. Women cannot conceive when they are already pregnant because their bodies suppress (7) _____ tion. The (8) com_____ pill fools the brain into acting as though the woman is already pregnant. The estrogen in the combination pill inhibits production of (9) F_____. The progestin inhibits the pituitary gland's secretion of (10) _____ hormone. Progestin also inhibits development of the (11) endo_____, so that a fertilized ovum could not become implanted in the uterus. The failure rate of the pill in perfect use is (12: Above *or* Below?) 1%. Oral contraception (13: Does *or* Does not?) interfere with sexual spontaneity or diminish sexual sensations. Birth-control pills appear to (14: Increase *or* Decrease?) the risk of pelvic inflammatory disease, ovarian cysts, fibrocystic breast growths, and some kinds of cancer. The pill (15: Does *or* Does not?) confer protection against STDs. The (16) _____ gen in combination pills may produce side effects such as nausea and vomiting, fluid retention, weight gain, and tenderness in the breasts. Women with (17) _____ cular disorders should probably not use oral contraception.

Morning-after pills have (18: High *or* Low?) doses of estrogen and progestin. They stop (19) _____ zation from taking place or prevent the fertilized egg from implanting itself in the uterus. (20) N_____ is a common side effect of morning-after pills.

Norplant consists of six matchstick-sized (21) _____ one tubes. The tubes contain (22) pro_____ and are surgically embedded in a woman's arm. Norplant provides continuous contraceptive protection for as long as (23) _____ years. Norplant (24: Is *or* Is not?) completely reversible. The main (25: Advantage *or* Disadvantage?) of Norplant is that the hormone is dispensed automatically.

(26)_____ ine devices (IUDs) are objects that are inserted into the uterus. IUDs may promote production of (27) _____ ies that may be toxic to sperm or to fertilized ova. They may produce (28) _____ tion that prevents implantation or proliferation of the endometrium. The IUD (29: Is *or* Is not?) highly effective. The IUD (30: Does *or* Does not?) diminish sexual spontaneity or sexual sensations. The IUD (31: Does *or* Does not?) interfere with the woman's natural hormonal production. The most common side effects of IUDs include (32) men_____ cramping, irregular (33) _____ ing between periods, and heavier than usual menstrual bleeding. The IUD may also (34) _____ ate the uterine or cervical walls.

The diaphragm is a shallow cup or dome made of (35) r_____. Diaphragms must be fitted to the contour of the (36) _____ na. The diaphragm forms a barrier against sperm when placed snugly over the (37) cer_____ opening. The diaphragm should be used along with a (38) _____ dal cream or jelly. The diaphragm (39: Is *or* Is not?) as effective as oral contraceptives or IUDs.

(40) _____ ides are chemical agents that kill sperm. Spermicides are placed within the vagina and coat the (41) _____ al opening, blocking the passage of sperm and killing sperm by chemical action. Spermicides (42: Are *or* Are not?) as effective as oral contraceptives. Spermicides that contain (43) no_____ -9 provide some protection against organisms that give rise to STDs.

The (44) _____ cal cap, like the diaphragm, is a dome-shaped rubber cup. The cervical cap is (45: Larger *or* Smaller?) than the diaphragm and is meant to fit snugly over the cervical opening. The cap (46: Is *or* Is not?) intended to be used with a spermicide. Like the diaphragm, the cervical cap forms a (47) ba_____ to sperm and also holds a spermicide in place. The failure rate in typical use is estimated to be (48: High *or* Low?).

Condoms are also called "rubbers," "safes," (49) pro_____ tics, and (50) "_____ ns" (referring to those that are made from lamb intestines). Condoms are (51: More *or* Less?) effective than the pill or IUD, may disrupt sexual spontaneity, and can (52: Increase *or* Decrease?) sexual sensations. Condoms have been making a comeback because those made of (53) la_____ _____ er can help prevent the spread of AIDS and other STDs. Unmarried women are (54: More *or* Less?) likely to report using condoms than are married women. A condom is a cylindrical sheath that serves as a (55) _____ er. The failure rate of the male condom is (56: Higher *or* Lower?) than that of oral contraceptives. The effectiveness of a condom and (57) _____ cide combined rivals that of the birth-control pill when used correctly and consistently. The condom tends to make sex (58: More *or* Less?) spontaneous.

Douching is (59: Effective *or* Ineffective?) as a method of birth control. The withdrawal (coitus interruptus) method has a (60: High *or* Low?) failure rate. The text characterizes both douching and withdrawal as (61) _____thods of contraception.

(62) Fer_____ _____ness, or rhythm, methods rely on awareness of the fertile segments of the woman's menstrual cycle. In such methods, sexual intercourse is avoided on days when conception is (63: Most *or* Least?) likely to occur. Since the rhythm method does not employ (64) _____cial devices, it is acceptable to the Roman Catholic Church. The (65) _____dar method assumes that ovulation occurs 14 days prior to menstruation. In the basal (66) b_____ _____ture (BBT) method, the woman tracks her body temperature upon awakening each morning. A woman's BBT sometimes (67: Rises *or* Dips?) slightly just before ovulation and then tends to (68: Rise *or* Dip?) between 0.4 and 0.8 degree Fahrenheit just before, during, and after ovulation. The cervical mucus (ovulation) method tracks changes in the (69) vis_____ of the cervical mucus. On days when conception is (70: Likely *or* Unlikely?), vaginal mucus tends to become slippery or stringy. Ovulation-prediction kits allow women to test their urine daily for the level of luteinizing hormone, which (71: Rises *or* Dips?) about 12 to 24 hours prior to ovulation. Rhythm methods (72: Do *or* Do not?) appeal to many people who, for religious or other reasons, prefer not to use artificial means. Rhythm methods (73: Do *or* Do not?) have side effects. Rhythm methods (74: Do *or* Do not?) decrease sexual sensations during lovemaking. The main drawback to rhythm methods is (75: High *or* Low?) effectiveness.

With the exception of abstinence, (76) _____za-tion is the most effective form of contraception. Sterilization is the most widely used form of birth control among (77: Single *or* Married?) couples age 30 and above. The male sterilization procedure used today is the (78) _____tomy. Each (79) _____ is cut, a small segment is removed, and the ends are tied off or cauterized. Vasectomy (80: Does *or* Does not?) diminish sex drive or result in any change in sexual arousal, erectile or ejaculatory ability, or sensations of ejaculation. There is a question as to whether there is a link between vasectomy and cancer of the (81) p_____. The operation to reverse a vasectomy is called a (82) vaso_____.

The success of a vasovasotomy (83: Can *or* Cannot?) be guaranteed.

Tubal sterilization, also called (84) tu_____ _____tion, is the most common method of female sterilization. In a (85) mini_____, a small incision is made in the abdomen. Each (86) _____pian tube is cut and tied back or clamped with a clip. In a (87) _____scopy, the fallopian tubes are approached through a small incision in the abdomen just below the navel. In a (88) _____tomy, the fallopian tubes are approached through an incision in the back wall of the vagina. These methods (89: Do *or* Do not?) disrupt sex drive or sexual response. Tubal ligation (90: Should *or* Should not?) be considered irreversible.

The female (91) c_____ is a polyurethane sheath that lines the vagina during intercourse. The female condom serves as a (92) ba_____ against sperm.

Abortion

An (93) _____ed abortion is the purposeful termination of a pregnancy. Nearly 90% of abortions in the United States occur during the (94: First, Second, *or* Third?) trimester. Women of color in the United States have proportionally (95: More *or* Fewer?) abortions than White women do. Abortion (96: Is *or* Is not?) a controversial social issue. The (97) right-to-_____ (pro-life) movement asserts that human life begins at conception and views abortion as the murder of an unborn child. (98) The pro-_____ movement contends that abortion is a matter of personal choice and that the government has no right to interfere with a woman's right to terminate a pregnancy.

(99) Va_____ _____tion, or suction curettage, is the safest and most common method of abortion. It can be done only during the (100: First, Second, *or* Third?) trimester. The cervix is usually dilated first by insertion of progressively larger metal rods or a stick of seaweed that expands as it absorbs (101) _____cal moisture. The uterine contents are then emptied by (102) s_____.

Dilation and (103) _____age (the D&C) is usually performed 8 to 20 weeks following the last menstrual period (LMP). Once the cervix has been dilated, the uterine contents are (104) _____ped from the uterine lining.

Dilation and evacuation (the D&E) is used most commonly during the (105: First, Second, *or* Third?) trimester. The D&E combines (106) _____tion and the D&C.

Second-trimester abortions are sometimes performed by instillation, or (107) in_____-_____tic infusion. A salt solution or a solution of (108) _____an-dins is injected into the amniotic sac. The prostaglandins induce (109) _____ine contractions.

The (110) _____tomy is, in effect, a cesarean section. A hysterotomy is major surgery that must be carried out under general (111) an_____ in a hospital.

The RU-486 abortion pill contains (112) mif_____, a chemical that induces early abortion by blocking the effects of (113) pro_____, the hormone that stimulates proliferation of the endometrium. A combination of the cancer drug (114) meth_____ and the ulcer drug misoprostol can also be used to terminate early pregnancy. Methotrexate is toxic to the embryo, and (115) _____stol causes uterine contractions.

Chapter Quiz

1. Birth-control pills appear to reduce the risk of
   (a) pelvic inflammatory disease.
   (b) sexually transmitted diseases.
   (c) blood clots.
   (d) nausea and vomiting.
2. Which of the following is termed a "nonmethod" of birth control in the text?
   (a) Sterilization.
   (b) Abortion.
   (c) Withdrawal.
   (d) Fertility awareness techniques.
3. Which of the following is the most effective method of birth control?
   (a) The female condom.
   (b) Oral contraceptives.
   (c) The diaphragm (without spermicide).
   (d) Douching.
4. Which of the following methods of birth control has the most side effects?
   (a) The intrauterine device (IUD).
   (b) The male condom.
   (c) The diaphragm (with or without spermicide).
   (d) Abstinence.
5. Which of the following methods of birth control is acceptable to the Roman Catholic Church?
   (a) Abortion during the first trimester.
   (b) Oral contraceptives.
   (c) The intrauterine device.
   (d) Fertility awareness techniques.
6. Which of the following is least likely to be reversible?
   (a) The intrauterine device.
   (b) Fertility awareness techniques.
   (c) Tubal ligation.
   (d) Oral contraceptives.
7. Which of the following is most likely to make the woman feel nauseous?
   (a) The intrauterine device.
   (b) The morning-after pill.
   (c) The cervical cap.
   (d) The minilaparotomy.
8. The male sterilization procedure used today is the
   (a) vasovasotomy.
   (b) vasectomy.
   (c) laparoscopy.
   (d) culpotomy.
9. Which of the following is true of attitudes toward abortion in the United States?
   (a) The majority of people favor abortion under some circumstances.
   (b) The majority of people favor abortion for women who cannot financially afford children.
   (c) The majority of Roman Catholics are opposed to abortion under any circumstances.
   (d) White Americans are more likely than African Americans to support abortion.
10. The most common method of abortion practiced in the United States today is
    (a) the D&C.
    (b) the D&E.
    (c) vacuum aspiration.
    (d) ectopic pregnancy.

Answers to Chapter Review

1. *Contraception*
2. *Abortion*
3. Oral
4. Combination
5. Multiphasic
6. Progestin
7. Ovulation
8. Combination
9. FSH (Follicle-stimulating hormone)
10. Luteinizing
11. Endometrium
12. Below
13. Does not
14. Decrease
15. Does not
16. Estrogen
17. Cardiovascular
18. High
19. Fertilization
20. Nausea
21. Silicone
22. Progestin (Progesterone)
23. Five
24. Is
25. Advantage
26. Intrauterine
27. Antibodies
28. Inflammation
29. Is
30. Does not
31. Does not
32. Menstrual
33. Bleeding or spotting
34. Perforate or tear
35. Rubber
36. Vagina
37. Cervical
38. Spermicidal
39. Is not
40. Spermicides
41. Cervical
42. Are not
43. Nonoxynol
44. Cervical
45. Smaller
46. Is
47. Barrier
48. High
49. Prophylactics
50. Skins
51. Less
52. Decrease
53. Latex rubber
54. More
55. Barrier
56. Higher
57. Spermicide
58. Less
59. Ineffective
60. High
61. Nonmethods
62. Fertility awareness
63. Most
64. Artificial
65. Calendar
66. Body temperature
67. Dips
68. Rise
69. Viscosity
70. Likely
71. Rises
72. Do
73. Do not
74. Do not
75. Low
76. Sterilization
77. Married
78. Vasectomy
79. Vas (Vas deferens)
80. Does not
81. Prostate
82. Vasovasotomy
83. Cannot
84. Tubal ligation
85. Minilaparotomy
86. Fallopian
87. Laparoscopy
88. Culpotomy
89. Do not
90. Should
91. Condom
92. Barrier or barricade
93. Induced
94. First
95. More
96. Is
97. Right-to-life
98. Pro-choice
99. Vacuum aspiration
100. First
101. Cervical
102. Suction
103. Curettage
104. Scraped
105. Second
106. Suction
107. Intra-amniotic
108. Prostaglandins
109. Uterine
110. Hysterotomy
111. Anesthesia
112. Mifepristone
113. Progesterone
114. Methotrexate
115. Misoprostol

Answers to Chapter Quiz

1. (a)
2. (c)
3. (b)
4. (a)
5. (d)
6. (c)
7. (b)
8. (b)
9. (a)
10. (c)

CHAPTER 11

Sexuality Across the Life Span

OUTLINE

Childhood
Infancy (0 to 2 Years)
Early Childhood (3 to 8 Years)
Preadolescence (9 to 13 Years)
Sex Education and Miseducation

Adolescence
Puberty
Sexual Behavior
Teenage Pregnancy

Adulthood
Singlehood
Cohabitation: Darling, Would You Be My POSSLQ?
Marriage
Marital Sexuality

Extramarital Sex
Divorce

Sex in the Later Years
Physical Changes
Sexual Behavior

Sex and Disability
Physical Disabilities
Psychological Disabilities

Applications
Talking to Your Children About Sex
Combating Teenage Pregnancy: A Role for the Schools?

A World of Diversity
Ethnic Differences in Premarital Intercourse, Adolescent Use
    of Contraception, and Resolution of Unwanted Pregnancies

- Many boys are born with erections?
- Most children learn the facts of life from their friends?
- Nocturnal emissions in boys are not necessarily accompanied by "wet dreams"?
- Nearly 1 million adolescent girls in the United States become pregnant each year?
- In some school districts, condoms are distributed to adolescents without parental consent?
- "Singlehood" (forgive the word) has become a more common U.S. lifestyle over the past few decades?
- The numbers of U.S. households consisting of cohabiting adults doubled between 1980 and the early 1990s?
- Most of today's sophisticated young people condemn extramarital affairs?
- Many people who are paralyzed due to spinal-cord injuries can become sexually aroused and engage in sexual intercourse?

This chapter chronicles sexual behavior across the life span. Within children's personal and social experiences lie the seeds of later sexual competence and self-esteem—or the seeds of incompetence, guilt, and shame. Sexuality remains an integral, potentially joyful part of our lives from childhood through advanced age. ■

Childhood

Infancy (0 to 2 Years)

Boys are often born with erections. Many sexual reflexes are present even before we are born. For example, fetuses also have erections. Fetuses suck their fingers. The sucking reflex allows babies to gain nourishment, which is necessary for survival. But as Sigmund Freud hypothesized, infants also seem to reap sensual pleasure from sucking fingers, pacifiers, nipples, or whatever else fits into the mouth. This is not surprising, given the sensitivity of the mouth's mucosal lining.

Stimulation of the genitals in infancy may also produce sensations of pleasure. Parents who touch their infants' genitals while changing or washing them may discover the infants smiling or becoming excited. Infants discover the pleasure of self-stimulation (masturbation) for themselves when they gain the capacity to manipulate their genitals with their hands.

Signs of sexual arousal in infant girls, such as vaginal lubrication, are less readily detected. Yet evidence of lubrication and genital swelling has been reported (Martinson, 1976).

Do not interpret children's responses according to adult concepts of sexuality, however. Lubrication and erection are reflexes, not necessarily signals of "interest" in sex. Infants have the biological capacity for these reflexes, but we cannot say what, if anything, the reflexes "mean" to them.

Kinsey and his colleagues (1953) noted that baby boys show behaviors that resemble adult orgasm by as early as 5 months; baby girls, as early as 4 months. Orgasmic responses in boys are similar to those in men—but without ejaculation. Ejaculation occurs only after puberty.

Masturbation is typical for infants and young children and tends to start between 6 and 12 months. At early ages children usually masturbate by rubbing the genitals against a soft object, such as a towel, bedding, or a doll. As the child matures and becomes capable of more coordinated hand movements, direct manual stimulation of the genitals often becomes preferred.

Masturbation to orgasm is rare until the second year, however (Reinisch, 1990). Some children begin masturbating to orgasm later. Some never do. All in all, however, an orgasmic response from masturbation is common among children, as it is among adults (Reinisch, 1990).

Children in the United States typically do not engage in genital play with others until about the age of 2. Then, as an expression of their curiosity about their environment and other people, they may investigate other children's genitals, or hug, cuddle, kiss, or climb on top of them. Rough-and-tumble play, including touching the genitals, is common among children.

Early Childhood (3 to 8 Years)

In early childhood many children masturbate and engage in sexual play with other children. Because of the difficulties in conducting research, statistics concerning the incidence of masturbation in children are largely speculative. Parents may not wish to respond to questions concerning the sexual conduct of their children. Or if they do, they may have a tendency to present their children as little "gentlemen" and "ladies" and underreport their sexual activity. If we are asked to look back as adults, our memories may be less than accurate. We can only conclude that some children masturbate, and others do not.

Three- and 4-year-olds commonly express affection through kissing. Curiosity about the genitals may also occur by this stage. Sex games like "show" and "playing doctor" may begin earlier but become common between the ages of 6 and 10 (Reinisch, 1990). Much of this sexual activity takes place in same-gender groups, although mixed-gender sex games are not uncommon. Children may exhibit their genitals to each other, touch each other's genitals, or even masturbate together.

Same-gender sexual play in childhood does not presage adult sexual orientation (Reinisch, 1990). It may, in fact, be more common than male–female play. It typically involves handling the other child's genitals, although it may include oral or anal contact. It may also include an outdoor variation of the game of "show" in which boys urinate together and see who can reach farthest or attain the highest trajectory.

Preadolescence (9 to 13 Years)

During preadolescence children typically form relationships with a close "best friend" that enable them to share secrets and confidences. The friends are usually peers of the same gender. Preadolescents also tend to socialize with larger networks of friends in gender-segregated groups. At this stage boys are likely to think that girls are "dorks." To girls at this stage, "dork" is too good a word to apply to most boys.

Preadolescents grow increasingly preoccupied with and self-conscious about their bodies. Their peers pressure preadolescents to conform to dress codes, standards of "cor-

Childhood Sexuality?
Children are naturally inquisitive about sexual behavior and anatomy.

rect" slang, and to group standards concerning sex and drugs. Peer disapproval can be an intense punishment.

Sexual urges are experienced by many preadolescents, but they may not emerge until adolescence. Sigmund Freud had theorized that sexual impulses are hidden, or latent, during preadolescence, but many preadolescents are quite active sexually during the so-called latency period.

Kinsey and his colleagues (1948, 1953) reported that masturbation is the primary means of achieving orgasm during preadolescence for both genders. They found that 45% of males and 15% of females masturbated by age 13.

Preadolescent sex play often involves mutual display of the genitals, with or without touching. Such sexual experiences are quite common and do not appear to impair future sexual adjustment (Leitenberg et al., 1989).

Although preadolescents tend to socialize in same-gender groups, interest in the other gender among heterosexuals tends to gradually increase as they approach puberty. Group dating and mixed-gender parties often provide preadolescents with their first exposure to heterosexual activities. Couples may not begin to pair off until early or midadolescence.

Much preadolescent sexual behavior among members of the same gender is simply exploration. As with younger children, experiences with children of the same gender during preadolescence may be more common than heterosexual experiences (Leitenberg et al., 1989). These activities are usually limited to touching of each other's genitals or mutual masturbation. Since preadolescents generally socialize within their genders, it is not surprising that their sexual explorations may also be within their genders. Most same-gender sexual experiences involve single episodes or short-lived relationships and are not signs of a budding gay orientation.

Sex Education and Miseducation

How do people learn about sex? Studies have consistently shown that in the United States, peers are the main source of sexual information for both genders. According to an ABC News *Nightline* poll (1995), 53% of American adults had learned about sex from their friends. Thirty percent had learned from their parents. Ten percent had learned from school sex-education programs. When asked where teenagers today learn about sex, five of six (83%) said from friends.

School-based sex-education programs were relatively rare as late as the early 1970s, despite the fact that an overwhelming majority of parents supported sex education in the schools (Norman & Harris, 1981). Sex-education programs became more common in the 1970s and 1980s. By the late 1980s, about six in ten teenagers received some form of sex education in the schools (Kenney et al., 1989).

The *Nightline* poll (1995) found that most American adults believe that sex-education programs should teach students to use contraceptives if they are going to engage in premarital sexual activity (91%), that condoms can prevent AIDS (85%), and that early sex is a bad idea (80%). On the other hand, there is great disagreement as to whether school sex-education programs should discuss masturbation, abortion, and sexual orientation.

Today, nearly all states mandate or recommend sex-education programs. The content and length of sex-education programs vary widely. Most programs emphasize the biological aspects of puberty and reproduction (Haffner, 1993). In keeping with parents' preferences, few focus on abortion, masturbation, and sexual orientation. Sexual pleasure is rarely mentioned.

Sex education in the schools, especially about value-laden topics, remains a source of controversy. Some people argue that sex education ought to be left to parents and religious authorities. But the data suggest that the real alternatives to the schools are peers and the corner newsstand, which sells more copies of "adult" magazines than of textbooks. Many parents are also concerned that teaching subjects such as sexual techniques and contraception encourages sexual experimentation. Yet research has failed to demonstrate that sex education increases early sexual experimentation (Eisen & Zellman, 1987; Hayes, 1987).

A P P L I C A T I O N S

TALKING TO YOUR CHILDREN ABOUT SEX

"Daddy, where do babies come from?"

"What are you asking me for? Go ask your mother."

Most children do not find it easy to talk to their parents about sex (Coles & Stokes, 1985). The parents may not find it any easier. Nearly half (47%) of the teens polled in a national survey said they would ask their friends, siblings, or sex partners if they desired information about sex. Only about a third (36%) would turn to their parents (Coles & Stokes, 1985). Three out of four say that it is hard to talk about sex with their fathers. More than half (57%) find it difficult to approach their mothers. Regrettably, information received from peers is likely to be strewn with inaccuracies. Misinformed teenagers run a higher risk of unwanted pregnancies and STDs.

Most young children are curious about where babies come from, about what makes little girls different from little boys, and so on. Parents who avoid answering such questions convey their own uneasiness about sex and may teach children that sex is something to be ashamed of, not something they should discuss openly.

Some parents resist talking about sex with their children because they are insecure in their own knowledge. Reinisch (1990) argues that parents need not be sex experts to talk to their children about sex, however. Parents can turn to books in the local bookstore to fill in gaps in knowledge, or to books that are intended for parents to read to their children. They can also admit that they do not know the answer to a particular question.

In answering children's questions, parents need to be sensitive to what their children can understand. The 4-year-old who wants to know where babies come from is probably not interested in detailed biological information. It may be sufficient to say "from Mommy's uterus" and then point to the mother's abdominal region. Why

say "tummy"? "Tummy" is wrong and confusing.

In their *Family Book About Sexuality*, Calderone and Johnson (1989) offer parents some pointers:

1. *Be willing to answer your child's questions about sex.* Parents who respond by saying, "Why do you want to know that?" squelch questioning. The child is likely to interpret the parent's response as meaning "You shouldn't be interested in that."

2. *Use appropriate language.* As children develop awareness of their sexuality, they need to learn the names of their sex organs. They also need to learn that the "dirty words" that others use to refer to the sexual parts of the body are not acceptable in most situations.

3. *Give advice in the form of information that the child can use to make sound decisions, not as an imperial edict.* State your own convictions, but label your beliefs as your own rather than as something you are trying to impose on your child. Provide information and encourage discussion.

    Parents of teenagers often react to sexual experimentation with threats or punishments, which may cause adolescents to rebel or tune them out. Or the adolescent may learn to associate sex with fear and anger, which may persist even in adult relationships. Parents may find it more constructive to convey concern about the consequences of children's actions in a loving and nonthreatening way that invites an open response. Say, for example, "I'm worried about the way you are experimenting, and I'd like to give you some information that you may not have. Can we talk about it?" (Calderone & Johnson, 1989, p. 141).

4. *Share information in small doses.* Pick a time and place that feels natural for such discussions, such as when the child is preparing for bed or when you are riding in the car.

5. *Encourage the child to talk about sex.* Children may feel embarrassed about talking about sex, especially with family members. Make the child aware that you are always available to answer questions. Be "askable." But let the child postpone talking about a sensitive topic until the two of you are alone or the child feels comfortable. Books about sexuality may help a child open up. They can be left lying around or given to the child with a suggestion such as "This is a good book about sex, or at least I thought so. If you read it, then maybe we can talk about it" (Calderone & Johnson, 1989, p. 136).

6. *Respect privacy rights.* Most of us, parents and children alike, value our privacy at certain times. A parent who feels uncomfortable sharing a bathroom with a child can simply tell the child that Daddy (or Mommy) likes to be alone when using the bathroom. Or the parent might explain, "I like my privacy, so please knock and I'll tell you if it's okay to come in. I'll do the same for you" (Calderone & Johnson, 1989, p. 137). This can be said without a scolding or harsh tone. Privacy rights in the bedroom can be established by saying in a clear and unthreatening way, "Please knock when the door's closed and wait to be invited in" (Calderone & Johnson, 1989, p. 138). It is important for the parent to respect the same rights to privacy that the parent expects from the child.

Many school programs that offer information about contraception and other sensitive topics are limited to high school juniors and seniors. Sexual experimentation often begins earlier, however. Most sexually active teens in Coles and Stokes's (1985) sample began engaging in intercourse by age 15. Fifty percent of the sexually active teenage boys and 18% of the sexually active teenage girls began by age 13.

Accurate information in preadolescence might prevent various sexual mishaps (Coles & Stokes, 1985). Many teens, for example, erroneously believe that a female cannot get pregnant from her first coital experience. Others believe that douching protects them from sexually transmitted diseases (STDs) or unwanted pregnancies.

Adolescence

Adolescence is bounded by the advent of puberty at the lower end and the capacity to take on adult responsibilities at the upper end. In our society adolescents are "neither fish nor fowl," as the saying goes—neither children nor adults. Adolescents may be able to reproduce and be taller than their parents, but they may not be allowed to get driver's licenses or attend R-rated films. They are prevented from working long hours and must usually stay in school until age 16. They cannot marry until they reach the "age of consent." The message is clear: Adults see adolescents as impulsive, and they must be restricted for "their own good." Given these restrictions, a sex drive heightened by surges of sex hormones, and media inundation with sexual themes, it is not surprising that many adolescents are in conflict with their families about "going around" with certain friends, sex, and using the family car.

Puberty

Menarche
The onset of menstruation; first menstruation. (From Greek roots meaning "month" [*men*] and "beginning" [*arche*].)

Puberty
The stage of development during which reproduction first becomes possible. Puberty begins with the appearance of *secondary sex characteristics* and ends when the long bones make no further gains in length. (From the Latin *puber*, meaning "of ripe age.")

Secondary sex characteristics
Physical traits that distinguish men from women but are not directly involved in reproduction.

Primary sex characteristics
Physical characteristics that differentiate males and females and are directly involved in reproduction, such as the sex organs.

I'll never forget seventh grade when it seemed all my friends were menstruating but me. At first I was thinking of coming to school one day and telling them I had gotten my first period but I was afraid that they'd know I was lying so I didn't. Pretty soon no one talked about it much so by the time I did get my first period no one really cared—except my mother who told me I was now a woman.

I began menstruating when I was twelve. I remember feeling great ambivalence about it. I was a little frightened by the blood, and resented having to wear a "diaper." I was sure everyone would be able to tell I had a belt and pad on! On the other hand, I was excited to know that I could become pregnant—that I had become a woman.

My mother showed me how to roll up and wrap a used sanitary napkin in Kleenex. I really did it perfectly my first try and went out to show my mother, who had company in the living room. They giggled; though I got no negative messages about it, I felt embarrassed.

(Morrison et al., 1980, *Growing Up Sexual*, pp. 70–73)

These recollections of college women reflect common attitudes toward menstruation. Some pubescent girls see it as a sign of "becoming a woman." They anxiously await **menarche** (the onset of menstruation). They compete with friends to see who will be first to arrive on the doorstep of adulthood. The second quotation shows that many people mistakenly believe that menstruation signals reproductive capacity. Yet such capacity may lag behind menarche by more than a year.

Menarche is one of the key events of puberty in girls. **Puberty** begins with the appearance of **secondary sex characteristics** and ends when the long bones make no further gains in length (see Table 11.1 on page 272). The appearance of strands of pubic hair are often the first visible signs of puberty. Pubic hair tends to be light colored, sparse, and straight at first. Then it spreads and grows darker, thicker, and coarser. Puberty also involves changes in **primary sex characteristics.** Once puberty begins, most major changes occur within three years in girls and within four years in boys (Etaugh & Rathus, 1995).

Toward the end of puberty, reproduction becomes possible. The two principal markers of reproductive potential are menarche in the girl and the first ejaculation in the boy. But these events do not generally herald immediate fertility.

Girls typically experience menarche between the ages of 10 and 18. In the mid-1800s, European girls typically achieved menarche by about age 17 (see Figure 11.1). The age of menarche has declined sharply since then among girls in Western nations, most likely because of improved nutrition and health care. In the United States, the average age of menarche by the 1960s and 1970s had dropped to between 12½ and 13 (Etaugh & Rathus, 1995).

One view is that a critical body weight (perhaps 103 to 109 pounds) triggers pubertal changes such as menarche, and children today do tend to achieve larger body sizes sooner. Menarche may also be triggered by the accumulation of a certain percentage of body fat. This theory is supported by the finding that menarche comes later to girls who have a lower percentage of body fat, such as athletes (Frisch, 1983). Whatever the exact triggering mechanism, the average age at which girls experience menarche has leveled off in recent years.

Pubertal Changes in the Female   First menstruation, or menarche, is the most obvious sign of puberty in girls. Yet other, less obvious changes have already taken place that have set the stage for menstruation. Between 8 and 14 years of age, release of FSH (follicle-stimulating hormone) by the pituitary gland causes the ovaries to begin to secrete estrogen. Estrogen has several major effects on pubertal development. For one, it stimulates the growth of breast tissue ("breast buds"), perhaps as early as age 8 or 9. The breasts usually begin to enlarge during the tenth year.

Estrogen also promotes the growth of the uterus and the thickening of the vaginal lining. It also stimulates growth of fatty and supporting tissue in the hips and buttocks. This tissue and the widening of the pelvis cause the hips to become rounded and permit childbearing. But growth of fatty deposits and connective tissue varies considerably. Some women may have pronounced breasts; others may have relatively large hips.

Small amounts of androgens produced by the female's adrenal glands, along with estrogen, stimulate development of pubic and underarm hair, beginning at about age 11. Excessive androgen production can darken or thicken facial hair.

Estrogen causes the labia to grow during puberty, but androgens cause the clitoris to develop. Estrogen stimulates growth of the vagina and uterus. Estrogen typically brakes the female growth spurt some years before that of the male. Girls deficient in estrogen during their late teens may grow quite tall, but most tall girls reach their heights because of normal genetically determined variations, not estrogen deficiency.

Estrogen production becomes cyclical in puberty and regulates the menstrual cycle. Following menarche, a girl's early menstrual cycles are typically **anovulatory.** Girls cannot become pregnant until ovulation occurs, which may lag behind menarche by as much as two years. At first ovulation may not be reliable, so a girl may be relatively infertile. Some teenagers are highly fertile soon after menarche, however (Reinisch, 1990).

Anovulatory

Without ovulation.

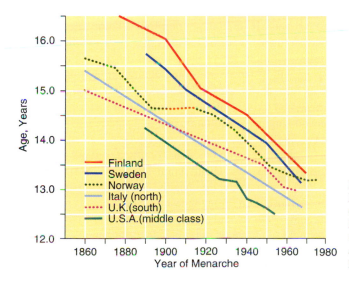

Figure 11.1.   Age at Menarche. The age at menarche has been declining since the mid-1800s among girls in Western nations apparently because of improved nutrition and health care. Menarche may be triggered by the accumulation of a critical percentage of body fat. *Source:* Etaugh, C., and Rathus, S. A. [1995]. *The World of Children.* Fort Worth: Harcourt Brace.

TABLE 11.1 Stages of pubertal development

IN FEMALES

Beginning sometime between ages 8 and 11	Pituitary hormones stimulate ovaries to increase production of estrogen.
	Internal reproductive organs begin to grow.
Beginning sometime between ages 9 and 15	First the areola (the darker area around the nipple) and then the breasts increase in size and become more rounded.
	Pubic hair becomes darker and coarser.
	Growth in height continues.
	Body fat continues to round body contours.
	A normal vaginal discharge becomes noticeable.
	Sweat and oil glands increase in activity, and acne may appear.
	Internal and external reproductive organs and genitals grow, which makes the vagina longer and the labia more pronounced.
Beginning sometime between ages 10 and 16	Areola and nipples grow, often forming a second mound sticking out from the rounded breast mound.
	Pubic hair begins to grow in a triangular shape and to cover the center of the mons.
	Underarm hair appears.
	Menarche occurs.
	Internal reproductive organs continue to develop.
	Ovaries may begin to release mature eggs capable of being fertilized.
	Growth in height slows.
Beginning sometime between ages 12 and 19	Breasts near adult size and shape.
	Pubic hair fully covers the mons and spreads to the top of the thighs.
	The voice may deepen slightly (but not as much as in males).
	Menstrual cycles gradually become more regular.
	Some further changes in body shape may occur into the young woman's early 20s.

This table is a general guideline. Changes may normally appear sooner or later than shown, and not always in the indicated sequence.

Pubertal Changes in the Male   At puberty the hypothalamus signals the pituitary to increase production of FSH and LH (luteinizing hormone). These releasing hormones stimulate the testes to increase their output of testosterone. Testosterone prompts growth of the male genitals: the testes, scrotum, and penis. It fosters differentiation of male secondary sex characteristics: the growth of facial, body, and pubic hair, and the deepening of the voice. Testicle growth, in turn, accelerates testosterone production and pubertal changes. The testes continue to grow, and the scrotal sac becomes larger and hangs loosely from the body. The penis widens and lengthens, and pubic hair appears.

By age 13 or 14, erections become frequent. Indeed, many junior high school boys dread that they may be caught between classes with erections, or asked to stand before the class. Under the influence of testosterone, the prostate and seminal vesicles—the organs that produce semen—increase in size, and semen production begins. Boys typically experience their first ejaculation by age 13 or 14, most often through masturbation. There is much variation, however. First ejaculations may occur as early as age 8 or not until the early 20s (Reinisch, 1990). Mature sperm are not usually found in the ejaculate until about a year after the first ejaculation, at age 14 on the average (Kulin et al., 1989). But sperm may be present in the first ejaculate (Reinisch, 1990), so pubertal boys should not assume that they have an

IN MALES

Beginning sometime between ages 9 and 15	Testicles begin to grow. Skin of the scrotum becomes redder and coarser. A few straight pubic hairs appear at the base of the penis. Muscle mass develops, and the boy begins to grow taller. The areola grows larger and darker.
Beginning sometime between ages 11 and 16	The penis begins to grow longer. The testicles and scrotum continue to grow. Pubic hair becomes coarser, more curled, and spreads to cover the area between the legs. The body gains in height. The shoulders broaden. The hips narrow. The larynx enlarges, resulting in a deepening of the voice. Sparse facial and underarm hair appears.
Beginning sometime between ages 11 and 17	The penis begins to increase in circumference as well as in length (though more slowly). The testicles continue to increase in size. The texture of the pubic hair is more like an adult's. Growth of facial and underarm hair increases. Shaving may begin. First ejaculation occurs. In nearly half of all boys, gynecomastia (breast enlargement) occurs, which then decreases in a year or two. Increased skin oils may produce acne.
Beginning sometime between ages 14 and 18	The body nears final adult height, and the genitals achieve adult shape and size, with pubic hair spreading to the thighs and slightly upward toward the belly. Chest hair appears. Facial hair reaches full growth. Shaving becomes more frequent. For some young men, further increases in height, body hair, and muscle growth and strength continue into their early 20s.

Source: Copyright © 1990 by the Kinsey Institute for Research in Sex, Gender, and Reproduction. From THE KINSEY INSTITUTE NEW REPORT ON SEX. Reprinted with permission from St. Martin's Press, New York, NY.

Nocturnal emission
Involuntary ejaculation of seminal fluid while asleep. Also referred to as a "wet dream," although the individual need not be dreaming about sex, or dreaming at all, at the time.

Larynx
A structure of muscle and cartilage at the upper end of the trachea that contains the vocal cords; the voice box.

Gynecomastia
Overdevelopment of a male's breasts. (From Greek roots meaning "woman" [*gyne*] and "breast" [*mastos*].)

infertile "grace period" following first ejaculation. About a year after first ejaculation, boys may also begin **nocturnal emissions,** which are also called "wet dreams" because of the belief that nocturnal emissions accompany erotic dreams—which need not be so.

Underarm hair appears at about age 15. Facial hair is at first a fuzz on the upper lip. A beard does not appear for another two or three years. Only half of U.S. boys shave (of necessity) by age 17. The beard and chest hair continue to develop past the age of 20. At age 14 or 15 the voice deepens because of the growth of the **larynx** and the lengthening of the vocal cords. Development is gradual, and the voices of adolescent boys sometimes crack embarrassingly.

Boys and girls undergo general growth spurts during puberty. Girls usually shoot up before boys. Individuals differ, however, and some boys spurt sooner than some girls.

Increases in muscle mass produce increases in weight. The shoulders and the circumference of the chest widen. At the age of 18 or so, men stop growing taller because estrogen prevents the long bones from making further gains in length (Smith et al., 1994). Males normally produce some estrogen in the adrenal glands and testes. Nearly one in two boys experiences temporary enlargement of the breasts, or **gynecomastia,** during puberty, which is also caused by estrogen.

Sexual Behavior

Masturbation is a major sexual outlet during adolescence. About half of the adolescent boys (46%) in Coles and Stokes's (1985) national survey of 1,067 teenagers and about a quarter of the girls (24%) reported masturbating. The average age at which teenagers in the Coles and Stokes survey reported they started to masturbate was 11 years 8 months.

A southern California survey of 641 teenagers showed that boys who masturbate do so two to three times a week, on the average, as compared to about once a month for girls (Hass, 1979). Researchers find no links between adolescent masturbation and early sexual activity (for example, frequency of intercourse, number of different partners, or age upon first intercourse) and sexual adjustment during young adulthood (Leitenberg et al., 1993).

Many teens still think of masturbation as shameful (Coles & Stokes, 1985). Only about one in three (31%) of the teens surveyed by Coles and Stokes reported feeling completely free of guilt over masturbation. One in five felt a "large amount" or "a great deal" of guilt. The others felt a "small" or "medium" amount of guilt.

Young people today start dating and "going steady" earlier than in past generations. These changes have implications for teenage pregnancy. Teens who date earlier (by age 14) are more likely to engage in coitus during high school (Miller et al., 1986). Teens who initiate sexual intercourse earlier are also less likely to use contraception and more likely to incur an unwanted pregnancy. If the young woman decides to keep her baby, she is also more likely to have to leave school and scuttle educational and vocational plans. Early dating does not always lead to early coitus, however. Nor does early coitus always lead to unwanted pregnancies. Still, some young women find their options in adulthood restricted by a chain of events that began in early adolescence.

Petting   Many adolescents use petting to express affection, satisfy their curiosities, heighten their sexual arousal, and reach orgasm while avoiding pregnancy and maintaining virginity.

An overwhelming majority (97%) of teenagers sampled in the Coles and Stokes (1985) survey had engaged in kissing (a form of light petting) by the age of 15 (Coles & Stokes, 1985). Girls tended to engage in kissing earlier than boys, perhaps because girls tend to mature faster. By age 13, 73% of the girls and 66% of the boys had engaged in kissing.

Oral Sex   The incidence of premarital oral sex has increased two- or threefold since Kinsey's time. About four in ten (41%) of the 17- and 18-year-old girls in the Coles and Stokes (1985) survey of the 1980s reported that they had performed fellatio. About a third of the boys reported performing cunnilingus. Many girls reported they had engaged in fellatio for the partner's pleasure, not their own. Some couples maintain *technical virginity* by substituting oral sex for intercourse (Gagnon & Simon, 1987).

Some adolescent couples use oral sex as a means of birth control. As one 17-year-old New York girl put it, "That's what we used to do before we could start having sex, because we didn't have protection and stuff" (Coles & Stokes, 1985, p. 60).

Premarital Intercourse   In the 1990s, more than half of our teenagers engage in coitus (Haffner, 1993). Many young people feel as if they are caught betwixt and between. On the one hand, adults tell them to wait until they're older, to "just say no." On the other hand, the movies and television programs they see, and the stories they hear from their peers, reinforce the belief that everybody's "doing it."

The incidence of premarital intercourse, especially for females, has increased dramatically since Kinsey's day. In Kinsey's time, the sexual double standard held firm. Women were expected to remain virgins until marriage, but society looked the other way for men. Not surprisingly, Kinsey and his colleagues found a much greater incidence of premarital coitus among men. By the age of 20, 77% of the single men but only 20% of the single women reported that they had engaged in premarital coitus. Of those still single by age 25, the figures rose to 83% for men but only 33% for women. Rates of premarital coitus among young women should not be confused with sexual promiscuity. Kinsey found that 53% of the females who had engaged in premarital coitus had done so with one partner only (Kinsey et al., 1953).

Surveys in the early 1970s found that about half (46% to 57% across studies) of the women sampled had engaged in premarital sex by the age of 19 (Kantner & Zelnik, 1972; Sorensen, 1973). This figure compares to fewer than 20% in Kinsey's day. By 1979, 65%—nearly two out of three—young, never-married women 19 years of age who lived in metropolitan areas of the United States had engaged in sexual intercourse (Zeman, 1990). By 1988, among 19-year-old, never-married adolescents living in metropolitan areas of the United States, 78% of the girls and 86% of boys had initiated sexual intercourse (Zeman, 1990).

Young people today are also initiating sexual intercourse at younger ages. Kinsey found that 7% of White females had engaged in intercourse by the age of 16. If surveys can be trusted, the average age of first intercourse among girls in the United States is 16; for boys, 15.5 (USDHHS, 1990b). Note, however, that sexual activity among teenagers tends to be episodic. Only half of the sexually experienced adolescents in one survey reported engaging in sexual intercourse during the month before the interview (Leigh et al., 1994).

In sum, the incidence of premarital sex has increased since Kinsey's day, dramatically so among females. Rates of premarital sex among young men have traditionally been higher, but the gender gap has narrowed considerably.

Motives for Intercourse   Premarital intercourse is motivated by a number of factors. Sex hormones, especially testosterone, activate sexual arousal. Thus the pubertal surge of hormones directly activates sexual arousal, at least among boys (Brooks-Gunn & Furstenberg, 1989). About half of the men (51%) and one quarter of the women (24%) in the NHSLS study report that their primary reason for the first coital experience was curiosity, or "readiness for sex" (Michael et al., 1994, p. 93). For some adolescents, sexual intercourse is perceived as the natural outgrowth of love (Thompson, 1995). Adolescents may consider intercourse a sign of maturity, a way for girls to reward a boyfriend for remaining loyal, or a means of punishing parents (Thompson, 1995). Some adolescents engage in coitus in response to peer pressure, especially from close friends.

Factors in Premarital Intercourse   Many young people abstain from premarital coitus for religious or moral reasons (Coles & Stokes, 1985; Miller & Bingham, 1989). Family influences and religious values are important determinants of adolescent sexual experience (White & DeBlassie, 1992). Other reasons include fear of being caught, fear of pregnancy, or fear of disease.

A study of 142 low-income, African American adolescent females (ages 13–18) at an inner-city health clinic in Dallas found that girls who were not sexually active tended to be younger and more career oriented, to have a father at home, to hold more conservative values about sexuality, and to be more influenced by family values, than sexually active girls (Keith et al., 1991).

Teens who have higher educational goals and do better in school are less likely to engage in coitus than less academically oriented teens (Brooks-Gunn & Furstenberg, 1989; Hofferth & Hayes, 1987). The causal connection between school performance and premarital sex is difficult to discern, because adolescents who do well in school are also more likely to come from better-functioning families.

Other researchers focus on relationships between family factors and premarital intercourse. Children whose parents are separated or divorced are more likely than those from intact homes to engage in premarital intercourse (Coles & Stokes, 1985). Perhaps parents who have "failed" in their marital relationships lack credibility in advising their adolescent children (Coles & Stokes, 1985). Single parents, because of time constraints, may also be less capable of supervising their children. Teenagers from single-parent homes may have greater opportunities for privacy, especially when the parent works (Coles & Stokes, 1985). Moreover, a teenager may interpret a single parent's becoming sexually active with dates as tacit approval of premarital sex.

The quality of the relationship between teens and their parents may also be important (Brooks-Gunn & Furstenberg, 1989). Teens who feel that they can talk to their parents are less likely to engage in coitus than those who describe communication with their parents as poor.

A WORLD OF DIVERSITY

ETHNIC DIFFERENCES IN PREMARITAL INTERCOURSE, ADOLESCENT USE OF CONTRACEPTION, AND RESOLUTION OF UNWANTED PREGNANCIES

African American teenagers become sexually active two years earlier, on the average, than White teenagers. They are more likely in dating relationships to progress directly from light petting to intercourse (Brooks-Gunn & Furstenberg, 1989). Earlier initiation to coitus and more rapid progression from petting to intercourse may place African American females at greater risk of unwanted pregnancies (Brooks-Gunn & Furstenberg, 1989; Smith & Udry, 1985).

A review of the available research on ethnicity and sexual behavior in college students shows Asian American and Hispanic American students to be somewhat more conservative sexually than their African American or (non-Hispanic) White American counterparts (Baldwin et al., 1992; Padilla & O'Grady, 1987).

There are also informative ethnic group differences in the use of contraception. Hispanic American adolescents, for example, are less likely than non-Hispanics to use contraception (Darabi et al., 1986). The low rate of use of contraceptives by Hispanic American teens may be due to conflict between sexual activity and the conservative sexual values with

Ethnic Differences in Use of Contraception. Researchers find ethnic differences in contraceptive use among sexually active adolescents. How do sociocultural factors affect use of contraceptives?

which they are reared. A survey of Mexican American and Anglo undergraduates at a southern California state university with a large Mexican American enrollment found that Mexican American students were more conservative and traditional in their sexual attitudes and reported *less* sexual experience than their Anglo counterparts (Padilla & O'Grady, 1987). Mexican American women also engage in first intercourse later than non-Hispanic White women (Slonim-Nevo, 1992).

The survey by Padilla and O'Grady (1987) also revealed that Mexican American students held more conservative attitudes than Anglo students concerning masturbation, abortion, and premarital and extramarital relationships. Mexican American students less frequently engaged in sexual intercourse, had fewer coital partners, and reported masturbating less often than their Anglo counterparts. They also identified more strongly than Anglo students with a traditional Judeo-Christian value system.

Adolescents whose parents are very permissive and impose very few rules and restrictions are also more likely to engage in premarital intercourse (Hogan & Kitigawa, 1985; Miller et al., 1986). Parents who show an interest in their children's behavior and communicate their concerns and expectations with understanding and respect may best influence their children to show sexual restraint.

Teenage Pregnancy

About 10% of American girls of ages 15 to 19 become pregnant each year ("Rate of births," 1995). This amounts to one in five sexually active girls and nearly 1 million pregnancies a year. About 40% of teenage pregnancies, or nearly 400,000 annually, end in abortion. Although some of the remainder of these pregnancies result in miscarriages, nearly 500,000 produce live births (Kantrowitz, 1990a).

Although these figures are cause for concern, the rate of births for teenagers was actually dropping modestly during the mid-1990s ("Rate of births," 1995). The proportion of out-of-wedlock births among teenagers shot up during the 1970s and 1980s. Among young women 15 to 17 years of age in the period 1985–1989, 81% of births occurred out of wedlock, as compared to 41% in 1965–1969 and 59% in 1975–1979 (Pear, 1991). Two of three teenage mothers in the 1990s are unmarried, as compared to 15% in 1960. Among African American teenage mothers, 92% are unmarried (National Research Council, 1993). Nine in ten pregnancies among unmarried teenagers are unplanned (Alan Guttmacher Institute, 1991).

There are ethnic and social class differences in rates of teenage pregnancy. Rates of teenage pregnancy are higher among women of color, women from lower socioeconomic classes, and urbanites (Hechtman, 1989). Poverty is an especially strong predictor of teenage pregnancy (Jencks & Mayer, 1990). African American and Hispanic American teenagers, many of whom are poor, are twice as likely as White teenagers to become pregnant (Alan Guttmacher Institute, 1991). African American girls have the highest birth rate overall. The majority of residents of the District of Columbia are African American, and this state had the highest rate of teenage pregnancy in the mid-1990s: 208 per 1,000 female teenagers ("Rate of births," 1995). Among the states, the rate varied from 54 per 1,000 in largely White Wyoming to 107 per 1,000 in Georgia ("Rate of births," 1995).

Consequences of Teenage Pregnancy   The consequences of unplanned teenage pregnancies can devastate young mothers, their children, and society at large. Even young people themselves perceive teenage parenthood to be disastrous (Moore & Stief, 1992). Teenage mothers are more likely to live in poverty and to receive welfare than their peers (Grogger & Bronars, 1993). Poverty, joblessness, and lack of hope for the future are recurrent themes in adolescent pregnancy (Desmond, 1994). Half of teenage mothers quit school and go on public assistance (Kantrowitz, 1990a). Few receive consistent emotional or financial help from the fathers, who generally cannot support themselves, much less a family. Working teenage mothers earn just half as much as those who give birth in their 20s (National Research Council, 1993). Barely able to cope with one baby, many young mothers who give birth at age 15 or 16 have at least one more baby by the time they are 20.

Medical complications associated with teenage childbearing are highest of any group of fertile women except for those in their late 40s (Hess et al., 1993). In addition to high rates of miscarriage and stillbirths, children born to teenagers are at greater risk of prematurity, birth complications, and infant mortality (Fraser et al., 1995; Goldenberg & Klerman, 1995). These problems are often the result of inadequate prenatal care. However, even when prenatal care is taken into consideration, the children of teenagers are at greater risk than those of women in their 20s.

Children of teenage mothers are at greater risk of physical, emotional, and intellectual problems in their preschool years, due to poor nutrition and health care, family instability, and inadequate parenting (Furstenberg et al., 1989; Hechtman, 1989). They are more aggressive and impulsive as preschoolers than are children of older mothers (Furstenberg et al., 1989). They do more poorly in school. They are also more likely to suffer maternal abuse or neglect (Felsman et al., 1987; Kinard & Reinherz, 1987).

A number of factors have contributed to the increase in teenage pregnancy, including a loosening of traditional taboos on adolescent sexuality (Hechtman, 1989). Impaired family relationships, problems in school, emotional problems, misunderstandings about reproduction or contraception, and lack of contraception also play roles (Hechtman, 1989). Some adolescent girls believe that a baby will elicit a commitment from their partners or fill an emotional void. Some become pregnant as a way of rebelling against parents. The largest number become pregnant because of misunderstandings about reproduction and contraception, or failure to use contraception consistently (Hechtman, 1989).

More attention has been focused on teenage mothers, but young fathers bear an equal responsibility for teenage pregnancies. A survey based on a nationally representative sample of 1,880 young men ages 15 through 19 showed that socioeconomically disadvantaged young men in particular appeared to view paternity as a source of self-esteem and were

APPLICATIONS

COMBATING TEENAGE PREGNANCY: A ROLE FOR THE SCHOOLS?

Various means have been recommended to combat the problem of teenage pregnancy, including universal sex education, free contraceptive services for teenagers, open discussion of sex between parents and children, and dissemination of information about responsible sex practices and contraception through the media. Many helping professionals believe that the rate of teenage pregnancy and the spread of sexually transmitted diseases in the United States could be curtailed through sex education about contraception and provision of contraceptives.

Pregnancy prevention programs in the schools range from encouraging teens to delay sex ("saying no to early sex") to providing information about contraception, distributing condoms, or referring students to contraceptive clinics (Furstenberg et al., 1989; Hayes, 1987). The vast majority of sex educa-

tors (86%) recommend abstinence to their students as the best way to prevent pregnancy and AIDS (Kantrowitz, 1990b). Fewer than half inform their students about how to obtain contraceptives. Three out of four large school districts in the United States provide some instruction about the methods of contraception and the use of condoms to prevent the spread of AIDS and other sexually transmitted diseases. About four in ten provide information about clinics or doctors through whom students can receive contraceptives (Kenney et al., 1989).

Evidence supports the effectiveness of programs that counsel abstinence, at least among younger teens. A school-based sex-education program focused on the development of skills needed to resist social and peer pressure to initiate sexual activity encouraged younger (junior high school) teens to postpone sexual involvement

(Howard & McCabe, 1990). Program participants also had fewer pregnancies than students who did not participate in the program. However, programs that rely on the "just say no" model to encourage abstinence are less effective in persuading high school students to abstain from sexual activity (Wilson & Sanderson, 1988).

Alarmed by the threat of AIDS and the epidemic of teenage pregnancy, some school districts now distribute contraceptives, such as condoms, to students. Most school districts require parental consent. Others, such as the New York City school system, do not. Whether public schools should make contraceptives available to sexually active teens is the focus of heated debate among parents, educators, health officials, and other public officials in the United States and Canada.

---

consequently more likely than more affluent young men to say that fathering a child would make them feel like a real man and that they would be pleased, or at least not as upset, with an unplanned pregnancy (Marsiglio, 1993a). Consistent with these attitudes, poor young men were less likely to use a contraceptive.

Various factors determine use of contraceptives. Teenage girls who engage in more frequent intercourse are more likely to use contraception and to use more effective methods (DuRant & Sanders, 1989). Older teenagers are more likely than younger ones to use contraception (Mosher & Bachrach, 1987). Younger teens who are sexually active may be less likely to use contraception because they lack information about contraception and because they do not always perceive the repercussions of their actions (Handler, 1990). Younger teens may also have less access to contraceptives.

Teenage boys are more likely than teenage girls to know how to obtain and use condoms correctly, according to the results of a California survey of more than 1,000 high school students (Leland & Barth, 1992). Boys are also more likely to have used birth control during their first or most recent sexual experience. It appears that girls are more uncomfortable than boys in obtaining or using contraception, especially condoms (Leland & Barth, 1992).

Poor family relationships and poor communication with parents are associated with inconsistent contraceptive use (Brooks-Gunn & Furstenberg, 1989). Poor performance in school and low educational ambitions predict irregular contraceptive use, as they also predict early sexual initiation. For many teenagers, coitus is an unplanned, "spur of the moment" experience.

Myths also decrease likelihood of using birth control. Some adolescents believe that they are too young to become pregnant. Others believe that pregnancy results only from repeated coitus or will not occur if they are standing up. Still other adolescents simply do not admit to themselves that they are engaging in coitus.

Teenagers who focus on the long-term consequences of their actions are more likely to use contraceptives. The quality of the relationship is also a factor. Satisfaction with the relationship is associated with more frequent intercourse *and* more consistent use of contraception (Jorgensen et al., 1980). More consistent contraceptive use is found in relationships in which the young woman takes the initiative in making decisions and resolving conflicts.

Let us note that many adolescents today who use condoms do so more because of fear of AIDS than to protect themselves against unwanted pregnancies (Lewin, 1991). A reduction in teenage pregnancies may be a side effect of this trend.

Adulthood

People entering adulthood today face a wider range of sexual choices and lifestyles than those of earlier generations. The sexual revolution loosened traditional constraints on sexual choices, especially for women. Couples experiment with lifestyles that would have been unthinkable in earlier generations. An increasing number of young people choose to remain single as a way of life, not merely as a way station preceding the arrival of Mr. or Ms. Right.

In this section, we discuss diverse forms of adult sexuality in the United States today, including singlehood, marriage, and cohabitation. Let us begin as people begin—with singlehood.

Singlehood

Recent years have seen a sharp increase in the numbers of single young people in our society. "Singlehood," not marriage, is now the most common lifestyle among people in their early 20s. Though marriages may be made in heaven, many Americans are saying heaven can wait. By the early 1990s, one in four people in the United States 18 years of age and older had never married, as compared to about one in six in 1970 and one in five in 1980 (Barringer, 1992a, 1992b). The rate of marriages had also fallen off. The proportion of people tying the knot reached a 25-year low (Barringer, 1992b). The proportion of people who remain single into their late 20s and early 30s has more than doubled since 1970 (U.S. Bureau of the Census, 1990a).

Several factors contribute to the increased proportion of singles. For one thing, more people are postponing marriage to pursue educational and career goals (Barringer, 1991). Many young people are deciding to "live together" (cohabit), at least for a while, rather than get married. Also, people are getting married at later ages (Lamanna & Riedman, 1997). The increased prevalence of divorce also swells the ranks of single adults.

Less social stigma is attached to remaining single today. Though single people are less likely today to be perceived as socially inadequate or as failures, some unmarried people still encounter stereotypes. Men who have never married may be suspected of being gay. Single women may feel that men perceive them as "loose."

Many single people do not choose to be single. Some remain single because they have not yet found Mr. or Ms. Right. Yet many young people see singlehood as an alternative, open-ended way of life, however—not just a temporary stage that precedes marriage. As career options for women have expanded, they are not as financially dependent on men as were their mothers and grandmothers. A number of career women, like young career-oriented men, choose to remain single (at least for a time) to focus their energies on their careers.

Singlehood is not without its problems. Many singles are lonely. Some singles express concerns about a lack of a steady, meaningful social relationship. Others, usually women, worry about their physical safety. Some people living alone may find it difficult to satisfy their needs for intimacy, companionship, sex, and emotional support. Despite these concerns, most singles are well adjusted and content. Singles who have a supportive social network tend to be more satisfied with their lifestyles.

Singles. There is no one "singles scene" today. While some singles meet in singles' bars, many singles meet in more casual settings, such as the neighborhood laundromat. Some singles advertise in newspapers and magazines, or online.

Serial monogamy

A pattern of involvement in one exclusive relationship after another, as opposed to engaging in multiple sexual relationships at the same time.

Celibacy

Complete sexual abstinence. (Sometimes used to describe the state of being unmarried, especially in the case of people who take vows to remain single.)

Cohabitation

Living together as though married but without legal sanction.

There is no single "singles scene." Single people differ in their sexual interests and lifestyles. Many achieve emotional and psychological security through a network of intimate relationships with friends. Most are sexually active, and many practice **serial monogamy.** Other singles have a primary sexual relationship with one steady partner but occasional flings with others. A few, even in this age of AIDS, are "swinging singles." That is, they pursue casual sexual encounters, or "one-night stands."

Some singles remain celibate, either by choice or for lack of opportunity. Nuns and priests choose **celibacy** for religious reasons. Others believe that celibacy allows them to focus their energies and attention on work or to commit themselves to an important cause. They see celibacy as a temporary accommodation to other pursuits. Others remain celibate because they view sex outside of marriage as immoral. Still others remain celibate because they find the prospects of sexual activity aversive or unalluring, or because of fears of STDs.

Cohabitation: Darling, Would You Be My POSSLQ?

There is nothing I would not do

If you would be my POSSLQ.

(Charles Osgood)

POSSLQ? This unromantic abbreviation was introduced by the U.S. Bureau of the Census to refer to **cohabitation.** It stands for People of Opposite Sex Sharing Living Quarters and applies to unmarried couples who live together.

Some social scientists believe that cohabitation has become accepted within the social mainstream (Bumpass, 1995). Whether or not this is so, society in general has become more tolerant of it. We seldom hear cohabitation referred to as "living in sin" or "shacking up" as we once did. People today are more likely to refer to cohabitation with value-free expressions such as "living together."

The numbers of households consisting of unmarried adults of the other gender living together in the United States doubled between 1980 and the early 1990s (Steinhauer, 1995). They grew from 1.6 million couples in 1980 to 2.9 million couples in 1990 and 3.3 million in 1992.

Who Are the Cohabitors? Much of the attention on cohabitation has been focused on college students living together, but cohabitation is more prevalent among the less well educated and less affluent classes (Willis & Michael, 1994). The cohabitation rate is about twice as high among African American couples as White couples. Fifty-five percent of male cohabitors and 41% of female cohabitors have never been married (U.S. Bureau of the Census, 1990a). Children live with about one cohabiting couple in three (Saluter, 1992).

About one cohabitor in three is divorced. Divorced people are more likely than people who never married to enter cohabiting relationships. Perhaps the experience of divorce makes some people more willing to share their lives than their bank accounts—the second or third time around (Steinhauer, 1995).

Willingness to cohabit is related to more liberal attitudes toward sexual behavior, nontraditional views of marriage, and nontraditional views of gender roles (Huffman et al., 1994). Cohabitors are less likely than noncohabitors to attend church regularly (Laumann et al., 1994). Six out of ten male cohabitors and nearly seven out of ten female cohabitors are under 35 years of age (U.S. Bureau of the Census, 1990a). Yet the greatest increase since 1980 in the numbers of people cohabiting has not been among young romantics, but among people age 35 and above (Bumpass, 1995).

Reasons for Cohabitation   Why do people cohabit? Cohabitation, like marriage, is an alternative to loneliness. Romantic partners may have deep feelings for each other but not be ready to get married. Some couples prefer cohabitation because it provides a consistent relationship without the legal and economic entanglements of marriage (Steinhauer, 1995).

Many cohabitors feel less commitment toward their relationships than married people do (Nock, 1995). Ruth, an 84-year-old woman, has been living with her partner, age 85, for four years. "I'm a free spirit," she says. "I need my space. Sometimes we think of marriage, but then I think that I don't want to be tied down" (cited in Steinhauer, 1995, p. C7).

Economic factors come into play as well. Emotionally committed couples may decide to cohabit because of the economic advantages of sharing household expenses. Cohabiting individuals who receive public assistance (social security or welfare checks) risk losing support if they get married (Steinhauer, 1995). Some older people live together rather than marry because of resistance from adult children (Yorburg, 1995). Some children fear that a parent will be victimized by a needy senior citizen. Others may not want their inheritances to come into question or may not want to decide where to bury the remaining parent. Younger couples may cohabit secretly to maintain parental support that they might lose if they were to get married or to openly reveal their living arrangements.

Cohabitation and Later Marriage: Benefit or Risk?   Cohabiting couples may believe that cohabitation will strengthen eventual marriage by helping them iron out the kinks in their relationship. Yet cohabitors who later marry may run a greater—not lesser—risk of divorce than noncohabitors. Statistics from a national survey of households reveal that the likelihood of divorce within ten years of marriage is nearly twice as great among married couples who cohabited before marriage (Riche, 1988). A Swedish study found that the likelihood of marital dissolution was 80% greater among women who had cohabited before a first marriage than among women who had not (Bennett et al., 1988).

We must be cautious about drawing causal conclusions from correlational data, however. None of the couples in these studies were *randomly assigned* to cohabitation or noncohabitation. Therefore, *selection factors*—the factors that lead some couples to cohabit and others not to cohabit—may explain the results (see Figure 11.2 on page 282). Cohabitors tend to be more committed to personal independence (Bumpass, 1995). They also tend to be less traditional and less religious than noncohabitors. All in all, people who cohabit prior to marriage tend to be less committed to the values and interests traditionally associated with the institution of marriage. The attitudes of cohabitors, and not cohabitation itself, may thus account for their higher rates of marital dissolution.

About 40% of cohabiting couples eventually marry (Laumann et al., 1994). The majority of couples break up within three years. Termination of the relationship, not marriage, is the more likely outcome of cohabitation (Willis & Michael, 1994).

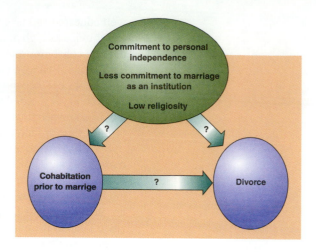

Figure 11.2. Does Cohabitation Prior to Marriage Increase the Risk of Eventual Divorce? There is a correlational relationship between cohabitation prior to marriage and the risk of divorce later on. Does cohabitation increase the risk of divorce, or do other factors—such as a commitment to personal independence—contribute to both the likelihood of cohabitation and eventual divorce?

Marriage

Marriage is found in all human societies. Most people in every known society, sometimes nearly all, get married at least once (Ember & Ember, 1990; Kammeyer, 1990).

In the United States, about 65% of the adult men and 60% of the adult women are married and living with their spouses (U.S. Bureau of the Census, 1990a). With more people delaying marriage in favor of pursuing educational and career goals, the average (median) age of first marriage has been rising steadily over the past few decades and is now 26.5 years for men and 24.4 years for women (Saluter, 1992). This represents an increase of three years for both men and women since 1975.

Whom Do We Marry: Are Marriages Made in Heaven or in the Neighborhood?
Most preliterate societies regulate the selection of spouses in some way. The universal incest taboo proscribes matings between close relatives. Societal rules and customs also determine which persons are desirable mates and which are not.

In Western cultures, mate selection is presumably free. Parents today seldom arrange marriages, although they may still encourage their child to date that wonderful son or daughter of the solid churchgoing couple who live down the street. Nevertheless, factors such as race, social class, and religion often determine the categories of persons within which we may seek mates (Laumann et al., 1994). People in our culture tend to marry others from the same geographical area and social class. Since neighborhoods are often made up of people from a similar social class, storybook marriages like Cinderella's are the exception to the rule.

Because we make choices, we tend to marry people who attract us. These people are usually similar to us in physical attractiveness and attitudes, even in minute details. We are more often than not similar to our mates in characteristics such as height, weight, personality traits, and intelligence (Buss, 1994; Lesnik-Oberstein & Cohen, 1984; Schafer & Keith, 1990). Those we marry also seem likely to meet our material, sexual, and psychological needs.

The concept of "like marrying like" is termed **homogamy.** We usually marry people of the same racial/ethnic background, educational level, and religion. Interracial marriages account for fewer than 1 in every 200 marriages (U.S. Bureau of the Census, 1991). Moreover, more than 9 of 10 marriages are between people of the same religion. Marriages between individuals who are alike may stand a better chance of survival, since the partners are more likely to share their values and attitudes (Michael et al., 1994).

We also tend to follow *age homogamy* (Michael et al., 1994). Age homogamy—the selection of a partner who falls in one's own age range—may reflect the tendency to marry early in adulthood. Persons who marry late or who remarry tend not to select partners so close in age.

Homogamy
The practice of marrying people who are similar in social background and standing. (From Greek roots meaning "same" [*homos*] and "marriage" [*gamos*].)

Some marriages also show a **mating gradient.** The stereotype has been that an economically established older man would take an attractive, younger woman as his wife. But by and large, with boring predictability, we are attracted to and marry the boy or girl (almost) next door. Most marriages seem to be made not in heaven, but in the neighborhood.

Marital Sexuality

Patterns of marital sexuality vary across cultures, yet anthropologists have noted some common threads (Ember & Ember, 1990). Privacy for sexual relations is valued in almost all cultures. Most cultures also place restrictions on coitus during menstruation, during at least some stages of pregnancy, and for a time after childbirth.

Until the sexual revolution of the 1960s and 1970s, Western culture could be characterized as sexually restrictive, even toward marital sex. Hunt noted that "Western civilization has long had the rare distinction of contaminating and restricting the sexual pleasure of married couples more severely than almost any other" (1974, p. 175).

The Sexual Revolution Hits Home   We usually think of the sexual revolution in terms of the changes in sexual behaviors and attitudes that occurred among young, unmarried people. It also ushered in profound changes in marital sexuality, however. Compared to Kinsey's "prerevolution" samples from the late 1930s and 1940s, married couples today engage in coitus more frequently, with greater variety, and for longer durations of time. They report higher levels of sexual satisfaction.

The sexual revolution also helped dislodge traditional male dominance in sexual behavior. In essence, male dominance is the view that sexual pleasure is meant for men but not women and that it is the duty of women to satisfy their husbands' sexual needs and serve as passive "receptacles."

Liberalizing trends were communicated through popular media. Hundreds if not thousands of books and magazines with sexual content crammed bookstore shelves and supermarket display cases. During Kinsey's day, books like Henry Miller's *Tropic of Cancer* and D. H. Lawrence's *Lady Chatterley's Lover* were censored in the United States. Now they are readily available but so tame when compared to today's explicit books and magazines that they barely raise an eyebrow. Similarly, since the late 1960s pornographic films have been shown in adult theaters across the nation. In many places the audiences include middle-class couples and college students, not just "dirty old men." The VCR has brought sexually explicit films into middle-class suburban homes.

Scientific findings were also liberalizing influences. Kinsey's and Masters and Johnson's findings that normal women were capable not only of orgasm but also of multiple orgasms punctured traditional beliefs that sexual gratification was the birthright of men alone. TV shows, films, and radio talk shows began to portray women as sexual initiators who enjoy sex. All of these influences have encouraged U.S. women to forgo the traditional passive approach to sexuality.

The development of effective contraceptives also separated sex from reproduction. Motives for sexual pleasure became more open. The term *recreational sex* came into play. All these liberalizing forces have led to changes in the frequency of marital sex and in techniques of foreplay and coitus since Kinsey's day.

Duration and Techniques of Foreplay   Married women in Kinsey's sample reported an average (median) length of foreplay of about 12 minutes. This figure rose to nearly 15 minutes among the wives in the *Playboy* survey (Hunt, 1974). Couples in more recent surveys report using a wider variety of foreplay techniques, including oral stimulation of the breasts and oral–genital contact (Blumstein & Schwartz, 1983; Hunt, 1974).

Frequency of Marital Coitus   According to data reported by the NHSLS study (see Table 11.2 on page 284), the majority of married men and women in the United States now report engaging in sexual relations either a few times per month or two to three times a week (Laumann et al., 1994). The average is seven times a month (Michael et al., 1994, p. 136).

TABLE 11.2 Median weekly frequency of marital coitus, male and female estimates combined (Kinsey and *Playboy* surveys)

KINSEY (1948, 1953)		PLAYBOY (1974)	
Age	Frequency	Age	Frequency
16–25	2.45	18–24	3.25
26–35	1.95	25–34	2.55
36–45	1.40	35–44	2.00
46–55	0.85	45–54	1.00
55–60	0.50	55 and over	1.00

Source: Hunt, M. (1974). *Sexual Behavior in the 1970's.* New York: Dell Books, p. 191.

Studies consistently find that the frequency of sexual relations declines with age (Call et al., 1995; Laumann et al., 1994). At the ages of 50–59, for example, people reported an average of four to five times per month. Regardless of a couple's age, sexual frequency also appears to decline with years of marriage (Blumstein & Schwartz, 1990).

Techniques and Duration of Coitus   In coitus, as in foreplay, the marital bed since Kinsey's day has become a stage on which the players act more varied roles. Today's couples use greater variety in coital positions. As many as 70% of Kinsey's males used the male-superior position exclusively (Kinsey et al., 1948). Perhaps three couples in ten used the female-superior position frequently. One in four or five used the lateral-entry position frequently, and about one in ten, the rear-entry position. Younger and more highly educated men showed greater variety, however. Hunt (1974), by comparison, found that three quarters of the married couples in the *Playboy* survey used the female-superior position at least occasionally. More than half had used the lateral-entry position, and about four in ten had used the rear-entry position.

An often overlooked but important difference between Kinsey's and current samples involves the length of intercourse. In Kinsey's time it was widely believed that the "virile" man ejaculated rapidly during intercourse. Kinsey estimated that most men reached orgasm within 2 minutes after penetration, many within 10 or 20 seconds. Kinsey recognized that women usually took longer to reach orgasm through coitus, and that some clinicians were already asserting that a man's ejaculation was "premature" unless he delayed it until "the female (was) ready to reach orgasm" (1948, p. 580)

Even today's less-educated couples appear to be more sophisticated than Kinsey's in their recognition of the need for sexual variety and their focus on exchanging sexual pleasure rather than rapidly reaching orgasm (Michael et al., 1994). According to the NHSLS study, the "duration of the last sexual event" of three out of four married couples was 15 minutes to an hour. Eight percent to 9% of couples exceeded an hour (Michael et al., 1994). (About one unmarried, noncohabiting couple in three made love for an hour or more, suggesting that novelty and youth have their motivational aspects.)

Sexual Satisfaction   One index by which researchers measure sexual satisfaction is orgasmic consistency. Men tend to reach orgasm more consistently than women do. After 15 years of marriage, 45% of the wives in Kinsey's study reported reaching orgasm 90% to 100% of the time. After 15 years of marriage, 12% of the wives in Kinsey's study had not experienced orgasm.

Orgasmic consistency now seems higher than in Kinsey's day. The NHSLS study found that more than 90% of the men and about 70% of women reported reaching orgasm "always" or "usually" with their primary partner during the 12 months prior to the survey (Laumann et al., 1994; Michael et al., 1994) (see Table 11.3). Three of four men (75%) and nearly three women in ten (28.6%) reported reaching orgasm on every occasion (not shown in Table 11.3). Only 2% of the married women reported never reaching orgasm with their husbands during the past year (not shown).

Women in their 40s were somewhat more likely to reach orgasm consistently than younger and older women. Perhaps women in their 40s have had more time to get in touch with their sexuality and may be more secure in their relationships as compared with younger women. Security in the relationship may promote orgasmic consistency. There do not seem to be notable racial or ethnic differences.

Orgasm is not the only criterion for measuring pleasure or satisfaction in marital sex. The NHSLS study asked participants whether they had been extremely physically satisfied with their primary partners during the past year. It is apparent, from Table 11.3, that men's and women's general physical satisfaction is comparable—about 47% and 41%, respectively. Orgasm, then, is not a guarantee of satisfaction. And lack of orgasm is not necessarily a sign of dissatisfaction.

The emotional satisfaction in a marital relationship is also linked to sexual satisfaction. Table 11.3 shows that about 40% of men and women report being extremely emotionally satisfied with their primary partners. Closer relationships are connected with more consistent orgasm.

TABLE 11.3 Sociocultural factors and sexual satisfaction in primary relationship during past year

Sociocultural Characteristics	Always or Usually Had an Orgasm with Partner		Has Been Extremely Physically Satisfied with Partner		Has Been Extremely Emotionally Satisfied with Partner	
	Men (%)	Women (%)	Men (%)	Women (%)	Men (%)	Women (%)
Age						
18–24	92	61	44	44	41	39
25–29	94	71	50	39	46	40
30–39	97	70	45	41	39	38
40–49	97	78	44	42	38	42
50–59	91	73	53	32	52	32
Marital Status						
Noncohabiting	94	62	39	40	32	31
Cohabiting	95	68	44	46	35	44
Married	95	75	52	41	49	42
Race/Ethnicity*						
White (non-Hispanic)	96	70	47	40	43	38
African American	90	72	43	44	43	38
Hispanic American	96	68	51	39	43	39

*The numbers of Asian Americans and Native Americans were too small to report reliable statistics.

Source: Combined from Laumann, E. O., Gagnon, J. H., Michael, R. T., & Michaels, S. (1994). *The Social Organization of Sexuality: Sexual Practices in the United States.* Chicago: University of Chicago Press, Table 3.7, pp. 116–117, and Michael, R. T., Gagnon, J. H., Laumann, E. O., & Kolata, G. (1994). *Sex in America: A Definitive Survey.* Boston: Little, Brown, Table 9, pp. 128–129.

Sexual Satisfaction. Marital closeness is linked to sexual satisfaction. Perhaps sexual pleasure contributes to marital closeness, or perhaps closeness helps couples achieve greater sexual satisfaction.

Extramarital Sex

Extramarital sex

Sexual relations between a married person and someone other than his or her spouse.

Conventional adultery

Extramarital sex that is kept clandestine (hidden) from one's spouse.

Consensual adultery

Extramarital sex that is engaged in openly with the knowledge and consent of one's spouse.

Swinging

A form of consensual adultery in which both spouses share extramarital sexual experiences. Also referred to as *mate-swapping*.

Extramarital sex (or "affairs") is usually conducted without the spouse's knowledge or approval. Such clandestine affairs are referred to as **conventional adultery,** infidelity, or simply "cheating." Some extramarital affairs are "one-night stands." Others persist for years.

In **consensual adultery,** extramarital relationships are conducted openly with the knowledge and consent of the partner and sometimes even with the partner's participation, as in **swinging.**

Some people engage in extramarital sex for variety (Lamanna & Riedmann, 1997). Some have affairs to break the routine of a confining marriage. Others enter affairs for reasons similar to the nonsexual reasons adolescents often have for coitus: as a way of expressing hostility toward a spouse or retaliating for injustice. Husbands and wives who engage in affairs often report that they are not satisfied with, or fulfilled by, their marital relationships.

Sometimes the sexual motive is less pressing than the desire for emotional closeness. Some women say they are seeking someone whom they could talk to or communicate with (Lamanna & Riedmann, 1997). Curiosity and desire for personal growth were more prominent motives for affairs than marital dissatisfaction. Middle-aged people may have affairs to boost their self-esteem or prove that they are still attractive.

Men (whether single, married, or cohabiting) are generally more approving of extramarital affairs than are women (Glass & Wright, 1992). Men who have had affairs are more likely to cite a need for sexual excitement as a justification than women are—75% versus 55% (Glass & Wright, 1992). Women are less accepting of sex without emotional involvement (Townsend, 1995). Women are more likely to cite "falling in love" as a justification for their affairs than do men: 77% versus 43%. These data support the widely held view that "men separate sex and love; women appear to believe that love and sex go together and that falling in love justifies sexual involvement" (Glass & Wright, 1992, p. 361).

Patterns of Extramarital Sex How many people "cheat" on their spouses? Viewers of TV talk shows may get the impression that everyone cheats, but surveys paint a different picture. In a study conducted between 1988 and 1992 by the respected National Opinion Research Center, 21% of the husbands and 12% of the wives acknowledged marital infidelity ("Cheating," 1993). More than 90% of the married women and 75% of the married men in the NHSLS study reported remaining loyal to their spouses (Laumann et al., 1994). The vast majority of those who were cohabiting also reported that they were loyal to their partners while they were living together (Laumann et al., 1994).

Having presented the percentages of reported extramarital sex, let us note one compelling limitation to these data. These reports cannot be verified. People may be reluctant to reveal they have "cheated" on their spouses even when they are assured of anonymity. There is likely to be an overall tendency to underreport the incidence of extramarital sex.

Attitudes Toward Extramarital Sex   The sexual revolution does not seem to have changed attitudes toward extramarital sex. Most people in the United States disapprove of it. Eighty percent to 98% of the *Playboy* sample reported that they would object to their mates' engaging in affairs (Hunt, 1974). Moreover, only 20% of those in the sample who reported having had affairs said that their mates were aware of them. Most married couples espouse the value of monogamy as the cornerstone of their marital relationship (Blumstein & Schwartz, 1990).

Effects of Extramarital Sex   The discovery of infidelity can evoke a range of emotional responses. The spouse may be filled with anger, jealousy, even shame. Feelings of inadequacy and doubts about one's attractiveness and desirability may surface. Infidelity may be seen by the betrayed spouse as a serious breach of trust and intimacy. Marriages that are not terminated in the wake of the disclosure may survive in a damaged condition (Charny & Parnass, 1995).

The harm an affair does to a marriage may reflect the meaning of the affair to the individual and his or her spouse. If a person has an affair because the marriage is deeply troubled, the affair may be one more factor that speeds its dissolution. The effects on the marriage may depend on the nature of the affair. It may be easier to understand that a spouse has fallen prey to an isolated, unplanned encounter than to accept an extended affair (Charny & Parnass, 1995). In some cases the discovery of infidelity stimulates the couple to work to improve their relationship. If the extramarital activity continues, however, it may undermine the couple's efforts to restore their relationship.

Divorce

Nearly half of the marriages in the United States end in divorce (Davies & Cummings, 1994; Laumann et al., 1994). The divorce rate in the United States rose steadily through much of the twentieth century (see Figure 11.3) before leveling off in the 1980s. About one quarter (26%) of children below the age of 18 live in single-parent households (Barringer, 1991). Divorced women outnumber divorced men, in part because men are more likely to remarry following divorce (Saluter, 1992).

The relaxation of legal restrictions on divorce, especially the introduction of the so-called no-fault divorce, has made divorces easier to obtain. Until the mid-1960s, adultery

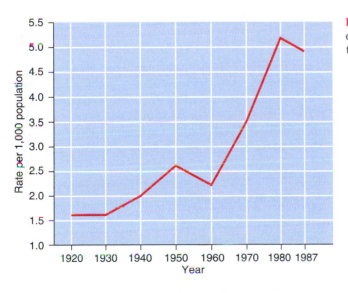

Figure 11.3.   Divorce Rates in the United States. The divorce rate in the United States rose steadily through much of the twentieth century before leveling off in the 1980s.

was the only legal grounds for divorce in New York State. Other states were equally strict. But now no-fault divorce laws have been enacted in nearly every state, allowing a divorce to be granted without a finding of marital misconduct. The increased economic independence of women has also contributed to the rising divorce rate. More women today have the economic means of breaking away from a troubled marriage. Today, more people consider marriage an alterable condition than in prior generations. People today hold higher expectations of marriage than did their parents or grandparents. They expect it to be personally fulfilling as well as meet the traditional expectation of marriage as an institution for rearing children. The most common reasons given for a divorce today are problems in communication and a lack of understanding. Years ago it was more likely to be lack of financial support.

The Cost of Divorce   Divorce is often associated with financial and emotional problems. When a household splits, the resources often cannot maintain the earlier standard of living for each partner. A woman who has not pursued a career may struggle to compete with younger, more experienced workers. Divorced mothers often face the combined stress of the sole responsibility for rearing their children (women receive custody in the majority of divorce cases) and the need to increase their incomes to make ends meet. Divorced fathers may also find it difficult to pay alimony and child support while attempting to establish a new lifestyle.

Divorce may also prompt feelings of failure as a spouse and parent, loneliness and uncertainty about the future, and depression. Married people appear to be better able to cope with the stresses and strains of life, perhaps because they can rely on each other for emotional support. Divorced and separated people have the highest rates of physical and mental illness in the population (Bloom et al., 1978; Nevid et al., 1997). Divorced people also have higher rates of suicide than married people (Trovato, 1986). On the other hand, divorce may be a time of personal growth and renewal. It can provide an opportunity for people to take stock of themselves and establish a new, more rewarding life for themselves.

Although children suffer in a divorce, marital conflict also causes problems for children (Amato & Keith, 1991; Davies & Cummings, 1994). Marital relations spill over into parent–child relations and affect children's behavior (Erel & Burman, 1995). Boys tend to show greater problems in adjusting to conflict or divorce, such as conduct problems at school and increased anxiety and dependence (Grych & Fincham, 1993; Holden & Ritchie, 1991). Children's adjustment is enhanced when parents maintain their parenting responsibilities and set aside their differences long enough to agree upon child-rearing practices (Wallerstein & Blakeslee, 1989).

Despite the difficulties in adjusting to a divorce, most divorced people eventually bounce back. Many remarry. Among older people, divorced men are more likely than divorced women to remarry—in part because men usually die earlier than women (and so fewer prospective husbands are available), in part because older men tend to remarry younger women.

Remarriages are even more likely than first marriages to end in divorce (Lown & Dolan, 1988). One reason is the selection factor. That is, divorced people may be less inclined than others to persist in a troubled marriage. Many divorced people who remarry are also encumbered with alimony and child-support payments that strain their new marriages. Many bring children from their earlier marriages to their new ones.

By the beginning of the next century, the stepfamily may be the most common family unit in the United States (CBS News, 1991). Six of ten stepfamilies eventually disband, often under the weight of the financial and emotional pressures of coping with the demands of a reconstituted family (CBS News, 1991).

Sex in the Later Years

Which is the fastest growing segment of the U.S. population? People age 65 and older. More than 30 million people in the United States are senior citizens, and their number is growing fast.

Researchers find that sexual daydreaming, sex drive, and sexual activity tend to decline with age, whereas negative sexual attitudes tend to increase (Purifoy et al., 1992). However, research does not support the belief that people lose their sexuality as they age. Nearly all (95%) of the older people in one sample reported that they liked sex, and 75% reported that orgasm was essential to their sexual fulfillment (Starr & Weiner, 1981). People who are exposed to cultural views that sex among older people is deviant may renounce sex as they age, however. Those who remain sexually active may be bothered by guilt (Reiss, 1988).

Sexual activity among older people, as among other groups, is influenced not only by physical structures and changes, but by psychological well-being, feelings of intimacy (Shaw, 1994), and cultural expectations.

Physical Changes

Although many older people retain the capacity to respond sexually, physical changes do occur as the years pass (see Table 11.4). If we are aware of them, we will not view them as abnormal or find ourselves unprepared to cope with them. Many potential problems can be averted by changing our expectations or making some changes to accommodate the aging process.

Changes in the Female   Many of the physical changes in women stem from decline in the production of estrogen around the time of menopause. The vaginal walls lose much elasticity and the thick, corrugated texture of the childbearing years. They grow paler and thinner. Coitus may become irritating. The thinning of the walls may also place greater pressure against the bladder and urethra during coitus, leading in some cases to urinary urgency and burning urination.

The vagina also shrinks in size. The labia majora lose much of their fatty deposits and become thin. The introitus becomes relatively constricted, and penile entry may become somewhat difficult. This "problem" has a positive aspect: increased friction between the penis and vaginal walls may heighten sexual sensations. The body of the uterus decreases in size after menopause and no longer becomes so congested during sexual arousal. Following menopause, women also produce less vaginal lubrication, and the lubrication that is produced may take minutes, not seconds, to appear. Lack of adequate lubrication is also a major reason for painful coitus.

Many of these changes may be slowed or reversed through estrogen-replacement therapy. Natural lubrication may also be increased through more elaborate foreplay. The need

---

TABLE 11.4 Changes in sexual arousal often associated with aging

Changes in the Female	Changes in the Male
Reduced myotonia (muscle tension)	Longer time to erection and orgasm
Reduced vaginal lubrication	Need for more direct stimulation for erection and orgasm
Reduced elasticity of the vaginal walls	Less semen emitted during ejaculation
Smaller increases in breast size during sexual arousal	Erections may be less firm
Reduced intensity of muscle spasms at orgasm	Testicles may not elevate as high into scrotum
	Less intense orgasmic contractions
	Lessened feeling of a need to ejaculate during sex
	Longer refractory period

Source: Copyright © 1990 by The Kinsey Institute for Research in Sex, Gender, and Reproduction. From THE KINSEY INSTITUTE NEW REPORT ON SEX. Reprinted with permission from St. Martin's Press, New York, NY.

Sexuality and Aging. Despite stereotypes that stigmatize older people who are sexually active as abnormal or deviant, it is normal for older people to have sexual urges and maintain an active sex life.

for more foreplay may encourage the man to become a more considerate lover. (He too will likely need more time to become aroused.) An artificial lubricant may also ease problems posed by difficult entry or painful thrusting.

Women's breasts show smaller increases in size with sexual arousal as they age, but the nipples still become erect. Because the muscle tone of the urethra and anal sphincters decreases, the spasms of orgasm become less powerful and fewer in number. They may feel less intense. The uterine contractions that occur during orgasm may become discouragingly painful for some postmenopausal women. Despite these changes, women can retain their ability to achieve orgasm well into their advanced years. The subjective experience of orgasm also remains highly satisfying, despite the lessened intensity of muscular contractions.

Changes in the Male Age-related changes tend to occur more gradually in men than in women and are not clearly connected with any one biological event, as they are with menopause in the woman. Male adolescents may achieve erection in a matter of seconds through sexual fantasy alone. After about age 50, men take progressively longer to achieve erection. Erections become less firm, perhaps because of lowered testosterone production. Older men may require minutes of direct stimulation of the penis to achieve an erection. Couples can adjust to these changes by extending the length and variety of foreplay.

Most men remain capable of erection throughout their lives. Erectile dysfunction is not inevitable with aging. Men generally require more time to reach orgasm as they age, however, which may also reflect lowered testosterone production. In the eyes of their sex partners, however, delayed ejaculation may make them better lovers.

The testes may decrease slightly in size and produce less testosterone. Testosterone production usually declines gradually from about age 40 to age 60 and then begins to level off. Sperm production tends to decline as the seminiferous tubules degenerate, but viable sperm may be produced quite late in life. Men in their 70s, 80s, and even 90s have fathered children.

Nocturnal erections tend to diminish in intensity, duration, and frequency as men age, but they do not normally disappear in healthy men (Reinisch, 1990; Schiavi et al., 1990). The refractory period tends to lengthen. An adolescent may require only a few minutes to regain erection and ejaculate again after a first orgasm, whereas a man in his 30s may require half an hour. Past age 50, the refractory period may increase to several hours.

Older men produce less ejaculate, and it may seep rather than shoot out. Though the contractions of orgasm still begin at 0.8-second intervals, they become weaker and fewer. Still, the number and strength of spasms do not translate precisely into subjective pleasure.

An older male may enjoy orgasm as thoroughly as he did at a younger age. Attitudes and expectations can be as important as the contractions themselves.

Following orgasm, erection subsides more rapidly than it does in a younger man. A study of 65 healthy men ages 45 to 74 showed an age-related decline in sexual desire, arousal, and activity. Yet there were no differences between younger and older men in level of sexual satisfaction or enjoyment (Schiavi et al., 1990).

In sum, most physical changes do not bring a man's or a woman's sex life to a grinding halt. People's attitudes, sexual histories, and partners are usually more important factors in sexual behavior and enjoyment.

Sexual Behavior

Despite the decline in certain physical functions, older people can continue to lead a vibrant, fulfilling sex life. In fact, years of sexual experience may more than compensate for any diminution of physical responsiveness (Hodson & Skeen, 1994). In one survey of 800 people in the United States, ages 60 through 91, nearly three out of four who had remained sexually active reported that lovemaking had become more rewarding over the years (Starr & Weiner, 1981). Unfortunately, people who overreact to expected changes in sexual response may conclude that their sex lives are over and give up on sexual activity or even on expressing any physical affection (Reinisch, 1990).

Ninety-four percent of the men and 84% of the women in Kinsey's samples remained sexually active at the age of 60. Half of the 60- to 91-year-olds surveyed by Starr and Weiner (1981) reported sexual relations on a regular basis; and half of these, at least once a week. A study of 200 healthy 80- to 102-year olds reported that 30% of the women and 62% of the men still engaged in intercourse (Bretschneider & McCoy, 1988). A study of 100 older men in England found that the key factor in whether they continued to engage in sexual activity was the availability of a partner—not physical condition (Jones et al., 1994).

Couples may accommodate to the physical changes of aging by broadening their sexual repertoire to include more diverse forms of stimulation. Many respondents to a *Consumer Reports* survey reported using oral–genital stimulation, sexual fantasy, sexually explicit materials, anal stimulation, vibrators, and other sexual techniques to offset problems in achieving lubrication or erection (Brecher, 1984).

The availability of a sexually interested and supportive partner may be the most important determinant of continued sexual activity. Many women discontinue sexual activity because of the death of their husbands.

Sex and Disability

Like older people, people with disabilities (especially those whose physical disabilities render them dependent on others) are often seen as sexless and childlike (Nosek et al., 1994). Such views are based on misconceptions about the sexual functioning of people with disabilities. Some of these myths and stereotypes may be eroding, however, in part due to the success of the civil and social rights movements of the disabled in the 1970s and the attention focused on the sexuality of people with disabilities in films such as *Coming Home, Born on the Fourth of July,* and *My Left Foot.*

A person may have been born with or acquire a bodily impairment, or suffer a loss of function or a disfiguring change in appearance. Although the disability may require the person to make adjustments in order to perform sexually, most people with disabilities have the same sexual needs, feelings, and desires as people without disabilities. Their ability to express their sexual feelings and needs depends on the physical limitations imposed by their disabilities, their adjustment to their disabilities, and the availability of partners. The establishment of mature sexual relationships generally demands some distance from one's parents. Therefore, persons with disabilities who are physically dependent on their parents may find it especially difficult to develop sexual relationships (Knight, 1989).

Physical Disabilities

According to Margaret Nosek and her colleagues (1994), sexual wellness, even among the disabled, involves five factors:

- Positive sexual self-concept; seeing oneself as valuable sexually and as a person
- Knowledge about sexuality
- Positive, productive relationships
- Coping with barriers to sexuality (social, environmental, physical, and emotional)
- Maintaining the best possible general and sexual health, given one's limitations

This model applies to all of us, of course. Let us now consider aspects of specific physical disabilities and human sexuality.

Cerebral palsy
A muscular disorder that is caused by damage to the central nervous system (usually prior to or during birth) and characterized by spastic paralysis.

Cerebral Palsy   **Cerebral palsy** does not generally impair sexual interest, capacity for orgasm, or fertility (Reinisch, 1990). Depending on the nature and degree of muscle spasticity or lack of voluntary muscle control, however, afflicted people may be limited to certain types of sexual activities and coital positions.

People with disabilities such as cerebral palsy often suffer social rejection during adolescence and perceive themselves as unfit or unworthy of intimate sexual relationships, especially with people who are not disabled. They are often socialized into an asexual role. Sensitive counseling can help them understand and accept their sexuality, promote a more positive body image, and provide the social skills to establish intimate relationships (Edmonson, 1988).

Sex and Disabled People.
Most people with disabilities have the same sexual needs, feelings, and desires as people without disabilities. They are capable of expressing their sexuality in ways that can be pleasurable for themselves and their partners.

Spinal-Cord Injuries Spinal-cord injuries affect about 6,000 to 10,000 people annually in the United States (Seftel et al., 1991). The majority of persons who suffer disabling spinal-cord injuries are young, active males. Automobile or pedestrian accidents account for about half of these cases. Other common causes include stabbing or bullet wounds, sports injuries, and falls. Depending on the location of the injury to the spinal cord, a loss of voluntary control (paralysis) can occur in either the legs (*paraplegia*) or all four limbs (*quadriplegia*). A loss of sensation may also occur in parts of the body that lie beneath the site of injury.

The effect of spinal-cord injuries on sexual response depends on the site and severity of the injury. Overall, researchers find that about three of four men with spinal-cord injuries are able to achieve erections, but only about one in ten continues to ejaculate naturally (Geiger, 1981; Spark, 1991). Others can be helped to ejaculate with the aid of a vibrator (Szasz & Carpenter, 1989).

Women may lose the ability to experience genital sensations or to lubricate normally during sexual stimulation. However, breast sensations may remain intact, making this area even more erotogenic. Most women with spinal-cord injuries can engage in coitus, become impregnated, and deliver vaginally. A survey of 27 spinal-cord-injured women showed that about half were able to experience orgasm (Kettl et al., 1991). Some also report "phantom orgasms" that provide intense psychological pleasure and that are accompanied by non-genital physical sensations similar to those experienced by nondisabled women (Perduta-Fulginiti, 1992). Spinal-cord-injured women can heighten their sexual pleasure by learning to use fantasized orgasm, orgasmic imagery, and amplification of their physical sensations (Perduta-Fulginiti, 1992).

Couples facing the challenge of spinal-cord injury may expand their sexual repertoire to focus less on genital stimulation (except to attain the reflexes of erection and lubrication) and more on the parts of the body that retain sensation. Stimulation of some areas of the body, such as the ears, the neck, and the breasts (in both men and women) can yield pleasurable erotic sensations (Knight, 1989; Seftel et al., 1991).

Sensory Disabilities Sensory disabilities, such as blindness or deafness, do not directly affect genital responsiveness. Still, sexuality may be affected in many ways. A person who has been blind since birth or early childhood may have difficulty understanding a partner's anatomy. Sex-education curricula have been designed specifically to enable visually impaired people to learn about sexual anatomy via models. Anatomically correct dolls may be used to simulate positions of intercourse.

Deaf persons, too, often lack knowledge about sex. Their ability to comprehend the social cues involved in forming and maintaining intimate relationships may also be impaired. Sex-education programs based on sign language are helping many hearing-impaired people become more socially perceptive as well as knowledgeable about the physical aspects of sex. Persons with visual and hearing impairments often lack self-esteem and self-confidence, which makes it difficult for them to establish intimate relationships. Sexual counseling may help them become more aware of their sexuality and develop social skills.

Arthritis
A progressive disease that is characterized by inflammation or pain in the joints.

Other Physical Disabilities and Impairments Specific disabilities pose particular challenges to, and limitations on, sexual functioning. **Arthritis** may make it difficult or painful for sufferers to bend their arms, knees, and hips during sexual activity (Ehrlich, 1988). Coital positions that minimize discomfort and the application of moist heat to the joints before sexual relations may be helpful.

A male amputee may find that he is better balanced in the lateral or female-superior position than in the male-superior position (Knight, 1989). A woman with limited hand function may find it difficult or impossible to insert a diaphragm and may need to request assistance from her partner or switch to another contraceptive (Cole, 1988). Sensitivity to each other's needs is as vital to couples in which one member has a disability as it is to nondisabled couples.

Psychological Disabilities

Persons with psychological disabilities, such as mental retardation, are often stereotyped as incapable of understanding their sexual impulses. Retarded people are sometimes assumed to maintain childlike innocence through their lives, or to be devoid of sexuality. Some stereotype retarded people in the opposite direction: as having stronger-than-normal sex drives and being incapable of controlling them (Reinisch, 1990). Some mentally retarded people do act inappropriately—by masturbating publicly, for example. The stereotypes are exaggerated, however, and even many of those who act inappropriately can be trained to follow social rules (Reinisch, 1990).

Parents and caretakers often discourage retarded people from learning about their sexuality or teach them to deny or suppress their sexual feelings. Although the physical changes of puberty may be delayed in mentally retarded people, most develop normal sexual needs (Edmonson, 1988). Most are capable of learning about their sexuality and can be guided into rewarding and responsible intimate relationships.

One of the greatest impediments to sexual fulfillment among people with disabilities is finding a loving and supportive partner. Some people engage in sexual relations with people with disabilities out of sympathy. By and large, however, the partners are other people with disabilities or nondisabled people who have overcome stereotypes that portray disabled people as undesirable.

Chapter Review

Childhood

Boys (1: Are *or* Are not?) born with the capacity for erections. There (2: Is *or* Is not?) also evidence of lubrication and genital swelling in newborn girls. Kinsey and his colleagues noted that babies (3: Do *or* Do not?) show behaviors that resemble orgasm during the first year after birth. Masturbation tends to start (4: During *or* After?) the first year. Children in the United States typically begin to engage in genital play with others at about the age of (5) _____.

Sex games like "show" and "playing doctor" become common at about the age of (6) _____. Sexual play with children of the same gender (7: Is *or* Is not?) a predictor of adult sexual orientation.

During (8) pre_____ children typically form relationships with a close "best friend" that enable them to share secrets and confidences. Preadolescents tend to prefer friends of the (9: Same *or* Other?) gender. Preadolescents grow (10: More *or* Less?) self-conscious about their bodies. Kinsey and his colleagues reported that (11) _____tion is the primary means of achieving orgasm during preadolescence. (12) G_____

dating and parties often provide preadolescents with their first exposure to heterosexual activities. Much preadolescent sexual activity with members of the same gender is (13) _____tion.

Studies show that in the United States, (14) _____rs are the main source of sexual information. A 1995 ABC News *Nightline* poll found that most Americans believe that sex-education programs should teach students to use (15) _____tives if they are going to engage in premarital sexual activity (91%), that (16) _____ms can prevent AIDS (85%), and that early sex is a bad idea (80%).

Adolescence

Adolescence is bounded by the advent of (17) p_____ and the capacity to take on adult responsibilities. Many adolescents are in (18) c_____ with their families about "going around" with certain friends, sex, and using the family car. (19) Me_____ is the onset of menstruation. Puberty begins with the appearance of (20) _____ary sex characteristics and ends when the long bones make no further gains in length. Toward the end of puberty, (21) re_____ becomes possible. The two main markers of reproductive potential are menarche in the girl and the first (22) _____tion in the boy. Menarche may be triggered by the accumulation of a certain percentage of body (23) _____t.

Between 8 and 14 years of age, release of FSH by the (24) p_____ gland causes the ovaries to begin to secrete estrogen. (25) _____gen stimulates the growth of breast tissue, the uterus, and fatty tissue in the hips and buttocks. (26) _____gens produced by the female's adrenal glands stimulate development of pubic and underarm hair. Girls cannot become pregnant until (27) _____tion occurs, which may lag behind menarche by two years.

FSH and LH stimulate the testes to increase their output of (28) _____one. Testosterone prompts growth of the male genitals and differentiation of male (29) _____ary sex characteristics, such as the growth of facial, body, and pubic hair. Mature sperm are not usually found in the ejaculate until about a year after the first (30) _____tion. About a year after first ejaculation, boys may begin (31) noc_____ _____sions, which are also called "wet dreams."

Boys and girls undergo general (32) g_____ spurts during puberty. Many boys experiences temporary enlargement of the breasts, or (33) gyn_____, during puberty, which is caused by estrogen.

(34) _____tion is a major sexual outlet during adolescence. (35: Boys or Girls?) are more likely to report masturbating. (36: Most or Only a few?) teens have at least some feelings of guilt over masturbation. Teens who begin dating (37: Earlier or Later?) are more likely to engage in coitus during high school. The incidence of premarital oral sex has (38: Increased or Decreased?) since Kinsey's time. Kinsey and his colleagues found a much greater incidence of premarital coitus among (39: Men or Women?). Common reasons for first intercourse include (40) cur_____ and the natural expression of love. Family influences and religious values (41: Are or Are not?) important determinants of adolescent sexual experience. African American teenagers become sexually active two years (42: Earlier or Later?), on the average, than White teenagers. Asian American and Hispanic American college students are (43: More or Less?) conservative sexually than African American or (non-Hispanic) White American students.

Children whose parents are separated or divorced are (44: More or Less?) likely than those from intact homes to engage in premarital intercourse. Teens who feel that they can talk to their parents are (45: More or Less?) likely to engage in coitus than those who describe communication with their parents as poor.

About (46) _____% of American girls of ages 15 to 19 become pregnant each year. The rate of births for teenagers has been (47: Rising or Dropping?) during the 1990s. African American teenagers have the (48: Highest or Lowest?) birth rate overall.

Adulthood

The numbers of single young people in our society have been (49: Increasing or Decreasing?). (50: More or Fewer?) people are postponing marriage to pursue educational and career goals than in previous generations. (51: More or Less?) social stigma is attached to remaining single today. Most single people practice (52) ser_____ _____gamy. So-called (53) _____ing singles pursue casual sexual encounters. Nuns and priests choose to remain (54) ce_____ for religious reasons.

The term (55) _____tion applies to unmarried couples who live together. In recent years, society has become (56: More or Less?) tolerant of cohabitation. Cohabitation is more prevalent among (57: More or Less?) well educated and (58: More or Less?) affluent people. Divorced people are (59: More or Less?) likely than people who never married to subsequently cohabit. Willingness to cohabit is related to (60: Traditional or Nontraditional?) attitudes toward sexual behavior, marriage, and gender roles. Cohabitors who later marry may run a (61: Greater or Lesser?) risk of divorce than noncohabitors.

The average age of first marriage has been (62: Rising or Declining?) steadily over the past few decades. People in our culture tend to marry partners from (63: The same or Another?) geographical area and social class. The concept of "like marrying like" is termed (64) _____gamy. Yet some marriages show a (65) ma_____ _____ent, in which an economically established older man marries an attractive, younger woman.

Compared to Kinsey's samples from the late 1930s and 1940s, married couples today engage in coitus with (66: More or Less?) frequency, variety, and sexual satisfaction. The development of effective contraceptives separated sex from (67) _____tion. According to the NHSLS study, the average married couple engage in sexual relations (68) _____ times a month. Among married couples, the frequency of sexual relations (69: Increases *or* Declines?) with age. Women in their 40s are (70: More *or* Less?) likely to reach orgasm consistently than younger and older women.

Secret extramarital affairs are referred to as (71) con_____ _____tery. In (72) con_____ adultery, extramarital relationships are conducted openly with the knowledge and sometimes participation of the partner. In (73) _____ing, both spouses share extramarital sexual experiences. Men are generally (74: More *or* Less?) approving of affairs than women are. Women are (75: More *or* Less?) more likely to cite "falling in love" as a justification for affairs than men are. Most people in the United States (76: Approve *or* Disapprove?) of affairs.

The divorce rate in the United States (77: Rose *or* Declined?) steadily through much of the twentieth century. Now no-fault divorces are available, but until the mid-1960s, (78) ad_____ was the only legal grounds for divorce in New York State. The most common reasons given today for divorce are problems in (79) _____tion and lack of understanding. (80: Boys *or* Girls?) tend to show greater problems in adjusting to parental conflict or divorce. Remarriages are (81: More *or* Less?) likely than first marriages to end in divorce.

Sex in the Later Years

Sexual activity (82: Rises *or* Declines?) with age. The great majority of older people report that they (83: Do *or* Do not?) like sex. Many of the physical changes in women stem from decline in estrogen production at (84) _____use. The vaginal walls become (85: More *or* Less?) elastic. Following menopause,

women produce (86: More *or* Less?) vaginal lubrication. Many of these changes may be slowed or reversed through (87) hor_____-_____ment therapy. In late adulthood, men attain erections (88: More *or* Less?) rapidly. Erectile dysfunction (89: Is *or* Is not?) inevitable with aging. As men age, the (90) _____tory period following orgasm lengthens. Despite physical changes, there (91: Are *or* Are no?) differences between younger and older men in level of sexual satisfaction or enjoyment. The availability of a sexually interested and supportive (92) p_____ may be the most important determinant of continued sexual activity.

Sex and Disability

Most people with disabilities (93: Do *or* Do not?) have sexual needs, feelings, and desires. Cerebral palsy (94: Does *or* Does not?) generally impair sexual interest, capacity for orgasm, or fertility. The effect of (95) sp_____-_____rd injury on sexual response depends on the site and severity of the injury. The majority of men with spinal-cord injuries are able to achieve (96) _____tions, but only about one in ten continues to ejaculate naturally. Women with spinal-cord injuries may lose the ability to experience sexual (97) _____tions or to lubricate. (98: Most *or* Only a few?) women with spinal-cord injuries can engage in coitus, become impregnated, and deliver vaginally.

Persons with mental (99) re_____ are often stereotyped as incapable of understanding their sexual impulses. Most retarded people (100: Are *or* Are not?) capable of learning about their sexuality. One of the greatest impediments to sexual fulfillment among people with disabilities is finding a loving and supportive (101) p_____.

Chapter Quiz

1. According to Kinsey and his colleagues, children first engage in behaviors that resemble orgasm
   (a) during the first year.
   (b) between the ages of 2 and 5.
   (c) between the ages of 5 and 8.
   (d) between the ages of 8 and adolescence.
2. All of the following are true about teenage pregnancy in the United States EXCEPT

   (a) about 10% of teenage girls ages 15 to 19 become pregnant each year.
   (b) about 40% of teenage pregnancies end in abortion.
   (c) African American teenagers are more likely than White teenagers to become pregnant.
   (d) babies born to teenage mothers are healthier than babies born to mothers in their 20s.

3. Most people in the United States first learn about the "facts of life" (reproduction) from
   (a) school sex-education programs.
   (b) popular media—TV, movies, magazines, and the like.
   (c) friends.
   (d) parents.
4. Puberty ends
   (a) with the appearance of primary sex characteristics.
   (b) with the appearance of secondary sex characteristics.
   (c) when people take on adult responsibilities.
   (d) when the long bones make no further gains in length.
5. Estrogen is the main cause of all of the following EXCEPT
   (a) growth of the uterus.
   (b) growth of fatty and supporting tissue in the breasts and buttocks.
   (c) growth of underarm and pubic hair.
   (d) thickening of the vaginal lining.
6. Which of the following is connected with abstaining from premarital sexual intercourse among teenagers?
   (a) Curiosity about sex.
   (b) High educational goals.
   (c) Peer pressure.
   (d) Poor communcation with one's parents.
7. All of the following are connected with getting married at later ages today EXCEPT
   (a) living together first to test compatibility.
   (b) the desire of many women to focus on careers during the 20s.
   (c) social pressure to remain single.
   (d) lengthy educations.
8. The text suggests that people who cohabit before getting married are more likely to get divorced later on because of
   (a) selection factors.
   (b) recognition that they were incompatible.
   (c) traditional religious values.
   (d) societal condemnation of cohabitation.
9. According to the text, all of the following have contributed to the high divorce rate in the United States EXCEPT
   (a) higher expectations from marriage.
   (b) relaxation of legal restrictions on divorce.
   (c) the increased economic independence of women.
   (d) sexual dysfunctions.
10. In late adulthood
   (a) men's testes increase slightly in size.
   (b) most men do not remain capable of erection.
   (c) most men still like sex.
   (d) testosterone production increases.

Answers to Chapter Review

1. Are	21. Reproduction	42. Earlier	63. The same	83. Do
2. Is	22. Ejaculation	43. More	64. *Homogamy*	84. Menopause
3. Do	23. Fat	44. More	65. Mating gradient	85. Less
4. During	24. Pituitary	45. Less	66. More	86. Less
5. 2	25. Estrogen	46. 10	67. Reproduction	87. Hormone-
6. Any answer from 6	26. Androgens	47. Dropping	68. Seven	replacement
to 10	27. Ovulation	48. Highest	69. Declines	88. Less
7. Is not	28. Testosterone	49. Increasing	70. More	89. Is not
8. Preadolescence	29. Secondary	50. More	71. Conventional	90. Refractory
9. Same	30. Ejaculation	51. Less	adultery	91. Are no
10. More	31. Nocturnal emissions	52. Serial monogamy	72. Consensual	92. Partner
11. Masturbation	32. Growth	53. Swinging	73. Swinging	93. Do
12. Group	33. Gynecomastia	54. Celibate	74. More	94. Does not
13. Exploration	34. Masturbation	55. *Cohabitation*	75. More	95. Spinal-cord
14. Peers	35. Boys	56. More	76. Disapprove	96. Erections
15. Contraceptives	36. Most	57. Less	77. Rose	97. Sensations
16. Condoms	37. Earlier	58. Less	78. Adultery	98. Most
17. Puberty	38. Increased	59. More	79. Communication	99. Retardation
18. Conflict	39. Men	60. Nontraditional	80. Boys	100. Are
19. Menarche	40. Curiosity	61. Greater	81. More	101. Partner
20. Secondary	41. Are	62. Rising	82. Declines	

Answers to Chapter Quiz

1. (a)	3. (c)	5. (c)	7. (c)	9. (d)
2. (d)	4. (d)	6. (b)	8. (a)	10. (c)

CHAPTER 12

Sexual Dysfunctions

OUTLINE

Types of Sexual Dysfunctions
Sexual Desire Disorders
Sexual Arousal Disorders
Orgasmic Disorders
Sexual Pain Disorders

Origins of Sexual Dysfunctions
Organic Causes
Psychosocial Causes

Treatment of Sexual Dysfunctions
The Masters and Johnson Approach
The Helen Singer Kaplan Approach
Treatment of Sexual Desire Disorders

Treatment of Sexual Arousal Disorders
Treatment of Orgasmic Disorders
Treatment of Sexual Pain Disorders
Evaluation of Sex Therapy
Biological Treatments of Premature Ejaculation and Erectile Disorder

Chapter Review

Chapter Quiz

A World of Diversity
Inis Beag and Mangaia—Worlds Apart

Applications
Finding a Qualified Sex Therapist

- About one woman in three reports being uninterested in sex?
- About three men in ten report reaching climax too soon?
- The most common cause of painful intercourse in women is inadequate vaginal lubrication?
- Many people have difficulty performing sexually and then find that anxiety over performance makes it yet more difficult to perform the next time?
- In sex therapy, men with erectile disorder are taught that they should not *try* to obtain an erection?
- Many sex therapists recommend masturbation as the treatment for women who have never been able to reach orgasm?
- A man can be prevented from ejaculating by squeezing his penis when he feels that he is about to do so?
- Drugs are available to treat premature ejaculation and erectile disorder?

Sexual dysfunctions

Persistent or recurrent difficulties in becoming sexually aroused or reaching orgasm.

 exual dysfunctions are problems in becoming sexually aroused or reaching orgasm. Many of us are troubled by sexual problems from time to time. Men occasionally cannot obtain an erection, or they ejaculate more rapidly than they would like. Most women occasionally have difficulty reaching orgasm or becoming sufficiently lubricated. People are not considered to have a sexual dysfunction unless the problem is persistent and causes distress, however.

Many people with sexual dysfunctions find it difficult to talk about them, even with their spouses or helping professionals. A woman who cannot reach orgasm with her husband may fake orgasms rather than "make a fuss." A man may find it difficult to admit erectile problems to his physician during a physical. Many physicians are also uncomfortable talking about sexual matters. They may never inquire about sexual problems.

Because many people are reluctant to admit to sexual problems, we do not have precise figures on their frequencies. The best current information we have may be based on the National Health and Social Life Survey (Laumann et al., 1994) (see Table 12.1). The NHSLS group asked respondents, "During the last 12 months has there ever been a period of several months or more when you lacked interest in having sex; were unable to come to a climax; came to a climax too quickly; experienced physical pain during intercourse; did not find sex pleasurable; felt anxious about your ability to perform sexually; or (for men) had trouble achieving or maintaining an erection or (for women) had trouble lubricating?" Women reported more problems than men in the areas of painful sex, lack of pleasure, inability to reach orgasm, and lack of interest in sex. Men were more likely than women to report reaching climax too early and being anxious about their performance. Difficulty keeping an erection (erectile disorder) increases with age from about 6% in the 18- to 24-year-old age group to about 20% in the 55- to 59-year-old age group. The NHSLS figures represent persistent current problems. The incidences of occasional problems and of lifetime problems would be higher. ■

Types of Sexual Dysfunctions

The most widely used system of classification of sexual dysfunctions is based upon the American Psychiatric Association's *Diagnostic and Statistical Manual of Mental Disor-*

TABLE 12.1 Current sexual dysfunctions according to the NHSLS study (respondents reporting the problem within the past year)

	Men (%)	Women (%)
Pain during sex	3.0	14.4
Sex not pleasurable	8.1	21.2
Unable to reach orgasm	8.3	24.1
Lack of interest in sex	15.8	33.4
*Anxiety about performance**	17.0	11.5
Reaching climax too early	28.5	10.3
Unable to keep an erection	10.4	—
Having trouble lubricating	—	18.8

*Anxiety about performance is not itself a sexual dysfunction. However, it figures prominently in sexual dysfunctions.

Source: Adapted from Tables 10.8A and 10.8B, pp. 370–371, in Laumann, E. O., Gagnon, J. H., Michael, R. T., & Michaels, S. (1994). *The Social Organization of Sexuality: Sexual Practices in the United States.* Chicago: University of Chicago Press.

Sexual desire disorders
Sexual dysfunctions in which people have persistent or recurrent lack of sexual desire or aversion to sexual contact.

Sexual arousal disorders
Sexual dysfunctions in which people persistently or recurrently fail to become adequately sexually aroused to engage in or sustain sexual intercourse.

Orgasmic disorders
Sexual dysfunctions in which people persistently or recurrently have difficulty reaching orgasm or reach orgasm more rapidly than they would like, despite attaining a level of sexual stimulation of sufficient intensity to normally result in orgasm.

Sexual pain disorders
Sexual dysfunctions in which people persistently or recurrently experience pain during coitus.

Dyspareunia
A sexual dysfunction characterized by persistent or recurrent pain during sexual intercourse. (From roots meaning "badly paired.")

Vaginismus
A sexual dysfunction characterized by involuntary contraction of the muscles surrounding the vaginal barrel, preventing penile penetration or rendering penetration painful.

ders (the DSM of 1994). The DSM, which is now in its fourth edition, groups sexual dysfunctions into four categories:

1. **Sexual desire disorders.** These involve dysfunctions in sexual desire, interest, or drive, in which the person experiences a lack of sexual desire or an aversion to genital sexual contact.
2. **Sexual arousal disorders.** In men, sexual arousal disorders involve recurrent difficulty in achieving or sustaining erections sufficient to successfully engage in sexual intercourse. In women, they typically involve failure to become sufficiently lubricated.
3. **Orgasmic disorders.** Men or women may encounter difficulties achieving orgasm or may reach orgasm more rapidly than they would like. Women are more likely to have trouble reaching orgasm; men are more likely to experience overly rapid orgasm (premature ejaculation).
4. **Sexual pain disorders.** Both men and women may suffer from **dyspareunia** (painful intercourse). Women may experience **vaginismus,** which prevents penetration by the penis or renders penetration painful.

Sexual dysfunctions may also be classified as either lifelong or acquired. *Lifelong* dysfunctions have existed throughout the person's lifetime. *Acquired* dysfunctions develop following a period of normal functioning. They also may be classified as generalized or situational. *Generalized* dysfunctions affect a person's general sexual functioning. *Situational* dysfunctions affect sexual functioning only in some sexual situations (such as during coitus but not during masturbation) or occur with some partners but not with others. For example, a man may not be able to achieve an erection for sexual relations with a partner but can do so during masturbation. His dysfunction would be classified as situational.

Sexual Desire Disorders

Sexual desire disorders involve lack of sexual desire or interest or aversion to genital sexual activity. Sex therapists report an increase in their frequency over the past generation (Schmidt, 1994).

Lack of Sexual Desire   People with little or no sexual interest or desire are said to have *hypoactive sexual desire disorder*. They also often report an absence of sexual fantasies. According to the NHSLS Study (Laumann et al., 1994), the problem is more common among women than men. Nevertheless, the belief that men are always eager and willing to engage in sexual activity is no more than a myth.

Lack of sexual desire does not imply that a person is unable to achieve erection, lubricate adequately, or reach orgasm. Some people with low sexual desire do have such problems. Others can become sexually aroused and reach orgasm when stimulated adequately. Many enjoy sexual activity, even if they are unlikely to initiate it. Many appreciate the affection and closeness of physical intimacy, but have no interest in genital stimulation.

How much sexual interest or desire is "normal"? There is no standard level of sexual desire—no 98.6 degree reading on the "sexual thermometer." Lack of desire is usually considered a problem when couples recognize that their level of sexual interest has seriously declined. Sometimes the lack of desire is limited to one partner. When one member of a couple is more interested in sex than the other, sex therapists often recommend that couples try to reach a compromise. They also try to uncover and resolve problems in the relationship that may dampen sexual ardor.

Biological and psychosocial factors—hormonal deficiencies, depression, marital dissatisfaction, and so on—contribute to lack of desire. A gradual decline in sexual desire, at least among men, may be explained in part by the reduction in testosterone levels that occurs in middle and later life (Brody, 1995c). Abrupt changes in sexual desire, however, are more often explained by psychological and interpersonal factors such as depression, emotional stress, and problems in the relationship (Leiblum & Rosen, 1988; Schreiner-Engle & Schiavi, 1986). Lingering anxiety and a history of sexual assault have also been linked to low sexual desire (Letourneau & O'Donohue, 1993).

Sexual Aversion Disorder   People with low sexual desire may have little or no interest in sex, but they are not repelled by genital contact. Some people, however, find sex disgusting or aversive and avoid genital contact.

Sexual aversions are less common than lack of desire and remain poorly understood (Spark, 1991). Some researchers consider sexual aversion to be a *sexual phobia* or *sexual panic state*. It is characterized by intense, irrational fears of sexual contact and a pressing desire to avoid sexual situations (Kaplan, 1987). A history of sexual trauma, such as rape or childhood sexual abuse or incest, often figures prominently in cases of sexual aversion, especially in women.

Sexual Arousal Disorders

When we are sexually stimulated, our bodies normally respond with **vasocongestion,** which produces erection in the male and vaginal lubrication in the female. People with sexual arousal disorders, however, fail to achieve or sustain the lubrication or erection necessary to facilitate sexual activity. Or they do not feel the sexual pleasure and excitement that normally accompany sexual arousal (American Psychiatric Association, 1994).

Male Erectile Disorder   Sexual arousal disorder in the male is called **male erectile disorder** or *erectile dysfunction*. It is characterized by persistent difficulty in achieving or maintaining an erection sufficient to allow the completion of sexual activity. In most cases the failure is limited to sexual activity with partners, or with some partners and not others. It can thus be classified as *situational*. In rare cases the dysfunction is found during any sexual activity, including masturbation. In such cases, it is considered *generalized*. Some men with erectile disorder are unable to attain an erection at all. Others can achieve erection but not sustain it (or recover it) long enough for penetration and ejaculation.

Perhaps 10 to 15 million men in the United States suffer from erectile disorder (Leary, 1992). Another 10 million may suffer from partial dysfunction. The incidence of erectile disorder increases with age and is believed to affect one in three men over the age of 60. Men with *lifelong* erectile disorder never had adequate erectile functioning. Erectile disorder far more commonly develops after a period of normal functioning and is classified as *acquired erectile disorder*.

Vasocongestion
The swelling of the genital tissues with blood, which causes erection of the penis and engorgement of the area surrounding the vaginal opening.

Male erectile disorder
Persistent difficulty achieving or maintaining an erection sufficient to allow the man to engage in or complete sexual intercourse. Also termed *erectile dysfunction*.

Performance anxiety
Feelings of dread and foreboding experienced in connection with sexual activity (or any other activity that might be judged by another person).

Occasional problems in achieving or maintaining erection are quite common. Fatigue, alcohol, anxiety over impressing a new partner, and other factors may account for a transient episode. Even an isolated occurrence can lead to a persistent problem if the man fears recurrence, however. The more anxious and concerned the man becomes about his sexual ability, the more likely he is to suffer **performance anxiety.** This anxiety can contribute to repeated failure, and a vicious cycle of anxiety and failure may develop.

A man with erectile difficulties may try to "will" an erection, which can compound the problem. Each failure may further demoralize him. He may ruminate about his sexual inadequacy, setting the stage for yet more anxiety. His partner may try to comfort and support him by saying things like "It can happen to anyone," "Don't worry about it," or "It will get better in time." But attempts at reassurance may be to no avail. As one client put it,

> I always felt inferior, like I was on probation, having to prove myself. I felt like I was up against the wall. You can't imagine how embarrassing this (erectile failure) was. It's like you walk out in front of an audience that you think is a nudist convention and it turns out to be a tuxedo convention.

(The Authors' Files)

The vicious cycle of anxiety and erectile failure may be interrupted if the man does not overreact to occasional problems. The emphasis in our culture on men's sexual prowess may spur them to view occasional failures as catastrophes rather than transient disappointments, however.

Performance anxiety is a prominent cause of erectile disorder. So are other psychological factors such as depression, lack of self-esteem, and problems in the relationship (Leary, 1992). Biological factors can also play a causative role.

Female Sexual Arousal Disorder   Women with sexual arousal disorder may have trouble becoming sexually excited or sufficiently lubricated in response to sexual stimulation. The problem can be lifelong or acquired, generalized or situational.

Female sexual arousal disorder, like its male counterpart, may have physical causes (Graber, 1993). A thorough evaluation by a medical specialist (a urologist in the case of a male; a gynecologist in the case of a female) is recommended. Any neurological, vascular, or hormonal problem that interferes with the lubrication or swelling response of the vagina to sexual stimulation may contribute to female sexual arousal disorder. For example, diabetes mellitus may lead to diminished sexual excitement in women because of the degeneration of the nerves servicing the clitoris and blood vessel (vascular) damage. Reduced estrogen production can also result in vaginal dryness.

Female sexual arousal disorder more commonly has psychological causes, however. In some cases, women harbor deep-seated anger and resentment toward their partners. They thus find it difficult to turn off these feelings when they go to bed. In other cases, sexual trauma is involved. Survivors of sexual abuse—especially child sexual abuse—often find it difficult to respond sexually to their partners (Morokoff, 1993). Feelings of helplessness, anger, or guilt, or even flashbacks of the abuse, may surface when the woman begins sexual activity. Other psychosocial causes include anxiety or guilt about sex and ineffective stimulation by the partner (Morokoff, 1993).

Orgasmic Disorders

Three disorders concern the orgasm phase of the sexual response cycle: (1) female orgasmic disorder, (2) male orgasmic disorder, and (3) premature ejaculation.

In female or male orgasmic disorder, the woman or man is persistently delayed in reaching orgasm or does not reach orgasm at all, despite achieving sexual stimulation of sufficient intensity to normally result in orgasm. The problem is more common among women than men. In some cases a person can reach orgasm without difficulty while engaging in sexual relations with one partner, but not with another.

Male Orgasmic Disorder   Male orgasmic disorder may be lifelong or acquired, generalized or situational. In most cases the disorder is limited to coitus. The man may be capable of ejaculating during masturbation or oral sex, but find it difficult, if not impossible—despite high levels of sexual excitement—to ejaculate during intercourse.

Male orgasmic disorder is not common (Dekker, 1993). Research on the problem has been scarce (Dekker, 1993). Only a few case reports have appeared in the literature (e.g., Masters & Johnson, 1970; Rathus, 1978).

Male orgasmic disorder may be caused by physical problems such as multiple sclerosis (Kedia, 1983) or neurological damage that interferes with neural control of ejaculation. It may also be a side effect of certain drugs. Psychological factors, including performance anxiety, sexual guilt, and hostility toward the partner, may play a role. Helen Singer Kaplan (1974) suggests that some men with male orgasmic disorder may be unconsciously "holding back" their ejaculate from their partners because of underlying hostility or resentment. Masters and Johnson (1970) found that men with this problem frequently have strict religious backgrounds that may leave a residue of unresolved guilt about sex, which inhibits ejaculation. Fear of pregnancy or anger toward one's partner can also play a role.

Female Orgasmic Disorder

Female Orgasmic Disorder   Women with female orgasmic disorder are unable to reach orgasm or have difficulty reaching orgasm following what would usually be an adequate amount of sexual stimulation. Women who have never achieved orgasm through any means are sometimes labeled **anorgasmic** or *preorgasmic*.

A woman who reaches orgasm through masturbation or oral sex may not necessarily reach orgasm dependably during coitus with her partner (Stock, 1993). Penile thrusting during coitus may not provide sufficient clitoral stimulation to facilitate orgasm. Women who try to force an orgasm may also find themselves unable to do so. They may assume a **spectator role** and observe, rather than fully participate in, their sexual encounters. "Spectatoring" may further decrease the likelihood of orgasm.

Premature Ejaculation

Premature Ejaculation   **Premature ejaculation** was the most common male sexual dysfunction reported in the NHSLS study (see Table 12.1). Men with this problem ejaculate too rapidly to permit their partners or themselves to fully enjoy sexual relations. The degree of prematurity varies. Some men ejaculate during foreplay, even at the sight of their partner disrobing. But most ejaculate either just prior to or immediately upon penetration, or following a few coital thrusts (Kaplan, 1974).

Just what makes an ejaculation "premature"? Some definitions focus on a particular time period during which a man should be able to control ejaculation. Is ejaculation within 30 seconds of intromission premature? Within one minute? Ten minutes? There is no clear cutoff. Some scholars argue that the focus should be on whether the couple is satisfied with the duration of coitus rather than on a specific time period.

Rapid Female Orgasm: Can Women Reach Orgasm Too Quickly?

The female counterpart to premature ejaculation, *rapid orgasm,* is so rarely recognized as a problem that it is generally ignored by clinicians and is not classified as a sexual dysfunction in the DSM. Still, some women experience orgasm rapidly and show little interest in continuing sexual activity so that their partners can achieve gratification. Other women who reach orgasm rapidly are open to continued sexual stimulation and capable of experiencing successive orgasms.

Sexual Pain Disorders

For most of us, coitus is a source of pleasure. For some of us, however, coitus gives rise to pain and discomfort.

Dyspareunia

Dyspareunia   Dyspareunia, or painful coitus, can afflict men or women. Dyspareunia is one of the most common sexual dysfunctions and is also a common complaint of women seeking gynecological services (Quevillon, 1993).

Pain is a sign that something is wrong—physically or psychologically. Dyspareunia may result from physical causes, emotional factors, or an interaction of the two (Meana & Binik, 1994). The most common cause of coital pain in women is inadequate lubrication.

Anorgasmic
Never having reached orgasm. (Literally, "without orgasm.")

Spectator role
A role, usually taken on because of performance anxiety, in which people observe rather than fully participate in their sexual encounters.

Premature ejaculation
A sexual dysfunction in which the male persistently ejaculates too early to afford the couple adequate sexual gratification.

In such a case, additional foreplay or artificial lubrication may help. Vaginal infections or sexually transmitted diseases (STDs) may also produce coital pain, however. Allergic reactions to spermicides, even the latex material in condoms, can give rise to coital pain or irritation. Pain during deep thrusting may be caused by endometriosis or pelvic inflammatory disease (PID), from other diseases or structural disorders of the reproductive organs (Reid & Lininger, 1993), or by penile contact with the cervix.

Psychological factors such as unresolved guilt or anxiety about sex or the lingering effects of sexual trauma may also be involved. These factors may inhibit lubrication and cause involuntary contractions of the vaginal musculature, making penetration painful or uncomfortable.

Painful intercourse is less common in men and is generally associated with genital infections that cause burning or painful ejaculation. Smegma under the penile foreskin of uncircumcised men may also irritate the penile glans during sexual contact.

Vaginismus   Vaginismus involves an involuntary contraction of the pelvic muscles that surround the outer third of the vaginal barrel. Vaginismus occurs reflexively during attempts at vaginal penetration, making entry by the penis painful or impossible. These reflexive contractions are accompanied by a deep-seated fear of penetration (Beck, 1993). Some women with vaginismus are unable to tolerate penetration by any object, including a finger, tampon, or a physician's speculum. Nevertheless, the woman with vaginismus usually is not aware that she is contracting her vaginal muscles.

Vaginismus is caused by a psychological fear of penetration, not by a physical injury or defect. Women with vaginismus often have histories of sexual trauma, rape, or botched abortions. They may desire sexual relations. They may be capable of becoming sexually aroused and achieving orgasm. However, fear of penetration triggers an involuntary spasm of the vaginal musculature at the point of penile insertion.

Vaginismus can also be a cause or an effect of dyspareunia. Fear leads to involuntary vaginal contractions. Women with vaginismus may also experience pain if the couple tries to force penetration. Vaginismus and dyspareunia may also give rise to, or result from, erectile disorder in men (Speckens et al., 1995). Feelings of failure and anxiety come to overwhelm both partners.

Table 12.2 shows differences between white Americans and African Americans in the incidences of current sexual dysfunctions and other problems, according to the NHSLS study (Laumann et al., 1994). The African American men report a higher incidence than

TABLE 12.2 White and African American differences in the incidence of current sexual problems (respondents reporting the problem within the past year)

	White Men (%)	African American Men (%)	White Women (%)	African American Women (%)
Pain during sex	3.0	3.3	14.7	12.5
Sex not pleasurable	7.0	15.2	19.7	30.0
Unable to reach orgasm	7.4	9.9	23.2	29.2
Lack of interest in sex	14.7	20.0	30.9	44.5
Anxiety about performance	16.8	23.7	10.5	14.5
Reaching climax too early	27.7	33.8	7.5	20.4
Unable to keep an erection	9.9	14.5	—	—
Having trouble lubricating	—	—	20.7	13.0

Source: Adapted from Tables 10.8A and 10.8B, pp. 370–371, in Laumann, E. O., Gagnon, J. H., Michael, R. T., & Michaels, S. (1994). *The Social Organization of Sexuality: Sexual Practices in the United States.* Chicago: University of Chicago Press.

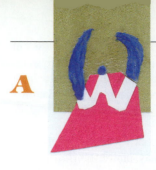

INIS BEAG AND MANGAIA—WORLDS APART

Let us invite you on a journey to two islands that are a world apart—sexually as well as geographically. The sexual attitudes and practices within these societies will shed some light on the role of cultural values in determining what is sexually normal and what is sexually dysfunctional.

Our first stop is the island of Inis Beag, which lies off the misty coast of Ireland. From the air Inis Beag is a green jewel, fertile and inviting. At ground level things do not appear quite so warm, however.

The residents of this Irish folk community do not believe that it is normal for women to experience orgasm. Anthropologist John Messenger (1971), who visited Inis Beag in the 1950s and 1960s, reported that any woman who finds pleasure in sex—especially the intense waves of pleasure that can accompany orgasm—is viewed as deviant. *Should women on Inis Beag, then, be diagnosed as orgasmically impaired?*

Premarital sex is all but unknown on Inis Beag. Prior to marriage, men and women socialize apart. Marriage comes relatively late—usually in the middle 30s for men and the middle 20s for women. Mothers teach their daughters that they will have to submit to their husbands' animal cravings in order to obey God's injunction to "be fruitful and multiply." *After this indoctrination, women show little interest in sex. Should they be diagnosed as having hypoactive sexual desire disorder?*

Polynesia. Cultural expectations affect our judgments as to what kinds of sexual behavior are functional and dysfunctional. Some Polynesian cultures are sexually permissive. They encourage children to explore their sexuality. Men may be expected to bring their partners to orgasm several times before ejaculating. In such cultures, should men who ejaculate before their partners have multiple orgasms be diagnosed with premature ejaculation?

White men of each of the sexual dysfunctions surveyed. African American women report a higher incidence of most sexual dysfunctions, with the exceptions of painful sex and trouble lubricating.

Origins of Sexual Dysfunctions

Since sexual dysfunctions involve the sex organs, it was once assumed that they stemmed largely from organic or physical causes. Today the pendulum has swung. It is now widely believed that many or most cases reflect psychosocial factors such as sexual anxieties, lack of sexual knowledge, or marital dissatisfaction. Many cases involve the interaction of organic and psychological factors (Meisler & Carey, 1990; Mohr & Beutler, 1990).

Organic Causes

Physical factors, such as fatigue and lowered testosterone levels, can dampen sexual desire and reduce responsiveness. Testosterone deficiencies, thyroid problems, and epilepsy can

The women of Inis Beag need not be overly concerned about frequent sexual intercourse, however, since the men of the island believe, erroneously, that sexual activity will drain their strength. Consequently, men avoid sex on the eve of sporting activity or strenuous work. Because of taboos against nudity, married couples engage in intercourse with their underclothes on. Intercourse takes place in the dark—literally as well as figuratively.

During intercourse the man takes the male-superior position. The male is always the initiator. Foreplay is brief, rarely involving manual stimulation of the breasts and never including oral stimulation of the genitals. *Should people who have difficulty becoming sexually aroused under these circumstances be diagnosed as having sexual arousal disorders?* The man ejaculates as rapidly as he can, in the belief that he is the only partner with sexual needs and to spare his wife as best he can. Then he turns over and rapidly falls asleep. Once more the couple have done their duty. *Since the man ejaculates rapidly, should he be diagnosed as having premature ejaculation?*

Our next stop is Mangaia. Mangaia is a Polynesian pearl of an island. It lifts languidly out of the blue waters of the Pacific. It lies on the other side of the world from Inis Beag—in more ways than one.

From an early age, Mangaian boys and girls are encouraged to get in touch with their own sexuality through sexual play and masturbation (Marshall, 1971). At about the age of 13, Mangaian boys are initiated into manhood by adults who instruct them in sexual techniques. Mangaian males are taught the merit of bringing their female partners to multiple orgasms before ejaculating. *Are Mangaian males who ejaculate before their partners have multiple orgasms suffering from premature ejaculation?*

Boys practice their new techniques with girlfriends on secluded beaches or beneath the listing fronds of palms. They may visit girlfriends in the evening in the huts where they sleep with their families. Parents often listen for their daughters to laugh and gasp so that they will know that their daughters have reached orgasm with a visiting young man, called a "sleepcrawler." Usually they pretend to be asleep so as not to interfere with courtship and impede their daughters' chances of finding a suitable mate. Daughters may receive a nightly succession of sleepcrawlers.

Girls, too, learn techniques of coitus from their elders. Typically they are initiated by an experienced male relative. Mangaians look on virginity with disdain, because virgins do not know how to provide sexual pleasure. Thus, the older relative makes his contribution to the family by initiating the girl.

Mangaians, by the way, expressed concern when they learned that many European and U.S. women do not regularly experience orgasm during coitus. Orgasm is apparently universal among Mangaian women. Therefore, Mangaians could only assume that Western women suffered from some abnormality of the sex organs. *Do they?*

All in all, the sharp contrasts between Inis Beag and Mangaia illustrate how concepts of normality are embedded within a cultural context. Behavior that is judged to be normal in one culture may be regarded as abnormal in another. How might our own cultural expectations influence our judgments about sexual dysfunction?

---

all diminish sexual desire (Kresin, 1993). Sexual desire is stoked by testosterone, which is produced by men in the testes and by both genders in the adrenal glands. Women may experience less sexual desire when their adrenal glands are surgically removed. Low sexual interest, along with erectile difficulties, are also common among men with **hypogonadism**. (Hypogonadism is treated with testosterone [Brody, 1995c; Carani et al., 1990].) Women with low sexual desire usually have normal levels of the hormones testosterone, estrogen, and progesterone, however (Schreiner-Engle et al., 1989; Stuart et al., 1987). The role of hormones in lack of desire among healthy people remains unclear.

Hypogonadism
An endocrine disorder that reduces the output of testosterone.

Some medications, such as those used to control anxiety, allergies, or hypertension, may also reduce desire. Changing medications or dosage levels may return the person's previous level of desire.

Fatigue may cause erectile disorder and orgasmic disorder in men. It can cause orgasmic disorder and inadequate lubrication in women. These will be isolated incidents unless the person attaches too much meaning to them and becomes concerned about future performances. Various medical conditions can affect orgasmic functioning in both men and women, including diabetes mellitus, multiple sclerosis, spinal-cord injuries, complications from certain surgical procedures (such as removal of the prostate in men), endocrinological problems, and use of some pharmacological agents, such as drugs used to treat hypertension and psychiatric disorders (Segraves & Segraves, 1993). Painful coitus, however, often reflects organic problems such as infections.

It was once believed that 95% of cases of erectile disorder resulted from psychological causes (Masters & Johnson, 1970). It is now thought that organic factors are also widely involved (Rajfer et al., 1992). Psychological factors such as anxiety or depression may serve to perpetuate or exacerbate the problem even when there are underlying organic causes.

Organic causes of erectile disorder affect the flow of blood to and through the penis or damage to nerves involved in erection (Appell, 1986; Spark, 1991). Rajfer and his colleagues (1992) believe that most cases of erectile disorder involve failure of the body to produce sufficient quantities of the substance nitric oxide. When nitric oxide comes into contact with the muscles encircling blood vessels in the penis, the muscles relax, allowing vasocongestion to occur and causing the penis to swell. One treatment approach to erectile disorder is to inject the penis with a chemical that raises nitric oxide levels and thus relaxes the penile muscles to permit blood to flow more freely. Erectile problems can also arise from clogged or narrow arteries to the penis (Lipshultz, 1996), diabetes, multiple sclerosis, syphilis, kidney disease, hypertension, cancer, emphysema, heart disease, and endocrine disorders.

Prescription drugs and illicit drugs are believed to account for one in four cases of erectile disorder (Leary, 1992b). Antidepressant medication and antipsychotic drugs may impair erectile functioning and cause orgasmic disorders (Segraves, 1988b; Spark, 1991). Tranquilizers like Valium and Xanax may cause orgasmic disorder in either gender (Segraves, 1988b).

Women may also encounter vascular or nerve disorders that impair genital blood flow, reducing lubrication and sexual excitement, rendering intercourse painful, and reducing their ability to reach orgasm.

People with sexual dysfunctions are advised to undergo a physical examination to determine whether their problems are biologically based. Men with erectile disorder may be evaluated in a sleep center to determine whether they attain erections while asleep. Healthy men usually have erections during rapid-eye-movement (REM) sleep, which occurs every 90 to 100 minutes. Men with organically based erectile disorder often do not have nocturnal erections. However, this technique, called nocturnal penile **tumescence** (NPT), may lead to misleading results in perhaps 20% of cases (Meisler & Carey, 1990). NPT may thus be helpful but not definitive in suggesting whether erectile disorder is organically based (Mohr & Beutler, 1990).

Central nervous system depressants such as alcohol, heroin, and morphine can reduce sexual desire and impair sexual arousal (Segraves, 1988a). Heavy drinking can damage the nerves that control erection and ejaculation (Spark, 1991). Narcotics also depress testosterone production, which can further reduce sexual desire and lead to erectile failure (Spark, 1991).

Psychosocial Causes

Psychosocial factors are connected with sexual dysfunctions. These include cultural influences, psychosexual trauma, marital dissatisfaction, lack of sexual skills, and performance anxiety.

Cultural Influences   Children reared in sexually repressive cultural or home environments may learn to respond to sex with feelings of anxiety and shame, rather than sexual arousal and pleasure. People whose parents instilled in them a sense of guilt over touching their genitals may find it difficult to accept their sex organs as sources of pleasure.

Despite the sexual revolution, women are more likely than men in our culture to be taught to repress their sexual desires and even to fear their sexuality (Nichols, 1990). Self-control and vigilance—not sexual awareness and acceptance—become identified as feminine virtues. Many women who are exposed to negative attitudes about sex during childhood and adolescence find it difficult to suddenly view sex as a source of pleasure and

Tumescence

Swelling; erection. (From the Latin *tumere*, meaning "to swell." *Tumor* has the same root.)

satisfaction once they are married. A lifetime of inhibiting sexual impulses may lead to problems in sexual response when an acceptable opportunity arises (Morokoff, 1993).

Psychosexual Trauma   Sexual stimuli may bring about anxiety when they have been paired with painful experiences, such as rape, incest, or sexual molestation. Strong conditioned anxiety can stifle sexual arousal. Unresolved anger and misplaced guilt can also make it difficult for victims of rape and other sexual traumas to respond sexually, even years afterward. Persons who have been sexually victimized may harbor feelings of disgust and revulsion toward sex, or deep-seated fears of sex that make it difficult for them to respond sexually, even with loving partners.

Ineffective Sexual Techniques   In some marriages couples practice a narrow range of sexual techniques. Perhaps they have fallen into a routine. A woman who remains unknowledgeable about the erotic importance of her clitoris may be unlikely to seek direct clitoral stimulation. The couple who fail to communicate their sexual preferences or to experiment with altering their sexual techniques may find themselves losing interest. Brevity of foreplay and coitus may contribute to female orgasmic disorder.

Emotional Factors   Orgasm involves a sudden loss of voluntary control. Fear of losing control or "letting go" may block sexual arousal. Other emotional factors, especially depression, are often implicated in sexual dysfunctions (Beck, 1988). People who are depressed frequently report lessened sexual interest and may find it difficult to respond sexually. Stress may also lessen sexual interest and response.

Problems in the Relationship   Problems in the relationship are important and often pivotal factors in sexual dysfunctions (Catalan et al., 1990; Fish et al., 1994; Leiblum & Rosen, 1991). Couples usually find that their sexual relationships are no better than the other facets of their relationships. Couples who harbor resentments toward one another may make sex their arena of combat. They may fail to become aroused by their partners or "withhold" orgasm to make their partners feel guilty or inadequate.

Troubled relationships are usually characterized by poor communication. Partners who have difficulty communicating about other matters may be unlikely to communicate their sexual desires to each other.

Psychological Conflicts   Within Freud's psychoanalytic theory, sexual dysfunctions are rooted in the failure to successfully resolve the Oedipus or Electra complexes of early childhood. Sexual encounters in adulthood arouse unconscious anxieties and hostilities that are believed to reflect unresolved conflicts, thereby inhibiting sexual response.

A modern psychoanalytic theorist, Helen Singer Kaplan (1974), believes that sexual dysfunctions represent an interaction of *immediate* causes (such as poor techniques, mari-

A Failure to Communicate. Problems in communication cause or exacerbate sexual problems. It is irrational to believe that one's partner would know what to do if she or he "really loved me." Sex therapy enhances communication skills.

tal conflict, performance anxiety, and lack of effective communication) and deep-seated or *remote* causes (such as unresolved childhood conflicts that predispose people to encounter sexual anxiety and hostility in adulthood). Kaplan recommends combining direct behavioral techniques, which deal with the immediate causes of sexual dysfunctions, with psychoanalytic techniques that deal with the remote causes.

Lack of Sexual Skills   Sexual competency involves the acquisition of sexual knowledge and skills. We generally learn what makes us and others feel good through trial and error and by talking and reading about sex. Some people may not develop sexual competency because of a lack of opportunity to acquire knowledge and experience—even within marriage. People with sexual dysfunctions may have been reared in families in which discussions of sexuality were off limits and early sexual experimentation was harshly punished. Such early influences may have squelched the young person's sexual learning and experimentation or led her or him to associate anxiety or guilt with sex.

Irrational Beliefs   Psychologist Albert Ellis (1962, 1977) points out that irrational beliefs and attitudes may contribute to sexual dysfunctions. Negative feelings like anxiety and fear, Ellis submits, do not stem directly from the events we experience, but rather from our interpretations of these events. If a person encounters a certain event, like an erectile or orgasmic disorder on a given day, and then *believes* that the event is awful or catastrophic, he or she will exaggerate feelings of disappointment and set the stage for future problems.

Performance Anxiety   Anxiety—especially performance anxiety—plays important roles in the development of sexual dysfunctions. Performance anxiety occurs when a person becomes overly concerned with how well he or she performs a certain act or task. Performance anxiety may place a dysfunctional individual in a spectator rather than a performer role. Rather than focusing on erotic sensations and allowing involuntary responses like erection, lubrication, and orgasm to occur naturally, he or she focuses on self-doubts and fears, and thinks, "Will I be able to do it this time? Will this be another failure?"

Performance anxiety can set the stage for a vicious cycle in which a sexual failure increases anxiety. Anxiety then leads to repeated failure, and so on. Sex therapists emphasize the need to break this vicious cycle by removing the need to perform.

In men, performance anxiety can inhibit erection while also triggering a premature ejaculation. (Erection, mediated by the parasympathetic nervous system, can be blocked by activation of the sympathetic nervous system in the form of anxiety. Since ejaculation, like anxiety, is mediated by the sympathetic nervous system, arousal of this system in the form of anxiety can increase the level of stimulation and thereby heighten the potential for premature ejaculation.)

In women, performance anxiety can reduce vaginal lubrication and contribute to orgasmic disorder. Women with performance anxieties may try to force an orgasm, only to find that the harder they try, the more elusive it becomes.

Treatment of Sexual Dysfunctions

When Kinsey conducted his surveys in the 1930s and 1940s, there was no effective treatment for sexual dysfunctions. At the time the predominant model of therapy for sexual dysfunctions was long-term psychoanalysis. Psychoanalysts believed that the sexual problem would abate only if the presumed unconscious conflicts that lay at the root of the problem were resolved through long-term therapy. Evidence of the effectiveness of psychoanalysis in treating sexual dysfunctions is still lacking, however.

Since that time behavioral models of short-term treatment, collectively called **sex therapy,** have emerged. These models aim to modify the dysfunctional behavior as directly as possible. Sex therapists also recognize the roles of childhood conflicts, self-defeating attitudes, and the quality of the partners' relationship. Therefore, they draw upon various forms of therapy, as needed (LoPiccolo, 1994; Rosen et al., 1994).

Sex therapy
A collective term for short-term behavioral models for treatment of sexual dysfunctions.

Although the particular approaches vary, sex therapies aim to:

1. Change self-defeating beliefs and attitudes
2. Teach sexual skills
3. Enhance sexual knowledge
4. Improve sexual communication
5. Reduce performance anxiety

Sex therapy usually involves both partners, although individual therapy is preferred in some cases. Therapists find that granting people "permission" to sexually experiment or discuss negative attitudes about sex helps many people overcome sexual problems without the need for more intensive therapy.

Let us begin with the groundbreaking work of Masters and Johnson.

The Masters and Johnson Approach

Masters and Johnson pioneered the use of direct behavioral approaches to treating sexual dysfunctions (Masters & Johnson, 1970). A female–male therapy team focuses on the couple as the unit of treatment during a two-week residential program. Masters and Johnson consider the couple, not the individual, dysfunctional. A couple may describe the husband's erectile disorder as the problem, but this problem is likely to have led to problems in the couple by the time they seek therapy. Similarly, a man whose wife has an orgasmic disorder is likely to be anxious about his ability to provide effective sexual stimulation.

The dual-therapist team permits each partner to discuss problems with a member of his or her own gender. It reduces the chance of therapist bias in favor of the female or male partner. It allows each partner to hear concerns expressed by another member of the other gender. Anxieties and resentments are aired, but the focus of treatment is behavioral change. Couples perform daily sexual homework assignments, such as **sensate focus exercises,** in the privacy of their own rooms.

Sensate focus exercises

Exercises in which sex partners take turns giving and receiving pleasurable stimulation in non-genital areas of the body.

Sensate focus sessions are carried out in the nude. Partners take turns giving and receiving stimulation in nongenital areas of the body. Without touching the breasts or genitals, the giver massages or fondles the receiving partner in order to provide pleasure under relaxing and nondemanding conditions. Since genital activity is restricted, there is no pressure to "perform." The giving partner is "freed" to engage in trial-and-error learning about the receiving partner's sensate preferences. The receiving partner is also "freed" to enjoy the experience without feeling rushed to reciprocate or obliged to perform by becoming sexually aroused. The receiving partner's only responsibility is to direct the giving partner as needed. In addition to these general sensate focus exercises, Masters and Johnson used specific assignments designed to help couples overcome particular sexual dysfunctions.

Masters and Johnson were pioneers in the development of sex therapy. Yet many sex therapists have departed from the Masters and Johnson format. Many do not treat clients in an intensive residential program. Many question the necessity of female–male therapist teams. Researchers find that one therapist is about as effective as two, regardless of her or his gender (Libman et al., 1985). Nor does the therapeutic benefit seem to depend to any great extent on whether the sessions are conducted within a short period of time, as in the Masters and Johnson approach, or spaced over time (Libman et al., 1985). Therapists have also departed from the Masters and Johnson approach by working individually with pre-orgasmic women rather than the couple.

The Helen Singer Kaplan Approach

Kaplan (1974) calls her approach *psychosexual therapy.* Psychosexual therapy combines behavioral and psychoanalytic methods. Kaplan, as noted, believes that sexual dysfunctions have both *immediate* causes and *remote* causes (childhood conflicts). Kaplan begins therapy with the behavioral approach. She focuses on improving the couple's communication, eliminating performance anxiety, and fostering sexual skills and knowledge. She uses a brief form of insight-oriented therapy when it appears that remote causes impede response to the behavioral program. In so doing, she hopes to bring to awareness unconscious conflicts that are believed to have stifled the person's sexual desires or responsiveness. Although Kaplan reports a number of successful case studies, there are no controlled studies demonstrating that the combination of behavioral and insight-oriented, or psychoanalytic, techniques is more effective than the behavioral techniques alone.

Let us now consider some of the specific techniques that sex therapists have introduced in treating several of the major types of sexual dysfunction.

Treatment of Sexual Desire Disorders

Some sex therapists help kindle the sexual appetites of people with hypoactive sexual desire by prescribing self-stimulation exercises combined with erotic fantasies (LoPiccolo & Friedman, 1988). Sex therapists may also assist dysfunctional couples by prescribing sensate focus exercises, enhancing communication, and expanding the couple's repertoire of sexual skills. Sex therapists recognize that hypoactive sexual desire is often a complex problem that requires more intensive treatment than do problems of the arousal or orgasm phases (Leiblum & Rosen, 1988). Helen Singer Kaplan (1987) argues that insight-oriented approaches are especially helpful in the treatment of hypoactive sexual desire and sexual aversion to help people with deep-seated conflicts.

When lack of desire is connected with depression, sexual interests may rebound when the depression lifts. Treatment in such cases may involve psychotherapy or chemotherapy, not sex therapy per se. When problems in the relationship are involved, marital or couples therapy may be indicated to improve the relationship. Once interpersonal problems are ironed out, sexual interest may return.

Treatment of sexual aversion disorder may involve medications to reduce anxiety and psychological treatments designed to help the individual overcome the underlying sexual phobia. Couples therapy may be used in cases in which sexual aversions arise from problems in relationships (Gold & Gold, 1993). Sensate focus exercises may be used to lessen generalized anxiety about sexual contact. But fears of specific aspects of the sexual act may need to be overcome through behavioral exercises in which the client learns to manage the stimuli that evoke fears of sexual contact:

> Bridget, 26, and Bryan, 30, were married for four years but had never consummated their relationship because Bridget would panic whenever Bryan attempted coitus with her. While she enjoyed foreplay and was capable of achieving orgasm with clitoral stimulation, her fears of sexual contact were triggered by Bryan's attempts at vaginal penetration. The therapist employed a program of gradual exposure to the feared stimuli to allow Bridget the opportunity to overcome her fears in small, graduated steps. First she was instructed to view her genitals in a mirror when she was alone—this in order to violate her long-standing prohibition against looking at and enjoying her body. While this exercise initially made her feel anxious, with repeated exposure she became comfortable performing it and then progressed to touching her genitals directly. When she became comfortable with this step, and reported experiencing pleasurable erotic sensations, she was instructed to insert a finger into the vagina. She encountered intense anxiety at this step and required daily practice for two weeks before she could tolerate inserting her finger into her vagina without discomfort. Her husband was then brought into the treatment process. The couple was instructed to have Bridget insert her own finger in her vagina while Bryan watched. When she was comfortable with this exercise, she then guided his finger into her vagina. Later he placed one and then two fingers into her vagina, while she controlled the depth, speed and duration of penetration. When she felt ready, they proceeded to attempt penile penetration in the female superior position, which allowed her to maintain control over penetration. Over time, Bridget became more comfortable with penetration to the point that the couple developed a normal sexual relationship.
>
> (Adapted from Kaplan, 1987, pp. 102–103)

Treatment of Sexual Arousal Disorders

Men with chronic erectile disorder may believe that they have "forgotten" how to have an erection. They may ask their therapists to "teach" them or "show them" how. Erection is an involuntary reflex, however, not a skill. A man need not learn how to have an erection any more than he need learn how to breathe.

In sex therapy, women who have trouble becoming lubricated and men with erectile problems learn that they need not "do" anything to become sexually aroused. As long as their problems are psychologically and not organically based, they need only receive sexual stimulation under relaxed circumstances so that anxiety does not inhibit their natural reflexes.

In order to reduce performance anxiety, the partners engage in nondemanding sexual contacts: contacts that do not demand lubrication or erection. They may start with nongenital sensate focus exercises in the style of Masters and Johnson. After a couple of sessions, sensate focus extends to the genitals. The position shown in Figure 12.1 allows the woman easy access to her partner's genitals. She repeatedly "teases" him to erection and allows the erection to subside. Thus she avoids creating performance anxiety that could lead to loss of erection. By repeatedly regaining his erection, the man loses the fear that loss of erection means it will not return. He learns also to focus on erotic sensations for their own sake. He experiences no demand to perform, as the couple is instructed to refrain from coitus.

When the dysfunctional partner can reliably achieve sexual excitement (denoted by erection in the male and lubrication in the female), the couple does not immediately attempt coitus, since this might rekindle performance anxiety. Rather, the couple engages in a series of nondemanding, pleasurable sexual activities, eventually culminating in coitus.

In Masters and Johnson's approach, the couple begin coitus after about 10 days of treatment. The woman teases the man to erection while she is sitting above him, straddling

Figure 12.1. **The Training Position Recommended by Masters and Johnson for Treatment of Erectile Disorder and Premature Ejaculation.** By lying in front of her partner who has his legs spread, the woman has ready access to his genitals. In one part of a program designed to overcome erectile disorder, she repeatedly "teases" him to erection and allows the erection to subside. Thus she avoids creating performance anxiety that could lead to loss of erection. Through repeated regaining of erection, the man loses the fear that loss of erection means it will not return.

his thighs. When he is erect, *she* inserts the penis—to avoid fumbling attempts at entry—and moves slowly back and forth in a *nondemanding way.* Neither attempts to reach orgasm. If erection is lost, teasing and coitus are repeated. Once the couple become confident that erection can be retained—or reinstated if lost—they may increase coital thrusting gradually to reach orgasm.

Treatment of Orgasmic Disorders

Women who have never experienced orgasm often harbor negative sexual attitudes that cause anxiety and inhibit sexual response. Treatment in such cases may first address these attitudes.

Masters and Johnson use a couples-oriented approach in treating anorgasmic women. They begin with sensate focus exercises. Then, during genital massage and later during coitus, the woman guides her partner in the caresses and movements that she finds sexually exciting. Taking charge helps free the woman, psychologically speaking, from the traditional stereotype of the passive, subordinate female role.

Masters and Johnson recommend a training position (see Figure 12.2) that gives the man access to his partner's breasts and genitals. She can guide his hands to show him the types of

Figure 12.2. **The Training Position for Nondemanding Stimulation of the Female Genitals.**
This position gives the man access to his partner's breasts and genitals. She can guide his hands to show him the types of stimulation she enjoys.

stimulation she enjoys. The genital play is *nondemanding*. The goals are to learn to provide and enjoy effective sexual stimulation, not to reach orgasm. The clitoris is not stimulated early, since doing so may produce a high level of stimulation before the woman is prepared.

After a number of occasions of genital play, the couple undertake coitus in the female-superior position (see Figure 12.3). This position allows the woman freedom of movement and control over her genital sensations. She is told to regard the penis as her "toy." The couple engages in several sessions of deliberately slow thrusting to sensitize the woman to sensations produced by the penis and break the common counterproductive pattern of desperate, rapid thrusting.

Orgasm cannot be willed or forced. When a woman receives effective stimulation, feels free to focus on erotic sensations, and feels that nothing is being demanded of her, she will generally reach orgasm. Once the woman is able to attain orgasm in the female-superior position, the couple may extend their sexual repertoire to other positions.

Masters and Johnson prefer working with the couple in cases of anorgasmia, but other sex therapists prefer to begin working with the woman individually through masturbation (Barbach, 1975; Heiman & LoPiccolo, 1987). This approach assumes that the woman accepts masturbation as a therapy tool. Masturbation provides women with opportunities to learn about their own bodies at their own pace. It frees them of the need to rely on partners or to please partners. The sexual pleasure they experience helps counter lingering sexual anxieties. Although there is some variation among therapists, the following elements are commonly found in directed masturbation programs:

1. *Education.* The woman and her sex partner (if she has one) are educated about female sexuality.
2. *Self-exploration.* Self-exploration is encouraged as a way of increasing the woman's sense of body awareness. She may hold a mirror between her legs to locate her sexual anatomic features. Exercises may be prescribed to help tone and strengthen the pubococcygeus (PC) muscle that surrounds the vagina and increase her awareness of genital sensations and sense of control.
3. *Self-massage.* Once the woman feels comfortable about exploring her body, she creates a relaxing setting for self-massage. She chooses a time and place where she is free from external distractions. She begins to explore the sensitivity of her body to touch, discovering and then repeating the caresses that she finds pleasurable. At first

Figure 12.3. **Coitus in the Female-Superior Position.** In treatment of female orgasmic disorder, the couple undertake coitus in the female-superior position after a number of occasions of genital play. This position allows the woman freedom of movement and control over her genital sensations. She is told to regard the penis as her "toy." The couple engages in several sessions of deliberately slow thrusting to sensitize the woman to sensations produced by the penis and to break the common counterproductive pattern of desperate, rapid thrusting.

self-massage is not concentrated on the genitals. It encompasses other sensitive parts of the body. She may incorporate stimulation of the nipples and breasts and then direct genital stimulation, focusing on the clitoral area and experimenting with hand movements. Nonalcohol-based oils and lotions may be used to enhance the sensuous quality of the massage and to provide lubrication for the external genitalia. Some women use their dominant hand to stimulate their breasts while the other hand massages the genitals. No two women approach masturbation in quite the same way. During the first few occasions the woman does not attempt to reach orgasm, so as to prevent performance anxiety.

4. *Giving oneself permission.* The woman may be advised to practice assertive thoughts to dispel lingering guilt and anxiety about masturbation. For example, she might repeat to herself, "This is my body. I have a right to learn about my body and receive pleasure from it."

5. *Use of fantasy.* Arousal is heightened through the use of sexual images, fantasies, and fantasy aids, such as erotic written or visual materials.

6. *Allowing, not forcing, orgasm.* It may take weeks of masturbation to reach orgasm, especially for women who have never achieved orgasm. By focusing on her erotic sensations and fantasies, but not demanding orgasm, the woman lowers performance anxiety and creates the stimulating conditions needed to reach orgasm.

7. *Use of a vibrator.* A vibrator may be recommended to provide more intense stimulation, especially for women who find that manual stimulation is insufficient.

8. *Involvement of the partner.* Once the woman is capable of regularly achieving orgasm through masturbation, the focus may shift to the woman's sexual relationship with her partner. Nondemanding sensate focus exercises may be followed by nondemanding coitus. The female-superior position is often used. It enables the woman to control the depth, angle, and rate of thrusting. She thus ensures that she receives the kinds of stimulation needed to reach orgasm.

Kaplan (1974) suggests a bridge maneuver to assist couples who are interested in making the transition from a combination of manual and coital stimulation to coital stimulation alone as a means for reaching orgasm. Manual stimulation during coitus is used until the woman senses that she is about to reach orgasm. Manual stimulation is then stopped and the woman thrusts with her pelvis to provide the stimulation necessary to reach orgasm. Over time the manual clitoral stimulation is discontinued earlier and earlier. Although some couples may prefer this "hands-off" approach to inducing orgasm, Kaplan points out that there is nothing wrong with combining manual stimulation and penile thrusting. There is no evidence that reliance on clitoral stimulation means that women are sexually immature. (Evidence has not borne out the theoretical psychoanalytic distinction between clitoral and vaginal orgasms.)

Our focus has been on sexual techniques, but it is worth noting that a combination of approaches that focus on sexual techniques and underlying interpersonal problems may be more effective than focusing on sexual techniques alone, at least for couples whose relationships are troubled (Killmann et al., 1987; LoPiccolo & Stock, 1986).

Male Orgasmic Disorder   Treatment of male orgasmic disorder generally focuses on increasing sexual stimulation and reducing performance anxiety (LoPiccolo & Stock, 1986). Masters and Johnson instruct the couple to practice sensate focus exercises for several days, during which the man makes no attempt to ejaculate. The couple is then instructed to bring the man to orgasm in any way they can, usually by the woman's stroking his penis. Once the husband can ejaculate in the woman's presence, she brings him to the point at which he is about to ejaculate. Then, in the female-superior position, she inserts the penis and thrusts vigorously to bring him to orgasm. If he loses the feeling he is about to ejaculate, the process is repeated. Even if ejaculation occurs at the point of penetration, it often helps break the pattern of inability to ejaculate within the vagina.

Premature Ejaculation   In the Masters and Johnson approach, sensate focus exercises are followed by practice in the training position shown in Figure 12.1. The woman teases her partner to erection and uses the **squeeze technique** when he indicates that he is about to ejaculate. She squeezes the tip of the penis, which temporarily prevents ejaculation. This process is repeated three or four times in a 15- to 20-minute session before the man purposely ejaculates.

In using the squeeze technique (which should be used only following personal instruction from a sex therapist), the woman holds the penis between the thumb and first two fingers of the same hand. The thumb presses against the frenulum. The fingers straddle the coronal ridge on the other side of the penis. Squeezing the thumb and forefingers together fairly hard for about 20 seconds (or until the man's urge to ejaculate passes) prevents ejaculation. The erect penis can withstand fairly strong pressure without discomfort, but erection may be partially lost.

After two or three days of these sessions, Masters and Johnson have the couple begin coitus in the female-superior position because it creates less pressure to ejaculate. The woman inserts the penis. At first she contains it without thrusting, allowing the man to get used to intravaginal sensations. If he signals that he is about to ejaculate, she lifts off and squeezes the penis. After some repetitions, she begins slowly to move backward and forward, lifting off and squeezing as needed. The man learns gradually to tolerate higher levels of sexual stimulation without ejaculating.

The alternate "stop-start" method for treating premature ejaculation was introduced by urologist James Semans (1956). The method can be applied to manual stimulation or coitus. For example, the woman can manually stimulate her partner until he is about to ejaculate. He then signals her to suspend sexual stimulation and allows his arousal to subside before stimulation is resumed. This process enables the man to recognize the cues that precede his point of ejaculatory inevitability or "point of no return," and to tolerate longer periods of sexual stimulation. When the stop-start technique is applied to coitus, the couple begin with simple vaginal containment with no pelvic thrusting, preferably in the female-superior position. The man withdraws if he feels he is about to ejaculate. As the man's sense of control increases, thrusting can begin, along with variations in coital positions. The couple again stop when the man signals that he is approaching ejaculatory inevitability.

Treatment of Sexual Pain Disorders

Dyspareunia   Dyspareunia, or painful intercourse, generally calls for medical intervention to ascertain and treat any underlying physical problems, such as genital infections, that might give rise to pain. When dyspareunia is caused by vaginismus, treatment of vaginismus through a behavioral approach, described below, may eliminate pain.

Vaginismus   Vaginismus is generally treated with behavioral exercises in which plastic vaginal dilators of increasing size are inserted to help relax the vaginal musculature. A gynecologist may first demonstrate insertion of the narrowest dilator. Later the woman herself practices insertion of wider dilators at home. The woman increases the size of the dilator as she becomes capable of tolerating insertion and containment (for 10 or 15 minutes) without discomfort or pain. The woman herself—not her partner or therapist—controls the pace of treatment (LoPiccolo & Stock, 1986). The woman's or her partner's fingers (first the littlest finger, then two fingers and so on) may be used in place of the plastic dilators, with the woman controlling the speed and depth of penetration. When the woman is able to tolerate dilators (or fingers) equivalent in thickness to the penis, the couple may attempt coitus. Still, the woman should control insertion. Circumstances should be relaxed and nondemanding. The idea is to avoid resensitizing her to fears of penetration. Since vaginismus often occurs among women with a history of sexual trauma, such as rape or incest, treatment for the psychological effects of these experiences may also be in order (LoPiccolo & Stock, 1986).

Evaluation of Sex Therapy

Masters and Johnson (1970) reported an overall success rate of about 80% in treating sexual dysfunctions in their two-week intensive program. Some dysfunctions proved more difficult to treat than others. An analysis of treatment results from 1950 to 1977 showed success rates ranging from 67% for primary erectile disorder to 99% for vaginismus (Kolodny, 1981). A follow-up of 226 initial successes after a five-year period showed that 16 people, or 7%, experienced a "treatment reversal."

Yet, Masters and Johnson's sample may also have been biased in at least two ways. It consisted only of people who were willing and could afford to spend two weeks at their institute for full-time therapy. These people were better educated, more affluent, and more highly motivated than the general population. So some of the success of treatment may have been due to the clients' high level of motivation rather than to the treatment they received.

Other researchers have reported more modest levels of success in treating erectile disorder than those reported at the Masters and Johnson Institute (Barlow, 1986). Nevertheless, long-term follow-up evaluations support the general effectiveness of sex therapy for erectile disorder (Everaerd, 1993). The addition of biological treatments to the arsenal of treatments for erectile disorder has improved success rates to the point that virtually all erection problems can be successfully treated in one way or another (Reinisch, 1990).

Sex therapy approaches to treating vaginismus and premature ejaculation have produced more consistent levels of success (Beck, 1993; O'Donohue et al., 1993). Reported success in treating vaginismus has ranged as high as 80% (Hawton & Catalan, 1990) to 100% in Masters and Johnson's (1970) original research. Treatment of premature ejaculation has resulted in success rates above 90% using the squeeze or stop-start techniques (Killmann & Auerbach, 1979). Because the squeeze technique carries with it some risk of discomfort, many therapists prefer using the stop-start method.

LoPiccolo and Stock (1986) found that 95% of a sample of 150 previously anorgasmic women were able to achieve orgasm through a directed masturbation program. About 85% of these women were able to reach orgasm through manual stimulation by their partners. Only about 40% were able to achieve orgasm during coitus, however. Generally speaking, couples-oriented treatment helps facilitate orgasm during coitus but is no guarantee (Heiman & LoPiccolo, 1987; LoPiccolo & Stock, 1986). Nevertheless, the goal of achieving orgasm through some form of genital stimulation with a cooperative partner, as through oral sex or by direct manual clitoral stimulation, is realistic for most women (LoPiccolo & Stock, 1986).

Biological Treatments of Premature Ejaculation and Erectile Disorder

Sex therapy is by definition psychological or behavioral. However, biological treatments are also being used, especially in the cases of premature ejaculation and male erectile disorder.

Premature Ejaculation   Drugs that are usually used for psychological problems have been helpful in treating premature ejaculation. One, clomipramine, is normally used to treat people with obsessive–compulsive disorder or schizophrenia. However, in a pilot study with 15 couples, low doses of clomipramine helped men engage in coitus five times longer than usual without ejaculating (Althof, 1994). So-called antidepressant drugs have also been helpful in treatment of premature ejaculation (Forster & King, 1994; Waldinger et al., 1994; Wise, 1994).

Erectile Disorder   Biological or biomedical approaches may also be helpful in treating erectile disorder, especially in cases in which organic factors are involved. Treatments include penile implants, hormone treatments, vascular surgery, and self-injections of drugs that induce erections.

A *penile implant* is surgically implanted. Two types of implants are currently used: semirigid and inflatable. The semirigid implant is made of two rods of silicone rubber that remain in a *permanent* semirigid position. The inflatable type requires more extensive surgery. Cylinders are implanted in the penis, a fluid reservoir is placed near the bladder, and a tiny pump is inserted in the scrotum. To attain erection, the man squeezes the pump, releasing fluid into the cylinders. When the erection is no longer needed, a release valve returns the fluid to the reservoir, deflating the penis (DATTA, 1988). The inflatable type more closely duplicates the normal processes of tumescence and detumescence.

Some adverse side effects of penile implants have also been reported, including infection, pain, and damage to the spongy tissues of the penis. Yet most men who receive penile implants, and their partners, are generally pleased with them (Anderson & Wold, 1986; LoPiccolo & Stock, 1986; Spark, 1991).

Vascular Surgery   *Vascular surgery* may be helpful when the blood vessels that supply the penis are blocked, or when structural defects in the penis restrict blood flow (Carmignani et al., 1987; Goldstein, 1987; Mohr & Beutler, 1990).

Hormone Treatments   Hormone (testosterone) treatments may help restore sex drive and erectile ability in men with abnormally low levels of testosterone (Bagatell & Bremner, 1996; Carani et al., 1990; Spark, 1991). There is no evidence for its effectiveness in men with normal hormone levels. Testosterone has been shown to help women who complain of lack of desire after their adrenal glands and ovaries have been removed (Bagatell & Bremner, 1996).

Penile Injection   The muscle relaxants *papaverine* and *alprostadil* work after injection into the corpus cavernosum of the penis. A physician teaches the man how to inject himself. The drugs work by relaxing the muscles that surround the small blood vessels in the penis. The majority of men with erectile failure achieve an erection sufficient for coitus through injection (Linet & Ogrinc, 1996). A six-month study of self-injections with alprostadil in 296 men found that 94% of the men reported erections adequate for sexual activity (Linet & Ogrinc, 1996).

Penile injections may have side effects, including local pain and prolonged, painful erections (*priapism*) (Linet & Ogrinc, 1996; Lipschultz, 1996). Many men find the idea of

APPLICATIONS

FINDING A QUALIFIED SEX THERAPIST

How would you find a sex therapist if you had a sexual dysfunction? You might find advertisements for "sex therapists" in the Yellow Pages. But beware. Most states do not restrict usage of the term "sex therapist" to recognized professionals. In these states, anyone who wants to use the label may do so, including quacks and prostitutes.

Thus, it is essential to determine that a sex therapist is a member of a recognized profession (such as psychology, social work, medicine, or marriage and family counseling) with training and supervision in sex therapy. Professionals are usually licensed or certified by their states.

If you are uncertain as to how to locate a qualified sex therapist in your area, you may obtain names of local practitioners from various sources, such as your university or college psychology department, health department, or counseling center; a local medical or psychological association; a family physician; or your instructor. You may also contact the American Association of Sex Educators, Counselors, and Therapists (AASECT), a professional organization that certifies sex therapists. They can provide you with the names of certified sex therapists in your area. They are located at 11 Dupont Circle, N.W., Washington, DC.

Ethical professionals are not annoyed or embarrassed if you ask them (1) what their profession is, (2) where they earned their advanced degree, (3) whether they are licensed or certified by the state, (4) their fees, (5) their plans for treatment, and (6) the nature of their training in human sexuality and sex therapy. If the therapist hems and haws, asks why you are asking such questions, or fails to provide a direct answer, beware.

Professionals are also restricted by the ethical principles of their professions from engaging in unethical practices, such as sexual relations with their clients. Any therapist who makes a sexual overture toward a client, or tries to persuade a client to engage in sexual relations, is acting unethically.

penile injections distasteful and reject them out of hand or drop out after a trial (Lipschultz, 1996). Researchers are investigating alternatives to injections, such as creams that can be rubbed on the penis.

Vacuum Constriction Device   A noninvasive *vacuum constriction device (VCD)* helps men achieve erections through vacuum pressure. The device (brand name: ErecAid) consists of a cylinder that is connected to a hand-operated vacuum pump. The vacuum increases the flow of blood into the penis, inducing an erection. Rubber bands placed around the base of the penis can maintain the erection for as long as 30 minutes. However, side effects such as pain and black-and-blue marks are common (Spark, 1991). The rubber bands can also injure penile tissue and prevent normal ejaculation, so semen remains trapped in the urethra until the bands are released (Spark, 1991).

Chapter Review

Sexual (1) _____tions are problems in becoming sexually aroused or reaching orgasm. People are not considered to have a sexual dysfunction unless the problem is (2) per_____ and causes (3) dis_____. In the NHSLS survey, (4: Women *or* Men?) reported more problems than (5: Women *or* Men?) in the areas of painful sex, lack of pleasure, inability to reach orgasm, and lack of sexual desire. (6: Women *or* Men?) were more likely to report reaching climax too early and being anxious about their performance.

Types of Sexual Dysfunctions

The text groups sexual dysfunctions into four categories: sexual (7) d_____ disorders, sexual (8) a_____ disorders, orgasmic disorders, and sexual pain disorders. (9) Dys_____ and (10) _____mus are sexual pain disorders. Sexual dysfunctions may be (11) _____-long or acquired. They may also be generalized or (12) _____onal.

Sexual desire disorders involve lack of sexual desire or (13) av_____ to genital sexual activity. People with little or no sexual interest or desire are said to have (14) _____tive sexual desire disorder. Sexual (15) _____sions are characterized by intense, irrational fears of sexual contact.

People with sexual arousal disorders fail to achieve or sustain adequate (16) lu_____ or erection. Male

(17) _____ile disorder is characterized by persistent difficulty in achieving or maintaining an erection sufficient to allow the completion of sexual activity. (18) Ac_____ erectile disorder is more common than lifelong erectile disorder. Occasional problems in achieving or maintaining erection (19: Are *or* Are not?) quite common. (20) Per_____ anxiety is a prominent cause of erectile disorder. Women with female sexual (21) _____sal disorder have trouble becoming sexually excited or lubricated enough in response to sexual stimulation.

Three disorders concern the orgasm phase of the sexual response cycle: female (22) _____mic disorder, male orgasmic disorder, and premature (23) _____tion. Orgasmic disorder is more common among (24: Men *or* Women?). Women who have never reached orgasm are sometimes labeled (25) _____smic or preorgasmic. (26) Pre_____ ejaculation was the most common male sexual dysfunction reported in the NHSLS study.

The most common cause of coital pain in women is inadequate (27) _____tion. Vaginismus involves involuntary (28) _____tion of the muscles that surround the vaginal barrel.

Origins of Sexual Dysfunctions

Sexual desire is stoked by the hormone (29) _____one. Women may experience less sexual desire when their

(30) _____al glands have been surgically removed. Fatigue may cause (31) _____ile disorder in men and (32) or_____ disorder in women. Nervous system (33) _____sants such as alcohol, heroin, and morphine can reduce sexual desire and response.

People whose parents instilled in them feelings of (34) g_____ over touching their genitals may find it difficult to accept their sex organs as sources of pleasure. (35: Men *or* Women?) in our culture remain more likely than (36: Men *or* Women?) to be taught to repress their sexual desires or even to fear their sexuality. Sexual stimuli may bring about (37) anx_____ when they are connected with painful experiences, such as rape, incest, or sexual molestation. The couple who fail to (38) _____cate their sexual preferences or to experiment with altering their sexual techniques may find themselves losing interest. Within (39) _____tic theory, sexual dysfunctions are rooted in the failure to successfully resolve the Oedipus or Electra complexes of early childhood. Helen Singer (40) _____n believes that sexual dysfunctions represent an interaction of *immediate* causes and deep-seated, or *remote,* causes. (41) _____ance anxiety occurs when a person becomes overly concerned with how well he or she performs a certain act or task. Performance anxiety may place an individual in a (42) _____tor rather than a performer role.

Treatment of Sexual Dysfunctions

Sex therapy aims to modify the dysfunctional behavior (43: Directly *or* Indirectly?). Sex therapies aim to change (44) self-_____ing beliefs and attitudes, teach sexual skills, enhance sexual knowledge, improve sexual (45) com_____, and reduce performance anxiety.

(46) M_____ and Johnson pioneered the use of a female–male therapy team in a two-week residential program. Masters and Johnson treat the (47: Individual *or* Couple?). Couples perform daily sexual homework assignments, such as (48) sen_____ _____us exercises. With these exercises, there (49: Is *or* Is not any?) pressure to perform. Kaplan's (50) _____ual therapy combines behavioral and psychoanalytic methods.

Erection and lubrication are involuntary (51) _____xes, not skills. In sex therapy, people learn that they (52: Do *or* Do not?) need to "do" something to become sexually aroused. In order to reduce performance anxiety, the partners engage in (53) non_____ sexual contacts.

Masters and Johnson begin to treat (54) an_____ women with sensate focus exercises. The woman guides her partner to show him the types of (55) stim_____ she enjoys. Orgasm (56: Can *or* Cannot?) be willed or forced. Other sex therapists begin working with the woman individually through (57) _____bation.

In the Masters and Johnson approach to treating premature ejaculation, the woman teases her partner to erection and uses the (58) s_____ technique when he indicates that he is about to ejaculate. An alternative is the (59) s_____-s_____ method.

(60) Dys_____ calls for medical evaluation to treat underlying physical problems that might give rise to pain. Vaginismus is generally treated with the insertion of (61) _____tors of increasing size.

(62) _____sant drugs have been helpful in treatment of premature ejaculation. Treatments for (63) _____ile disorder include penile implants, hormone treatments, vascular surgery, and self-injections of drugs that induce erections. The two types of penile implants are (64) semi_____ and inflatable. Injected muscle (65) _____ants work by relaxing the muscles that surround the blood vessels in the penis so that blood can flow into the penis more freely.

Chapter Quiz

1. According to the NHSLS study, the most common male sexual dysfunction is
   (a) male orgasmic disorder.
   (b) erectile disorder.
   (c) premature ejaculation.
   (d) performance anxiety.

2. Which of the following is most likely to have organic causes?
   (a) Dyspareunia.
   (b) Vaginismus.
   (c) Female orgasmic disorder.
   (d) Performance anxiety.

3. According to the NHSLS study, the most common female sexual dysfunction is
   (a) dyspareunia.
   (b) lack of interest in sex.
   (c) reaching climax too early.
   (d) having trouble lubricating.
4. Masters and Johnson used all of the following treatment methods EXCEPT
   (a) sensate focus exercises.
   (b) a male-and-female therapy team.
   (c) a two-week residential program.
   (d) guided masturbation.
5. According to the text, which of the following is most likely to be connected with a history of sexual trauma?
   (a) Dyspareunia.
   (b) Rapid ejaculation.
   (c) Performance anxiety.
   (d) Vaginismus.
6. Papaverine is used in the treatment of
   (a) premature ejaculation.
   (b) male erectile disorder.
   (c) female orgasmic disorder.
   (d) hypoactive sexual desire.
7. According to the text, a low level of _____ has been connected with lack of sexual desire.

   (a) testosterone
   (b) estrogen
   (c) Depo-Provera
   (d) alprostadil
8. Helen Singer Kaplan's approach to sex therapy is termed
   (a) couples therapy.
   (b) family therapy.
   (c) medical therapy.
   (d) psychosexual therapy.
9. All of the following are sex therapy methods, with the exception of
   (a) penile implants.
   (b) improving sexual communication.
   (c) reducing performance anxiety.
   (d) sensate focus exercises.
10. Under what circumstances may a sex therapist ethically engage in sexual relations with a client?
    (a) When the client requests it.
    (b) When the client is an adult.
    (c) When the client does not have a partner of his or her own.
    (d) Under no circumstances, ever.

Answers to Chapter Review

1. Dysfunctions
2. Persistent
3. Distress (Discomfort is not as good an answer)
4. Women
5. Men
6. Men
7. Desire
8. Arousal
9. Dyspareunia
10. Vaginismus
11. Lifelong
12. Situational
13. Aversion
14. Hypoactive
15. Aversions
16. Lubrication
17. Erectile
18. Acquired
19. Are
20. Performance
21. Arousal
22. Orgasmic
23. Ejaculation
24. Women
25. Anorgasmic
26. Premature
27. Lubrication
28. Contraction
29. Testosterone
30. Adrenal
31. Erectile
32. Orgasmic
33. Depressants
34. Guilt
35. Women
36. Men
37. Anxiety
38. Communicate
39. Psychoanalytic
40. Kaplan
41. Performance
42. Spectator
43. Directly
44. Defeating
45. Communication
46. Masters
47. Couple
48. Sensate focus
49. Is not any
50. Psychosexual
51. Reflexes
52. Do not
53. Nondemanding
54. Anorgasmic
55. Stimulation
56. Cannot
57. Masturbation
58. Squeeze
59. Stop-start
60. Dyspareunia
61. Dilators
62. Antidepressant
63. Erectile
64. Semirigid
65. Relaxants

Answers to Chapter Quiz

1. (c)
2. (a)
3. (b)
4. (d)
5. (d)
6. (b)
7. (a)
8. (d)
9. (a)
10. (d)

C H A P T E R   *13*

Sexually Transmitted Diseases

O U T L I N E

Bacterial Diseases
Gonorrhea
Syphilis
Chlamydia
Other Bacterial Diseases

Vaginal Infections
Bacterial Vaginosis
Candidiasis
Trichomoniasis

Viral Diseases
AIDS
Herpes
Viral Hepatitis
Genital Warts

Ectoparasitic Infestations
Pediculosis
Scabies

Chapter Review

Chapter Quiz

A World of Diversity
Ethnicity and AIDS in the United States

Applications
How HIV Is *Not* Transmitted
Preventing AIDS and Other Sexually Transmitted Diseases

■ More people in the United States are infected with human papilloma virus each year than with the organisms that cause syphilis, genital herpes, and AIDS combined?

■ The majority of women who contract gonorrhea do not develop symptoms?

■ A number of sexually transmitted diseases actually can be contracted from toilet seats in public rest rooms?

■ Although a syphilitic sore goes away by itself, the infection still requires treatment?

■ As you are reading this page, you are engaged in search-and-destroy missions against foreign agents within your body?

■ Most people who are infected by HIV remain symptom-free and appear healthy for years?

■ Genital herpes can be transmitted at any time, not only during flare-ups of the disease?

■ Pubic lice may be referred to as "crabs," but they are not of the same family of animals?

Today, for the first time, a generation of young people are becoming sexually active with the threat of a lethal disease hanging over every sexual encounter. AIDS has changed the expression of human sexuality. Innocence and complete spontaneity are things of the past.

AIDS is indeed a scary thing, yet other **sexually transmitted diseases** (STDs) pose much wider threats. In a study of more than 16,000 students on 19 U.S. college campuses, HIV (the virus that causes AIDS) was found in 30 blood samples (Gayle et al., 1990), or 0.2% of the students in the sample. *Chlamydia trachomatous* (the bacterium that causes chlamydia) and *human papilloma virus* (HPV) (the organism that causes genital warts) were each found in 1 sample in 10, or 10% of the college population! HPV is estimated to be present in one third of college women and 8% of men ages 15 to 49 (Cannistra & Niloff, 1996).

College students are reasonably well versed about AIDS, but many are unaware that chlamydia can go undetected for years. Moreover, if it is left untreated, it can cause pelvic inflammation and infertility. Many, perhaps most, students were completely ignorant of HPV, which is linked to cervical cancer. Yet as many as 1 million new cases of HPV infection occur each year in the United States—more than cases of syphilis, genital herpes, and AIDS combined. Whereas 1 to 1.5 million Americans are thought to be infected with HIV, about 56 million are infected with other STD-causing viruses, such as those causing genital warts, herpes, and hepatitis (Barringer, 1993a).

Sexually transmitted diseases (STDs) are transmitted through sexual means, such as vaginal or anal intercourse or oral sex. They were formerly called *venereal diseases* (VD)—after Venus, the Roman goddess of love. In this chapter we discuss STDs that are caused by bacteria, viruses, protozoa, and parasites. ■

Bacterial Diseases

Bacteria are one-celled microorganisms that cause many diseases such as pneumonia, tuberculosis, and meningitis—along with the common STDs gonorrhea, syphilis, and chlamydia.

Sexually transmitted diseases

Diseases that are communicated through sexual contact. Abbreviated *STDs.*

Bacteria

Plural of *bacterium,* a class of one-celled microorganisms that have no chlorophyll and can give rise to many illnesses. (From the Greek *baktron,* meaning "stick," referring to the fact that many bacteria are rod-shaped.)

Gonorrhea

An STD caused by the *Neisseria gonorrhoeae* bacterium and characterized by a discharge and burning urination. Left untreated, gonorrhea can give rise to pelvic inflammatory disease (PID) and infertility. (From the Greek *gonos,* meaning "seed," and *rheein,* meaning "to flow," referring to the fact that in ancient times the penile discharge characteristic of the illness was erroneously interpreted as a loss of seminal fluid.)

Gonorrhea

Nearly a million cases of **gonorrhea**—also known as "the clap" or "the drip"—are reported each year (Centers for Disease Control [CDC], 1990a). Many cases go unreported, however. Gonorrhea is caused by the *gonococcus* bacterium (see Table 13.1 on page 326).

Transmission   Gonococcal bacteria require a warm, moist environment, like that found along the mucous membranes of the urinary tract in both genders or the cervix in women. Outside the body, they die in about a minute. Gonorrhea is almost always transmitted by unprotected vaginal, oral, or anal sexual activity, or from mother to newborn during delivery (Reinisch, 1990).

A person who performs fellatio on an infected man may develop **pharyngeal gonorrhea,** which produces a throat infection. Mouth-to-mouth kissing and cunnilingus are less likely to spread gonorrhea. The eyes provide a good environment for the bacterium. Thus, a person whose hands come into contact with infected genitals and who inadvertently touches his or her eyes afterward may infect them. Babies have contracted gonorrhea of the eyes **(ophthalmia neonatorum)** when passing through the birth canals of infected mothers. This disorder may cause blindness but has become rare because the eyes of newborns are treated routinely with silver nitrate or penicillin ointment, which are toxic to gonococcal bacteria.

A gonorrheal infection may be spread from the penis to the partner's rectum during anal intercourse. A cervical gonorrheal infection can be spread to the rectum if an infected woman and her partner follow vaginal intercourse with anal intercourse. Gonorrhea is less likely to be spread by vaginal than penile discharges.

Symptoms   Most men experience symptoms within two to five days after infection. Symptoms include a penile discharge that is clear at first. Within a day it turns yellow to yellow-green, thickens, and becomes puslike. The urethra becomes inflamed, and urination is accompanied by a burning sensation. Thirty percent to 40% of males have swelling and tenderness in the lymph glands of the groin. Inflammation and other symptoms may become chronic if left untreated.

The initial symptoms of gonorrhea usually abate within a few weeks without treatment, leading people to think of gonorrhea as being no worse than a bad cold. However, the gonococcus bacterium will usually continue to damage the body even though the early symptoms fade.

In women the primary site of the infection is the cervix, where it causes **cervicitis.** Cervicitis may cause a yellowish to yellow-green puslike discharge that irritates the vulva. If the infection spreads to the urethra, women may also note burning urination. About 80% of the women who contract gonorrhea are **asymptomatic** during the early stages of the disease, however. Unfortunately, therefore, many infected women do not seek treatment until more serious symptoms develop. They may also inadvertently infect another sex partner.

When gonorrhea is not treated early, it may spread through the urogenital systems in both genders and strike the internal reproductive organs. In men, it can lead to **epididymitis,** which can cause fertility problems. Swelling and feelings of tenderness or pain in the scrotum are the principal symptoms of epididymitis. Fever may also be present. Occasionally the kidneys are affected.

In women, the bacterium can spread through the cervix to the uterus, fallopian tubes, ovaries, and other parts of the abdominal cavity, causing **pelvic inflammatory disease** (PID). Symptoms of PID include cramps, abdominal pain and tenderness, cervical tenderness and discharge, irregular menstrual cycles, coital pain, fever, nausea, and vomiting. PID may also be asymptomatic. PID can cause scarring that blocks the fallopian tubes, leading to infertility. PID is a serious illness that requires aggressive treatment with antibiotics or surgery to remove infected tissue.

Diagnosis and Treatment   When diagnosed and treated early, gonorrhea clears up rapidly in more than 90% of cases. Diagnosis of gonorrhea involves clinical inspection of the genitals by a physician and the culturing and examination of a sample of genital discharge.

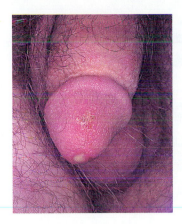

Gonorrheal Discharge. Gonorrhea in the male often causes a thick, yellowish, pus-like discharge from the penis.

Pharyngeal gonorrhea
A gonorrheal infection of the pharynx (the cavity leading from the mouth and nasal passages to the larynx and esophagus) that is characterized by a sore throat.

Ophthalmia neonatorum
A gonorrheal infection of the eyes of newborn children who contract the disease by passing through an infected birth canal. (From the Greek *oph-thalmos*, meaning "eye.")

Cervicitis
Inflammation of the cervix.

Asymptomatic
Without symptoms.

Epididymitis
Inflammation of the epididymis.

Pelvic inflammatory disease
Inflammation of the pelvic region—possibly including the cervix, uterus, fallopian tubes, abdominal cavity, and ovaries—that can be caused by organisms such as *Neisseria gonorrhoeae*. Its symptoms are abdominal pain, tenderness, nausea, fever, and irregular menstrual cycles. The condition may lead to infertility. Abbreviated *PID*.

TABLE 13.1 Causes, modes of transmission, symptoms, diagnosis, and treatment of major sexually transmitted diseases (STDs)

STD and Pathogen	Modes of Transmission	Symptoms	Diagnosis	Treatment
Bacterial Diseases				
Gonorrhea ("clap," "drip"): gonococcus bacterium (*Neisseria gonorrhoeae*).	Transmitted by vaginal, oral, or anal sexual activity, or from mother to newborn during delivery.	In men, yellowish, thick penile discharge; burning urination. In women, increased vaginal discharge, burning urination, irregular menstrual bleeding (most women show no early symptoms).	Clinical inspection, culture of sample discharge.	Antibiotics: ceftriaxone, spectinomycin, penicillin.
Syphilis: *Treponema pallidum.*	Transmitted by vaginal, oral, or anal sexual activity, or by touching an infectious chancre.	In primary stage, a hard, round painless chancre or sore appears at site of infection within 2 to 4 weeks. May progress through secondary, latent, and tertiary stages, if left untreated.	Primary-stage syphilis is diagnosed by clinical examination and by examination of fluid from a chancre. Secondary-stage syphilis is diagnosed by blood test (the VDRL).	Penicillin; or doxycycline, tetracycline, or erythromycin for nonpregnant, penicillin-allergic patients.
Chlamydia and non-gonococcal urethritis (NGU): *Chlamydia trachomatous* bacterium; NGU in men may also be caused by *Ureaplasma urealycticum* bacterium and other pathogens.	Transmitted by vaginal, oral, or anal sexual activity; to the eye by touching one's eyes after touching the genitals of an infected partner, or to newborns passing through the birth canal of an infected mother.	In women, frequent and painful urination, lower abdominal pain and inflammation, and vaginal discharge (but most women are symptom-free). In men, symptoms are similar to but milder than those of gonorrhea—burning or painful urination, slight penile discharge (most men are also asymptomatic). Sore throat may indicate infection from oral–genital contact.	The Abbott Testpack analyzes a cervical smear in women; in men, an extract of fluid from the penis is analyzed.	Antibiotics: doxycycline, tetracycline , or erythromycin.
Vaginitis				
Bacterial vaginosis: *Gardnerella vaginalis* bacterium and others.	Can arise by overgrowth of organisms in vagina, allergic reactions, etc.; also transmitted by sexual contact.	In women, thin, foul-smelling vaginal discharge. Irritation of genitals and mild pain during urination. In men, inflammation of penile foreskin and glans, urethritis, and cystitis. May be asymptomatic in both genders.	Culture and examination of bacterium.	Oral treatment with metronidazole (brand name: Flagyl).

STD and Pathogen	Modes of Transmission	Symptoms	Diagnosis	Treatment
Candidiasis (moniliasis, thrush, "yeast infection"): *Candida albicans*—a yeastlike fungus.	Can arise by overgrowth of fungus in vagina; may also be transmitted by sexual contact or by sharing a washcloth with an infected person.	In women, vulval itching; white, cheesy, foul-smelling discharge; soreness or swelling of vaginal and vulval tissues. In men, itching and burning on urination, or a reddening of the penis.	Diagnosis usually made on basis of symptoms.	Vaginal suppositories, creams, or tablets containing miconazole, clotrimazole , or terconazole; modification of use of other medicines and chemical agents; keeping infected area dry.
Trichomoniasis ("trich"): *Trichomonas vaginalis*—a protozoan (one-celled animal).	Almost always transmitted sexually.	In women, foamy, yellowish, odorous vaginal discharge; itching or burning sensation in vulva. Many women are asymptomatic. In men, usually asymptomatic, but mild urethritis is possible.	Microscopic examination of a smear of vaginal secretions, or of culture of the sample (latter method preferred).	Metronidazole (Flagyl).

Viral Diseases

STD and Pathogen	Modes of Transmission	Symptoms	Diagnosis	Treatment
Acquired immunodeficiency syndrome (AIDS): *Human immunodeficiency virus (HIV)*	HIV is transmitted by sexual contact, by infusion with contaminated blood, from mother to fetus during pregnancy, or through childbirth or breast-feeding.	Infected people may initially be asymptomatic or develop mild flulike symptoms, which may then disappear for many years prior to the development of AIDS. AIDS is symptomized by fever, weight loss, fatigue, diarrhea, and opportunistic infections such as rare forms of cancer (Kaposi's sarcoma) and pneumonia (PCP).	Blood, saliva, or urine tests detect HIV antibodies. The Western blot blood test may be used to confirm the results when HIV antibodies are present. The diagnosis of AIDS is usually made on the basis of antibodies, a low count of CD4 cells, and/or presence of indicator diseases.	Nucleoside analogues such as AZT, ddI, ddC, d4T, and 3TC may delay the progress of HIV infection to AIDS. Protease inhibitors in combination with nucleoside analogues have decreased the amount of HIV in the blood to undetectable levels in many people with HIV infection and AIDS.
Oral herpes: *Herpes simplex* virus-type 1 (HSV-1).	Touching, kissing, sexual contact with sores or blisters; sharing cups, towels, toilet seats.	Cold sores or fever blisters on the lips, mouth, or throat; herpetic sores on the genitals	Usually clinical inspection.	Over-the-counter lip balms, cold-sore medications; check with your physician, however.
Genital herpes: *Herpes simplex* virus-type 2 (HSV-2).	Almost always by means of vaginal, oral, or anal sexual activity; most contagious during active outbreaks of the disease.	Painful, reddish bumps around the genitals, thighs, or buttocks; in women, may also be in the vagina or on the cervix. Bumps become blisters or sores that fill with pus and break, shedding viral particles. Other possible symptoms: burning urination, fever, aches and pains, swollen glands; in women, vaginal discharge.	Clinical inspection of sores; culture and examination of fluid drawn from the base of a genital sore.	The antiviral drug acyclovir (brand name: Zovirax) may provide relief and prompt healing, but is not a cure; people with herpes often profit from counseling and group support as well.

(continued)

TABLE 13.1 Causes, modes of transmission, symptoms, diagnosis, and treatment of major sexually transmitted diseases (STDs) *(continued)*

STD and Pathogen	Modes of Transmission	Symptoms	Diagnosis	Treatment
Viral hepatitis: hepatitis A, B, C, and D type viruses.	Sexual contact, especially involving the anus (especially for hepatitis A); contact with infected fecal matter; transfusion of contaminated blood (especially for hepatitis B and C).	Ranges from being asymptomatic to mild flu-like symptoms and more severe symptoms including fever, abdominal pain, vomiting, and "jaundiced" (yellowish) skin and eyes.	Examination of blood for hepatitis antibodies; liver biopsy.	Treatment usually involves bed rest, intake of fluids, and, sometimes, antibiotics to ward off bacterial infections that might take hold because of lowered resistance. Alpha interferon is sometimes used in treating hepatitis C.
Genital warts (venereal warts): *human papilloma virus (HPV)*.	Transmission is by sexual and other forms of contact, such as with infected towels or clothing.	Appearance of painless warts, often resembling cauliflowers, on the penis, foreskin, scrotum, or internal urethra in men; on the vulva, labia, wall of the vagina, or cervix in women. May occur around the anus and in the rectum of both genders.	Clinical inspection.	Methods include cryotherapy (freezing), podophyllin, burning, surgical removal.
Ectoparasitic Infestations				
Pediculosis ("crabs"): *Pthirus pubis* (pubic lice).	Transmission is by sexual contact, or by contact with an infested towel, sheet, or toilet seat.	Intense itching in pubic area and other hairy regions to which lice can attach.	Clinical examination.	Lindane (brand name: Kwell)—a prescription shampoo; nonprescription medications containing pyrethrins or piperonal butoxide (brand names: RID, Triple X).
Scabies: *Sarcoptes scabiei*.	Transmission is by sexual contact, or by contact with infested clothing, bed linen, towels, and other fabrics.	Intense itching; reddish lines on skin where mites have burrowed in; welts and pus-filled blisters in affected areas.	Clinical inspection.	Lindane (Kwell).

Source: Adapted from Rathus, S. A. (1996). *Psychology,* 6th ed. Fort Worth: Harcourt Brace College Publishers.

Antibiotics are the standard treatment for gonorrhea. Penicillin was once the favored antibiotic, but the rise of penicillin-resistant strains of *Neisseria gonorrhoeae* has required that alternative antibiotics be used (Goldstein & Clark, 1990). Since gonorrhea and chlamydia often occur together, persons infected with gonorrhea are usually also treated for chlamydia through the use of another antibiotic. Sex partners of people with gonorrhea should also be examined.

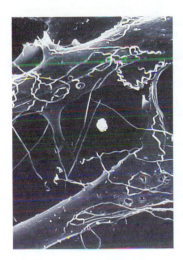

Figure 13.1. *Treponema Pallidum. Treponema pallidum* is the bacterium that causes syphilis. Because of its spiral shape, *T. pallidum* is also called a *spirochete*.

Syphilis

A sexually transmitted disease that is caused by a bacterial infection.

Chancre

A sore or ulcer.

Congenital syphilis

A syphilis infection that is present at birth.

Neurosyphilis

Syphilitic infection of the central nervous system, which can cause brain damage and death.

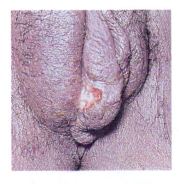

Syphilis Chancre. The first, or primary, stage of a syphilis infection is marked by the appearance of a painless sore or chancre at the site of infection.

Syphilis

The bacterium that causes **syphilis** is *Treponema pallidum* (*T. pallidum,* for short). Because of its spiral shape, *T. pallidum* is also called a *spirochete,* from Greek roots meaning "spiral" and "hair." (See Figure 13.1).

The incidence of syphilis decreased in the United States with the introduction of penicillin (Zenker & Rolfs, 1990) but rose again during the 1980s (Rolfs & Nakashima, 1990). About 45,000 cases of syphilis are reported each year (CDC, 1989a). Many cases go unreported. Cocaine users risk contracting syphilis through sex with multiple partners or with prostitutes, not through cocaine use per se (Rolfs et al., 1990).

Transmission   Syphilis, like gonorrhea, is most often transmitted by vaginal or anal intercourse, or oral–genital or oral–anal contact with an infected person. The spirochete is usually transmitted when open lesions on an infected person come into contact with the mucous membranes or skin abrasions of the partner's body during sexual activity. The chance of contracting syphilis from one sexual contact with an infected partner is estimated at one in three (Reinisch, 1990). Syphilis may also be contracted by touching an infectious **chancre,** but not from using the same toilet seat as an infected person.

Pregnant women may transmit syphilis to their fetuses, because the spirochete can cross the placental membrane. Miscarriage, stillbirth, or **congenital syphilis** may result. Congenital syphilis may impair vision and hearing or deform bones and teeth. Blood tests are administered routinely during pregnancy to diagnose syphilis in the mother so that congenital problems in the baby may be averted. The fetus will probably not be harmed if an infected mother is treated before the fourth month of pregnancy.

Symptoms and Course of Illness   Syphilis develops through several stages. In the first or *primary stage* of syphilis, a painless chancre (a hard, round, ulcerlike lesion with raised edges) appears at the site of infection two to four weeks after contact. When women are infected, the chancre usually forms on the vaginal walls or the cervix. It may also form on the external genitalia, most often on the labia. When men are infected, the chancre usually forms on the penile glans. It may also form on the scrotum or penile shaft. If the mode of transmission is oral sex, the chancre may appear on the lips or tongue. If the infection is spread by anal sex, the rectum may serve as the site of the chancre. The chancre disappears within a few weeks, but if the infection remains untreated, syphilis will continue to work within the body.

The *secondary stage* begins a few weeks to a few months later. A skin rash develops, consisting of painless, reddish, raised bumps that darken after a while and burst, oozing a discharge. Other symptoms include sores in the mouth, painful swelling of joints, a sore throat, headaches, and fever. A person with syphilis may thus wrongly assume that he or she has the flu.

These symptoms also disappear. Syphilis then enters the *latent stage* and may lie dormant for 1 to 40 years. But spirochetes continue to multiply and burrow into the circulatory system, central nervous system (brain and spinal cord), and bones. The person may no longer be contagious to sex partners after several years in the latent stage, but a pregnant woman may pass along the infection to her newborn.

In many cases the disease eventually progresses to the late or *tertiary stage.* A large ulcer may form on the skin, muscle tissue, digestive organs, lungs, liver, or other organs. This destructive ulcer can often be successfully treated, but still more serious damage can occur as the infection attacks the central nervous system or the cardiovascular system (the heart and the major blood vessels). Either outcome can be fatal. **Neurosyphilis** can cause brain damage, resulting in paralysis or the mental illness called **general paresis.**

The primary and secondary symptoms of syphilis inevitably disappear. Infected people may thus be tempted to believe that they are no longer at risk and fail to see a doctor. This is indeed unfortunate, because failure to eradicate the infection through proper treatment may lead to dire consequences.

Diagnosis and Treatment   Primary-stage syphilis is diagnosed by clinical examination. If a chancre is found, fluid drawn from it can be examined under a microscope. The spirochetes are usually quite visible. Blood tests are not definitive until the secondary stage begins. The most frequently used blood test is the **VDRL.** The VDRL tests for the presence of **antibodies** to *Treponema pallidum* in the blood.

Penicillin is the treatment of choice for syphilis, although other antibiotics are sometimes used. Sex partners of persons infected with syphilis should also be evaluated by a physician.

Chlamydia

Although you may be more familiar with gonorrhea and syphilis, chlamydia, another bacterial STD, is actually more common in the United States (CDC, 1993a). Chlamydial infections are caused by the *Chlamydia trachomatis* bacterium. This bacterium can cause several different types of infection, including *nongonococcal urethritis (NGU)* in men and women, *epididymitis* (infection of the epididymis) in men, and *cervicitis* (infection of the cervix), *endometritis* (infection of the endometrium), and PID in women.

As many as 4 million cases may occur annually (Toomey & Barnes, 1990). The incidence of chlamydial infections is especially high among teenagers and college students (Shafer et al., 1993). Researchers estimate that between 8% and 40% of teenage women become infected (Yarber & Parillo, 1992).

Transmission   *Chlamydia trachomatis* is usually transmitted through sexual intercourse—vaginal or anal. It may also cause an eye infection if a person touches his or her eyes after handling the genitals of an infected partner. Oral sex with an infected partner can infect the throat. Newborns can acquire potentially serious chlamydial eye infections as they pass through the cervix of an infected mother during birth. Even newborns delivered by cesarean section may be infected if the amniotic sac breaks before delivery (Reinisch, 1990). Each year more than 100,000 infants are infected with the bacterium during birth (Graham & Blanco, 1990). Of these, about 75,000 develop eye infections and 30,000 develop pneumonia.

Symptoms   Chlamydial infections usually produce symptoms that are similar to, but milder than, those of gonorrhea. In men, *Chlamydia trachomatis* can lead to nongonococcal urethritis (NGU). *Urethritis* is an inflammation of the urethra. NGU refers to forms of urethritis that are not caused by the gonococcal bacterium. (NGU is generally diagnosed only in men. In women, an inflammation of the urethra caused by *Chlamydia trachomatis* is called a chlamydial infection or simply chlamydia.) NGU was formerly called nonspecific urethritis or NSU. Many organisms can cause NGU. *Chlamydia trachomatis* accounts for about half of the cases among men (CDC, 1985).

NGU in men may give rise to a thin, whitish discharge from the penis and some burning or other pain during urination. These contrast with the yellow-green discharge and more intense pain produced by gonorrhea. There may be soreness in the scrotum and feelings of heaviness in the testes. NGU is about two to three times as prevalent among American men as gonorrhea (CDC, 1989a; Reinisch, 1990).

In women, chlamydial infections usually give rise to infections of the urethra or cervix. Women, like men, may experience burning when they urinate, genital irritation, and a mild (vaginal) discharge. Women are also likely to encounter pelvic pain and irregular menstrual cycles. The cervix may look swollen and inflamed.

Yet, as many as 25% of men and 70% of women infected with chlamydia are asymptomatic (Cates & Wasserheit, 1991). For this reason, chlamydia has been dubbed the "silent disease." People without symptoms may go untreated and unknowingly pass along their infections to their partners. In women, an untreated chlamydial infection can spread throughout the reproductive system, leading to PID and to scarring of the fallopian tubes, resulting in infertility (Garland et al., 1990; Hodgson et al., 1990). About half of the more than 1 million annual cases of PID are attributed to chlamydia (Schachter, 1989). Women with a history of exposure to *Chlamydia trachomatis* also stand twice the normal chance of incurring an ectopic (tubal) pregnancy (Sherman et al., 1990).

Untreated chlamydial infections can also damage the internal reproductive organs of men. About 50% of cases of epididymitis are caused by chlamydial infections (Crum & Ellner, 1985). Yet only about 1% or 2% of men with untreated NGU caused by *Chlamydia trachomatis* go on to develop epididymitis (Bowie, 1990). The long-term effects of untreated chlamydial infections in men remain undetermined.

Chlamydial infections also frequently occur together with other STDs, most often gonorrhea. As many as 45% of cases of gonorrhea involve coexisting chlamydial infections (CDC, 1985; CDC, 1989a).

Diagnosis and Treatment   The Abbott Testpack permits physicians to verify a diagnosis of chlamydia in women in about half an hour (Reichart et al., 1990; Reinisch, 1990). The test analyzes a cervical smear (like a Pap smear) and identifies 75% to 80% of infected cases. There are relatively few **false positives** (incorrect positive findings). In men, a swab is inserted through the penile opening, and the extracted fluid is analyzed to detect the presence of *Chlamydia trachomatis*.

Antibiotics other than penicillin are highly effective in eradicating chlamydial infections (CDC, 1989b; Toomey & Barnes, 1990). (Penicillin, effective in treating gonorrhea, is ineffective against *Chlamydia trachomatis*.) Treatment of sex partners is considered critical regardless of whether the partner shows symptoms, so as to prevent the infection from bouncing back and forth (Martin, 1990).

Other Bacterial Diseases

Several other types of bacterial STDs occur less commonly in the United States and Canada. These include chancroid, shigellosis, granuloma inguinale, and lymphogranuloma venereum.

Chancroid   **Chancroid,** or "soft chancre," is caused by the bacterium *Hemophilus ducreyi*. It is more commonly found in the tropics and Eastern nations than in Western countries. The chancroid sore consists of a cluster of small bumps or pimples on the genitals, perineum (the area of skin that lies between the genitals and the anus), or the anus itself. These lesions usually appear within seven days of infection. Within a few days the lesion ruptures, producing an open sore or ulcer. Several ulcers may merge with other ulcers, forming giant ulcers. There is usually an accompanying swelling of a nearby lymph node. In contrast to the syphilis chancre, the chancroid ulcer has a soft rim (hence the name) and is painful in men. Women frequently do not experience any pain and may be unaware of being infected. The bacterium is typically transmitted through sexual or bodily contact with the lesion or its discharge. Diagnosis is usually confirmed by culturing the bacterium, which is found in pus from the sore, and examining it under a microscope. Antibiotics (erythromycin or ceftriaxone) are usually effective in treating the disease.

Shigellosis   **Shigellosis** is caused by the *Shigella* bacterium and is characterized by fever and severe abdominal symptoms, including diarrhea and inflammation of the large intestine. About 25,000 cases of shigellosis are reported annually (CDC, 1989a). It is often contracted by oral contact with infected fecal material, which may occur as the result of oral–anal sex. It can be treated with antibiotics, such as tetracycline or *ampicillin*.

Granuloma Inguinale   Rare in the United States, **granuloma inguinale,** like chancroid, is more common in tropical regions. It is caused by the bacterium *Calymmatobacterium granulomatous* and is not as contagious as many other STDs. Primary symptoms are painless red bumps or sores in the groin area that ulcerate and spread. Like chancroid, it is usually spread by intimate bodily or sexual contact with a lesion or its discharge. Diagnosis is confirmed by microscopic examination of tissue of the rim of the sore. The antibiotics tetracycline and streptomycin are effective in treating this disorder. If left untreated, however, the disease may lead to the development of fistulas (holes) in the rec-

False positive
An erroneous positive test result or clinical finding.

Chancroid
An STD caused by the *Hemophilus ducreyi* bacterium. Also called *soft chancre.*

Shigellosis
An STD caused by the *Shigella* bacterium.

Granuloma inguinale
A tropical STD caused by the *Calymmatobacterium granulomatous* bacterium.

Elephantiasis
A disease characterized by enlargement of parts of the body, especially the legs and genitals, and by hardening and ulceration of the surrounding skin. (From the Greek *elephas*, meaning "elephant," referring to the resemblance of the affected skin areas to elephant hide.)

Lymphogranuloma venereum
A tropical STD caused by the *Chlamydia trachomatis* bacterium.

Vaginitis
Vaginal inflammation.

Bacterial vaginosis
A form of vaginitis usually caused by the *Gardnerella vaginalis* bacterium.

Candidiasis
A form of vaginitis caused by a yeastlike fungus, *Candida albicans*.

tum or bladder, destruction of the tissues or organs that underlie the infection, or scarring of skin tissue that results in a condition called **elephantiasis,** a condition that afflicted the so-called Elephant Man in the nineteenth century.

Lymphogranuloma venereum (LGV)   Lymphogranuloma venereum (LGV) is another tropical STD that occurs only rarely in the United States and Canada. Some U.S. soldiers returned home from Vietnam with cases of LGV. It is caused by several strains of the *Chlamydia trachomatis* bacterium. LGV usually enters the body through the penis, vulva, or cervix, where a small, painless sore may form. The sore may go unnoticed, but a nearby lymph gland in the groin swells and grows tender. Other symptoms mimic those of flu: chills, fever, and headache. Other symptoms that may occur include backache (especially in women) and arthritic complaints (painful joints). If LGV is untreated, complications such as growths and fistulas in the genitals and elephantiasis of the legs and genitals may occur. Diagnosis is made by skin tests and blood tests. The antibiotic doxycycline is the usual treatment.

Vaginal Infections

Vaginitis refers to any kind of vaginal infection or inflammation. Women with vaginitis may encounter genital irritation or itching and burning during urination, but the most common symptom is an odious discharge.

Most cases of vaginitis are caused by organisms that reside in the vagina or by sexually transmitted organisms. Organisms that reside in the vagina may overgrow and cause symptoms when the environmental balance of the vagina is upset by factors such as birth-control pills, antibiotics, dietary changes, excessive douching, or nylon underwear or pantyhose. Still other cases are caused by sensitivities or allergic reactions to various chemicals.

As many as 90% of vaginal infections involve bacterial vaginosis (BV), candidiasis (commonly called a "yeast" infection), or trichomoniasis ("trich"). Bacterial vaginosis is the most common form of vaginitis, followed by candidiasis, then by trichomoniasis (Reinisch, 1990), but some cases involve combinations of the three.

The microbes causing vaginal infections in women can also infect the man's urethral tract. In some cases, a "vaginal infection" can be passed back and forth between sex partners.

Bacterial Vaginosis

Bacterial vaginosis (BV—formerly called *nonspecific vaginitis*) is most often caused by the bacterium *Gardnerella vaginalis*. The bacterium is primarily transmitted through sexual contact. The most characteristic symptom in women is a thin, foul-smelling vaginal discharge, but infected women are often asymptomatic. Accurate diagnosis requires culturing the bacterium in the laboratory (Reinisch, 1990). Besides causing troublesome symptoms in some cases, BV may increase the risk of various gynecological problems, including infections of the reproductive tract (Hillier & Holmes, 1990). Oral treatment with *metronidazole* (brand name: Flagyl) for seven days is recommended (CDC, 1989b) and is effective in about 90% of cases (Reinisch, 1990). Recurrences are common, however.

Questions remain about whether the male partner should also be treated. The bacterium can usually be found in the male urethra but does not generally cause symptoms (Reinisch, 1990). Lacking symptoms, the male partner may unknowingly transmit the bacterium to others. There is no evidence that treating the male with metronidazole benefits either partner, however (CDC, 1989b; Moi et al., 1989).

Candidiasis

Also known as *moniliasis, thrush,* or, most commonly, a yeast infection, **candidiasis** is caused by a yeastlike fungus, *Candida albicans*. Candidiasis commonly produces soreness, inflammation, and intense (sometimes maddening!) itching around the vulva that is accompanied by a white, thick, curdlike vaginal discharge. Yeast generally produces no symptoms when the vaginal environment is normal (Reinisch, 1990). Yeast infections can also occur in the mouth in both men and women and in the penis in men.

Infections most often arise from changes in the vaginal environment that allow the fungus to overgrow. Factors such as the use of antibiotics or birth-control pills, pregnancy, and diabetes may alter the vaginal balance, allowing the fungus that causes yeast infections to grow to infectious levels. Wearing nylon underwear and tight, restrictive, poorly ventilated clothing may also set the stage for a yeast infection.

Diet may play a role in recurrent yeast infections. Reducing one's intake of substances that produce excessive excretion of urinary sugars (such as dairy products, sugar, and artificial sweeteners) apparently reduces the frequency of recurrent yeast infections (Friedrich, 1985). In one study, daily ingestion of one pint of yogurt containing active bacterial (*Lactobacillus acidophilus*) cultures actually helped reduce the rate of recurrent infections (Hilton et al., 1992).

Candidiasis can be passed back and forth between sex partners through vaginal intercourse. It may also be passed back and forth between the mouth and the genitals through oral–genital contact and infect the anus through anal intercourse. However, most infections in women are believed to be caused by an overgrowth of "yeast" normally found in the vagina, not by sexual transmission. Still, it is advisable to evaluate both partners simultaneously. Whereas most men with *Candida* are asymptomatic (Hillier & Holmes, 1990), some may develop NGU or a genital thrush that is accompanied by sensations of itching and burning during urination, or a reddening of the penis (Hillier & Holmes, 1990). Candidiasis may also be transmitted by nonsexual means, as between women who share a washcloth.

About 75% of women will experience an episode of candidiasis at some point during their reproductive years (Reinisch, 1990). About half of these women will have recurrent infections. Three days of treatment with vaginal suppositories, creams, or tablets containing miconazole (brand name: Monistat), clotrimazole (brand names: Lotrimin and Mycelex), or terconazole (brand name: Terazol) is usually recommended (CDC, 1989b). Some of these medications are now available without a prescription. Even so, women with vaginal complaints should consult their physicians before taking any medication, to ensure that they receive the proper diagnosis and treatment.

Trichomoniasis

Trichomoniasis

A form of vaginitis caused by the protozoan *Trichomonas vaginalis*.

Trichomoniasis ("trich") is caused by *Trichomonas vaginalis*, a parasitic animal that consists of only one cell (technically, a protozoan). Trichomoniasis is the most common parasitic STD (Levine, 1991). It accounts for some 8 million cases a year among women in the United States (Martens & Faro, 1989). Symptoms in women include burning or itching in the vulva, mild pain during urination or coitus, and an odorous, foamy whitish to yellowish green discharge. Lower abdominal pain is reported by 5% to 12% of infected women (Rein & Muller, 1990). Many women notice symptoms appearing or worsening during, or just following, their menstrual periods. Trichomoniasis is also linked to the development of tubal adhesions that can result in infertility (Grodstein et al., 1993). As with many other STDs, about half of infected women are asymptomatic (Reinisch, 1990).

Unlike, candidiasis, trichomoniasis is almost always sexually transmitted (CDC, 1989b). Because the parasite may survive for several hours on moist surfaces outside the body, trich can be communicated from contact with infected semen or vaginal discharges on towels, washcloths, and bedclothes. This parasite is one of the few disease agents that can be picked up from a toilet seat, but it would have to directly touch the penis or vulva (Reinisch, 1990).

Trichomonas vaginalis can cause NGU in the male, which can be asymptomatic or cause a slight penile discharge that is usually noticeable only upon awakening before one first urinates in the morning. There may be tingling, itching, and other irritating sensations in the urethral tract. Yet most infected men are symptom-free (Rein & Muller, 1990). Therefore, they may unwittingly transfer the organism to their sex partners. Perhaps three or four in ten male partners of infected women are found to harbor *Trichomonas vaginalis* themselves (Reinisch, 1990). Diagnosis is frequently made by microscopic examination of a smear of a woman's vaginal fluids in a physician's office (Levine, 1991). Diagnosis based on examination of cultures grown from the vaginal smear is considered more reliable, however (Thomason & Gelbart, 1989).

Except during the first three months of pregnancy, trichomoniasis is treated in both genders with metronidazole (brand name: Flagyl). Both partners are treated, whether or not they report symptoms. When both partners are treated simultaneously, the success rate approaches 100% (Thomason & Gelbart, 1989).

Viral Diseases

Viruses are tiny particles of DNA coated by protein. They cannot reproduce on their own. When they invade a body cell, however, they can direct the cell's own reproductive machinery to spin off new viral particles that spread to other cells, causing infection. In this section we discuss several viral STDs: AIDS, herpes, viral hepatitis, and genital warts.

AIDS

AIDS is the acronym for **acquired immunodeficiency syndrome.** AIDS is a fatal disease that is caused by the **human immunodeficiency virus** (HIV). HIV attacks and disables the immune system, the body's natural line of defense, stripping it of its ability to fend off disease-causing organisms. No one knows where HIV originated, but some investigators suspect that it may be a variant of viruses found in monkeys and chimpanzees.

Prevalence   Fewer than 100 Americans had died of AIDS in 1981 when the syndrome was first described in the medical journals (Gottlieb, 1991). By June 30, 1996, more than 548,000 Americans would be diagnosed as having AIDS. More than 338,000 would die from it (CDC, 1996). In 1995 alone there were more than 74,000 new cases of AIDS in the United States (CDC, 1996). AIDS had become the leading killer of Americans of ages 25 to 44.

As many as 1.5 million people in the United States are infected with HIV (Fisher et al., 1995). The World Health Organization (WHO) estimated that 20 million people around the world were infected with HIV in 1995. Nearly 4.5 million of them had developed AIDS (WHO, 1995). WHO estimates that the number of persons infected with HIV may soar to 30 to 40 million by the year 2000.

In 1981, when AIDS-related problems were first described in medical journals, they were labeled as problems that affected gay males. For many years, at least three out of four cases of AIDS were found among the gay male population. But by midyear 1996, only 51% of Americans with AIDS were infected by male–male sexual contact (CDC, 1996). Between July 1995 and June 1996, only 41% of the new cases of AIDS were reported to be due to male–male sexual contact (CDC, 1996). During the same one-year period, another 26% of new cases were infected by sharing contaminated needles when injecting illicit drugs (see Figure 13.2a). Male–female sexual contact is the fastest-growing exposure category. Among women, however, 40% of the new cases of AIDS reported between July 1995 and June 1996 were thought to be due to male–female sexual contact (see Figure 13.2b).

The Immune System and AIDS   AIDS attacks the body's **immune system—** the body's natural line of defense against disease. The immune system combats disease in a number of ways. It produces white blood cells that envelop and kill **pathogens** such as bacteria, viruses, and funguses; worn-out body cells; and cancer cells. White blood cells are referred to as **leukocytes.** Leukocytes engage in microscopic warfare. They undertake search-and-destroy missions. They identify and eradicate foreign agents and debilitated cells.

Acquired immunodeficiency syndrome (AIDS)
A sexually transmitted disease that destroys white blood cells in the immune system, leaving the body vulnerable to various opportunistic diseases.

Human immunodeficiency virus (HIV)
A sexually transmitted virus that destroys white blood cells in the immune system, leaving the body vulnerable to life-threatening diseases.

Immune system
A term for the body's complex of mechanisms for protecting itself from disease-causing agents such as pathogens.

Pathogen
An agent, especially a microorganism, that can cause a disease. (From the Greek *pathos,* meaning "suffering" or "disease," and *genic,* meaning "forming" or "coming into being.")

Leukocytes
White blood cells that are essential to the body's defenses against infection. (From the Greek *leukos,* meaning "white," and *kytos,* meaning "a hollow," and used in combination with other word forms to mean *cell.*)

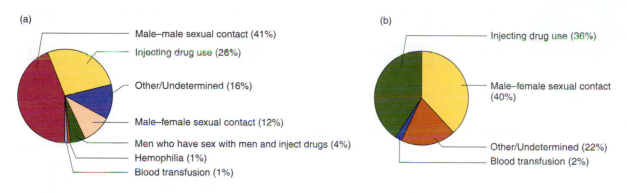

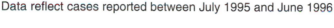

Data reflect cases reported between July 1995 and June 1996

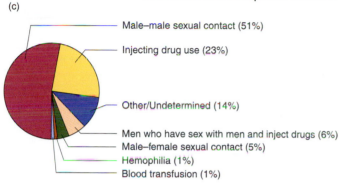

Figure 13.2. **AIDS Cases by Exposure Category (1996).** Part A shows men and women combined; Part B, women; and Part C, men. Overall, 12% of cases of AIDS reported between July 1995 and June 1996 were believed to have been transmitted by male–female sexual contact (Part A). Among women, however, two cases in five (40%) were attributed to male–female sexual contact (Part B). By contrast, only 5% of cases of AIDS among men were attributed to male–female sexual contact (Part C). *Source:* Table 3, Centers for Disease Control and Prevention (1996). *HIV/AIDS Surveillance Report*, Year-end Edition (U.S. HIV and AIDS cases reported through June 1996), Vol. 8, No. 1.

Antigen

A protein, toxin, or other substance to which the body reacts by producing antibodies. (Combined word formed from *anti*body *gen*erator.)

Inflammation

Redness and warmth that develop at the site of an injury, reflecting dilation of blood vessels that permits the expanded flow of leukocytes to the region.

Leukocytes recognize foreign agents by their shapes. The shapes are termed **antigens** because the body develops antibodies in response to them. Antibodies attach themselves to the foreign bodies, inactivate them, and mark them for destruction.

Other lymphocytes, called "memory lymphocytes," are held in reserve. Memory lymphocytes can remain in the bloodstream for years, and they form the basis for a quick immune response to an invader the second time around.[1]

Another function of the immune system is to promote **inflammation.** When you suffer an injury, blood vessels in the region initially contract to check bleeding. Then they dilate. Dilation expands blood flow to the injured region, causing the redness and warmth that identify inflammation. The elevated blood supply also brings in an army of leukocytes to combat invading microscopic life forms, like bacteria, that might otherwise use the local injury to establish a beachhead into the body.

Like other viruses, HIV uses the cells it invades to spin off copies of itself. HIV uses the enzyme *reverse transcriptase* to cause the genes in the cells it attacks to make proteins that the virus needs in order to reproduce.

HIV directly attacks the immune system by invading and destroying a type of lymphocyte called the CD4 cell (or helper T-cell).[2] The CD4 cell is the "quarterback" of the immune system. CD4 cells "recognize" invading pathogens and signal B-lymphocytes, or B-cells—another kind of white blood cell—to produce antibodies that inactivate pathogens

---

[1]Vaccination is the placement of a weakened form of an antigen in the body, which activates the creation of antibodies and memory lymphocytes. Smallpox has been annihilated by vaccination, and researchers are trying to develop a vaccine against the virus that causes AIDS.

[2]CD4 cells are also know as T_4 cells. The terms are synonymous and interchangeable.

ETHNICITY AND AIDS IN THE UNITED STATES

Disproportionately high numbers of African Americans and Hispanic Americans have contracted AIDS (Amaro, 1995). Forty-eight percent of the men and 76% of the women with AIDS in the United States are African American or Hispanic American (CDC, 1996). Yet these groups comprise only 21% of the population. Figure 13.3 shows the cumulative totals for men and women combined, through June 1996, according to ethnic background. Death rates due to AIDS are more than twice as great among African Americans and Hispanic Americans (especially Hispanic people of Puerto Rican origin) than among White Americans (CDC, 1996).

Ethnic differences in rates of transmission of HIV appear linked to injection of illicit drugs. People who share needles with HIV-infected people when they inject drugs can become infected themselves. They can then also transmit the virus to their sex partners. People who share needles now account for one in four AIDS cases. African Americans constitute about 58% of the people who apparently became infected with HIV by injecting drugs (CDC, 1996). Hispanic Americans account for another 19% of cases (CDC, 1996). Drug abuse and the related problem of prostitution occur disproportionately in poor, urban communities with large populations of people of color. Thus, it is not surprising that HIV infection and AIDS have affected these groups disproportionately.

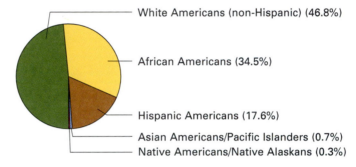

White Americans (non-Hispanic) (46.8%)

African Americans (34.5%)

Hispanic Americans (17.6%)

Asian Americans/Pacific Islanders (0.7%)

Native Americans/Native Alaskans (0.3%)

Figure 13.3. AIDS Cases by Race. The figure reflects cumulative totals for men and women combined, through June 1996. *Source:* Table 8, Centers for Disease Control and Prevention (1995). *HIV/AIDS Surveillance Report*, (U.S. HIV and AIDS cases reported through June 1996), Vol. 8, No. 1.

and mark them for annihilation. CD4 cells also signal another class of T-cells, called killer T-cells, to destroy infected cells. By attacking and destroying helper T-cells, HIV disables the very cells that the body relies on to fight off this and other diseases.

The blood normally contains about 1,000 CD4 cells per cubic millimeter. The numbers of CD4 cells may remain at about this level for years following HIV infection. Many people show no symptoms and appear healthy while CD4 cells remain at this level. Then, for reasons that are not clearly understood, the levels of CD4 cells begin to drop off, although symptoms may not appear for a decade or more. As the numbers of CD4 cells decline, symptoms generally increase, and people fall prey to diseases that their weakened immune systems are unable to fight off. People become most vulnerable to opportunistic infections when the level of CD4 cells falls below 200 per cubic millimeter.

Progression of HIV Infection and AIDS   Most people who are infected with HIV remain symptom-free for years. Some have symptoms such as chronically swollen lymph nodes and intermittent weight loss, fever, fatigue, and diarrhea. The severity of symptomatic HIV infection depends on various factors, such as the person's general health. This symptomatic state does not constitute full-blown AIDS, but shows that HIV is undermining the integrity of the person's immune system.

The beginnings of full-blown cases of AIDS are often marked by symptoms such as swollen lymph nodes, fatigue, fever, "night sweats," diarrhea, and weight loss that cannot

Opportunistic diseases
Diseases that take hold only when the immune system is weakened and unable to fend them off.

be attributed to dieting or exercise. People with AIDS develop **opportunistic diseases** such as *Pneumocystis carinii* pneumonia, other forms of pneumonia, Kaposi's sarcoma (an otherwise rare form of cancer), toxoplasmosis of the brain (a parasitic infection), *herpes simplex* with chronic ulcers, invasive cancer of the cervix, and tuberculosis. AIDS has almost always resulted in death within a few years. Whether current treatments will make a dent in the mortality rate remains to be seen.

Transmission   HIV can be transmitted by certain contaminated bodily fluids—blood, semen, vaginal secretions, or breast milk. The first three of these may enter the body through vaginal, anal, or oral–genital intercourse with an infected partner. Other avenues of infection include sharing a hypodermic needle with an infected person (as do many people who inject drugs), transfusion with contaminated blood, transplants of organs and tissues that have been infected with HIV, artificial insemination with infected semen, or being stuck by a needle used previously on an infected person. HIV may enter the body through tiny cuts or sores in the mucosal lining of the vagina, rectum, and even the mouth. These cuts or sores may be so tiny that you may not be aware of them.

What of kissing? There need be no concern about closed-mouth kissing. Moreover, saliva does not transmit HIV. However, deep (open-mouth) kissing may pose a threat because blood mixed with saliva may be transmitted from person to person, if there were blood in an infected person's mouth, (e.g., from active gum disease or vigorous toothbrushing) and cuts or sores in the partner's mouth. Though the risk of passing HIV through deep kissing is extremely small, it may be prudent to avoid the practice with partners not known to be HIV-negative.

When a person injects drugs, a small amount of his or her blood remains inside the needle and syringe. If the person is HIV-infected, the virus may be found in the blood remaining in the needle or syringe. When others use the same needle, they inject the infected blood into their bloodstreams. HIV may also be spread by sharing needles used for other purposes, such as injecting steroids, ear piercing, or tattooing.

HIV may also be transmitted from mother to fetus during pregnancy or from mother to child through childbirth or breast-feeding (Peckham & Gibb, 1995). Transmission is most likely to occur during the birth process.

Male-to-female transmission through vaginal intercourse is about twice as likely as female-to-male transmission (Allen & Setlow, 1991), partly because more of the virus is found in the ejaculate than in vaginal secretions. A man's ejaculate may also remain for many days in the vagina, providing greater opportunity for infection to occur. Male–female or male–male anal intercourse is especially risky, particularly to the recipient, since it often tears or abrades rectal tissue, facilitating entry of the virus into the bloodstream (Caceres & van-Griensven, 1994). Worldwide, male–female sexual intercourse accounts for 75% of cases of HIV infection. In the United States, male–female transmission of HIV accounts for about 12% of AIDS cases reported between July 1995 and June 1996 (CDC, 1996).

In the early years of the AIDS epidemic, HIV spread rapidly among hemophiliacs who had unknowingly been transfused with contaminated blood. In 1985, the test to detect HIV antibodies (revealing the presence of HIV infection) became available, and blood banks began universal screening of donor blood. Medical authorities today consider the risk of HIV transmission through transfusion of screened blood to be negligible (Lackritz et al., 1995; Schreiber et al., 1996; Vyas et al., 1996).

Some people seem more likely to communicate HIV, and others seem to be especially vulnerable to HIV infection. Why, for instance, are some people infected by one sexual contact with an infected partner, whereas others are not infected during months or years of unprotected sex? Several factors appear to affect the risk of HIV infection and development of AIDS:

- The number of sexual contacts with an infected partner
- The type of sexual activity (Anal intercourse, for example, provides a convenient port of entry for HIV because it often tears or abrades the rectal lining.)
- The amount of virus in semen
- Unprotected sex during menses (It increases the probability of female-to-male transmission.)

APPLICATIONS

HOW HIV IS NOT TRANSMITTED

Much misinformation has been spread about the transmission of HIV. Although knowledge about transmission of HIV is valuable, even lifesaving, many people have needless concerns. Let us set aside some of these concerns by considering some of the ways in which HIV is *not* transmitted:

1. *Closed-mouth kissing.*
2. *Donating blood.* AIDS cannot be contracted by donating blood because needles are discarded after a single use.
3. *Casual, everyday contact.* There is no evidence of transmission of HIV through hugging someone, shaking hands, bumping into strangers on buses and trains; handling money, doorknobs, or other objects that have been touched by infected people; sharing drinking fountains, public telephones, public toilets, or swimming pools; or by trying on clothing that has been worn by an infected person.
4. *Massage.*
5. *Insect bites.*
6. *Airborne germs or contact with contaminated food.* People do not contract HIV from contact with airborne germs, as by sneezing or coughing, or by contact with contaminated food or eating food prepared by a person infected with HIV (CDC, 1992).
7. *Sharing work or home environments.* HIV has not been shown to be transmitted from infected people to family members or others they live with through any form of casual contact, such as hugging or touching, or through sharing bathrooms, food, or eating utensils, so long as there is no exchange of blood or genital secretions (CDC, 1992; Hatcher et al., 1990). But do *not* share razor blades or toothbrushes with an infected person.

- Presence of other STDs (Many STDs either inflame the genital region or produce genital ulcers, both of which heighten vulnerability to HIV infection.)
- Circumcision (It *decreases* the risk of infection.)
- Genetic factors (HIV apparently enters cells in the immune system through certain receptors. About 1% of people of western European descent have a gene that prevents development of these receptors from both parents and are apparently immune to HIV infection. Perhaps 20% of individuals of western European descent have inherited the gene from one parent. HIV disease appears to progress more slowly in these people. Some prostitutes in Thailand and Africa, where HIV infection has been running rampant, also appear to be immune to HIV infection ["Genes that protect," 1996].)

Diagnosis   The most widely used test for HIV infection is the *enzyme-linked immunosorbent assay* (ELISA, for short). ELISA detects HIV antibodies in the blood, saliva, or urine.[3] Saliva and urine tests are not as accurate as blood tests, but they are less expensive and may encourage people who avoid blood tests to be tested. Positive ELISA results may be confirmed by the Western blot test, which detects a pattern of protein bands that are linked to the virus.

Treatment

We can really say "Get tested, get into care." We have more to offer people, so the concept of getting into care and getting treatment becomes more important.

(Margaret Chesney, Center for AIDS Prevention Studies, University of California–San Francisco; cited in Freiberg, 1996)

For many years, researchers were frustrated by failure in the effort to develop effective vaccines and treatments for HIV infection and AIDS. There is still no safe, effective vaccine, but recent developments in drug therapy have raised hopes about treatment.

---

[3]HIV itself is not found in measurable quantities in saliva or urine. However, HIV *antibodies* may be.

Caring for People with AIDS. People with AIDS need love and support, but are often rejected by others, even family members, who fear contracting the disease by touching or hugging them. However, HIV is not transmitted by hugging or touching an infected person, or by being in the same room.

Zidovudine (AZT) has been the most widely used HIV/AIDS drug. AZT is one of a number of so-called nucleoside analogues that inhibit replication (reproduction) of HIV by targeting the enzyme called reverse transcriptase. Other nucleoside analogues include ddI, ddC, d4T, and 3TC. Most studies suggest that AZT can delay the progression of infection from the symptom-free to the symptomatic state (Cooper et al., 1993) and increase the blood count of CD4 cells (Kinloch-de Loes et al., 1995).

Researchers also found that AZT administered to HIV-infected pregnant women reduced the rate of HIV infection in their newborns by two thirds (Connor et al., 1994). AZT may help prevent transmission during childbirth by reducing the amount of the virus in the mother's bloodstream. Only 8% of the babies born to the AZT-treated women became infected with HIV, compared to 25% of the babies born to women in the placebo group.

Although AZT is helpful, it may eventually lose effectiveness. Researchers have thus also studied the effectiveness of combining AZT with other antiviral drugs, such as didanosine (ddI) and zalcitabine (ddC). Studies reported in the *New England Journal of Medicine* have found that AZT in combination with either ddI or ddC is more effective in delaying the progression of HIV infection to AIDS than is AZT alone (Hammer et al., 1996; Katzenstein et al., 1996; Saravolatz et al., 1996). AZT and ddI may be the most potent combination of nucleoside analogues, delaying the rate of progression to AIDS or death by about 40% to 50% (Hammer et al., 1996; Katzenstein et al., 1996).

A new generation of drugs that block the replication of HIV, called *protease inhibitors*, shows yet greater promise in treating HIV infection and AIDS (Corey & Holmes, 1996). Protease inhibitors block reproduction of HIV particles by targeting the protease enzyme. A cocktail of antiviral drugs such as AZT, 3TC, and protease inhibitors has reduced HIV below detectable levels in many infected people. The drugs have created hope that AIDS will become "increasingly manageable, a chronic disease as opposed to a terminal illness" (Chesney, 1996). However, drug therapy is expensive, and many people who could benefit from it cannot afford it (Kolata, 1996b). In addition, many people with AIDS are too ill to profit from the drug cocktail.

Promising results are also reported in treating the opportunistic infections, such as PCP (Bozzette et al., 1995) and fungal infections (Powderly et al., 1995), that take hold in people with weakened immune systems (Clumeck, 1995).

Although there is more hope than there has been, make no mistake: AIDS is a killer.

Herpes

There are some 500,000 new cases of genital herpes each year (Brody, 1993a). Once you get herpes, it's yours for life. After the initial attack, it remains an unwelcome guest in your body. It causes recurrent outbreaks that often happen at the worst times, such as around final exams. This is not just bad luck. Stress can depress the functioning of the immune

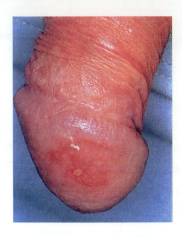

Herpes Lesion on the Male Genitals. Herpes lesions or sores can appear on the genitals in women or men and be associated with flu-like symptoms.

Herpes simplex **virus type 1**
The virus that causes oral herpes, which is characterized by cold sores or fever blisters on the lips or mouth. Abbreviated *HSV-1*.

Genital herpes
An STD caused by the *Herpes simplex* virus type 2 and characterized by painful shallow sores and blisters on the genitals.

Herpes simplex **virus type 2**
The virus that causes genital herpes. Abbreviated *HSV-2*.

Ocular herpes
A herpes infection of the eye, usually caused by touching an infected area of the body and then touching the eye.

system and heighten the likelihood of outbreaks. On the other hand, some people have no recurrences. Still others have mild, brief recurrences that become less frequent over time.

Different types of herpes are caused by variants of the *Herpes simplex* virus. The most common type, *Herpes simplex* **virus type 1** (HSV-1 virus), causes oral herpes. Oral herpes is denoted by cold sores or fever blisters on the lips or mouth. It can also be transferred to the genitals by the hands or by oral–genital contact. **Genital herpes** is caused by a related but distinct virus, the *Herpes simplex* **virus type 2** (HSV-2). This virus produces painful shallow sores and blisters on the genitals. HSV-2 can also be transferred to the mouth through oral–genital contact. Both types of herpes can be transmitted sexually.

It is estimated that more than 100 million people in the United States are infected with oral herpes and perhaps 30 million with genital herpes (Brody, 1993a).

Transmission   Herpes can be transmitted through oral, anal, or vaginal sexual activity with an infected person (Mertz et al., 1992; Wald et al., 1995). The herpes viruses can also survive for several hours on toilet seats or other objects, where they can be picked up by direct contact. Oral herpes is easily contracted by drinking from the same cup as an infected person, by kissing, even by sharing towels. But genital herpes is generally spread by coitus or by oral or anal sex.

Many people do not realize that they are infected. They can thus unknowingly transmit the virus through sexual contact. Though genital herpes is most contagious during active flare-ups, it may also be transmitted when an infected partner has no symptoms (genital sores or feelings of burning or itching in the genitals) (Mertz et al., 1992; Wald et al., 1995). Any intimate contact with an infected person carries some risk of transmission of the virus, even if the infected person never has another outbreak.

Herpes may also be spread from one part of the body to another by touching the infected area and then touching another body part. One potentially serious result is a herpes infection of the eye: **ocular herpes.** Thorough washing with soap and water after touching an infected area may reduce the risk of spreading the infection to other parts of the body.

Women with genital herpes are more likely than the general population to have miscarriages. Passage through the birth canal of an infected mother can infect babies with genital herpes, damaging or killing them (Whitley et al., 1991). Obstetricians thus often perform cesarean sections if the mother has herpes (Osborne & Adelson, 1990). Herpes also appears to place women at greater risk of genital cancers, such as cervical cancer (Graham et al., 1982).

Symptoms   Genital lesions or sores appear about six to eight days after infection with genital herpes. At first they appear as reddish, painful bumps, or papules, along the penis or the vulva. They may also appear on the thighs or buttocks, in the vagina, or on the cervix. These papules turn into groups of small blisters that are filled with fluid containing infectious viral particles. The blisters are attacked by the body's immune system (white blood cells). They fill with pus, burst, and become extremely painful, shallow sores or ulcers that are surrounded by a red ring. People are especially infectious during such outbreaks, as the ulcers shed millions of viral particles. Other symptoms may include headaches and muscle aches, swollen lymph glands, fever, burning urination, and a vaginal discharge. The blisters crust over and heal within one to three weeks. Internal sores in the vagina or on the cervix may take ten days longer than external (labial) sores to heal completely.

Although the symptoms disappear, the virus burrows into nerve cells in the base of the spine, where it may lie dormant for years or a lifetime. The infected person is least contagious during this dormant stage.

Recurrences may be related to factors such as infections, stress, fatigue, depression, exposure to the sun, and hormonal changes, such as those that occur during pregnancy or menstruation. Recurrences tend to occur within 3 to 12 months of the initial episode and to affect the same part of the body.

Diagnosis and Treatment   Genital herpes is first diagnosed by clinical inspection of herpetic sores or ulcers in the mouth or on the genitals. A sample of fluid may be taken from the base of a genital sore and cultured in the laboratory to detect the growth of the virus.

There is no cure or safe, effective vaccine for herpes. Viruses, unlike the bacteria that cause gonorrhea or syphilis, do not respond to antibiotics. The antiviral drug *acyclovir* (brand name: Zovirax) is applied directly to sores in ointment form. It can relieve pain, speed healing, and reduce the duration of viral shedding. Acyclovir must be administered orally to combat internal lesions in the vagina or on the cervix. Oral acyclovir may reduce the severity of the initial episode and, if taken regularly, the frequency and duration of outbreaks (Brody, 1993a; Goldberg et al., 1993).

Warm baths, loose fitting clothing, aspirin, and cold, wet compresses may relieve pain during flare-ups. People with herpes are advised to maintain regular sleeping habits and to learn to manage stress.

Viral Hepatitis

Hepatitis

An inflammation of the liver. (From the Greek *hepar*, meaning "liver.")

Jaundice

A yellowish discoloration of the skin and the whites of the eyes. (From the French *jaune*, meaning "yellow.")

Hepatitis is an inflammation of the liver that may be caused by factors such as chronic alcoholism and exposure to toxic materials. Viral hepatitis refers to several different types of hepatitis caused by related, but distinct, viruses. The major types are *hepatitis A* (formerly called infectious hepatitis), *hepatitis B* (formerly called serum hepatitis), *hepatitis C* (formerly called hepatitis non-A, non-B), and *hepatitis D.*

Most people with acute hepatitis have no symptoms. When symptoms do appear, they often include **jaundice,** feelings of weakness and nausea, loss of appetite, abdominal discomfort, whitish bowel movements, and brownish or tea-colored urine. The symptoms of hepatitis B tend to be more severe and long-lasting than those of hepatitis A or C. In about 10% of cases, hepatitis B can lead to chronic liver disease. Hepatitis C tends to have milder symptoms but often leads to chronic liver disease such as cirrhosis or cancer of the liver. Hepatitis D—also called *delta hepatitis* or type D hepatitis—occurs only in the presence of hepatitis B. Hepatitis D, which has symptoms similar to those of hepatitis B, can produce severe liver damage and often leads to death.

The hepatitis A virus is transmitted through contact with infected fecal matter found in contaminated food or water, and by oral contact with fecal matter, as through oral–anal sexual activity (licking or mouthing the partner's anus). (It is largely because of the risk of hepatitis A that restaurant employees are required to wash their hands after using the toilet.) Ingesting uncooked, infested shellfish is also a frequent means of transmission of hepatitis A (Lemon & Newbold, 1990).

Hepatitis B can be transmitted sexually through anal, vaginal, or oral intercourse with an infected partner; through transfusion with contaminated blood supplies; by the sharing of contaminated needles or syringes; and by contact with contaminated saliva, menstrual blood, nasal mucus, or semen (Lemon & Newbold, 1990). Sharing razors, toothbrushes, or other personal articles with an infected person may also transmit hepatitis B. Hepatitis C and hepatitis D may also be transmitted sexually or through contact with contaminated blood. A person can transmit the viruses that cause hepatitis even if he or she is unaware of having any symptoms of the disease.

Hepatitis is usually diagnosed by testing blood samples for the presence of hepatitis antigens and antibodies. There is no cure for viral hepatitis. Bed rest and fluids are usually recommended until the acute stage of the infection subsides, generally in a few weeks. Full recovery may take months. A vaccine provides protection against hepatitis B and also against hepatitis D, since hepatitis D can occur only if hepatitis B is present. In 1992, the federal government and the American Academy of Pediatrics recommended that all adolescents and young adults be immunized against hepatitis B. No vaccine is yet available for hepatitis C or A (Lemon & Newbold, 1990).

Genital Warts

Genital warts

An STD that is caused by the human papilloma virus and takes the form of warts that appear around the genitals and anus.

The *human papilloma virus* (HPV) causes **genital warts** (formerly termed *venereal warts*). HPV is extremely widespread, possibly infecting as many as 20% to 30% of sexually active people in the United States (Blakeslee, 1992). Though the warts may appear in visible areas of the skin, in perhaps 7 of 10 cases they appear in areas that cannot be seen, such as

Genital Warts. Genital warts are caused by the *human papilloma virus* (HPV) and often have a cauliflower appearance.

on the cervix in women or in the urethra in men (Reinisch, 1990). Within a few months following infection, the warts are usually found in the genital and anal regions. Women are more susceptible to HPV infection because cells in the cervix divide swiftly, facilitating the multiplication of HPV (Blakeslee, 1992). Women who initiate coitus prior to the age of 18 and who have many sex partners are particularly susceptible to infection (Blakeslee, 1992). A study of University of California at Berkeley women revealed that nearly half—46%!—had contracted HPV (Blakeslee, 1992). Similarly, it is estimated that nearly half of the sexually active teenage women in some U.S. cities are infected with HPV (Blakeslee, 1992).

Genital warts are similar to common plantar warts—itchy bumps that vary in size and shape. Genital warts are hard and yellow-gray when they form on dry skin. They take on pink, soft, cauliflower shapes in moist areas such as the lower vagina. In men they appear on the penis, foreskin, and scrotum, and within the urethra. They appear on the vulva, along the vaginal wall, and on the cervix in women. They can occur outside the genital area in either gender—for example, in the mouth; on the lips, eyelids, or nipples; around the anus; or in the rectum.

Genital warts may not cause any symptoms, but those that form on the urethra can cause bleeding or painful discharges. HPV itself is believed to be harmless in most cases (Penn, 1993), but it has been implicated in cancers of the genital organs, particularly cervical cancer and penile cancer. Cervical cancer is linked to HPV (Cannistra & Niloff, 1996; Ochs, 1994). Moreover, women whose husbands visit prostitutes or have many sex partners are 5 to 11 times as likely as other married women to develop cervical cancer ("Roving mates," 1996).

HPV can be transmitted sexually through skin-to-skin contact during vaginal, anal, or oral sex (Penn, 1993). It can also be transmitted by other forms of contact, such as touching infected towels or clothing. The incubation period may vary from a few weeks to a couple of years.

Freezing the wart (*cryotherapy*) with liquid nitrogen is the preferred treatment (CDC, 1989b). One alternative treatment involves painting the warts over a period of several days with an alcohol-based podophyllin solution, which causes them to dry up and fall off. The warts may also be treated (by a doctor!) with electrodes (burning) or surgery (by laser or surgical removal). Although such treatments may remove the warts, they do not rid the body of the virus (CDC, 1989b). There may thus be recurrences. Podophyllin is not recommended for use with pregnant women or for treatment of warts that form on the cervix (CDC, 1989b).

Unfortunately, no vaccine against HPV exists or appears to be in the offing. Latex condoms help reduce the risk of contracting HPV. They do not eliminate the risk entirely because the virus may be transmitted from areas of the skin not protected by condoms, such as the scrotum (Ochs, 1994). People with active warts should probably avoid sexual contact until the warts are removed and the area heals completely.

Ectoparasitic Infestations

Ectoparasites, as opposed to *endoparasites,* live on the outer surfaces of animals (*ecto* means "outer"). *Trichomonas vaginalis,* which causes trichomoniasis, is an endoparasite (*endo* means "inner"). Ectoparasites are larger than the agents that cause other STDs. In this section we consider two types of STDs caused by ectoparasites: pediculosis and scabies.

Pediculosis

Pediculosis is caused by *Pthirus pubis* (pubic lice). Pubic lice are commonly called "crabs" because under the microscope they are somewhat similar in appearance to crabs (see Figure 13.4). In the adult stage, pubic lice are large enough to be seen with the naked eye. They are spread sexually but may also be transmitted by contact with an infested towel, sheet, or—yes—toilet seat. They can survive for only about 24 hours without a human host,

Ectoparasites
Parasites that live on the outside of the host's body—as opposed to *endo*parasites, which live within the body. (From the Greek *ektos,* meaning "outside.")

Pediculosis
A parasitic infestation by pubic lice (*Pthirus pubis*) that causes itching.

Figure 13.4. Pubic Lice. Pediculosis is an infestation by pubic lice (*Pthirus pubis*). Pubic lice are commonly called "crabs" because of their appearance under a microscope.

Scabies

A parasitic infestation caused by a tiny mite (*Sarcoptes scabiei*) that causes itching.

but they may deposit eggs that can take up to seven days to hatch in bedding or towels (Reinisch, 1990). Therefore, all bedding, towels, and clothes that have been used by an infested person must be washed in hot water and dried on the hot cycle, or dry-cleaned. Fingers may also transmit the lice from the genitals to other hair-covered parts of the body, including the scalp and armpits. Sexual contact should be avoided until the infestation is eradicated.

Itching, ranging from the mildly irritating to the intolerable, is the most prominent symptom of a pubic lice infestation. The itching is caused when "crabs" attach themselves to the pubic hair and pierce the skin to feed on the blood of their hosts. The life span of these insects is only about one month, but they are prolific egg-layers and may spawn several generations before they die.

An infestation can be treated effectively with a prescription medication, a 1% solution of lindane (brand name: Kwell), which is available as a cream, lotion, or shampoo. Nonprescription medications containing pyrethrins or piperonyl butoxide (brand names: RID, Triple X, and others) will also do the job (Reinisch, 1990). Kwell is not recommended for use by pregnant or lactating women (CDC, 1989b).

Scabies

Scabies (short for *Sarcoptes scabiei*) is a parasitic infestation caused by a tiny mite that may be transmitted through sexual contact or contact with infested clothing, bed linen, towels, and other fabrics. The mites attach themselves to the base of pubic hair and burrow into the skin, where they lay eggs and subsist for the duration of their 30-day life span. Like pubic lice, scabies are often found in the genital region and cause itching and discomfort. They are also responsible for reddish lines (created by burrowing) and sores, welts, or blisters on the skin. Unlike lice, they are too tiny to be seen by the naked eye. Diagnosis is made by detecting the mite or its by-products on microscopic examination of scrapings from suspicious-looking areas of skin. Scabies are most often found on the hands and wrists, but they may also appear on the genitals, buttocks, armpits, and feet (Reinisch, 1990).

Scabies, like pubic lice, may be treated effectively with 1% lindane (Kwell). The entire body from the neck down must be coated with a thin layer of the medication, which should not be washed off for eight hours (CDC, 1989b). But lindane should not be used by women who are pregnant or lactating. To avoid reinfection, sex partners and others in close bodily contact with infected persons should also be treated. Clothing and bed linen used by the infected person must be washed and dried on the hot cycle or dry-cleaned. As with "crabs," sexual contact should be avoided until the infestation is eliminated.

A P P L I C A T I O N S

PREVENTING AIDS AND OTHER SEXUALLY TRANSMITTED DISEASES

Make no mistake about it. Although protease inhibitors have brought new hope to people infected with HIV, AIDS remains a deadly disease. Other STDs are also connected with serious health problems.

What, then, can we do to curb the spread of AIDS and other STDs? Given that many STDs have no vaccine or cure, prevention is our best hope.

Most prevention efforts focus on education. Sexually active people have been advised to alter their sexual behavior either by practicing abstinence, by limiting their sexual experiences to a lifelong monogamous relationship, or by practicing "safe sex"—which, as we shall see, could be more accurately dubbed "safer sex."

1. *Consider abstinence or monogamy.* The only fully effective strategies to prevent the sexual transmission of STDs are abstinence or maintaining a monogamous sexual relationship with an uninfected partner.

2. *Be aware of the risks involved in sexual behavior.* Don't use denial. Many of us try to put the

(continued)

Encouraging Safer Sex. AIDS prevention programs encourage sexually active people to engage in safer sex. However, many young people, including college students, continue to engage in risky sex.

dangers of STDs out of our minds —especially in moments of passion. Refuse to play the dangerous game of pretending that you are immune to the threat of STDs.

3. *Stay sober.* Alcohol and some other drugs increase the likelihood of engaging in risky sexual behavior.

4. *Avoid high-risk sexual behaviors, unless you are absolutely certain that your partner is not infected.* Use latex condoms ("protection"). Latex condoms block nearly all sexually transmissible organisms. Latex condoms may be even more effective in preventing STDs when used along with spermicides containing the ingredient nonoxynol-9, which kills STD-causing microorganisms including the viruses that cause AIDS and genital herpes.

   Unprotected anal intercourse is one of riskiest practices. Other high-risk behaviors include unprotected oral–genital activity, oral–anal activity, insertion of a hand or fist into someone's rectum or vagina, or any activity in which you or your partner would come into contact with the other's blood, semen, or vaginal secretions.

5. *Be selective.* Choose partners carefully. Avoid sexual contact with someone who has engaged in high-risk sexual or drug-use practices and is not known to be uninfected with STDs. It is not enough to ask your partner about past sexual behavior and drug use. You need to know the person well enough to judge the truthfulness of his or her answers.

6. *Limit your number of sex partners.* The more sexual contacts you have, the greater your risk of exposing yourself to STDs. Also avoid sex with a partner who has had multiple partners.

7. *Inspect your sex organs and those of your partner.* Inspect yourself for a discharge, bumps, rashes, warts, blisters, chancres, sores, lice, or foul odors. Check out any unusual feature with a physician before you engage in sexual activity.

   You may be able to work an inspection of your partner into foreplay—a reason for making love the first time with the lights on. In particular, a woman may hold her partner's penis firmly, pulling the loose skin up and down, as if "milking" it. Then she can check for a discharge at the penile opening. The man may use his fingers to detect any sign of a vaginal discharge. Other visible features of STDs include herpes blisters, genital warts, syphilitic chancres or rashes, and pubic lice.

8. *Engage in "outercourse," not "intercourse."* Hugging, massage, caressing, mutual masturbation, and rubbing bodies together without vaginal, anal, or oral contact are low-risk ways of finding sexual pleasure, so long as semen or vaginal fluids do not come into contact with mucous membranes or breaks in the skin. These activities may be termed *outercourse* to distinguish them from sexual intercourse.

9. *Use barrier devices when practicing oral sex (fellatio or cunnilingus).* Use a condom before practicing fellatio and a dental dam (a square piece of latex rubber used by dentists during oral surgery) to cover the vagina before engaging in cunnilingus.

10. *Wash the sex organs before and after sex.* Washing removes many potentially harmful agents, but is not an effective substitute for safer sex.

11. *Have regular medical checkups.* Many people are symptomless carriers of STDs, especially of chlamydial infections. Medical checkups enable them to learn about and treat "silent" diseases.

12. *Consult your physician if you suspect that you have been exposed to an STD.* Early intervention may prevent serious health problems.

13. *Avoid sex when in doubt.* None of the previous practices guarantees protection. Avoid sex when you are in doubt.

Chapter Review

In a study of more than 16,000 college students, (1) _____ (the virus that causes AIDS) was found in 30 blood samples. (2) *Chl*_____ _____tous (the bacterium that causes chlamydia) was found in 1 sample in 10, or 10% of the college population. (3) Hu_____ _____oma virus (HPV) (the organism that causes genital warts) is estimated to be present in one third of college women and 8% of men of ages 15 to 49. As many as 1 million new cases of (4) _____ infection occur each year in the United States—more than cases of syphilis, genital herpes, and AIDS combined. Sexually transmitted diseases (STDs) were formerly called (5) v_____ diseases (VDs), after (6) _____us, the Roman goddess of love.

Bacterial Diseases

(7) G_____ is also known as "the clap" or "the drip." Gonorrhea is almost always transmitted by unprotected (8) v_____, oral, or anal sexual activity, or from mother to newborn during (9) _____th. A person who performs fellatio on an infected man may develop (10) ph_____ _____rhea, which produces a throat infection. Babies have contracted gonorrhea of the eyes—(11) oph_____ _____rum—during childbirth. Most infected men develop a penile discharge and burning (12) _____tion. In women, the primary site of the infection is the (13) c_____. Most women (14: Do *or* Do not?) have symptoms during the early stages of the disease. In women, the bacterium can spread throughout the reproductive system and cause (15) p_____ _____tory disease (PID), which can lead to infertility. Gonorrhea is treated with (16) _____tics.

The bacterium that causes (17) s_____ is *Treponema pallidum*. Syphilis, like gonorrhea, is most often transmitted by (18) _____nal or anal intercourse, or oral–genital or oral–anal contact with an infected person. The syphilis spirochete (19: Can *or* Cannot?) cross the placental membrane. Syphilis develops through (20: Two, Three, *or* Four?) stages. In the first or primary stage, a painless (21) ch_____ appears at the site of infection. The chancre (22: Does *or* Does not?) disappear by itself. In the secondary stage, a (23) s_____ _____sh develops. The rash (24: Does *or* Does not?) disappear by itself. If the disease progresses to the late, or (25) _____tiary stage, it can attack the (26) ce_____ _____ous system or the cardiovascular system. Tertiary syphilis (27: Can *or* Cannot?) be fatal. The most frequently used blood test for syphilis is the (28) V_____. (29) Pe_____ is the treatment of choice for syphilis.

Chlamydia is (30: More *or* Less?) common than gonorrhea and syphilis in the United States. The *Chlamydia trachomatous* bacterium can cause (31) non_____ _____itis (NGU) in men and women, (32) epi_____tis in men, and cervicitis, (33) endo_____, and PID in women. Chlamydia is usually transmitted through sexual (34) _____se. Chlamydial infections usually produce symptoms that are similar to but (35: Milder *or* More intense?) than those of gonorrhea. Because many people are asymptomatic, chlamydia has been dubbed the (36) "si_____ _____se." In women, an untreated chlamydial infection can result in (37) _____tility. Chalmydia in women is diagnosed by means of the (38) Ab_____ _____pack. Antibiotics (39: Including *or* Other than?) penicillin are effective in chlamydial infections.

Other, rarer bacterial STDs include (40) chan_____, shigellosis, (41) gran_____ _____nale, and lymphogranuloma venereum.

Vaginal Infections

(42) _____itis refers to any vaginal infection or inflammation that tends to cause soreness and itching. Most vaginal infections involve (43) bac_____

_____sis (BV), (44) cand_____, or (45) _____iasis ("trich").

Bacterial vaginosis is most often caused by the bacterium (46) Gar_____ _____alis, which is primarily transmitted through sexual contact. Oral treatment with (47) met_____ (brand name: Flagyl) is used.

Candidiasis is also known as moniliasis, thrush, or, simply, a (48) y_____ infection. It is caused by a yeastlike fungus, (49) Can_____ _____cans. A yeast infection can produce soreness and intense (50) _____ing that is accompanied by a vaginal discharge. Infections most often arise from changes in the vaginal environment that allow the fungus to (51) _____grow. Treatment with vaginal suppositories, creams, or tablets containing (52) mi_____, clotrimazole, or terconazole is usually recommended.

"Trich" is caused by the protozoan parasite (53) Tri_____ _____lis. Trichomoniasis (54: Is or Is not?) usually sexually transmitted. Most infected men (55: Are or Are not?) symptom-free. Trichomoniasis is treated with (56) _____azole (brand name: Flagyl).

Viral Diseases

Viruses are tiny particles of (57) _____ coated with protein.

AIDS is the acronym for (58) ac_____ _____-deficiency syndrome. AIDS is a fatal disease that is caused by the (59) _____ _____ virus (HIV). HIV attacks and disables the (60) im_____ _____tem, the body's natural line of defense. The World Health Organization estimates that the number of persons infected with HIV may soar to (61) _____ million by the year 2000. For many years after AIDS was discovered, at least three out of four cases of AIDS were found among the (62) g_____ male population. The percentage of new cases among gay males has been (63: Increasing or Decreasing?) in recent years. Disproportionately (64: High or Low?) numbers of African Americans and Hispanic Americans have contracted AIDS. Ethnic differences in rates of transmission of HIV appear to be linked to (65) in_____ing illicit drugs.

HIV uses the enzyme (66) re_____ _____tase to cause the genes in the cells it attacks to make proteins that the virus needs in order to reproduce. HIV attacks the immune system by destroying a type of (67) _____cyte called the CD4 cell (or helper T-cell). The blood normally contains about (68) _____ CD4 cells per cubic millimeter. People become most vulnerable to opportunistic infections when the level of CD4 cells falls below (69) _____ per cubic millimeter. People with AIDS develop (70) oppor_____ _____ses such as PCP, Kaposi's sarcoma, and invasive cancer of the cervix. HIV can be transmitted by contaminated bodily fluids—(71) b_____, (72) s_____, vaginal and cervical secretions, or breast milk. Saliva (73: Does or Does not?) transmit HIV.

The most widely used test for HIV infection is the (74) en_____-_____ked immunosorbent assay (ELISA, for short). ELISA detects HIV (75) _____ dies in the blood, saliva, or urine. The (76) W_____ blot test detects the virus itself.

(77) Zi_____ (AZT) has been the most widely used HIV/AIDS drug. AZT in combination with other antiviral drugs is (78: As or More?) effective in delaying the progression of HIV infection to AIDS than is AZT alone. A new generation of drugs that block the replication of HIV, called (79) pro_____ _____tors, shows yet greater promise in treating HIV infection and AIDS.

Different types of herpes are caused by variants of the (80) He_____ _____ex virus. Herpes simplex virus type 1 causes (81) _____al herpes. Herpes simplex virus type 2 causes (82) _____al herpes. Herpes can be transmitted through oral, anal, or (83) _____nal sexual activity with an infected person. Genital herpes is (84: Most or Least?) contagious during flare-ups. Symptoms of genital herpes include (85) gen_____ _____res and feelings of burning or itching in the genitals. Women with genital herpes are more likely than the general population to have (86) _____ages. Passage through the birth canal of an infected mother (87: Can or Cannot?) infect babies with genital herpes. Genital lesions or sores at first appear as reddish, painful bumps, or (88) _____les. They turn into (89) _____ters that fill with pus and burst. Genital herpes is first diagnosed by clinical inspection or the culturing of a sample of (90) f_____ from a sore. The antiviral drug (91) _____vir can relieve pain, speed healing, and reduce the duration of viral shedding.

Hepatitis is an inflammation of the (92) l_____. Symptoms of hepatitis include (93) _____ice, weakness, nausea, loss of appetite, abdominal discomfort, whitish bowel movements, and brownish urine. The hepatitis A virus is transmitted through contact with infected (94) f_____ matter found in contaminated food or water, and by oral contact with fecal matter, as through oral–anal sexual activity. Hepatitis (95) _____ can be transmitted sexually through anal, vaginal, or oral intercourse with an infected partner; through transfusion with contaminated blood supplies; by the sharing of contaminated needles or syringes; and by contact with contaminated saliva, menstrual blood, nasal mucus, or semen. Hepatitis C and hepatitis D (96: May or May not?) be transmitted sexually or through contact with contaminated blood.

The human papilloma virus (HPV) causes genital (97) _____ts. (98: Most or Only a few?) warts appear in areas that cannot be seen, such as on the cervix in women or in the urethra in men. Women who have (99: Many or Only a few?) sex partners are particularly susceptible to infection. Genital warts are similar to common (100) p_____ warts. HPV has been implicated in cancers of the genital organs, particularly

(101) _____cal cancer and penile cancer. HPV can be transmitted sexually and by other forms of contact, such as touching infected towels or clothing. (102) _____zing the wart with liquid nitrogen is the preferred treatment.

Ectoparasitic Infestations

(103) _____sites, as opposed to endoparasites, live on the outer surfaces of animals. (104) _____losis is caused by *Pthirus pubis* (pubic lice), or "crabs." Pubic lice are spread sexually; they (105: May or May not?) be transmitted by contact with an infested towel, sheet, or toilet seat. The main symptom of pediculosis is (106) _____ing. An infestation can be cured with a prescription of (107) lin_____ (brand name: Kwell) or nonprescription medications containing pyrethrins or piperonyl butoxide (brand names: RID, Triple X, and others).

Scabies is a parasitic infestation caused by a (108) m_____ that may be transmitted through sexual contact or contact with infested clothing, bed linen, towels, and other fabrics. The mites cause (109) _____ing and discomfort. Scabies, like pubic lice, is treated with (110) _____ane (Kwell).

Chapter Quiz

1. Which of the following is the most widespread STD?
   (a) AIDS.
   (b) Syphilis.
   (c) Genital herpes.
   (d) Genital warts.
2. Silver nitrate is used to prevent
   (a) PCP.
   (b) ophthalmia neonatorum.
   (c) general paresis.
   (d) hepatitis C.
3. In women the primary site of a gonorrhea infection is the
   (a) cervix.
   (b) endometrium.
   (c) perineum.
   (d) introitus.
4. *Treponema pallidum* is the organism that causes
   (a) gonorrhea.
   (b) syphilis.

   (c) chlamydia.
   (d) genital herpes.
5. The Abbott Testpack is used to diagnose _____ in women.
   (a) trichomoniasis
   (b) HIV infection
   (c) chlamydia
   (d) candidiasis
6. Miconazole is used to treat
   (a) candidiasis.
   (b) hepatitis.
   (c) pediculosis.
   (d) syphilis.
7. Protease inhibitors in combination with nucleoside analogues have been shown to decrease the amount of _____ in the bloodstream.
   (a) *Herpes simplex* virus, type 1
   (b) HPV

(c) HIV

(d) *Pthirus pubis*

8. Which of the following is an antiviral drug?

(a) Acyclovir.

(b) Podophyllin.

(c) Lindane.

(d) Penicillin.

9. General paresis may develop during the _____ stage of syphilis.

(a) primary

(b) secondary

(c) tertiary

(d) all of the above

10. The World Health Organization estimates that _____ people may be infected with HIV by the year 2000.

(a) 300,000 to 400,000

(b) 3 million to 4 million

(c) 30 million to 40 million

(d) 300 million to 400 million

Answers to Chapter Review

1. HIV (Human immunodeficiency virus)
2. *Chlamydia trachomatous*
3. Human papilloma
4. HPV (Human papilloma virus)
5. Venereal
6. Venus
7. Gonorrhea
8. Vaginal
9. Childbirth
10. Pharyngeal gonorrhea
11. Ophthalmia neonatorum
12. Urination
13. Cervix
14. Do not
15. Pelvic inflammatory
16. Antibiotics
17. Syphilis
18. Vaginal
19. Can
20. Three

21. Chancre
22. Does
23. Skin rash
24. Does
25. Tertiary
26. Central nervous
27. Can
28. VDRL
29. Penicillin
30. More
31. Nongonococcal urethritis
32. Epididymitis
33. Endometritis
34. Intercourse
35. Milder
36. Silent disease
37. Infertility
38. Abbott Testpack
39. Other than
40. Chancroid
41. Granuloma inguinale
42. Vaginitis
43. Bacterial vaginosis
44. Candidiasis

45. Trichomoniasis
46. *Gardnerella vaginalis*
47. Metronidazole
48. Yeast
49. *Candida albicans*
50. Itching
51. Overgrow
52. Miconazole
53. *Trichomonas vaginalis*
54. Is
55. Are
56. Metronidazole
57. DNA (Deoxyribonucleic acid)
58. Acquired immunodeficiency
59. Human immunodeficiency
60. Immune system
61. 30 to 40 (Be in the ballpark)
62. Gay
63. Decreasing

64. High
65. Injecting
66. Reverse transcriptase
67. Lymphocyte
68. 1,000
69. 200
70. Opportunistic diseases
71. Blood
72. Semen
73. Does not
74. Enzyme-linked
75. Antibodies
76. Western
77. Zidovudine
78. More
79. Protease inhibitors
80. *Herpes simplex*
81. Oral
82. Genital
83. Vaginal
84. Most
85. Genital sores
86. Miscarriages
87. Can

88. Papules
89. Blisters
90. Fluid
91. Acyclovir
92. Liver
93. Jaundice
94. Fecal
95. B
96. May
97. Warts
98. Most
99. Many
100. Plantar
101. Cervical
102. Freezing
103. Ectoparasites
104. Pediculosis
105. May
106. Itching
107. Lindane
108. Mite
109. Itching
110. Lindane

Answers to Chapter Quiz

1. (d)
2. (b)
3. (a)
4. (b)
5. (c)
6. (a)
7. (c)
8. (a)
9. (c)
10. (c)

CHAPTER 14

Atypical Sexual Variations

O U T L I N E

Normal Versus Deviant Sexual Behavior

The Paraphilias
Fetishism
Transvestism
Exhibitionism
Obscene Telephone Calling
Voyeurism
Sexual Masochism
Sexual Sadism
Frotteurism
Other Paraphilias

Theoretical Perspectives
Biological Perspectives
Psychoanalytic Perspectives

Learning Perspectives
Sociological Perspectives
An Integrated Perspective: The "Lovemap"

Treatment of the Paraphilias
Psychotherapy
Behavior Therapy
Biochemical Approaches

Chapter Review

Chapter Quiz

A World of Diversity
Nymphomania, Satyriasis, and the Sexual Double Standard

Applications
How to Respond to an Exhibitionist

- Nude sunbathers and stripteasers are not considered exhibitionists?
- It is normal—not voyeuristic—to enjoy watching one's sex partner undress?
- Exhibitionists and voyeurs are sometimes violent?
- Some people cannot become sexually aroused unless they are bound, flogged, or humiliated by their sex partners?
- It is considered normal to enjoy some mild forms of pain during sexual activity?
- There is a subculture in the United States in which sexual sadists and sexual masochists form liaisons to inflict and receive pain and humiliation during sexual activity?

What is normal, and what is abnormal or deviant sexual behavior? In this chapter we explore a number of sexual behaviors that deviate from the norm in one sense or another. ■

Normal Versus Deviant Sexual Behavior

One common approach to defining normality is based on a statistical norm. From this perspective, rare or unusual sexual behaviors are considered abnormal or deviant. In our own culture, sexual practices such as oral sex and masturbation were once considered to be deviant or abnormal. Today, however, they are practiced so widely in our society that few people would label them as deviant practices.

Another basis for determining sexual deviance is to classify sexual practices as deviant when they involve the persistent preference for nongenital sexual outlets. If a man prefers fondling a woman's panties to engaging in sexual relations with her, or prefers to masturbate against her foot rather than engage in coitus, his behavior is likely to be labeled deviant.

Because of the confusing array of meanings of the terms *deviant* and *abnormal,* we prefer to speak about unusual patterns of sexual arousal or behavior as "atypical variations" in sexual behavior rather than as "sexual deviations." Atypical patterns of sexual arousal or behavior that become problematic in the eyes of the individual or society are labeled *paraphilias* by the American Psychiatric Association (1994).

Paraphilia
A diagnostic category used by the American Psychiatric Association to describe atypical patterns of sexual arousal or behavior that become problematic in the eyes of the individual or society, such as fetishism or exhibitionism. (From Greek roots meaning "to the side of" [*para-*] and "loving" [*philos*].)

The Paraphilias

Paraphilias involve sexual arousal in response to unusual stimuli such as children or other nonconsenting persons (such as unsuspecting people whom one watches or to whom one exposes one's genitals), nonhuman objects (such as shoes, leather, rubber, or undergarments), or pain or humiliation. Psychiatrists diagnose paraphilias when the person has acted on the urges or is distinctly distressed by them.

People with paraphilias often feel that their urges have an insistent, demanding, or compulsory quality (Brody, 1990a; Money, 1988). People with paraphilias tend to experience their urges as beyond their control, much as drug addicts or compulsive gamblers might regard themselves as helpless to avert irresistible urges to gamble or use drugs.

Paraphilias vary in severity. In some cases the person can function sexually in the absence of paraphilic stimuli and seldom if ever acts upon paraphilic urges. In other cases the person resorts to paraphilic behavior only in times of stress. In more extreme forms the person may not be able to become sexually aroused without either fantasizing about the paraphilic stimulus or having it present. For some people paraphilic behavior is the only means of attaining sexual gratification.

The person with a paraphilia typically replays the paraphilic act in sexual fantasies to stimulate arousal during masturbation or sexual relations. It is as if he or she is mentally replaying a videotape of the paraphilic scene. The scene grows stale after a while, however. According to sex researcher John Money, "the tape wears out and he has to perform another paraphilic act, in effect, to create a new movie" (quoted in Brody, 1990a, p. C12). Except in the case of sexual masochism, paraphilias are believed to occur almost exclusively among men (Money & Wiedeking, 1980).

Fetishism

In **fetishism,** an inanimate object elicits sexual arousal. Articles of clothing (for example, women's panties, bras, lingerie, stockings, gloves, shoes, or boots) and materials made of rubber, leather, silk, or fur are common fetishistic objects. Leather boots and high-heeled shoes are popular ones.

The fetishist may act on the urges to engage in fetishistic behavior, such as by masturbating by stroking an object or while fantasizing about it, or he may be distressed about such urges or fantasies but not act upon them. In a related paraphilia, **partialism,** people are excessively aroused by a particular body part, such as the feet, breasts, or buttocks.

Most fetishes and partialisms are harmless. Fetishistic practices are almost always private and involve masturbation or are incorporated into coitus with a willing partner. Only rarely have fetishists coerced others into paraphilic activities. Yet some partialists have touched parts of women's bodies in public. And some fetishists have committed burglaries to acquire the fetishistic objects (Sargent, 1988).

Transvestism

Transvestism may be viewed as a type of fetish. Transvestites become excited by wearing articles of clothing—the fetishistic objects—of the other gender. Transvestites are almost always males. Most are married and otherwise masculine in behavior and style of dress.

Fetishism
A paraphilia in which an inanimate object, such as an article of clothing or items made of rubber, leather, or silk, elicits sexual arousal.

Partialism
A paraphilia related to fetishism, in which sexual arousal is exaggeratedly associated with a particular body part, such as feet, breasts, or buttocks.

Transvestism
A paraphilia in which a person repeatedly cross-dresses to achieve sexual arousal or gratification, or is troubled by persistent, recurring urges to cross-dress. (From the Latin roots *trans-*, meaning "cross," and *vestis*, meaning "garment.")

Fetishism. In fetishism, inanimate objects such as leather shoes or boots elicit sexual arousal. Fetishists may derive sexual gratification by fondling, manipulating, or fantasizing about the object during masturbation. They may want the object to be present during sexual activity with, or to be worn by, their partners.

Transvestism. Transvestites cross-dress for the purpose of sexual gratification. Some transvestites sport feminine attire in public. Others cross-dress only in the privacy of their own homes.

The origins of transvestism are unknown. Family relationships appear to play a role, however. Transvestites are more likely than other people to be oldest children or only children (Schott, 1995). They also report closer relationships with their mothers than their fathers (Schott, 1995). Some transvestites report a history of "petticoat punishment" during childhood. That is, they were humiliated by being dressed in girl's attire. Perhaps the adult transvestite is trying psychologically to convert humiliation into mastery by achieving an erection and engaging in sexual activity despite being attired in female clothing (Geer et al., 1984). Transvestism can also be looked at as an attempt by males to escape the narrow confines of the masculine role (Bullough, 1991).

Transvestism ranges from wearing a single female garment when alone to sporting dresses, wigs, makeup, and feminine mannerisms at a transvestite club. Most transvestites do not engage in antisocial or illegal behavior. Most practice their sexual inclination in private and would be horrified or embarrassed to be discovered by associates while dressed as women.

Some transvestites persuade their female partners to permit them to wear feminine attire during their sexual activities. Most keep their transvestism a secret.

Exhibitionism

Exhibitionism

A paraphilia characterized by persistent, powerful urges and sexual fantasies involving exposing one's genitals to unsuspecting strangers to achieve sexual arousal or gratification.

Exhibitionism ("flashing") involves persistent, powerful urges and sexual fantasies involving exposing one's genitals to unsuspecting strangers for the purpose of achieving sexual arousal or gratification. The urges are either acted upon or are disturbing to the individual. Exhibitionists are almost always males. What we know of exhibitionists is almost entirely derived from studies of men who have been apprehended or treated by mental health professionals. Such knowledge may yield a biased picture of exhibitionists. Relatively few reported incidents result in apprehension and conviction (Cox, 1988).

The prevalence of exhibitionism in the general population is unknown, but a survey of 846 college women at nine randomly selected U.S. universities found exposure to exhibitionism to be widespread. A third of the women reported that they had run into a "flasher" (Cox, 1988). Only 15 of the women had reported these incidents to the police.

The urge to exhibit oneself, if not the actual act, usually begins in early adolescence, generally between the ages of 13 and 16 (Freund et al., 1988). The frequency of exhibitionism declines markedly after the age of 40 (American Psychiatric Association, 1994). The typical exhibitionist does not attempt further sexual contact with the victim. Thus, he does not usually pose a physical threat (American Psychiatric Association, 1994).

PPLICATIONS

HOW TO RESPOND TO AN EXHIBITIONIST

It is understandable that an unsuspecting woman who is exposed to an exhibitionist may react with shock, surprise, or fear. Unfortunately, her display of shock or fear may reinforce the flasher's tendencies to expose himself. She may fear that the flasher is likely to assault her physically as well. Fortunately, most exhibitionists do not seek actual sexual contact with their victims and run away before they can be caught.

Some women may respond with anger, insults, even arguments that the offender should feel ashamed. A display of anger may reinforce exhibitionism. We do not recommend that the victim insult the flasher, lest it provoke a violent response. Although most exhibitionists are nonviolent, about one in ten has considered or attempted rape (Gebhard et al., 1965).

When possible, showing no reaction or simply continuing on one's way

may be the best response. If women do desire to respond to the flasher, they might calmly say something like "You really need professional help. You should see a professional to help you with this problem." They should report the incident to police, so that they can catch the offender.

Victims of exhibitionism may feel violated and be bothered by recurrent images or nightmares. They may harbor misplaced guilt that they had somehow tempted the exhibitionist. They may also develop fears of venturing out on their own.

Geer and his colleagues (1984) see exhibitionism as an indirect means of expressing hostility toward women. Exposure may be an attempt by the exhibitionist to strike back at women because of a belief that women have wronged him or damaged his self-esteem by failing to notice him or take him seriously.

Other studies show exhibitionists to be shy, dependent, passive, lacking in sexual and social skills, even inhibited (Dwyer, 1988). They tend to be self-critical, to have doubts about their masculinity, and to suffer from feelings of inadequacy and inferiority (Blair & Lanyon, 1981; Dwyer, 1988). Many have had poor relationships with their fathers and have overprotective mothers (Dwyer, 1988). Exhibitionists who are socially shy or inadequate may be using exhibitionism as a substitute for the intimate relationships they cannot develop.

The preferred victims are typically girls or young women (Freund & Blanchard, 1986). Exhibitionists may also need to risk being caught to experience a heightened erotic response (Stoller, 1977). The exhibitionist may even situate himself to increase the risk. For example, he may repeatedly expose himself in the same location or while sitting in his own easily identifiable car.

Courts nowadays tend to be hard on exhibitionists, partly because of evidence that shows that some exhibitionists progress to more serious crimes of sexual aggression. In one sample, about 10% of rapists and child molesters had begun their "sexual careers" by exposing themselves to strangers (Abel et al., 1984).

Definitions of exhibitionism also bring into focus the boundaries between normal and abnormal behavior. Are exotic dancers (stripteasers) or nude sunbathers exhibitionists? After all, aren't they also exposing themselves to strangers? But exotic dancers—male or female—usually remove their clothes to sexually excite or entertain an expectant audience, not themselves. Their motive is to earn a living or (arguably) to express themselves in dance. Sunbathers in their "birthday suits" may also seek to sexually arouse others, not themselves. Of course, they may also be seeking an all-over tan or trying to avoid feeling encumbered by clothing. In any case, stripteasers and sunbathers do not expose themselves to unsuspecting others. Thus these behaviors are not regarded as exhibitionistic.

It is also normal to become sexually excited while stripping before one's sex partner. Such stripping is done to elicit a positive response from one's partner, not to surprise or shock a stranger.

Obscene Telephone Calling

Telephone scatologia

A paraphilia characterized by the making of obscene telephone calls. (From the Greek *skatos*, meaning "excrement.")

Like exhibitionists, obscene phone callers (almost all of whom are male) seek to become sexually aroused by shocking their victims. The American Psychiatric Association (1994) labels this type of paraphilia **telephone scatologia** (lewdness).

Obscene phone callers are generally motivated by a desire for sexual excitement and usually choose their victims randomly from the phone book or by chance dialing. They typically masturbate during the phone call or shortly afterwards. Most obscene phone callers are not dangerous. Most do not make repeat calls to the same person (Reinisch, 1990).

There are many patterns of obscene phone calling (Matek, 1988). Some callers limit themselves to obscenities. Others make sexual overtures. Some just breathe heavily. Others describe their masturbatory activity. Some profess to have previously met the victim at a social gathering or through a mutual acquaintance. Some even present themselves as "taking a sex survey" and ask provocative questions.

The typical obscene phone caller is a socially inadequate heterosexual male. The relative safety and anonymity of the telephone may shield him from the risk of rejection. A reaction of shock or fright from his victims may fill him with feelings of power and control that are lacking in his life, especially in his relationships with women. The obscenities may vent the rage that he holds against women who have rejected him.

What should a woman do if she receives an obscene phone call? Advice generally parallels that given to women who are victimized by exhibitionists. Above all, women are advised to remain calm and not reveal shock or fright, since such reactions tend to reinforce the caller and increase the probability of repeat calls. If she should receive repeated calls, the woman might request an unlisted number, obtain caller ID from the telephone company, or contact the police about tracing the calls.

Voyeurism

Voyeurism

A paraphilia characterized by strong, repetitive urges and related sexual fantasies of observing unsuspecting strangers who are naked, disrobing, or engaged in sexual relations. (From the French verb *voir*, meaning "to see.")

Voyeurism involves strong, repetitive urges to observe unsuspecting strangers who are naked, disrobing, or engaged in sexual relations (American Psychiatric Association, 1994). The voyeur becomes sexually aroused by the act of watching and typically does not seek sexual relations with the observed person. Like fetishism and exhibitionism, voyeurism is found almost exclusively among males. It usually begins before the age of 15 (American Psychiatric Association, 1994).

The voyeur may masturbate while "peeping" or afterward while "replaying" the incident. The voyeur may fantasize about making love to the observed person but have no intention of actually doing so.

Are people voyeurs who become sexually aroused by the sight of their lovers undressing? What about people who enjoy watching pornographic films or stripteasers? No, no, and no. The people being observed are not unsuspecting strangers. The lover knows that his or her partner is watching. Porn actors and strippers know that others will be viewing them. They would not be "performing" if they did not expect or have an audience.

It is perfectly normal for men and women to be sexually stimulated by the sight of other people who are nude, undressing, or engaged in sexual relations. Voyeurism is characterized by urges to "peep" on *unsuspecting* strangers.

Voyeurs often put themselves in risky situations in which they face the prospect of being discovered or apprehended. They may risk physical injury by perching themselves in trees or otherwise assuming precarious positions to catch a preferred view of their target. They will occupy rooftops and fire escapes in brutal winter weather. Peepers can be patient. They may wait hour after hour, night after night, for a glimpse of an unsuspecting person. One 25-year-old recently married man secreted himself in his mother-in-law's closet, waiting for her to disrobe. Part of the sexual excitement seems to stem from the risks voyeurs run.

Although most voyeurs are nonviolent, some commit violent crimes like assault and rape (Langevin et al., 1985). Voyeurs who break into and enter homes or buildings, or who tap at windows to gain the attention of victims, are among the more dangerous.

Compared to other types of sex offenders, voyeurs tend to be less sexually experienced and are less likely to be married (Gebhard et al., 1965). Like exhibitionists, voyeurs tend to harbor feelings of inadequacy and to lack social and sexual skills (Dwyer, 1988). They may thus have difficulty forming romantic relationships with women. Yet not all voyeurs are socially awkward and inept with women.

Sexual Masochism

Although pleasure and pain may seem like polar opposites, some people experience sexual pleasure through having pain or humiliation inflicted on them by their sex partners. People who associate the receipt of pain or humiliation with sexual arousal are called **sexual masochists.** A sexual masochist either acts upon or is distressed by persistent urges and sexual fantasies involving the desire to be bound, flogged, humiliated, or made to suffer in some way by a sexual partner so as to achieve sexual excitement. In extreme cases the person is incapable of becoming sexually aroused unless pain or humiliation is incorporated into the sexual act.

Sexual masochism is the only paraphilia that is found among women with some frequency (American Psychiatric Association, 1994). Even sexual masochism is much more prevalent among men than women, however. Male masochists may outnumber females by a margin of 20 to 1 (American Psychiatric Association, 1994).

The word *masochism* is derived from the name of the Austrian storyteller Leopold von Sacher-Masoch (1835–1895). He wrote tales of men who derived sexual satisfaction from having a female partner inflict pain on them, typically by flagellation (beating or whipping).

Sexual masochists may derive pleasure from various types of punishing experiences, including being restrained (a practice known as **bondage**), blindfolded (*sensory* bondage), spanked, whipped, or made to perform humiliating acts, such as walking around on all fours and licking the boots or shoes of the sex partner, or being subjected to vulgar insults. Some masochists have their partners humiliate them by urinating or defecating on them. Some masochists seek pain. Sexual masochists and **sexual sadists** often form sexual relationships to meet each other's needs. Some sexual masochists enlist the services of prostitutes or obtain the cooperation of their regular sexual partners to enact their masochistic fantasies.

It may seem contradictory for pain to become connected with sexual pleasure. The association of sexual arousal with mildly painful stimuli is actually quite common, however. Kinsey and his colleagues (1953) reported that perhaps as many as one person in four has experienced erotic sensations from being bitten during lovemaking. The eroticization of mild forms of pain (love bites, hair pulls, minor scratches) may fall within the normal range of sexual variation.

Baumeister (1988a) proposes that independent and responsible selfhood becomes burdensome or stressful at times. Sexual masochism provides a temporary reprieve from the responsibilities of independent selfhood. It is a blunting of one's ordinary level of self-awareness that is achieved by "focusing on immediate sensations (both painful and pleasant) and on being a sexual object" (Baumeister, 1988a, p. 54).

Sexual masochism can range from relatively benign to potentially lethal practices, like **hypoxyphilia.** People who practice hypoxyphilia may place plastic bags over their heads or nooses around their necks during sexual acts to enhance their sexual arousal by being temporarily deprived of oxygen. Or they may apply pressure to their chests. Oxygen deprivation is usually accompanied by sexual fantasies of being strangled by a lover. People usually discontinue oxygen deprivation before they lose consciousness, but some miscalculations result in death by suffocation (Blanchard & Hucker, 1991; Cosgray et al., 1991).

Sexual Sadism

Sadism is named after the infamous Marquis de Sade (1774–1814), a Frenchman who wrote tales of becoming sexually aroused by inflicting pain or humiliation on others. The virtuous Justine, the heroine of his best-known novel of the same name, endures terrible suffering at the hands of fiendish men. She is at one time bound and spread-eagled so that bloodhounds

---

Sexual masochism
A paraphilia characterized by the desire or need for pain or humiliation to enhance sexual arousal so that gratification may be attained. (From the name of the author Leopold von Sacher-Masoch.)

Bondage
Ritual restraint, as by shackles, as practiced by many sexual masochists.

Sexual sadists
People who become sexually aroused by inflicting pain or humiliation on others.

Hypoxyphilia
A practice in which a person seeks to enhance sexual arousal, usually during masturbation, by becoming deprived of oxygen. (From the Greek root meaning "under" [*hypo-*].)

Sadism
A paraphilia characterized by the desire or need to inflict pain or humiliation on others to enhance sexual arousal so that gratification is attained. (From the name of the author Marquis de Sade.)

can savage her. She then seeks refuge with a surgeon who tries to dismember her. Later she falls into the clutches of a saber-wielding mass murderer, but Nature saves her with a timely thunderbolt.

Sexual sadism is characterized by persistent, powerful urges and sexual fantasies involving the inflicting of pain and suffering on others to achieve sexual excitement or gratification. The urges are acted on or are disturbing enough to cause personal distress. Some sexual sadists cannot become sexually aroused unless they make their sex partners suffer. Others can become sexually excited without such acts.

Some sadists hurt or humiliate willing partners, such as prostitutes or sexual masochists. Others—clearly a small minority—stalk and attack nonconsenting victims.

Sadomasochism

A mutually gratifying sexual interaction between consenting sex partners in which sexual arousal is associated with the infliction and receipt of pain or humiliation. Commonly known as *S&M*.

Sadomasochism   Sadomasochism (or *S&M*) involves *mutually gratifying sexual interactions* between *consenting partners*. Occasional S&M is quite common among the general population. Couples may incorporate mild or light forms of S&M in their love-making now and then, such as mild dominance and submission games or gentle physical restraint. It is also not uncommon for lovers to scratch or bite their partners to heighten their mutual arousal during coitus. They generally do not inflict severe pain or damage, however.

Twenty-two percent of the men and 12% of the women surveyed by Kinsey and his colleagues (1953) reported at least some sexual response to sadomasochistic stories. Although some milder forms of sadomasochism may fall within the boundaries of normal sexual variation, sadomasochism becomes pathological when such fantasies are acted upon in ways that become destructive, dangerous, or distressing to oneself or others, as we find in the following case example:

> A 25-year-old female graduate student described a range of masochistic experiences. She reported feelings of sexual excitement during arguments with her husband when he would scream at her or hit her in a rage. She would sometimes taunt him to make love to her in a brutal fashion, as though she were being raped. She found the brutality and sense of being punished to be sexually stimulating. She had also begun having sex with strange men and enjoyed being physically punished by them during sex more than any other type of sexual stimulus. Being beaten or whipped produced the most intense sexual experiences she had ever had. Although she recognized the dangers posed by her sexual behavior, and felt somewhat ashamed about it, she was not sure that she wanted treatment for "it" because of the pleasure that it provided her.
>
> (Adapted from Spitzer et al., 1989, pp. 87–88)

In one subculture, sadomasochism is the preferred or even the exclusive form of sexual gratification. People in this subculture seek one another out through mutual contacts, S&M social organizations, or personal ads in S&M magazines. The S&M subculture has spawned magazines and clubs catering to people who describe themselves as "into S&M," as well as sex shops that sell sadomasochistic paraphernalia. These include leather restraints and leather face masks that resemble the ancient masks of executioners.

Sadomasochists often engage in highly elaborate rituals involving dominance and submission. Rituals are staged like scenes in a play (Weinberg et al., 1984). In the "master and slave" game, the sadist leads the masochist around by a leash. The masochist performs degrading or menial acts. In "bondage and discipline" (B&D), the dominant partner restrains the submissive partner and flagellates (spanks or whips) or sexually stimulates the submissive partner. The erotic appeal of bondage seems connected with controlling or being controlled.

Various types of stimulation may be used to administer pain during S&M encounters, but pain is not always employed. When it is, it is usually mild or moderate. Psychological pain, or humiliation, may be as common as physical pain. Pain may also be used symbolically, as in the case of a sadist who uses a harmless, soft rubber paddle to spank the masochist. So the erotic appeal of pain for some S&M participants may derive from the ritual of control rather than from the pain itself (Weinberg, 1987).

S&M participants may be heterosexual, gay, or bisexual (Breslow et al., 1986). They may assume either the masochistic or the sadistic role, or may alternate roles. Persons who seek to enact both sadistic and masochistic roles are known as *sadomasochists*. In hetero-

S&M Paraphernalia. People who participate in S&M often incorporate handcuffs and other paraphernalia into their sadomasochistic encounters.

sexual relationships the partners may reverse traditional gender roles. The man may assume the submissive or masochistic role, and the woman may take the dominant or sadistic role (Reinisch, 1990).

The causes of sexual masochism and sadism, as of other paraphilias, are unclear. Ford and Beach (1951) speculated that humans may possess a physiological capacity to experience heightened sexual arousal from the receipt or infliction of pain (which may explain the prevalence of love bites). Mild pain may heighten physiological arousal both in the aggressor and victim, adding to the effects of sexual stimulation. Yet intense pain is likely to decrease rather than increase sexual arousal.

Pain may also have more direct biological links to pleasure. Natural chemicals called *endorphins,* similar to opiates, are released in the brain in response to pain and produce feelings of euphoria and general well-being. Perhaps, then, pleasure is derived from pain due to the release or augmentation of endorphins (Weinberg, 1987). This theory fails to explain the erotic appeal of sadomasochistic encounters that involve minimal pain, however. Nor does it explain the erotic appeal to the sadist of inflicting pain.

Whatever their causes, the roots of sexual masochism and sadism apparently date to childhood. Sadomasochistic behavior commonly begins in early adulthood, but sadomasochistic fantasies are likely to have been present during childhood (American Psychiatric Association, 1994; Breslow et al., 1986).

Frotteurism

Frotteurism

A paraphilia characterized by recurrent, powerful sexual urges and related fantasies involving rubbing against or touching a nonconsenting person. (From the French *frotter,* meaning "to rub.")

Toucherism

A practice related to frotteurism and characterized by the persistent urge to fondle nonconsenting strangers.

Frotteurism (also known as "mashing") is rubbing against or touching a nonconsenting person. As with other paraphilias, a diagnosis of frotteurism requires either acting upon these urges or being distressed by them. Mashing has been reported exclusively among males (Spitzer et al., 1989).

Most mashing takes place in crowded places, such as buses, subway cars, or elevators. The man finds the rubbing or the touching, not the coercive nature of the act, to be sexually stimulating. While rubbing against a woman, he may fantasize a consensual, affectionate sexual relationship with her. Typically the man incorporates images of his mashing within his masturbation fantasies. Mashing also incorporates a related practice, **toucherism:** fondling nonconsenting strangers.

Mashing may be so fleeting and furtive that the woman may not realize what has happened (Spitzer et al., 1989). Mashers thus stand little chance of being caught.

Many mashers have difficulties forming relationships with women and are handicapped by fears of rejection. Mashing provides sexual contact in a relatively nonthreatening context.

Other Paraphilias

Let us consider some other less common paraphilias.

Zoophilia
A paraphilia involving persistent or repeated sexual urges and related fantasies involving sexual contact with animals.

Necrophilia
A paraphilia characterized by desire for sexual activity with corpses. (From the Greek *nekros*, meaning "dead body.")

Klismaphilia
A paraphilia in which sexual arousal is derived from use of enemas.

Coprophilia
A paraphilia in which sexual arousal is attained in connection with feces. (From the Greek *copros*, meaning "dung.")

Urophilia
A paraphilia in which sexual arousal is associated with urine.

Nymphomania
An excessive, insatiable sexual appetite or drive in women. (From the Greek roots *nymphe*, meaning "a bride," and *mania*, which means "madness.")

Satyriasis
An excessive, insatiable sexual appetite or drive in men. (After *satyr*, a sexually insatiable, goat-legged creature with pointed ears and short horns in Greek mythology. Satyrs were part man, part beast.)

Don Juanism
An excessive, insatiable sexual appetite or drive in men. (After the fictional Spanish nobleman who was unable to obtain true sexual gratification despite numerous affairs.)

Hypersexuality
An excessive or apparently insatiable sex drive that disrupts the person's ability to concentrate on other needs or leads to self-defeating behavior, such as indiscriminate sexual contacts.

Zoophilia   A person with **zoophilia** experiences repeated, intense urges and related fantasies involving sexual contact with animals. As with other paraphilias, the urges may be acted upon or cause personal distress. A child or adolescent who shows some sexual response to an occasional episode of rough-and-tumble play with the family pet is thus not displaying zoophilia.

The term *bestiality* applies to actual sexual contact with an animal. Kinsey and his colleagues (1948, 1953) found that men more often had sexual contact with farm animals, such as calves and sheep. Women more often reported sexual contacts with household pets. Urban–rural differences also emerged.

Necrophilia   In **necrophilia,** a rare paraphilia, a person desires sex with corpses. Three types of necrophilia have been identified (Rosman & Resnick, 1989). In *regular necrophilia,* the person has sex with a deceased person. In *necrophilic homicide,* the person commits murder to obtain a corpse for sexual purposes. In *necrophilic fantasy,* the person fantasizes about sex with a corpse but does not actually carry out necrophilic acts. Necrophiles often obtain jobs that provide them with access to corpses, such as working in cemeteries, morgues, or funeral homes. The primary motivation for necrophilia appears to be the desire to sexually possess a completely nonresistant and nonrejecting partner (Rosman & Resnick, 1989). Many necrophiles are clearly mentally disturbed.

Less Common Paraphilias   In **klismaphilia,** sexual arousal is derived from use of enemas. Klismaphiles generally prefer the receiving role to the giving role. Klismaphiles may have derived sexual pleasure in infancy or childhood from the anal stimulation provided by parents giving them enemas.

In **coprophilia,** sexual arousal is connected with feces. The person may desire to be defecated on or to defecate on a sex partner. The association of feces with sexual arousal may also be a throwback to childhood. Many children appear to obtain anal sexual pleasure by holding in and then purposefully expelling feces. It may also be that the incidental connection between erections or sexual arousal and soiled diapers during infancy eroticizes feces.

In **urophilia,** sexual arousal is associated with urine. As with coprophilia, the person may desire to be urinated upon or to urinate upon a sexual partner. Also like coprophilia, urophilia may have childhood origins. Stimulation of the urethral canal during urination may become associated with sexual pleasure. Or urine may have become eroticized by experiences in which erections occurred while the infant was clothed in a wet diaper.

Theoretical Perspectives

The paraphilias are among the most fascinating and perplexing variations in sexual behavior. Let us consider explanations that have been advanced from the major theoretical perspectives.

Biological Perspectives

Little is known about whether there are biological factors in paraphilic behavior. Efforts to date to find concrete evidence of brain damage or abnormalities among people with paraphilias have failed (e.g., Langevin et al., 1989). Because testosterone is linked to sex drive, researchers have also focused on differences in testosterone levels between people with paraphilias and people without them. A study of hormonal differences between a group of 16 male exhibitionists and controls found no differences in overall levels of testosterone, but the exhibitionists had elevated levels of the measure of testosterone believed to be most closely linked to sex drive (Lang et al., 1989). Yet many of the people with paraphilias studied fell within the normal range.

NYMPHOMANIA, SATYRIASIS, AND THE SEXUAL DOUBLE STANDARD

Sarah R., a never-married, 39-year-old artist became sexually active in her junior year in high school and has rarely been without at least one or two lovers ever since. Whenever she has not had an opportunity for sexual intercourse for several weeks or longer, for one reason or another, she has felt quite uncomfortable, or as she put it, "horny and hard-up." She has had two unwanted pregnancies, both of which resulted in abortions, and has contracted gonorrhea on three separate occasions and has suffered several times from infestations of pubic lice. She continues to be troubled with recurrent episodes of genital herpes. She generally limits her sexual relationships to one or two partners, but has on occasion maintained sexual relationships at the same time with three or four men. She engages in sexual intercourse two or three times a week, on the average, and engages in masturbation to relieve her sexual urges when intercourse is not possible.

Both her family practitioner and gynecologist, who have treated her for years, consider her to be a nymphomaniac. Her gynecologist says of her, "Of course she has herpes. What can you expect with the kind of sexual excesses she indulges in? She's a real nympho."

(Goldberg, 1987, p. 204)

Would you have reached the same conclusion as Sarah's physicians did? Why, or why not? What criteria would you use to define **nymphomania**? Perhaps most readers have heard of nymphomania, but only a few are likely to be acquainted with the term describing the same condition in men, **satyriasis. Don Juanism** is another term for the condition.

The fact that nymphomania is more commonly used in our society than the male counterpart underscores the traditional double standard in Western society (Groneman, 1994). Greater sexual liberties are accorded to men than women. A man who has a number of flings is likely to be labeled a "playboy," a "Casanova," or even a "stud." A woman who does so is likely to be branded with labels that carry negative connotations, such as "nympho," "slut," or "whore."

Clinicians prefer to use the term **hypersexuality** to refer to nymphomania in women and satyriasis in men, thereby avoiding disparaging connotations. No absolute criteria exist for determining hypersexuality or establishing the boundary between normal sexuality and hypersexuality, however. Some people might consider a person who requires a sexual release through masturbation or coitus more than once daily to be hypersexual. Others draw the line at two, three, or perhaps six or ten or more times daily. Among some couples, the partner desiring less frequent sexual activity may label the other as "oversexed." But what defines "oversexed" in one relationship may be considered normal, or subnormal, in another.

Clinicians may weigh the compulsive or self-defeating nature of the behavior in determining the boundaries of hypersexuality, not the sheer frequency of sexual activity. Hypersexual people may use sex as a means of buttressing a flagging sense of self-esteem. They may feel driven to a series of sexual conquests or brief encounters to reassure themselves that they are desirable, or masculine or feminine enough. Because they lack true intimacy, however, the encounters leave them feeling empty and sexually unfulfilled. Such relationships provide only a temporary salve for feelings of self-doubt or unworthiness. The person quickly loses sexual interest in the new partner once the conquest or brief encounter has occurred and begins searching for another. Partners are treated like objects to be used and discarded.

Return to Sarah. Do the facts of her case suggest hypersexuality? Did Sarah feel a lack of control over her sexual urges? Did she feel compelled to engage in sexual behaviors that put herself at risk of incurring unwanted pregnancies or sexually transmitted diseases?

Goldberg (1987) argues that Sarah's physicians labeled her as a nymphomaniac because her behavior did not meet social expectations of female sexuality. Goldberg (1987) comments, "In all likelihood, a 39-year-old man living the sort of life that Sarah is living would not be regarded as suffering from satyriasis or, indeed, as being sexually abnormal in any way" (p. 204). Does the label of nymphomania represent a sexist tendency to judge women and men by different sets of social standards?

Psychoanalytic Perspectives

Classical psychoanalytic theory suggests that paraphilias are psychological defenses, usually against unresolved castration anxiety dating back to the Oedipus complex (Fenichel, 1945). To the transvestic man, the sight of a woman's vagina threatens to arouse castration anxiety. It reminds him that women do not have penises and that he might suffer the same fate. Sequestering his penis beneath women's clothing symbolically asserts that women do have penises, which provides unconscious reassurance against his own fears of castration.

By exposing his genitals, the exhibitionist unconsciously seeks reassurance that his penis is secure. It is as if he were asserting, "Look! I have a penis!" Shock or surprise on the victim's face acknowledges that his penis still exists, temporarily relieving unconscious castration anxiety.

Masturbation with a fetishistic object (a shoe, for example) allows the fetishist to gratify his sexual desires while keeping a safe distance from the fantasized dangers that he unconsciously associates with sexual contact with women. Or the fetishistic object itself—the shoe—may unconsciously symbolize the penis. Stroking a woman's shoe during sexual relations, or fantasizing about one, may unconsciously provide reassurance that the man's own penis, symbolically represented by the fetishistic object, is secure.

In one psychoanalytic view of voyeurism, the man is unconsciously denying castration by searching for a penis among women victims. Other psychoanalytic views suggest that the voyeur is identifying with the man in the observed couple as he had identified with his own father during childhood observations of the parental coitus—the so-called *primal scene*. Perhaps he is trying to "master" the primal scene by compulsively reliving it.

Psychoanalytic explanations of sadism suggest that sadists are attempting to defend themselves against unconscious feelings of impotence and powerlessness by inflicting pain on others. The recipients' shouts of pain or confessions of unworthiness make sadists feel masculine and powerful.

Psychoanalytic theory suggests that masochism in the male may be the turning inward of aggressive impulses originally aimed toward the powerful, threatening father. The flagellation or bondage may also be unconsciously preferred to castration as a form of punishment for having unacceptable sexual feelings. Like the child who experiences relief when punishment is over, the sexual masochist willingly accepts immediate punishment in the form of flagellation or bondage in place of the future punishment of castration. Or a woman who witnessed her parents having coitus at an early age may have misperceived the father to be assaulting the mother. Her masochism then represents her unconscious reliving of her mother's (imagined) role with her father. Sexual masochists of either gender may also have such high levels of sex guilt that they can permit themselves to experience sexual pleasure only if they are adequately punished for it during sex.

The paraphilias have provided a fertile ground for psychoanalytic theories. There is a lack of evidence to support the role of such unconscious processes as unresolved castration anxiety, however. The basic shortcoming of psychoanalytic theory is that many of its key concepts involve unconscious mechanisms that cannot be directly observed or measured. So psychoanalytic theories remain interesting but speculative hypotheses about the origins of atypical sexual behavior patterns.

Learning Perspectives

Learning theorists believe that fetishes and other paraphilias are learned behaviors that are acquired through experience. An object may acquire sexually arousing properties through association with sexual arousal or orgasm. Like Pavlov's dogs, who learned to salivate to the ringing of a bell that had been repeatedly paired with food, "an animal may become conditioned to respond not only to particular stimuli, but to objects and other phenomena which were associated with the original experience. . . . In the laboratory, male animals may respond to particular dishes, to particular boards, or to particular pieces of furniture with which some female has had contact" (Kinsey et al., 1953, p. 647).

According to the conditioning model, a boy who catches a glimpse of his mother's stockings hanging on the towel rack while he is masturbating may go on to develop a fetish for stockings (Breslow, 1989). Orgasm in the presence of the object would reinforce the erotic connection, especially if the experience occurs repeatedly.

Breslow (1989) proposes a learning theory explanation that describes the development of paraphilias in terms of the gradual acquisition of sexual arousal to an unusual object or activity through its incorporation in masturbatory fantasies. A transvestite, for example, may have achieved an erection while trying on his mother's panties in childhood. The paraphilic object or activity is then incorporated within masturbatory fantasies and is reinforced by orgasm. The paraphilic object or activity is then repeatedly used as a masturbatory aid, further strengthening the erotic bond.

Fetishistic interests can often be traced to early childhood. Some rubber fetishists, for example, recall erotic interests in rubber objects since early childhood. Reinisch (1990) speculates that for some rubber fetishists, the earliest awareness of sexual arousal or response (such as erection) may have been associated with the presence of rubber pants, diapers, and so forth, such that a connection was formed between the two. The fetishistic act may represent an attempt to recapture sexual or loving feelings from early childhood.

McGuire and his colleagues (1965) report a case that provides some support for the role of learning in the development of exhibitionism. Two young males were surprised by an attractive woman while urinating. Although embarrassed at the time, their memories of the incident were sexually stimulating, and they masturbated repeatedly while fantasizing about it. The fantasies persisted, possibly reinforced by frequent orgasms. After a while, the young men purposely began to expose themselves to rekindle the high level of sexual excitement.

Friedrich and Gerber (1994) studied five adolescent boys who practiced hypoxyphilia and found extensive early histories of choking in combination with physical or sexual abuse. The combination seems to have encouraged each of the boys to associate choking with sexual arousal.

Learning explanations of sexual masochism focus on the pairing of sexual excitement with punishment. For example, a child may be punished when discovered masturbating. Or a boy may reflexively experience an erection if his penis accidentally rubs against the parent's body as he is being spanked. With repeated encounters like these, pain and pleasure may become linked in the person's sexual arousal system. Another learning explanation focuses on the association of pain with parental affection (Breslow, 1989; Sue et al., 1981). A child with cold and indifferent parents may be hugged only following a spanking. The pain or humiliation associated with the spanking becomes associated with the affection of the hug, which leads in later life to pain becoming a prerequisite for sexual pleasure.

Why do some people who are exposed to early conditioning experiences develop paraphilic interests, whereas others do not? Predisposing factors may include poor self-esteem and difficulties forming intimate relationships. Many exhibitionists, voyeurs, frotteurs, and other people with paraphilias have few interpersonal skills in relating to women. They may avoid customary social interactions with women for fear of rejection. Their furtive, paraphilic behaviors may provide a sexual release with minimal risks of rejection or apprehension and be maintained because they represent the only available source of sexual gratification or reinforcement. Some paraphilias, such as voyeurism, exhibitionism, and frotteurism, may also be conceptualized as *courtship disorders,* involving an exaggeration or distortion of the steps normally taken during courtship in identifying, approaching, and becoming more intimate with new sexual partners (Freund & Blanchard, 1986).

Sociological Perspectives

Martin Weinberg (1987) proposes a sociological model that focuses on the social context of sadomasochism. Weinberg notes that S&M rituals generally involve some form of dominance and submission and attributes their erotic appeal to the opportunity to reverse the customary power relationships that exist between the genders and social classes in society at large. Within the confines of the carefully scripted S&M encounter, the meek can be powerful and the powerful meek (Geer et al., 1984). Dominance and submission games also allow opportunities to accentuate or reverse the gender stereotypes that identify masculinity with dominance and femininity with submissiveness.

Individual sadomasochistic interests may become institutionalized as an S&M subculture in societies (like ours) that have certain social characteristics: (1) dominance–submission relationships are embedded within the culture, and aggression is socially valued;

(2) there is an unequal distribution of power between people from different gender or social class categories; (3) there are enough affluent people to enable them to participate in such leisure-time activities; and (4) imagination and creativity, important elements in the development of S&M scripts and fantasies, are socially valued and encouraged (Weinberg, 1987).

An Integrated Perspective: The "Lovemap"

Lovemap
A representation in the mind and in the brain of the idealized lover and the idealized erotic activity with the lover.

The paraphilias may have multiple biological, psychological, and sociocultural origins (Money, 1994). Money and Lamacz (1989) trace the origins of paraphilias to childhood. They believe that childhood experiences etch a pattern in the brain, called a **lovemap,** that determines the types of stimuli and activities that become sexually arousing to the individual. In the case of paraphilias, these lovemaps become distorted or "vandalized" by early traumatic experiences, such as incest, overbearing antisexual upbringings, and physical abuse or neglect.

Research suggests that voyeurs and exhibitionists often were the victims of childhood sexual abuse (Dwyer, 1988). Not all children exposed to such influences develop paraphilic compulsions, however. A genetic predisposition, hormonal factors, brain abnormalities, or a combination of these and other factors may play a role in determining one's vulnerability to vandalized lovemaps (Brody, 1990a).

Treatment of the Paraphilias

The treatment of these atypical patterns of sexual behavior raises a number of issues. First, people with paraphilias usually do not want or seek treatment, at least not voluntarily. They are generally seen by mental health workers only when they come into conflict with the law or at the urging of their family members or sexual partners. Second, helping professionals traditionally help clients clarify or meet their own goals; it is not their role to impose societal goals on the individual. Many helping professionals believe that the criminal justice system, and not they, ought to enforce social standards. Third, unless the motivation to change is present, therapeutic efforts may be wasted. Fourth, most therapies require that people accept personal responsibility for their actions as a prelude to change. Yet sex offenders tend to claim that they are unable to control their urges.

Despite these issues, many offenders are referred for treatment by the courts. A few seek therapy themselves because they have come to see that their behavior is harmful. Let us consider some of the ways in which therapists treat people with these atypical sexual behaviors.

Psychotherapy

Psychoanalysis focuses on resolving the unconscious conflicts that are believed to originate in childhood and to give rise in adulthood to pathological problems such as paraphilias. The aim of therapy is to help bring unconscious conflicts, principally Oedipal conflicts, into conscious awareness so that they might be worked on. Although some favorable case results have been reported (e.g., Rosen, 1967), psychoanalytic therapy of the paraphilias has not been subjected to experimental analysis. We thus do not know whether successes are due to the psychoanalytic treatment itself or to other factors, such as spontaneous improvement or a client's willingness to change.

Behavior Therapy

Behavior therapy
The systematic application of the principles of learning to help people modify problem behavior.

Systematic desensitization
A method for terminating the connection between a stimulus (such as a fetishistic object) and an inappropriate response (such as sexual arousal to the paraphilic stimulus). Muscle relaxation is practiced in connection with each stimulus in a series of increasingly arousing stimuli, so that the person learns to remain relaxed (and not sexually aroused) in their presence.

Behavior therapy focuses directly on changing behavior. A number of techniques have been used to help eliminate paraphilic behaviors. **Systematic desensitization** attempts to break the link between the sexual stimulus (such as a fetishistic stimulus) and the inappropriate response (sexual arousal). The client is taught to relax muscle groups. Muscle relaxation is then paired repeatedly with paraphilic images or fantasies. Relaxation comes to replace sexual arousal in response to these stimuli. In one case study, a fetishistic transvestite who had become attracted to his mother's lingerie at age 13 was taught to relax when presented with audiotaped scenes representing transvestite or fetishistic themes (Fensterheim & Kantor, 1980). He played such tapes daily while remaining relaxed. He later reported a complete absence of transvestite thoughts or activities.

In **aversion therapy,** the undesirable sexual behavior (for example, masturbation to fetishistic fantasies) is paired repeatedly with an aversive stimulus (such as a harmless but painful electric shock or a nausea-inducing chemical) in the hope that the client will develop a conditioned aversion toward the paraphilic behavior.

Covert sensitization is a variation of aversion therapy in which paraphilic fantasies are paired with an aversive stimulus in imagination. In a broad-scale application, 38 **pedophiles** and 62 exhibitionists, more than half of whom were court referred, were treated by pairing imagined aversive odors with fantasies of the problem behavior (Maletzky, 1980). Clients were instructed to fantasize pedophiliac or exhibitionistic scenes. Then,

> at a point . . . when sexual pleasure is aroused, aversive images are presented. . . . Examples might include a pedophiliac fellating a child, but discovering a festering sore on the boy's penis; an exhibitionist exposing to a woman but suddenly being discovered by his wife or the police; or a pedophiliac laying a young boy down in a field, only to lie next to him in a pile of dog feces.
>
> (Maletzky, 1980, p. 308)

Maletzky used this treatment weekly for six months, then followed it with "booster sessions" every three months over a three-year period. The procedure resulted in at least a 75% reduction of the deviant activities and fantasies for over 80% of the study participants at follow-up periods of up to 36 months.

Social skills training focuses on helping the individual improve his ability to relate to other people and to develop appropriate sexual relationships.

Orgasmic reconditioning aims to increase sexual arousal to socially appropriate sexual stimuli by pairing culturally appropriate imagery with orgasmic pleasure. The person is instructed to become sexually aroused by masturbating to paraphilic images or fantasies. But as he approaches the point of orgasm, he switches to "appropriate imagery," such as photos of *Playboy* models. Orgasm is thus paired with socially acceptable images, which gain the capacity to elicit sexual arousal.

Biochemical Approaches

No drug or surgical technique eliminates paraphilic urges and behavior. Yet some progress has recently been reported in using the antidepressant Prozac (fluoxetine hydrochloride) in treating exhibitionism, voyeurism, and fetishism (Emmanuel et al., 1992; Lorefice, 1991; Miller, 1995). Why Prozac? In addition to treating depression, Prozac has been helpful in treating obsessive–compulsive disorder, a type of emotional disorder involving recurrent obsessions (intrusive ideas) and/or compulsions (urges to repeat a certain behavior or thought). Paraphilias involve obsessions and compulsions.

People who experience such intense urges that they are at risk of committing sexual offenses may be helped by **antiandrogen drugs,** which reduce the level of testosterone in the bloodstream (Marshall et al., 1991). *Medroxyprogesterone acetate* (MPA) (trade name: Depo-Provera), which can be administered in weekly injections, has been used extensively in the treatment of sex offenders. Antiandrogens reduce sexual desire and the frequencies of erections and ejaculations (Cooper, 1986; Money, 1987b). Yet Depo-Provera does not change the types of stimuli that the individual finds arousing.

Although we have amassed a great deal of research on atypical variations in sexual behavior, our understanding of and treatment approaches to them remain largely in their infancy.

Aversion therapy
A method for terminating undesirable sexual behavior in which the behavior is repeatedly paired with an aversive stimulus, such as electric shock, so that a conditioned aversion develops.

Covert sensitization
A form of aversion therapy in which thoughts of engaging in undesirable behavior are paired repeatedly with imagined aversive stimuli.

Pedophiles
Persons with pedophilia, a paraphilia involving sexual interest in children.

Social skills training
Behavior therapy methods for building social skills that rely on a therapist's coaching and practice.

Orgasmic reconditioning
A method for strengthening the connection between sexual arousal and appropriate sexual stimuli (such as fantasies about an adult of the other gender) by repeatedly pairing the desired stimuli with orgasm.

Antiandrogen drug
A chemical substance that reduces the sex drive by lowering the level of testosterone in the bloodstream.

Chapter Review

Normal Versus Deviant Sexual Behavior

One approach to defining normality is the (1) st_____ norm. We must also consider whether the sexual practice (2) _____ates from a social norm. Another approach is to classify sexual practices as deviant when they involve persistent preference for (3) non_____ sexual outlets. Atypical patterns of sexual arousal or behavior that become problematic in the eyes of the individual or society are labeled (4) _____lias by the American Psychiatric Association.

The Paraphilias

Paraphilias involve sexual (5) _____sal in response to unusual stimuli. People with paraphilias tend to experience their urges as (6: Under or Beyond?) their control. Except in the case of sexual masochism, paraphilias are believed to occur almost exclusively among (7: Men or Women?).

In (8) _____ism, an inanimate object such as an undergarment or rubber object elicits sexual arousal. In (9) _____ism, people are excessively aroused by a particular body part, such as the feet. (10) _____tites become excited by wearing articles of clothing of the other gender. Most transvestites (11: Do or Do not?) engage in antisocial behavior.

(12) _____nism ("flashing") involves urges and fantasies involving exposing one's genitals to unsuspecting strangers to achieve sexual arousal or gratification. (13) One _____ of a sample of college women reported that they had run into a "flasher." The typical exhibitionist is (14: Happily or Unhappily?) married and sexually repressed. The typical exhibitionist (15: Does or Does not?) attempt further sexual contact with the victim. Geer and his colleagues see exhibitionism as a way of expressing (16) hos_____ toward women. Stripteasers and nude sunbathers (17: Are or Are not?) exhibitionists. Like exhibitionists, (18) ob_____ phone callers seek to become sexually aroused by shocking their victims. The American Psychiatric Association labels this type of paraphilia telephone (19) _____logia.

(20) _____ism involves urges to observe unsuspecting strangers who are naked, disrobing, or engaged in sexual relations. It (21: Is or Is not?) normal for men and women to be sexually stimulated by the sight of other people who are nude, undressing, or engaged in sexual relations.

Sexual (22) _____ists associate the receipt of pain or humiliation with sexual arousal. Sexual masochists may derive pleasure from various types of punishing experiences, including (23) bon_____ (being restrained) or being blindfolded, spanked, whipped, or made to perform humiliating acts. Sexual masochists and sexual (24) _____ists often form sexual relationships to meet each other's needs. People who practice (25) _____philia may place plastic bags over their heads during sexual acts to enhance their sexual arousal. Sexual (26) _____ism involves inflicting pain and suffering on others to achieve sexual excitement or gratification. Participants in (27) _____chism often engage in highly elaborate rituals involving dominance and submission.

(28) _____rism (also known as "mashing") is rubbing against or touching a nonconsenting person. (29) _____philia involves urges and fantasies involving sexual contact with animals. The term (30) _____lity applies to actual sexual contact with an animal. In (31) nec_____, a person desires sex with corpses. In (32) _____philia, sexual arousal is derived from use of enemas. In (33) _____ilia, sexual arousal is connected with feces. In (34) uro_____, sexual arousal is associated with urine. Clinicians use the term (35) _____sexuality to refer to nymphomania in women and satyriasis in men. Clear standards (36: Do or Do not?) exist for establishing the boundary between normal sexuality and hypersexuality.

Theoretical Perspectives

There (37: Is a *or* Is no?) clear connection between biological factors and paraphilic behavior.

(38) _____tic theory suggests that paraphilias are psychological defenses, usually against castration anxiety. Shock or surprise on the victim's face acknowledges that the exhibitionist's penis still exists, temporarily relieving (39) _____tion anxiety. Perhaps (40) _____ists are defending themselves against feelings of powerlessness by inflicting pain on others. Sexual masochists may have high levels of (41) g_____ about sex that prevent them from experiencing sexual pleasure unless they are also punished for it during sex.

Learning theorists believe that paraphilias are learned through (42) _____ience. For example, a boy who catches a glimpse of his mother's stockings hanging on the towel rack while he is masturbating may develop a (43) fe_____ for stockings. Breslow proposes that paraphilias develop as people incorporate unusual objects or activities in (44) _____batory fantasies. Learning explanations of sexual masochism focus on the pairing of sexual excitement with (45) _____ment.

Weinberg notes that S&M rituals generally involve some form of (46) dom_____ and submission, and he attributes their erotic appeal to the opportunity to reverse the customary power relationships that exist between the genders and social classes in society.

Money and Lamacz believe that childhood experiences etch a pattern in the brain, called a (47) _____map, that determines the types of stimuli that become sexually arousing.

Treatment of the Paraphilias

People with paraphilias usually (48: Do *or* Do not?) seek treatment. Psychoanalysis focuses on resolving the unconscious (49) con_____s that are believed to give rise to paraphilias. (50) _____vior therapy focuses on directly changing behavior. (51) Sys_____ _____zation attempts to break the link between the sexual stimulus (such as a fetishistic stimulus) and the inappropriate response (sexual arousal). In (52) av_____ _____apy, the undesirable sexual behavior (for example, masturbation to fetishistic fantasies) is paired repeatedly with an aversive stimulus (such as electric shock). In (53) co_____ _____zation, paraphilic fantasies are paired with an aversive stimulus in imagination. (54) Or_____ _____tioning aims to increase sexual arousal to socially appropriate sexual stimuli by pairing culturally appropriate imagery with orgasmic pleasure.

Some progress has been reported in using the antidepressant (55) P_____ in treating exhibitionism, voyeurism, and fetishism. Men with intense urges to commit sexual offenses may be helped by (56) anti_____ drugs, which reduce the level of testosterone in the bloodstream.

Chapter Quiz

1. What is the most accurate statement about gender and paraphilias?
   (a) All people with paraphilias are male.
   (b) All people with paraphilias are female.
   (c) People with paraphilias are about equally divided among males and females.
   (d) The great majority of people with paraphilias are male.
2. People who are excessively aroused by a particular body part, such as the feet, breasts, or buttocks, are said to have
   (a) voyeurism.
   (b) frotteurism.
   (c) partialism.
   (d) transvestism.
3. Hypoxyphilia is an activity related to
   (a) sexual sadism.
   (b) sexual masochism.
   (c) fetishism.
   (d) zoophilia.
4. Which of the following is NOT a problem in treating people with paraphilias?
   (a) They usually do not see their behavior as undesirable.
   (b) They see their behavior is being beyond their control.
   (c) "Treatment" often requires encouragement to conform to social norms rather than therapy.
   (d) No treatments are available.

5. According to psychoanalytic theory, the _____ is declaring, "Look, I have a penis!"
   - (a) exhibitionist
   - (b) voyeur
   - (c) masher
   - (d) sexual sadist

6. A "lovemap" is most likely to become distorted or "vandalized" by
   - (a) alcohol.
   - (b) physical abuse or neglect.
   - (c) unconscious conflicts from the Oedipal period.
   - (d) the sadomasochistic subculture.

7. Transvestism is considered to be most closely related to
   - (a) fetishism.
   - (b) exhibitionism.
   - (c) mashing.
   - (d) sadomasochism.

8. Telephone scatalogia is considered to be most closely related to
   - (a) coprophilia.
   - (b) sexual sadism.
   - (c) voyeurism.
   - (d) exhibitionism.

9. Which of the following are most likely to need to risk capture to heighten their sexual arousal?
   - (a) Sadomasochists
   - (b) Coprophiliacs
   - (c) Exhibitionists
   - (d) Mashers

10. Which of the following are most likely to report a history of "petticoat punishment" during childhood?
    - (a) Transvestites
    - (b) Sexual sadists
    - (c) Sexual masochists
    - (d) Sadomasochists

Answers to Chapter Review

1. Statistical
2. Deviates
3. Nongenital
4. Paraphilias
5. Arousal
6. Beyond
7. Men
8. Fetishism
9. Partialism
10. Transvestites
11. Do not
12. Exhibitionism
13. Third
14. Unhappily
15. Does not
16. Hostility
17. Are not
18. Obscene
19. Scatalogia
20. Voyeurism
21. Is
22. Masochists
23. Bondage
24. Sadists
25. Hypoxyphilia
26. Sadism
27. Sadomasochism
28. Frotteurism
29. Zoophilia
30. *Bestiality*
31. Necrophilia
32. Klismaphilia
33. Coprophilia
34. Urophilia
35. *Hypersexuality*
36. Do not
37. Is no
38. Psychoanalytic
39. Castration
40. Sadists
41. Guilt
42. Experience
43. Fetish
44. Masturbatory
45. Punishment
46. Dominance
47. Lovemap
48. Do not
49. Conflicts
50. Behavior
51. Systematic desensitization
52. Aversion therapy
53. Covert sensitization
54. Orgasmic reconditioning
55. Prozac
56. Antiandrogen

Answers to Chapter Quiz

1. (d)
2. (c)
3. (b)
4. (d)
5. (a)
6. (b)
7. (a)
8. (d)
9. (c)
10. (a)

CHAPTER 15

Sexual Coercion

O U T L I N E

Rape
Incidence of Rape
Types of Rapes
Social Attitudes and Myths That Encourage Rape
Sociocultural Factors in Rape
Psychological Characteristics of Rapists
Adjustment of Rape Survivors
Treatment of Rape Survivors

Sexual Abuse of Children
What Is Child Sexual Abuse?
Patterns of Abuse
Pedophilia
Incest
Effects of Child Sexual Abuse
Treatment of Survivors of Child Sexual Abuse

**Treatment of Rapists and
Child Molesters**

Sexual Harassment

Chapter Review

Chapter Quiz

Applications
If You Are Raped . . .
Preventing Rape
Preventing Child Sexual Abuse
Resisting Sexual Harassment

A World of Diversity
Rape-Prone and Rape-Free Societies: Whither the
    United States?

- Any sexual activity with a child is coercive?
- A woman is raped nearly every three minutes in the United States?
- The prevalence of rape is 20 times greater in the United States than in Japan?
- The majority of rapes are committed by people known to the rapist, not by strangers in deserted neighborhoods or darkened alleyways?
- The great majority men who rape other men are heterosexual?
- The belief that women say no when they mean yes is the type of cultural myth that encourages rape?
- Most rapists are "normal" in the sense that they are neither mentally ill nor retarded?
- Women who plead with rapists are more likely to be raped than women who scream or try to run away?
- Brother–sister incest is the most common type of incest?

Sexual coercion includes rape and other forms of sexual pressure, including sexual harassment and sexual activity between an adult and a child. Sexual relations with children are coercive, even when children cooperate, because children are below the legal age of consent. ■

Rape

Rape

Sexual intercourse that takes place as a result of force or threats of force rather than consent. (The legal definition of rape varies from state to state.)

Forcible rape

Sexual intercourse with a nonconsenting person obtained by the use of force or the threat of force.

Statutory rape

Sexual intercourse with a person who is below the age of consent. Sexual intercourse under such conditions is considered statutory rape even though the person attacked may cooperate.

Sexual assault

Any sexual activity that involves the use of force or the threat of force.

Rape is the subjugation of women by men by force or threat of force. **Forcible rape** is defined as sexual intercourse with a nonconsenting person by the use of force or the threat of force. **Statutory rape** refers to sexual intercourse with a person who is below the age of consent, even though the person may cooperate. Many social scientists view rape as an act of violence that is more connected with domination, anger, power, and sadism than with passion or sexual desire (Tedeschi & Felson, 1994). Sexual motivation does play a role in rape. However, the use of sex to express domination and anger is more central to our understanding of rape.

Most states have rape statutes that permit the prosecution of husbands who rape their wives. Many states have also broadened the scope of rape laws to include forced sexual acts other than coitus, such as anal intercourse and oral–genital relations. Forcible rape is a form of **sexual assault**. Even when a sexual attack does not meet the legal definition of rape, it can be classified and prosecuted as a sexual assault (Powell, 1991).

Incidence of Rape

The government's National Crime Victimization Survey (1995) estimates that 500,000 women are sexually assaulted each year. This figure includes 170,000 rapes and 140,000 attempted rapes. This means that a woman was reported to be raped about every three minutes on the average. Moreover, the number of rapes has been swelling faster than the population (FBI, 1991; U.S. Senate Committee on the Judiciary, 1991).

Historical studies have seriously underreported the incidence of rape (Schafran, 1995). They have largely relied on crime statistics. However, the majority of rapes are not reported to the police or prosecuted. Many women choose not to report assaults because of concern that they will be humiliated by the criminal justice system. Others fear reprisal from their families or the rapist. Some simply assume that the offender will not be apprehended or prosecuted.

Other surveys report the following prevalences of rape or sexual assaults:

- Twenty-one percent of a sample of more than 5,000 female members of a health maintenance plan reported being sexually assaulted (Koss, 1988).
- Fifteen percent of the 3,187 women sampled in a national survey of college students reported that they had been raped. An additional 12% reported that they had been victims of an attempted rape (Koss et al., 1987).
- Nearly 22% of the women in the NHSLS study reported being forced to do something sexual by a man (Laumann et al., 1994).

It appears that between 14% and 25% of women in the United States are raped at some point during their lifetimes (Calhoun & Atkeson, 1991; Koss, 1993). The prevalence of reported rapes in the United States is 13 times greater than that in Great Britain and more than 20 times greater than that in Japan (*Newsweek,* 1990).

Women of all ages, races, and social classes are raped. Young women, however, are at greater risk than older women. Women of ages 16 to 24 are two to three times more likely to be raped than are women in general (National Crime Victimization Survey, 1995).

Types of Rapes

Are most rapes perpetrated by strangers lurking in dark alleyways or by intruders who climb through open windows in the middle of the night? No. Most women are raped by men they know—often by men they have come to trust. Figure 15.1 shows that only 4% of the women in the NHSLS study were "forced to do something sexual that they did not want to do" by a stranger. According to the National Crime Victimization Survey, 80% of rapes were committed by acquaintances of the victim (Schafran, 1995).

The types of rape include stranger rape, acquaintance rape, marital rape, male rape, and rape by females.

Stranger rape
Rape that is committed by an assailant previously unknown to the person who is assaulted.

Stranger Rape   **Stranger rape** refers to a rape that is committed by someone previously unknown. The stranger rapist often selects targets who seem vulnerable—women who live alone, who are older or retarded, who are walking down deserted streets, or who are asleep or intoxicated. After choosing a target, the rapist may search for a safe time and place to commit the crime—a deserted, run-down part of town, a darkened street, a second-floor apartment without window bars or locks.

Acquaintance Rape   Women are more likely to be raped by men they know, such as classmates, fellow office workers, and even their brothers' friends, than by strangers (Schafran, 1995). **Acquaintance rapes** are much less likely than stranger rapes to be reported to the police (Schafran, 1995). One reason is that rape survivors may not perceive sexual assaults by acquaintances as rapes. Only 27% of the women in the national college survey who had been sexually assaulted saw themselves as rape victims (Koss et al., 1987). Even when acquaintance rapes are reported to police, they are often treated as "misunderstandings" or lovers' quarrels rather than as violent crimes.

Acquaintance rape
Rape by an acquaintance of the person who is assaulted.

Date Rape   Date rape is a form of acquaintance rape. Studies of college women show a consistent trend: 10% to 20% of women report being forced into sexual intercourse by

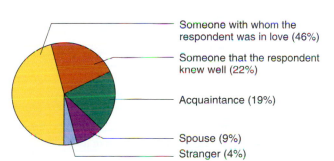

Someone with whom the respondent was in love (46%)

Someone that the respondent knew well (22%)

Acquaintance (19%)

Spouse (9%)

Stranger (4%)

Figure 15.1.   **Women's Relationships with Men Who Forced Them to Do Something Sexual That They Did Not Want to Do.**   Only 4% of the sexual assaults reported in the NHSLS study were perpetrated by strangers.   *Source:* Adapted from Laumann, E. O., Gagnon, J. H., Michael, R. T., & Michaels, S. (1994). *The Social Organization of Sexuality: Sexual Practices in the United States.* Chicago: University of Chicago Press, Figure 9.3, p. 338.

Combatting Rape on Campus. Many colleges and universities have instituted rape awareness programs to combat the problem of rape on campus. What is the prevalence of rape on your campus? What are you going to do about it?

dates (Tang et al., 1995). These figures hold at the Chinese University of Hong Kong as well as in the United States (Tang et al., 1995). Rapes are more likely to occur when the couple have had too much to drink and then park in the man's car or go back to his residence. The man tends to perceive his partner's willingness to return home with him as a signal of sexual interest, even if she resists his advances. Most of the men ignore women's protests and overcome their resistance by force.

Men who commit date rape may believe that acceptance of a date indicates willingness to engage in coitus. They may think that women should reciprocate with coitus if they are taken to dinner. Other men assume that women who frequent settings such as singles bars are expressing tacit agreement to engage in coitus with men who show interest in them.

The issue of consent lies at the heart of determining whether a sexual act is rape. Unlike stranger rape, date rape occurs within a context in which sexual relations could occur voluntarily. Thus, the issue of consent can become murky.

The Gang Rape Many men who participate in gang rapes are trying to conform to the stereotype of the tough, competent, "masculine" he-man. Exercise of power appears to be the major motive behind gang rapes, although some attackers may also be expressing anger against women. Gang members often believe that once women engage in coitus they are "whores." Thus, each offending gang member may become more aggressive as he takes his turn.

Male Rape The prevalence of male rape is unknown because most assaults are never reported. Some estimates suggest that perhaps 1 in 10 rape survivors is a man, however (Gibbs, 1991). Most men who rape other men are heterosexual. Their motives tend to include domination and control, revenge and retaliation, sadism and degradation, and (when the rape is carried out by a gang member) status and affiliation (Groth & Birnbaum, 1979). Sexual motives are generally absent.

Most male rapes occur in prison settings, but some occur outside prison walls. Males are more often attacked by multiple assailants, are held captive longer, and are more often reluctant to report the assault (Gerrol & Resick, 1988; Groth & Burgess, 1980; Myers, 1989). After all, victimization does not fit the male stereotype of capacity for self-defense. Men are expected to be not only strong but silent. Male rape survivors may suffer traumatic effects similar to those suffered by female rape survivors, however (Calhoun & Atkeson, 1991).

Marital Rape Marital rapes are probably more common than date rapes because a sexual relationship has already been established. A husband may believe that he is entitled to sexual access to his wife any time he desires it. He may believe it is his wife's duty to satisfy his sexual needs even when she is uninterested. Although there are no precise statistics on marital rape, a committee of the U.S. Congress estimated that one wife in seven is likely to be raped by her husband (Gibbs, 1991).

Marital rape goes largely unreported and unrecognized by survivors as rape (Russell, 1982). Women may fail to report marital rape because of fear that no one will believe them.

Motives for marital rape vary. Some men use sex to dominate their wives. Others degrade their wives through sex, especially after arguments. Sexual coercion often occurs within a context of marital violence, battering, and physical intimidation (Finkelhor & Yllo, 1982; Russell, 1982). In some cases, though, violence is limited to the sexual relationship (Finkelhor & Yllo, 1982). Some men see sex as the solution to all marital disputes. They think that if they can force their wives into coitus, "everything will be OK."

Survivors of marital rape may be as fearful as survivors of stranger rape of serious injury or death (Kilpatrick et al., 1987). The long-term effects of marital rape on survivors are also similar to those experienced by survivors of stranger rape (Calhoun & Atkeson, 1991), including fear, depression, and sexual dysfunctions (Kilpatrick et al., 1987). Moreover, the woman who is raped by her husband usually continues to live with her assailant and may fear repeated attacks.

Rape by Women   Rape by women is rare. When it does occur, it often involves aiding or abetting men who are attacking another woman. Rape by women may occur in gang rape in which women follow male leaders to gain their approval. In such cases, a woman may be used to lure another woman to a reasonably safe place for the rape. Or the woman may hold the other woman down while she is assaulted. But some men have actually been raped by women (Sarrel & Masters, 1982; Struckman-Johnson, 1988).

Social Attitudes and Myths That Encourage Rape

Many people believe a number of myths about rape, such as "women say no when they mean yes," "all women like a man who is pushy and forceful," "the way women dress, they are just asking to be raped," and "rapists are crazed by sexual desire" (Powell, 1996, p. 139). Yet another myth is that deep down inside, women want to be raped. Many women report rape fantasies, but they are in control of their fantasies. Rape is a complete lack of control, which no one wants (Powell, 1996). The belief that women desire to be overpowered and forced by men into sexual relations is a rationalization for violence (Powell, 1996).

Rape myths create a social climate that legitimizes rape. Though both men and women are susceptible to rape myths, researchers find that college men show greater acceptance of rape myths than do college women (Brady et al., 1991; Margolin et al., 1989). Men also cling more stubbornly to myths about date rape than do women, even following date rape education classes designed to challenges these views (Lenihan et al., 1992). College men who endorse rape myths are more likely to see themselves as likely to commit rape (Malamuth, 1981). Such myths do not occur in a social vacuum. They are related to other social attitudes, including gender-role stereotyping, the perception of sex as adversarial, and the acceptance of violence in interpersonal relationships (Burt, 1980).

Sociocultural Factors in Rape

Many observers contend that our society breeds rapists by socializing males into socially and sexually dominant roles (Lisak, 1991; Powell, 1996). Men are often reinforced from early childhood for stereotypical aggressive and competitive behavior (Lisak, 1991). Gender typing may also lead men to reject or repress traits that might restrain sexual aggression but are associated with the feminine gender role, such as tenderness and empathy (Lisak, 1991).

Research with college students supports the connection between stereotypical masculine identification and tendencies to rape or condone rape. One study compared college men who adhered strictly to stereotypical gender-role beliefs with men holding less rigid

RAPE-PRONE AND RAPE-FREE SOCIETIES: WHITHER THE UNITED STATES?

Cross-cultural studies suggest that sexual violence is not unique to our culture. It may in fact be culturally sanctioned in some societies. Rape is more common in violent cultures, especially in the minority of cultures in which violence toward women is legitimized (Ember & Ember, 1990; Powell, 1991). Among the Yanomamö people of the Amazon jungle, a tribe known to be among the fiercest and most aggressive people in the world, men often raid neighboring villages and literally carry away the women to keep as their wives (Ember & Ember, 1990). Wives are often savagely beaten, stabbed with sticks, or burned with glowing firewood by husbands as punishment for misbehavior. Wives come to accept punishment as part of their marital role. They may also come to regard the scars as signs that their husbands must care deeply for them to have beaten them so badly.

Sanday (1981) characterized 18% of the 156 cultures she studied as *rape-prone*. These rape-prone societies or "cultures of violence" tended to treat women as property. By contrast, Sanday found 45 "rape-free" cultures in which rape was absent or rare. Rape-free societies were characterized by sexual equality in which both genders shared power and were deemed to make important contributions, albeit in different ways, to the welfare of the society. In such societies, women did not economically depend on men and were able to control their own resources. Such societies also rear their children to be nurturant and to shun interpersonal violence. It thus appears that sexual violence occurs within the cultural context of interpersonal violence and male dominance (Stock, 1991).

Such cultural factors may help to explain the high rate of rape in the United States (Renzetti & Curran, 1989). The United States has both a high level of violent behavior, including the highest homicide rate among industrialized nations, and unequal gender relations.

---

attitudes. The stereotypical men expressed a greater likelihood of committing rape, were more accepting of violence against women, were more likely to blame rape survivors, and were more aroused by depictions of rape (Check & Malamuth, 1983). Other researchers found that college men who more closely identified with the traditional masculine gender role more often reported having engaged in verbal sexual coercion and forcible rape (Muehlenhard & Falcon, 1990).

Women may be socialized into assuming the helpless role. The stereotypical feminine gender role includes characteristics such as submissiveness, passivity, cooperativeness, even obedience to male authority. Such qualities may make it difficult for a woman to resist when faced with the possibility of rape. A woman may lack skills in aggressiveness and believe that physical resistance is inappropriate or that she is incapable of resisting. Women are also taught that is important to be sexually attractive to men. Women may thus unfairly blame themselves for the assault, believing that they somehow enticed the assailant.

Social influences may reinforce cultural themes that underlie rape, such as the belief that a truly masculine man is expected to be sexually aggressive and overcome a woman's resistance until she "melts" in his arms (Stock, 1991). The popular belief that women fantasize about being overpowered sanctions coercive tactics to "awaken" a woman's sexual desires. Images from popular books and movies reinforce these themes, such as that of Rhett Butler in *Gone with the Wind,* carrying a protesting Scarlett O'Hara up the stairs to her bedroom. Violent pornography, which fuses violence and erotic arousal, may also serve to legitimize rape (Stock, 1991).

Young men may come to view dates not as chances to get to know their partners but as opportunities for sexual conquest, in which the object is to overcome their partners' resistance. In one study, male college students expressed support for a man's right to kiss his female partner even if she resists (Margolin et al., 1989). Malamuth (1981) found that 35%

of the college men in his sample said they would force a woman into sexual relations if they knew they could get away with it.

The lessons learned in competitive sports may also predispose young Americans to sexual violence (Levy, 1991). Coaches often encourage boys to win at all costs. They are taught to be dominant and to vanquish their opponents, even if winning means injuring or "taking out" the opposition. This philosophy may be carried from the playing field into relationships with women. Some athletes distinguish between sports and dating relationships. Others do not. Evidence shows that student athletes commit a disproportionate number of sexual assaults (Eskenazi, 1990). Consider the aggressive competitiveness with which this male college student views dating relationships between men and women:

> A man is supposed to view a date with a woman as a premeditated scheme for getting the most sex out of her. Everything he does, he judges in terms of one criterion—"getting laid." He's supposed to constantly pressure her to see how far he can get. She is his adversary, his opponent in a battle, and he begins to view her as a prize, an object, not a person. While she's dreaming about love, he's thinking about how to conquer her.

(Powell, 1991, p. 55)

Psychological Characteristics of Rapists

Although sexual aggressiveness may be embedded within our social fabric, not all men are equally vulnerable to such cultural influences (Burkhart & Fromuth, 1991). Not all men become rapists. Personal factors are thus also involved. What are they? Are rapists mentally disturbed? Retarded? Driven by insatiable sexual urges?

Much of our knowledge of the psychological characteristics of rapists derives from studies of samples of incarcerated rapists (Harney & Muehlenhard, 1991). One conclusion that emerges is that there is no single type of rapist. Rapists vary in their psychological characteristics, family backgrounds, mental health, and criminal histories (Prentky & Knight, 1991). As a group, rapists are no less intelligent or more likely to be mentally ill than comparison groups (Renzetti & Curran, 1989). This does not mean that their behavior is "normal." It means that the great majority of rapists are in control of their behavior, and they know that it is illegal.

Some rapists feel socially inadequate and report that they cannot find willing partners. Some lack social skills and avoid social interactions with women (Overholser & Beck, 1986). Others are no less skillful socially than nonrapists in the same socioeconomic group, however (Segal & Marshall, 1985). Some rapists are basically antisocial and have long histories of violent behavior (Knight et al., 1991). They tend to act upon their impulses regardless of the cost to the person they attack. Some were sexually victimized or physically assaulted as children (Groth, 1978; Sack & Mason, 1980). As adults, they may be identifying with the aggressor role in interpersonal relationships. The use of alcohol may also dampen self-restraint and spur sexual aggressiveness.

For some rapists, violence and sexual arousal become enmeshed. Thus, they seek to combine sex and violence to enhance their sexual arousal (Quinsey et al., 1984). Some rapists are more sexually aroused (as measured by the size of erections) by verbal descriptions, films, or audiotapes that portray themes of rape than are other people (Barbaree & Marshall, 1991). Other researchers, however, have failed to find deviant patterns of arousal in rapists (e.g., Baxter et al., 1986; Hall, 1989). These researchers find that, as a group, rapists, like most other people, are more aroused by stimuli depicting mutually consenting sexual activity than by rape stimuli.

Harney and Muehlenhard (1991) summarized research findings on self-identified sexually aggressive men. They are more likely than other men to:

- Condone rape and violence against women
- Hold traditional gender-role attitudes
- Be sexually experienced
- Be hostile toward women
- Engage in sexual activity in order to express social dominance

- Be sexually aroused by depictions of rape
- Be irresponsible and lack a social conscience
- Have peer groups, such as fraternities, that pressure them into sexual activity

The Motives of Rapists: The Search for Types   Although sexual arousal is an obvious and important element in rape (Barbaree & Marshall, 1991), some researchers argue that sexual desire is not the basic motivation for rape (Gebhard et al., 1965; Groth & Birnbaum, 1979). Other researchers believe that sexual motivation plays a key role in at least some rapes (Hall & Hirschman, 1991). Based on their clinical work with more than 1,000 rapists, Groth and Birnbaum believe that there are three basic kinds of rape—anger rape, power rape, and sadistic rape:

Anger rape
A vicious, unplanned rape that is triggered by feelings of intense anger and resentment toward women.

Power rape
Rape that is motivated by the desire to control and dominate the person assaulted.

Sadistic rape
A highly ritualized, savage rape in which the person who is attacked is subjected to painful and humiliating experiences and threats.

1. *Anger rape.* The **anger rape** is a vicious, unplanned attack that is triggered by anger and resentment toward women. The anger rapist usually employs more force than is needed to obtain compliance. The person they rape is often coerced into performing degrading and humiliating acts, fellatio, or anal intercourse. Typically, the anger rapist reports that he had suffered humiliations at the hands of women and used the rape as a means of revenge.
2. *Power rape.* The man who commits a **power rape** is motivated by the desire to control and dominate the woman he rapes. Sexual gratification is secondary. The power rapist uses rape as an attempt "to resolve disturbing doubts about [his] masculine identity and worth, [or] to combat deep-seated feelings of insecurity and vulnerability" (Groth & Hobson, 1983, p. 165). Only enough force to subdue the woman is used.
3. *Sadistic rape.* The **sadistic rape** is a ritualized, savage attack. Sadistic rapists often carefully plan their assaults and use a "con" or pretext to approach their targets, such as asking for directions or offering or requesting assistance (Dietz et al., 1990). Some sadists bind their victims and subject them to humiliating and degrading experiences and threats. Some torture or murder their victims (Dietz et al., 1990). Mutilation of the victim is unfortunately common. Groth and Birnbaum (1979) suggest that sadistic rapists are often preoccupied with violent pornography but have little or no interest in nonviolent (consensual) pornography. Groth (Groth and Birnbaum, 1979) estimated that about 40% of rapes are anger rapes; 55%, power rapes; and 5%, sadistic rapes.

Adjustment of Rape Survivors

Many women who are raped fear for their lives during the attack (Calhoun & Atkeson, 1991). Whether or not weapons or threats are used, the experience of being dominated by an unpredictable and threatening assailant is terrifying. The woman does not know whether she will survive and may feel helpless to do anything about it. Afterwards, many survivors enter a state of **crisis**.

Crisis
A highly stressful situation that can involve shock, loss of self-esteem, and lessened capacity for making decisions.

Many survivors are extremely distraught in the days and weeks following the rape (Calhoun & Atkeson, 1991; Valentiner et al., 1996). They have trouble sleeping and cry frequently. They report eating problems, cystitis, headaches, irritability, mood changes, anxiety and depression, and menstrual irregularity. They may become withdrawn, sullen, and mistrustful (McArthur, 1990). People in the United States tend to believe that women who are raped are at least partly to blame for the assault (Bell et al., 1994). Therefore, some survivors experience feelings of guilt and shame (McArthur, 1990).

Rape survivors may also suffer physical injuries and sexually transmitted diseases, even AIDS, as a result of a sexual assault. In one study, concerns about contracting AIDS were reported by about 1 in 4 survivors (Baker et al., 1990).

Survivors may also encounter problems at work, such as problems relating to coworkers or bosses or difficulties in concentrating. Work adjustment, however, usually returns to normal levels within a year (Calhoun & Atkeson, 1991). Relationships with spouses or partners may also be impaired. Disturbances in sexual functioning are common and may last for years or a lifetime. Survivors often report a lack of sexual desire, fears of sex, and difficulty becoming sexually aroused (Becker et al., 1986). Some women simply do not experience the level of sexual enjoyment they found before the assault (Calhoun & Atkeson, 1991).

A P P L I C A T I O N S

IF YOU ARE RAPED . . .

Elizabeth Powell (1991) offers the following suggestions if you should be raped:

1. Don't change anything about your body—don't wash or even comb your hair. Leave your clothes as they are. Otherwise you could destroy evidence.

2. Strongly consider reporting the incident to police. You may prevent another woman from being assaulted, and you will be taking charge, starting on the path from victim to survivor.

3. Ask a relative or friend to take you to a hospital, if you can't get an ambulance or a police car. If you call the hospital, tell them why you're requesting an ambu-

lance, in case they are able to send someone trained to deal with rape cases.

4. Seek help in an assertive way. Seek medical help. Injuries you are unaware of may be detected. Insist that a written or photographic record be made to document your condition. If you decide to file charges, the prosecutor may need this evidence to obtain a conviction.

5. Question health professionals. Ask about your biological risks. Ask what treatments are available. Ask for whatever will help make you comfortable. Call the shots. Demand confidentiality if that's what you want. Refuse what you don't want.

You may also wish to call a rape hotline or rape crisis center for advice, if one is available in your area. A rape crisis volunteer may be available to accompany you to the hospital and help see you through the medical evaluation and police investigation if you report the attack. It is not unusual for rape survivors to try to erase the details of the rape from their minds. However, trying to remember details clearly will permit you to provide an accurate description of the rapist to the police, including his clothing, type of car, and so on. This information may help police apprehend the rapist and assist in the prosecution.

Posttraumatic stress disorder
A type of stress reaction brought on by a traumatic event and characterized by flashbacks of the experience in the form of disturbing dreams or intrusive recollections, a sense of emotional numbing or restricted range of feelings, and heightened body arousal. Abbreviated *PTSD*.

Rape trauma syndrome
A two-phase reaction to rape that is characterized by disruption of the survivor's lifestyle (the acute phase) and reorganization of the survivor's life (the long-term phase).

Rape and Psychological Disorders Rape survivors are at higher-than-average risk of developing psychological disorders such as depression, alcohol and substance abuse, and anxiety (Koss, 1993). **Posttraumatic stress disorder** (PTSD) is an anxiety disorder brought on by exposure to a traumatic event and is also often seen in soldiers who were in combat. Features of PTSD include flashbacks to the traumatic experience, disturbing dreams, emotional numbing, and nervousness. PTSD may persist for years. A person with the disorder may also develop fears of situations connected with the traumatic event. For example, a woman who was raped on an elevator may develop a fear of riding elevators by herself. Researchers also report that women who blame themselves for the rape tend to suffer more severe depression and adjustment problems, including sexual problems (Frazier, 1990; Wyatt et al., 1990).

Rape Trauma Syndrome Burgess and Holmstrom (1974) identified some common response patterns in survivors of rape, which they labeled the **rape trauma syndrome.** Through emergency room interviews with 92 women at Boston City Hospital, and telephone or in-person follow-up interviews, they found two phases in rape trauma syndrome:

The Acute Phase: Disorganization The acute phase typically lasts for several weeks following the attack. Many survivors are disorganized during this time and may benefit from rape trauma counseling. The woman may cry uncontrollably and experience feelings of anger, shame, fear, and nervousness.

Some women present a calm, composed face to the world, but inwardly have not yet come to terms with the traumatic experience. Calmness often gives way to venting of feelings later on.

The Long-Term Process: Reorganization The long-term reorganization phase may last for years. The woman gradually comes to deal with her feelings and to reorganize her life. Lingering fears may lead rape survivors to move to safer surroundings. Women

PREVENTING RAPE

The elimination of rape would probably require massive changes in cultural attitudes and socialization processes. Educational intervention on a smaller scale may reduce its incidence, however. A study of 276 undergraduates at Pitzer College in California showed that college men who were more knowledgeable about the trauma caused by rape were less likely to report that they might commit a rape (Hamilton & Yee, 1990). Many colleges and universities offer educational programs about date rape. The University of Washington, for example, offers students lectures and seminars on date rape (and also provides women with escorts to their homes or dorms after dark). Brown University requires all first-year students to attend orientation sessions on rape (Celis, 1991). The point of such programs is for men to learn that no means no, despite the widespread belief that some women like to be "talked into" sex.

Until the basic cultural attitudes that support rape change, however, "rape prevention" will require that women take a number of precautions. Why, a reader may wonder, should women be advised to take measures to avoid rape? Is not the very listing of such measures a subtle way of blaming the woman if she should fall prey to an attacker? No, providing the information does not blame the person who is attacked. The rapist is *always* responsible for the assault. However, *The New Our Bodies, Ourselves* (Boston Women's Health Book Collective, 1992) lists several suggestions that may help prevent rape:

- Establish a set of signals with other women in the building or neighborhood.
- List yourself in the phone directory and on the mailbox by your first initials only.
- Use dead-bolt locks.
- Lock windows, and install iron grids on first-floor windows.
- Keep doorways and entries well lit.
- Keep your keys handy when approaching the car or the front door.
- Do not walk by yourself after dark.
- Avoid deserted areas.
- Do not allow strange men into your house or apartment without first checking their credentials.
- Keep your car doors locked and the windows up.
- Check out the back seat of your car before entering.
- Don't live in a risky building. (We realize that this suggestion may be of little use to poor women who have relatively little choice as to where they live.)
- Don't give rides to hitchhikers (including women hitchhikers).
- Don't converse with strange men on the street.
- Shout "Fire!" not "Rape!" People are likely to flock to fires but to avoid scenes of violence.

Powell (1996) adds the following suggestions for avoiding date rape:

- Communicate your sexual limits to your date. Tell your partner how far you would like to go so that he will know what the limits are. For example, if your partner starts fondling you in ways that make you uncomfortable, you might say, "I'd prefer if you didn't touch me there. I really like you, but I prefer not getting so intimate at this point in our relationship."
- Meet new dates in public places, and avoid driving with a stranger or a group of people you've met. When meeting a new date, drive in your own car and meet your date at a public place. Don't drive with strangers or offer rides to strangers or groups of people. In some cases of date rape, the group disappears just prior to the assault.

---

who informed the police may fear retaliation by the rapist. They may change their phone numbers, often to unlisted numbers. Some take out-of-state trips, often visiting parents, although they do not necessarily tell them of the rape. Many survivors continue to be bothered by frightening dreams.

Burgess and Holmstrom note that survivors of rape who do not disclose their attacks may have a silent rape reaction. Unfortunately, concealing rape may keep them from receiving social support. If they are children or adolescents, their feelings may go unresolved for years.

Treatment of Rape Survivors

Treatment of rape survivors typically involves a two-stage process of helping the woman (the vast majority are female) through the crisis following the attack and then helping to

- State your refusal definitively. Be firm in refusing a sexual overture. Look your partner straight in the eye. The more definite you are, the less likely your partner will misinterpret your wishes.
- Become aware of your fears. Take notice of any fears of displeasing your partner that might stifle your assertiveness. If your partner is truly respect-ful of you, you need not fear an angry or demeaning response. But if your partner is not re-spectful, it is best to become aware of it and end the rela-tionship right there.
- Pay attention to your "vibes." Trust your gut-level feelings. Many victims of acquaintance rape said afterward that they had had a strange feeling about the man but failed to pay atten-tion to it.
- Be especially cautious if you are in a new environment, such as a college or a foreign country. You may be especially vulnerable to exploitation when you are becom-ing acquainted with a new envi-ronment, different people, and different customs.
- If you have broken off a rela-tionship with someone you don't

really like or feel good about, don't let him into your place. Many so-called date rapes are committed by ex-lovers and ex-boyfriends.

Confronting a Rapist: Should You Fight, Flee, or Plead?

But what if you are accosted by a rapist? Should you try to fight him off, flee, or try to plead with him to stop? Some women have thwarted attacks by pleading or crying. Yet re-search has shown that less forceful forms of resistance, such as pleading, begging, or reasoning, can be dan-gerous strategies. They may not fend off the attack and may heighten the probability of injury (Bart & O'Brien, 1985). Screaming may be particularly effective in warding off some attacks (Byers & Lewis, 1988). Running away is sometimes an ef-fective strategy for avoiding a rape (Bart & O'Brien, 1985), but running may not be effective if the woman is outnumbered by a group of as-sailants (Gidycz & Koss, 1990). No suggestion is likely to be helpful in all rape cases, however.

Self-defense training may help women become better prepared to fend off an assailant. Yet physical re-sistance may spur some rapists to be-come more aggressive (Powell, 1996).

Federal statistics show that women who resist increase their chances of preventing the completion of a rape by 80%. However, resistance increases the odds of being physically injured by as much as threefold (Brody, 1992a). A study of 116 rapes showed that women were more likely to physically resist if the attacker was a friend or relative, if the attacker made verbal threats, and if the attacker physically restrained her or injured her (Atkeson et al., 1989).

It is difficult, if not impossible, for people to think through their options clearly and calmly when they are sud-denly attacked. Rape experts recom-mend that women rehearse alternative responses to a rape attack. The Boston Police Department recommends that whatever form of self-defense a woman intends to use, she should carefully think through how it is used and practice using it (Brody, 1992a). Thompson (1991) suggests that effec-tive self-defense is built upon the use of multiple strategies, ranging from attempts to avoid potential rape situa-tions (such as installing home security systems or walking only in well-lit areas), to acquiescence when active resistance would seem too risky, to the use of more active verbal or physical forms of resistance in some low-risk situations.

foster long-term adjustment. Crisis intervention typically provides the survivor with sup-port and information to help her express her feelings and develop strategies for coping with the trauma (Resick & Schnicke, 1990). Psychotherapy, involving group or individual ap-proaches, can help the survivor cope with the emotional consequences of rape, avoid self-blame, improve self-esteem, validate the welter of feelings surrounding the experience, and help her establish or maintain loving relationships. Therapists also recognize the impor-tance of helping the rape survivor identify supportive social networks (Ledray, 1990; Valentiner et al., 1996). Family, friends, religious leaders, and health care specialists are all potential sources of help. In major cities and many towns, concerned men and women have formed rape crisis centers and hotlines, peer counseling groups, and referral agencies geared to assessing and treating survivors' needs after the assault. Some counselors are spe-cially trained to mediate between survivors of rape and their loved ones—husbands, lovers, and so forth. These counselors help people to discuss and work through the often complex

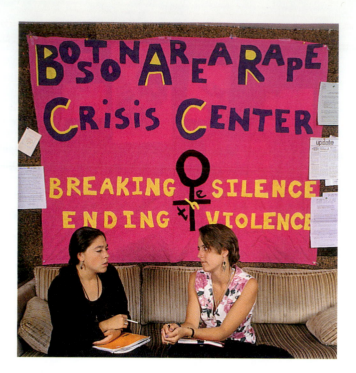

Rape Crisis Center. Rape crisis centers provide rape victims with emotional support to help them cope with the traumatic effects of rape. They also help victims obtain medical, legal, and psychological services.

emotional legacy of rape. Phone numbers for these services can be obtained from feminist groups (for example, your local office of the National Organization for Women [NOW]), the police department, or the telephone directory.

Sexual Abuse of Children

Many view child sexual abuse as among the most heinous of crimes. Children who are sexually assaulted often suffer social and emotional problems that impair their development and persist into adulthood, affecting their self-esteem and their ability to form intimate relationships.

No one knows how many children are sexually abused. Although most sexually abused children are girls (Knudsen, 1991), one quarter to one third are boys (Finkelhor, 1990). A randomized national telephone survey of more than 2,600 adults showed that 9.5% of the men and 14.6% of the women reported having been sexually abused (a completed or attempted act of sexual intercourse) prior to age 19 (Finkelhor et al., 1990). These estimates may underrepresent the actual prevalences, as people may fail to report such incidents due to faulty memories or because of shame or embarrassment. In addition, about one in four people refused to participate in the survey, casting doubt on the sample's representativeness. Other researchers estimate that the prevalence of sexual abuse among boys ranges from 4% to 16% (Genuis et al., 1991; Janus & Janus, 1993; Kohn, 1987) and among girls exceeds 20% (Janus & Janus, 1993; Kohn, 1987).

What Is Child Sexual Abuse?

Sexual abuse of children may range from exhibitionism, kissing, fondling, and sexual touching to oral sex and anal intercourse and, in the case of girls, vaginal intercourse (Knudsen, 1991). Any form of sexual contact between an adult and a child is abusive, even if the child is willing, since children are below the age of consent.

Voluntary sexual activity between children of similar ages is not sexual abuse. Children often engage in sex play with peers or siblings, as in "playing doctor" or mutual masturbation. When the experience involves coercion, however, or when the other child is

So there really was a monster in her bedroom.

For many kids, there's a real reason to be afraid of the dark.

Last year in Indiana, there were 6,912 substantiated cases of sexual abuse. The trauma can be devastating for the child and for the family. So listen closely to the children around you.

If you hear something you don't want to believe, perhaps you should. For helpful information on child abuse prevention, contact the LaPorte County Child Abuse Prevention Council, 7451 Johnson Road, Michigan City, IN 46360. (219) 874-0007

LaPorte County Child Abuse Prevention Council

The Monster in the Bedroom. Not all monsters are make-believe. Some, like perpetrators of incest, are members of the family.

significantly older or in a position of power over the younger child, the sexual contact may be considered sexual abuse.

Patterns of Abuse

Children from stable, middle-class families appear to be generally at lower risk of encountering sexual abuse than children from poorer, less cohesive families (Finkelhor, 1984). In most cases, children who are sexually abused are not accosted by the proverbial stranger lurking in the school yard. In perhaps 75% to 80% of cases, the molesters are relatives, steprelatives, family friends, and neighbors (Waterman & Lusk, 1986).

The average age at which most children are first sexually abused ranges from 6 to 12 years for girls and 7 to 10 years for boys (Knudsen, 1991). Parents who discover that their child has been abused by a family member are often reluctant to notify authorities. Some may feel that such problems are "family matters" that are best kept private. Others may be reluctant to notify authorities for fear that it may shame the family or that they may be held accountable for failing to protect the child.

Typically, the child initially trusts the abuser. Physical force is seldom needed to gain compliance, largely because of the child's helplessness, gullibility, and submission to adult authority. Whereas most sexually abused children are abused only once, those who are abused by family members are more likely to suffer repeated acts of abuse (Briere & Runtz, 1987; Dube & Hebert, 1988).

Genital fondling is the most common type of abuse (Knudsen, 1991). In one sample of women who had been molested in childhood, most of the contacts involved genital fondling (38% of cases) or exhibitionism (20% of cases). Intercourse occurred in only 4% of cases (Knudsen, 1991). Repeated abuse by a family member, however, commonly follows a pattern that begins with affectional fondling during the preschool years, progresses to oral sex or mutual masturbation during the early school years, and then to sexual penetration (vaginal or anal intercourse) during preadolescence or adolescence (Waterman & Lusk, 1986).

Abused children rarely report the abuse, often because of fear of retaliation from the abuser or because they believe they will be blamed for it. Adults may suspect abuse if a child shows sudden personality changes or develops fears, problems in school, or eating or sleeping problems. A pediatrician may discover physical signs of abuse during a medical exam.

Types of Abusers   Researchers find that the overwhelming majority of perpetrators of child sexual abuse of both boys and girls are males (Thomlison et al., 1991). Although most sexual abusers are adults, some are adolescents. Male adolescent sexual offenders are more likely than nonoffenders to have been molested themselves as young boys (Becker et al., 1989; Muster, 1992). Some adolescent sexual offenders may be imitating their own victimization. Adolescent child molesters also tend to feel socially inadequate and to be fearful of social interactions with age-mates of the other gender (Katz, 1990).

Why do men molest children? Banning (1989) suggests that males in our culture are socialized into seeking partners who are younger and weaker, whom they can easily dominate. This pattern of socialization may take the extreme form of development of sexual interest in children and adolescent girls, who because of their age are more easily dominated than adult women. Yet sexual interest in children may also be motivated by unusual patterns of sexual arousal in which children become the objects of sexual desire, sometimes to the exclusion of more appropriate (adult) stimuli.

Although the great majority of sexual abusers are male, the number of female sexual abusers may be greater than has been generally believed (Banning, 1989). Many female sexual abusers may go undetected because society accords women a much freer range of physical contact with children than it does men. A woman who fondles a child might be seen as affectionate, or at worst seductive, whereas a man would be more likely to be perceived as a child molester (Banning, 1989).

What motivates a woman to sexually abuse children, even her own children? Little research has been done to explore this question, but some factors have begun to emerge (Matthews et al., 1990). Some appear to have been manipulated into engaging in sexual abuse by their husbands. Others appear to have unmet emotional needs and low self-esteem and may have been seeking acceptance, closeness, and attention through sexual acts with children. Some, motivated by unresolved feelings of anger, revenge, powerlessness, or jealousy, may view their own and others' children as safe targets for venting these feelings. Some view their crimes as expressions of love.

Pedophilia

Pedophilia

A type of paraphilia that is defined by sexual attraction to unusual stimuli: children. (From the Greek *paidos*, meaning "child," not the Latin *pedis*, meaning "foot.")

Pedophilia is a paraphilia that involves persistent or recurrent sexual attraction to children. Although pedophiles are sometimes called child molesters, not all child molesters are pedophiles. Some molesters, however, may seek sexual contacts only with children when they are under unusual stress or lack other sexual outlets. Thus, they do not meet the clinical definition of pedophilia.

Research suggests that sexual attraction to children may be more common than is generally believed. Researchers in one study administered an anonymous survey to a sample of 193 college men (Briere & Runtz, 1989). A surprisingly high percentage of the students—21%—admitted to having been sexually attracted to small children. Nine percent reported sexual fantasies involving young children. Five percent reported masturbating to such fantasies. Seven percent reported that there was some likelihood that they would have sex with a young child if they knew they could avoid detection and punishment. Fortunately, most people with such erotic interests never act upon them.

Pedophiles are almost exclusively male, although some isolated cases of female pedophiles have been reported (Cooper et al., 1990). Some pedophiles are sexually attracted only to children. Others are sexually attracted to adults as well. Some pedophiles limit their sexual interest in children to incestuous relationships with family members. Others abuse children to whom they are unrelated. Some pedophiles limit their sexual interest in children to looking at them or undressing them. Others fondle them or masturbate in their presence. Some manipulate or coerce children into oral, anal, or vaginal intercourse.

Children tend not to be worldly-wise. They can often be "taken in" by pedophiles who tell them that they would like to "show them something," "teach them something," or do something with them that they would "like." Some pedophiles seek to gain the child's affection and discourage the child from disclosing the sexual activity by showering the child with attention and gifts. Others threaten the child or the child's family to prevent disclosure.

There is no consistent personality profile of the pedophile (Okami & Goldberg, 1992). Most pedophiles do not fit the common stereotype of the "dirty old man" in the trench coat who hangs around school yards. Most are otherwise law-abiding, well-respected citizens, generally in their 30s and 40s. Many are married or divorced, with children of their own.

Pedophilia may have complex and varied origins. Some pedophiles who are lacking in social skills may turn to children after failing to establish gratifying relationships with adult women (Overholser & Beck, 1986; Tollison & Adams, 1979). Research generally supports the stereotype of the pedophile as weak, passive, and shy—a socially inept, isolated man who feels threatened by mature relationships (Ames & Houston, 1990; Wilson & Cox, 1983).

Pedophiles who engage in incestuous relationships with their own children tend to present a somewhat different picture. They tend to fall on one or the other end of the dominance spectrum. Some are very dominant; others, very passive. Few are found between these extremes (Ames & Houston, 1990).

Some pedophiles were sexually abused as children and may be attempting to establish feelings of mastery by reversing the situation (De Young, 1982). Cycles of abuse may be perpetuated from generation to generation if children who are sexually abused become victimizers or partners of victimizers as adults.

Incest

Incest

Marriage or sexual relations between people who are so closely related (by "blood") that sexual relations are prohibited and punishable by law. (From the Latin *in-*, meaning "not," and *castus*, meaning "chaste.")

Incest applies to people who are related by blood, or *consanguineous*. The law may also proscribe coitus between, say, a stepfather and stepdaughter, however. Although a few societies have permitted incestuous pairings among royalty, all known cultures have some form of an incest taboo.

Most of our knowledge of incestuous relationships concerns father–daughter incest. Why? Most identified cases involve fathers who were eventually incarcerated.

About 1% of a sample of women in five American cities reported a sexual encounter with a father or stepfather (Cameron et al., 1986). Brother–sister incest, not parent–child incest, is the most common type of incest, however (Waterman & Lusk, 1986). Brother–sister incest is also believed to be greatly underreported, possibly because it tends to be transient and is apparently less harmful than parent–child incest. Finkelhor (1990) found that 21% of the college men in his sample, and 39% of the college women, reported incest with a sibling of the other gender. Only 4% reported incest with their fathers. Incest between siblings of the same gender is rare (Waterman & Lusk, 1986). Mother–daughter incest is the rarest form of incest (Waterman & Lusk, 1986).

Father–daughter incest often begins with affectionate cuddling or embraces and then progresses to teasing sexual play, lengthy caresses, hugs, kisses, and genital contact, even penetration. In some cases genital contact occurs more abruptly, usually when the father has been drinking, or arguing with his wife. Force is not typically used to gain compliance, but daughters are sometimes physically overcome and injured by their fathers.

In sibling incest, the brother usually initiates sexual activity and assumes the dominant role (Meiselman, 1978). Some brothers and sisters may view their sexual activity as natural and not know that it is taboo (Knox, 1988). Evidence on the effects of incest between brothers and sisters is mixed. In a study of college undergraduates, those who reported childhood incest with siblings did not reveal greater evidence of sexual adjustment problems than other undergraduates (Greenwald & Leitenberg, 1989). Sibling incest is most likely to be harmful when it is recurrent or forced or when parental response is harsh (Knox, 1988; Laviola, 1989).

Family Factors in Incest Incest frequently occurs within the context of general family disruption, as in families in which there is spouse abuse, a dysfunctional marriage, or alcoholic or physically abusive parents (Alter-Reid et al., 1986; Sirles & Franke, 1989; Waterman, 1986). Stressful events in the father's life, such as the loss of a job or problems at work, often precede the initiation of incest (Waterman, 1986).

Fathers who abuse older daughters tend to be domineering and authoritarian with their families (Waterman, 1986). Fathers who abuse younger, preschool daughters are more likely to be passive, dependent, and low in self-esteem. As Waterman (1986) notes:

> [The fathers] may need soothing and comforting, and may feel especially safe with preschool children: "I felt safe with her. . . . I didn't have to perform. She was so little that I knew she wouldn't and couldn't hurt me." (p. 215)

Marriages in incestuous families tend to be characterized by an uneven power relationship between the spouses. The abusive father is usually dominant. Another thread that frequently runs through incestuous families is a troubled sexual relationship between the spouses. The wife often rejects the husband sexually (Waterman, 1986).

Gebhard and his colleagues (1965) found that many fathers who committed incest with their daughters were religiously devout, fundamentalist, and moralistic. Perhaps such men, when sexually frustrated, are less likely to seek extramarital and extrafamilial sexual outlets or to turn to masturbation as a sexual release. In many cases the father is under stress but does not find adequate emotional and sexual support from his wife (Gagnon, 1977). He turns to a daughter as a wife surrogate, often when he has been drinking alcohol (Gebhard et al., 1965). The daughter may become, in her father's fantasies, the "woman of the house." This fantasy may become his justification for continuing the incestuous relationship. In some incestuous families, a role reversal occurs. The abused daughter assumes many of the mother's responsibilities for managing the household and caring for the younger children (Waterman, 1986).

Incestuous abuse is often repeated from generation to generation. One study found that in 154 cases of children who were sexually abused within the family, more than a third of the male offenders and about half of the mothers had either been abused themselves or were exposed to abuse as children (Faller, 1989b).

Sociocultural factors, such as poverty, overcrowded living conditions, and social or geographical isolation, may contribute to incest in some families (Waterman, 1986). Sibling incest may be encouraged by the crowded living conditions and open sexuality that occur among some economically disadvantaged families (Waterman, 1986).

Effects of Child Sexual Abuse

Child sexual abuse often inflicts great psychological harm on the child, whether the abuse is perpetrated by a family member, acquaintance, or stranger. Children who are sexually abused may suffer from a litany of short- and long-term psychological complaints, including anger, depression, anxiety, eating disorders, inappropriate sexual behavior, aggressive behavior, self-destructive behavior, sexual promiscuity, drug abuse, suicide attempts, posttraumatic stress disorder, low self-esteem, sexual dysfunction, mistrust of others, and feelings of detachment, (Beitchman, et al., 1992; Finkelhor, 1990; Goodwin et al., 1990; McLaren & Brown, 1989). Child sexual abuse may also have physical effects such as genital injuries and cause psychosomatic problems such as stomachaches and headaches.

Abused children commonly "act out." Younger children have tantrums or display aggressive or antisocial behavior. Older children turn to substance abuse (Finkelhor, 1990; Lusk & Waterman, 1986). Some abused children become withdrawn and retreat into fantasy

A P P L I C A T I O N S

PREVENTING CHILD SEXUAL ABUSE

Many of us were taught by our parents never to accept a ride or an offer of candy from a stranger. However, many instances of child sexual abuse are perpetrated by familiar adults, often a family member or friend. Prevention programs help children understand what sexual abuse is and how they can avoid it. A national survey showed that two of three children in the United States have participated in school-based sex-abuse prevention programs (Goleman, 1993). In addition to learning to avoid strangers, children need to recognize the differences between acceptable touching, as in an affectionate embrace or pat on the head, and unacceptable or "bad" touching. Even elementary-school-age children can learn the distinction between "good touching and bad touching" (Tutty, 1992). Good school-based programs are generally helpful in preparing children to handle an actual encounter with a potential molester (Goleman, 1993). Children who receive comprehensive training are more likely to use strategies such as running away, yelling, or saying no when they are threatened by an abuser. They are also more likely to report incidents to adults.

Researchers recognize that children can easily be intimidated or overpowered by adults or older children. Children may be unable to say no in a sexually abusive situation, even though they want to and know it is the right thing to do (Waterman et al., 1986). Although children may not always be able to prevent abuse, they can be encouraged to tell someone about it. Most prevention programs emphasize teaching children messages such as "It's not your fault," "Never keep a bad or scary secret," and "Always tell your parents about this, especially if someone says you shouldn't tell them" (Waterman et al., 1986).

Children also need to be alerted to the types of threats they might receive for disclosing the abuse. They are more likely to resist threats if they are reassured that they will be believed if they disclose the abuse, that their parents will continue to love them, and that they and their families will be protected from the molester.

School-based prevention programs focus on protecting the child. In most states, teachers and helping professionals are required to report suspected abuse to authorities. Tighter controls and better screening are needed to monitor the hiring of day care employees. Administrators and teachers in preschool and day care facilities also need to be educated to recognize the signs of sexual abuse and to report suspected cases (Waterman et al., 1986). Treatment programs to help people who are sexually attracted to children *before* they commit abusive acts would also be of use.

---

or refuse to leave the house. Regressive behaviors, such as thumb sucking, fear of the dark, and fear of strangers, are also common among sexually abused children. On the heels of the assault and in the ensuing years, many survivors of childhood sexual abuse—like many rape survivors—show signs of posttraumatic stress disorder. They have flashbacks, nightmares, numbing of emotions, and feelings of estrangement from others (Finkelhor, 1990).

Sexual development of abused children may also become shaped in dysfunctional ways. For example, the survivor may become prematurely sexually active or promiscuous in adolescence and adulthood (Finkelhor, 1988; Lusk & Waterman, 1986; Tharinger, 1990). Researchers find that adolescent girls who are sexually abused tend to engage in consensual coitus at earlier ages than nonabused peers (Wyatt, 1988).

Researchers generally find more similarities than differences between the genders with respect to the effects of sexual abuse in childhood (Finkelhor, 1990). For example, both boys and girls tend to suffer fears and sleep disturbance. There are some gender differences, however. The most consistent gender difference appears to be that boys more often "externalize" their problems, perhaps by becoming more physically aggressive. Girls more often "internalize" their difficulties, as by becoming depressed (Finkelhor, 1990; Gomez-Schwartz et al., 1990).

Late adolescence and early adulthood seem to pose especially difficult periods for survivors of childhood sexual abuse. Studies of women in these age groups reveal more psychological and social problems in abused women than are found among nonabused reference groups (Jackson et al., 1990; Roland et al., 1989).

Effects of childhood sexual abuse are often long-lasting. In one study, researchers found evidence of greater psychological distress in a group of 54 adult women, ranging from 23 to 61 years of age, who had been sexually abused as children than in a matched group of nonabused women (Greenwald et al., 1990). Women who blame themselves for the abuse apparently have relatively lower self-esteem and more depression than those who do not (Hoagwood, 1990).

Treatment of Survivors of Child Sexual Abuse

At least 75% of cases of child sexual abuse go unreported. Psychotherapy in adulthood often becomes the first opportunity for survivors to confront leftover feelings of pain, anger, and misplaced guilt (Alter-Reid et al., 1986; Ratican, 1992). Group or individual therapy can help improve survivors' self-esteem and ability to develop intimate relationships. Confronting the trauma within a supportive therapeutic relationship may also help prevent the cycle of abuse from perpetuating itself from one generation to another (Alter-Reid et al., 1986).

Special programs have begun to appear that provide therapeutic services to abused children and adolescents. Most therapists recommend a multicomponent treatment approach, which may involve individual therapy for the child, mother, and father; group therapy for the adolescent or even preadolescent survivor; art therapy or play therapy for the younger child (e.g., using drawings or puppets to express feelings); marital counseling for the parents; and family therapy for the entire family (de Luca et al., 1992; Waterman, 1986).

Treatment of Rapists and Child Molesters

What does *treatment* mean? When a helping professional treats someone, the goal is usually to help that individual. When we speak of treating a sex offender, the goal is as likely, or more likely, to help society by eliminating the problem behavior.

Rapists and child molesters are criminals, not patients. Most convicted rapists and child molesters are incarcerated as a form of punishment, not treatment. They may receive psychological treatment or rehabilitation in prison to help prepare them for release and reentry into society, however. The most common form of treatment is group therapy, which is based on the belief that though offenders may fool counselors, they do not easily fool one another (Kaplan, 1993). Yet the great majority of incarcerated sex offenders receive little or no treatment in prison (Goleman, 1992). In California, for example, which has 15,000 incarcerated sex offenders, treatment has been provided in but one experimental program for only 46 rapists and child molesters (Goleman, 1992).

The results of prison-based treatment programs are mixed at best. Consider a Canadian study of 54 rapists who participated in a treatment program. Following release from prison, 28% were later convicted of a sexual offense, and 43% were convicted of a violent offense (Rice et al., 1990). Treatment also failed to curb recidivism among a sample of 136 child molesters (Rice et al., 1991).

More promising findings resulted from innovative programs in prison facilities in California and Vermont (Goleman, 1992). In the Vermont program, the average rate of conviction for additional sex crimes following release was reduced by at least half in a group of sex offenders who received the treatment program, as compared to a control group who did not. These innovative programs used a variety of techniques. Empathy training was used to increase the offender's sensitivity to his victims. One empathy exercise had offenders write about their crimes from the perspective of the victim. The technique of covert sensitization was used to help offenders resist deviant sex fantasies, which often lead to deviant behavior. The offender would pair, in his imagination, scenes involving rape and molestation with aversive consequences. An exhibitionist, for example, might be asked to practice imagining that he is about to expose himself and is discovered in the act by his parents. A child molester might fantasize about sexually approaching a child, only to find himself confronted by police officers.

Another approach uses medical interventions to reduce testosterone levels and, consequently, offenders' sex drives. In a few European countries, some offenders who claimed they were unable to control their sex drives have been castrated to reduce testosterone levels (Wille & Beier, 1989). The effects of castration are mixed. Many castrated rapists report markedly lowered sex drives, but they may retain sexual interest and remain capable of erection, however. And some do repeat their crimes. Other researchers report lower recidivism rates among castrated offenders than among noncastrated offenders. In any event, the use of castration with sex offenders appears to be declining (Wille & Beier, 1989).

Antiandrogen drugs such as Depo-Provera induce "chemical castration" (Ayres, 1996). Unlike surgical castration, chemical castration is reversible (Ayres, 1996). In 1996, California passed a bill that requires repeat child molesters to undergo chemical castration upon release unless they have undergone voluntary surgical castration ("Injections approved," 1996).

Sexual Harassment

Many Americans were spellbound by the Michael Douglas–Demi Moore film *Disclosure*. In the film, Demi Moore plays Michael Douglas's supervisor. She uses her power over him to attempt to harass him into sexual activity.

Sexual harassment
Deliberate or repeated unsolicited verbal comments, gestures, or physical contact of a sexual nature that is considered unwelcome by the recipient.

What *is* **sexual harassment?** Definitions of sexual harassment vary, but its definition in the workplace as the "deliberate or repeated unsolicited verbal comments, gestures, or physical contact of a sexual nature that is considered to be unwelcome by the recipient" has been widely adopted (U.S. Merit Systems Protection Board, 1981, p. 2). Sexual harassment can range from unwelcome sexual jokes, overtures, suggestive comments, and sexual innuendos to outright sexual assault, and may include behaviors such as the following (Powell, 1996):

- Verbal harassment or abuse
- Subtle pressure for sexual activity
- Remarks about a person's clothing, body, or sexual activities

Disclosure. The film *Disclosure* revolved around a case in which a female supervisor (Demi Moore) sexually harassed a male employee (Michael Douglas). The film was of interest not only because of the "star power," but also because of the role reversals. That is, the great majority of sexual harassers are men.

APPLICATIONS

RESISTING SEXUAL HARASSMENT

What would you do if you were sexually harassed by an employer or a professor? How would you handle it? Would you try to ignore it and hope that it would stop? What actions might you take? We offer some suggestions, adapted from Powell (1996), that may be helpful. Recognize, however, that responsibility for sexual harassment always lies with the perpetrator and the organization that permits sexual harassment to take place, not with the person subjected to the harassment.

1. *Convey a professional attitude.* Harassment may be stopped cold by responding to the harasser with a businesslike, professional attitude.
2. *Discourage harassing behavior, and encourage appropriate behavior.* Harassment may also be stopped cold by shaping the harasser's behavior. Your reactions to the harasser may encourage businesslike behavior and discourage flirtatious or suggestive

behavior. If a harassing professor suggests that you come back after school to review your term paper so that the two of you will be undisturbed, set limits assertively. Tell the professor that you'd feel more comfortable discussing the paper during regular office hours. Remain task-oriented. Stick to business. The harasser should get the message that you wish to maintain a professional relationship. If the harasser persists, do not blame yourself. You are responsible only for your own actions. If the harasser persists, you may try a more direct response: "Professor Jones, I'd like to keep our relationship on a purely professional basis, okay?"

3. *Avoid being alone with the harasser.* If you are being harassed by your professor but need some advice about preparing your term paper, approach him or her after class when other students are milling about, not privately during office hours. Or bring a friend

to wait outside the office while you consult the professor.

4. *Maintain a record.* Keep a record of incidents of harassment as documentation in the event you decide to lodge a complaint. The record should include the following: (1) where the incident took place; (2) the date and time; (3) what happened, including the exact words that were used, if you can recall them; (4) how you felt; and (5) the names of witnesses. Some people who have been subjected to sexual harassment have carried a hidden tape recorder during contacts with the harasser. Such recordings may not be admissible in a court of law, but they are persuasive in organizational grievance procedures. A hidden tape recorder may be illegal in your state, however. It is thus advisable to check the law.

5. *Talk with the harasser.* It may be uncomfortable to address the issue with a harasser, but doing

- Leering at or ogling a person's body
- Unwelcome touching, patting, or pinching
- Brushing against a person's body
- Demands for sexual favors accompanied by implied or overt threats concerning one's job or student status
- Physical assault

Men or women can both commit, and be subjected to, sexual harassment. However, despite the plot of the film *Disclosure,* the great majority of harassers are men.

Charges of sexual harassment are often ignored or trivialized by coworkers and employers. The victim may hear, "Why make a big deal out of it? It's not like you were attacked in the street." Yet some find harassment on the job so unbearable that they resign. College women have dropped courses, switched majors, or changed graduate programs or even colleges because they were unable to stop professors from sexually harassing them (Dziech & Weiner, 1984; Fitzgerald, 1993a, 1993b).

One reason that sexual harassment is so stressful is that, as with so many other forms of sexual exploitation or coercion, the blame tends to fall on the victim (Powell, 1996). Some harassers seem to believe that charges of harassment were exaggerated or that the so puts the offender on notice that you want it to stop. It may be helpful to frame your approach in terms of a description of the offending actions (e.g., "When we were alone in the office, you repeatedly attempted to touch me or brush up against me"), your feelings about the offense ("It made me feel like my privacy was being violated. I'm very upset about this and haven't been sleeping well"), and what you would like the offender to do ("So I'd like you to agree never to attempt to touch me again, okay?"). Having a talk with the harasser may stop the harassment. If the harasser denies the accusations, it may be necessary to take further action.

6. *Write a letter to the harasser.* Set down on paper a record of the offending behavior, and put the harasser on notice that the harassment must stop. Your letter might (1) describe what happened ("Several times you have made sexist comments about my body"), (2) describe how you feel ("It made me feel like a sexual object when you talked to me that way"), and (3) describe what you would like the harasser to do ("I want you to stop making sexist comments to me").

7. *Seek support.* Support from people you trust can help you through the often trying process of resisting sexual harassment. Talking with others allows you to express your feelings and receive emotional support, encouragement, and advice. In addition, it may strengthen your case if you have the opportunity to identify and talk with other people who have been harassed by the offender.

8. *File a complaint.* Companies and organizations are required by law to respond reasonably to complaints of sexual harassment. In large organizations, a desig-

nated official (sometimes an ombudsman, affirmative action officer, or sexual harassment advisor) is usually charged to handle such complaints. Set up an appointment with this official to discuss your experiences. Ask about the grievance procedures in the organization and your right to confidentiality. Have available a record of the dates of the incidents, what happened, how you felt about it, and so on. The two major government agencies that handle charges of sexual harassment are the Equal Employment Opportunity Commission and your state's Human Rights Commission.

9. *Seek legal remedies.* Sexual harassment is illegal and actionable. If you are considering legal action, consult an attorney familiar with this area of law. You may be entitled to back pay (if you were fired for reasons arising from the sexual harassment), job reinstatement, and punitive damages.

---

victim "overreacted" or "took me too seriously." In our society, women are expected to be "nice"—to be passive and not "make a scene." The woman who assertively protects her rights may be seen as "strange" and disturbing, or a "troublemaker." "Women are damned if they assert themselves and victimized if they don't" (Powell, 1991, p. 114).

Sexual harassment may have more to do with the abuse of power than with sexual desire (Goleman, 1991; Tedeschi & Felson, 1994). Relatively few cases of sexual harassment involve outright requests for sexual favors. Most involve the expression of power as a tactic to control or frighten someone, usually a woman. The harasser is usually in a dominant position and abuses that position by exploiting the victim's vulnerability. Sexual harassment may be used as a tactic of social control, a means of keeping women "in their place." This is especially so in work settings that are traditional male preserves, such as the firehouse, the construction site, or the military academy. Sexual harassment expresses resentment and hostility toward women who venture beyond the boundaries of the traditional feminine role (Fitzgerald, 1993b).

Sexual harassment is not confined to the workplace or the university. It may also occur between patients and doctors and between therapists and clients. Therapists may use their power and influence to pressure clients into sexual relations. The harassment may be disguised, expressed in terms of the "therapeutic benefits" of sexual activity.

Chapter Review

Rape

(1) F_____ rape is defined in most states as sexual intercourse with a nonconsenting person by the use of force or the threat of force. (2) St_____ rape refers to sexual intercourse with a person who is below the age of consent, even though the person may cooperate. Most states (3: Do *or* Do not?) have rape statutes that permit the prosecution of husbands who rape their wives.

The U.S. National Crime Victimization Survey estimates that (4) _____ women are sexually assaulted each year. Studies tend to (5: Overreport *or* Underreport?) the incidence of rape. The majority of rapes (6: Are *or* Are not?) reported or prosecuted. The prevalence of reported rapes in the United States is (7: Greater *or* Lesser?) than that in Great Britain and Japan.

Most women (8: Are *or* Are not?) raped by acquaintances. Men who commit (9) d_____ rape may believe that acceptance of a date indicates willingness to engage in coitus. Many men who participate in (10) g_____ rapes are trying to conform to the stereotype of the tough he-man. Most male rapes occur in (11) p_____ settings. Some men engage in (12) _____tal rape to degrade their wives.

Rape myths create a social climate that (13) _____mizes rape. Many observers contend that our society breeds rapists by socializing males into socially and sexually (14) dom_____ roles. Men are often reinforced for (15) ag_____ behavior. Many young men come to view dates not as chances to get to know their partners but as opportunities for (16) con_____.

Rapists (17: Do *or* Do not?) vary in their psychological characteristics, family backgrounds, mental health, and criminal histories. Some rapists are (18) anti_____ and have long histories of violent behavior. Rapists are more likely than other men to hold (19: Traditional *or* Nontraditional?) gender-role attitudes and be (20) hos_____ toward women. Groth and

Birnbaum believe that there are three basic kinds of rape: (21) a_____ rape, power rape, and (22) _____tic rape.

Many rape survivors enter a state of (23) cri_____. Some survivors experience feelings of (24) g_____ and shame. Rape survivors often report a lack of sexual (25) d_____, fears of sex, and difficulty becoming sexually aroused. Burgess and Holmstrom identified some common response patterns in survivors of rape, which they labeled the (26) r_____ _____ma syndrome. Research has shown that pleading, begging or reasoning with an assailant may not prevent rape and (27: May *or* May not?) heighten the probability of injury. Screaming and running away are (28: More *or* Less?) likely than begging to ward off an attack.

Sexual Abuse of Children

Most sexually abused children are (29: Boys *or* Girls?). Any sexual contact between an adult and a child is abusive because the child is below the age of (30) _____sent. Children are most likely to be sexually abused by (31: Acquaintances *or* Strangers?). The most common type of abuse is (32) _____ling the genitals. Abused children (33: Usually *or* Rarely?) report the abuse.

The overwhelming majority of child abusers are (34: Males *or* Females?). Men may molest children because they can (35) _____nate children.

(36) _____philia is a paraphilia that involves persistent or recurrent sexual attraction to children. Pedophiles are almost exclusively (37: Male *or* Female?). Most pedophiles (38: Do *or* Do not?) fit the common stereotype of the "dirty old man" in the trench coat who hangs around school yards.

(39) In_____ is child molestation by people who are related by blood. Most of our knowledge of incestuous relationships concerns (40) _____–daughter incest. Yet (41) _____–sister incest is

the most common type of incest. Sibling incest appears to be (42: More *or* Less?) harmful than father–daughter incest. The abusive father is usually (43: Dominant *or* Submissive?). Incest (44: Is *or* Is not?) often repeated from generation to generation. The survivor of childhood sexual abuse may become prematurely sexually active or (45) _____cuous. At least (46) _____% of cases of child sexual abuse go unreported.

Treatment of Rapists and Child Molesters

Rapists and child molesters are (47) cr_____s, not patients. The most common form of treatment is (48) g_____ therapy. In a treatment program in Vermont, (49) _____thy training was used to in-crease the offender's sensitivity to his victims. Another approach uses medical interventions to reduce offenders' (50) tes_____ levels and sex drives.

Sexual Harassment

Sexual (51) _____ment is defined as "deliberate or repeated unsolicited verbal comments, gestures, or physical contact of a sexual nature that is considered to be unwelcome by the recipient." The great majority of harassers are (52: Men *or* Women?). With sexual harassment, as with other forms of sexual coercion, the blame often falls on the (53) vic_____. Sexual harassment may have more to do with the abuse of (54) p_____ than with sexual desire.

Chapter Quiz

1. All forms of sexual activity between adults and children are coercive because
   (a) the children resist.
   (b) the adults have a need to dominate the children.
   (c) the children are invariably hurt by the sexual activity.
   (d) the children are below the age of consent.
2. Which of the following is NOT a reason why the incidence of rape is underreported?
   (a) Some women fear that they will be humiliated by the criminal justice system.
   (b) Some women fear reprisal from their families or the rapist.
   (c) Some women assume that the offender will not be apprehended or prosecuted.
   (d) Some women are raped by total strangers.
3. The most common type of rape is
   (a) rape by an acquaintance.
   (b) rape by a stranger.
   (c) marital rape.
   (d) rape by females.
4. Most men who rape other men are
   (a) heterosexual.
   (b) gay.
   (c) pedophiles.
   (d) insane.
5. Which one of the following is NOT a cultural myth that encourages rape?
   (a) Women say no when they mean yes.
   (b) The way women dress, they are asking to be raped.
   (c) Women do not wish to forced into sexual activity.

   (d) Women want a truly masculine man—one who is sexually aggressive.
6. Which of the following is TRUE of rapists?
   (a) Rapists are opposed to violence as a way of encouraging other people to do their will.
   (b) Rapists are out of control of their behavior.
   (c) Rapists vary in their psychological characteristics and family backgrounds.
   (d) Rapists are less intelligent than most other people.
7. The term *rape trauma syndrome* was originated by
   (a) Money.
   (b) Burgess and Holmstrom.
   (c) Groth and Birnbaum.
   (d) Powell.
8. The most common type of incest is
   (a) father–daughter incest.
   (b) father–son incest.
   (c) mother–son incest.
   (d) brother–sister incest.
9. Which of the following is the most common form of child sexual abuse?
   (a) Genital fondling
   (b) Exhibitionism
   (c) Oral–genital sex
   (d) Sexual intercourse
10. Which of the following has been used to induce "chemical castration" in sex offenders?
    (a) Testosterone
    (b) Estrogen
    (c) Depo-Provera
    (d) Progesterone

Answers to Chapter Review

1. Forcible
2. Statutory
3. Do
4. 500,000
5. Underreport
6. Are not
7. Greater
8. Are
9. Date
10. Gang
11. Prison
12. Marital
13. Legitimizes
14. Dominant
15. Aggressive
16. Conquest
17. Do
18. Antisocial
19. Traditional
20. Hostile
21. Anger
22. Sadistic
23. Crisis
24. Guilt
25. Desire
26. Rape trauma
27. May
28. More
29. Girls
30. Consent
31. Acquaintances
32. Fondling
33. Rarely
34. Males
35. Dominate
36. Pedophilia
37. Male
38. Do not
39. Incest
40. Father
41. Brother
42. Less
43. Dominant
44. Is
45. Promiscuous
46. 75
47. Criminals
48. Group
49. Empathy
50. Testosterone
51. Harassment
52. Men
53. Victim
54. Power

Answers to Chapter Quiz

1. (d)
2. (d)
3. (a)
4. (a)
5. (c)
6. (c)
7. (b)
8. (d)
9. (a)
10. (c)

C H A P T E R 16

Commercial Sex

O U T L I N E

Prostitution
Types of Female Prostitutes
Characteristics of Female Prostitutes
Customers of Female Prostitutes
Male Prostitution
HIV, AIDS, and Prostitution

Pornography and Obscenity
What Is Pornographic?
Prevalence and Use of Pornography
Pornography and Sexual Coercion

Sex in Advertising
Advertising and Gender-Role Stereotypes

Chapter Review

Chapter Quiz

A World of Diversity
'Tis a Puzzlement: On AIDS and Prostitution in Thailand

DID YOU KNOW THAT . . .

- Prostitution is legal in parts of Nevada?
- Many massage parlors and escort services are fronts for prostitution?
- Many prostitutes enjoy sexual relations with at least some clients?
- Many prostitutes were sexually abused as children?
- One of the lures of prostitution is that it provides sex without the need to make a commitment?
- Sex with prostitutes is the key factor in the male–female transmission of HIV in Africa?
- It has not been shown that pornography causes crimes of violence?
- Both men and women are sexually aroused by pornography?
- Sexy ads can backfire in that viewers focus so much on the sexy imagery that they forget what the product is?

Sex as commerce runs the gamut from adult movie theaters and book-shops to strip shows, sex toy shops, erotic hotels and motels, escort/out-call services, "massage parlors," "900" telephone services, and the use of sex appeal in advertisements for legitimate products. The "world of commercial sex is a kind of X-rated amusement park—Disneyland for Adults" (Edgley, 1989, p. 372).

In this chapter, we discuss three commercial aspects of sexuality: prostitution, pornography, and the use of sex in advertising. Though the streetwalker, the purveyor of "adult" movies, and the Madison Avenue copywriter may otherwise have little else in common, they all have learned to use sex to make a profit. ■

Prostitution

Prostitution

The sale of sexual activity for money or goods of value, such as drugs. (From the Latin *prostituere*, meaning "to cause to stand in front of." The implication is that one is offering one's body for sale.)

Prostitution is illegal everywhere in the United States except for some rural counties in Nevada, where it is restricted to state-licensed brothels.

Soliciting the services of a prostitute is also illegal in many states. Police rarely crack down on customers, or "johns," however. The few who are arrested are usually penalized with a small fine. On occasion, the names of convicted johns are published in local newspapers, which may deter men who fear publicity. Although prostitutes and their clients can be male or female, most prostitutes are female and virtually all customers are male.

No one knows how many prostitutes there are in the United States. The little we know of prostitution derives from sex surveys. Almost two thirds of the White males in Kinsey's sample (Kinsey et al., 1948) reported visiting a prostitute at least once. About 15% to 20% visited them regularly. The use of prostitutes varied with educational level, however. By the age of 20, about 50% of Kinsey's non-college-educated single males, but only 20% of his college-educated males, had visited a prostitute. By the age of 25, the figures swelled to about two thirds for non-college-educated males but only slightly above 25% for college men.

Kinsey's data foreshadowed a falling off of experience with prostitutes that seems linked to the decay of the sexual double standard. Kinsey found that 20% of his college-educated men had been sexually initiated by prostitutes. This figure was more than cut in half among generations who came of age in the 1960s and 1970s (Hunt, 1974). Less than 10% of both college-educated *and* non-college-educated males in the *Playboy* survey (Hunt, 1974) of the 1970s reported being sexually initiated by a prostitute.

Why are young men less likely to visit prostitutes than they were in Kinsey's day? For one thing, young men in recent generations were more likely to become sexually initiated with their girlfriends. As Edgley (1989) put it, "An old and hallowed economic principle was at work; those who charge for a service cannot compete with those who give it away" (p. 392). Concern about sexually transmitted diseases, especially AIDS, has also limited the use of prostitution. Nevertheless, prostitution continues to flourish.

Types of Female Prostitutes

Female prostitutes—commonly called *hookers, whores, working girls,* or *escorts*—are usually classified according to the settings in which they work. The major types of prostitutes today are streetwalkers; brothel or "house" prostitutes, many of whom work in "massage parlors" and for "escort services" (often listed in the Yellow Pages); and call girls. Traditional brothel prostitution is much less common today than before World War II.

Streetwalkers   Most prostitutes are **streetwalkers**. They occupy the bottom rung in the hierarchy of prostitutes. They earn the lowest incomes and are usually the least desirable. They also incur the greatest risk of abuse by customers and **pimps.** Streetwalkers tend to come from poverty and to have had unhappy childhoods (Edgley, 1989). Perhaps as many as 80% are survivors of rape, sexual abuse, or incest (Gordon & Snyder, 1989). Many were teenage runaways who turned to prostitution to survive.

Streetwalkers operate in the open. They are thus more likely than other prostitutes to draw attention to themselves and risk arrest. To avoid arrest, streetwalkers may be indirect about their services. They may ask passersby if they are interested in a "good time" or some "fun" rather than sex per se. In many cities, streetwalkers dress in revealing or provocative fashions.

There is the stereotype of the prostitute as a sexually unresponsive woman who feigns sexual arousal with johns while she keeps one eye glued to the clock. Most street prostitutes in a Philadelphia sample, however, reported that some forms of sex with customers were "very satisfying" (Savitz & Rosen, 1988). More than 60% of the prostitutes reported achieving orgasm with customers at least occasionally. Most prostitutes also reported that they had enjoyable sexual relationships in their private lives and were regularly orgasmic. Not surprisingly, they garnered more sexual enjoyment from their personal relationships than from their customers.

In most locales, penalties for prostitution involve small fines or short jail terms. Many police departments, besieged by crimes such as drug peddling and violent crimes, consider prostitution a "minor" or "nuisance" crime (Carvajal, 1995). Many prostitutes find the criminal justice system a revolving door. They pay the fine. They spend a night or two in jail. They return to the streets.

A bar prostitute is a variation of the streetwalker. She approaches men in a bar she frequents, rather than on the streets. Payoffs to bar owners or managers secure their cooperation, although the women are sometimes tolerated because they draw customers. Some streetwalkers work X-rated, or "adult," movie houses and may service their patrons in their seats with manual or oral sex. Payoffs may secure the cooperation of the management.

Many streetwalkers support a pimp. A pimp acts as lover–father–companion–master. He provides streetwalkers with protection, bail, and sometimes room and board, in exchange for a high percentage of their earnings, often more than 90%. Prostitutes are often physically abused by their pimps, who may use threats and beatings as means of control. In a study of young streetwalkers in Boston, Price (1989) observed that as the relationship progressed, the beatings became more vicious. Romenesko and Miller (1989), who studied streetwalkers in Milwaukee, commented, "Clearly, 'men' are the rulers of the underworld" (p. 117).

Streetwalkers do not tend to remain in the business (sometimes referred to as "the life") very long (Edgley, 1989). Some make the transition to a more traditional life or get married. Others die young from drug abuse, disease, suicide, or physical abuse from pimps or customers. Those who survive become less marketable with age.

Streetwalkers
Prostitutes who solicit customers on the streets.

Pimps
Men who serve as agents for prostitutes and live off their earnings. (From the Middle French *pimper*, meaning "to dress smartly.")

Streetwalkers who work hotels and conventions generally hold a higher status than those that work the streets or bars. Clients are typically conventioneers or businessmen traveling away from home. Some hotel managers will tolerate known prostitutes (usually for a payoff under the table), so long as the woman conducts herself discreetly.

Brothel Prostitution

Cathouse, bordello, cat wagon, parlor house, whore-house, joy house, house of ill repute—these are but a handful of names given to brothels, houses in which many prostitutes work. Brothel prostitutes occupy a middle status in the hierarchy of prostitutes, between streetwalkers on one end and call girls on the other (Edgley, 1989). Some work in a massage parlor or for an "escort service."

The life of the brothel (or "house") prostitute is usually neither as lucrative as that of the call girl nor as degrading as that of the streetwalker. Some prostitutes in massage parlors or working for escort services may not consider themselves to be "real prostitutes" because they do not walk the streets and because their businesses present a legitimate front (Edgley, 1989). The heyday of the brothel is all but over in the United States. Formal brothels today are rare, except in Nevada, where they are legal but regulated.

Some brothel prostitutes lead lives of complete degradation. Many poor Asian women have been recently lured to the United States by promises of the good life. Upon arrival, they have found themselves enslaved in brothels—working for tips and not allowed to leave. Such a brothel was recently closed by police at 208 Bowery in New York City. It housed more than 30 women smuggled from Thailand and came to the attention of police when one woman jumped from a window (Goldberg, 1995).

The Massage Parlor

"Massage parlors" have sprung up from coast to coast to fill the vacuum left by the departure of the brothels. Many massage parlors are legitimate establishments that provide massage, and only massage, to customers. Masseuses and masseurs are licensed in many states, and laws restrict them from offering sexual services. Many localities require that the masseuse or masseur keep certain parts of her or his body clothed and not touch the client's genitals.

Many massage parlors serve as fronts for prostitution, however. Today they are often found in malls in middle-class suburbs, where there is ample parking (Carvajal, 1995). In these establishments, clients typically pay fees for a standard massage and then tip the workers for sexual extras.

Massage parlor prostitutes generally offer to perform manual stimulation of the penis ("a local"), oral sex, or less frequently, coitus. Some massage parlor prostitutes are better educated than streetwalkers and brothel workers and would not work in these other venues.

Brothel Prostitutes. In this Nevada brothel, customers typically select their sex partners from women who line up in a central area.

Escort Services   Conventioneers and businessmen are more likely to turn to the listings for "massage" and "escort services" in the telephone directory or under the personal ads in local newspapers than to seek hotel prostitutes. Services that provide "outcall" send masseuses (or masseurs) or escorts to the hotel room.

Escort services are typically (but not always) fronts for prostitution. Escort services are found in every major American city and present themselves as legitimate business providing escorts for men. Indeed, one will find female companionship for corporate functions and for unattached men traveling away from home under "escort services." Many escort services provide only prostitution, however, and clients of other escort services sometimes negotiate sexual services after formal escort duties are completed—or in their stead.

Prostitutes who work for escort services often come from middle-class backgrounds and are well educated—so much the better to help prepare them to hold their own in social conversation. Escort services may establish arrangements with legitimate companies to provide "escorts" for visiting customers or potential clients. They also provide female escorts to "entertain" at conventions.

Call Girls   Call girls occupy the highest status on the social ladder of female prostitution. Many of them overlap with escorts. Call girls tend to be the most attractive and well-educated prostitutes and tend to charge more for their services. Many come from middle-class backgrounds (Edgley, 1989). Unlike other types of prostitutes, call girls usually work on their own. Thus, they need not split their income with a pimp, escort service, or massage parlor. Many lead a luxurious lifestyle. They live in expensive neighborhoods, wear stylish clothes, and are more selective about customers. Yet they incur expenses for laundry services and for payoffs to landlords, doormen, and sometimes to police.

Call girls often escort their clients to dinner and social functions, and are expected not only to provide sex but also charming and gracious company and conversation (Edgley, 1989). Call girls often give clients the feeling that they are important and attractive. They may effectively simulate pleasure and orgasm and can create the illusion that time does not matter. It does, of course. To the call girl, as to other entrepreneurs, time is money.

Call girls may receive clients in their apartments or make "outcalls" to clients' homes and hotels. Call girls may trade or sell "black books" that list clients and their sexual preferences. To protect themselves from police and abusive clients, call girls may insist on reviewing a client's business card or learning his home telephone number before personal contact is made. They may investigate whether the customer is in fact the person he purports to be.

Call girls

Prostitutes who arrange for their sexual contacts by telephone. *Call* refers both to telephone calls and to being "on call."

Characteristics of Female Prostitutes

No single factor explains entry into female prostitution. Yet, poverty and sexual and/or physical abuse figure prominently in the backgrounds of many prostitutes. They often come from conflict-ridden or one-parent homes in poor urban areas or rural farming communities.

For young women of impoverished backgrounds and marginal skills, the life of the prostitute may seem alluring. It is an alternative to the menial and dismal work that is otherwise available. Based on their studies of streetwalkers in Milwaukee, Romensko and Miller (1989) concluded that

> poverty, and the many concomitants of poverty manifest in American society, were the factors pushing these women into the world of illicit work. Conversely, the bright lights, money, and independence that the street seemingly offered—things that were largely absent from these women's lives prior to their entrance into street life—were enticements that drew women to street life. (p. 112)

Researchers also find a high level of psychological disturbance among streetwalkers. In New York, Exner and his colleagues (1977) found that call girls and brothel prostitutes could not be distinguished from nonprostitutes on their psychological characteristics. Streetwalkers and drug-addicted prostitutes showed higher rates of psychological disturbance than comparison groups, however. In another study, teenage female prostitutes were more likely than normal female adolescents or delinquents who did not engage in prostitution to show signs of psychological disturbance and to have been placed in special-education classes in school (Gibson et al., 1988).

Poverty accounts for the entry of young women into prostitution in many countries. In some Third World nations, such as Thailand, rural, impoverished parents may in effect sell daughters to recruiters who place them in brothels in cities (Erlanger, 1991; Goldberg, 1995). Many of the women send home whatever money they can and also work hard to try to pay off the procurers and break free of their financial bonds.

In the United States and Canada, many initiates into prostitution are teenage runaways. The family backgrounds of teenage runaways vary in socioeconomic status (some come from middle-class or affluent homes, whereas others are reared in poverty). However, family discord and dysfunction frequently set the stage for their entry to street life and prostitution (Price, 1989). A study of teenage prostitutes in Boston found that a majority had come from broken homes and were reared by single parents or in reconstituted families consisting of half siblings and stepsiblings (Price, 1989).

Teenage runaways are at particularly high risk of unsafe sexual practices, such as unprotected sex with multiple partners. The average male teenage runaway in a New York City study reported having had 11 female sexual partners in his lifetime (Rotheram-Borus et al., 1992). Only 8% of the teenage boys reported using condoms consistently.

Teenage runaways with marginal skills and limited means of support may find few alternatives to prostitution. Adolescent prostitution results from the "necessities of street life—it is survival behavior more than it is sexual behavior" (Seng, 1989, p. 674). It is not long before the teenage runaway is approached by a pimp or a john. A study of 149 teenage runaways in Toronto found that 67% of the boys and 82% of the girls who had been away from home for more than a year had been offered money to engage in sexual activity with an adult (Hartman et al., 1987).

Studies of teenage prostitutes in the United States show that perhaps as many as one half to two thirds of female prostitutes had been sexually abused as children (Seng, 1989). One sample of 45 former prostitutes in Canada showed that 73% had been sexually abused in childhood (Bagley & Young, 1987).

Not all sexually abused children become prostitutes, of course. Only 12% of one sample of predominantly female 16- to 18-year-olds who had been sexually abused became involved in prostitution (Seng, 1989). Nor do all teenage runaways become prostitutes. A Boston study of homeless street youth in the mid-1980s found that fewer than 20% had engaged in prostitution (Price, 1989). Though most had been approached for prostitution within a few days of living on the streets, the overwhelming majority refused.

In sum, evidence suggests that most female prostitutes are survivors of sexual abuse or incest. Running away from home appears to funnel many survivors of childhood sexual abuse into prostitution, yet not all survivors of sexual abuse, nor all teenage runaways, become prostitutes.

Customers of Female Prostitutes

Many prostitutes refer to a customer as a "john" or a "trick." Terms such as *patron, meatball, sucker,* and *beefbuyer* are also heard. Men who use female prostitutes come from all walks of life and all socioeconomic and racial groups. Many, perhaps most, are married men of middle-class background. A study of the address listings of customers (seized by the local police) of an "escort service" in a southern city showed that most of the clients lived in relatively affluent neighborhoods consisting of a high percentage of well-educated, largely White, and married residents (Adams, 1987).

Most patrons are "occasional johns." Examples include traveling salesmen or military personnel who are stopping over in town and away from their regular sex partners. One study of 30 occasional johns showed that all had regular sex partners. They used prostitutes because they desired novelty or sexual variety, not because they lacked other sexual outlets (Holzman & Pines, 1982).

"Habitual johns" use prostitutes as their major or exclusive sexual outlet. Some habitual johns have never established an intimate sexual relationship. Some wealthy men who wish to avoid intimate relationships habitually patronize call girls.

"Compulsive johns" feel driven to prostitutes to meet some psychological or sexual need. They may repeatedly resolve to stop using prostitutes but feel unable to control their compulsions. Some compulsive johns engage in acts of fetishism or transvestism with prostitutes but would not inform their wives or girlfriends of their variant interests. Some men who are compulsive users of prostitutes suffer from a **whore–madonna complex.** They see women as either sinners or saints. They can permit themselves to enjoy sex only with prostitutes or would ask only prostitutes to engage in acts such as fellatio. They see marital coitus as a duty or obligation.

Motives for Using Prostitutes   Though the reasons for using prostitutes vary, researchers have identified six of the most common motives (Edgley, 1989; Gagnon, 1977):

1. *Sex without negotiation.* Prostitution may be attractive to men who do not want to spend the time, effort, and money involved in dating and getting to know someone simply to obtain sex.
2. *Sex without commitment.* Prostitutes require no commitment from the man other than payment for services rendered.
3. *Sex for eroticism and variety.* Many prostitutes offer "something extra" in the way of novel or kinky sex—for example, use of costumes (e.g., leather attire) and S&M rituals (bondage and discipline or spanking). Men may not be able to obtain such activities with their regular partners.
4. *Prostitution as sociability.* In the nineteenth and early twentieth centuries, the brothel served not only as a place to obtain sex, but also as a kind of "stopping off" place between home and work. At times, sex was secondary to the companionship and amiable conversation that men would find in brothels. Today, however, such sociability is more likely to be found among call girls and escort prostitutes who offer social companionship, with or without sex.
5. *Sex away from home.* The greatest contemporary use of prostitution occurs among men who are away from home, such as businessmen attending conventions and sports fans attending out-of-town sporting events.
6. *Problematical sex.* Persons with physical disabilities or disfiguring conditions sometimes seek the services of prostitutes because of difficulty attracting other partners or because of fears of rejection. Men with sexual dysfunctions may also turn to prostitutes to help them overcome their problems.

Male Prostitution

Male prostitution includes both male–male and male–female activities. Male prostitutes who service female clients—*gigolos*—are rare. Gigolos' clients are typically older, wealthy, unattached women. Gigolos may serve as escorts or as surrogate sons for the women, and may or may not offer sexual services. Many gigolos are struggling actors or models.

The overwhelming majority of male prostitutes service gay men. Men who engage in male prostitution are called **hustlers.** Their patrons are typically called **scores.** Hustlers average 17 to 18 years of age and become initiated into prostitution at an average age of 14 or so (Coleman, 1989). They typically have less than eleventh-grade educations and few, if any, marketable skills. The majority come from working-class and lower-class backgrounds. Many male prostitutes, like many female prostitutes, come from families troubled by conflict, alcoholism, or abuse (Boyer, 1989; Coleman, 1989).

Hustlers may be gay, bisexual, or heterosexual in orientation. At least half of the male prostitutes surveyed are gay.

The major motive for male prostitution, like female prostitution, is money. In one study, 69% of male prostitutes cited money as their principal motive (Fisher et al., 1982). Running away from home typically serves as an entry point for male as well as female prostitution. In one study, three of four male prostitutes had run away by an average age of 15 (Weisberg, 1985). Some had run away because of family problems; others, because of a desire for adventure or independence (Coleman, 1989). Some gay male prostitutes are literally thrown out because their families cannot accept their sexual orientation (Coleman, 1989; Kruks, 1991).

Heterosexual hustlers may try to psychologically detach themselves from male clients by refusing to kiss or hug them or to perform fellatio. Gagnon (1977) writes that, "As long as the [client's] head is below the [hustler's] belly button and contact is on the penis, it is the other person who is [gay]" (p. 264). To become aroused, heterosexual hustlers may fantasize about women while the "score" is fellating them.

Most hustlers are part-timers who continue some form of educational or vocational activity as they support themselves through prostitution. Drug dealing and drug use are also common among hustlers (Coleman, 1989).

Unlike female prostitutes, hustlers typically are not attached to a pimp (Luckenbill, 1985). They generally make contacts with clients in gay bars and social clubs, or by working the streets in areas frequented by gay men. They typically learn to hustle through their interactions with other hustlers and by watching other hustlers ply their trade (Luckenbill, 1985).

Coleman (1989) identifies several types of male prostitutes:

- *Kept boys* have relationships with older, economically secure men who keep them in an affluent lifestyle. The older male, or "sugar daddy," often assumes a parental role.
- *Call boys,* like call girls, may work on their own or through an agency or escort service.
- *Punks* are prison inmates who are used sexually by other inmates and rewarded with protection or goods such as cigarettes or drugs.
- *Drag prostitutes* are transvestites or presurgical male-to-female transsexuals who impersonate female prostitutes and have sex with men who may be unaware of their gender.
- *Brothel prostitutes* are rarer than their female counterparts. Fewer houses of male prostitution exist.
- *Bar hustlers* and *street hustlers,* like their female counterparts, occupy the lowest status and ply their trade in gay bars or on streets frequented by gay passersby. Street hustlers are the most common and typically the youngest subtype.

Male prostitutes typically have shorter careers than their female counterparts (Price, 1989). By and large, male prostitution is an adolescent enterprise.

HIV, AIDS, and Prostitution

The risk of HIV transmission has been linked to both male and female prostitution (Bloor et al., 1990; Campbell, 1991; Van den Hoek et al., 1990; Yates et al., 1991). Sex with prostitutes is the most important factor in the male–female transmission of HIV in Africa, where the infection is spread predominantly via male–female sexual intercourse. A Florida study showed that regular contact with female street prostitutes was a risk factor in the transmission of HIV in U.S. men (Castro et al., 1988). Prostitutes incur a greater risk of HIV transmission because they have sexual relations with a great many partners, often without protection (Quadagno et al., 1991). Moreover, many prostitutes and their clients and other sex partners inject drugs and share contaminated needles (Bloor et al., 1990; Freund et al., 1989). HIV may be spread by unprotected sex from prostitutes to customers, then to the customers' wives or lovers.

The rate of HIV infection is high among male prostitutes, and many, if not most, of their male customers describe themselves as either bisexual or heterosexual (Morse et al., 1992). One study found that the rate of HIV infection was 50% for gay male prostitutes, 36.5% for bisexual male prostitutes, and 18.5% for heterosexual male prostitutes (Boles & Elifson, 1994). Customers of such men may thus be exposing their wives and girlfriends to HIV.

Despite the danger of HIV transmission, many U.S. prostitutes have not altered either their sexual behavior or their patterns of drug use to any large extent. Only 30% of a sample of 20 street prostitutes in Camden, New Jersey, reported always using condoms (Freund et al., 1989). A study of 72 heroin-addicted female street prostitutes in southern California showed a high level of knowledge and fear about AIDS but a failure to change patterns of sexual behavior or drug use (Bellis, 1990). The prostitutes sampled did nothing to protect themselves or their clients from HIV. Their need for money led them to deny the

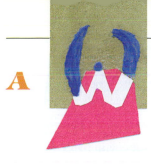 
'TIS A PUZZLEMENT: ON AIDS AND PROSTITUTION IN THAILAND

" 'Tis a puzzlement," sang the king in the Broadway musical *The King and I.* The king of nineteenth-century Thailand was referring to the importation of Western values and culture. Today it could be considered a puzzlement that so many Thais continue high-risk sexual behavior in the face of AIDS, which may be another import from the West.

HIV may have been brought to Thailand by gay Thais who lived for a while in the West (Erlanger, 1991). Through the 1980s, HIV was spread in Thailand mostly via gay male sexual activity and injectable drug use. In the 1990s, however—in a progression that is found in many other nations—the central route of infection has become male–female sexual intercourse.

Whereas only a minority of Westerners visit (or admit to visiting) prostitutes, prostitution is a way of life in Thailand. About 3 in 4 Thai men—at a rate of 450,000 a day—avail themselves of prostitutes. In many brothels in northwest Thailand, such as in the city of Chiang Mai, where the epidemic is most advanced, 80% of the "working women" test positive for HIV antibodies (Erlanger, 1991). In populous Bangkok, the figure now exceeds 20%. HIV is leapfrogging from prostitutes to customers to the customers' wives, lovers, and—often—to their children.

Yet there are some signs of hope. During the 1990s, for example, the Thai Ministry of Public Health began an educational program to encourage army recruits to use condoms during sexual contacts with prostitutes. In 1991 and 1993, soldiers from northern Thailand were found to have HIV infection rates of 10.4% and 12.5%, respectively (Nelson et al., 1996). Moreover, only 61% of the men reported using condoms during recent contacts with prostitutes. By 1995, however, 92.5% of the men were using condoms reliably, and the infection rate among new recruits had fallen to 6.7%.

Yet many Thai men still report that they never wear condoms. Nor do prostitutes always insist on them.

As says Daeng, a Bangkok bar girl, "If the man seems clean and healthy, I say, OK. If the man comes to me often and is nice to me, I say, OK. If he offers me more money, I say, OK" (Erlanger, 1991, p. 49).

'Tis a puzzlement.

Prostitution in Thailand. Many prostitutes in Thailand are infected with HIV. It is common for their customers to become infected and to then transmit HIV to their wives.

risks to which they were exposing themselves. Surveys of adolescent prostitutes show a similar pattern of denial, as Price (1989) observes:

> Some [adolescent prostitutes] simply believe it will not happen to them, while others say they are willing to take the risk. Still others do not care whether they live or die, and expect their lives to end shortly anyway. (p. 86)

Some changes in prostitution practices have taken place. Brothel owners in Nevada, for example, now require customers to wear condoms. But prostitutes who are bent on denial or are so filled with despair that they care nothing about their own or clients' lives may be most resistant to change.

Pornography and Obscenity

The production and distribution of sexually explicit materials has become a boom industry in the United States. In the United States, 20 million "adult" magazines are sold each month. X-rated or adult movies (also called *porn* movies) have moved from sleazy adult theaters to the living rooms of middle America in the form of videocassette rentals and sales. According to a Gallup poll, X-rated films account for about one in five video sales (Linsley, 1989).

Pornography is indeed popular, but also highly controversial. Many people in our society are opposed to pornography on moral grounds. Feminists oppose pornography on the grounds that it degrades and dehumanizes women. It portrays women as objects who are subservient to men's sexual wishes, as sexually insatiable nymphomaniacs, or as sexual masochists who enjoy being raped and violated. Moreover, feminists hold that depictions of women in sexually subordinate roles may encourage men to treat them as sex objects and may increase the potential for rape (Scott & Schwalm, 1988).

What is pornography? How is it defined? Who uses it? Why? How does it affect users?

What Is Pornographic?

Pornography

Written, visual, or audiotaped material that is sexually explicit and produced for purposes of eliciting or enhancing sexual arousal. (From Greek roots meaning "to write about prostitutes.")

Prurient

Tending to excite lust; lewd. (From the Latin *prurire*, meaning "to itch" in the sense of "to long for.")

Webster's Deluxe Unabridged Dictionary defines **pornography** as "writing, pictures, etc., intended to arouse sexual desire." The inclusion of the word *intended* places the determination of what is pornographic in the mind of the person composing the work. Applying this definition makes it all but impossible to determine what is pornographic. If a filmmaker admits that he or she wanted to arouse the audience sexually, we may judge the work to be pornographic, even if no naked bodies or explicit sex scenes are shown. On the other hand, explicit representations of people engaged in sexual activity would not be pornographic if the work was intended as an artistic expression, rather than created for its **prurient** value. Many works that were once prohibited in this country because of explicit sexual content, such as the novels *Tropic of Cancer* by Henry Miller, *Lady Chatterley's Lover* by D. H. Lawrence, and *Ulysses* by James Joyce, are now generally considered literary works rather than pornography. Even Mark Twain's *Huckleberry Finn,* John Steinbeck's *The Grapes of Wrath,* and Ernest Hemingway's *For Whom the Bell Tolls* have been banned from place to place because local citizens found them to be offensive, obscene, or morally objectionable (Linsley, 1989).

There is thus a subjective element in the definition of pornography. An erotic statue that sexually arouses viewers may not be considered pornographic if the sculptor's intent was artistic. A grainy photograph of a naked body that was intended to excite sexually may be pornographic. One alternative definition finds material pornographic when it is judged to be offensive by others. This definition, too, relies on the subjective judgment of the person exposed to the material. In other words, one person's pornography is another person's work of art.

Pornography is often classified as either "hard-core" (X-rated) or "soft-core" (R-rated). Hard-core pornography includes graphic and sexually explicit depictions of sex organs and sexual acts. Soft-core porn, as represented by R-rated films and *Playboy* or *Penthouse* photo spreads, features more stylized nude photos and suggestive (or simulated) rather than explicit sexual acts.

Obscenity

That which offends people's feelings or goes beyond prevailing standards of decency or modesty. (From the Latin *caenum*, meaning "filth.")

Legislative bodies usually write laws about **obscenity** rather than pornography. A landmark case in 1957 helped establish the legal basis of obscenity in the United States. In *Roth v. United States,* the U.S. Supreme Court ruled that portrayal of sexual activity was protected under the First Amendment to the Constitution unless its dominant theme dealt with "sex in a manner appealing to prurient interest" (*Roth v. United States,* 1957, p. 487). In a 1973 case, *Miller v. California,* the U.S. Supreme Court held that obscenity is based upon a determination of

> (a) whether the average person, applying contemporary community standards, would find that the work, taken as a whole, appeals to the prurient interest . . . ; (b) whether the work depicts or describes, in a patently offensive way, sexual conduct specifically defined by the

applicable state law; and (c) whether the work, taken as a whole, lacks serious literary, artistic, political, or scientific value.

(*Miller v. California*, 1973, p. 24).

Courts have since had to grapple with the *Miller* standard in judging whether material is obscene. *Miller* recognizes that judgments of obscenity may vary with "community standards." As a result, the same material may be considered obscene in one community but not in another.

Child pornography and violent, degrading, or dehumanizing pornography complicate matters further. People who do not find depictions, however explicit, of consensual sexual activity between adults to be obscene may regard child pornography or violent pornography to be obscene. Child pornography is clearly psychologically harmful to the juvenile actors (Silbert, 1989).

Prevalence and Use of Pornography

Most of us have been exposed to sexually explicit materials, whether in the form of a novel, an article in *Playboy* or *Playgirl* (purchased, no doubt, for its literary value), or an X-rated film. The NHSLS study found that about one man in four (23%) and one woman in ten (11%) had bought an X-rated movie or video within the past year (Michael et al., 1994). Sixteen percent of the men and 4% of the women had bought sexually explicit magazines or books.

People in the United States are typically introduced to pornography by their high school years, often by peers (Bryant & Brown, 1989). Females are more likely to have been exposed to pornography by their boyfriends than the reverse (Bryant & Brown, 1989).

Pornography is typically used to elicit or enhance sexual arousal, often as a masturbation aid (Michael et al., 1994). Pornographic materials may also be used by couples to enhance sexual arousal during lovemaking. Couples may find that running a soft- or hardcore video on the VCR, or reading an erotic story aloud, enlivens their sexual appetite or suggests novel sexual techniques.

Researchers have found that both men and women are physiologically sexually aroused by pornographic pictures, movies, or audiotaped passages (Goleman, 1995). That is, both men and women respond to pornographic stimuli with vasocongestion of the genitals and myotonia (muscle tension). However, there is a significant difference between

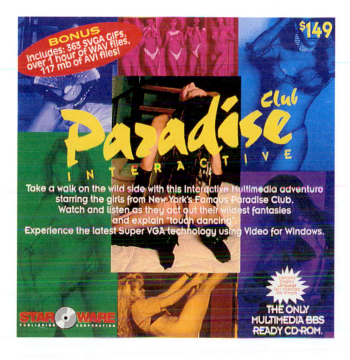

Adults Only: 2001. The VCR has already brought explicit sex from the red-light district into America's living rooms—or bedrooms. Now the home computer is getting involved as people purchase CD-ROM disks that play X-rated interactive videos.

PORNOGRAPHY AND OBSCENITY ~ **401**

physiological response and subjective feelings of arousal in women. Despite what is happening within their bodies, women tend to rate romantic scenes as more sexually arousing than sexually explicit scenes (Laan & Heiman, 1994).

Women are less accepting of sex without emotional involvement (Townsend, 1995). "Women like sex to come from an emotional connection," says marital and sex therapist Lonnie Barbach (1995). "For women there's a predisposition to allowing themselves to become turned on that romance allows. This wouldn't necessarily be measured by genital arousal."

Repeated exposure to the same pornographic materials progressively lessens the sexual response to them. People may become aroused by the familiar materials again if some time is allowed to go by. Novel materials are also likely to reactivate a sexual response (Meuwissen & Over, 1990; Zillmann, 1989).

Gender Differences in Response to Pornography   Both genders can become physiologically aroused by erotic materials. Yet men and women do not necessarily share the same subjective response to them or level of interest in them. Visual pornography (sexually explicit pictures or films) is actually largely a male preserve (Symons, 1995; Winick, 1985). The majority of erotic visual materials are produced by men for men. Attempts to market visual materials to females have been largely unsuccessful (Symons, 1995). Women may read erotic romance novels, but they show little interest in acquiring erotic pictures, films, or videotapes (Lawrence & Herold, 1988).

The reasons for these gender differences remain unclear (Bryant & Brown, 1989). Women may find such material a "turn-off" when it portrays women in unflattering roles, as "whorish," as subservient to the sexual demands of men, and as sexually aroused by male domination and coercion. Symons (1979), a sociobiologist, believes that a basic evolutionary process is at work. He argues that ancestral men who were more sexually aroused by the sight of a passing female may have had reproductive advantages over their less arousable peers:

> The male's desire to look at female genitals, especially genitals he has not seen before, and to seek out opportunities to do so, is part of the motivational process that maximizes male reproductive opportunities. (p. 181)

Women, however, have fewer mating opportunities than men and must make the most of any reproductive opportunity by selecting the best possible mate and provider. To be sexually aroused by the sight of male genitalia might encourage random matings, which would undermine their reproductive success.

Pornography and Sexual Coercion

Is pornography a harmless diversion or an impetus to sexual violence or other antisocial acts? Let us consider several sources of evidence in examining these highly charged questions, beginning with the findings of a 1970 government commission impaneled to review the evidence that was available at the time.

The Commission on Obscenity and Pornography   In the 1960s, Congress created the Commission on Obscenity and Pornography to study the effects of pornography. Upon reviewing the existing research, the commission (Abelson et al., 1970) concluded that there was no evidence that pornography led to crimes of violence or sexual offenses such as exhibitionism, voyeurism, or child molestation. Some people were sexually aroused by pornography and increased the frequency of their usual sexual activity, such as masturbation or coitus with regular partners, following exposure. They did not engage in antisocial behavior, however. These results have been replicated many times.

The commission found no causal link between pornography and delinquent behavior or sexual violence against women. Finding pornography basically harmless (Edgley, 1989), the commission recommended that "federal, state, and local legislation should not seek to interfere with the right of adults who wish to read, obtain, or view explicit sexual materials" (Abelson et al., 1970, p. 58). Congress and then-president Richard Nixon rejected the commission's findings and recommendation, however, on moral and political—not scientific—grounds.

Pornography and Sex Offenders   Another approach to examining the role of pornography in crimes of sexual violence involves comparing the experience of sex offenders and nonoffenders with pornographic materials. A review of the research literature found little or no difference in the level of exposure to pornography between incarcerated sex offenders and comparison groups of felons who were incarcerated for nonsexual crimes (Marshall, 1989).

Yet evidence also shows that as many as one in three rapists and child molesters use pornography to become sexually aroused immediately preceding, and during the commission of, their crimes (Marshall, 1989). These findings suggest that pornography may stimulate sexually deviant urges in certain subgroups of men who are predisposed to commit crimes of sexual violence (Marshall, 1989).

The Meese Commission Report   In 1985, President Ronald Reagan appointed a committee headed by Attorney General Edwin Meese to reexamine the effects of pornography. In 1986, the U.S. Attorney General's Commission on Pornography, known as the Meese commission, issued a report that reached very different conclusions than the 1970 commission. The Meese commission claimed to find a causal link between sexual violence and exposure to violent pornography (U.S. Department of Justice, 1986). The report concluded that exposure to pornography that portrayed women in degrading or subservient roles increased acceptability of rape in the minds of viewers. The commission found no evidence linking exposure to nonviolent, nondegrading pornography (consensual sexual activity between partners in equal roles) and sexual violence but noted that only a small fraction of the pornographic materials on the market was of this type.

The commission's findings are controversial. Critics claim that although the Meese commission did not falsify the data, its conclusions reflected an overgeneralization of laboratory-based findings (Wilcox, 1987). Two researchers in the area, Edward Donnerstein and Daniel Linz (1987), contended that the Meese commission failed to distinguish between the effects of sexually explicit materials per se and the effects of violent materials. Evidence of links between exposure to sexually explicit materials (without violent content) and sexual aggression is lacking. Donnerstein and Linz concluded that violence, not sex, is the obscenity. Let us take a look at the scientific evidence on the effects of violent and nonviolent pornography.

Violent Pornography   Laboratory-based studies have shown that men exposed to violent pornography are more likely to become aggressive against females and to show less sensitivity toward women who have been sexually assaulted (Donnerstein, 1980; Donnerstein & Berkowitz, 1981).

Exposure to violent pornography leads men to become more accepting of rape, less sensitive to women survivors of rape, and more accepting of the use of violence in interpersonal relationships (Donnerstein & Linz, 1987; Malamuth, 1984).

Yet research suggests that it is the violence in violent pornography, and not sexual explicitness, that hardens men's attitudes toward rape survivors. In one study (Donnerstein & Linz, 1987), college men were exposed to films consisting of either violent pornography, nonviolent pornography (a couple having consensual intercourse), or a violent film that was not sexually explicit. The violent pornographic and nonpornographic films both showed a woman being tied up and slapped at gunpoint, but the nonpornographic version contained no nudity or explicit sexual activity. The men had first been either angered or treated in a neutral manner by a female confederate of the experimenter. The results showed that, in comparison with nonviolent pornography, both violent pornographic films and violent *non*pornographic films produced greater acceptance of rape myths, increased reported willingness to force a woman into sexual activity, and greater reported likelihood of engaging in rape (if the man also knew that he could get away with it). These effects occurred regardless of whether the man was angered by the woman or not.

Based on a review of the research literature, Linz (1989) concluded that short-term and prolonged exposure to sexual violence, whether sexually explicit or not, lessens sensitivity toward survivors of rape and increases acceptance of the use of force in sexual encounters. Research on the effects of pornography should be interpreted with caution, however. Most of it has employed college students, whose behavior may or may not be typical of people in general or of people with tendencies toward sexual violence. Another issue is that most studies in this area are laboratory-based experiments that involve simulated aggression or judgments of sympathy toward hypothetical women who have been portrayed as rape victims. None measured *actual* violence against women outside the lab.

Nonviolent Pornography   Even nonviolent pornography typically portrays women in degrading or dehumanizing roles—as sexually promiscuous, insatiable, and subservient. Might such portrayals of women reinforce traditional stereotypes of women as sex objects? Might they lead viewers to condone acts of rape by suggesting that women are essentially promiscuous? Might the depiction of women as readily sexually accessible inspire men to refuse to "take no for an answer" on dates?

Zillmann and Bryant (1982, 1984) exposed male and female study participants to six sessions of pornography over six consecutive weeks. Participants were exposed to either a massive dose of pornography, consisting of six nonviolent pornographic films ("Swedish erotica") during each weekly session; to an intermediate dose consisting of three pornographic and three neutral films each session; or to a no-dose control, consisting of six nonsexual films each session. When later tested in a purportedly independent study, both males and females who received extended exposure to pornography, especially those receiving the massive dose, gave more lenient punishments to a rapist who was depicted in a newspaper article. Moreover, males became more callous in their attitudes toward women.

Zillmann and Weaver (1989) argue that making women appear sexually permissive and promiscuous increases men's callousness toward women who have been sexually assaulted. Once men brand women as promiscuous, they lose respect for them and see them as "public property" who have forfeited their rights to exercise choice in sex partners.

Not all researchers, however, find exposure to nonviolent pornography to increase callousness toward women. Some report finding that nonviolent pornography did not reduce the sensitivity of men (Linz et al., 1988) and women (Krafka, 1985) to female victims of sexual assault. Others report that nonviolent pornography did not increase men's aggression toward women in laboratory studies (Malamuth & Ceniti, 1986). Still others did not find repeated exposure to nonviolent pornography to make men adopt more callous attitudes toward women or increase their acceptance of rape myths (Padgett et al., 1989).

Given the inconsistencies in the research findings and the limited amount of research on nonviolent pornography, Linz (1989) concludes that

> . . . the data, *overall,* do not support the contention that exposure to nonviolent pornography has significant adverse effects on attitudes toward rape as a crime or more general evaluations of rape victims. (p. 74)

Moreover, if nonviolent pornography can be connected with negative attitudes toward women, Linz (1989) suggests that such attitudes may result from the demeaning portrayals of women as sexual playthings who are valued only for their physical attributes and sexual availability, rather than from sexual explicitness per se.

Zillmann (1989) argues that nonviolent pornography loosens traditional family values by projecting an image of sexual enjoyment without responsibility or obligations. Prolonged exposure to such pornography may also foster dissatisfaction with the physical appearance and sexual performance of one's intimate partners (Zillmann, 1989).

In sum, research on the effects of nonviolent pornography does not permit conclusions. The effects of nonviolent pornography may be more connected with whether or not women are presented in a dehumanizing manner than with sexual explicitness per se. No research has yet linked sexual explicitness itself with undesirable effects.

Sex in Advertising

In the 1980s a coquettish Brooke Shields was featured in a TV commercial that showed her spreading her denim-clad legs, smiling coyly at the camera, and murmuring that nothing came between her and her Calvins (Calvin Klein jeans, that is). The advertising campaign evoked a storm of complaints from viewers who felt that it was vulgar and obscene. Meanwhile, the sales of Calvin Klein jeans went through the roof. In short, sex sells.

Calvin Klein ads keep on "pushing the envelope" in the United States. That is, they keep on challenging the limits of what is acceptable to the public (see Figure 16.1).

The use of sexual imagery in advertising ranges from more subtle uses of innuendo and double entendre, such as slogans like "Take it off, take it all off" (for Noxema shave cream) and "*It's* better in the Bahamas," to the use of an attractive woman who says her men wear "English Leather or they wear nothing at all."

Sex in advertising operates according to the principle of association. Advertisers hope that people will link the product with the sexual imagery that is incorporated within the advertisement. Perhaps the use of a sexy ad will make consumers think that the product will make them more sexually alluring or enhance their sexual arousal, which, in turn, will prompt them to purchase the product rather than that of a competitor.

Researchers caution, however, that sexy ads can backfire. Viewers may pay such careful attention to the sexy imagery that they tune out the advertising message or product claims, or even forget what the product is (Edgley, 1989; Severn et al., 1990). Sexy advertising may not only be distracting. It may also turn people off to the advertisement and, by extension, to the product, especially if the sexual image is unrelated to the nature of the product.

Advertisers may also need to consider the gender of the target audience. Researchers find that men tend to react more positively and women more negatively toward various

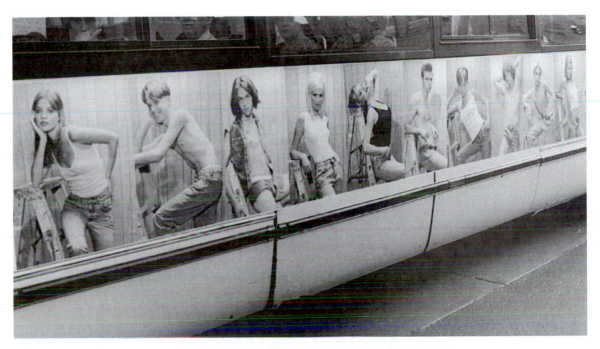

Figure 16.1. **"Pushing the Envelope."** Calvin Klein's ad campaigns have been accused of using child pornography to sell jeans. What do you think? How far is too far?

forms of sexual content in advertising, whether it be sexual innuendos uttered by female models in TV commercials (Bello et al., 1983) or female nudity in print advertising (La-Tour, 1990).

Advertising and Gender-Role Stereotypes

The frequent use of sexy female models in advertisements raises broader concerns about the depiction of women in advertising. As Edgley notes, "Despite years of feminist consciousness-raising about the issue, commercials still tend to depict women in stereotypical ways" (Edgley, 1989). What Komisar said of advertising in 1971 may be as true today as it was then:

> If television commercials are to be believed, most American women go into uncontrollable ecstasies at the sight and smell of tables and cabinets that have been lovingly caressed with long-lasting, satin-finish, lemon-scented, spray-on furniture polish. Or they glow with rapture at the blinding whiteness of their wash—to the green-eyed envy of their neighbors. . . . it is an amazing feat of hocus-pocus worthy of Tom Sawyer and P. T. Barnum to lovingly declare that domestic labor is the true vocation of women wearing wedding bands. (p. 209)

Studies of TV commercials in the United States, Canada, the United Kingdom, and Italy show a consistent pattern: Females are more likely to be portrayed visually on screen, whereas males are more likely to do voice-overs as the "voice of authority" (Ferrante et al., 1988; Furnham & Voli, 1989; Lovdal, 1989). A study of 320 U.S. TV commercials employing voice-overs showed that 91% used male voices. Only 9% used female voices (Lovdal, 1989).

TV commercials also tend to portray men in a wider variety of occupational roles than women (Bretl & Cantor, 1988; Lovdal, 1989). Women's roles are still generally stereotyped in traditional roles as wives, mothers, brides, waitresses, actresses, and so on. Rarely are they photographers, athletes, or businesswomen. Still, we can report some signs of change, at least with respect to the portrayal of men's roles. Men today are increasingly represented in commercials as spouses and parents (Bretl & Cantor, 1988). Women, however, are still more likely to be seen in domestic settings, advertising products that they can use in the home (Bretl & Cantor, 1988).

Chapter Review

Prostitution

Prostitution is illegal everywhere in the United States except for parts of (1) N_____, where it is restricted to state-licensed brothels. Most prostitutes are (2: Male *or* Female?) and virtually all customers are (3: Male *or* Female?). Young men today are (4: More *or* Less?) likely to visit prostitutes than they were in Kinsey's day.

Most prostitutes are (5) _____kers. Streetwalkers earn the (6: Highest *or* Lowest?) incomes among prostitutes. Many streetwalkers support a (7) p_____, who acts as lover–father–companion–master. The houses in which many prostitutes work are termed (8) _____els. Many (9) mas_____ parlors are legitimate establishments that provide only massage; others serve as fronts for (10) _____tion, however. Conventioneers and businessmen are likely to turn to the listings for (11) es_____ _____vices in the telephone directory. (12) C_____ girls occupy the highest status on the social ladder of female prostitution.

(13) Po_____ and sexual and/or physical (14) _____se are found in the backgrounds of many prostitutes. (15) Str_____s show high rates of psychological disturbance. In the United States and Canada, many teenagers who enter prostitution are (16) _____ways.

Many prostitutes refer to their customers as (17) "j_____s" or "tricks." Most patrons are (18) oc_____ johns. (19) _____ual johns use prostitutes as their major or exclusive sexual outlet. (20) _____lsive johns feel driven to prostitutes to meet some psychological or sexual need.

The (21: Majority *or* Minority?) of male prostitutes service gay men. Men who engage in male prostitution are called (22) _____lers.

The risk of HIV transmission (23: Has *or* Has not?) been linked to prostitution. Sex with prostitutes is the most important factor in the male–female transmission of HIV in (24) A_____.

Pornography and Obscenity

Feminists oppose (25) por_____ on the grounds that it degrades women. Pornography portrays women as objects who are subservient to men's sexual wishes, as (26) _____maniacs, or as sexual masochists. Pornography is "writing, pictures, etc., intended to (27) a_____ sexual desire." Pornography is often classified as either "hard-core" (X-rated) or (28) "_____-core" (R-rated). Laws usually refer to (29) ob_____ rather than pornography. In *Miller v. California,* the U.S. Supreme Court held that obscenity is based upon a determination of "whether the average person, applying contemporary (30) com_____ standards, would find that the work . . . appeals to the prurient interest."

Pornography is more likely to appeal to (31: Men *or* Women?). Pornography is typically used to enhance (32) sex_____ _____sal, often as a masturbation aid. Researchers have found that (33: Men, Women, *or* Men and women?) are physiologically sexually aroused by pornography. Women are (34: More *or* Less?) accepting than men of sex without emotional involvement. Repeated exposure to the same pornographic materials (35: Heightens *or* Lessens?) the sexual response to them.

The Commission on Obscenity and Pornography that there (36: Was *or* Was no?) evidence that pornography led to crimes of violence or sexual offenses. *The Meese Commission Report* claimed (37: To find *or* Not to find?) a causal link between sexual violence and exposure to violent pornography. Critics claim that the Meese commission failed to distinguish between the effects of sexually explicit materials per se and the effects of (38) vio_____ materials. Research suggests that the (39) _____ence in violent pornography, and not the sexual explicitness, hardens men's attitudes toward rape survivors. Linz concludes that "the data, overall, (40: Do *or* Do not?) support the contention that exposure to nonviolent pornography has significant adverse effects on attitudes toward rape as a crime or more general evaluations of rape victims."

Sex in Advertising

Sex in advertising operates according to the principle of (41) _____tion. Perhaps the sexy ad will enhance customers' (42) sex_____ _____sal, which will cause them to buy the product. Researchers find that men tend to react more (43: Positively *or* Negatively?) and women more (44: Positively *or* Negatively?) toward sexual content in advertising. TV commercials still depict women in (45) _____typical ways.

Chapter Quiz

1. Which kind of prostitute is most likely to support a pimp?
   (a) The streetwalker
   (b) The call girl
   (c) The brothel prostitute
   (d) The masseuse

2. Conventioneers and businessmen who desire prostitutes are most likely to seek
   (a) bar girls.
   (b) escorts.
   (c) streetwalkers.
   (d) hustlers.

3. The text notes that the following factors are frequently found in the backgrounds of prostitutes, EXCEPT for
   (a) poverty.
   (b) a conflict-ridden home.
   (c) sexual abuse.
   (d) a religious upbringing.
4. Most customers of prostitutes are
   (a) compulsive johns.
   (b) occasional johns.
   (c) habitual johns.
   (d) sexually dysfunctional.
5. The most common use of prostitution occurs among men who
   (a) are away from home.
   (b) are seeking variety.
   (c) want sex without commitment.
   (d) want sex without negotiation.
6. The overwhelming majority of male prostitutes service
   (a) heterosexual men.
   (b) heterosexual women.
   (c) gay men.
   (d) lesbians.
7. _____ are most likely to have "sugar daddies."
   (a) Punks
   (b) Drag prostitutes
   (c) Call boys
   (d) Kept boys

8. In _____, the U.S. Supreme Court held that obscenity is based upon a determination of "whether the average person, applying contemporary community standards, would find that the work . . . appeals to the prurient interest."
   (a) *Roe v. Wade*
   (b) *Roth v. United States*
   (c) *Miller v. California*
   (d) *Comstock v. New York*
9. Which of the following is true of women's response to pornography?
   (a) Women prefer explicit sex to romance.
   (b) Women are less accepting of sex without emotional involvement.
   (c) Women prefer violent pornography to nonviolent pornography.
   (d) Feminists claim that pornography is degrading to men.
10. Social scientists criticize *The Meese Commission Report* on the grounds that
   (a) it studied the effects of obscene materials.
   (b) it failed to review a high number of research studies.
   (c) it did not adequately sort out the effects of sex from those of violence.
   (d) its recommendations were consistent with a conservative, traditional point of view.

Answers to Chapter Review

1. Nevada	10. Prostitution	19. Habitual	28. Soft-core	37. To find
2. Female	11. Escort services	20. Compulsive	29. Obscenity	38. Violent
3. Male	12. Call	21. Majority	30. Community	39. Violence
4. Less	13. Poverty	22. Hustlers	31. Men	40. Do not
5. Streetwalkers	14. Abuse	23. Has	32. Sexual arousal	41. Association
6. Lowest	15. Streetwalkers	24. Africa	33. Men and women	42. Sexual arousal
7. Pimp	16. Runaways	25. Pornography	34. Less	43. Positively
8. Brothels	17. Johns	26. Nymphomaniacs	35. Lessens	44. Negatively
9. Massage	18. Occasional	27. Arouse	36. Was no	45. Stereotypical

Answers to Chapter Quiz

1. (a)	3. (d)	5. (a)	7. (d)	9. (b)
2. (b)	4. (b)	6. (c)	8. (c)	10. (c)

Glossary

ABCDE model   Levinger's view, which approaches romantic relationships in terms of five stages: attraction, building, continuation, deterioration, and ending.

Acquaintance rape   Rape by an acquaintance of the person who is assaulted.

Acquired immunodeficiency syndrome (AIDS)   A sexually transmitted disease that destroys white blood cells in the immune system, leaving the body vulnerable to various "opportunistic" diseases.

Activating effects   Those effects of sex hormones that influence the level of the sex drive but not sexual orientation.

Agape   (AH-gah-pay) Selfless love; a kind of loving that is similar to generosity and charity.

Age of viability   The age at which a fetus can sustain independent life.

Amenorrhea   The absence of menstruation.

Amniocentesis   A procedure for drawing off and examining fetal cells in the amniotic fluid to determine the presence of various disorders in the fetus.

Amniotic fluid   Fluid within the amniotic sac that suspends and protects the fetus.

Amniotic sac   The sac containing the fetus.

Ampulla   The wide segment of a fallopian tube near the ovary. (A Latin word meaning "bottle.") Also, a sac or dilated part of a tube or canal.

Analogous   Similar in function.

Anaphrodisiacs   Drugs or other agents that dull sexual arousal or sexual desire.

Androgen-insensitivity syndrome   A form of pseudohermaphroditism in which a genetic male is prenatally insensitive to androgens. As a result his genitals do not become normally masculinized.

Androgenital syndrome   A form of pseudohermaphroditism in which a genetic female has internal female sexual structures but masculinized external genitals.

Androgens   Male sex hormones. (From the Greek *andros,* meaning "man" or "males," and *-gene,* meaning "born.")

Anger rape   A vicious, unplanned rape that is triggered by feelings of intense anger and resentment toward women.

Anilingus   Oral stimulation of the anus.

Anorexia nervosa   A potentially life-threatening eating disorder characterized by refusal to maintain a healthy body weight, intense fear of being overweight, a distorted body image, and, in females, lack of menstruation (amenorrhea).

Anorgasmic   Never having reached orgasm. (Literally, "without orgasm.")

Anovulatory   Without ovulation.

Anoxia   Oxygen deprivation.

Antiandrogen   A substance that decreases the levels of androgens in the bloodstream.

Antiandrogen drug   A chemical substance that reduces the sex drive by lowering the level of testosterone in the bloodstream.

Antibodies   Specialized proteins produced by the white blood cells of the immune system in response to disease organisms and other toxic substances. Antibodies recognize and attack the invading organisms or substances.

Antigen   A protein, toxin, or other substance to which the body reacts by producing antibodies. (Combined word formed from *anti*body *gen*erator.)

Aphrodisiac   Any drug or other agent that is sexually arousing or increases sexual desire. (From *Aphrodite,* the Greek goddess of love and beauty.)

Areola   The dark ring on the breast that encircles the nipple.

Arthritis   A progressive disease that is characterized by inflammation or pain in the joints.

Artificial insemination   The introduction of sperm in the reproductive tract through means other than sexual intercourse.

Asexuals   Bell and Weinberg's term for gay people who live alone and have few sexual contacts.

Asymptomatic   Without symptoms.

Auto-immune response   The production of antibodies that attack naturally occurring substances that are (incorrectly) recognized as being foreign or harmful.

Autonomic nervous system   The division of the nervous system that regulates automatic bodily processes, such as heartbeat, pupil dilation, respiration, and digestion. Abbreviated *ANS.*

Aversion therapy   A method for terminating undesirable sexual behavior in which the behavior is repeatedly paired with an aversive stimulus, such as electric shock, so that a conditioned aversion develops.

Bacteria   Plural of *bacterium,* a class of one-celled microorganisms that have no chlorophyll and can give rise to many illnesses. (From the Greek *baktron,* meaning "stick," referring to the fact that many bacteria are rod-shaped.)

Bacterial vaginosis   A form of vaginitis usually caused by the *Gardnerella vaginalis* bacterium.

Bartholin's glands   Glands that lie just inside the minor lips and secrete fluid just before orgasm.

Basal body temperature (BBT) method   A fertility awareness method of contraception that relies on prediction of ovulation by tracking the woman's temperature during the course of the menstrual cycle.

Behavior therapy   The systematic application of the principles of learning to help people modify problem behavior.

Behaviorists   Learning theorists who argue that a scientific approach to understanding behavior must refer only to observable and measurable behaviors.

Benign   Doing little or no harm.

Benign prostatic hyperplasia   Enlargement of the prostate gland due to hormonal changes associated with aging and characterized by symptoms such as urinary frequency, urinary urgency, and difficulty starting the flow of urine.

Bisexual   Sexually responsive to either gender. (From the Latin *bi-,* meaning "two.")

Bisexuality   Erotic attraction to, and interest in developing romantic relationships with, both males and females.

Blastocyst   A stage within the germinal stage of prenatal development, in which the embryo is a sphere of cells surrounding a cavity of fluid.

Bondage   Ritual restraint, as by shackles, as practiced by many sexual masochists.

Braxton-Hicks contractions   So-called false labor contractions that are relatively painless.

Breech presentation   Emergence of the baby feet-first from the womb.

Bulbourethral glands   Another term for *Cowper's glands.*

Butch   A lesbian who assumes a traditional masculine gender role.

Calendar method   A fertility awareness (rhythm) method of contraception that relies on prediction of ovulation by tracking menstrual cycles, typically for a 10- to 12-month period, and assuming that ovulation occurs 14 days prior to menstruation.

Call girls   Prostitutes who arrange for their sexual contacts by telephone. *Call* refers both to telephone calls and to being "on call."

Candidiasis   A form of vaginitis caused by a yeastlike fungus, *Candida albicans.*

Case study   A carefully drawn, in-depth biography of an individual or a small group of individuals that may be obtained through interviews, questionnaires, and historical records.

Castration anxiety   In psychoanalytic theory, a man's fear that his genitals will be removed. Castration anxiety is an element of the Oedipus complex and is implicated in the directionality of erotic interests.

Celibacy   Complete sexual abstinence. (Sometimes used to describe the state of being unmarried, especially in the case of people who take vows to remain single.)

Cephalic presentation   Emergence of the baby headfirst from the womb.

Cephalocaudal   From the head downward. (From Latin roots meaning "head" and "tail.")

Cerebral palsy   A muscular disorder that is caused by damage to the central nervous system (usually prior to or during birth) and characterized by spastic paralysis.

Cervicitis   Inflammation of the cervix.

Cervix   The lower end of the uterus. (Latin for "neck.")

Cesarean section   A method of childbirth in which the fetus is delivered through a surgical incision in the abdomen.

Chancre   A sore or ulcer.

Chancroid   An STD caused by the *Hemophilus ducreyi* bacterium. Also called *soft chancre.*

Chromosome   One of the rodlike structures, found in the nucleus of every living cell, that carries the genetic code in the form of genes.

Cilia   Hairlike projections from cells that beat rhythmically to produce locomotion or currents.

Circumcision   Surgical removal of the foreskin of the penis. (From the Latin *circumcidere,* meaning "to cut around.")

Climacteric   A long-term process, including menopause, that involves the gradual decline in the reproductive capacity of the ovaries.

Clitoridectomy   Surgical removal of the clitoris.

Clitoris   A female sex organ consisting of a shaft and glans located above the urethral opening. It is extremely sensitive to sexual sensations.

Clomiphene   A synthetic hormone that is chemically similar to LH and induces ovulation.

Close couples   Bell and Weinberg's term for gay couples whose relationships resemble marriage in their depth of commitment and exclusiveness.

Cohabitation   Living together as though married but without legal sanction.

Coitus   (co-it-us or co-EET-us). Sexual intercourse.

Coitus interruptus   The practice of withdrawing the penis prior to ejaculation during sexual intercourse.

Combination pill   A birth-control pill that contains synthetic estrogen and progesterone.

Complete hysterectomy   Surgical removal of the ovaries, fallopian tubes, cervix, and uterus.

Concordance   Agreement.

Concubine   A secondary wife, usually of inferior legal and social status. (From Latin roots meaning "lying with.")

Condom   A sheath made of animal membrane or latex that covers the penis during coitus and serves as a barrier to sperm following ejaculation.

Congenital syphilis   A syphilis infection that is present at birth.

Consensual adultery   Extramarital sex that is engaged in openly with the knowledge and consent of one's spouse.

Control group   A group of study participants who do not receive the experimental treatment. However, other conditions are held comparable to those of individuals in the experimental group.

Conventional adultery   Extramarital sex that is kept clandestine (hidden) from one's spouse.

Coprophilia   A paraphilia in which sexual arousal is attained in connection with feces. (From the Greek *copros,* meaning "dung.")

Corona   The ridge that separates the glans from the body of the penis. (From the Latin for "crown.")

Corpora cavernosa   Masses of spongy tissue in the clitoral shaft that become engorged with blood and stiffen in response to sexual stimulation. (Latin for "cavernous bodies.") Also, cylinders of spongy tissue in the penis that become congested with blood and stiffen during sexual arousal.

Corpus luteum   The follicle that has released an ovum and then produces copious amounts of progesterone and estrogen during the luteal phase of a woman's cycle. (From Latin roots meaning "yellow body.")

Corpus spongiosum   The spongy body that runs along the bottom of the penis, contains the penile urethra, and enlarges at the tip of the penis to form the glans.

Correlation   A statistical measure of the relationship between two variables.

Correlation coefficient   A statistic that expresses the strength and direction (positive or negative) of the relationship between two variables.

Courtesan   A prostitute—especially the mistress of a noble or wealthy man. (From Italian roots meaning "court lady.")

Covert sensitization   A form of aversion therapy in which thoughts of engaging in undesirable behavior are paired repeatedly with imagined aversive stimuli.

Cowper's glands   Structures that lie below the prostate and empty their secretions into the urethra during sexual arousal.

Cremaster muscle   The muscle that raises and lowers the testicle in response to temperature changes and sexual stimulation.

Crisis   A highly stressful situation that can involve shock, loss of self-esteem, and lessened capacity for making decisions.

Critical period of vulnerability   A period of time during which an embryo or fetus is vulnerable to the effects of a teratogen.

Cruising   The name that gay people give to searching for a sex partner.

Crura   Anatomical structures resembling legs that attach the clitoris to the pubic bone. (Singular: crus. A Latin word meaning "leg" or "shank.")

Cryptorchidism   A condition in which one or two testicles fail to descend from the abdomen into the scrotum.

Culpotomy   A kind of tubal sterilization in which the fallopian tubes are approached through an incision in the back wall of the vagina.

Cunnilingus   Oral stimulation of the female genitals.

Cystitis   An inflammation of the urinary bladder. (From the Greek *kystis,* meaning "sac.")

Cysts   Saclike structures filled with fluid or diseased material.

D&C   Abbreviation for *dilation and curettage,* an operation in which the cervix is dilated and uterine contents are then gently scraped away.

D&E   Abbreviation for *dilation and evacuation,* an abortion method in which the cervix is dilated prior to vacuum aspiration.

Dartos muscle   The muscle in the middle layer of the scrotum that contracts and relaxes in response to temperature changes.

Defense mechanisms   In psychoanalytic theory, automatic processes that protect the ego from anxiety by disguising or ejecting unacceptable ideas and urges.

Dependent variables   The measured results of an experiment, which are believed to be a function of the independent variables.

DES   Diethylstilbestrol: an estrogen that was once given to women at risk for miscarriage to help maintain pregnancy.

Diaphragm   A shallow rubber cup or dome, fitted to the contour of a woman's vagina, that is coated with a spermicide and inserted prior to coitus to prevent conception.

Dilate   To open or widen.

Dildo   A penis-shaped object used in sexual activity.

Displacement   In psychoanalytic theory, a defense mechanism that allows one to transfer unacceptable wishes or desires onto more appropriate or less threatening objects.

Dizygotic (DZ) twins   Twins who develop from different fertilized ova; fraternal twins.

Dominican Republic syndrome   A form of pseudohermaphroditism in which a genetic enzyme disorder prevents testosterone from masculinizing the external genitalia.

Don Juanism   An excessive, insatiable sexual appetite or drive in men. (After the fictional Spanish nobleman who was unable to obtain true sexual gratification despite numerous affairs.)

Donor IVF   A variation of in vitro fertilization in which the ovum is taken from one woman, fertilized, and then injected into the uterus or fallopian tube of another woman.

Douche   Application of a jet of liquid to the vagina as a rinse. (From the Italian *doccia,* meaning "shower bath.")

Down syndrome   A chromosomal abnormality that leads to mental retardation, caused by an extra chromosome on the 21st pair.

Dysfunctionals   Bell and Weinberg's term for gay people who live alone and have sexual, social, or psychological problems.

Dysmenorrhea   Pain or discomfort during menstruation.

Dyspareunia   A sexual dysfunction characterized by persistent or recurrent pain during sexual intercourse. (From roots meaning "badly paired.")

Ectoparasites   Parasites that live on the outside of the host's body— as opposed to *endo*parasites, which live within the body. (From the Greek *ektos,* meaning "outside.")

Ectopic pregnancy   A pregnancy in which the fertilized ovum becomes implanted outside the uterus, usually in the fallopian tube. (*Ectopic* derives from Greek roots meaning "out of place.")

Efface   To become thin.

Ego   In Freud's theory, the second mental structure to develop, which is characterized by self-awareness, planning, and delay of gratification.

Ejaculatory duct   A duct formed by the convergence of a vas deferens with a seminal vesicle through which sperm pass through the prostate gland and into the urethra.

Elephantiasis   A disease characterized by enlargement of parts of the body, especially the legs and genitals, and by hardening and ulceration of the surrounding skin. (From the Greek *elephas,* meaning "elephant," referring to the resemblance of the affected skin areas to elephant hide.)

Embryo   The stage of prenatal development that begins with implantation of a fertilized ovum in the uterus and concludes with development of the major organ systems at about two months after conception.

Embryonic stage   The stage of prenatal development that lasts from implantation through the eighth week and is characterized by the differentiation of the major organ systems.

Embryonic transfer   A method of conception in which a woman volunteer is artificially inseminated by the male partner of the intended mother, after which the embryo is removed from the volunteer and inserted within the uterus of the intended mother.

Emission stage   The first phase of ejaculation, which involves contractions of the prostate gland, seminal vesicles, and the upper part of the vas deferens.

Endocrine gland   A ductless gland that releases its secretions directly into the bloodstream.

Endometriosis   A condition caused by the growth of endometrial tissue in the abdominal cavity or elsewhere outside the uterus. Characterized by menstrual pain, it may cause infertility.

Endometrium   The innermost layer of the uterus. (From Latin and Greek roots meaning "within the uterus.")

Epididymis   A tube that lies against the back wall of each testicle and serves as a storage facility for sperm. (From Greek roots meaning "upon testicles.")

Epididymitis   Inflammation of the epididymis.

Episiotomy   A surgical incision in the perineum that widens the birth canal, preventing random vaginal tearing during childbirth. (From the Greek roots *epision,* meaning "pubic region," and *tome,* meaning "cutting.")

Erection   The enlargement and stiffening of the penis as a consequence of engorgement with blood.

Erogenous zones   Parts of the body, including but not limited to the sex organs, that are responsive to sexual stimulation.

Eros   The kind of love that is closest in meaning to the modern-day concept of passion.

Erotic   Arousing sexual feelings or desires. (From the Greek word for love, *eros.*)

Estrogen   A generic term for female sex hormones (including estradiol, estriol, estrone, and others) or synthetic compounds that promote the development of female sex characteristics and regulate the menstrual cycle. (From the roots meaning "generating" [*-gen*] and "estrus.")

Excitement phase   The first phase of the sexual response cycle, which is characterized by erection in the male, vaginal lubrication in the female, and muscle tension and increases in heart rate in both males and females.

Exhibitionism   A paraphilia characterized by persistent, powerful urges and sexual fantasies involving exposing one's genitals to unsuspecting strangers to achieve sexual arousal or gratification.

Experiment   A scientific method that seeks to confirm cause-and-effect relationships by manipulating independent variables and observing their effects on dependent variables.

Experimental group   A group of study participants who receive a treatment.

Expulsion stage   The second stage of ejaculation, during which muscles at the base of the penis and elsewhere contract rhythmically, forcefully expelling semen and providing pleasurable sensations.

Extramarital sex   Sexual relations between a married person and someone other than his or her spouse.

Fallopian tubes   Tubes that extend from the upper uterus toward the ovaries and conduct ova to the uterus. (After the Italian anatomist Gabriel Fallopio, who is credited with their discovery.)

False positive   An erroneous positive test result or clinical finding.

Fellatio   Oral stimulation of the male genitals.

Female-superior position   A coital position in which the woman is on top.

Femme   A lesbian who assumes a traditional feminine gender role.

Fetal alcohol syndrome   A cluster of symptoms caused by maternal drinking, in which the child shows developmental lags and characteristic facial features such as an underdeveloped upper jaw, flattened nose, and widely spaced eyes.

Fetishism   A paraphilia in which an inanimate object, such as an article of clothing or items made of rubber, leather, or silk, elicits sexual arousal.

Fibroadenoma   A benign, fibrous tumor.

Fimbriae   Projections from a fallopian tube that extend toward an ovary. (Singular: fimbria. Latin for "fiber" or "fringe.")

Follicle   A capsule within an ovary that contains an ovum. (From a Latin word meaning "small bag.")

Follicle-stimulating hormone (FSH)   A gonadotropin that stimulates development of follicles in the ovaries.

Forcible rape   Sexual intercourse with a nonconsenting person obtained by the use of force or the threat of force.

Foreplay   Mutual sexual stimulation that precedes sexual intercourse.

Foreskin   The loose skin that covers the penile glans. Also referred to as the *prepuce.*

Frenulum   The sensitive strip of tissue that connects the underside of the penile glans to the shaft. (From the Latin *frenum,* meaning "bridle.")

Frequency   The number of times an action is repeated within a given period.

Frotteurism   A paraphilia characterized by recurrent, powerful sexual urges and related fantasies involving rubbing against or touching a nonconsenting person. (From the French *frotter,* meaning "to rub.")

Functionals   Bell and Weinberg's term for gay people who live alone, have adapted well to a swinging lifestyle, and are sociable and well adjusted.

Fundus   The uppermost part of the uterus. (*Fundus* is a Latin word meaning "base.")

Gamete intrafallopian transfer (GIFT)   A method of conception in which sperm and ova are inserted into a fallopian tube to encourage conception.

Gay bashing   Violence against homosexuals.

Gay males   Males who are erotically attracted to and desire to form romantic relationships with other males.

Gender   One's personal, social, and legal status as male or female.

Gender assignment   The labeling of a newborn as a male or female.

Gender constancy   The concept that people's genders do not change, even if they alter their dress or behavior.

Gender dysphoria   The subjective experience of incongruity between genital anatomy and gender identity or role.

Gender identity   The psychological sense of being male or female.

Gender roles   Complex clusters of ways in which males and females are expected to behave within a given culture.

Gender schema   A cluster of mental representations about male and female physical qualities, behaviors, and personality traits.

Gender stability   The concept that people retain their genders for a lifetime.

Gender typing   The process by which children acquire behavior that is deemed appropriate to their gender.

General anesthesia   The use of drugs to put people to sleep and eliminate pain, as during childbirth.

General paresis   A progressive form of mental illness caused by neurosyphilis and characterized by gross confusion.

Generalize   To go from the particular to the general.

Genes   The basic units of heredity, which consist of chromosomal segments of DNA.

Genital herpes   An STD caused by the *Herpes simplex* virus type 2 and characterized by painful shallow sores and blisters on the genitals.

Genital warts   An STD that is caused by the human papilloma virus and takes the form of warts that appear around the genitals and anus.

Germ cell   A cell from which a new organism develops. (From the Latin *germen,* meaning "bud" or "sprout.")

Germinal stage   The period of prenatal development prior to implantation in the uterus.

Gonadotropin-releasing hormone (Gn-RH)   A hormone secreted by the hypothalamus that stimulates the pituitary gland to release gonadotropins.

Gonadotropins   Pituitary hormones that stimulate the gonads. (Literally, "that which 'feeds' the gonads.")

Gonorrhea   An STD caused by the *Neisseria gonorrhoeae* bacterium and characterized by a discharge and burning urination. Left untreated, gonorrhea can give rise to pelvic inflammatory disease (PID) and infertility. (From the Greek *gonos,* meaning "seed," and *rheein,* meaning "to flow," referring to the fact that in ancient times the penile discharge characteristic of the illness was erroneously interpreted as a loss of seminal fluid.)

Grafenberg spot   A part of the anterior wall of the vagina, whose prolonged stimulation is theorized to cause particularly intense orgasms and a female ejaculation. Abbreviated *G-spot.*

Granuloma inguinale   A tropical STD caused by the *Calymmatobacterium granulomatous* bacterium.

Gynecologist   A physician who treats women's diseases, especially of the reproductive tract. (From the Greek *gyne,* meaning "woman.")

Gynecomastia   Overdevelopment of a male's breasts. (From Greek roots meaning "woman" [*gyne*] and "breast" [*mastos*].)

Hegar's sign   Softness of a section of the uterus between the uterine body and the cervix, which indicates that a woman is pregnant.

Hepatitis   An inflammation of the liver. (From the Greek *hepar,* meaning "liver.")

Hermaphrodites   People who possess both ovarian and testicular tissue. (From the names of the male and female Greek gods *Hermes* and *Aphrodite.*)

***Herpes simplex* virus type 1**   The virus that causes oral herpes, which is characterized by cold sores or fever blisters on the lips or mouth. Abbreviated *HSV-1.*

***Herpes simplex* virus type 2**   The virus that causes genital herpes. Abbreviated *HSV-2.*

Heteroerotic   Of an erotic nature and involving members of the other gender.

Heterosexual orientation   Erotic attraction to, and preference for, developing romantic relationships with members of the other gender.

Homoerotic   Of an erotic nature and involving members of one's own gender.

Homogamy   The practice of marrying people who are similar in social background and standing. (From Greek roots meaning "same" [*homos*] and "marriage" [*gamos*].)

Homologous   Similar in structure; developing from the same embryonic tissue.

Homophobia   A cluster of negative attitudes and feelings toward gay people, including intolerance, hatred, and fear. (From Greek roots meaning "fear" [of members of the] "same" [gender].)

Homosexual orientation   Erotic attraction to, and preference for, developing romantic relationships with members of one's own gender. (From the Greek *homos,* meaning "same," not the Latin *homo,* which means "man").

Hormone   A substance secreted by an endocrine gland that regulates various body functions. (From the Greek *horman,* meaning "to stimulate" or "to excite.")

Hormone-replacement therapy (HRT)   Replacement of naturally occurring estrogen, or estrogen and progesterone, with synthetic equivalents, following menopause.

Human chorionic gonadotropin   A hormone produced by women shortly after conception, which stimulates the corpus luteum to continue to produce progesterone. The presence of HCG in a woman's urine indicates that she is pregnant.

Human immunodeficiency virus (HIV)   A sexually transmitted virus that destroys white blood cells in the immune system, leaving the body vulnerable to life-threatening diseases.

Human sexuality   The ways in which we experience and express ourselves as sexual beings.

Hustlers   Men who engage in prostitution with male customers.

Hyaluronidase   An enzyme that briefly thins the zona pellucida, enabling one sperm to penetrate. (From roots meaning "substance that breaks down a glasslike fluid.")

Hymen   A fold of tissue across the vaginal opening that is usually present at birth and remains at least partly intact until a woman engages in coitus. (Greek for "membrane.")

Hypersexuality   An excessive or apparently insatiable sex drive that disrupts the person's ability to concentrate on other needs or leads to self-defeating behavior, such as indiscriminate sexual contacts.

Hypogonadism   An endocrine disorder that reduces the output of testosterone.

Hypothalamus   A bundle of neural cell bodies near the center of the brain that are involved in regulating body temperature, motivation, and emotion.

Hypoxyphilia   A practice in which a person seeks to enhance sexual arousal, usually during masturbation, by becoming deprived of oxygen. (From the Greek root meaning "under" [*hypo-*].)

Hysterectomy   Surgical removal of the uterus.

Hysterotomy   An abortion method in which the fetus is removed by cesarean section.

Id   In Freud's theory, the mental structure that is present at birth, embodies physiological drives, and is fully unconscious.

Identification   In psychoanalytic theory, the process of incorporating within ourselves our perceptions of the behaviors, thoughts, and feelings of others.

Immune system   A term for the body's complex of mechanisms for protecting itself from disease-causing agents such as pathogens.

In vitro fertilization   A method of conception in which mature ova are surgically removed from an ovary and placed in a laboratory dish along with sperm.

Incest   Marriage or sexual relations between people who are so closely related (by "blood") that sexual relations are prohibited and punishable by law. (From the Latin *in-,* meaning "not," and *castus,* meaning "chaste.")

Incest taboo   The prohibition against intercourse and reproduction among close blood relatives.

Incidence   A measure of the occurrence or the degree of occurrence of an event.

Independent variable   A condition in a scientific study that is manipulated so that its effects may be observed.

Induced abortion   The purposeful termination of a pregnancy before the embryo or fetus is capable of sustaining independent life. (From the Latin *abortio,* meaning "that which is miscarried.")

Infatuation   A state of intense absorption in or focus on another person, which is usually accompanied by sexual desire, elation, and general physiological arousal or excitement; passion.

Infertility   Inability to conceive a child.

Inflammation   Redness and warmth that develop at the site of an injury, reflecting dilation of blood vessels that permits the expanded flow of leukocytes to the region.

Infundibulum   The outer, funnel-shaped part of a fallopian tube. (A Latin word meaning "funnel.")

Inguinal canal   A fetal canal that connects the scrotum and the testes, allowing their descent. (From the Latin *inguinus,* meaning "near the groin.")

Interstitial cells   Cells that lie between the seminiferous tubules and secrete testosterone. (*Interstitial* means "set between.")

Intimacy   Feelings of closeness and connectedness that are marked by sharing of inmost thoughts and feelings.

Intra-amniotic infusion   An abortion method in which a substance is injected into the amniotic sac to induce premature labor. Also called *instillation.*

Intracytoplasmic injection   A method of conception in which sperm is injected directly into an ovum.

Intrauterine device   A small object that is inserted into the uterus and left in place to prevent conception. Abbreviated *IUD.*

Introitus   The vaginal opening. (From the Latin for "entrance.")

Isthmus   The segment of a fallopian tube closest to the uterus. (A Latin word meaning "narrow passage.")

Jaundice   A yellowish discoloration of the skin and the whites of the eyes. (From the French *jaune,* meaning "yellow.")

Klinefelter's syndrome   A sex-chromosomal disorder caused by an extra X sex chromosome.

Klismaphilia   A paraphilia in which sexual arousal is derived from use of enemas.

Labia majora   Large folds of skin that run downward from the mons along the sides of the vulva. (Latin for "large lips" or "major lips.")

Labia minora   Hairless, light-colored membranes, located between the labia majora. (Latin for "small lips" or "minor lips.")

Lactation   Production of milk by the mammary glands.

Lamaze method   A childbirth method in which women learn about childbirth, learn to relax and to breathe in patterns that conserve energy and lessen pain, and have a coach (usually the father) present at childbirth. Also termed *prepared childbirth.*

Laparoscopy   (1) A medical procedure in which a long, narrow tube (laparoscope) is inserted through an incision in the navel, permitting the visual inspection of organs in the pelvic cavity. (From the Greek *lapara,* meaning "flank."); (2) Tubal sterilization by means of a *laparoscope,* which is inserted through a small incision just below the navel and used to cauterize, cut, or clamp the fallopian tubes. Sometimes referred to as "belly button surgery."

Larynx   A structure of muscle and cartilage at the upper end of the trachea that contains the vocal cords; the voice box.

Lesbians   Females who are erotically attracted to and desire to form romantic relationships with other females. (After *Lesbos,* the Greek island on which, legend has it, female–female sexual activity was idealized.)

Leukocytes   White blood cells that are essential to the body's defenses against infection. (From the Greek *leukos,* meaning "white," and *kytos,* meaning "a hollow," and used in combination with other word forms to mean *cell.*)

Leydig's cells   Another term for *interstitial cells.*

Local anesthesia   Anesthesia that eliminates pain in a specific area of the body, as during childbirth.

Lovemap   A representation in the mind and in the brain of the idealized lover and the idealized erotic activity with the lover.

Lumpectomy   Surgical removal of a lump from the breast.

Luteinizing hormone (LH)   A gonadotropin that helps regulate the menstrual cycle by triggering ovulation.

Lymphogranuloma venereum   A tropical STD caused by the *Chlamydia trachomatis* bacterium.

Male erectile disorder   Persistent difficulty achieving or maintaining an erection sufficient to allow the man to engage in or complete sexual intercourse. Also termed *erectile dysfunction.*

Male-superior position   A coital position in which the man is on top.

Malignant   Lethal; causing or likely to cause death.

Mammary glands   Milk-secreting glands. (From the Latin *mamma,* which means both "breast" and "mother.")

Mammography   A special type of X-ray test that detects cancerous lumps in the breast.

Mastalgia   A swelling of the breasts that sometimes causes premenstrual discomfort.

Mastectomy   Surgical removal of the entire breast.

Masturbation   Sexual self-stimulation.

Matching hypothesis   The concept that people tend to develop romantic relationships with people who are similar to themselves in attractiveness.

Mating gradient   The tendency for women to "marry up" (in social or economic status) and for men to "marry down."

Menarche   The onset of menstruation; first menstruation. (From Greek roots meaning "month" [*men*] and "beginning" [*arche*].)

Menopause   The cessation of menstruation.

Menstrual phase   The fourth phase of the menstrual cycle, during which the endometrium is sloughed off in the menstrual flow.

Menstruation   The cyclical bleeding that stems from the shedding of the uterine lining (endometrium).

Minilaparotomy   A kind of tubal sterilization in which a small incision is made in the abdomen to provide access to the fallopian tubes.

Minipill   A birth-control pill that contains synthetic progesterone but no estrogen.

Miscarriage   A spontaneous abortion.

Missionary position   The coital position in which the man is on top. Also termed the *male-superior position.*

Mittelschmerz   Pain that occurs during ovulation. (German for "middle pain," reflecting the fact that the pain occurs midway between menstrual periods).

Modeling   Acquiring knowledge and skills by observing others.

Monozygotic (MZ) twins   Twins who develop from the same fertilized ovum; identical twins.

Mons veneris   A mound of fatty tissue that covers the joint of the pubic bones in front of the body, below the abdomen and above the clitoris. (The name is a Latin phrase meaning "hill" or "mount of Venus," the Roman goddess of love. Also known as the *mons pubis,* or simply *mons.*)

Morning sickness   Symptoms of pregnancy, including nausea, aversions to specific foods, and vomiting.

Motility   Self-propulsion. A measure of the viability of sperm cells.

Multiple orgasms   One or more additional orgasms following the first, which occur within a short period of time and before the body has returned to a pre-plateau level of arousal.

Mutuality   A phase in building a relationship in which members of a couple come to regard themselves as "we," no longer two "I's" who happen to be in the same place at the same time.

Myometrium   The middle, well-muscled layer of the uterus. (*Myo-* stems from the Greek *mys,* meaning "muscle.")

Myotonia   Muscle tension.

Natural childbirth   A method of childbirth in which women use no anesthesia but are given other strategies for coping with discomfort and are educated about childbirth.

Naturalistic observation   A method in which organisms are observed in their natural environments.

Necrophilia   A paraphilia characterized by desire for sexual activity with corpses. (From the Greek *nekros,* meaning "dead body.")

Neurosyphilis   Syphilitic infection of the central nervous system, which can cause brain damage and death.

Nocturnal emission   Involuntary ejaculation of seminal fluid while asleep. Also referred to as a "wet dream," although the individual need not be dreaming about sex, or dreaming at all, at the time.

Nymphomania   An excessive, insatiable sexual appetite or drive in women. (From the Greek roots *nymphe,* meaning "a bride," and *mania,* which means "madness.")

Obscenity   That which offends people's feelings or goes beyond prevailing standards of decency or modesty. (From the Latin *caenum,* meaning "filth.")

Observer effect   A distortion of individuals' behavior caused by the act of observation.

Ocular herpes   A herpes infection of the eye, usually caused by touching an infected area of the body and then touching the eye.

Oedipus complex   In psychoanalytic theory, a conflict of the phallic stage in which the boy wishes to possess his mother sexually and perceives his father as a rival in love. (The analogous conflict for girls is the *Electra complex.*)

Open couples   Bell and Weinberg's term for gay couples who live together but engage in secret affairs.

Ophthalmia neonatorum   A gonorrheal infection of the eyes of newborn children who contract the disease by passing through an infected birth canal. (From the Greek *ophthalmos,* meaning "eye.")

Opportunistic diseases   Diseases that take hold only when the immune system is weakened and unable to fend them off.

Oral contraceptive   A contraceptive, consisting of sex hormones, which is taken by mouth.

Orgasm   The climax of sexual excitement.

Orgasmic disorders   Sexual dysfunctions in which people persistently or recurrently have difficulty reaching orgasm or reach orgasm more rapidly than they would like, despite attaining a level of sexual stimulation of sufficient intensity to normally result in orgasm.

Orgasmic platform   The thickening of the walls of the outer third of the vagina, due to vasocongestion, that occurs during the plateau phase of the sexual response cycle.

Orgasmic reconditioning   A method for strengthening the connection between sexual arousal and appropriate sexual stimuli (such as fantasies about an adult of the other gender) by repeatedly pairing the desired stimuli with orgasm.

Os   The opening in middle of the cervix. (Latin for "mouth.")

Osteoporosis   A condition caused by estrogen deficiency and characterized by a decline in bone density, such that bones become porous and brittle. (From the Greek *osteon,* meaning "bone," and the Latin *porus,* meaning "pore.")

Ova   Egg cells. (Singular: *ovum.*)

Ovariectomy   Surgical removal of the ovaries.

Ovaries   Almond-shaped organs that produce ova and the hormones estrogen and progesterone.

Ovulation   The release of an ovum from an ovary.

Ovulation method   A fertility awareness method of contraception that relies on prediction of ovulation by tracking the viscosity of the cervical mucus.

Ovulatory phase   The second stage of the menstrual cycle, during which a follicle ruptures and releases a mature ovum.

Oxytocin   A pituitary hormone that stimulates uterine contractions in labor and the ejection of milk during nursing.

Pap test   A test of a sample of cervical cells that screens for cervical cancer and other abnormalities. (Named after the originator of the technique, Dr. Papanicolaou.)

Paraphilia   A diagnostic category used by the American Psychiatric Association to describe atypical patterns of sexual arousal or behavior that become problematic in the eyes of the individual or society, such as fetishism or exhibitionism. (From Greek roots meaning "to the side of" [*para-*] and "loving" [*philos*].)

Paraplegic   A person with sensory and motor paralysis of the lower half of the body.

Parasympathetic   The branch of the ANS most active during processes that restore the body's reserves of energy, such as digestion. The parasympathetic ANS largely controls erection.

Partialism   A paraphilia related to fetishism, in which sexual arousal is exaggeratedly associated with a particular body part, such as feet, breasts, or buttocks.

Participant observation   A method in which observers interact with the people they study as they collect data.

Pathogen   An agent, especially a microorganism, that can cause a disease. (From the Greek *pathos,* meaning "suffering" or "disease," and *genic,* meaning "forming" or "coming into being."

Peak days   The days during the menstrual cycle during which a woman is most likely to be fertile.

Pederasty   Sexual love of boys. (From the Greek *paidos,* meaning "boy.")

Pediculosis   A parasitic infestation by pubic lice (*Pthirus pubis*) that causes itching.

Pedophiles   Persons with pedophilia, a paraphilia involving sexual interest in children.

Pedophilia   A type of paraphilia that is defined by sexual attraction to unusual stimuli: children. (From the Greek *paidos,* meaning "child," not the Latin *pedis,* meaning "foot.")

Pelvic inflammatory disease Inflammation of the pelvic region—possibly including the cervix, uterus, fallopian tubes, abdominal cavity, and ovaries—that can be caused by organisms such as *Neisseria gonorrhoeae.* Its symptoms are abdominal pain, tenderness, nausea, fever, and irregular menstrual cycles. The condition may lead to infertility. Abbreviated *PID.*

Penis The male organ of sexual intercourse. (From the Latin for "tail.")

Penis envy In psychoanalytic theory, the girl's wish to have a penis.

Performance anxiety Feelings of dread and foreboding experienced in connection with sexual activity (or any other activity that might be judged by another person).

Perimetrium The outer layer of the uterus. (From roots meaning "around the uterus.")

Perineum The skin and underlying tissue that lie between the vaginal opening and the anus. (From Greek roots meaning "around" and "to empty out.")

Period of the ovum Germinal stage.

Peyronie's disease An abnormal condition characterized by an excessive curvature of the penis that can make erections painful.

Phallic symbols Images of the penis.

Phallic worship Worship of the penis as a symbol of generative power.

Pharyngeal gonorrhea A gonorrheal infection of the pharynx (the cavity leading from the mouth and nasal passages to the larynx and esophagus) that is characterized by a sore throat.

Pheromones Chemical substances secreted externally by certain animals, which convey information to, or produce specific responses in, other members of the same species. (From the Greek *pherien,* meaning "to bear [a message]" and *hormone.*)

Philia (FEEL-yuh) Friendship love, which is based on liking and respect rather than sexual desire.

Phimosis An abnormal condition in which the foreskin is so tight that it cannot be withdrawn from the glans. (From the Greek *phimos,* meaning "muzzle.")

Pimps Men who serve as agents for prostitutes and live off their earnings. (From the Middle French *pimper,* meaning "to dress smartly.")

Pituitary gland The gland that secretes growth hormone, prolactin, oxytocin, and others.

Placenta An organ connected to the fetus by the umbilical cord. The placenta serves as a relay station between mother and fetus, allowing the exchange of nutrients and wastes.

Plateau phase The second phase of the sexual response cycle, which is characterized by increases in vasocongestion, muscle tension, heart rate, and blood pressure in preparation for orgasm.

Polymorphously perverse In psychoanalytic theory, being receptive to all forms of sexual stimulation.

Population A complete group of organisms or events.

Pornography Written, visual, or audiotaped material that is sexually explicit and produced for purposes of eliciting or enhancing sexual arousal. (From Greek roots meaning "to write about prostitutes.")

Postpartum Following birth.

Postpartum depression Persistent and severe mood changes during the postpartum period, involving feelings of despair and apathy and characterized by changes in appetite and sleep, low self-esteem, and difficulty in concentrating.

Posttraumatic stress disorder A type of stress reaction brought on by a traumatic event and characterized by flashbacks of the experience in the form of disturbing dreams or intrusive recollections, a sense of emotional numbing or restricted range of feelings, and heightened body arousal. Abbreviated *PTSD.*

Power rape Rape that is motivated by the desire to control and dominate the person assaulted.

Premature ejaculation A sexual dysfunction in which the male persistently ejaculates too early to afford the couple adequate sexual gratification.

Premenstrual syndrome (PMS) A combination of physical and psychological symptoms (e.g., anxiety, depression, irritability, weight gain from fluid retention, and abdominal discomfort) that regularly afflicts many women during the four- to six-day interval that precedes their menses each month.

Prepuce The fold of skin covering the glans of the clitoris (or penis). (From Latin roots meaning "before a swelling.")

Preterm Born prior to 37 weeks of gestation.

Primary amenorrhea Lack of menstruation in a woman who has never menstruated.

Primary dysmenorrhea Menstrual pain or discomfort that occurs in the absence of known organic problems.

Primary erogenous zones Erogenous zones that are particularly sensitive because they are richly endowed with nerve endings.

Primary sex characteristics Physical characteristics that differentiate males and females and are directly involved in reproduction, such as the sex organs.

Progesterone A steroid hormone secreted by the corpus luteum or prepared synthetically that stimulates proliferation of the endometrium and is involved in regulation of the menstrual cycle. (From the root *pro-,* meaning "promoting," and the words *gestation, steroid,* and *one.*)

Prolactin A pituitary hormone that stimulates production of milk.

Proliferative phase The first phase of the menstrual cycle, which begins with the end of menstruation and lasts about 9 or 10 days. During this phase, the endometrium proliferates.

Prophylactic An agent that protects against disease.

Prostaglandins Hormones that cause muscle fibers in the uterine wall to contract, as during labor.

Prostate gland The gland that lies beneath the bladder and secretes prostatic fluid, which gives semen its characteristic odor and texture.

Prostatitis Inflammation of the prostate gland.

Prostitution The sale of sexual activity for money or goods of value, such as drugs. (From the Latin *prostituere,* meaning "to cause to stand in front of." The implication is that one is offering one's body for sale.)

Proximodistal From the central axis of the body outward. (From Latin roots meaning "near" and "far.")

Prurient Tending to excite lust; lewd. (From the Latin *prurire,* meaning "to itch" in the sense of "to long for.")

Pseudohermaphrodites People who possess the gonads of one gender but external genitalia that are ambiguous or typical of the other gender.

Psychoanalysis The theory of personality originated by Sigmund Freud, which proposes that human behavior represents the outcome of clashing inner forces.

Psychological androgyny Possession of stereotypical masculine traits, such as assertiveness and instrumental skills, along with stereotypical feminine traits, such as expressiveness, nurturance, and cooperation.

Psychosexual development   In psychoanalytic theory, the process by which sexual feelings shift from one erogenous zone to another as a human being matures.

Puberty   The stage of development during which reproduction first becomes possible. Puberty begins with the appearance of *secondary sex characteristics* and ends when the long bones make no further gains in length. (From the Latin *puber,* meaning "of ripe age.")

Pudendum   The external female genitals.

Radiotherapy   Treatment of a disease by X-rays or by emissions from a radioactive substance.

Random sample   A sample in which every member of a population has an equal chance of participating.

Rape   Sexual intercourse that takes place as a result of force or threats of force rather than consent. (The legal definition of rape varies from state to state.)

Rape trauma syndrome   A two-phase reaction to rape that is characterized by disruption of the survivor's lifestyle (the acute phase) and reorganization of the survivor's life (the long-term phase).

Recessive trait   A trait that is not expressed when the gene or genes involved have been paired with dominant genes. Recessive traits are transmitted to future generations, however, and are expressed if they are paired with other recessive genes.

Reciprocity   Mutual exchange.

Reflex   A simple, unlearned response to a stimulus that is mediated by the spine rather than the brain.

Refractory period   A period of time following a response (e.g., orgasm) during which an individual is no longer responsive to stimulation (e.g., sexual stimulation).

Reliability   The consistency or accuracy of a measure.

Repression   The automatic ejection of anxiety-evoking ideas from consciousness.

Resolution phase   The fourth phase of the sexual response cycle, during which the body gradually returns to its prearoused state.

Respiratory distress syndrome   A cluster of breathing problems, including weak and irregular breathing, to which preterm babies are especially vulnerable.

Retrograde ejaculation   Ejaculation in which the ejaculate empties into the bladder. (From the Latin *retrogradi,* meaning "to go backward.")

Rh incompatibility   A condition in which antibodies produced by a pregnant woman are transmitted to the fetus and may cause brain damage or death.

Romantic love   A kind of love characterized by feelings of passion and intimacy.

Root   The base of the penis, which extends into the pelvis.

Rubella   A viral infection that can cause mental retardation and heart disease in an embryo. Also called *German measles.*

Sadism   A paraphilia characterized by the desire or need to inflict pain or humiliation on others to enhance sexual arousal so that gratification is attained. (From the name of the author Marquis de Sade.)

Sadistic rape   A highly ritualized, savage rape in which the person who is attacked is subjected to painful and humiliating experiences and threats.

Sadomasochism   A mutually gratifying sexual interaction between consenting sex partners in which sexual arousal is associated with the infliction and receipt of pain or humiliation. Commonly known as *S&M.*

Sample   Part of a population.

Satyriasis   An excessive, insatiable sexual appetite or drive in men. (After *satyr,* a sexually insatiable, goat-legged creature with pointed ears and short horns in Greek mythology. Satyrs were part man, part beast.)

Scabies   A parasitic infestation caused by a tiny mite (*Sarcoptes scabiei*) that causes itching.

Scores   Customers of hustlers.

Scrotum   The pouch of loose skin that contains the testes. (From the same linguistic root as the word *shred,* meaning "a long, narrow strip," and probably referring to the long furrows on the scrotal sac.)

Secondary amenorrhea   Lack of menstruation in a woman who has previously menstruated.

Secondary dysmenorrhea   Menstrual pain or discomfort that is caused by identified organic problems.

Secondary erogenous zones   Parts of the body that become erotically sensitized through experience.

Secondary sex characteristics   Physical traits that distinguish men from women but are not directly involved in reproduction.

Secretory phase   The third phase of the menstrual cycle, which follows ovulation. Also referred to as the *luteal phase,* after the *corpus luteum,* which begins to secrete large amounts of progesterone and estrogen following ovulation.

Selection factor   A bias that may operate in research when people are allowed to determine whether or not they will receive a treatment.

Self-disclosure   The revelation of personal, perhaps intimate, information.

Semen   The whitish fluid that constitutes the ejaculate, consisting of sperm and secretions from the seminal vesicles, prostate, and Cowper's glands.

Seminal vesicles   Small glands that lie behind the bladder and secrete fluids that combine with sperm in the ejaculatory ducts.

Seminiferous tubules   Tiny, winding, sperm-producing tubes that are located within the lobes of the testes. (From Latin roots meaning "seed bearing.")

Sensate focus exercises   Exercises in which sex partners take turns giving and receiving pleasurable stimulation in nongenital areas of the body.

Serial monogamy   A pattern of involvement in one exclusive relationship after another, as opposed to engaging in multiple sexual relationships at the same time.

Sex flush   A reddish rash that appears on the chest or breasts late in the excitement phase of the sexual response cycle.

Sex skin   Reddening of the labia minora that occurs during the plateau phase.

Sex therapy   A collective term for short-term behavioral models for treatment of sexual dysfunctions.

Sexism   The prejudgment that because of gender, a person will possess negative traits.

Sexologist   A person who engages in the scientific study of sexual behavior.

Sexual arousal disorders   Sexual dysfunctions in which people persistently or recurrently fail to become adequately sexually aroused to engage in or sustain sexual intercourse.

Sexual assault   Any sexual activity that involves the use of force or the threat of force.

Sexual desire disorders Sexual dysfunctions in which people have persistent or recurrent lack of sexual desire or aversion to sexual contact.

Sexual differentiation The process by which males and females develop distinct reproductive anatomy.

Sexual dysfunctions Persistent or recurrent difficulties in becoming sexually aroused or reaching orgasm.

Sexual harassment Deliberate or repeated unsolicited verbal comments, gestures, or physical contact of a sexual nature that is considered unwelcome by the recipient.

Sexual masochism A paraphilia characterized by the desire or need for pain or humiliation to enhance sexual arousal so that gratification may be attained. (From the name of the author Leopold von Sacher-Masoch.)

Sexual orientation The direction of one's sexual interests—toward members of the same gender, the other gender, or both genders.

Sexual pain disorders Sexual dysfunctions in which people persistently or recurrently experience pain during coitus.

Sexual response cycle Masters and Johnson's model of sexual response, which consists of four phases.

Sexual sadists People who become sexually aroused by inflicting pain or humiliation on others.

Sexually transmitted diseases Diseases that are communicated through sexual contact. Abbreviated *STDs*.

Shaft The body of the penis, which expands as a result of vasocongestion.

Shigellosis An STD caused by the *Shigella* bacterium.

Small talk A superficial kind of conversation that allows exchange of information but stresses breadth of topic coverage rather than in-depth discussion.

Social desirability A response bias to a questionnaire or interview, in which the person provides a socially acceptable response.

Social skills training Behavior therapy methods for building social skills that rely on a therapist's coaching and practice.

Social-exchange theory The view that the development of a relationship reflects the unfolding of social exchanges—that is, the rewards and costs of maintaining the relationship as opposed to ending it.

Social-learning theory A cognitively oriented learning theory in which observational learning, values, and expectations play key roles in determining behavior.

Socialization The process of guiding people into socially acceptable behavior patterns by means of information, rewards, and punishments.

Sociobiology The theory that dispositions toward behavior patterns that enhance reproductive success may be genetically transmitted.

Spectator role A role, usually taken on because of performance anxiety, in which people observe rather than fully participate in their sexual encounters.

Sperm The male germ cell. (From a Greek root meaning "seed.")

Spermatic cord The cord that suspends a testicle within the scrotum and contains a vas deferens, blood vessels, nerves, and the cremaster muscle.

Spermatids Cells formed by the division of spermatocytes. Each spermatid has 23 chromosomes.

Spermatocyte An early stage in the development of sperm cells, in which each parent cell has 46 chromosomes, including one X and one Y sex chromosome.

Spermatogenesis Process by which sperm cells are produced and developed.

Spermatozoa Mature sperm cells.

Sphincters Ring-shaped muscles that surround body openings and open or close them by expanding or contracting. (From the Greek for "that which draws close.")

Squeeze technique A method for treating premature ejaculation whereby the tip of the penis is squeezed temporarily to prevent ejaculation.

Statutory rape Sexual intercourse with a person who is below the age of consent. Sexual intercourse under such conditions is considered statutory rape even though the person attacked may cooperate.

Stereotype A fixed, conventional idea about a group of people.

Sterilization Surgical procedures that render people incapable of reproduction without affecting sexual activity.

Stillbirth The birth of a dead fetus.

Storge (STORE-gay) Loving attachment and nonsexual affection; the type of emotion that binds parents to children.

Stranger rape Rape that is committed by an assailant previously unknown to the person who is assaulted.

Stratified random sample A random sample in which known subgroups in a population are represented in proportion to their numbers in the population.

Streetwalkers Prostitutes who solicit customers on the streets.

Superego In Freud's theory, the third mental structure, which functions as a moral guardian and sets forth high standards for behavior.

Surfactants Substances that prevent the walls of the airways from sticking together.

Surrogate mother A woman who is impregnated through artificial insemination, with the sperm of a prospective father, carries the embryo and fetus to term, and then gives the child to the prospective parents.

Survey A detailed study of a sample obtained by means such as interviews and questionnaires.

Swinging A form of consensual adultery in which both spouses share extramarital sexual experiences. Also referred to as *mate-swapping*.

Sympathetic The branch of the ANS most active during emotional responses, such as fear and anxiety, that spend the body's reserves of energy. The sympathetic ANS largely controls ejaculation.

Sympathetic pregnancy The experiencing of a number of signs of pregnancy by the father.

Syphilis A sexually transmitted disease caused by a bacterial infection.

Systematic desensitization A method for terminating the connection between a stimulus (such as a fetishistic object) and an inappropriate response (such as sexual arousal to the paraphilic stimulus). Muscle relaxation is practiced in connection with each stimulus in a series of increasingly arousing stimuli, so that the person learns to remain relaxed (and not sexually aroused) in their presence.

Tampon A cylindrical plug of cotton that is inserted into the vagina and left in place to absorb menstrual fluid. (A French word, meaning a gun barrel "plug.")

Telephone scatologia A paraphilia characterized by the making of obscene telephone calls. (From the Greek *skatos*, meaning "excrement.")

Teratogens Environmental influences or agents that can damage an embryo or fetus. (From the Greek *teras*, meaning "monster.")

Testes The male gonads. (Singular: testis.)

Testicles Testes.

Testosterone The male sex hormone that fosters the development of male sex characteristics and is connected with the sex drive.

Toucherism A practice related to frotteurism and characterized by the persistent urge to fondle nonconsenting strangers.

Toxemia A life-threatening condition that is characterized by high blood pressure.

Transition The process during which the cervix becomes nearly fully dilated and the head of the fetus begins to move into the birth canal.

Transsexuals People who have a gender-identity disorder in which they feel trapped in the body of the wrong gender.

Transverse position A crosswise birth position.

Transvestism A paraphilia in which a person repeatedly cross-dresses to achieve sexual arousal or gratification, or is troubled by persistent, recurring urges to cross-dress. (From the Latin roots *trans-*, meaning "cross," and *vestis*, meaning "garment.")

Treatment In experiments, an intervention that is administered to participants (e.g., a test, a drug, or a sex education program) so that its effects may be observed.

Trichomoniasis A form of vaginitis caused by the protozoan *Trichomonas vaginalis*.

Tubal sterilization The most common method of female sterilization, in which the fallopian tubes are surgically blocked to prevent the meeting of sperm and ova. Also called *tubal ligation*.

Tumescence Swelling; erection. (From the Latin *tumere*, meaning "to swell." *Tumor* has the same root.)

Turner syndrome A sex-chromosomal disorder caused by loss of some X chromosome material.

Umbilical cord A tube that connects the fetus to the placenta.

Unconscious mind Those parts or contents of the mind that lie outside of conscious awareness.

Urethral bulb The small tube that makes up the prostatic part of the urethral tract, which balloons out as muscles close at either end, trapping semen prior to ejaculation.

Urethral opening The opening through which urine passes from the female's body.

Urethritis An inflammation of the bladder or urethra.

Urologist A physician who specializes in the diagnosis and treatment of diseases of the urogenital system.

Urophilia A paraphilia in which sexual arousal is associated with urine.

Uterus The hollow, muscular, pear-shaped organ in which a fertilized ovum becomes implanted and develops until birth.

Vacuum aspiration Removal of the uterine contents by suction. An abortion method used early in pregnancy. (From the Latin *aspirare*, meaning "to breathe upon.")

Vagina The tubular female sex organ that contains the penis during sexual intercourse and through which a baby is born. (Latin for "sheath.")

Vaginismus A sexual dysfunction characterized by involuntary contraction of the muscles surrounding the vaginal barrel, preventing penile penetration or rendering penetration painful.

Vaginitis Vaginal inflammation.

Validity With respect to tests, the degree to which a particular test measures the constructs or traits it purports to measure.

Vas deferens A tube that conducts sperm from the testicle to the ejaculatory duct of the penis. (From Latin roots meaning "a vessel" that "carries down.")

Vasectomy A male sterilization procedure in which the vas deferens is severed, preventing sperm from reaching the ejaculatory duct.

Vasocongestion The swelling of the genital tissues with blood, which causes erection of the penis and engorgement of the area surrounding the vaginal opening.

Vasovasotomy The surgical method of reversing vasectomy in which the cut or cauterized ends of the vas deferens are sewn together.

VDRL The test named after the Venereal Disease Research Laboratory of the U.S. Public Health Service that tests for the presence of antibodies to *Treponema pallidum* in the blood.

Vestibular bulbs Cavernous structures that extend downward along the sides of the introitus and swell during sexual arousal.

Viscosity Stickiness, consistency.

Volunteer bias A slanting of research data that is caused by the characteristics of individuals who volunteer to participate, such as willingness to discuss intimate behavior.

Voyeurism A paraphilia characterized by strong, repetitive urges and related sexual fantasies of observing unsuspecting strangers who are naked, disrobing, or engaged in sexual relations. (From the French verb *voir*, meaning "to see.")

Vulva The external sexual structures of the female.

Whore–madonna complex A rigid stereotyping of women as either sinners or saints.

Zona pellucida A gelatinous layer that surrounds an ovum. (From roots meaning "zone that light can shine through.")

Zoophilia A paraphilia involving persistent or repeated sexual urges and related fantasies involving sexual contact with animals.

Zygote A fertilized ovum (egg cell).

Zygote intrafallopian transfer (ZIFT) A method of conception in which an ovum is fertilized in a laboratory dish and then placed in a fallopian tube.

References

ABC News *Nightline* Poll. (1995, February 17). *Most favor sex ed. in schools, believing it changes behavior.* New York: ABC News.

Abel, G. G., et al. (1984). Complications, consent, and cognitions in sex between children and adults. *International Journal of Law and Psychiatry, 7,* 89–103.

Abelson, H., et al. (1970). Public attitudes toward and experience with erotic materials. In *Technical reports of the commission on obscenity and pornography,* (Vol. 6). Washington, DC: U.S. Government Printing Office.

Abramowitz, S. (1986). Psychosocial outcomes of sex reassignment surgery. *Journal of Consulting and Clinical Psychology, 54,* 183–189.

Acker, M., & Davis, M. H. (1992). Intimacy, passion and commitment in adult romantic relationships: A test of the triangular theory of love. *Journal of Social and Personal Relationships, 9,* 21–50.

Adams, R. (1987). The role of prostitution in AIDS and other STDs. *Medical Aspects of Human Sexuality, 21,* 27–33.

Adelson, A. (1990, November 19). Study attacks women's roles in TV. *The New York Times,* p. C18.

Ahmed, R. A. (1991). Women in Egypt and the Sudan. In L. L. Adler (Ed.), *Women in cross-cultural perspective* (pp. 107–134). New York: Praeger.

Alan Guttmacher Institute. (1991). *Facts in brief.* New York: Author.

Allen, J. R., & Setlow, V. P. (1991). Heterosexual transmission of HIV: A view of the future. *Journal of the American Medical Association, 266,* 1695–1696.

Alter-Reid, K., et al. (1986). Sexual abuse of children: A review of the empirical findings. *Clinical Psychology Review, 6,* 249–266.

Althof, S. E. (1994). Paper presented to the annual meeting of the American Urological Association. San Francisco, CA.

Altman, L. K. (1991, April 15). Study challenges federal research on risks of IUD's. *The New York Times,* p. A1.

Altman, L. K. (1993a, February 17). 2 new studies link vasectomy to higher prostate cancer risk. *The New York Times,* p. C12.

Altman, L. K. (1993b, February 21). New caution, and some reassurance, on vasectomy. *The New York Times,* Section 4, p. 2.

Altman, L. K. (1993c, June 8). World health official says AIDS spread could be controlled. *The New York Times,* p. C6

Alzate, H. (1985). Vaginal eroticism: A replication study. *Archives of Sexual Behavior, 14,* 529–537.

Amaro, H. (1995). Love, sex, and power: Considering women's realities in HIV prevention. *American Psychologist, 50,* 437–447.

Amato, P. R., & Keith, B. (1991). Parental divorce and the well-being of children: A meta-analysis. *Psychological Bulletin, 110,* 26–46.

American Cancer Society. (1991). *Cancer facts and figures.* New York: Author.

American Cancer Society. (1994). *Cancer facts and figures.* Atlanta: Author.

American Cancer Society. (1995a). America Online. Document ID: ACS049.

American Cancer Society. (1995b). America Online. Document ID: ACS050.

American Cancer Society. (1995c). America Online. Document ID: ACS052.

American Cancer Society. (1995d). America Online. Document ID: ACS053.

American Cancer Society. (1995e). America Online. Document ID: ACS058.

American Psychiatric Association. (1994). *Diagnostic and statistical manual of mental disorders* (4th ed.). Washington, DC: Author.

American Psychological Association, Committee on Gay and Lesbian Concerns. (1991). Avoiding heterosexual bias in language. *American Psychologist, 46,* 973–974.

Ames, M. A., & Houston, D. A. (1990). Legal, social, and biological definitions of pedophilia. *Archives of Sexual Behavior, 19,* 333–342.

Anderson, B. J., & Wold, F. M. (1986). Chronic physical illness and sexual behavior. *Journal of Consulting and Clinical Psychology, 54,* 168–175.

Anderson, J. L., et al. (1992). Was the Duchess of Windsor right? A cross-cultural review of the socioecology of ideals of female body shape. *Ethology and Sociobiology, 13,* 197–227.

Angier, N. (1990, July 19). Scientists say gene on Y chromosome makes a man a man. *The New York Times,* pp. A1, 19.

Angier, N. (1991, August 30). Zone of brain linked to men's sexual orientation. *The New York Times,* A1, D18.

Angier, N. (1993a). Future of the pill may lie just over the counter. *The New York Times,* Section 4, p. 5.

Antill, J. K. (1983). Sex role complementarity versus similarity in married couples. *Journal of Personality and Social Psychology, 52,* 260–267.

Antonarakas, S. E., et al. (1991). Prenatal origin of the extra chromosome in trisomy 21 as indicated by analysis of DNA polymorphisms. *New England Journal of Medicine, 324,* 872–876.

Appell, R. A. (1986). Importance of the neurological examination in erectile dysfunction. *Medical Aspects of Human Sexuality, 20,* 32–36.

Asbell, B. (1995). *The pill: A biography of the drug that changed the world.* New York: Random House.

Asso, D., & Magos, A. (1992). Psychological and physiological changes in severe premenstrual syndrome. *Biological Psychology, 33,* 115–132.

Astley, S. J., et al. (1992). Analysis of facial shape in children gestationally exposed to marijuana, alcohol, and/or cocaine. *Pediatrics, 89,* 67–77.

Atkeson, B. M., et al. (1989). Victim resistance to rape: The relationship of previous victimization, demographics, and situational factors. *Archives of Sexual Behavior, 18,* 497–507.

Ayres, B. D. (1996, August 27). California bill would require "chemical castration" for repeat sex offenders. *The New York Times.*

Bach, G. R., & Deutsch, R. M. (1970). *Pairing.* New York: Peter H. Wyden.

Bagatell, C. J., & Bremner, W. J. (1996). Drug therapy: Androgens in men—Uses and abuses. *New England Journal of Medicine, 334,* 707–714.

Bagley, C., & Young, L. (1987). Juvenile prostitution and child sexual abuse: A controlled study. *Canadian Journal of Community Mental Health, 6,* 5–26.

Bailey, J. M., and Pillard, R. C. (1991). A genetic study of male sexual orientation. *Archives of General Psychiatry, 48,* 1089–1096.

Bailey, J. M., et al. (1993). Heritable factors influence sexual orientation in women. *Archives of General Psychiatry, 50,* 217–223.

Baker, T. C., et al. (1990). Rape victims' concerns about possible exposure to HIV infection. *Journal of Interpersonal Violence, 5,* 49–60.

Baldwin, J. D., & Baldwin, J. I. (1989). The socialization of homosexuality and heterosexuality in a non-Western society. *Archives of Sexual Behavior, 18,* 13–29.

Baldwin, J. D., et al. (1992). The effect of ethnic group on sexual activities related to contraception and STDs. *Journal of Sex Research, 29,* 189–205.

Bancroft, J. (1990). Commentary: Biological contributions to sexual orientation. In D. P. McWhirter, et al. (Eds.), *Homosexuality/heterosexuality: Concepts of sexual orientation* (pp. 101–111). New York: Oxford University Press.

Banning, A. (1989). Mother–son incest: Confronting a prejudice. *Child Abuse and Neglect, 13,* 563–570.

Barbach, L. G. (1975). *For yourself: The fulfillment of female sexuality.* New York: Doubleday.

Barbach, L. G. (1995). Cited in Goleman, D. (1995, June 14). Sex fantasy research said to neglect women. *The New York Times,* p. C14.

Barbaree, H. E., & Marshall, W. L. (1991). The role of male sexual arousal in rape: Six models. *Journal of Consulting and Clinical Psychology, 59,* 621–630.

Barlow, D. H. (1986). Causes of sexual dysfunction: The role of anxiety and cognitive interference. *Journal of Consulting and Clinical Psychology, 54,* 140–148.

Barlow, D. H., & Durand, V. M. (1995). *Abnormal psychology.* Pacific Grove, CA: Brooks/Cole.

Barr, H. M., et al. (1990). Prenatal exposure to alcohol, caffeine, tobacco, and aspirin. *Developmental Psychology, 26,* 339–348.

Barringer, F. (1992a, July 17). Rate of marriage continues decline. *The New York Times,* p. A20.

Barringer, F. (1992b, July 19). More Americans are saying, "I don't." *The New York Times,* p. E2.

Barringer, F. (1993a, April 1). Viral sexual diseases are found in 1 of 5 in U.S. *The New York Times,* pp. A1, B9.

Bart, P. B., & O'Brien, P. B. (1985). *Stopping rape: Successful survival strategies.* Elmsford, NY: Pergamon Press.

Bar-Tal, D., & Saxe, L. (1976). Perceptions of similarly and dissimilarly physically attractive couples and individuals. *Journal of Personality and Social Psychology, 33,* 772–781.

Baumeister, R. F. (1988a). Gender differences in masochistic scripts. *Journal of Sex Research, 25,* 478–499.

Baumeister, R. F. (1988b). Masochism as escape from self. *Journal of Sex Research, 25,* 28–59.

Baxter, D. J., et al. (1986). Sexual responses to consenting and forced sex in a large sample of rapists and nonrapists. *Behaviour Research and Therapy, 17,* 215–222.

Beck, A. (1988). *Love is never enough.* New York: Harper & Row.

Beck, J. G. (1993). Vaginismus. In W. O'Donohue & J. H. Geer (Eds.), *Handbook of sexual dysfunctions: Assessment and treatment* (pp. 381–397). Boston: Allyn & Bacon.

Becker, J. V., et al. (1986). Level of postassault sexual functioning in rape and incest victims. *Archives of Sexual Behavior, 15,* 37–49.

Becker, J. V., et al. (1989). Factors associated with erection in adolescent sex offenders. *Journal of Psychopathology and Behavioral Assessment, 11,* 353–362.

Beitchman, J. H., et al. (1992). A review of the long-term effects of child sexual abuse. *Child Abuse and Neglect, 16,* 101–118.

Bell, A. P., & Weinberg, M. S. (1978). *Homosexualities: A study of diversity among men and women.* New York: Simon & Schuster.

Bell, A. P., et al. (1981). *Sexual preference: Its development in men and women.* Bloomington: University of Indiana Press.

Bell, S., et al. (1994). Understanding attributions of blame in stranger rape and date rape situations: An examination of gender, race, identification, and students' social perceptions of rape victims. *Journal of Applied Social Psychology, 24* (19), 1719–1734.

Bellis, D. J. (1990). Fear of AIDS and risk reduction among heroin-addicted female street prostitutes: Personal interviews with 72 Southern California subjects. *Journal of Alcohol and Drug Education, 35,* 26–37.

Bello, D. C., et al. (1983). The communications effects of controversial sexual content in television programs and commercials. *Journal of Advertising, 12*(3), 32–42.

Bem, S. L. (1975). Sex role adaptability: One consequence of psychological androgyny. *Journal of Personality and Social Psychology, 31,* 634–643.

Bem, S. L. (1981). Gender schema theory: A cognitive account of sex typing. *Psychological Review, 88,* 354–364.

Bem, S. L. (1985). Androgyny and gender schema theory: A conceptual and empirical integration. In T. B. Sonderegger (Ed.), *Nebraska symposium on motivation, 1984: Psychology and gender.* Lincoln: University of Nebraska Press.

Bem, S. L. (1993). *The lenses of gender.* New Haven: Yale University Press.

Bem, S. L., et al. (1976). Sex typing and androgyny: Further explorations of the expressive domain. *Journal of Personality and Social Psychology, 34,* 1016–1023.

Bennett, N. G., et al. (1988). Commitment and the modern union: Assessing the link between premarital cohabitation and subsequent marital stability. *American Sociological Review, 53,* 127–138.

Berlin, F. S. (1983). Sex offenders: A biomedical perspective and a status report of biomedical treatment. In J. G. Greer & I. R. Stuart (Eds.), *The sexual aggressor* (pp. 83–123). New York: Van Nostrand Reinhold.

Berliner, D. (1993). Cited in Blakeslee, S. (1993, September 7). Human nose may hold an additional organ for a real sixth sense. *The New York Times,* p. C3.

Bernstein, W. M., et al. (1983). Causal ambiguity and heterosexual affiliation. *Journal of Experimental Social Psychology, 19,* 78–92.

Berscheid, E. (1988). Some comments on love's anatomy: Or, whatever happened to old-fashioned lust? In R. J. Sternberg & M. L. Barnes (Eds.), *The psychology of love* (pp. 359–374). New Haven: Yale University Press.

Berscheid, E., & Walster, E. (1978). *Interpersonal attraction.* Reading, MA: Addison-Wesley.

Beutler, L. E., et al. (1986). Inflatable and noninflatable penile prostheses: Comparative follow-up evaluation. *Urology, 28,* 136–143.

Bieber, I. (1976). A discussion of "Homosexuality: The ethical challenge." *Journal of Consulting and Clinical Psychology, 44,* 163–166.

Bieber, I., et al. (1962). *Homosexuality.* New York: Basic Books.

Billy, J. O. G., et al. (1993). The sexual behavior of men in the United States. *Family Planning Perspectives, 25,* 52–60.

Bixler, R. H. (1989). Diversity: A historical/comparative perspective. *Behaviorial and Brain Sciences, 12,* 15–16.

Bjorklund, D. F., & Kipp, K. (1996). Parental investment theory and gender differences in the evolution of inhibition mechanisms. *Psychological Bulletin, 120,* 163–188.

Blair, C. D., & Lanyon, R. I. (1981). Exhibitionism: A critical review of the etiology and treatment. *Psychological Bulletin, 89,* 439–463.

Blakeslee, S. (1992, January 22). An epidemic of genital warts raises concern but not alarm. *The New York Times,* p. C12.

Blanchard, R., & Hucker, S. J. (1991). Age, transvestism, bondage, and concurrent paraphilic activities in 117 fatal cases of autoerotic asphyxia. *British Journal of Psychiatry, 159,* 371–377.

Blanchard, R., et al. (1985). Gender dysphoria, gender reorientation, and the clinical management of transsexualism. *Journal of Consulting and Clinical Psychology, 53,* 295–304.

Blenner, J. L. (1992). Stress and mediators: Patients' perceptions of infertility treatment. *Nursing Research, 41,* 92–97.

Bloom, B. J., et al. (1978). Marital disruption as a stressor: A review and analysis. *Psychological Bulletin, 85,* 867–894.

Bloor, M., et al. (1990). An ethnographic study of HIV-related risk practices among Glasgow rent boys and their clients: Report of a pilot study. *AIDS Care, 2,* 17–24.

Blumstein, P., & Schwartz, P. (1983). *American couples: Money, work, sex.* New York: William Morrow.

Blumstein, P. & Schwartz, P. (1990). Intimate relationships and the creation of sexuality. In D. P. McWhirter, et al. (Eds.), *Homosexuality/heterosexuality: Concepts of sexual orientation* (pp. 307–320). New York: Oxford University Press.

Boles, J., & Elifson, K. W. (1994). Sexual identity and HIV: The male prostitute. *Journal of Sex Research, 31,* 39–46.

Boston Women's Health Book Collective. (1992). *The new our bodies, ourselves.* New York: Simon & Schuster.

Both-Orthman, B., et al. (1988). Menstrual cycle phase: Related changes in appetite in patients with premenstrual syndrome and in control subjects. *American Journal of Psychiatry, 145,* 628–631.

Bowie, W. R. (1990). Approach to men with urethritis and urologic complications of sexually transmitted diseases. *Medical Clinics of North America, 74,* 1543–1557.

Bozzette, S. A., et al. (1995). A randomized trial of three anti-pneumocystitis agents in patients with advanced human immunodeficiency virus infection. *New England Journal of Medicine, 332,* 693–699.

Brady, E. C., et al. (1991). Date rape: Expectations, avoidance strategies, and attitudes toward victims. *Journal of Social Psychology, 131,* 427–429.

Breast fears fade. (1993, November). *Prevention,* 19–20.

Brecher, E. M, and the Editors of Consumer Reports Books. (1984). *Love, sex, and aging.* Boston: Little, Brown.

Breslow, N. (1989). Sources of confusion in the study and treatment of sadomasochism. *Journal of Social Behavior and Personality, 4,* 263–274.

Breslow, N., et al. (1986). Comparisons among heterosexual, bisexual and homosexual male sadomasochists. *Journal of Homosexuality, 13,* 83–107.

Bretl, D. J., & Cantor, J. (1988). The portrayal of men and women in U.S. television commercials: A recent content analysis and trends over 15 years. *Sex Roles, 18,* 595–609.

Bretschneider, J., & McCoy, N. (1988). Sexual interest and behavior in healthy 80- to 102-year-olds. *Archives of Sexual Behavior, 17,* 109.

Briere, J., & Runtz, M. (1987). Post sexual abuse trauma: Data and implications for clinical practice. *Journal of Interpersonal Violence, 2,* 367–379.

Briere, J., & Runtz, M. (1989). University males' sexual interest in children: Predicting potential indices of "pedophilia" in a non-forensic sample. *Child Abuse and Neglect, 13,* 65–75.

Brody, J. E. (1989, January 5). How women can begin to cope with premenstrual syndrome, a biological mystery. *The New York Times,* p. B12.

Brody, J. E. (1990a, January 23). Scientists trace aberrant sexuality. *The New York Times,* pp. C11, C12.

Brody, J. E. (1990b, August 2). In fight against breast cancer, mammograms are a crucial tool, but not foolproof. *The New York Times,* p. B5.

Brody, J. E. (1992a, April 29). How to outwit a rapist: Rehearse. *The New York Times,* p. C13.

Brody, J. E. (1992b, May 20). Alternatives to hormone therapy after menopause. *The New York Times,* p. C14.

Brody, J. E. (1992c, November 11). PMS is a worldwide phenomenon. *The New York Times,* p. C14.

Brody, J. E. (1993a, July 7). Genital herpes drug found safe for daily use. *The New York Times,* p. C11.

Brody, J. E. (1993b, August 4). A new look at an old quest for sexual stimulants. *The New York Times,* p. C12.

Brody, J. E. (1995a, May 3). Breast scans may indeed help women under 50. *The New York Times,* p. C11.

Brody, J. E. (1995b, August 30). Hormone replacement therapy for men: When does it help? *The New York Times,* p. C8.

Brody, J. E. (1996, August 28). PMS need not be the worry it was just decades ago. *The New York Times,* p. C9.

Brooks, V. R. (1982). Sex differences in student dominance behavior in female and male professors' classrooms. *Sex Roles, 8,* 683–690.

Brooks-Gunn, J., & Furstenberg, F. F. (1989). Adolescent sexual behavior. *American Psychologist, 44,* 249–257.

Brooks-Gunn, J., & Matthews, W. S. (1979). *He and she: How children develop their sex-role identity.* Englewood Cliffs, NJ: Spectrum.

Brown, R. A. (1994). Romantic love and the spouse selection criteria of male and female Korean college students. *Journal of Social Psychology, 134*(2), 183–189.

Bryant, J., & Brown, D. (1989). Uses of pornography. In D. Zillmann & J. Bryant (Eds.), *Pornography: Research advances and policy considerations* (pp. 25–55). Hillsdale, NJ: Erlbaum.

Bullough, V. L. (1990). The Kinsey Scale in historical perspective. In D. P. McWhirter, et al. (Eds.), *Homosexuality/heterosexuality: Concepts of sexual orientation* (pp. 3–14). New York: Oxford University Press.

Bullough, V. L. (1991). Transvestism: A reexamination. *Journal of Psychology and Human Sexuality, 4,* 53–67.

Bumiller, E. (1990, October 25). Japan's abortion agony: In a country that prohibits the pill, reality collides with religion. *The Washington Post.*

Bumpass, L. (1995). Cited in Steinhauer, J. (1995, July 6). No marriage, no apologies. *The New York Times,* pp. C1, C7.

Burgess, A. W., & Holmstrom, L. L. (1974). Rape trauma syndrome. *American Journal of Psychiatry, 131,* 981–986.

Burkhart, B., & Fromuth, M. E. (1991). Individual psychological and social psychological understandings of sexual coercion. In E. Grauerholz & M. A. Koralewski (Eds.), *Sexual coercion: A sourcebook on its nature, causes, and prevention* (pp. 7–89). Lexington, MA: Lexington Books.

Buss, D. M. (1994). *The evolution of desire: Strategies of human mating.* New York: Basic Books.

Buxton, A. P. (1994). *The other side of the closet.* New York: Wiley.

Byers, E. S., & Lewis, K. (1988). Dating couples' disagreements over the desired level of sexual intimacy. *Journal of Sex Research, 24,* 15–29.

Byrnes, J., & Takahira, S. (1993). Explaining gender differences on SAT-math items. *Developmental Psychology, 29,* 805–810.

Caceres, C. F., & van-Griensven, G. J. P. (1994). Male homosexual transmission of HIV-1. *AIDS, 8* (8), 1051–1061.

Calderone, M. S., & Johnson, E. W. (1989). *Family book about sexuality* (rev. ed.). New York: Harper & Row.

Calhoun, K. S., & Atkeson, B. M. (1991). *Treatment of rape victims: Facilitating social adjustment.* New York: Pergamon Press.

Call, V., et al. (1995). The incidence and frequency of marital sex in a national sample. *Journal of Marriage and the Family, 57,* 639–652.

Cameron, P., et al. (1986). Child molestation and homosexuality. *Psychological Reports, 58,* 327–337.

Campbell, C. A. (1991). Prostitution, AIDS, and preventive health behavior. *Social Science and Medicine, 32,* 1367–1378.

Campbell, S. B., & Cohn, J. F. (1991). Prevalence and correlates of postpartum depression in first-time mothers. *Journal of Abnormal Psychology, 100,* 594–599.

Cannistra, S. A., & Niloff, J. M. (1996). Cancer of the uterine cervix. *New England Journal of Medicine, 334,* 1030–1038.

Cappella, J. N., & Palmer, M. T. (1990). Attitude similarity, relational history, and attraction: The mediating effects of kinesic and vocal behaviors. *Communication Monographs, 5,* 161–183.

Carani, C., et al. (1990). Effects of androgen treatment in impotent men with normal and low levels of free testosterone. *Archives of Sexual Behavior, 19,* 223–234.

Carmignani, G., et al. (1987). Cavernous artery revascularization in vasculogenic impotence: New simplified technique. *Urology, 30,* 23–26.

Carrera, M. (1981). *Sex: The facts, the acts and your feelings.* New York: Crown.

Cartwright, R. D., et al. (1983). The traditional-liberated woman dimension: Social stereotype and self-concept. *Journal of Personality and Social Psychology, 44,* 581–588.

Carvajal, D. (1995). Oldest profession's newest home. *The New York Times,* pp. L29, L32.

Castro, K. G., et al. (1988). Transmission of HIV in Belle Glade, Florida: Lessons for other communities in the United States. *Science, 239,* 193–197.

Catalan, J., et al. (1990). Couples referred to a sexual dysfunction clinic: Psychological and physical morbidity. *British Journal of Psychiatry, 156,* 61–67.

Catalona, W. J., et al. (1993). Detection of organ-confined prostate cancer is increased through prostate-specific antigen-based screening. *Journal of the American Medical Association, 270,* 948–954.

Catania, J. A., et al. (1991). Changes in condom use among homosexual men in San Francisco. *Health Psychology, 10,* 190–199.

Cates, W., Jr., & Stone, K. M. (1992a). Family planning, sexually transmitted diseases, and contraceptive choice: A literature update. *Family Planning Perspectives, 24,* 75–84.

Cates, W., Jr., & Stone, K. M. (1992b). Family planning, sexually transmitted diseases, and contraceptive choice: A literature update—Part II. *Family Planning Perspectives, 24,* 122–127.

Cates, W., Jr., & Wasserheit, J. N. (1991). Genital chlamydial infections: Epidemiology and reproductive sequelae. *American Journal of Obstetrics and Gynecology, 164,* 1171–1181.

CBS News. (1991, May 22). *48 hours: For better or worse.*

Celis, W. (1991, January 2). Students trying to draw line between sex and an assault. *The New York Times,* pp. 1, B8.

Centers for Disease Control. (1985). Chlamydia trachomatis infections. *Morbidity and Mortality Weekly Report, 34,* 53.

Centers for Disease Control. (1989a). Summaries of identifiable diseases in the United States.

Centers for Disease Control. (1989b). Treatment guidelines for sexually transmitted diseases. *Morbidity and Mortality Weekly Report, 38,* No. S-8.

Centers for Disease Control. (1990a). Progress toward achieving the 1990 objectives for the nation for sexually transmitted diseases. *Morbidity and Mortality Weekly Report 39,* 53–57.

Centers for Disease Control. (1990b). Update: Acquired immunodeficiency syndrome—United States, 1989. *Journal of the American Medical Association, 263,* 1191–1192.

Centers for Disease Control, Division of Sexually Transmitted Diseases/HIV Prevention. (1991b). *Annual Report.* Atlanta: Author.

Centers for Disease Control. (1992, January). *HIV infection and AIDS: Are you at risk?* Atlanta: Author.

Centers for Disease Control. (1993a). Evaluation of surveillance for *Chlamydia trachomatis* infections in the United States, 1987 to 1991. *Mortality and Morbidity Weekly Report, 42* (SS-3), 21–27.

Centers for Disease Control. (1993b). Selected behaviors that increase risk for HIV infection, other sexually transmitted diseases, and unintended pregnancy among high school students—United States, 1991. *Mortality and Morbidity Weekly Report, 41,* 945–950.

Centers for Disease Control. AIDS Hotline Communication. (1996). April 1, 1996.

Centers for Disease Control and Prevention. (1996, September 1). AIDS Hotline.

Chan, C. (1992). Cultural considerations in counseling Asian American lesbians and gay men. In S. Dworkin & F. Gutierrez (Eds.), *Counseling gay men and lesbians: Journey to the end of the rainbow.* Alexandria, VA: American Association for Counseling and Development.

Chance of breast cancer is figured at 1 in 8. (1992, September 27). *The New York Times,* p. A30.

Charny, I. W., & Parnass, S. (1995). The impact of extramarital relationships on the continuation of marriages. *Journal of Sex and Marital Therapy, 21,* 100–115.

Cheating going out of style but sex is popular as ever. (1993, October 19). *New York Newsday,* p. 2.

Check, J. V. P., & Malamuth, N. M. (1983). Sex-role stereotyping and reactions to depictions of stranger versus acquaintance rape. *Journal of Personality and Social Psychology, 45,* 344–356.

Choi, P. Y. (1992). The psychological benefits of physical exercise: Implications for women and the menstrual cycle. [Special issue: The menstrual cycle]. *Journal of Reproductive and Infant Psychology, 10,* 111–115.

Clark, M. S., et al. (1989). Keeping track of needs and inputs of friends and strangers. *Personality and Social Psychology Bulletin, 15,* 533–542.

Clumeck, N. (1995). Primary prophylaxis against opportunistic infections in patients with AIDS. *New England Journal of Medicine, 332,* 739–740.

Cobb, M., & Jallon, J. M. (1990). Pheromones, mate recognition and courtship stimulation in the *Drosophila melanogaster* species sub-group. *Animal Behaviour, 39,* 1058–1067.

Colditz, G. A., et al. (1995). The use of estrogens and progestins and the risk of breast cancer in postmenopausal women. *New England Journal of Medicine, 332,* 1589–1593.

Cole, S. S. (1988). Women's sexuality, and disabilities. *Women and Therapy, 7,* 277–294.

Coleman, E. (1989). The development of male prostitution activity among gay and bisexual adolescents [Special issue: Gay and lesbian youth]. *Journal of Homosexuality, 17,* 131–149.

Coleman, M., & Ganong, L. H. (1985). Love and sex role stereotypes: Do macho men and feminine women make better lovers? *Journal of Personality and Social Psychology, 49,* 170–176.

Coles, C. (1994). Critical periods for prenatal alcohol exposure: Evidence from animal and human studies. *Alcohol Health and Research World, 18*(1), 22–29.

Coles, R., & Stokes, G. (1985). *Sex and the American teenager.* New York: Harper & Row.

Collaer, M. L., & Hines, M. (1995). Human behavioral sex differences: A role for gonadal hormones during early development? *Psychological Bulletin, 118,* 55–107.

Collins, G., & Kinder, B. (1984). Adjustment following surgical implantation of a penile prosthesis: A critical overview. *Journal of Sex and Marital Therapy, 10,* 255–271.

Collins, N. L., & Miller, L. C. (1994). Self-disclosure and liking: A meta-analytic review. *Psychological Bulletin, 116,* 457–475.

Condon, J. W., & Crano, W. D. (1988). Inferred evaluation and the relation between attitude similarity and interpersonal attraction. *Journal of Personality and Social Psychology, 54,* 789–797.

Connor, E. M., et al. (1994). Reduction of maternal–infant transmission of human immunodeficiency virus type 1 with zidovudine treatment. *New England Journal of Medicine, 331,* 1173–1180.

Consumer's Union. (1995, May). Consumer reports: How reliable are condoms? America Online.

Cooper, A. J. (1986). Progestogens in the treatment of male sex offenders: A review. *Canadian Journal of Psychiatry, 31,* 73–79.

Cooper, A. J., et al. (1990). A female sex offender with multiple paraphilias: A psychologic, physiologic (laboratory sexual arousal) and endocrine case study. *Canadian Journal of Psychiatry, 35,* 334–337.

Cooper, D. A., et al. (1993). Zidovudine in persons with asymptomatic HIV infection and CD4 cell counts greater than 400 per cubic millimeter. *New England Journal of Medicine, 329,* 297–303.

Corey, L., & Holmes, K. K. (1996). Therapy for HIV infection—What have we learned? *New England Journal of Medicine, 335,* 1142–1144.

Cosgray, R. E., et al. (1991). Death from auto-erotic asphyxiation in a long-term psychiatric setting. *Perspectives in Psychiatric Care, 27,* 21–24.

Cox, D. J. (1988). Incidence and nature of male genital exposure behavior as reported by college women. *Journal of Sex Research, 24,* 227–234.

Cronin, A. (1993, June 27). Two viewfinders, two views of Gay America. *The New York Times,* Section 4, p. 10.

Crum, C., & Ellner, P. (1985). Chlamydia infections: Making the diagnosis. *Contemporary Obstetrics and Gynecology, 25,* 153–159, 163, 165, 168.

Cunningham, M. R., et al. (1995). "Their ideas of beauty are, on the whole, the same as ours": Consistency and variability in the cross-cultural perception of female physical attractiveness. *Journal of Personality and Social Psychology, 68*(2), 261–279.

Curtis, R. C., & Miller, K. (1986). Believing another likes or dislikes you: Behavior making the beliefs come true. *Journal of Personality and Social Psychology, 51,* 284–290.

Cutrona, C. E. (1983). Causal attributions and perinatal depression. *Journal of Abnormal Psychology, 92,* 161–172.

Dabbs, J. M., Jr., & Morris, R. (1990). Testosterone, social class, and antisocial behavior in a sample of 4,462 men. *Psychological Science, 1,* 1–3.

Darabi, K. F., et al. (1986). Hispanic adolescent fertility. *Hispanic Journal of Behavioral Sciences, 8,* 157–171.

Darling, C. A., et al. (1991). The female sexual response revisited: Understanding the multiorgasmic experience in women. *Archives of Sexual Behavior, 20,* 527–540.

DATTA (Diagnostic and Theapeutic Technology Assessment). (1988). Questions and answers: Penile implants for erectile impotence. *Journal of the American Medical Association, 260,* 997–1000.

Davenport, W. (1977). Sex in cross-cultural perspective. In F. Beach (Ed.), *Human sexuality in four perspectives* (pp. 115–163). Baltimore: Johns Hopkins University Press.

Davidson, J. K., & Hoffman, L. E. (1986). Sexual fantasies and sexual satisfaction: An empirical analysis of erotic thought. *Journal of Sex Research, 22,* 184–205.

Davidson, K. J., et al. (1989). The role of the Grafenberg spot and female ejaculation in the female orgasmic response: An empirical analysis. *Journal of Sex and Marital Therapy, 15,* 102–119.

Davidson, N. E. (1995). Hormone-replacement therapy—breast versus heart versus bone. *New England Journal of Medicine, 332,* 1638–1639.

Davies, P. T., & Cummings, E. M. (1994). Marital conflict and child adjustment. *Psychological Bulletin, 116,* 387–411.

Davis, J. A., & Smith, T. (1987). *General social surveys, 1972–1987: Cumulative data.* Storrs, CT: University of Connecticut, Roper Center for Public Opinion Research.

Dawes, R. M. (1989). Statistical criteria for establishing a truly false consensus effect. *Journal of Experimental Social Psychology, 25,* 1–17.

Day, N. L., & Richardson, G. A. (1994). Comparative teratogenicity of alcohol and other drugs. *Alcohol Health and Research World, 18*(1), 42–48.

Deaux, K. (1985). Sex and gender. *Annual Review of Psychology, 36,* 49–81.

Deaux, K., & Lewis, L. L. (1983). Assessment of gender stereotypes: Methodology and components. *Psychological Documents, 13,* 25 (Ms. No. 2583).

Defense dept. suspends its policy on homosexuals. (1993, October 8). *The New York Times,* p. A25.

Dekker, J. (1993). Inhibited male orgasm. In W. O'Donohue & J. H. Geer (Eds.), *Handbook of sexual dysfunctions: Assessment and treatment* (pp. 279–301). Boston: Allyn & Bacon.

Del Priore, G., et al. (1995). Risk of ovarian cancer after treatment for infertility. *New England Journal of Medicine, 332,* 1300.

de Luca, R. V., et al. (1992). Group treatment for child sexual abuse [Special issue: Violence and its aftermath]. *Canadian Psychology, 33,* 168–179.

Denny, N., et al. (1984). Sex differences in sexual needs and desires. *Archives of Sexual Behavior, 13,* 233–245.

de Raad, B., & Doddema-Winsemius, M. (1992). Factors in the assortment of human mates: Differential preferences in Germany and the Netherlands. *Personality and Individual Differences, 13,* 103–114.

Desmond, A. M. (1994). Adolescent pregnancy in the United States: Not a minority issue. *Health Care for Women International, 15* (4), 325–331.

Deutsch, F. M., et al. (1987). What is in a smile? *Psychology of Women Quarterly, 11,* 341–352.

de Young, M. (1982). *The sexual victimization of children.* Jefferson, NC: McFarland & Company.

Dick-Read, G. (1944). *Childbirth without fear: The principles and practices of natural childbirth.* New York: Harper & Bros.

Dietz, P. E., et al. (1990). The sexually sadistic criminal and his offenses. *Bulletin of the American Academy of Psychiatry and the Law, 18,* 163–178.

DiMatteo, M. R., et al. (1996). Cesarean childbirth and psychosocial outcomes: A meta-analysis. *Health Psychology, 15,* 303–314.

Dindia, K., & Allen, M. (1992). Sex differences in self-disclosure: A meta-analysis. *Psychological Bulletin, 112,* 106–124.

Doctors tie male mentality to shorter life span. (1995, June 14). *The New York Times,* p. C14.

Donnerstein, E. I., & Linz, D. G. (1987). *The question of pornography.* New York: The Free Press.

Drews, C. D., et al. (1996, April). *Pediatrics.* Cited in "Smokers more likely to bear retarded babies, study says." (1996, April 10). *The New York Times,* p. B7.

Dube, R., & Hebert, M. (1988). Sexual abuse of children 12 years of age: A review of 511 cases. *Child Abuse and Neglect, 12,* 321–330.

Duffy, S. M., & Rusbult, C. E. (1985/1986). Satisfaction and commitment in homosexual and heterosexual relationships. *Journal of Homosexuality, 12,* 1–24.

Dugger, C. W. (1996a, September 11). A refugee's body is intact but her family is torn. *The New York Times,* pp. A1, B6.

Dugger, C. W. (1996b, October 12). New law bans genital cutting in the United States. *The New York Times,* pp. A1, A28.

Dunn, M. E., & Trost, J. E. (1989). Male multiple orgasms: A descriptive study. *Archives of Sexual Behavior, 18,* 377–387.

DuRant, R. H., & Sanders, J. M. (1989). Sexual behavior and contraceptive risk taking among sexually active adolescent females. *Journal of Adolescent Health Care, 10,* 1–19.

Dwyer, M. (1988). Exhibitionism/voyeurism. *Journal of Social Work and Human Sexuality, 7,* 101–112.

Dziech, B. W., & Weiner, L. (1984). *The lecherous professor: Sexual harassment on campus.* Boston: Beacon Press.

Early prostate surgery is found very effective. (1996, August 28). *The New York Times,* p. C9.

Edgley, C. (1989). Commercial sex: Pornography, prostitution, and advertising. In K. McKinney & S. Sprecher (Eds.), *Human sexuality: The societal and interpersonal context* (pp. 370–424). Norwood, NJ: Ablex Publishing Corporation.

Edmonson, B. (1988). Disability and sexual adjustment. In V. B. Van Hasselt, et al. (Eds.), *Handbook of developmental and physical disabilities* (pp. 91–106). New York: Pergamon Press.

Eggert, A. K., & Muller, J. K. (1989). Mating success of pheromone-emitting necrophorus males: Do attracted females discriminate against resource owners? *Behaviour, 110,* 248–257.

Ehrlich, G. (1988, March). Sexual concerns of patients with arthritis. *Medical Aspects of Human Sexuality, 10,* 281–300.

Eisen, M., & Zellman, G. (1987). Changes in incidence of sexual intercourse of unmarried teenagers following a community-based sex education program. *Journal of Sex Research, 23,* 527–544.

Ellis, A. (1962). *Reason and emotion in psychotherapy.* New York: Lyle Stuart.

Ellis A. (1977). The basic clinical theory of rational–emotive therapy. In A. Ellis & R. Grieger (eds.), *Handbook of rational–emotive therapy.* New York: Springer.

Ellis, L., & Ames, M. A. (1987). Neurohormonal functioning and sexual orientation: A theory of homosexuality–heterosexuality. *Psychological Bulletin, 101,* 233–258.

Elmer-Dewitt, P. (1991, September 30). Making babies. *Time,* 56–63.

Emmanuel, N. P., et al. (1992). Fluoxetine treatment of voyeurism. *American Journal of Psychiatry, 148,* 950.

Ember, C. R., & Ember, M. (1990). *Anthropology* (6th ed., instructor's edition). Englewood Cliffs, NJ: Prentice-Hall.

English, P. B., & Eskenazi, B. (1992). Reinterpreting the effects of maternal smoking on infant birthweight and perinatal mortality: A multivariate approach to birthweight standardization. *International Journal of Epidemiology, 21,* 1097–1105.

Erel, O., & Burman, B. (1995). Interrelatedness of marital relations and parent–child relations: A meta-analytic review. *Psychological Bulletin, 118,* 108–132.

Erlanger, S. (1991, July 14). A plague awaits. *The New York Times Magazine,* pp. 24, 26, 49, 53.

Eskenazi, G. (1990, June 3). The male athlete and sexual assault. *The New York Times,* pp. L1, L4.

Etaugh, C., & Rathus, S. A. (1995). *The world of children.* Fort Worth, TX: Harcourt Brace College Publishers.

Everaerd, W. (1993). Male erectile disorder. In W. O'Donohue & J. H. Geer (Eds.), *Handbook of sexual dysfunctions: Assessment and treatment* (pp. 201–224). Boston: Allyn & Bacon.

Everson, S. A., et al. (1995). Effects of surgical menopause on psychological characteristics and lipid levels: The healthy women study. *Health Psychology, 14,* 435–443.

Exner, J. E., et al. (1977). Some psychological characteristics of prostitutes. *Journal of Personality Assessment, 41,* 474–485.

Faller, K. C. (1989a). The role relationship between victim and perpetrator as a predictor of characteristics of intrafamilial sexual abuse. *Child and Adolescent Social Work Journal, 6,* 217–229.

Faller, K. C. (1989b). Why sexual abuse? An exploration of the intergenerational hypothesis. *Child Abuse and Neglect, 13,* 543–548.

Fallon, A. E., & Rozin, P. (1985). Sex differences in perceptions of desirable body shape. *Journal of Abnormal Psychology, 94,* 102–105.

Federal Bureau of Investigation. (1991). *Uniform crime reports.* Washington, DC: U.S. Department of Justice.

Federman, D. D. (1994). Life without estrogen. *New England Journal of Medicine, 331,* 1088–1089.

Feingold, A. (1991). Sex differences in the effects of similarity and physical attractiveness on opposite-sex attraction. *Basic and Applied Social Psychology, 12,* 357–367.

Feingold, A. (1994). Gender differences in personality: A meta-analysis. *Psychological Bulletin, 116,* 429–456.

Felsman, D., et al. (1987). Control theory in dealing with adolescent sexuality and pregnancy. *Journal of Sex Education and Therapy, 13,* 15–16.

Feng, T. (1993). Substance abuse in pregnancy. *Current Opinions in Obstetrics and Gynecology, 5,* 16–23.

Fenichel, O. (1945). *The psychoanalytic theory of neurosis.* New York: Norton.

Fensterheimn, H., & Kantor, J. S. (1980). Behavioral approach to sexual disorders. In B. Wolman & J. Money (Eds.), *Handbook of human sexuality.* Englewood Cliffs, NJ: Prentice-Hall.

Ferrante, C. L., et al. (1988). Image of women in television advertising. *Journal of Broadcasting and Electronic Media, 32,* 231–237.

Fichner-Rathus, L. (1995). *Understanding art* (4th ed.). Englewood Cliffs, NJ: Prentice Hall.

Finkelhor, D. (1984). *Child sexual abuse: Theory and research.* New York: The Free Press.

Finkelhor, D. (1988). The trauma of child sexual abuse: Two models. In G. E. Wyatt & G. J. Powell (Eds.), *The lasting effects of child sexual abuse* (pp. 61–82). Newburg Park, CA: Sage.

Finkelhor, D. (1990). Early and long-term effects of child sexual abuse: An update. *Professional Psychology: Research and Practice, 21,* 325–330.

Finkelhor, D., & Yllo, K. (1982). Rape in marriage: A sociological view. In D. Finkelhor, et al. (Eds.), *The dark side of families: Current family violence research* (pp. 119–130). Beverly Hills, CA: Sage.

Finkelhor, D., et al. (1990). Sexual abuse in a national survey of adult men and women: Prevalence, characteristics, and risk factors. *Child Abuse and Neglect, 14,* 19–28.

Fish, L. S., et al. (1994). Structural couple therapy in the treatment of inhibited sexual drive. *American Journal of Family Therapy, 22*(2), 113–125.

Fisher, B., et al. (1982). *Report on adolescent male prostitution.* San Francisco: Urban and Rural Systems Associates.

Fisher, W. A., et al. (1995). Understanding and promoting AIDS-preventive behavior: Insights from the theory of reasoned action. *Health Psychology, 14,* 255–264.

Fitzgerald, L. F. (1993a). *Sexual harassment in higher education: Concepts and issues.* Washington, DC: National Education Association.

Fitzgerald, L. F. (1993b). Sexual harassment: Violence against women in the workplace. *American Psychologist, 48,* 1070–1076.

Floyd, R. L., et al. (1993). A review of smoking in pregnancy: Effects on pregnancy outcomes and cessation efforts. *Annual Review of Public Health, 14,* 379–411.

Ford, C. S., & Beach, F. A. (1951). *Patterns of sexual behavior.* New York: Harper & Row.

Forrest, J. D., & Fordyce, R. R. (1993). Women's contraceptive attitudes and use in 1992. *Family Planning Perspectives, 25,* 175–179.

Forster, P., & King, J. (1994). Fluoxetine for premature ejaculation. *American Journal of Psychiatry, 151*(10), 1523.

Franzoi, S. L., & Herzog, M. E. (1987). Judging physical attractiveness: What body aspects do we use? *Personality and Social Psychology Bulletin, 13,* 19–33.

Fraser, A. M., et al. (1995). Association of young maternal age with adverse reproductive outcomes. *New England Journal of Medicine, 332,* 1113–1117.

Frayser, S. (1985). *Varieties of sexual experience: An anthropological perspective on human sexuality.* New Haven: Human Relations Area Files Press.

Frazier, P. A. (1990). Victim attributions and post-rape trauma. *Journal of Personality and Social Psychology, 59,* 298–304.

Freiberg, P. (1995). Psychologists examine attacks on homosexuals. *APA Monitor, 26*(6), 30–31.

Freiberg, P. (1996). New drugs give hope to AIDS patients. *APA Monitor, 27*(6), 28.

Freud, S. (1922/1959). Analysis of a phobia in a 5-year-old boy. In A. & J. Strachey (Ed. & Trans.), *Collected papers* (Vol. 3). New York: Basic Books. (Original work published 1909.)

Freund, J., & Blanchard, R. (1986). The concept of courtship disorder. *Journal of Sex and Marital Therapy, 12,* 79–92.

Freund, K., et al. (1988). The value of self-reports in the study of voyeurism and exhibitionism. *Annals of Sex Research, 1,* 243–262.

Freund, M., et al. (1989). Sexual behavior of resident street prostitutes with their clients in Camden, New Jersey. *Journal of Sex Research, 26,* 460–478.

Fried, P. A. (1986). Marijuana use in pregancy. In I. J. Chasnott (Ed.), *Drug use in pregancy: Mother and child.* Boston: MTP Press.

Friedman, L. C., et al. (1994). Dispositional optimism, self-efficacy, and health beliefs as predictors of breast self-examination. *American Journal of Preventive Medicine, 10* (3), 130–135.

Friedman, R. C., & Downey, J. I. (1994). Homosexuality. *New England Journal of Medicine, 331,* 923–930.

Friedrich, E. (1985). Vaginitis. *American Journal of Obstetrics and Gynecology, 152,* 247–251.

Friedrich, W. N., & Gerber, P. N. (1994). Autoerotic asphyxia: The development of a paraphilia. *Journal of the American Academy of Child and Adolescent Psychiatry, 33*(7), 970–974.

Frisch, R. E. (1983). Fatness, puberty and fertility: The effects of nutrition and physical training on menarche and ovulation. In J. Brooks-Gunn & A. C. Petersen (Eds.), *Girls at puberty: Biological and psychosocial aspects.* New York: Plenum.

Fuchs, C. S., et al. (1995). Alcohol consumption and mortality among women. *New England Journal of Medicine, 332,* 1245–1250.

Furnham, A., & Voli, V. (1989). Gender stereotypes in Italian television advertisements. *Journal of Broadcasting and Electronic Media, 33,* 175–185.

Furstenberg, F. F., Jr., et al. (1989). Teenaged pregnancy and childbearing. *American Psychologist, 44,* 313–320.

Gabriel, T. (1995a, April 23). When one spouse is gay and a marriage unravels. *The New York Times,* pp. A1, A22.

Gabriel, T. (1995b, June 12). A new generation seems ready to give bisexuality a place in the spectrum. *The New York Times,* p. A12.

Gagnon, J. H. (1977). *Human sexualities.* Glenview, IL: Scott, Foresman.

Gagnon, J. H. (1990). Gender preferences in erotic relations: The Kinsey scale and sexual scripts. In D. P. McWhirter, et al. (Eds.), *Homosexuality/heterosexuality: Concepts of sexual orientation* (pp. 177–207). New York: Oxford University Press.

Gagnon, J. H., & Simon, W. (1973). *Sexual conduct: The social origins of human sexuality.* Chicago: Aldine.

Gagnon, J. H., & Simon, W. (1987). The sexual scripting of oral genital contacts. *Archives of Sexual Behavior, 16,* 1–25.

Ganitsch, C. (1992, January 14). Personal communication.

Garber, M. (1995). *Vice versa.* New York: Simon & Schuster.

Garland, S. M., et al. (1990). Chlamydia trachomatis: Role in tubal infertility. *Australian and New Zealand Journal of Obstetrics and Gynaecology, 30,* 83–86.

Garnets, L., & Kimmel, D. (1991). In J. D. Goodchilds (Ed.). *Psychological perspectives on human diversity in America.* Washington, DC: American Psychological Association.

Garwood, S. G., et al. (1980). Beauty is only "name deep": The effect of first name in ratings of physical attraction. *Journal of Applied Social Psychology, 10,* 431–435.

Gayle, J., et al. (1990). Surveillance for AIDS and HIV infection among Black and Hispanic children and women of childbearing age, 1981–1989. *Morbidity and Mortality Weekly Report: Progress in Chronic Disease Prevention, 39,* 23–29. Washington, DC: U.S. Department of Health and Human Services.

Gebhard, P. H. (1976). The institute. In M. S. Weinberg (Ed.), *Sex research: Studies from the Kinsey Institute.* New York: Oxford University Press.

Gebhard, P. H. (1977). *Memorandum on the incidence of homosexuals in the United States.* Bloomington, IN: Indiana University Institute for Sex Research.

Gebhard, P. H., et al. (1965). *Sex offenders: An analysis of types.* New York: Harper & Row.

Geer, J., et al. (1984). *Human sexuality.* Englewood Cliffs, NJ: Prentice-Hall.

Geiger, R. (1981). Neurophysiology of sexual response in spinal cord injury. In D. Bullard & S. Knight (Eds.), *Sexuality and physical disability: Personal perspectives.* St. Louis: C. V. Mosby.

Gelles, R. J., & Cornell, C. P. (1985). *Intimate violence in families.* Beverly Hills, CA: Sage.

Gelman, D., with P. Kandell. (1993, January 18). Isn't it romantic? *Newsweek,* 60–61.

Genes that protect against AIDS. (1996, August 14). *The New York Times,* p. A18.

Genuis, M., et al. (1991, Fall). Male victims of child sexual abuse: A brief overview of pertinent findings [Special issue: Child sexual abuse]. *Journal of Child and Youth-Care,* 1–6.

Gerrol, R., & Resick, P. A. (1988, November). *Sex differences in social support and recovery from victimization.* Paper presented at the meeting of the Association for Advancement of Behavior Therapy, New York, NY.

Gibbs, N. (1991, June 3). When is it rape? *Time,* 48–54.

Gibson, A. I., et al. (1988). Adolescent female prostitutes. *Archives of Sexual Behavior, 17,* 431–438.

Gidycz, C. A., & Koss, M. P. (1990). A comparison of group and individual sexual assault victims. *Psychology of Women Quarterly, 14,* 325–342.

Gilbert, S. (1996, September 25). No long-term link is found between pill and breast cancer. *The New York Times,* p. C9.

Gillis, J. S., & Avis, W. E. (1980). The male-taller norm in mate selection. *Personality and Social Psychology Bulletin, 6,* 396–401.

Giovannucci, E., et al. (1993a). A prospective cohort study of vasectomy and prostate cancer in U.S. men. *Journal of the American Medical Association, 269,* 873–877.

Giovannucci, E., et al. (1993b). A retrospective cohort study of vasectomy and prostate cancer in U.S. men. *Journal of the American Medical Association, 269,* 878–882.

Gitlin, M. J., & Pasnau, R. O. (1989). Psychiatric syndromes linked to reproductive function in women: A review of current knowledge. *American Journal of Psychiatry, 146,* 1413–1422.

Glass, S. P., & Wright, T. L. (1992). Justifications of extramarital relationships: The association between attitudes, behaviors, and gender. *Journal of Sex Research, 29,* 361–387.

Gold, S. R., & Gold, R. G. (1993). Sexual aversions: A hidden disorder. In W. O'Donohue & J. H. Geer (Eds.), *Handbook of sexual dysfunctions: Assessment and treatment* (pp. 83–102). Boston: Allyn & Bacon.

Goldberg, C. (1995, September 11). Sex slavery, Thailand to New York. *The New York Times,* pp. B1, B6.

Goldberg, L. H., et al. (1993). Longterm suppression of recurrent genital herpes with acyclovir. *Archives of Dermatology, 129,* 582–587.

Goldberg, M. (1987). Understanding hypersexuality in men and women. In G. R. Weeks and Larry Hof (Eds.), *Integrating sex and marital therapy: A clinical guide* (pp. 202–220). New York: Brunner/Mazel.

Goldenberg, R. L., & Klerman, L. V. (1995). Adolescent pregnancy—another look. *New England Journal of Medicine, 332,* 1161–1162.

Goldstein, A. M., & Clark, J. H. (1990). Treatment of uncomplicated gonococcal urethritis with single-dose ceftriaxone. *Sexually Transmitted Diseases, 17,* 181–183.

Golestein, I. (1987). Penile revascularization. *Urologic Clinics of North America, 14,* 805–813.

Goleman, D. (1991, October 22). Sexual harassment: It's about power, not lust. *The New York Times,* pp. C1, C12.

Goleman, D. (1992). Therapies offer hope for sex offenders. *The New York Times,* pp. C1, C11.

Goleman, D. (1993, October 6). Abuse-prevention efforts aid children. *The New York Times,* p. C13.

Goleman, D. (1995, June 14). Sex fantasy research said to neglect women. *The New York Times,* p. C14.

Gomez, J., & Smith, B. (1990). Taking the home out of homophobia: Black lesbian health. In E. C. White (Ed.), *The Black women's health book: Speaking for ourselves.* Seattle: Seal Press.

Gomez-Schwartz, B., et al. (1990). *Child sexual abuse: The initial effects.* Newbury Park, CA: Sage.

Goodwin, J. M., et al. (1990). Borderline and other severe symptoms in adult survivors of incestuous abuse. *Psychiatric Annals, 20,* 22–32.

Gordon, S., & Snyder, C. W. (1989). *Personal issues in human sexuality: A guidebook for better sexual health* (2nd ed.). Boston: Allyn & Bacon.

Gottlieb, M. S. (1991, June 5). AIDS—the second decade: Leadership is lacking. *The New York Times,* p. A29.

Graber, B. (1993). Medical aspects of sexual arousal disorders. In W. O'Donohue & J. H. Geer (Eds.), *Handbook of sexual dysfunctions: Assessment and treatment* (pp. 103–156). Boston: Allyn & Bacon.

Graca, L. M., et al. (1991). Acute effects of maternal cigarette smoking on fetal heart rate and fetal body movements felt by the mother. *Journal of Perinatal Medicine, 19,* 385–390.

Graham, J. M., & Blanco, J. D. (1990). Chlamydial infections. *Primary Care: Clinics in Office Practice, 17,* 85–93.

Graham, S., et al. (1982). Sex patterns and herpes simplex virus type 2 in the epidemiology of cancer of the cervix. *American Journal of Epidemiology, 115,* 729–735.

Green, R. (1978). Sexual identity of 37 children raised by homosexual or transsexual parents. *American Journal of Psychiatry, 135,* 692–697.

Greene, B. (1994). Ethnic-minority lesbians and gay men: Mental health and treatment issues. *Journal of Consulting and Clinical Psychology, 62,* 243–251.

Greenwald, E., & Leitenberg, H. (1989). Long-term effects of sexual experiences with siblings and non-siblings during childhood. *Archives of Sexual Behavior, 18,* 389–399.

Greenwald, E., et al. (1990). Childhood sexual abuse: Long-term effects on psychological and sexual functioning in a nonclinical and nonstudent sample of adult women. *Child Abuse and Neglect, 14,* 503–513.

Griffin, E., & Sparks, G. G. (1990). Friends forever: A longitudinal exploration of intimacy in same-sex friends and platonic pairs. *Journal of Social and Personal Relationships, 7,* 29–46.

Grodstein, F., et al. (1993). Relation of tubal infertility to history of sexually transmitted diseases. *American Journal of Epidemiology, 137,* 577–584.

Grodstein, F., et al. (1996). Postmenopausal estrogen and progestin use and the risk of cardiovascular disease. *New England Journal of Medicine, 335,* 453–461.

Grogger, J., & Bronars, S. (1993). The socioeconomic consequences of teenage childbearing: Findings from a natural experiment. *Family Planning Perspectives, 25,* 156–161.

Groneman, C. (1994). Nymphomania: The historical construction of female sexuality. *Signs, 19*(2), 337–367.

Groth, A. N. (1978). Patterns of sexual assault against children and adolescents. In A. W. Burgess, et al. (Eds.), *Sexual assault of children and adolescents.* Toronto: Lexington Books.

Groth, A. N., & Birnbaum, H. J. (1979). *Men who rape: The psychology of the offender.* New York: Plenum.

Groth, A. N., & Burgess, A. W. (1980). Male rape: Offenders and victims. *American Journal of Psychiatry, 137,* 806–810.

Groth, A. N., & Hobson, W. (1983). The dynamics of sexual assault. In L. Schlesinger & E. Revitch (Eds.), *Sexual dynamics of antisocial behavior.* Springfield, IL: Thomas.

Grych, J. H., & Fincham, F. D. (1993). Children's appraisals of marital conflict. *Child Development, 64,* 215–230.

Guinan, M. E. (1992). Cited in Leary, W. E. (1992, February 1). U.S. panel backs approval of first condom for women. *The New York Times,* p. 7.

Gupta, M. (1994). Sexuality in the Indian subcontinent. *Sexual and Marital Therapy, 9*(1), 57–69.

Haffner, D. (1993, August). *Sex education: Trends and issues.* Paper presented at the meeting of the American Psychological Association, Toronto, Canada.

Haglund, B., & Cnattingius, S. (1990). Cigarette smoking as a risk factor for sudden infant death syndrome: A population based study. *American Journal of Public Health, 80,* 29–32.

Hall, C. S. (1984). "A ubiquitous sex difference in dreams" revisited. *Journal of Personality and Social Psychology, 46,* 1109–1117.

Hall, G. C. N. (1989). Sexual arousal and arousability in a sexual offender population. *Journal of Abnormal Psychology, 98,* 145–149.

Hall, G. C. N., & Hirschman, R. (1991). Toward a theory of sexual aggression: A quadripartite model. *Journal of Consulting and Clinical Psychology, 59,* 662–669.

Hamer, D. H., et al. (1993, July 16). A linkage between DNA markers on the X chromosome and male sexual orientation. *Science, 261,* 321–327.

Hamilton, M., & Yee, J. (1990). Rape knowledge and propensity to rape. *Journal of Research in Personality, 24,* 111–122.

Hammer, S. M., et al. (1996). A trial comparing nucleoside monotherapy with combination therapy in HIV-infected adults with CD4 cell counts from 200 to 500 per cubic millimeter. *New England Journal of Medicine, 335,* 1081–1090.

Handler, A. (1990). The correlates of the initiation of sexual intercourse among young urban Black females. *Journal of Youth and Adolescence, 19,* 159–170.

Hanrahan, J. P., et al. (1992). The effect of maternal smoking during pregnancy on early infant lung function. *American Review of Respiratory Disease, 145,* 1129–1135.

Harding, J. J. (1989). Postpartum psychiatric disorders: A review. *Comprehensive Psychiatry, 30,* 109–112.

Harney P. A., & Muehlenhard, C. L. (1991). Rape. In E. Grauerholz & M. A. Koralewski (Eds.), *Sexual coercion: A sourcebook on its nature, causes, and prevention* (pp. 3–16). Lexington, MA: Lexington Books.

Hart, J., et al. (1991). Sexual behavior in pregnancy: A study of 219 women. *Journal of Sex Education and Therapy, 17,* 86–90.

Hartman, C. R., et al. (1987). Pathways and cycles of runaways: A model for understanding repetitive runaway behavior. *Hospital and Community Psychiatry, 38,* 292–299.

Harvey, S. (1987). Female sexual behavior: Fluctations during the menstrual cycle. *Journal of Psychosomatic Research, 31,* 101–110.

Hass, A. (1979). *Teenage sexuality.* New York: Macmillan.

Hatcher, R. A., et al. (1990). *Contraceptive technology 1990–1992* (15th rev. ed.). New York: Irvington Publishers.

Hatcher, R. A., et al. (1994). *Contraceptive technology 1992–1994* (16th rev. ed.). New York: Irvington Publishers.

Hatfield, E. (1988). Passionate and companionate love. In R. J. Sternberg & M. L. Barnes (Eds.), *The psychology of love* (pp. 191–217). New Haven: Yale University Press.

Hatfield, E., & Sprecher, S. (1986). Measuring passionate love in intimate relationships. *Journal of Adolescence, 9,* 383–410.

Hausknecht, R. U. (1995). Methotrexate and misoprostol to terminate early pregnancy. *New England Journal of Medicine, 333,* 537–540.

Havemann, E., & Lehtinen, M. (1990). *Marriages and families: New problems, new opportunities* (2nd ed.). Englewood Cliffs, NJ: Prentice-Hall.

Hawton, K., and Catalan, J. (1990). Sex therapy for vaginismus: Characteristics of couples and treatment outcomes. *Sexual and Marital Therapy, 5,* 39–48.

Hayes, C. D. (Ed.). (1987). *Risking the future* (Vol. 1). Washington, DC: National Academy Press.

Hazan, C., & Shaver, P. (1987). Love conceptualized as an attachment process. *Journal of Personality and Social Psychology, 52,* 511–524.

Hechtman, L. (1989). Teenage mothers and their children: Risks and problems: A review. *Canadian Journal of Psychiatry, 34,* 569–575.

Heiman, J. R., & LoPiccolo, J. (1987). *Becoming orgasmic* (2nd ed.). Englewood Cliffs, NJ: Prentice-Hall.

Hendrick, C., & Hendrick, S. S. (1986). A theory and method of love. *Journal of Personality and Social Psychology, 50,* 392–402.

Hendrick, S. S., et al. (1988). Romantic relationships, love, satisfaction, and staying together. *Journal of Personality and Social Psychology, 54,* 980–988.

Hensley, W. E. (1992). Why does the best-looking person in the room always seem to be surrounded by admirers? *Psychological Reports, 70,* 457–458.

Hensley, W. E. (1994). Height as a basis for interpersonal attraction. *Adolescence, 29,* 469–474.

Herdt, G. H. (1981). *Guardians of the flutes: Idioms of masculinity.* New York: McGraw-Hill.

Herzog, L. (1989). Urinary tract infections and circumcision. *American Journal of Diseases of Children, 143,* 348–350.

Hess, B. B., et al. (1993). *Sociology* (4th ed.). New York: Macmillan.

Hillier, S., & Holmes, K. K. (1990). Bacterial vaginosis. In K. K. Holmes, et al. (Eds.), *Sexually transmitted diseases* (2nd ed.) (pp. 547–560). New York: McGraw-Hill.

Hillier, S. L., et al. (1995). Association between baterial vaginosis and preterm delivery of a low-birth-weight infant. *The New England Journal of Medicine, 333* (26), 1737–1742.

Hilton, E., et al. (1992). Ingestion of yogurt containing *Lactobacillus acidophilus* as prophylaxis for candidal vaginitis. *Annals of Internal Medicine, 116,* 353–357.

Hite, S. (1976). *The Hite report.* New York: Macmillan.

Hoagwood, K. (1990). Blame and adjustment among women sexually abused as children. *Women and Therapy, 9,* 89–110.

Hodgson, R., et al. (1990). Chlamydia trachomatis: The prevalence, trend and importance in initial infertility management. *Australian and New Zealand Journal of Obstetrics and Gynaecology, 30,* 251–254

Hodson, D. S., & Skeen, P. (1994). Sexuality and aging: The hammerlock of myths. *Journal of Applied Gerontology, 13*(3), 219–235.

Hofferth, S. L., & Hayes, C. D. (Eds.). (1987). *Risking the future: Adolescent sexuality, pregnancy, and childbearing: Vol. 2. Working papers and statistical reports.* Washington, DC: National Academy Press.

Hoffman, J. (1993, January 10). The morning after pill: A well-kept secret. *The New York Times Sunday Magazine,* p. 12.

Holden, G. W., & Ritchie, K. L. (1991). Linking extreme marital discord, child rearing, and child behavior problems. *Child Development, 62,* 311–327.

Holzman, H. R., & Pines, S. (1982). Buying sex: The phenomenology of being a john. *Deviant Behavior, 4,* 89–116.

Howard, J. A., et al. (1987). Social or evolutionary theories: Some observations on preferences in mate selection. *Journal of Personality and Social Psychology, 53,* 194–200.

Howard, M., & McCabe, J. B. (1990). Helping teenagers postpone sexual involvement. *Family Planning Perspectives, 22,* 21–26.

Howards, S. S. (1995). Current concepts: Treatment of male infertility. *New England Journal of Medicine, 332,* 312–317.

Hsu, B., et al. (1994). Gender differences in sexual fantasy and behavior in a college population: A ten-year replication. *Journal of Sex and Marital Therapy, 20* (2), 103–118.

Hubbard, R., & Wald, E. (1993). *Exploding the gene myth.* Boston: Beacon Press.

Huffman, T., et al. (1994). Gender differences and factors related to the disposition toward cohabitation. *Family Therapy, 21*(3), 171–184.

Hunt, M. (1974). *Sexual behavior in the 1970's.* New York: Dell.

Hunter, D. J., et al. (1996). Cohort studies of fat intake and the risk of breast cancer–A pooled analysis. *New England Journal of Medicine, 334,* 356–361.

Hyde, J. S., & Linn, M. C. (1988). Gender differences in verbal ability: A meta-analysis. *Psychological Bulletin, 104,* 53–69.

Hyde, J. S., & Plant, E. A. (1995). Magnitude of psychological gender differences: Another side to the story. *American Psychologist, 50,* 159–161.

Hyde, J. S., et al. (1990). Gender differences in mathematics performance: A meta-analysis. *Psychological Bulletin, 107,* 139–155.

Imperato-McGinley, J., et al. (1974). Steroid 5 reductase deficiency in man: An inherited form of male pseudohermaphroditism. *Science, 186,* 1213–1215.

Injections approved for child molesters. (1996, August 31). *The New York Times,* p. L7.

Isay, R. A. (1990). Psychoanalytic theory and the therapy of gay men. In D. P. McWhirter, et al. (Eds.), *Homosexuality/heterosexuality: Concepts of sexual orientation* (pp. 283–303). New York: Oxford University Press.

Isay, R. A. (1993, April 23). Sex survey may say most about society's attitudes to gays [Letter]. *The New York Times,* Section 4, p. 16.

Jacklin, C. N., et al. (1984). Sex-typing behavior and sex-typing pressure in child–parent interaction. *Archives of Sexual Behavior, 13,* 413–425.

Jackson, J., et al. (1990). Young adult women who report childhood intrafamilial sexual abuse: Subsequent adjustment. *Archives of Sexual Behavior, 19,* 211–221.

Jackson, L. A., & Ervin, K. S. (1992). Height stereotypes of women and men: The liabilities of shortness for both sexes. *Journal of Social Psychology, 132,* 433–445.

Jacobson, J. L., & Jacobson, S. W. (1994). Prenatal alcohol exposure and neurobehavioral development: Where is the threshold? *Alcohol Health and Research World, 18*(1), 30–36.

Jamison, P. L., & Gebhard, P. H. (1988). Penis size increase between flaccid and erect states: An analysis of the Kinsey data. *Journal of Sex Research, 24,* 177–183.

Jankowiak, W. R., & Fischer, E. F. (1992). A cross-cultural perspective on romantic love. *Ethnology, 31,* 149–155.

Janus, S. S., & Janus, C. L. (1993). *The Janus report on sexual behavior.* New York: Wiley.

Jencks, C., & Mayer, S. E. (1990). Residential segregation, job proximity, and Black job opportunities. In L. E. Lynn and M. McGeary (Eds.), *Inner-city poverty in the United States.* Washington, DC: National Academy Press.

Job rights for homosexuals backed in poll. (1992, September 7). *The New York Times,* p. L10.

Johnson, K. A., & Williams, L. (1993). Risk of breast cancer in the nurses' health study: Applying the Gail model. *Journal of the American Medical Association, 270,* 2925–2926.

Jones, H. W., & Toner, J. P. (1993). The infertile couple. *New England Journal of Medicine, 329,* 1710–1715.

Jorgensen, S. R., et al. (1980). Dyadic and social network influences on adolescent exposure to pregnancy risk. *Journal of Marriage and the Family, 42,* 141–155.

Kalick, S. M. (1988). Physical attractiveness as a status cue. *Journal of Experimental Social Psychology, 24,* 469–489.

Kammeyer, K. C. W. (1990). *Marriage and family: A foundation for personal decisions* (2nd ed.). Boston: Allyn & Bacon.

Kammeyer, K. C. W., et al. (1990). *Sociology: Experiencing changing societies.* Boston: Allyn & Bacon.

Kantner, J. F., & Zelnik, M. (1972). Sexual experience of young unmarried women in the United States. *Family Planning Perspectives, 4,* 9–18.

Kantrowitz, B. (1990a, Summer/Fall Special Issue). High school homeroom. *Newsweek,* 50–54.

Kantrowitz, B. (1990b, Summer/Fall Special Issue). The push for sex education. *Newsweek,* 52.

Kaplan, D. (1993, January 18). The incorrigibles. *Newsweek,* 48–50.

Kaplan, H. S. (1974). *The new sex therapy: Active treatment of sexual dysfunctions.* New York: Brunner/Mazel.

Kaplan, H. S. (1987). *Sexual aversion, sexual phobias, and panic disorder.* New York: Brunner/Mazel.

Karney, B. R., & Bradbury, T. N. (1995). The longitudinal course of marital quality and stability: A review of theory, method, and research. *Psychological Bulletin, 118,* 3–34.

Katz, J. N. (1995). *The invention of heterosexuality.* New York: Dutton.

Katz, R. C. (1990). Psychosocial adjustment in adolescent child molesters. *Child Abuse and Neglect, 14,* 567–575.

Katzenstein, D. A., et al. (1996). The relation of virologic and immunologic markers to clinical outcomes after nucleoside therapy in HIV-infected adults with 200 to 500 CD4 cells per cubic millimeter. *New England Journal of Medicine, 335,* 1091–1098.

Kedia, K. (1983). Ejaculation and emission: Normal physiology, dysfunction, and therapy. In R. J. Krane, et al. (Eds.), *Male sexual dysfunction* (pp. 37–54). Boston: Little, Brown.

Keith, J. B., et al. (1991). Sexual activity and contraceptive use among low-income urban Black adolescent females. *Adolescence, 26,* 769–785.

Kellerman, J., et al. (1989). Looking and loving: The effects of mutual gaze on feelings of romantic love. *Journal of Research in Personality, 23,* 145–161.

Kenney, A. M., et al. (1989). Sex education and AIDS education in the schools. *Family Planning Perspectives, 21,* 56–64.

Kerns, J. G., & Fine, M. A. (1994). The relation between gender and negative attitudes toward gay men and lesbians: Do gender role attitudes mediate this relation? *Sex Roles, 31*(5–6), 297–307.

Kettl, P., et al. (1991). Female sexuality after spinal cord injury. *Sexuality and Disability, 9,* 287–295.

Killmann, P. R., & Auerbach, R. (1979). Treatments of premature ejaculation and psychogenic impotence: A critical review of the literature. *Archives of Sexual Behavior, 8,* 81–100.

Killmann, P. R., et al. (1987). The treatment of secondary orgasmic dysfunction II. *Journal of Sex and Marital Therapy, 13,* 93–105.

Kilpatrick, D. G., et al. (1987, January). *Rape in marriage and dating relationships: How bad are they for mental health?* Paper presented at the meeting of the New York Academy of Science, New York, NY.

Kimlicka, T., et al. (1983). A comparison of androgynous, feminine, masculine, and undifferentiated women on self-esteem, body satisfaction, and sexual satisfaction. *Psychology of Women Quarterly, 1,* 291–294.

Kinard, E., & Reinherz, H. (1987). School aptitude and achievement in children of adolescent mothers. *Journal of Youth and Adolescence, 16,* 69–78.

King, L. (1988). Editorial comment in response to Wisell et al., 1987. *Journal of Urology, 139,* 883.

Kinloch-de Loes, S., et al. (1995). A controlled trial of zidovudine in primary human immunodeficiency virus infection. *New England Journal of Medicine, 333,* 408–413.

Kinsey, A. C., et al. (1948). *Sexual behavior in the human male.* Philadelphia: W. B. Saunders Co.

Kinsey, A. C., et al. (1953). *Sexual behavior in the human female.* Philadelphia: W. B. Saunders Co.

Knapp, M. L. (1978). *Social intercourse: A behavioral approach to counseling.* Champaign, IL: Research Press.

Knight, R. A., et al. (1991). *Antisocial personality disorder and Hare assessments of psychopathy among sexual offenders.* Manuscript in preparation.

Knight, S. E. (1989). Sexual concerns of the physically disabled. In B. W. Heller, et al. (Eds.), *Psychosocial interventions with physically disabled persons* (pp. 183–199). New Brunswick, NJ: Rutgers University Press.

Knox, D. (1988). *Choices in relationships.* St. Paul: West.

Knudsen, D. D. (1991). Child sexual coercion. In E. Grauerholz & M. A. Koralewski (Eds.), *Sexual coercion: A sourcebook on its nature, causes, and prevention* (pp. 17–28). Lexington, MA: Lexington Books.

Knussman, R., et al. (1986). Relations between sex hormone levels and sexual behavior in men. *Archives of Sexual Behavior, 15,* 429–445.

Kockott, G., & Fahrner, E. (1987). Transsexuals who have not undergone surgery: A follow-up study. *Archives of Sexual Behavior, 16,* 511–522.

Kohlberg, L. (1966). A cognitive–developmental analysis of children's sex-role concepts and attitudes. In E. E. Maccoby (Ed.),

The development of sex differences. Stanford, CA: Stanford University Press.

Kohn, A. (1987, February). Shattered innocence. *Psychology Today,* 54–58.

Komisar, L. (1971). The image of women in advertising. In V. Gornick & B. Moran (Eds.), *Women in sexist society.* New York: Basic Books.

Kon, I. S. (1995). *The sexual revolution in Russia.* New York: The Free Press.

Koss, M. P. (1988). Stranger and acquaintance rape: Are there differences in the victim's experience? *Psychology of Women Quarterly, 12,* 1–24.

Koss, M. P. (1993). Rape: Scope, impact, interventions, and public policy responses. *American Psychologist, 48,* 1062–1069.

Koss, M. P., et al. (1987). The scope of rape: Incidence and prevalence of sexual aggression and victimization in a national sample of higher education students. *Journal of Consulting and Clinical Psychology, 55,* 162–170.

Krafka, C. L. (1985). *Sexually explicit, sexually violent, and violent media: Effects of multiple naturalistic exposures and debriefing on female viewers.* Unpublished doctoral dissertation, University of Wisconsin-Madison.

Kresin, D. (1993). Medical aspects of inhibited sexual desire disorder. In W. O'Donohue & J. H. Geer (Eds.), *Handbook of sexual dysfunctions: Assessment and treatment* (pp. 15–52). Boston: Allyn & Bacon.

Kruesi, M. J. P., et al. (1992). Paraphilias: A double-blind crossover comparison of clomipramine versus desipramine. *Archives of Sexual Behavior, 21,* 587–594.

Kruks, G. (1991). Gay and lesbian homeless/street youth: Special issues and concerns [Special issue: Homeless youth]. *Journal of Adolescent Health, 12,* 515–518.

Kuhn, D., et al. (1978). Sex-role concepts of two- and three-year olds. *Child Development, 49,* 445–451.

Kuiper, B., & Cohen-Kettenis, P. (1988). Sex reassignment surgery: A study of 141 Dutch transsexuals. *Archives of Sexual Behavior, 17,* 439–457.

Kulin, H., et al. (1989). The onset of sperm production in pubertal boys. *American Journal of Diseases of Children, 143,* 190–193.

Laan, E., & Heiman, J. (1994). *Archives of Sexual Behavior.*

Lackritz, E. M., et al. (1995). Estimated risk of transmission of the human immunodeficiency virus by screened blood in the United States. *New England Journal of Medicine, 333,* 1721–1725.

Lamanna, M. A., & Riedmann, A. (1997). *Marriages and families,* 6th ed. Belmont, CA: Wadsworth.

Lamaze, F. (1981). *Painless childbirth.* New York: Simon & Schuster.

Lamke, L. K. (1982b). The impact of sex-role orientation on self-esteem in early adolescence. *Child Development, 53,* 1530–1535.

Lang, R. A., et al. (1989). An examination of sex hormones in genital exhibitionists. *Annals of Sex Research, 2,* 67–75.

Langevin, R., et al. (1985). Sexual aggression: Constructing a predictive equation. In R. Langevin (Ed.), *Erotic preference, gender identity, and aggression in men: New research studies* (pp. 39–76). Hillsdale, NJ: Erlbaum.

Langevin, R., et al. (1989). Characteristics of sex offenders who were sexually victimized as children. *Annals of Sex Research, 2,* 227–253.

LaTour, M. S. (1990). Female nudity in print advertising: An analysis of gender differences in arousal and ad response. *Psychology and Marketing, 7,* 65–81.

Laumann, E. O., et al. (1994). *The social organization of sexuality: Sexual practices in the United States.* Chicago: University of Chicago Press.

Laviola, M. (1989). Effects of older brother–younger sister incest: A review of four cases. *Journal of Family Violence, 4,* 259–274.

Lavoisier, P., et al. (1995). Clitoral blood flow increases following vaginal pressure stimulation. *Archives of Sexual Behavior, 24,* 37–45.

Lawrence, K., & Herold, E. S. (1988). Women's attitudes toward and experience with sexually explicit materials. *Journal of Sex Research, 24,* 161–169.

Leary, W. E. (1990, September 13). New focus on sperm brings fertility successes. *The New York Times,* p. B11.

Leary, W. E. (1992, December 10). Medical panel says most sexual impotence in men can be treated without surgery. *The New York Times,* p. D20.

Leary, W. E. (1993, April 28). Screening of all newborns urged for sickle cell disease. *The New York Times,* p. C11.

Ledray, L. E. (1990). Counseling rape victims: The nursing challenge. *Perspectives in Psychiatric Care, 26,* 21–27.

Lee, J. A. (1988). Love-styles. In R. J. Sternberg & M. L. Barnes (Eds.), *The psychology of love* (pp. 38–67). New Haven: Yale University Press.

Leiblum, S. R., & Rosen, R. C. (1991). Couples therapy for erectile disorders: Conceptual and clinical considerations [Special issue: The treatment of male erectile disorders]. *Journal of Sex and Marital Therapy, 17,* 147–159.

Leigh, B. C., et al. (1994). Sexual behavior of American adolescents: Results from a U.S. national survey. *Journal of Adolescent Health, 15* (2) 117–125.

Leitenberg, H., & Henning, K. (1995). Sexual fantasy. *Psychological Bulletin, 117,* 469–496.

Leitenberg, H., et al. (1989). The relation between sexual activity among children during preadolescence and/or early adolescence and sexual behavior and sexual adjustment in young adulthood. *Archives of Sexual Behavior, 18,* 299–313.

Leitenberg, H., et al. (1993). Gender differences in masturbation and the relation of masturbation experience in preadolescence and/or early adolescence to sexual behavior and sexual adjustment in young adulthood. *Archives of Sexual Behavior, 22,* 87–98.

Leland, N. L., & Barth, R. P. (1992). Gender differences in knowledge, intentions, and behaviors concerning pregnancy and sexually transmitted disease prevention among adolescents. *Journal of Adolescent Health, 13,* 589–599.

Lemon, S. J., & Newbold, J. E. (1990). Viral hepatitis. In K. K. Holmes, et al. (Eds.), *Sexually transmitted diseases* (2nd ed.) (pp. 449–466). New York: McGraw-Hill.

Lenihan, G., et al. (1992). Gender differences in rape supportive attitudes before and after a date rape education intervention. *Journal of College Student Development, 33,* 331–338.

Lesnik-Oberstein, M., & Cohen, L. (1984). Cognitive style, sensation seeking, and assortive mating. *Journal of Personality and Social Psychology, 46,* 57–66.

Letourneau, E., & O'Donohue, W. (1993). Sexual desire disorders. In W. O'Donohue & J. H. Geer (Eds.), *Handbook of sexual dysfunctions: Assessment and treatment.* (pp. 53–81). Boston: Allyn & Bacon.

LeVay, S. (1991). A difference in hypothalamic structure between heterosexual and homosexual men. *Science, 253,* 1034–1037.

Lever, J., et al. (1992). Behavior patterns and sexual identity of bisexual males. *Journal of Sex Research, 29,* 141–167.

Levine, G. I. (1991). Sexually transmitted parasitic diseases. *Primary Care: Clinics in Office Practice, 18,* 101–128.

Levinger, G. (1980). Toward the analysis of close relationships. *Journal of Experimental Social Psychology, 16,* 510–544.

Levy, D. S. (1991, September 16). Why Johnny might grow up violent and sexist. *Time,* 16–19.

Levy, J. (1985). Right brain, left brain: Fact and fiction. *Psychology Today, 19,* (5), 38–44.

Lewin, T. (1991, February 8). Studies on teen-age sex cloud condom debate. *The New York Times,* p. A14.

Libman, E., et al. (1985). The role of therapeutic format in the treatment of sexual dysfunction: A review. *Clinical Psychology Review, 5,* 103–117.

Lief, H. I., & Hubschman, L. (1993). Orgasm in the postoperative transsexual. *Archives of Sexual Behavior, 22,* 145–155.

Lipshultz, L. I. (1996). Injection therapy for erectile dysfunction. *New England Journal of Medicine, 334,* 913–914.

Linsley, W. A. (1989). The case against censorship of pornography. In D. Zillmann & J. Bryant (Eds.), *Pornography: Research advances and policy considerations* (pp. 343–359). Hillsdale, NJ: Erlbaum.

Linz, D., et al. (1988). The effects of long-term exposure to violent and sexually degrading depictions of women. *Journal of Personality and Social Psychology, 55,* 758–767.

Lohr, J. (1989). The foreskin and urinary tract infections. *Journal of Pediatrics, 114,* 502–504.

LoPiccolo, J. (1994). The evolution of sex therapy. *Sexual and Marital Therapy, 9*(1), 5–7.

LoPiccolo, J., & Friedman, J. (1988). Broad-spectrum treatment of low sexual desire: Integration of cognitive, behavioral, and systemic therapy. In S. Leiblum & R. Rosen (Eds.), *Sexual desire disorders.* New York: Guilford Press.

LoPiccolo, J., & Stock, W. E. (1986). Treatment of sexual dysfunction. *Journal of Consulting and Clinical Psychology, 54,* 158–167.

Lorefice, L. S. (1991). Fluoxetine treatment of a fetish. *Journal of Clinical Psychiatry, 52.*

Lottes, I. L., & Kuriloff, P. J. (1992). The effects of gender, race, religion, and political orientation on the sex role attitudes of college freshmen. *Adolescence, 27,* 675–688.

Lovdal, L. T. (1989). Sex role messages in television commercials: An update. *Sex Roles, 21,* 715–724.

Lown, J., & Dolan, E. (1988). Financial challenges in remarriage. *Lifestyles: Family and Economic Issues, 9,* 73–88.

Luckenbill, D. F. (1985). Entering male prostitution. *Urban Life, 14,* 131–153.

Lundstrom, B., et al. (1984). Outcome of sex reassignment surgery. *Acta Psychiatrica Scandinavica, 70,* 289–294.

Maccoby, E. E. (1990). Gender and relationships: A developmental account. *American Psychologist, 45,* 513–520.

Maccoby, E. E., & Jacklin, C. N. (1974). *The psychology of sex differences.* Stanford, CA: Stanford University Press.

MacFarquhar, N. (1996, August 8). Mutilation of Egyptian girls: Despite ban, it goes on. *The New York Times,* p. A3.

Malamuth, N. M. (1981). Rape proclivity among males. *Journal of Social Issues, 37,* 138–157.

Malamuth, N. M. (1984). Aggression against women: Cultural and individual causes. In N. M. Malamuth & E. Donnerstein (Eds.), *Pornography and sexual aggression* (pp. 19–52). Orlando, FL: Academic Press.

Malamuth, N. M., & Ceniti, J. (1986). Repeated exposure to violent and nonviolent pornography: Likelihood of raping ratings and laboratory aggression against women. *Aggressive Behavior, 12,* 129–137.

Male birth control. (1995, August 1). *New York Newsday,* p. B31.

Maletzky, B. M. (1980). Self-referred vs. court-referred sexually deviant patients: Success with assisted covert sensitization. *Behavior Therapy, 11,* 306–314.

Malinowski, B. (1929). *The sexual life of savages in north-western Melanesia.* New York: Eugenics.

Malloy, M. H., et al. (1992). Sudden infant death syndrome and maternal smoking. *American Journal of Public Health, 82,* 1380–1382.

Marchbanks, P., et al. (1988). Risk factors for ectopic pregnancy. *Journal of the American Medical Association, 259,* 1823–1827.

Margolin, L., et al. (1989). When a kiss is not just a kiss: Relating violations on consent in kissing to rape myth acceptance. *Sex Roles, 20,* 231–243.

Marks, G., et al. (1981). Effect of targets' physical attractiveness on assumption of similarity. *Journal of Personality and Social Psychology, 41,* 198–206.

Marshall, W. L. (1989). Pornography and sex offenders. In D. Zillmann & J. Bryant (Eds.), *Pornography: Research advances and policy considerations* (pp. 185–214). Hillsdale, NJ: Erlbaum.

Marshall, W. L., et al. (1991). Treatment outcome with sex offenders. *Clinical Psychology Review, 11,* 465–485.

Marsiglio, W. (1993b). Attitudes toward homosexual activity and gays as friends: A national survey of heterosexual 15- to 19-year-old males. *Journal of Sex Research, 30,* 12–17.

Martens, M., & Faro, S. (1989, January). Update on trichomoniasis: Detection and management. *Medical Aspects of Human Sexuality,* 73–79.

Martin, C. L., & Halverson, C. F., Jr. (1981). A schematic processing model of sex typing and stereotyping in children. *Child Development, 54,* 1119–1134.

Martin, C. L., & Halverson, C. F., Jr. (1983). The effects of sex-typing schemas on young children's memory. *Child Development, 54,* 563–574.

Martin, D. H. (1990). Chlamydial infections. *Medical Clinics of North America, 74,* 1367–1387.

Martinez, F. D., et al. (1992). Increased incidence of asthma in children of smoking mothers. *Pediatrics, 89,* 21–26.

Martinson, F. M. (1976). Eroticism in infancy and childhood. *The Journal of Sex Research, 2,* 251–262.

Mason, R. T., et al. (1989). Sex pheromones in snakes. *Science, 245,* 290–293.

Masters, W. H., & Johnson, V. E. (1966). *Human sexual response.* Boston: Little, Brown.

Masters, W. H., & Johnson, V. E. (1970). *Human sexual inadequacy.* Boston: Little, Brown.

Masters, W. H., & Johnson, V. E. (1979). *Homosexuality in perspective.* Boston: Little, Brown.

Matek, O. (1988). Obscene phone callers. *Journal of Social Work and Human Sexuality, 7,* 113–130.

Matthews, K. A., et al. (1990). Influences of natural menopause on psychological characteristics and symptoms of middle-aged healthy women. *Journal of Consulting and Clinical Psychology, 58,* 345–351.

Maybach, K. L., & Gold, S. R. (1994). Hyperfemininity and attraction to macho and non-macho men. *Journal of Sex Research, 31*(2), 91–98.

Mayer, J. P., et al. (1990). A randomized evaluation of smoking cessation interventions for pregnant women at a WIC [women, infants, and children] clinic. *American Journal of Public Health, 80,* 76–79.

McArthur, M. J. (1990). Reality therapy with rape victims. *Archives of Psychiatric Nursing, 4,* 360–365.

McConaghy, M. J. (1979). Gender performance and the genital basis of gender: Stages in the development of constancy of gender. *Child Development, 50,* 1223–1226.

McGuire, R. J., et al. (1965). Sexual deviation as conditioned behavior: A hypothesis. *Behaviour Research and Therapy, 2,* 185–190.

McLaren, J., & Brown, R. E. (1989). Childhood problems associated with abuse and neglect. *Canada's Mental Health, 37*(3), 1–6.

McLaughlin, F. J., et al. (1992). Randomized trial of comprehensive prenatal care for low-income women: Effect on infant birth weight. *Pediatrics, 89,* 128–132.

McMahon, M. J., et al. (1996). Comparison of a trial of labor with an elective second cesarean section. *The New England Journal of Medicine, 335,* 689–695.

Mead, M. (1935). *Sex and temperament in three primitive societies.* New York: Dell.

Mead, M. (1967). *Male and female: A study of the sexes in a changing world.* New York: Morrow.

Meana, M., & Binik, Y. M. (1994). Painful coitus: A review of female dyspareunia. *Journal of Nervous and Mental Disease, 182*(5), 264–272.

Meiselman, K. C. (1978). *Incest: A psychological study of causes and effects with treatment recommendations.* San Francisco: Jossey-Bass.

Meisler, A. W., & Carey, M. P. (1990). A critical reevaluation of nocturnal penile tumescence monitoring in the diagnosis of erectile dysfunction. *Journal of Nervous and Mental Disease, 178,* 78–89.

Mertz, G. J., et al. (1992). Risk factors for the sexual transmission of genital herpes. *Annals of Internal Medicine, 116,* 197–202.

Messenger, J. C. (1971). Sex and repression in an Irish folk community. In D. S. Marshall and R. C. Suggs (Eds.), *Human sexual behavior: Variations in the ethnographic spectrum* (pp. 3–37). New York: Basic Books.

Meston, C. M., & Gorzalka, B. B. (1992). Psychoactive drugs and human sexual behavior: The role of serotonergic activity. *Journal of Psychoactive Drugs, 24,* 1–40.

Meuwissen, I., & Over, R. (1990). Habituation and dishabituation of female sexual arousal. *Behaviour Research and Therapy, 28,* 217–226.

Meyer-Bahlburg, H. F. L., et al. (1995). Prenatal estrogens and the development of homosexual orientation. *Developmental Psychology, 31*(1), 12–21.

Michael, R. T., et al. (1994). *Sex in America: A definitive survey.* Boston: Little, Brown.

Miller, B. C., & Bingham, C. R. (1989). Family configuration in relation to the sexual behavior of female adolescents. *Journal of Marriage and the Family, 51,* 499–506.

Miller, B. C., et al. (1986). Dating age and stage as correlates of adolescent sexual attitudes and behavior. *Journal of Adolescent Research, 1,* 361–371.

Miller, D. (1995). Personal communication.

Miller, S. M., et al. (1996). Applying cognitive–social theory to health-protective behavior: Breast self-examination in cancer screening. *Psychological Bulletin, 199,* 70–94.

Mills, J. L. (1995). Protecting the embryo from X-rated drugs. *New England Journal of Medicine, 333,* 124–125.

Minai, N. (1981). *Women in Islam: Tradition and transition in the Middle East.* London: John Murray.

Mishell, D. R., Jr. (1989). Medical progress: Contraception. *New England Journal of Medicine, 320,* 777–787.

Mohr, D. C., & Beutler, L. E. (1990). Erectile dysfunction: A review of diagnostic and treatment procedures. *Clinical Psychology Review, 10,* 123–150.

Moi, H., et al. (1989). Should male consorts of women with bacterial vaginosis be treated? *Genitourinary Medicine, 65,* 263–268.

Money, J. (1987a). Sin, sickness or status—Homosexual gender identity and psychoneuroendocrinology. *American Psychologist, 42,* 384–399.

Money, J. (1987b). Treatment guidelines: Antiandrogen and counseling of paraphiliac sex offenders. *Journal of Sex and Marital Therapy, 13,* 219–223.

Money, J. (1988). *Gay, straight, and in-between.* New York: Oxford University Press.

Money, J. (1990). Agenda and credenda of the Kinsey Scale. In D. P. McWhirter, et al. (Eds.), *Homosexuality/heterosexuality: Concepts of sexual orientation* (pp. 41–60). New York: Oxford University Press.

Money, J. (1994). The concept of gender identity disorder in childhood and adolescence after 39 years. *Journal of Sex and Marital Therapy, 20*(3), 163–177.

Money, J., & Ehrhardt, A. (1972). *Man and woman, boy and girl.* Baltimore: Johns Hopkins University Press.

Money, J., & Lamacz, M. (1989). *Vandalized lovemaps.* Buffalo, NY: Prometheus Books.

Money, J., & Wiedeking, C. (1980). Gender identity/role: Normal differentiation and its transpositions. In B. Wolman & J. Money (Eds.), *Handbook of human sexuality* (pp. 269–284). Englewood Cliffs, NJ: Prentice-Hall.

Money, J., et al. (1984). Micropenis: Adult follow-up and comparison of size against new norms. *Journal of Sex and Marital Therapy, 10,* 105–116.

Moore, K. A., & Stief, T. M. (1992). Changes in marriage and fertility behavior: Behavior versus attitudes of young adults. *Youth and Society, 22,* 362–386.

Morales, E. (1992). Latino gays and Latina lesbians. In S. Dworkin & F. Gutierrez (Eds.), *Counseling gay men and lesbians: Journey to the end of the rainbow.* Alexandria, VA: American Association for Counseling and Development.

Morgan, T. O., et al. (1996). Age-specific reference ranges for serum prostate-specific antigen in black men. *New England Journal of Medicine, 335,* 304–310.

Morse, E., et al. (1992). Sexual behavior patterns of customers of male street prostitutes. *Archives of Sexual Behavior, 21,* 347.

Mosher, W. D., & Bachrach, C. A. (1987). First premarital contraceptive use. *Studies in Family Planning, 18,* 83.

Muehlenhard, C. L., & Falcon, P. L. (1990). Men's heterosocial skill and attitudes toward women as predictors of verbal sexual coercion and forceful rape. *Sex Roles, 23,* 241–259.

Mueser, K. T., et al. (1984). You're only as pretty as you feel: Facial expression as a determinant of physical attractiveness. *Journal of Personality and Social Psychology, 46,* 469–478.

Murstein, B. I. (1988). A taxonomy of love. In R. J. Sternberg & M. L. Barnes (Eds.), *The psychology of love* (pp. 13–37). New Haven: Yale University Press.

Muster, N. J. (1992). Treating the adolescent victim-turned-offender. *Adolescence, 27,* 441–450.

Myers, A. M., & Gonda, G. (1982). Utility of the masculinity–femininity construct: Comparison of traditional and androgyny ap-

proaches. *Journal of Personality and Social Psychology, 43,* 514–523.

Myers, M. F. (1989). Men sexually assaulted as adults and sexually abused as boys. *Archives of Sexual Behavior, 18,* 203–215.

Nakanishi, M. (1986). Perceptions of self-disclosure in initial interaction: A Japanese sample. *Human Communication Research, 13,* 167–190.

National Academy of Sciences, Institute of Medicine. (1982). *Marijuana and health.* Washington, DC: National Academy Press.

National Crime Victimization Survey. (1995). U.S. Bureau of Justice Statistics. Washington, DC: U.S. Department of Justice.

National Research Council. (1993). *Losing generations: Adolescents in high risk settings.* Washington, DC: National Academy Press.

Nelson, K. E. (1996). Changes in sexual behavior and a decline in HIV infection among young men in Thailand. *New England Journal of Medicine, 335,* 297–303.

Nevid, J. S. (1984). Sex differences in factors of romantic attraction. *Sex Roles, 11,* 401–411.

Newcomb, P. A., & Storer, B. E. (1995). Postmenopausal hormone use and risk of large-bowel cancer. *Journal of the National Cancer Institute, 87*(14), 1067–1071.

Nichols, M. (1990a). Lesbian relationships: Implications for the study of sexuality and gender. In D. P. McWhirter, et al. (Eds.), *Homosexuality/heterosexuality: Concepts of sexual orientation* (pp. 350–364). New York: Oxford University Press.

Norman, J., & Harris, M. (1981). *The private life of the American teenager.* New York: Rawson Wade.

Nosek, M. A., et al. (1994). Wellness models and sexuality among women with physical disabilities. *Journal of Applied Rehabilitation Counseling, 25*(1), 50–58.

Ochs, R. (1993a, December 7). Breast cancer risk: What the numbers mean. *New York Newsday,* pp. 72–75.

Ochs, R. (1993b, December 7). Prostate cancer jolt: 16% increase attributed to wider screening. *New York Newsday,* p. 7.

Ochs, R. (1994, January 11). Cervical cancer comeback. *New York Newsday,* pp. 55, 57.

O'Donohue, W., et al. (1993). Premature ejaculation. In W. O'Donohue & J. H. Geer (Eds.), *Handbook of sexual dysfunctions: Assessment and treatment.* (pp. 303–333). Boston: Allyn & Bacon.

O'Hara, M. W., et al. (1984). Prospective study of postpartum depression: Prevalence, course, and predictive factors. *Journal of Abnormal Psychology, 93,* 158–171.

O'Hara, M. W., et al. (1991). Prospective study of postpartum blues: Biological and psychosocial factors. *Archives of General Psychiatry, 48,* 801–806.

Okami, P., & Goldberg, A. (1992). Personality correlates of pedophilia: Are they reliable indicators? *Journal of Sex Research, 29,* 297–328.

Osborne, N. G., & Adelson, M. D. (1990). Herpes simplex and human papillomavirus genital infections: Controversy over obstetric management. *Clinical Obstetrics and Gynecology, 33,* 801–811.

Overholser, J. C., & Beck, S. (1986). Multimethod assessment of rapists, child molesters, and three control groups on behavioral and psychological measures. *Journal of Consulting and Clinical Psychology, 54,* 682–687.

Padgett, V. R., et al. (1989). Pornography, erotica, and attitudes toward women: The effects of repeated exposure. *Journal of Sex Research, 26,* 479–491.

Padilla, E. R., & O'Grady, K. E. (1987). Sexuality among Mexican Americans: A case of sexual stereotyping. *Journal of Personality and Social Psychology, 52,* 5–10.

Palace, E. M. (1995). Modification of dysfunctional patterns of sexual arousal through autonomic arousal and false physiological feedback. *Journal of Consulting and Clinical Psychology, 63,* 604–615.

"Panel says Pap tests could almost end cervical cancer deaths." (April 4, 1996). *The New York Times,* p. A18.

Paul, R. H. (1996). Toward fewer cesarean sections—The role of a trial of labor. *The New England Journal of Medicine, 335,* 735–736.

Pauly, I. B. (1974). Female transsexualism: Part 1. *Archives of Sexual Behavior, 3,* 487–508.

Pear, R. (1991, December 4). Larger number of new mothers are unmarried. *The New York Times,* p. A20.

Pearson, C. A. (1992). Cited in Leary, W. E. (1992, February 1). U.S. panel backs approval of first condom for women. *The New York Times,* p. 7.

Peckham, C., & Gibb, D. (1995). Mother-to-child transmission of the human immunodeficiency virus. *New England Journal of Medicine, 333,* 298–302.

Penn, F. (1993, October 21). Cancer confusion: The risks and realities of human papilloma virus. *Manhattan Spirit,* pp. 14–15.

Peplau, L. A., & Cochran, S. D. (1990). A relationship perspective on homosexuality. In D. P. McWhirter, et al. (Eds.), *Homosexuality/heterosexuality: Concepts of sexual orientation* (pp. 321–349). New York: Oxford University Press.

Perduta-Fulginiti, P. S. (1992). Sexual functioning of women with complete spinal cord injury: Nursing implications [Special issue: Nursing roles and perspectives]. *Sexuality and Disability, 10,* 103–118.

Perrett, D. I. (1994). *Nature.* Cited in Brody, J. E. (1994, March 21). Notions of beauty transcend culture, new study suggests. *The New York Times,* p. A14.

Perry, D. G., & Bussey, K. (1979). The social learning theory of sex differences: Imitation is alive and well. *Journal of Personality and Social Psychology, 37,* 1699–1712.

Perry, J. D., & Whipple, B. (1981). Pelvic muscle strength of female ejaculation: Evidence in support of a new theory of orgasm. *Journal of Sex Research, 17,* 22–39.

Person, E. S., et al. (1989). Gender differences in sexual behaviors and fantasies in a college population. *Journal of Sex and Marital Therapy, 15,* 187–198.

Pillard, R. C. (1990). The Kinsey Scale: Is it familial? In D. P. McWhirter, et al. (Eds.), *Homosexuality/heterosexuality: Concepts of sexual orientation* (pp. 88–100). New York: Oxford University Press.

Pillard, R. C., & Weinrich, J. D. (1986). Evidence of familial nature of male homosexuality. *Archives of Sexual Behavior, 43,* 808–812.

Pines, A., & Aronson, E. (1983). Antecedents, correlates, and consequences of sexual jealousy. *Journal of Personality, 51,* 108–109.

Population Council. (1995). Cited in Brody, J. E. (1995, August 31). Abortion method using two drugs gains in a study. *The New York Times,* pp. A1, B12.

Porter, N., et al. (1985). Androgyny and leadership in mixed-sex groups. *Journal of Personality and Social Psychology, 49,* 808–823.

Poussaint, A. (1990, September). An honest look at Black gays and lesbians. *Ebony, 124, 126,* 130–131.

Powderly, W. G., et al. (1995). A randomized trial comparing fluconazole with clotrimazole troches for the prevention of fungal infections in patients with advanced human immunodeficiency virus infection. *New England Journal of Medicine, 332,* 700–705.

Powell, E. (1991). *Talking back to sexual pressure.* Minneapolis: CompCare Publications.

Powell, E. (1996). *Sex on your terms.* Boston: Allyn & Bacon.

Prentky, R. A., & Knight, R. A. (1991). Identifying critical dimensions for discriminating among rapists. *Journal of Consulting and Clinical Psychology, 59,* 643–661.

Price, V. A. (1989). Characteristics and needs of Boston street youth: One agency's response [Special issue: Runaway, homeless, and shut-out children and youth in Canada, Europe, and the United States]. *Children and Youth Services Review, 11,* 75–90.

Proctor, F., et al. (1974). The differentiation of male and female orgasm: An experimental study. In N. Wagner (Ed.), *Perspectives on human sexuality.* New York: Behavioral Publications.

Purifoy, F. E., et al. (1992). The relationship of sexual daydreaming to sexual activity, sexual drive, and sexual attitudes for women across the life-span. *Archives of Sexual Behavior, 21,* 369–375.

Quadagno, D., et al. (1991). Women at risk for human immunodeficiency virus. *Journal of Psychology and Human Sexuality, 4,* 97–110.

Quevillon, R. P. (1993). Dyspareunia. In W. O'Donohue & J. H. Geer (Eds.), *Handbook of sexual dysfunctions: Assessment and treatment* (pp. 367–380). Boston: Allyn & Bacon.

Quinsey, V. L., et al. (1984). Sexual arousal to nonsexual violence and sadomasochistic themes among rapists and non-sex-offenders. *Journal of Consulting and Clinical Psychology, 52,* 651–657.

Radlove, S. (1983). Sexual response and gender roles. In E. R. Allgeier & N. B. McCormick (Eds.), *Changing boundaries: Gender roles and sexual behavior.* Palo Alto, CA: Mayfield.

Rajfer, J., et al. (1992). Nitric oxide as a mediator of relaxation of the corpus cavernosum in response to nonadrenergic, noncholinergic neurotransmission. *New England Journal of Medicine, 326,* 90–94.

Rate of births for teen-agers drops again. (1995, September 22). *The New York Times,* p. A18.

Rathus, S. A. (1978). Treatment of recalcitrant ejaculatory incompetence. *Behavior Therapy, 9,* 962.

Rathus, S. A., & Fichner-Rathus, L. (1994). *Making the most of college* (2nd ed.). Englewood Cliffs, NJ: Prentice-Hall.

Ratican, K. L. (1992). Sexual abuse survivors: Identifying symptoms and special treatment considerations. *Journal of Counseling and Development, 71,* 33–38.

Reichart, C. A., et al. (1990). Evaluation of Abbott Testpack Chlamydia for detection of chlamydia trachomatis in patients attending sexually transmitted diseases clinics. *Sexually Transmitted Diseases, 17,* 147–151.

Reid, T. R. (1990, December 24). Snug in their beds for Christmas Eve: In Japan, December 24th has become the hottest night of the year. *The Washington Post.*

Rein, M. F., & Muller, M. (1990). *Trichomonas vaginalis* and trichomoniasis. In K. K. Holmes, et al. (Eds.), *Sexually transmitted diseases* (2nd ed.) (pp. 481–492). New York: McGraw-Hill.

Reinisch, J. M. (1990). *The Kinsey Institute new report on sex: What you must know to be sexually literate.* New York: St. Martin's Press.

Reiss, B. F. (1988, Spring/Summer). The long-lived person and sexuality. *Dynamic Psychotherapy, 6,* 79–86.

Reiss, I. L. (1980). *Family systems in America.* New York: Holt, Rinehart & Winston.

Remafedi, G. (1990). Study group report on the impact of television portrayals of gender roles on youth. *Journal of Adolescent Health Care, 11*(1), 59–61.

Renzetti, C. M., & Curran, D. J. *Women, men, and society: The sociology of gender.* Boston: Allyn & Bacon.

Resick, P. A., & Schnicke, M. K. (1990). Treating symptoms in adult victims of sexual assault. *Journal of Interpersonal Violence, 5,* 488–506.

Reuter. (1996, September 18). The RU-486 abortion pill got a tentative seal of approval. America Online.

Rice, M. E., et al. (1990). A follow-up of rapists assessed in a maximum-security psychiatric facility. *Journal of Interpersonal Violence, 5,* 435–448.

Rice, M. E., et al. (1991). Sexual recidivism among child molesters released from a maximum security psychiatric institution. *Journal of Consulting and Clinical Psychology, 59,* 381–386.

Riche, M. (1988, November 23–26). Postmarital society. *American Demographics, 60.*

Riggio, R. E., & Woll, S. B. (1984). The role of nonverbal cues and physical attractiveness in the selection of dating partners. *Journal of Social and Personal Relationships, 1,* 347–357.

Roberto, L. G. (1983). Issues in diagnosis and treatment of transsexualism. *Archives of Sexual Behavior, 12,* 445–473.

Roland, B., et al. (1989). MMPI correlates of college women who reported experiencing child/adult sexual contact with father, stepfather, or with other persons. *Psychological Reports, 64,* 1159–1162.

Rolfs, R. T., & Nakashima, A. K. (1990). Epidemiology of primary and secondary syphilis in the United States: 1981 through 1989. *Journal of the American Medical Association, 264,* 1432–1437.

Rolfs, R. T., et al. (1990) Risk factors for syphilis: Cocaine use and prostitution. *American Journal of Public Health, 80,* 853–857.

Romenesko, K., & Miller, E. M. (1989). The second step in double jeopardy: Appropriating the labor of female street hustlers. *Crime and Delinquency, 35,* 109–135.

Roper Organization. (1985). *The Virginia Slims American women's poll.* New York: Author.

Rose, P. G. (1996). Endometrial carcinoma. *New England Journal of Medicine, 335,* 640–649.

Rose, R. J. (1995). Genes and human behavior. *Annual Review of Psychology, 46,* 625–654.

Rosen, I. (1967). *Pathology and treatment of sexual deviations.* London: Oxford University Press.

Rosen, R. C., et al. (1994). Psychologically based treatment for male erectile disorder: A cognitive–interpersonal model. *Journal of Sex and Marital Therapy, 20*(2), 67–85.

Rosenthal, A. M. (1994, September 6). A victory in Cairo. *The New York Times,* p. A19.

Rosenthal, A. M. (1995, June 13). The possible dream. *The New York Times,* p. A25.

Rosenthal, E. (1992, July 22). Her image of his ideal, in a faulty mirror. *The New York Times,* p. C12.

Rosman, J. P., & Resnick, P. J. (1989). Sexual attraction to corpses: A psychiatric review of necrophilia. *Bulletin of the American Academy of Psychiatry and the Law, 17,* 153–163.

Rotheram-Borus, M. J., et al. (1992). Lifetime sexual behaviors among predominantly minority male runaways and gay/bisexual adolescents in New York City. *AIDS Education and Prevention,* (Fall Suppl.), 34–42.

Rovet, J., & Ireland, L. (1994). Behavioral phenotype in children with Turner syndrome. *Journal of Pediatric Psychology, 19,* 779–790.

Roving mates called factor in cancer. (1996, August 7). *The New York Times,* p. A10.

Rozin, P., & Fallon, A. (1988). Body image, attitudes to weight, and misperceptions of figure preferences of the opposite sex: A comparison of men and women in two generations. *Journal of Abnormal Psychology, 97,* 342–345.

Rubinow, D. R., & Schmidt, P. J. (1995). The treatment of premenstrual syndrome—forward into the past. *New England Journal of Medicine, 332,* 1574–1575.

Ruble, D. N., & Ruble, T. L. (1982). Sex stereotypes. In A. G. Miller (Ed.), *In the eye of the beholder: Contemporary issues in stereotyping.* New York: Praeger.

Russell, D. (1982). *Rape in marriage.* New York: Macmillan.

Sack, W. H., & Mason, R. (1980). Child abuse and conviction of sexual crimes: A preliminary finding. *Law and Human Behavior, 4,* 211–215.

Sadalla, E. K., et al. (1987). Dominance and heterosexual attraction. *Journal of Personality and Social Psychology, 52,* 730–738.

Sadker, M., & Sadker, D. (1994). *How America's schools cheat girls.* New York: Scribners.

Sagan, C., & Dryan, A. (1990, April 22). The question of abortion: A search for answers. *Parade Magazine,* 4–8.

Saluter, A. F. (1992). Marital status and living arrangements: March 1992. *Current Population Reports,* Series P20–468.

Samuels, M., & Samuels, N. (1986). *The well pregnancy book.* New York: Simon & Schuster.

Sanday, P. R. (1981). The socio-cultural context of rape: A cross-cultural study. *Journal of Social Issues, 37,* 5–27.

Sanders, S. A., et al. (1990). Homosexuality/heterosexuality: An overview. In D. P. McWhirter, et al. (Eds.), *Homosexuality/heterosexuality: Concepts of sexual orientation* (pp. xix–xxvii). New York: Oxford University Press.

Saravolatz, L. D., et al. (1996). Zidovudine alone or in combination with didanosine or zalcitabine in HIV-infected patients with the acquired immunodeficiency syndrome or fewer than 200 CD4 cells per cubic millimeter. *New England Journal of Medicine, 335,* 1099–1106.

Sargent, T. O. (1988). Fetishism. *Journal of Social Work and Human Sexuality, 7,* 27–42.

Sarrel, P., & Masters, W. (1982). Sexual molestation of men by women. *Archives of Sexual Behavior, 11,* 117–131.

Savitz, L., & Rosen, L. (1988). The sexuality of prostitutes: Sexual enjoyment reported by "streetwalkers." *Journal of Sex Research, 24,* 200–208.

Schachter, J. (1989). Why we need a program for the control of *Chlamydia trachomatis. New England Journal of Medicine, 320,* 802–804.

Schafer, R. B., & Keith, P. M. (1990). Matching by weight in married couples: A life cycle perspective. *Journal of Social Psychology, 130,* 657–664.

Schafran, L. H. (1995, August 26). Rape is still underreported. *The New York Times,* p. A19.

Schiavi, R. C., et al. (1990). Healthy aging and male sexual function. *American Journal of Psychiatry, 147,* 766–771.

Schillinger, L. (1995, June 10). More sex please, we're Russian. *The New York Times Book Review,* p. 49.

Schmidt, G. (1994). Sex therapy, 1970–1994. *Nordisk-Sexologi, 12*(3), 178–183.

Schmitt, E. (1996, September 11). Senators reject both job-bias ban and gay marriage. *The New York Times,* pp. A1, A16.

Schoendorf, K. C., & Kiely, J. L. (1992). Relationship of sudden infant death syndrome to maternal smoking during and after pregnancy. *Pediatrics, 90,* 905–908.

Schork, K. (1990, August 19). The despair of Pakistan's women: Not even Benazir Bhutto could stop the repression. *The Washington Post.*

Schreiber, G. B., et al. (1996). The risk of transfusion-transmitted viral infections. *The New England Journal of Medicine, 334,* 1685–1690.

Schreiner-Engle, P., & Schiavi, R. (1986). Lifetime psychopathology in individuals with low sexual desire. *Journal of Nervous and Mental Disease, 174,* 646–651.

Schreiner-Engle, P., et al. (1989). Low sexual desire in women: The role of reproductive hormones. *Hormones and Behavior, 23,* 221–234.

Schultz, N. R., Jr., & Moore, D. W. (1984). Loneliness: Correlates, attributions, and coping among older adults. *Personality and Social Psychology Bulletin, 10,* 67–77.

Schwartz, M. F., & Masters, W. H. (1984). The Masters and Johnson treatment program for dissatisfied homosexual men. *American Journal of Psychiatry, 141,* 173–181.

Scott, J. E., & Schwalm, L. A. (1988). Rape rates and the circulation rates of adult magazines. *Journal of Sex Research, 24,* 241–250.

Seftel, A. D., et al. (1991). Disturbed sexual function in patients with spinal cord disease. *Neurologic Clinics, 9,* 757–778.

Segal, Z. V., & Marshall, W. L. (1985). Heterosexual social skills in a population of rapists and child molesters. *Journal of Consulting and Clinical Psychology, 53,* 55–63.

Segraves, R. T. (1988a). Drugs and desire. In S. Leiblum & R. Rosen (Eds.), *Sexual desire disorders.* New York: Guilford Press.

Segraves, R. T. (1988b). Sexual side-effects of psychiatric drugs. *International Journal of Psychiatry in Medicine, 18,* 243–252.

Segraves, R. T., & Segraves, K. B. (1993). Medical aspects of orgasm disorders. In W. O'Donohue & J. H. Geer (Eds.), *Handbook of sexual dysfunctions: Assessment and treatment* (pp. 225–252). Boston: Allyn & Bacon.

Self. (1995, June). 75.

Sell, R. L., et al. (1995). The prevalence of homosexual behavior and attraction in the United States, the United Kingdom, and France: Results of national, population-based samples. *Archives of Sexual Behavior, 24,* 235–248.

Selvin, B. W. (1993, June 1). Transsexuals are coming to terms with themselves and Society. *New York Newsday,* pp. 55, 58, 59.

Semans, J. (1956). Premature ejaculation: A new approach. *Southern Medical Journal, 49,* 353–358.

Seng, M. J. (1989). Child sexual abuse and adolescent prostitution: A comparative analysis. *Adolescence, 24,* 665–675.

Severn, J., et al. (1990). The effects of sexual and non-sexual advertising appeals and information level on cognitive processing and communication effectiveness. *Journal of Advertising, 19,* 14–22.

Shafer, M. A., et al. (1993). Evaluation of urine-based screening strategies to detect *Chlamydia trachomatis* among sexually active asymptomatic young men. *Journal of the American Medical Association, 270,* 2065–2070.

Shaver, P., et al. (1988). Love as attachment. In R. J. Sternberg & M. L. Barnes (Eds.), *The psychology of love* (pp. 68–99). New Haven: Yale University Press.

Sheehy, G. (1995). *New passages: Mapping your life across time.* New York: Random House.

Shenon, P. (1995, July 15). New Zealand seeks causes of suicides by young. *The New York Times*, p. A3.

Sheppard, J. A., & Strathman, A. J. (1989). Attractiveness and height: The role of stature in dating preference, frequency of dating, and perceptions of attractiveness. *Personality and Social Psychology Bulletin, 15,* 17–627.

Sherman, K. J., et al. (1990). Sexually transmitted diseases and tubal pregnancy. *Sexually Transmitted Diseases, 17,* 115–121.

Sherwin, B. B., et al. (1985). Androgen enhances sexual motivation in females: A prospective, crossover study of sex steroid administration in the surgical menopause. *Psychosomatic Medicine, 47,* 339–351.

Siegel, K., et al. (1988). Patterns of change in sexual behavior among gay men in New York City. *Archives of Sexual Behavior, 17,* 481–497.

Signorielli, N. (1990). Children, television, and gender roles: Messages and impact. *Journal of Adolescent Health Care, 11*(1), 50–58.

Silber, S. J. (1991). *How to get pregnant with the new technology.* New York: Time Warner.

Silbert, M. H. (1989). The effects on juveniles of being used for pornography and prostitution. In D. Zillmann & J. Bryant (Eds.), *Pornography: Research advances and policy considerations* (pp. 215–234). Hillsdale, NJ: Erlbaum.

Simpson, J. A., et al. (1986). The association between romantic love and marriage: Kephart (1967) twice revisited. *Personality and Social Psychology Bulletin,* 363–372.

Singh, D. (1994a). Body fat distribution and perception of desirable female body shape by young Black men and women. *International Journal of Eating Disorders, 16*(3) 289–294.

Singh, D. (1994b). Is thin really beautiful and good? Relationship between waist-to-hip ratio (WHR) and female attractiveness. *Personality and Individual Differences, 16*(1) 123–132.

Singh, G. K., & Yu, S. M. (1995). Cited in Pear, R. (1995, July 10). Infant mortality rate drops but racial disparity grows. *The New York Times*, p. B9.

Sirles, E. A., & Franke, P. J. (1989). Factors influencing mother's reactions to intrafamily sexual abuse. *Child Abuse & Neglect, 13,* 131–139.

Slattery, M. L., & Kerber, R. A. (1993). A comprehensive evalution of family history and breast cancer risk: The Utah population database. *Journal of the American Medical Association, 270,* 1563–1568.

Slonim-Nevo, V. (1992). First premarital intercourse among Mexican-American and Anglo-American adolescent women: Interpreting ethnic differences. *Journal of Adolescent Research, 7,* 332–351.

Smith, E. A., & Udry, J. R. (1985). Coital and non-coital sexual behaviors of white and black adolescents. *American Journal of Public Health, 75,* 1200–1203.

Smith, E. P., et al. (1994). Estrogen resistance caused by a mutation in the estrogen-receptor gene in a man. *The New England Journal of Medicine, 331,* 1056–1061.

Smolowe, J. (1993, June 14). New, improved and ready for battle. *Time*, pp. 48–51.

Solano, C. H., et al. (1982). Loneliness and patterns of self-disclosure. *Journal of Personality and Social Psychology, 43,* 524–531.

Sonenstein, F. L., et al. (1989). Sexual activity, condom use and AIDS awareness among adolescent males. *Family Planning Perspectives, 21,* 152–157.

Sorensen, R. C. (1973). *Adolescent sexuality in contemporary America.* New York: World.

Sourander, L. B. (1994). Geriatric aspects on estrogen effects and sexuality. *Gerontology, 40* (Suppl. 3), 14–17.

Southerland, D. (1990, May 27). Limited "sexual revolution" seen in China: Nationwide survey shows more liberal attitudes developing in conservative society. *The Washington Post.*

Spark, R. F. (1991). *Male sexual health: A couple's guide.* Mount Vernon, NY: Consumer Reports Books.

Speckens, A. E. M., et al. (1995). Psychosexual functioning of partners of men with presumed non-organic erectile dysfunction: Cause or consequence of the disorder? *Archives of Sexual Behavior, 24,* 157–172.

Spitzer, R. L., et al. (1989). *DSM-III-R casebook.* Washington, DC: American Psychiatric Press.

Sprecher, S., et al. (1994). Mate selection preferences: Gender differences examined in a national sample. *Journal of Personality and Social Psychology, 66* (6), 1074–1080.

Stampfer, M. J., et al. (1991, June). Ten-year follow-up study of estrogen replacement therapy in relation to cardiovascular disease and mortality. Paper presented at the 24th annual meeting of the Society for Epidemiologic Research, Buffalo, New York.

Starr, B. D., & Weiner, M. B. (1981). *The Starr-Weiner report on sex and sexuality in the mature years.* New York: Stein & Day.

Steele, C. M., & Josephs, R. A. (1990). Alcohol myopia: Its prized and dangerous effects. *American Psychologist, 45,* 21–933.

Steiner, M., et al. (1995). Fluoxetine in the treatment of premenstrual dysphoria. *New England Journal of Medicine, 332,* 1529–1534.

Steinhauer, J. (1995, July 6). No marriage, no apologies. *The New York Times*, pp. C1, C7.

Stericker, A., & LeVesconte, S. (1982). Effect of brief training on sex-related differences in visual–spatial skill. *Journal of Personality and Social Psychology, 43,* 1018–1029.

Sternberg, R. J. (1986). A triangular theory of love. *Psychological Review, 93,* 119–135.

Sternberg, R. J. (1987). Liking versus loving: A comparative evaluation of theories. *Psychological Bulletin, 102,* 331–345.

Sternberg, R. J. (1988). *The triangle of love: Intimacy, passion, commitment.* New York: Basic Books.

Sternberg, R. J., & Grajek, S. (1984). The nature of love. *Journal of Personality and Social Psychology, 47,* 312–329.

Stewart, F. H. (1992). Cited in Leary, W. E. (1992, February 1). U.S. panel backs approval of first condom for women. *The New York Times*, p. 7.

Still no pill for Japan. (1992, March 22). *The New York Times*, Section 4, p. 7.

Stock, W. E. (1991). Feminist explanations: Male power, hostility, and sexual coercion. In E. Grauerholz & M. A. Koralewski (Eds.), *Sexual coercion: A sourcebook on its nature, causes, and prevention* (pp. 61–73). Lexington, MA: Lexington Books.

Stock, W. E. (1993). Inhibited female orgasm. In W. O'Donohue & J. H. Geer (Eds.), *Handbook of sexual dysfunctions: Assessment and treatment* (pp. 253–301). Boston: Allyn & Bacon.

Stoller, R. J. (1969). Parental influences in male transsexualism. In R. Green & J. Money (Eds.), *Transsexualism and sex reassignment.* Baltimore: Johns Hopkins University Press.

Stoller, R. J. (1977). Sexual deviations. In R. Beach (Ed.), *Human sexuality in four perspectives* (pp. 190–214). Baltimore: Johns Hopkins University Press.

Stoller, R. J., & Herdt, G. H. (1985). Theories of origins of male homosexuality. *Archives of General Psychiatry, 42,* 399–404.

Storms, M. D. (1980). Theories of sexual orientation. *Journal of Personality and Social Psychology, 38,* 783–792.

Strickland, B. R. (1995). Research on sexual orientation and human development: A commentary. *Developmental Psychology, 31,* 137–140.

Struckman-Johnson, C. (1988). Forced sex on dates: It happens to men, too. *Journal of Sex Research, 24,* 234–241.

Stuart, F., et al. (1987). Inhibited sexual desire in women. *Archives of Sexual Behavior, 16,* 91–106.

Sue, D., et al. (1981). *Understanding abnormal behavior.* Boston: Houghton Mifflin Co.

Swann, W. B., Jr., et al. (1987). Cognitive–affective crossfire: When self-consistency meets self-enhancement. *Journal of Personality and Social Psychology, 52,* 881–889.

Symons, D. (1979). *The evolution of human sexuality.* New York: Oxford University Press.

Symons, D. (1995). Cited in Goleman, D. (1995, June 14). Sex fantasy research said to neglect women. *The New York Times*, p. C14.

Szasz, G., & Carpenter, C. (1989). Clinical observations in vibratory stimulation of the penis of men with spinal cord injury. *Archives of Sexual Behavior, 18,* 461–474.

Tanfer, K., et al. (1993). Condom use among U.S. men, 1991. *Family Planning Perspectives, 25,* 61–66.

Tang, C. S., et al. (1995). Sexual aggression and victimization in dating relationships among Chinese college students. *Archives of Sexual Behavior, 24,* 47–53.

Tannahill, R. (1980). *Sex in history.* Briarcliff Manor, NY: Stein & Day.

Tannen, D. (1990). *You just don't understand.* New York: Ballantine.

Tedeschi, J. T., & Felson, R. B. (1994). *Violence, aggression, & coercive actions.* Washington, DC: American Psychological Association.

Tharinger, D. (1990). Impact of child sexual abuse on developing sexuality. *Professional Psychology: Research and Practice, 21,* 331–337.

Thomason, J. L., & Gelbart, S. M. (1989). Trichomonas vaginalis. *Obstetrics and Gynecology, 74,* 536–541.

Thomlison, B., et al. (1991, Fall). Characteristics of Canadian male and female child sexual abuse victims [Special issue: Child sexual abuse]. *Journal of Child and Youth Care,* 65–76.

Thompson, D. S. (Ed.). (1993). *Every woman's health: The complete guide to body and mind.* New York: Simon & Schuster.

Thompson, J. K., & Tantleff, S. (1992). Female and male ratings of upper torso: Actual, ideal, and stereotypical conceptions. *Journal of Social Behavior and Personality, 7,* 345–354.

Thompson, M. E. (1991). Self-defense against sexual coercion: Theory, research, and practice. In E. Grauerholz & M. A. Koralewski (Eds.), *Sexual coercion: A sourcebook on its nature, causes, and prevention* (pp. 111–121). Lexington, MA: Lexington Books.

Tobias, S. (1982). Sexist equations. *Psychology Today, 16*(1), pp. 14–17.

Tollison, C. D., & Adams, H. E. (1979). *Sexual disorders: Treatment, theory, and research.* New York: Gardner Press.

Toner, J. P., et al. (1991). Basal follicle-stimulating hormone level is a better predictor of in vitro fertilization performance than age. *Fertility and Sterility, 55,* 784–791.

Toomey, K. E., & Barnes, R. C. (1990). Treatment of chlamydia trachomatis genital infection. *Reviews of Infectious Diseases* (Suppl. 6), S645–S655.

Toubia, N. (1994). Female circumcision as a public health issue. *New England Journal of Medicine, 331,* 712–716.

Touchette, N. (1991). HIV-1 link prompts circumspection of circumcision. *Journal of NIH Research, 3,* 44–46.

Townsend, J. M. (1995). Sex without emotional involvement: An evolutionary interpretation of sex differences. *Archives of Sexual Behavior, 24,* 173–206.

Trovato, F. (1986). The relationship between marital dissolution and suicide: The Canadian case. *Journal of Marriage and the Family, 48,* 341–348.

Trujillo, C. (Ed.). (1991). *Chicana lesbians: The girls our mothers warned us about.* Berkeley, CA: Third Woman Press.

Trussell, J., et al. (1993). Contraceptive efficacy of the diaphragm, the sponge, and the cervical cap. *Family Planning Perspectives, 25,* 100–105.

Tutty, L. M. (1992). The ability of elementary school children to learn child sexual abuse prevention concepts. *Child Abuse and Neglect, 16,* 369–384.

Udry, J. R., & Billy, J. O. G. (1987). Initiation of coitus in early adolescence. *American Sociological Review, 52,* 841–855.

Udry, J. R., et al. (1985). Serum androgenic hormones motivate sexual behavior in adolescent boys. *Fertility and Sterility, 43,* 90–94.

Udry, J. R., et al. (1986). Biosocial foundations for adolescent female sexuality. *Demography, 23*(2), 217–230.

Ulbrich, P. M., et al. (1990) Involuntary childlessness and marital adjustment: His and hers. *Journal of Sex & Marital Therapy, 16,* 147–158.

U.S. Bureau of the Census. (1990a). Marital status and living arrangements: March 1990. *Current Population Reports,* Series P-20, No. 450. Washington, DC: U.S. Government Printing Office.

U.S. Bureau of the Census. (1990b). *Statistical abstract of the United States.* Washington, DC: U.S. Government Printing Office.

U.S. Department of Health and Human Services (USDHHS). (1990). *The health benefits of smoking cessation: A report of the Surgeon General.* (DHHS Publication No. CDC 90–8416). Rockville, MD: Public Health Service, Centers for Disease Control, Center for Chronic Disease Prevention and Health Promotion, Office on Smoking and Health.

U.S. Department of Health and Human Services (USDHHS). (1991). *Strategies to control tobacco use in the United States: A blueprint for public health action in the 1990's.* (NIH Publication No. 92–3316). Washington, DC: National Cancer Institute, Public Health Service, National Institutes of Health, National Cancer Institute.

U.S. Department of Health and Human Services (USDHHS). (1992). *Smoking and health in the Americas.* (DHHS Publication No. [CDC] 92–8419). Atlanta: Public Health Service, Centers for Disease Control, National Center for Chronic Disease Prevention and Health Promotion, Office on Smoking and Health.

U.S. Department of Justice. (1986). *Attorney general's commission on pornography: Final report.* Washington, DC: U.S. Government Printing Office.

U.S. Merit Systems Protection Board. (1981). *Sexual harassment in the federal workplace: Is it a problem?* Washington, DC: Office of Merit Systems Review and Studies.

U.S. Senate Committee on the Judiciary. (1991). Violence against women: The increase of rape in America 1990. *Response to the Victimization of Women and Children, 14*(79, No. 2), 20–23.

Valentiner, D. P., et al. (1996). Coping strategies and posttraumatic stress disorder in female victims of sexual and nonsexual assault. *Journal of Abnormal Psychology, 105,* 455–458.

Van den Hoek, A., et al. (1990). Heterosexual behaviour of intravenous drug users in Amsterdam: Implications for the AIDS epidemic. *AIDS, 4,* 449–453.

Van Steirteghem, A. C., et al. (1993). High fertilization and implantation rates after intracytoplasmic sperm injection. *Human Reproduction, 8,* 1061–1066.

Vazi, R., et al. (1989). Evaluation of a testicular cancer curriculum for adolescents. *Journal of Pediatrics, 114,* 150–162.

Vinacke, W., et al. (1988). Similarity and complementarity in intimate couples. *Genetic, Social, and General Psychology Monographs, 114,* 51–76.

Voeller, B. (1991). AIDS and heterosexual anal intercourse. *Archives of Sexual Behavior, 20,* 33–276.

Voyer, D., et al. (1995). Magnitude of sex differences in spatial abilities: A meta-analysis and consideration of critical variables. *Psychological Bulletin, 117,* 250–270.

Vyas, G. N., et al. (1996). The risk of HIV transmission by screened blood. *New England Journal of Medicine, 334,* 992.

Wald, A., et al. (1995). Virologic characteristics of subclinical and symptomatic genital herpes infections. *New England Journal of Medicine, 333,* 770–775.

Waldinger, M. D., et al. (1994). Paroxetine treatment of premature ejaculation: A double-blind, randomized, placebo-controlled study. *American Journal of Psychiatry, 151* (9), 1377–1379.

Walfish, S., & Mayerson, M. (1980). Sex role identity and attitudes toward sexuality. *Archives of Sexual Behavior, 9,* 199–204.

Wallerstein, J. S., & Blakeslee, S. (1989). *Second chances: Women and children a decade after divorce.* New York: Ticknor & Fields.

Walsh, P. C. (1996). Treatment of benign prostatic hyperplasia. *New England Journal of Medicine, 335,* 586–587.

Walster, E., & Walster, G. W. (1978). *A new look at love.* Reading, MA: Addison-Wesley.

Walt, V. (1993, July 26). Some 2nd thoughts on Depo. *New York Newsday,* p. 13.

Waterman, J. (1986). Overview of treatment issues. In K. MacFarlane et al. (Eds.), *Sexual abuse of young children: Evaluation and treatment* (pp. 197–203). New York: Guilford Press.

Waterman, J., & Lusk, R. (1986). Scope of the problem. In K. MacFarlane et al. (Eds.), *Sexual abuse of young children: Evaluation and treatment* (pp. 3–14). New York: Guilford Press.

Weinberg, M. S., et al. (1984). The social constituents of sadomasochism. *Social Problems, 31,* 379–389.

Weinberg, M. S., et al. (1994). *Dual attraction.* New York: Oxford University Press.

Weinberg, T. S. (1987). Sadomasochism in the United States: A review of recent sociological literature. *Journal of Sex Research, 23,* 50–69.

Weisberg, D. K. (1985). *Children of the night: A study of adolescent prostitution.* Lexington, MA: Heath.

Weiss, R. D., & Mirin, S. M. (1987). *Cocaine.* Washington, DC: American Psychiatric Press.

Whalen, R. E., et al. (1990). Models of sexuality. In D. P. McWhirter, et al. (Eds.), *Homosexuality/Hetero-sexuality: Concepts of sexual orientation* (pp. 61–70). New York: Oxford University Press.

Whiffen, V. E. (1992). Is postpartum depression a distinct diagnosis? *Clinical Psychology Review, 12,* 485–508.

Whipple, B., & Komisaruk, B. R. (1988). Analgesia produced in women by genital self-stimulation. *Journal of Sex Research, 24,* 130–140.

Whitam, F. L., et al. (1993). Homosexual orientation in twins: A report on 61 pairs and three triplet sets. *Archives of Sexual Behavior, 22,* 187–206.

White, G. L. (1981). Some correlates of romantic jealousy. *Journal of Personality, 49,* 129–146.

White, J. W. (1983). Sex and gender issues in aggression research. In R. G. Green & E. I. Donnerstein (Eds.), *Aggression: Theoretical and empirical reviews* (Vol. 2). New York: Academic Press.

White, S. D., & DeBlassie, R. R. (1992). Adolescent sexual behavior. *Adolescence, 27,* 183–191.

Whitley, B. E., Jr. (1983). Sex role orientation and self-esteem: A critical meta-analysis. *Journal of Personality and Social Psychology, 44,* 765–788.

Whitley, R., et al. (1991). Predictors of morbidity and mortality in infants with herpes simplex virus infections. *New England Journal of Medicine, 324,* 450–454.

Whittemore, A. S. (1994). The risk of ovarian cancer after treatment for infertility. *New England Journal of Medicine, 331,* 805–806.

WHO (1995). Cited in "Rise in STDs concerns group." (1995, September 12). *Newsday,* p. B27.

Wilcox, A. J., et al. (1995). Timing of sexual intercourse in relation to ovulation: Effects on the probability of conception, survival of the pregancy, and sex of the baby. *New England Journal of Medicine, 333,* 1517–1521.

Wilcox, B. L. (1987). Pornography, social science and politics: When research and ideology collide. *American Psychologist, 42,* 941, 943.

Wildman, B. G., & White, P. A. (1986). Assessment of dysmenorrhea using the Menstrual Symptom Questionnaire: Factor structure and validity. *Behaviour Research & Therapy, 24,* 547–551.

Wille, R., & Beier, K. M. (1989). Castration in Germany. *Annals of Sex Research, 2,* 103–133.

Williams, D. E., & D'Alessandro, J. D. (1994). A comparison of three measures of androgyny and their relationship to psychological adjustment. *Journal of Social Behavior and Personality, 9* (3) 469–480.

Willis, R. J., & Michael, R. T. (1994). Innovation in family formation: Evidence on cohabitation in the United States. In J. Eruisch & K. Ogawa (Eds.), *The family, the market and the state in aging societies.* London: Oxford University Press.

Wilson, G., & Cox, D. (1983). Personality of pedophile club members. *Personality and Individual Differences, 4,* 323–329.

Wilson, M. R., & Filsinger, E. E. (1986). Religiosity and marital adjustment: Multidimensional interrelationships. *Journal of Marriage and the Family, 48,* 147–151.

Wilson, S. N., & Sanderson, C. A. (1988). The sex report curriculum: Is "just say no" effective? *SIECUS Report, 17,* 10–11.

Winick, C. (1985). A content analysis of sexually explicit magazines sold in an adult bookstore. *Journal of Sex Research, 21,* 206–210.

Wise, T. N. (1994). Sertraline as a treatment for premature ejaculation. *Journal of Clinical Psychiatry, 55*(9), 417.

Wisell, T. E., et al. (1987). Declining frequency of circumcision: Implications for changes in the absolute incidence and male to female sex ratio of urinary tract infections in early infancy. *Pediatrics, 79,* 338–342.

Wortman, C. B., et al. (1976). Self-disclosure: An attributional perspective. *Journal of Personality and Social Psychology, 33,* 184–191.

WuDunn, S. (1996, January 25). In Japan, a ritual of mourning for abortions. *The New York Times,* A1, A8.

Wyatt, G. E. (1985). The sexual abuse of Afro-American and white American women in childhood. *Child Abuse and Neglect, 9,* 507–519.

Wyatt, G. E. (1988). The relationship between child sexual abuse and adolescent sexual functioning in Afro-American and white American women. *Annals of the New York Academy of Sciences, 528,* 111–122.

Wyatt, G. E. (1989). Reexamining factors predicting Afro-American and white American women's age at first coitus. *Archives of Sexual Behavior, 18,* 271–298.

Wyatt, G. E., et al. (1988a). Kinsey revisited, Part I: Comparisons of the sexual socialization and sexual behavior of white women over 33 years. *Archives of Sexual Behavior, 17*(3), 201–209.

Wyatt, G. E., et al. (1988b). Kinsey revisited, Part II: Comparisons of the sexual socialization and sexual behavior of black women over 33 years. *Archives of Sexual Behavior, 17*(4), 289–332.

Wyatt, G. E., et al. (1990). Internal and external mediators of women's rape experiences. *Psychology of Women Quarterly, 14,* 153–176.

Yarber, W. L., & Parillo, A. V. (1992). Adolescents and sexually transmitted diseases. *Journal of School Health, 62,* 331–338.

Yates, G. L., et al. (1991). A risk profile comparison of homeless youth involved in prostitution and homeless youth not involved [Special issue: Homeless youth]. *Journal of Adolescent Health, 12,* 545–548.

Yorburg, B. (1995, July 9). Why couples choose to live together. *The New York Times,* p. 14.

Zaviacic, M., & Whipple, B. (1993). Update on the female prostate and the phenomenon of female ejaculation. *Journal of Sex Research, 30,* 148–151.

Zaviacic, M., et al. (1988a). Concentrations of fructose in female ejaculate and urine: A comparative biochemical study. *Journal of Sex Research, 24,* 319–325.

Zaviacic, M., et al. (1988b). Female urethral expulsions evoked by local digitial stimulation of the G-spot: Differences in the response patterns. *Journal of Sex Research, 24,* 311–318.

Zeman, N. (1990, Summer/Fall). The new rules of courtship [Special Edition]. *Newsweek,* 24–27.

Zenker, P. N., & Rolfs, R. T. (1990). Treatment of syphilis, 1989. *Reviews of Infectious Diseases* (Suppl. 6), S590-S609.

Zhang, J., & Fried, D. B. (1992). Relationship of maternal smoking during pregnancy to placenta previa. *American Journal of Preventative Medicine, 8,* 278–282.

Zilbergeld, B. (1978). *Male sexuality.* Boston: Little, Brown.

Zillmann, D., & Bryant, J. (1982, Autumn). Pornography, sexual callousness, and the trivialization of rape. *Journal of Communication,* 10–21.

Zillmann, D., & Bryant, J. (1984). Effects of massive exposure to pornography. In N. M. Malamuth & E. Donnerstein (Eds.), *Pornography and sexual aggression* (pp. 115–138). New York: Academic Press.

Zillmann, D., & Weaver, J. B. (1989). Pornography and men's sexual callousness toward women. In D. Zillmann & J. Bryant (Eds.), *Pornography: Research advances and policy considerations* (pp. 95–125). Hillsdale, NJ: Erlbaum.

Name Index

Abel, G., 353
Abelson, H., 402, 403
Abramowitz, S., 118
Acker, M., 149
Acton, W., 8
Adams, H., 117, 186, 381
Adams, R., 396
Adelson, A., 125
Adelson, M., 340
Aeschylus, 6
Allen, J., 337
Allen, M., 122, 160
Alter-Reid, K., 382, 384
Althof, S., 318
Altman, L., 239, 251, 252
Alzate, H., 90
Amaro, H., 336
Amato, P. 288
Ames, M., 188, 381
Anderson, B., 319
Anderson, J., 136
Angier, N., 111, 189, 234
Antill, J., 128
Antonarakas, S., 217
Appell, R., 308
Archimedes, 6
Aristophanes, 6
Aristotle, 6
Aronson, E., 161
Asbell, D., 10
Asso, D., 51
Astley, S., 216
Atkeson, B., 369, 370, 371, 374, 377
Auerbach, R., 318
Augustine, saint, 6
Avis, W., 136
Ayres, B., 385

Bachrach, C., 279
Bagatell, C., 319
Bagley, C., 396
Bailey, J., 187, 188
Baker, T., 374
Baldwin, J. D., 184, 276
Baldwin, J. I., 184
Bancroft, J., 188
Banning, A., 380
Bar-Tal, D., 141
Barbach, L., 96, 315, 402
Barbaree, H., 373
Barlow, D., 188, 318
Barnes, R., 331
Barr, H., 216
Barrett, 193
Barringer, F., 279, 287, 324
Bart, P., 377

Barth, R., 279
Baumeister, R., 355
Baxter, D., 373
Beach, F., 11, 122, 136, 139, 183, 184, 357
Beck, J., 305, 309, 318
Beck, S., 373, 381
Becker, J., 374, 380
Beier, K., 385
Beitchman, J., 382
Bell, A., 16, 191, 192, 193, 194, 195
Bell, S., 374
Bellis, D., 399
Bello, D., 406
Bem, S., 125, 127, 178
Bennett, N., 281
Berkowitz, 403
Berlin, F., 83
Berliner, D., 80
Bernstein, W., 141
Berscheid, E., 144
Beutler, L., 306, 308, 319
Bieber, I., 190, 192
Billy, J., 16, 83
Bingham, C., 275
Binik, Y., 304
Birnbaum, H., 370, 374
Bixler, R., 140
Bjorklund, D., 10, 122, 139
Blakeslee, S., 80, 288, 341, 342
Blanchard, R., 118, 353, 355, 361
Blanco, J., 330
Blenner, J., 206
Bloom, B., 288
Bloor, M., 399
Blumstein, P., 20, 195, 196, 283, 284
Boles, J., 399
Bowie, W., 331
Boyer, 397
Bozzette, S., 339
Bradbury, T., 156
Brady, E., 371
Bremner, W., 319
Breslow, N., 356, 360–361
Bretl, D. 406
Bretschneider, J., 291
Briere, J., 379, 380
Brody, J., 40, 49, 51, 52, 62, 80, 81, 302, 307, 339, 340, 350, 351, 362, 377, 406
Bronars, S., 277
Brooks, V., 122
Brooks-Gunn, J., 116, 275, 276, 278
Brown, D., 401
Brown, R. A., 139
Brown, R. E., 382
Bryant, J., 401, 405

Bullough, V., 181, 352
Bumiller, E., 5
Bumpass, L., 280, 281
Burgess, A., 370, 375, 376
Burkhart, B., 373
Burman, B., 288
Burt, 371
Buss, D., 140, 141, 282
Bussey, K., 124
Buxton, A., 193
Byers, E., 377
Byrnes, J., 121

Caceres, C., 337
Calderone, M., 269
Calhoun, K., 369, 370, 371, 374
Caligula, 6
Call, V., 284
Calvin, J., 8
Cameron, P., 381
Campbell, C., 399
Campbell, S., 226
Cannistra, S., 35, 324, 342
Cantor, E., 165
Cantor, J., 406
Cappella, J., 142
Carani, C., 307, 319
Carey, M., 306, 308
Carmignani, G., 319
Carpenter, C., 293
Carrera, M., 186
Cartwright, R., 118
Carvajal, D., 393, 394
Castro, K., 399
Catalan, J., 309, 318
Catalona, W., 67
Catania, J., 194
Cates, W., 245, 254, 330
Celis, W., 376
Ceniti, J., 405
Chan, C., 185
Charny, I., 287
Check, J., 372
Chesney, C., 338, 339
Clark, M., 143
Clinton, W., 195
Clumeck, N., 339
Cnattingius, S., 216
Cobb, M., 80
Cochran, S., 195
Cohen, L., 282
Cohen-Kettenis, P., 118
Cohn, J., 226
Colditz, G., 39, 40, 48
Cole, S., 293
Coleman, E., 397, 398

Coleman, M., 128
Coleman, S., 257
Coles, C., 216
Coles, R., 16, 269, 270, 274, 275
Collaer, M., 116, 123, 188
Collins, N., 159
Condon, J., 143
Cooper, A., 363, 381
Cooper, D., 339
Corey, L., 339
Cornell, C., 184
Cosgray, R., 355
Cox, D., 352, 381
Crano, W., 143
Crews, 188
Cronin, A., 181, 192
Crum, C., 331
Cummings, E., 287, 288
Cunningham, M., 138
Curran, D., 372, 373
Curtis, R., 143
Cutrona, C., 226

Dabbs, J., 83
D'Alessandro, J., 127
Dante, 144
Darabi, K., 276
Darling, C., 88
Darwin, C., 138
Davenport, W., 4
Davidson, J., 101
Davidson, K., 48
Davidson, N., 90
Davies, P., 287, 288
Davis, J., 184
Davis, M., 149
Dawes, R., 142
Day, N., 216
de Luca, R., 384
de Raad, B., 139
de Young, M., 381
Deaux, K., 122
DeBlassie, R., 275
Dekker, J., 304
Del Priore, G., 38
Denny, N., 96
Desmond, A., 277
Deutsch, F., 137
Dick-Read, G., 223
Dietz, P., 374
DiMatteo, M., 224
Dindia, K., 122, 160
Doddema-Winsemius, M., 139
Dolan, E., 288
Donnerstein, E., 403
Douglas, M., 385
Downey, J., 188
Drews, C., 216
Dryan, A., 256
Dube, R., 379
Dugger, C., 30, 31
Dunn, M., 89
Durand, V., 188
DuRant, R., 279
Dwyer, M., 353, 355, 362
Dziech, B., 386

Edgerton, 118
Edgley, C., 392, 393, 394, 395, 397, 402, 405, 406
Edmonson, B., 292, 294

Eggert, A., 80
Ehrhardt, A., 115, 116
Ehrlich, G., 293
Eisen, M., 268
Elifson, K., 399
Ellis, A., 310
Ellis, H., 10
Ellis, L., 188
Ellner, P., 331
Elmer-Dewitt, P., 63
Ember, C., 5, 282, 283, 372
Ember, M., 5, 282, 283, 372
Emmanuel, N., 363
English, P., 216
Erel, O., 288
Erlanger, S., 396, 399
Ervin, K., 136
Eskenazi, G., 216, 373
Etaugh, C., 113, 217, 270, 271
Everaerd, W., 318
Everson, S., 48
Exner, J., 395

Fahrner, E., 118
Falcon, P., 372
Faller, K., 382
Fallon, A., 136
Fallopio, G., 36
Faro, S., 333
Feingold, A., 121, 142
Felsman, D., 277
Felson, R., 369, 387
Feng, T., 216
Fenichel, O., 359
Fensterheim, H., 363
Ferrante, C., 406
Fichner-Rathus, L., 4, 150
Filsinger, E., 20
Fincham, F., 288
Fine, M., 186
Finkelhor, D., 371, 378, 379, 381, 382, 383
Fischer, E., 143
Fish, L., 309
Fisher, B., 397
Fisher, W., 334
Fitzgerald, L., 386, 387
Floyd, R., 216
Ford, C., 11, 122, 136, 139, 183, 184, 357
Forster, P., 318
Franke, P., 382
Franzoi, S., 136
Fraser, A., 277
Frayser, S., 136
Frazier, P., 375
Freiberg, P., 186
Freud, S., 10, 11–13, 16, 89, 124, 189–190, 266, 268, 309
Freund, J., 353, 361
Freund, K., 352, 399
Fried, D., 216
Friedman, J., 312
Friedman, L., 41
Friedman, R., 188
Friedrich, E., 333
Friedrich, W., 361
Fromuth, M., 373
Fuchs, C., 40
Furnham, A., 406
Furstenberg, F., 275, 276, 277, 278

Gabriel, T., 193
Gagnon, J., 14, 17, 18, 91, 93, 98, 28, 191, 195, 274, 305, 382, 397, 398
Ganitsch, C., 223
Ganong, L., 128
Garber, M., 183
Garland, S., 330
Garnets, L., 185
Garwood, S., 139
Gayle, J., 324
Gebhard, P., 10, 61, 181, 353, 355, 382
Geer, J., 352, 353, 361
Geiger, R., 293
Gelbart, S., 334
Gelles, R., 184
Gelman, D., 143
Genuis, M., 378
Gerber, P., 361
Gerrol, R., 370
Gibb, D., 214, 337
Gibbs, N., 370, 371
Gibson, A., 396
Gidycz, C., 377
Gilbert, S., 40, 234, 235, 236
Gillis, J., 136
Giovanucci, E., 252
Gitlin, M., 226
Glass, S., 286
Gold, R., 312
Gold, S., 137, 312
Goldberg, A., 381
Goldberg, C., 394, 396
Goldberg, L., 341
Goldberg, M., 359
Goldenberg, R., 277
Goleman, D., 383, 384, 387, 401
Gomez, J., 185
Gomez-Schwartz, B., 383
Gonda, G., 118
Goodwin, J., 382
Gordon, S., 145, 184, 393
Gorzalka, B., 81
Gottlieb, M., 334
Graber, B., 303
Grafenberg, E., 90
Graham, J., 330
Graham, S., 8, 340
Grajek, S., 145
Green, R., 184
Greene, B., 185
Greenwald, E., 382, 384
Griffin, E., 142
Grodstein, F., 36, 48, 49, 333
Grogger, J., 277
Groneman, C., 359
Groth, A., 370, 373, 374
Grych, J., 288
Gudykunst, 159
Guinan, M., 254
Gupta, M., 7

Haffner, D., 268, 274
Haglund, B., 216
Hall, C., 122
Hall, G., 373, 374
Halverson, C., 125
Hamer, D., 181, 188
Hamilton, M., 376
Hammer, S., 339
Handler, A., 279
Harahap, 60

Harding, J., 226
Harney, P. 373
Harris, M., 268
Hart, J., 207
Hartman, C., 396
Harvey, S., 47
Hatcher, R., 204, 235, 236, 237, 238, 239,
    241, 242, 243, 244, 247, 248, 250, 253,
    254, 255, 338
Hatfield, E., 136, 140, 145
Hausknecht, R., 214, 259
Havemann, E., 123, 165
Hawton, K., 318
Hayes, C., 268, 275, 279
Hazan, C., 143
Hebert, M., 379
Hechtman, L., 277
Heiman, J., 315, 318, 402
Hemingway, E., 400
Hendrick, C., 146
Hendrick, S., 146
Henning, K., 95, 96
Hensley, W., 136
Herdt, G., 184
Herold, E., 402
Herzog, L., 60
Herzog, M., 136
Hess, B., 277
Hillier, S., 332
Hillingdon, A., 8
Hilton, E., 333
Hines, M., 116, 123, 188
Hirschman, R., 374
Hite, S., 92, 94, 95, 99
Hoagwood, K., 384
Hobson, W., 374
Hodgson, R., 330
Hodson, D., 291
Hofferth, S., 275
Hoffman, J., 238
Hoffman, L., 101
Hogan, 276
Holden, G., 288
Holmes, K., 332, 339
Holmstrom, L., 375, 376
Holzman, H., 396
Houston, D., 381
Howard, J., 139
Howard, M., 279
Howards, S., 204, 206
Hsu, B., 95
Hubbard, R., 218
Hubschman, L., 118
Hucker, S., 355
Hunt, M., 16, 90, 96, 283, 284, 287, 392
Hunter, D., 40
Hyde, J., 121

Imperato-McGinley, J., 115
Ireland, L., 113
Isay, R., 181, 193, 194

Jacklin, C., 120, 122, 124
Jackson, J., 383
Jackson, L., 136
Jacobson, J., 216
Jacobson, S., 216
Jallon, J., 80
Jamison, P. 61
Jankowiak, W., 143
Janus, C., 16, 143, 144, 181, 378

Janus, S., 16, 143, 144, 181, 378
Javier, R., 119
Jencks, C., 277
Johnson, E., 269
Johnson, K., 39
Johnson, V., 18–19, 50, 61, 72, 83, 88, 89,
    92, 96, 192, 194, 283, 304, 308, 311,
    313–314, 315, 316, 317, 318
Jones, 291
Jones, H., 204
Jorgensen, C., 116
Jorgensen, S., 279
Josephs, R., 81
Joyce, J., 400

Kalick, S., 141
Kammeyer, K., 4, 163, 282
Kantner, J., 275
Kantor, J., 363
Kantrowitz, B., 277, 278
Kaplan, D., 31, 384
Kaplan, H., 88. 302, 304, 309, 311–312, 316
Karney, B., 156
Katz, J., 184, 186
Katz, R., 380
Katzenstein, D., 339
Kedia, K., 304
Keith, B., 288
Keith, J., 275
Keith, P., 141, 282
Kellerman, J., 164
Kellogg, J., 91
Kenney, A., 268, 278
Kerber, R., 39
Kerns, J., 186
Kettl, P., 293
Kiely, J., 216, 217
Killmann, P., 316, 318
Kilpatrick, D., 371
Kimlicka, T., 128
Kimmel, D., 185
Kinard, E., 277
King, J., 318
King, L., 60
Kinloch-de Loes, S., 339
Kinsey, A., 10, 16, 17, 79, 90, 92, 93, 94, 95,
    96, 97, 180–183, 194, 266, 268, 274, 283,
    284, 310, 355, 356, 358, 360, 392
Kipp, 10, 122, 139
Kite, 186
Kitigawa, 276
Klein, C., 405
Klerman, L., 277
Knight, R., 373
Knight, S., 291, 292
Knox, D., 381, 382
Knudsen, D., 378, 379, 380
Knussman, R., 83
Kockott, G., 118
Kohlberg, L., 125
Kohn, A., 378
Kolata, G., 18, 285, 339
Kolodny, 318
Komisar, L., 406
Komisaruk, B., 90
Kon, I., 5
Koss, M., 369, 375, 377
Krafft-Ebing, R., 10
Krafka, C., 405
Kresin, D., 47, 307
Kruks, G., 397

Kuhn, D., 124
Kuiper, B., 118
Kulin, H., 272
Kuriloff, P., 186

Laan, E., 402
Lackritz, E., 337
Lamacz, M., 362
Lamanna, M., 279, 286
Lamaze, F., 223
Lamke, K., 128
Landon, A., 15
Lang, R., 358
Langevin, R., 354, 358
LaTour, M., 406
Laumann, E., 13, 14, 16, 17, 18, 91, 92, 93,
    95, 97, 98, 102, 103, 142, 181, 183, 184,
    281, 282, 283, 284, 285, 286, 287, 302,
    305, 369
Laviola, M., 382
Lavoisier, P., 89
Lawrence, D.H., 283, 400
Lawrence, K., 402
Leary, W., 62, 204, 218, 302, 303, 308
Ledray, L., 377
Lee, J., 143, 144
Lehtinen, M., 123, 165
Leiblum, S., 302, 309, 312
Leigh, B., 275
Leitenberg, H., 92, 95, 96, 268, 274, 382
Leland, N., 279
Lemon, S., 341
Lenihan, G., 371
Lesnik-Oberstein, M., 282
Letourneau, E., 302
LeVay, S., 188
Lever, J., 179
LeVesconte, S., 121
Levine, G., 333, 334
Levinger, G., 156, 160
Levy, D., 373
Lewin, T., 279
Lewis, K., 377
Lewis, S., 143
Libman, E., 311
Lief, H., 118
Linet, 319
Lininger, 305
Linsley, W., 400
Linz, D., 403, 404
Lipschultz, L., 308, 319, 320
Lisak, 371
Lohr, J., 60
LoPiccolo, J., 310, 312, 315, 316, 317, 318,
    319
Lorefice, L., 363
Lottes, I., 186
Lovdal, T., 406
Lown, J., 288
Luckenbill, D., 398
Lundstrom, B., 118
Lusk, J., 382, 383
Lusk, R., 379, 380, 381
Luther, M., 8

Maccoby, E., 120, 121, 122
MacFarquhar, N., 30, 31
Magos, A., 51
Malamuth, N., 371, 372, 405
Maletzky, B., 363
Malinowski, B., 10, 11

Malloy, M., 216
Marchbanks, P., 37
Margolin, L., 371, 372
Marks, G., 142
Marshall, W., 307, 363, 373, 403
Marsiglio, W., 184, 186, 279
Martens, M., 333
Martin, C., 125
Martin, D., 331
Martinez, F., 216
Martinson, F., 266
Mason, R., 80, 373
Masters, W., 18–19, 50, 61, 72, 83, 88, 89,
     92, 96, 192, 194, 283, 304, 308, 311,
     313–314, 315, 316, 317, 318, 371
Matek, O., 354
Matthews, K., 380
Matthews, W., 116
Maybach, K., 137
Mayer, J., 216
Mayer, S., 277
Mayerson, M., 128
McArthur, M., 374
McCabe, J., 279
McConaghy, M., 113
McCoy, N., 291
McGuire, R., 361
McLaren, J., 382
McLaughlin, F., 225
McMahon, M., 224
Mead, M., 10, 11, 122, 123, 140
Meana, M. 304
Meese, E., 403
Meiselman, K., 381
Meisler, A., 306, 308
Mertz, G., 340
Messenger, J., 306
Meston, C., 81
Meuwissen, I., 402
Meyer-Bahlburg, H., 188
Michael, R., 14, 17, 18, 91, 92, 93, 98, 142,
     156, 275, 281, 282, 283, 284, 285, 305,
     401
Michaels, S., 14, 17, 91, 93, 98, 285, 305
Miller, B., 275, 276
Miller, D., 363
Miller, E., 393, 395
Miller, H., 283, 400
Miller, K., 143
Miller, L., 159
Miller, S., 39
Mills, J., 215
Minai, N., 7
Mirin, S., 82
Mishell, D., 235, 237, 239, 244
Mohr, D., 306, 308, 319
Moi, H., 332
Money, J., 61, 83, 115, 116, 117, 123, 184,
     188, 191, 350, 351, 362, 363
Moore, D., 150, 385
Moore, K., 277
Morales, E., 185
Morgan, T., 67
Morokoff, 303, 309
Morris, R., 83
Morrison, 270
Morse, E., 399
Mosher, W., 279
Muehlenhard, C., 372, 373
Mueser, K., 137
Muhammad, 7

Muller, J., 80
Muller, M., 333
Murstein, B., 149
Muster, N., 380
Myers, A., 118
Myers, M., 370

Nakamura, R., 189
Nakanishi, M., 159
Nakashima, A., 329
Nelson, K., 399
Nevid, J., 139, 288
Newbold, J., 341
Newcomb, P., 48
Nichols, M., 308
Niloff, J., 35, 324, 342
Nishida, 159
Norman, J., 268
Nosek, M., 291, 292

O'Brien, P., 377
Ochs, R., 39, 67, 342
O'Donohue, W., 302, 318
O'Grady, K., 276
Ogrinc, 319
O'Hara, M., 226
Okami, P., 381
Osborne, N., 340
Over, R., 402
Overholser, J., 373, 381

Padesky, 193
Padgett, V., 405
Padilla, E., 276
Palace, E., 82
Palmer, M., 142
Parnass, S., 287
Pasnau, R., 226
Paul, R., 224
Paul, saint, 6
Pauly, I., 117, 118
Pear, R., 277
Pearson, C., 254
Peckham, C., 214, 337
Penn, F., 342
Peplau, L., 195
Perduta-Fulginiti, P., 293
Perrett, D., 138
Perry, D., 124
Perry, J., 90
Person, E., 96
Pillard, R., 113, 187, 188, 190
Pines, A., 161
Pines, S., 396
Plant, E., 121
Plato, 6
Porter, N., 127
Poussaint, A., 185
Powderly, W., 339
Powell, E., 369, 371, 372, 373, 375,
     376–377, 385, 386, 387
Prentky, R., 373
Price, V., 393, 396, 398
Purifoy, F., 289

Quadagno, D., 399
Quevillon, R., 304
Quinsey, V., 373

Radlove, S., 128
Rajfer, J., 308

Raskin, R., 116
Rathus, S., 12, 113, 150, 217, 270, 271, 304
Ratican, K., 384
Reagan, R., 403
Reichart, C., 331
Reid, 305
Rein, M., 333
Reinherz, H., 277
Reinisch, J., 61, 66, 95, 205, 235, 237, 240,
     241, 242, 243, 247, 248, 249, 250, 251,
     252, 253, 267, 269, 272, 290, 292, 294,
     319, 329, 330, 331, 332, 333, 334, 342,
     343, 354, 357, 361
Reiss, B., 289
Reiss, I., 192
Remafedi, G., 125
Renzetti, C., 372, 373
Resick, P., 370, 377
Resnick, P., 358
Reuter, 259
Rice, 384
Richards, R., 116
Richardson, G., 216
Riche, M., 281
Riedmann, A., 279, 286
Riggio, R., 137
Ritchie, K., 288
Roberto, L., 117
Roland, B., 383
Rolfs, R., 329
Rolfs, R., 329
Romenesko, K., 393, 395
Roosevelt, F., 15
Rose, P., 187
Rose, R., 36
Rosen, I., 362
Rosen, L., 393
Rosen, R., 302, 309, 310, 312
Rosenthal, A., 31
Rosenthal, E., 136
Rosman, J., 358
Rotheram-Borus, M., 396
Rovet, J., 113
Rozin, P., 136
Rubinow, D., 51
Ruble, D., 124
Ruble, T., 124
Runtz, M., 379, 380
Russell, D., 371
Russo, 256

Sacher-Masoch, L., 355
Sack, W., 373
Sadalla, E., 137
Sade, M. de, 355
Sadker, D., 122
Sadker, M., 122
Sagan, C., 256
Saluter, A., 281, 282, 287
Samuels, M., 207, 226
Samuels, N., 207, 226
Sanday, P., 372
Sanders, J., 279
Sanders, S., 181, 182
Sanderson, C., 279
Sappho, 187
Saravolatz, L., 339
Sargent, T., 351
Sarrel, P., 371
Savitz, L., 393
Saxe, L., 141

Schachter, J., 330
Schafer, R., 141, 282
Schafran, L., 369
Schiavi, R., 290, 291, 302
Schillinger, L., 5
Schmidt, P., 51
Schmitt, E., 186
Schnicke, M., 377
Schoendorf, K., 216, 217
Schork, K., 4
Schott, 352
Schreiber, G., 337
Schreiner-Engle, P., 302, 307
Schroeder, P., 31
Schultz, N., 150
Schwalm, L., 400
Schwartz, M., 192
Schwartz, P., 20, 195, 196, 283, 284
Scott, J., 400
Seftel, A., 293
Segal, Z., 373
Segraves, K., 308
Segraves, R., 308
Sell, R., 181
Seltzer, 186
Selvin, B., 116
Semans, J., 317
Seng, M., 396
Setlow, V., 337
Severn, J., 405
Shaver, P., 143
Shaw, 289
Sheehy, G., 204
Shenon, P., 193
Sheppard, J., 136
Sherman, K., 331
Sherwin, B., 83
Shields, B., 405
Siegel, K., 195
Signorielli, M., 125
Silber, S., 204
Silbert, M., 401
Simon, W., 191, 274
Simpson, J., 144
Singh, D., 136
Singh, G., 224, 225
Siregar, 60
Sirles, E., 382
Skeen, P., 291
Skinner, B., 13
Slattery, M., 39
Slonim-Nevo, V., 276
Smith, B., 185
Smith, E. A., 276
Smith, E. P., 273
Smith, T., 184
Smolowe, J., 255, 259
Snyder, C., 145, 184, 393
Socrates, 6
Solano, C., 150
Solon, 6
Sonenstein, F., 194
Sophocles, 6
Sourander, L., 37, 48
Southerland, D., 5
Spark, R., 71, 293, 302, 308, 319, 320
Sparks, G., 142
Speckens, A., 305
Spitzer, R., 357

Sprecher, S., 136, 139, 140
Stampfer, M., 49
Starr, B., 289, 291
Steele, C., 81
Steinbeck, J., 400
Steiner, M., 50, 51
Steinhauer, J., 280, 281
Stericker, A., 121
Sternberg, R., 145, 146–149, 162
Stewart, F., 254
Stief, T., 277
Stock, W., 316, 317, 318, 319, 372
Stokes, G., 16, 269, 270, 274, 275
Stoller, R., 117, 184, 353
Stone, K., 245, 254
Storer, B., 48
Storms, M., 126, 182
Strathman, A., 136
Strickland, B., 191
Struckman-Johnson, C., 371
Stuart, F., 307
Sue, D., 361
Sugimoto, Y., 256
Sullivan, Q., 140
Swann, W., 143
Symons, D., 139, 402
Szasz, G., 293

Takahira, S., 121
Tanfer, K., 16
Tang, C., 370
Tannahill, R., 5, 8
Tannen, D., 159, 163, 164
Tantleff, S., 136
Tedeschi, J., 369, 387
Thabit, S., 30
Thomason, J., 334
Thomlison, B., 380
Thompson, D., 63, 207, 212, 258, 275
Thompson, J., 136
Thompson, M., 377
Tobias, S., 121
Tollison, C., 117, 381
Toner, J., 204, 206
Toomey, K., 331
Toubia, N., 31
Touchette, N., 60
Townsend, J., 286, 402
Trost, J., 89
Trovato, F., 288
Trujillo, C., 185
Trussell, J., 242, 245, 246
Tutty, L., 383
Twain, M., 400

Udry, J., 83, 276
Ulbrich, P., 207

Valentiner, D., 374, 377
Van den Hoek, A., 399
Van Steirteghem, A., 206
van-Griensven, G., 337
Vatsyayana, 7
Vazi, R., 65
Victoria, queen, 8, 219
Vinci, L. da, 16
Voeller, B., 103
Voli, V., 406
Voyer, D., 121
Vyas, G., 337

Wald, A., 340
Wald, E., 218
Waldinger, M., 318
Walfish, S., 128
Walker, A., 30, 31
Wallerstein, J., 288
Walsh, P., 66
Walt, V., 255
Wasserheit, J., 330
Waterman, J., 379, 380, 381, 382, 383
Watson, J., 13
Weaver, J., 405
Weinberg, M., 183, 192, 193, 194, 195, 361–362
Weinberg, T., 356, 357
Weiner, L., 386
Weiner, M., 289, 291
Weinrich, J., 113, 187, 190
Weisberg, D., 397
Weiss, R., 82
Whalen, R., 188
Whiffen, V., 226
Whipple, B., 90
Whitam, F., 188
White, G., 161
White, J., 122
White, P., 50
White, S., 275
Whitley, B., 127, 186
Whitley, R., 340
Whittemore, A., 38
Wiedeking, C., 351
Wilcox, A., 215
Wilcox, B., 403
Wildman, B., 50
Wille, R., 385
Williams, D., 127
Williams, L., 39
Willis, R., 281
Wilson, 67
Wilson, G., 381
Wilson, M., 20
Wilson, S., 279
Winick, C., 402
Wise, T., 318
Wisell, T., 60
Wold, F., 319
Woll, S., 137
Wortman, C., 159
Wright, T., 286
WuDunn, S., 256
Wyatt, G., 16, 375, 383

Yates, G., 399
Yee, J., 376
Yllo, K., 371
Yorburg, B., 281
Young, L., 396
Yu, S., 224, 225

Zaviacic, M., 90
Zellman, G., 268
Zelnik, M., 275
Zeman, N., 275
Zenker, P. 329
Zhang, J., 216
Zilbergeld, B., 60
Zillmann, D., 402, 405
Zuwera, H., 30

Subject Index

ABCDE model of relationships, 156–162
Abkhasians, sexuality among, 4
Abortion
    controversy about, 256–257
    cross-cultural views of, 256–257
    drugs to cause, 259
    incidence of, 255
    in Japan, 5, 256–257
    methods of, 257–259
Abstinence, 249
Accentuating the positive, 168
Acculturation, 119
Acne medication, effects on fetus, 215
Acquaintance rape, 369–370
Acquired dysfunctions, 301
Acquired erectile disorder, 302
Acquired immunodeficiency syndrome. *See*
    AIDS; HIV
Activating effects, 82, 188
Active listening, 167
Acyclovir, 341
Adolescence, 270
    contraceptive use in, 276
    puberty, 270–273
    sexual behavior in, 274–276
    sexuality in, 4, 270–279
Adoption, 206
Adultery, 286
Adulthood, 279
    sexuality in, 279–288
Advertising
    sex in, 405–406
    stereotyping in, 406
Advocate, 187
Africa, genital mutilation in, 30
African Americans
    AIDS among, 336
    attitudes about sexual orientation, 185
    infant mortality among, 225
    teen pregnancy among, 277
    teen sex among, 276
Agape, 143, 146
Age, sex and, 13
Age homogamy, 282
Age of viability, 212
Aggression
    gender differences in, 122
    and rape, 374, 403
Agreeing to disagree, 172
AIDS, 327, 334
    diagnosis of, 338
    epidemiology of, 335
    ethnicity and, 336
    fetal effects of, 214
    and gay bashing, 186
    immune system and, 334–336

incidence of, 334
prevention of, 343
progression of, 336–337
prostitution and, 398–399
sexual behavior changed by threat of, 194,
    195–196
transmission of, 337–338
treatment of, 338–339
Alcohol
    effects on fetus, 216
    and sexuality, 81
Alimony, 288
Amenorrhea, 50
Amitriptyline, 81
Amniocentesis, 219
Amniotic fluid, 210
Amniotic sac, 210
Amphetamines, 82
Amphett people, sexuality among, 11
Ampulla, 37, 72
Amyl nitrate, 80
Anal intercourse, 102–103
    infection risk from, 32
Analogous, defined, 30
Anaphrodisiacs, 80
Androgen-insensitivity syndrome, 115
Androgenital syndrome, 114–115
Androgens, 61, 62, 82–83, 111
    function of, 271
Androgyny, 126
Anencephaly, 217
Anesthesia, 223
Anger rape, 374
Anilingus, 103
Animal experimentation, 22
Anorexia nervosa, 136
    infertility and, 205
Anorgasmic, defined, 304
Anovulatory, defined, 271
Anoxia, 224
Anthropology, 18
Antiandrogens, 80, 363
Antibodies
    defined, 330
    effects on fetus, 215
Antigen, defined, 335
Antihistamines, effects on fetus, 215
Antihypertensives, 81
Antroverted, defined, 36
Aphrodisiacs, 78, 80–81
Arapesh people, sex roles in, 123
Arctic, wife sharing in, 4
Areola, 38
Arousal, love as, 145–146
Arthritis, 293
Artificial insemination, 204

Asexuals, defined, 196
Asian Americans
    AIDS among, 336
    attitudes about sexual orientation, 185
    infant mortality among, 225
    teen sex among, 276
Aspirin, effects on fetus, 215
Assertiveness, importance of, 150
Asymptomatic, defined, 325
Attraction
    cultural factors in, 136–137
    inherited preferences and, 139–141
    matching hypothesis and, 141–143
    physical, 135–139
    reciprocity in, 143
    stage of relationship, 156
Auto-immune response, 204
Autonomic nervous system, 70–71
Aversion therapy, 363
AZT, 339

B&D, 356
Bacteria, 324
Bacterial vaginosis, 326, 332
Bar hustlers, 399
Bar prostitutes, 393
Barbiturates, 81
Bartholin's glands, 33–34
Basal body temperature (BBT), 44
    chart, 203
    contraceptive method, 249
Beauty, cross-cultural aspects of, 138
Behavior therapy, 362
Behaviorists, 13
Benign, defined, 40
Benign prostatic hyperplasia, 66–67
Bestiality, 358
    defined, 10
Birth control, 249. *See also* Contraception
Bisexual, defined, 6
    defined, 6, 178
Blastocyst, 209
Bondage, 355
Born on the Fourth of July, 291
Bottle-feeding, 227
Brain
    sexual differentiation of, 113, 123
    and sexual orientation, 188–189
Braxton-Hicks contractions, 220
Breast self-examination, 41
Breast-feeding, 226
Breasts, 38–41
    attraction to, 38, 136
    cancer of, 39–41
    stimulation of, 97
Breech presentation, 212, 224

Britain
  incidence of rape in, 369
  laws about homosexuality, 186
Brothel prostitutes, 394
  male, 398
Brother-sister incest, 381–382
Building, stage of relationship, 157–160
Bulbourethral glands, 64–65
Bupropion, 80
Butch, defined, 187

Calendar method, 249
Call boys, 399
Call girls, 395
Calymmatobacterium granulomatus, 331
Canada, laws about homosexuality, 186
Candida albicans, 327, 332
Candidiasis, 327, 332–333
Cantharidin, 80
Caring, in intimacy, 162–163
Case study, defined, 16
Castration, 82
Castration anxiety, 189
Catholicism, sexuality in, 8, 15
Cause and effect, 21
CD4 cells, 335
Celibacy, 280
  historical views of, 7
Cephalic presentation, 212
Cephalocaudal development, 209
Cerebral palsy, 292
Cervical cancer, 36
Cervical cap, 244–245
Cervical mucus method, 250
Cervicitis, 325, 330
Cervix, 35
Cesarean section, 223–224
Chancre, 329
Chancroid, 331
Chattel, defined, 6
Child sexual abuse
  defined, 378–379
  effect of, 382–384
  incest, 381–382
  incidence of, 378
  patterns of, 379–380
  perpetrators of, 380
  prevention of, 383
  treatment for perpetrators of, 384–385
  treatment for victims of, 384
Childbirth
  methods of, 222–224
  postpartum period, 226–227
  problems in, 224–226
  signs of, 220
  stages of, 220–222
Childbirth Without Fear, 223
Childhood, sexuality in, 266–270
China
  premarital sex in, 5
  self-disclosure in, 159
  sexuality in, 7
Chlamydia trachomatis, 324, 326, 330–331
Chorionic villus sampling (CVS), 219
Christianity
  sexuality in, 6–7
  views on homosexuality, 183
Christmas Eve, in Japan, 5
Chromosomes, 110
  abnormalities of, 113, 217–219

Cigarette smoke, effects on fetus, 215, 216–217
Cilia, 37, 64
Circumcision, 60
Climeracteric, 47
Clitoral glans, 29, 30
Clitoral orgasm, 89
Clitoridectomy, 30–31
Clitoris, 28, 29
  stimulation of, 97, 99–100
Clomid (clomiphene), 44, 205
Clomipramine, 318
Close couples, defined, 196
Clotrimazone, 333
Cocaine, 82
Cognition, gender differences in, 120–122
Cognitive-developmental theory, 125
Cohabitation, 8, 279, 280–281
Coitus
  anal, 102–103
  defined, 3
  duration of, 284
  fantasy in, 101
  foreplay in, 283
  frequency of, 11, 17, 20, 283–284
  techniques of, 100–104, 284
Coitus interruptus, 248
Colpotomy, 253
Combination pill, 234, 235
Coming Home, 291
Coming out, 193
Commercial sex
  advertising, 405–406
  pornography, 400–405
  prostitution, 392–399
Commission on Obscenity and Pornography, 402–403
Commitment, in intimacy, 163
Communication
  criticism as, 170–171
  gender differences in, 122
  in intimacy, 163
  nonverbal, 164–165
  problems of, 163–164, 171–172
  providing information, 168–169
  reinforcement in, 167
  requests in, 169–171
  sexual, 165–172
Companionate love, 147, 148
Complete hysterectomy, 36, 37
Conception, 210
  defined, 202
  promotion of, 203
Concordance, defined, 188
Concubine, defined, 6
Condoms, 245–248, 344, 399
  female, 254
Congenital syphilis, 329
Consanguineous, defined, 381
Consensual adultery, 286
Consummate love, 147, 148, 149
Continuation, stage of relationship, 160
Contraception
  cervical cap, 244–245
  condoms, 245–248
  diaphragm, 241–243
  douching, 248
  effectiveness of, 236–237
  fertility awareness methods, 248–251
  implantable, 238–239
  IUDs, 239–241

  male, 255
  new methods of, 254–255
  oral, 234–238
  reversibility of, 236
  selecting a method of, 238
  spermicidal, 243–244
  and STDs, 236
  sterilization, 251–254
  teen use of, 278
  withdrawal, 248
Control group, 21
Conventional adultery, 286
Copper T, 239, 240
Coprophilia, 358
Corona, 59
Corpora cavernosa, 29, 58
Corpus luteum, 42, 45
Corpus spongiosum, 58
Correlation, 20
Correlation coefficient, 20
Correlational method, 20–21
Counseling, taking advantage of, 150
Courtesan, defined, 6
Courtship disorders, 361
Covert sensitization, 363
Cowper's glands, 64–65
Crab lice, 328, 343
Cremaster muscle, 61
Crisis, defined, 374
Critical periods of vulnerability, 213
Critical thinking, defined, 3
Criticism, delivering and receiving, 170–171
Cruising, 195
Crura, 33
Cryotherapy, 342
Cryptorchidism, 66, 112
Cunnilingus, 97, 274
  techniques of, 99–100
Cystic fibrosis, 217, 219
Cystitis, 32
Cysts, 40

d4T, 339
Dartos muscle, 61
Date rape, 369–370
  preventing, 376–377
Date-seeking skills, 150, 158
Daughters of Bilitis, 187
ddC, 339
ddI, 339
Decision/commitment, as aspect of love, 146
Decoding, 163
Deep kissing, 96
Defense mechanisms, 12
Delta hepatitis, 341
Dental dams, 344
Dependent variable, 21
Depo-Provera, 254–255, 363
Depression, postpartum, 226
DES, 66, 188
Deterioration, of relationship, 161
Diaphragm, 241–243
Didanosine, 339
Diet
  and cancer, 67
  fetal effects of, 212
Diethylstilbestrol, 66, 188
  effects on fetus, 215
Dihydrotestosterone, 111
Dilate, defined, 220
Dilation and curettage (D&C), 258

Dilation and evacuation (D&E), 258
Disability, sexuality and, 291–294
Disclosure, 386
Diseases, fetal effects of, 212
Displacement, 189
Divorce
    consequences of, 288
    historical views of, 7
    incidence of, 287
Dizygotic twins, 188
Dominican Republic syndrome, 115, 116
Don Juanism, 358, 359
Donor IVF, 205
Douche, 35
    as contraceptive, 248
Dowager's hump, 48
Down syndrome, 217, 219
    risk of, 218
Drag prostitutes, 399
Dream interpretation, 12
Drugs
    effects on fetus, 215
    effects on sexuality, 307, 308
Dry orgasm, 89
Ductus deferens, 63
Dysfunctionals, defined, 196
Dysmenorrhea, 49–50
    coping with, 51–52
Dyspareunia, 301, 304
    treatment of, 317

Eclampsia, 214
Ectoparasites, 342–343
Ectopic pregnancy, 37, 214
Educational level, sexuality and, 13
Efface, defined, 220
Ego, defined, 11
Egypt
    brother-sister marriages in, 5–6
    sexuality in, 5
Ejaculation, 71–72, 85–86
    female, 90
    premature, 304, 310, 313
Ejaculatory duct, 64
Elavil, 81
Elderly, sexuality in, 288–291
Electra complex, 124, 189–190
Elephantiasis, 332
ELISA (enzyme-linked immunosorbent
    assay), 338
Embryo, 211
    defined, 110
    development of, 110–111
Embryonic stage, of prenatal development,
    208, 209–211
Embryonic transfer, 206
Emission stage, 72
Empty love, 147, 148
Encoding, 163
Ending, of relationship, 161–162
Endocrine glands, 42
Endometrial cancer, 36
Endometriosis, 36, 205
Endometrium, 36
Endoparasites, 342
Endorphins, 357
Epididymis, 63
Epididymitis, 325, 330, 331
Epidural block, 223
Episiotomy, 33, 220
ErecAid, 320

Erectile dysfunction, 302, 308
    treatment of, 313, 316, 318–320
Erection, 12, 68–69, 79
Eros, 144, 146
Erotic, defined, 3
ERT, 83
Escort services, 395
Estrogen, 37
    function of, 271
    and sexual differentiation, 113
Estrogen replacement therapy (ERT; HRT),
    83
Ethnicity
    and sexual behavior, 15
    and sexual orientation, 185
Excitement phase, 84, 85, 86
Exhibitionism, 352–353, 361
    responding to, 353
Experiment, defined, 21
Experimental group, 21
Experimental method, 21–22
Expulsion stage, 72
Extramarital sex, 286
    attitudes towards, 287
    effects of, 287
    patterns of, 286–287
Eyes, importance of, 164

Facial preferences, 138
Failure, realistic view of, 150
Fallopian tubes, 36, 37
False positive, defined, 331
Family, and sexual orientation, 189–190
Family Planning in Japanese Society,
    257
Fantasy, 316
    in coitus, 101–102
    in masturbation, 95–96
Father-daughter incest, 381
Father-son relationship, 190
Fatigue, and sexual desire, 307
Fatuous love, 147, 148
Fellatio, 97, 274
    techniques of, 98–99
Female condom, 254
Female orgasmic disorder, 304
Female sexual arousal disorder, 303
Female-superior position, 100–101, 102,
    104, 126, 315
Femme, defined, 187
Fertility, 202
    enhancing, 203
    female problems of, 205–206
    male problems of, 204
Fertility awareness methods, 248–251
Fertilization, 202
Fetal alcohol syndrome, 216
Fetal erythroblastosis, 215
Fetal stage, of prenatal development, 208,
    211–212
Fetishism, 351, 360, 360
Fetus, 211
    abnormalities of, 217–219
Fibroadenoma, 40
Fidelity, as cultural phenomenon, 4
Field study, 18
Fighting, fair, 150
Fimbriae, 37
Fisting, 194
Flagyl, 332, 333, 334
Fluoxetine, 81, 363

Follicle, 37
    development of, 46
Follicle-stimulating hormone (FSH), 43, 62
Food, as aphrodisiac, 80
For Whom the Bell Tolls, 400
Forcible rape, 369
Foreplay, 96, 283
Foreskin, 60
France, laws about homosexuality, 186
French kissing, 96
Frenulum, 59
Frequency, 17
Freudian theory, 11–13
Friendship, as love, 146
Frotteurism, 357
FSH, 43, 62
Functionals, defined, 196
Fundus, 36

G-spot, 90
Game-playing love, 146
Gang rape, 370
Gardnerella vaginalis, 326, 332
Gay activism, 186
Gay bashing, 184
    AIDS and, 186
Gay males
    adjustment of, 192–194
    attitudes towards, 184, 186–187
    cross-cultural perspective on, 183–184
    defined, 178
    lifestyles of, 195–196
    sexual behavior of, 194
Gay marriages, 186
Gay rights organizations, 195
Gazing, 164
Gender
    and attitudes towards pornography, 402
    cognitive differences by, 120–122
    defined, 2
    and health-care behavior, 122
    and mate preferences, 141
    self-disclosure and, 159–160
    sex and, 13
Gender assignment, 113
Gender constancy, 125
Gender dysphoria, 116
Gender identity, 113, 125
    defined, 3
    nature and nurture and, 113–114
    variations in, 115–118
Gender reassignment surgery, 117–118
Gender roles, 118, 120
    attractiveness and, 137
    defined, 3
    and homophobia, 186
Gender schema, 125
Gender schema theory, 125–126
Gender stability, 125
Gender typing
    biological perspectives on, 122–123
    cross-cultural perspectives on, 123
    psychological perspectives on, 124–126
General anesthesia, 223
General paresis, 329, 330
Generalize, defined, 15
Generalized dysfunctions, 301
Genes, defined, 10
Genetic abnormalities, 217–218
    averting, 219
    sex-linked, 218–219

Genetic counseling, 219
Genital herpes, 327
    diagnosis of, 340
    incidence of, 339
    symptoms of, 340
    transmission of, 340
    treatment of, 340
Genital mutilation, 30
Genital warts, 328, 341–342
Genitals
    development of, 111–113
    female, 28–38
    male, 58–65
    manual stimulation of, 96–97
    nondemanding stimulation of,
        314–316
    oral stimulation of, 97–100, 274
Germ cells, 61, 62
German measles, 213–214
Germinal stage, of prenatal development,
    208, 209
GIFT (gamete intrafallopian transfer),
    205
Gigolos, 397
Glans penis, 59
GnRH (Gonadotropin-releasing hormone),
    43
Gonadotropins, 43
Gonads, 61
Gone with the Wind, 372
Gonorrhea, 324, 325, 326, 328
Gossypol, 255
Graafian follicle, 44
Grafenberg spot, 90
Graham crackers, 8
Granuloma inguinale, 331
Grapes of Wrath, 400
Greece, ancient
    love in, 143
    sexuality in, 6, 102
Greeting, 157
Group sampling, 17
Gynecologist, defined, 32
Gynecomastia, 273

H-Y antigen, 111
Hallucinogens, 82
    effects on fetus, 216
Headaches, 50
Health care behavior, gender differences in,
    122
Hearing, and sexuality, 80
Hebrews, ancient, sexuality among, 6
Hegar's sign, 206
Hemispheres, brain, 123
Hemophilia, 217, 219
Hemophilus ducreyi, 331
Hepatitis, 328
    types of, 341
Hermaphrodites, 114–115
Herpes simplex types 1 and 2, 327, 340
Heteroerotic, defined, 182
Heterosexual orientation, defined, 178
Hindus, sexuality among, 7
Hispanic Americans
    AIDS among, 336
    attitudes about sexual orientation, 185
    infant mortality among, 225
    stereotypes in, 119
    teen pregnancy among, 277
    teen sex among, 276

HIV, 327, 334
    contraceptives as protection against, 245,
        247
    contraction of, 103
    diagnosis of, 338
    fetal effects of, 214
    prostitution and, 398–399
    sexual behavior changed by threat of,
        194
    transmission of, 337–338
    treatment of, 338–339
Holland, laws about homosexuality, 186
Homoerotic, defined, 182
Homogamy, 282
Homologous, defined, 30
Homophile, defined, 178
Homophobia, 184
Homosexual Citizen, 187
Homosexual orientation, defined, 178
Homosexualities: A Study of Diversity
        Among Men and Women, 195
Homosexuality
    in ancient Greece, 6
    coming out, 193
    historical views of, 6, 7
    "treatment" of, 192–194
    See also Gay males; Lesbians
Homosexuality in Perspective, 19
Honesty, in intimacy, 163
Hopi people, sexuality among, 11
Hormone replacement therapy (HRT), 48
Hormones, 82
    defined, 42
    effects on fetus, 215
    and sexual differentiation, 111–112
    and sexual orientation, 188
    and sexuality, 82–83
    to treat erectile dysfunction, 319
Hot flashes, 47
HPV, 324, 328, 341–342
HRT, 48
Huckleberry Finn, 400
Hudood Ordinance, 4
Human chorionic gonadotropin (HCG),
    206
Human growth hormone, 62
Human immunodeficiency virus. See AIDS;
    HIV
Human papilloma virus (HPV), 324, 328,
    341–342
Human Sexual Response, 18
Human sexuality. See Sexuality
Huntington's chorea, 217, 219
Hustlers, 397
Hyaluronidase, 202
Hymen, 32, 33
Hypersexuality, 358, 359
Hypoactive sexual desire, 301
Hypogonadism, 307
Hypothalamus, 42
    and sexual orientation, 189
Hypoxyphilia, 355, 361
Hysterectomy, 36–37, 253
Hysterotomy, 259

I-talk, 169–171
ICSH, 62
Id, defined, 11
Identification, 117
Imipramine, 81
Immune system, 334

In vitro fertilization (IVF), 205
Incest
    defined, 381
    family factors in, 382
    incidence of, 381
Incest taboo, 5, 282
Incidence, 17
Independent variable, 21
Individuality, in intimacy, 163
Induced abortion, 255
Infancy, sexuality in, 266–267
Infant mortality, ethnicity and, 225
Infertility
    defined, 202
    female, 205–206
    male, 204
Infibulation, 31
Infidelity, 286
    consequences of, 287
Inflammation, defined, 335
Infundibulum, 37
Inguinal canal, 112
Inis Beag, sexuality in, 306–307
Instillation, 258
Intercourse
    anal, 102–103
    defined, 3
    duration of, 284
    fantasy in, 101
    foreplay in, 283
    frequency of, 11, 17, 20, 283–284
    techniques of, 100–104, 284
Interstitial cells, 61, 63
Interstitial-cell-stimulating hormone,
    62
Interview method, 16
Intimacy
    as aspect of love, 146
    aspects of, 162–165
    defined, 162
Intra-amniotic infusion, 258–259
Intracytoplasmic injection, 206
Intrauterine devices (IUDs), 239–241
Introitus, 32
Islam
    circumcision in, 60
    clitoridectomy in, 30, 31
    sexuality in, 7
Isthmus, 37
Italy, laws about homosexuality, 186
IUDs, 239–241

Japan
    abortion in, 5, 256–257
    incidence of rape in, 369
    self-disclosure in, 159
    sexual customs of, 5
Jaundice, 341
Jealousy, 160–161
Jews
    circumcision among, 60
    views on homosexuality, 183

Kama Sutra, 7
Kaposi's sarcoma, 337
Karma, 8
Kept boys, 399
King and I, 399
Kinsey continuum, 180–182
    challenges to, 182–183

Kissing, 96
  in adolescence, 274
  in childhood, 267
  as cultural phenomenon, 4, 11
  and HIV transmission, 337
Klinefelter's syndrome, 113
Klismaphilia, 358
Kwell, 343

L-dopa, 80
Labia majora, 28, 29
Labia minora, 28, 29
Laboratory observation, 18–19
Lactation, 227
Lactobacillus acidophilus, 333
Ladder, 187
Lady Chatterley's Lover, 283, 400
Lamaze method, 223
Laminaria digitata, 258, 259
Laparoscopy, 205, 252, 253
Larynx, 273
Lateral-entry position, 101, 102, 104
Law, sexual orientation and, 186
Left brain, 123
Lesbians
  adjustment of, 192–194
  attitudes towards, 187
  cross-cultural perspective on, 184
  defined, 178
  lifestyles of, 195–196
  sexual behavior of, 194
Leukocytes, function of, 334
Leydig's cells, 61, 63
LH, 43, 62
  assaying for, 203, 250
LH-releasing hormone, 62
Librium, effects on fetus, 216
Lice, 328, 342–343
Lifelong dysfunctions, 301
Liking, 147, 148
Lindane, 343
Listening, 166–168
  importance of, 150
Local anesthesia, 223
Loneliness, coping with, 150
Lotrimin, 333
Love
  models of, 145–149
  romantic, 144–145
  styles of, 146
  types of, 143–144
Lovemap, 362
Low birth weight infants, 225
LSD, effects on fetus, 216
Ludus, 146
Lumpectomy, 40
Luteal phase, 45
Luteinizing hormone (LH), 43, 62
  assaying for, 203, 250
Lymphogranuloma venereum, 332
Lytta vesicatoria, 80

Machismo, 119
Maidenhead, 32
Male erectile disorder, 302, 308
  treatment of, 313, 316, 318–320
Male orgasmic disorder, 303–304
Male prostitution, 397–398
Male rape, 370
Male-superior position, 100, 104, 126
  fertility enhancement and, 203

Malignant, defined, 40
Mammary glands, 38
Mammography, 39, 40
Man-on-top position, 100, 104
Mangaia, sexuality in, 307
Mania, 146
"Manopause," 62
Marianismo, 119
Marijuana, effects on fetus, 215, 216
Marital rape, 370–371
Marriage
  cohabitation and, 281, 282
  ending of, 287–288
  gay, 186
  infidelity in, 286–288
  love in, 149
  partner choice for, 156, 157, 282–283
  satisfaction in, 20
  sexual satisfaction in, 283–285
  sexuality in, 282–288
Mashing, 357
Masochism, 355, 360, 361
Massage parlors, 394
Mastalgia, 50
Mastectomy, 40
Masturbation, 91
  in adolescence, 274
  in childhood, 267, 268
  cultural views of, 11, 13
  female techniques of, 94–95
  frequency of, 93
  historical views of, 7, 8
  incidence of, 92
  in infancy, 266–267
  infection risk from, 32
  male techniques of, 92–94
  reasons for, 91
  as component of therapy, 315
Matching hypothesis, 141
Mate preferences, 139–141
Math ability, gender differences in, 121
Mating gradient, 283
Mattachine Newsletter, 187
Mattachine Society, 187
Meatus, 58
Medroxyprogesterone acetate (MPA),
  254–255, 363
Men
  age-related changes in, 290–291
  hormones and, 82–83
  reproductive system of, 58–65
  secondary sex characteristics of, 61, 63,
    272–273
  sexual function of, 68–72
Menarche, 42, 270, 271
Menopause, 47–49, 289
  and sexuality, 48
Menstrual cycle, 42
  cessation of, 47–49
  changes occurring in, 45
  phases of, 43–47
  regulation of, 42–43
Menstrual phase, 46–47
Menstruation, 42
  problems of, 49–50
  sex during, 47
Mental retardation, sexuality and, 294
Methotrexate, 214, 259
Metronidazole, 332, 333, 334
Mexico, laws about homosexuality, 186
Miconazole, 333

Middle East, genital mutilation in, 30
Mifepristone, 259
Migraines, 50
Milk ducts, 38
Miller v. California, 400–401
Minilaparotomy, 252
Minipills, 234, 235
Miscarriage, 207, 214
Misoprostol, 259
Missionary position, 100, 104
Mittelschmerz, 44
Modeling, 13
Mongolism, 217
Moniliasis, 327, 332
Monistat, 333
Monozygotic twins, 187
Mons veneris, 28, 29
Morning after pill, 238
Morning sickness, 207
Motility, 204
Müllerian ducts, 110, 111
Müllerian inhibiting substance, 111
Multiphasic pills, 234
Multiple orgasms, 88
Mundugumor people, sex roles in, 123
Muscular dystrophy, 219
Mutuality, 160
My Left Foot, 291
Mycelex, 333
Myometrium, 36
Myotonia, 83–84

Nagele's rule, 208
Nama people, standards of attractiveness in,
  136
Names, attractiveness of, 139
Narcotics, effects on fetus, 215
Native Americans, AIDS in, 336
Natural childbirth, 223
Natural family planning, 248
Naturalistic observation, 18
Necrophilia, 358
  defined, 10
Negative correlation, 20
Neisseria gonorrhoeae, 324, 326
Neural-tube defects, 217, 219
Neurosyphilis, 329
New Guinea
  sex roles in, 123
  sexuality in, 183
NHSLS study, 17
Nicotine, 81
Nipples, 38
Nitric oxide, 308
Nocturnal emissions, 273
Nocturnal penile tumescence (NPT), 308
Nongonococcal urethritis (NGU), 326, 330
Nonlove, 148
Nonoxynol-9, 242, 244, 247, 344
Nonspecific vaginitis, 332
Nonverbal communication, 164–165
Nonverbal cues, 169
Norplant, 238–239
Nymphomania, 358, 359

Obesity, as unattractive trait, 136
Obscene phone calls, 354
Obscenity, defined, 400
Observation, methods of, 16
Observer effect, 19
Ocular herpes, 340

Oedipus complex, 13, 124, 189
Open couples, defined, 196
Opening line, 157
Ophthalmia neonatorum, 325
Opportunistic diseases, 337
Oral contraceptives
    advantages and disadvantages of, 235–238
    effectiveness of, 235
    mechanism of action of, 234–235
    "morning after pill," 238
    reversibility of, 235
    types of, 234–235
Oral herpes, 327
Oral sex, 97
    in adolescence, 274
    sociocultural factors in, 98
    techniques of, 98–100
Organizing effects, 82
Orgasm
    controversies about, 88–90
    cross-cultural views of, 306
    female, 86–87
    frequency of, 284–285
    male, 71, 85–86
    types of, 89
Orgasmic disorders, 301, 303–304
    treatment of, 314–317
Orgasmic phase, 85–86
Orgasmic platform, 85
Orgasmic reconditioning, 363
Os, 35
Osteoporosis, 48
Outercourse, 344
Ova, 28
Ovarian cancer, 37–38
Ovariectomy, 83
Ovaries, 37–38
Ovulation, 42
    failure of, 205
    prediction of, 250
Ovulation method, 250
Ovulatory mucus, 250
Ovulatory phase, 44
Ovum, period of the, 209
Oxytocin, 43
    function of, 220

Pakistan, Hudood Ordinance of, 4
Pap test, 36
ParaGard, 239, 240
Paraphilias
    biological perspectives on, 358
    defined, 350
    learning perspectives on, 360–361
    psychoanalytic perspectives on, 359–360
    sociological perspectives on, 361–362
    treatment of, 362–363
    types of, 351–358
Paraphrasing, 167
Paraplegia, 293
Paraplegic, defined, 71
Parasites, STDs caused by, 342–343
Parasympathetic nervous system, 70–71
Partialism, 351
Participant observation, 18
Passion, as aspect of love, 146
Pathogen, defined, 334
Peak days, defined, 250
Pederasty, 6
Pediculosis, 328, 342
Pedophilia, 363, 380–381

Pelvic inflammatory disease (PID), 205, 241
    causes of, 325, 330
Penile cancer, 60
Penile implant, 318
Penile injection, 319–320
Penis, 58–61
    stimulation of, 97, 98–99
Penis envy, 189–190
Performance anxiety, 69, 303, 310
Pergonal, 205
Perimetrium, 36
Perineum, 33, 221
Period of the ovum, 209
Permission, giving and receiving, 166, 168
Personality, gender differences in, 121–122
Pessimism, combating, 150
Petting, 274
Peyronie's disease, 71
Phallic symbols, 5
Phallic worship, 5
Pharaonic circumcision, 31
Pharyngeal gonorrhea, 325
Phenobarbital, effects on fetus, 216
Phenylketonuria, 217
Pheromones, 80
Philia, 144, 146
Phimosis, 60
Physical attractiveness, 136
    perceptions of, 137, 138, 139
Physical disability, sexuality and, 292–293
PID. See Pelvic inflammatory disease
Pimps, 393
Piperonyl butoxide, 343
Pituitary gland, 42
Placenta, 210
Plateau phase, 84–85, 86, 87
PMS, 50–51
    coping with, 51–52
Pneumocystis pneumonia, 337
Pneumonia, 337
Podophyllin, 342
Polymorphously perverse, defined, 189
Poppers, 80
Population, defined, 15
Population of interest, 15
Pornography, 399
    changing standards of, 400–401
    gender differences in appreciation of, 402
    nonviolent, 404–405
    and sexual coercion, 402–405
    use and prevalence of, 401–402
    violent, 403–404
Positive correlation, 20
Possessing the Secret of Joy, 30, 31
Possessive love, 146
POSSLQ, 280
Postcoital contraceptive, 238
Postpartum depression, 226
Postpartum period, 226–227
Posttraumatic stress disorder (PTSD), 375
Power rape, 374
Preadolescence, sexuality in, 267
Preeclampsia, 214
Pregnancy
    early signs of, 207
    ectopic, 37
    psychological changes in, 207–208
    sex in, 207
    signs of, 206
    term of, 224
    tests for, 206–207

Premarital intercourse, 274–275
    cultural factors in, 276
    factors in, 275
    motives for, 275
Premature ejaculation, 60, 304, 310
    treatment of, 81, 313, 316–317, 318
Premenstrual syndrome, 50–51
    coping with, 51–52
Prenatal development, 208
    critical periods of, 213
    environmental influences on, 212–217
    stages of, 208–212
Preorgasmic, defined, 304
Prepuce, 29, 30
Preterm babies, 224–226
Priapism, 71, 319
Primal scene, 360
Primary amenorrhea, 50
Primary dysmenorrhea, 49
Primary erogenous zones, 79
Probe, defined, 16
Progestasert, 239, 240
Progesterone, 37
Progestin, 234, 235
    effects on fetus, 215
Prolactin, 43
    function of, 227
Proliferative phase, 43–44
Prophylactics, 245
Prostaglandins, 50
    function of, 220
Prostate gland, 64
    cancer of, 67–68
    disorders of, 66–68
Prostatitis, 68
Prostitutes
    characteristics of, 395–396
    male, 397–398
    types of, 393–395
Prostitution, 392–393
    customers of, 396–397
    settings for, 393–395
    and STDs, 398–399
Protease inhibitors, 339
Protestant Reformation, sexuality in, 8
Proximodistal development, 209, 210
Prozac, 81, 363
Prurient, defined, 400
Pseudohermaphrodites, 114, 115
    and gender identity, 115–116
Psychoactive drugs, and sexuality, 81–82
Psychoanalysis, 11, 12
    on gender typing, 124
    on sexual orientation, 189–190
Psychological androgyny, 126
    benefits of, 127–128
    model of, 127
    and sexuality, 128
Psychological disability, sexuality and, 294
Psychopathia Sexualis, 9
Psychosexual development, 12
Psychosexual therapy, 311–312
Psychosexual trauma, 309
Psychotherapy, for paraphilias, 362
Pthirus pubis, 328, 342
Puberty, 270
    changes in female, 271, 272
    changes in male, 272–273
Pubococcygeus muscle, 315
Pudendal block, 223
Pudendum, 28

Punks, 399
Pyrethrins, 343

Quadriplegia, 293
Questionnaires, 16

Radiotherapy, 36
Random assignment, 21
Random sample, defined, 15
Rape
    blaming the victim, 4
    cross-cultural view of, 372
    incidence of, 368–369
    preventing, 376–377
    social attitudes that encourage, 371
    sociocultural factors in, 371–373
    treatment of victim of, 374–378
    types of, 368, 369–371
    by women, 371
Rape trauma syndrome, 375
Rapid female orgasm, 304
Rapist
    characteristics of, 373–374
    motives of, 374
    pornography and, 403
    treatment of, 384–395
Rapport, defined, 16
Rear-entry position, 101, 103, 104
Recessive traits, 218
Recreational sex, 283
Rectal examination, importance of, 67
Reflex, 70
    defined, 69
Reflex arc, 69–70
Reformation, sexuality in, 8
Refractory period, 88
Reinforcement, in communication, 167
Relationship, criteria for partner, 139
Reliability, 17
Religion, sexuality and, 13, 20, 103
Rely tampon, 47
Representative sample, 15
Repression, 12, 308–309
    defined, 190
Reproductive system
    female, 32–38
    male, 58–65
Requests, making, 169
Resolution phase, 85, 86, 87–88
Respiratory distress syndrome, 225, 226
Retina blastoma, 217
Retrograde ejaculation, 72
Retroverted, defined, 36
Reverse transcriptase, 335
Rh incompatibility, 214
Rhythm method, 248
Right brain, 123
Romantic love, 144–145, 146, 147, 148
Rome, ancient, sexuality in, 6
Root, penile, 59
Roth v. United States, 400
RU-486, 259
Rubella, 213–214
Russia, sexuality in, 5

S&M, 356–357, 361–362
Sadism, 355–356, 360
Sadistic rape, 374
Sadomasochism, 356–357, 361–362
    defined, 10
Saltpeter, 81

Sambian people, sexuality among, 183
Sample, defined, 15
Sampling, methods of, 15–16
Sanitary napkin, 46
Sarcoptes scabei, 328, 343
Satyriasis, 358, 359
Scabies, 328, 343
Scandinavia, laws about homosexuality, 186
Science, as liberalizing force, 283
Scores, 397
Scrotum, 61
Secondary amenorrhea, 50
Secondary dysmenorrhea, 49
Secondary erogenous zones, 79
Secondary sex characteristics, 38, 61, 63, 270
Secretory phase, 45–46
Selection factor, 21
Self-disclosure, 159–160
    and sexuality, 168
Self-esteem, 162
    cultivating, 150
Self-massage, 315–316
Semen, 65
    sperm in, 202
Seminal vesicles, 64
Seminiferous tubules, 62, 63
Sensate focus exercises, 311
Senses, and sexuality, 78–80
Sensory bondage, 355
Serial monogamy, 280
Serotonin, 50
Sex and Temperament in Three Primitive Societies, 11
Sex, defined, 2
Sex education, 268, 270
Sex flush, 84
Sex in America, 18
Sex partners, number of, 13, 14
Sex skin, 85
Sex talk, 165
Sex therapy, 310–311
    finding a practitioner for, 319
Sex-change operations, 116
Sex-linked genetic abnormalities, 218–219
Sexism, 120
Sexologist, 10
Sexual arousal disorders, 301, 302–303
    treatment of, 312–314
Sexual assault, 369
Sexual behavior, 90
    deviant, 350–363
    with others, 96–103
    solitary, 91–96
Sexual Behavior in the Human Female, 9
Sexual Behavior in the Human Male, 9
Sexual coercion
    child abuse, 378–384
    harassment, 385–388
    rape, 368–378
    therapy for perpetrators of, 384–385
Sexual desire disorders, 301–302
    treatment of, 312
Sexual differentiation, 110–111
    abnormalities of, 113
    of brain, 113
    hormones and, 111–112
Sexual dysfunctions, 300
    organic causes of, 306–308
    psychosocial causes of, 308–310

treatment of, 310–320
    types of, 301–310
Sexual fantasy, 316
    in coitus, 101–102
    in masturbation, 95–96
Sexual harassment
    defined, 385–386
    incidence of, 387
    resisting, 386–387
Sexual intercourse
    anal, 102–103
    defined, 3
    duration of, 284
    fantasy in, 101
    foreplay in, 283
    frequency of, 11, 17, 20, 283–284
    techniques of, 100–104, 284
Sexual jealousy, 160–161
Sexual masochism, 355, 360, 361
Sexual orientation
    attitudes about, 184, 186–187
    biological perspectives on, 187–189
    brain and, 188–189
    classification of, 179–183
    cross-cultural view of, 183–184
    defined, 178
    ethnicity and, 185
    genes and, 187–188
    historical view of, 183
    hormones and, 188
    psychological perspectives on, 188–192
Sexual pain disorders, 301, 304–306
    treatment of, 317
Sexual response cycle, 83–88
Sexual revolution, 9
Sexual sadism, 355–356, 360
Sexuality
    in adolescence, 270–279
    in adulthood, 279–288
    biology of, 9–10
    in childhood, 266–270
    commercial, 392–406
    communicating with children about, 269
    communication of, 165–172
    cross-cultural perspective of, 10–11
    defined, 3
    disorders of, 300–320
    of elderly, 288–291
    gender roles in, 126
    in infancy, 266–267
    irrational beliefs about, 165–166, 310
    learning about your partner, 168
    in marriage, 282–288
    in preadolescence, 267
    in pregnancy, 207
    postpregnancy, 227
    prehistoric, 3–6
    psychological perspectives on, 11–13
    research methods in, 15–22
    scientific study of, 9
    senses and, 78–80
    sociocultural perspectives on, 13–15
Sexually transmitted diseases. *See* STDs
Shaft, penile, 59
Shigellosis, 331
Sibling incest, 381–382
Sickle cell anemia, 217, 218, 219
Side-entry position, 101, 102, 104
SIDS (sudden infant death syndrome), 216
Simple kissing, 96
Singlehood, 279–280

Situational dysfunctions, 301
Sixty nine, 99–100
Skepticism, defined, 3
Small talk, 157
Smell, and sexuality, 78
Smile, attractiveness of, 137
Smoke, effects on fetus, 215, 216–217
Social contacts, importance of, 150
Social desirability, 18
Social Organization of Sexuality, 17–18
Social skills training, 363
Social-exchange theory, on relationships, 156
Social-learning theory, 13, 124–125
Socialization, 124
Sociobiology, 10
   on gender typing, 122–123
Sodomy, 183
Soul kissing, 96
Spain, laws about homosexuality, 186
Spanish fly, 80
Spatial ability, gender differences in, 121
Specificity, in communication, 169
Spectator role, 304
Sperm, 61, 62–63
   defects of, 204
Spermatic cord, 61
Spermatids, 63
Spermatocytes, 62, 63
Spermatogenesis, 62, 63
Spermatozoa, 63, 64
Spermicides, 243–244
Sphincter, 33
Spina bifida, 217, 219
Spinal block, 223
Spinal injury, sexuality and, 293
Spinal reflexes, 69
Sponge, contraceptive, 254
Squeeze technique, 317
Staphylococcus aureus, 46
Staring, 164
Statutory rape, 369
STDs
   bacterial, 325–334
   contraceptives as protection against, 236, 245, 247
   fetal effects of, 214
   incidence of, 324
   parasitic, 328, 342–343
   prevention of, 343
   types of, 326–328
   viral, 327–328, 334–342
Stereotypes, 160
   advertising and, 406
   defined, 118
   examples of, 119
   of gay people, 184, 186
   and rape, 371–372
   and sexual behavior, 187
Sterilization, 251
   female, 252–254
   male, 251–252
Stillbirth, 214
Stimulants, 82
Stone age, art of, 4
Storge, 143, 146
Straight, defined, 178
Stranger rape, 369
Stratified random sample, 15, 16
Street hustlers, 399
Streetwalkers, 393–394

Stripping, distinguished from exhibitionism, 353
Studies in the Psychology of Sex, 9
Successive approximation, 158
Sudan, 31
Sudden infant death syndrome, 216
Superego, 12
Surfactants, 225
Surrogate motherhood, 206
Surveys, 16–18
   defined, 16
Survivor anxiety, 374
Swinging, 286
Sympathetic nervous system, 70
Sympathetic pregnancy, 208
Syphilis, 326, 329–330
   fetal effects of, 214
Systematic desensitization, 362

T-cells, 336
Tampon, 46
Taoism, sexuality in, 7
Target population, 15
Taste, and sexuality, 79
Tay-Sachs disease, 217, 218, 219
Tchambuli people, sex roles in, 123
Technical virginity, 274
Teenage pregnancy
   combating, 278
   consequences of, 277–279
   incidence of, 276–277
Telephone scatologia, 354
Tenderness, 163
Teratogens, 212
Terazol, 333
Terconazole, 333
Testes (testicles), 42, 61, 62
   stimulation of, 97
Testicular cancer, 65–66
Testicular self-examination, 66
Testosterone, 42, 61, 62, 111
   as aphrodisiac, 80
   as contraceptive, 255
   function of, 272, 307
   and sexual differentiation, 111, 113
Tetracycline, effects on fetus, 215
Thailand, prostitution in, 399
THC, effects on fetus, 216
Thonga people, 11
3TC, 339
Thrush, 327, 332
Tobacco, effects on fetus, 215, 216–217
Tofranil, 81
Togo, genital mutilation in, 30
Tolerance, in communication, 172
Toucherism, 357
Touching
   as communication, 164
   as foreplay, 96
   and sexuality, 79
Toxemia, 214
Toxic shock syndrome (TSS), 46, 241
Toxoplasmosis of the brain, 337
Tranquilizers, 81
   effects on fetus, 216
Transition, defined, 220
Transsexualism, 116–118
Transverse presentation, 224
Transvestism, 351–352, 359–360, 360–361
Treatment, defined, 21

Treponema pallidum, 326, 329
Triangular theory of love, 146–149
Trichomoniasis, 327, 333–334, 342
Trobriand Islands, sexuality in, 11, 13
Tropic of Cancer, 283, 400
Trust, in intimacy, 162–163
Tubal ligation (sterilization), 252, 253
Tumescence, defined, 308
Tunica albuginea, 68
Turner syndrome, 113
Twin studies, on sexual orientation, 187–188

Ultrasound
   as contraceptive, 255
   of fetus, 219
Ulysses, 400
Umbilical cord, 210
Unconscious mind, 12
United States
   incidence of rape in, 369, 372
   marriage statistics in, 282
   sexuality in, 13
Urethral bulb, 72
Urethral opening, 31
Urethritis, 65, 330
   nongonococcal, 326, 330
Urinary urgency, 32
Urogenital system, diseases of, 65–68
Urologist, 65
Urophilia, 358
Uterus, 36–37

Vaccination, 335
Vacuum aspiration, 257–258
Vacuum constriction device, 320
Vagina, 28, 29, 32–33, 34–35
   stimulation of, 97
Vaginal mucus, tracking, 203
Vaginal orgasm, 89
Vaginal ring, 254
Vaginal suppositories, 243
Vaginismus, 301, 305–306
   treatment of, 317
Vaginitis, 35, 326, 332
Valentine's Day, 5
Validating information, in communication, 172
Validity, 17
Valium, effects on fetus, 216
Variables, 21
Vas deferens, 61, 63–64
Vascular surgery, to treat erectile dysfunction, 319
Vasectomy, 64, 251
Vasocongestion, 83, 302
Vasomotor instability, 47
Vasovasotomy, 252
VDRL test, 330
Venereal disease, 324
Venereal warts, 328, 341
Verbal ability, gender differences in, 121
Verbal cues, 169
Vestibular bulbs, 33
Vestibule, 31
Viability, 212
Vibrator, 316
Victorian period, 8
Violent pornography, effects of, 403
Viscosity, defined, 250

Vision, and sexuality, 78
Vitamins, effects on fetus, 215
Volunteer bias, 16
Voyeurism, 354–355, 360
Vulva, 28, 29

Warrior Marks, 30, 31
Warts, genital, 328, 341–342
Wellbutrin, 80
Western blot test, 338
Wet dreams, 273
White Americans
　AIDS among, 336
　teen pregnancy among, 277
　teen sex among, 276

Whore-madonna complex, 397
Withdrawal, as contraceptive, 248
Wolffian ducts, 110
Woman-on-top position, 100–101,
　104
Women
　age-related changes in, 289–290
　hormones and, 83
　menstrual cycle of, 42–47
　reproductive system of, 32–38
　secondary sex characteristics of, 38,
　271
Women's rights, 8

X-rays, effects on fetus, 217

Yanomamo people, rape among,
　372
Yeast infections, 327, 332
Yohimbine, 80

Zalcitabine, 339
Ziduvodine, 339
ZIFT (zygote intrafallopian transfer),
　205
Zona pellucida, 202
Zoophilia, 358
Zovirax, 341
Zygote, 44, 110, 205